THE ENCYCLOPEDIA
OF
MENTAL HEALTH

THE ENCYCLOPEDIA
OF
MENTAL HEALTH

Ada P. Kahn, M.P.H.
and
Jan Fawcett, M.D.

Facts On File

The Encyclopedia of Mental Health

Facts On File, Inc.
460 Park Avenue South
New York, NY 10016
USA

Library of Congress Cataloging-in-Publication Data
Kahn, Ada P.
  The encyclopedia of mental health / Ada P. Kahn and Jan Fawcett.
      p.   cm.
  Includes bibliographical references and index.
  ISBN 0-8160-2694-7
  1. Psychiatry—Encyclopedias.   2. Mental health—Encyclopedias.
I. Fawcett, Jan, 1934–   .   II. Title.
RC437.K34   1993
616.89′003—dc20   92-35148

A British CIP catalogue record for this book is available from the British Library.

Facts On File books are available at special discounts when purchased in bulk quantities for businesses, associations, institutions or sales promotions. Please call our Special Sales Department in New York at 212/683-2244 or 800/322-8755.

Composition and manufacturing by The Maple-Vail Book Manufacturing Group
Printed in the United States of America

10 9 8 7 6 5 4 3 2 1

This book is printed on acid-free paper.

CONTENTS

ACKNOWLEDGMENTS

We thank the following for providing information and materials useful in preparation of this manuscript: Bennett G. Braun, M.D., Director, Dissociative Disorders Program, Rush North Shore Medical Center, Skokie, IL (dissociative disorders and multiple personality disorder); Linda Hughey Holt, M.D., Chair, Department of Obstetrics and Gynecology, Rush North Shore Medical Center, Skokie, IL (childbirth, pregnancy, menopause); Dorothy Riess, M.D., Pasadena, CA (burnout, stress); Ray Ulmer, Ph.D., Noncompliance Institute of Los Angeles (noncompliance); Marlene Wilson, Volunteer Management Associates, Boulder, CO (volunteerism); and H. Michael Zal, D.O., Bala Cynwd, PA (panic disorder).

We also thank Hope Apple and Susan Sherman for research and editorial assistance, Lenore Opasinski for production assistance and Joel Spitzer for computer services.

Ada P. Kahn, M.P.H., Evanston, IL   Jan Fawcett, M.D., Chicago, IL

PREFACE

Why do readers need an encyclopedia of mental health? As there seem to be more situations than ever before that affect our everyday emotions and overall mental health, there are also more words and terms to explain those situations. Today we face a vast range of concerns, including the normal and more than normal stresses, such as those involving relationships, family and marital disputes, sexual problems, job or school-related challenges, and needs for better ways to cope with age-related situations. As a society, we are increasingly mobile and fragmented, with fewer people being able to rely on family for guidance and emotional support. Additionally, there are more options concerning choice of life-style; with choices come additional stresses. All of these factors have contributed to the vast vocabulary related to mental well-being.

Most of us seem to understand the meaning of good physical health. By good mental well-being, we refer to one's ability to get through daily challenges and social interactions of life without experiencing undue emotional or behavioral incapacity.

Modern life cannot be stress-free. However, a healthy life-style, for good mental and physical well-being, includes personal ways to reduce stress. Major elements also include no smoking, moderate or no alcohol consumption, planned exercise and recreation, an ability to relax, maintaining moderate weight, healthy choices of nutritional foods, daily breakfast with minimal snacking, sufficient sleep, enjoyment of one's chosen career, school or life track and, because the human being is a social animal, a feeling of relatedness to loved ones, chosen friends or social groups.

Good mental health is a continuum. Most of us have good days and bad; we experience stresses brought on by family and work, with moods feeling better on some days than others. Sometimes we have anger, frustration, fears and "the blues." For those with chronic illnesses, the challenges to maintain a healthy mental outlook are unique and special.

There is a connection between the mind and the body, our mental and physical well-being. Each acts on the other. Mental outlook often has a direct effect on physical health or illness. For example, research has shown that an optimistic attitude can affect the immune system and increase killer cells that attack malignant tumors. Contrarily, depression can lower immune system activity and possibly invite physical illness. Being in excellent physical condition because of a regular exercise habit is good not only for your cardiovascular system but also for your sense of self-mastery and self-esteem, essential components of good mental health.

Many people discover that physical symptoms can be related to their mental outlook. Some who visit their primary care physicians really have psychosocial problems rather than strictly medical ones. For many, the underlying cause is stress. Symptoms of stress can be varied, confusing and frustrating. In many cases, when the mental aspects are uncovered, and can be described and discussed, physical symptoms improve, too.

A good mental outlook as a result of good mental health can give you a sense of optimism that will help you deal with disappointments, rebuffs, unfair treatment or failures, all of which are stressors. The secret to success seems to be to place these factors in perspective, to realize that they are usually transitory rather than permanent and to learn not to generalize from one adverse event to your whole life. Keep the big pictures in mind. Keep your sense of humor; avoid letting unimportant things get to you.

In addition to the countless millions of people who experience occasional emotional upheaval simply because of the human condition, more than 20 percent of our population at any time is affected with some form of specifically diagnosable psychiatric disorder. These disorders range from the least severe to the most severe forms of illness—from mild anxiety, alcoholism and substance abuse through depression and schizophrenia.

Mental health concerns face all age groups. For example, among young people under the age of 18, 12 million suffer from hyperactivity, autism and depression. Among children, suicide is the third leading cause of death, and in the age group 25–44 years old, suicide is the fifth leading cause of death. Among all age groups, some 8 million to 14 million Americans have serious depression each year; statistics show that about two out of every 10 Americans have at least one episode of major depression during their lifetime. Among all age groups, about 13 million Americans, including 3 million children, suffer from alcohol abuse or dependence and another 12.5 million suffer from substance abuse or dependence. Among the elderly, about 25 percent of those who were once labeled "senile" actually have some form of mental illness that can be effectively treated. Among all age groups, 1.4 million Americans suffer from schizophrenic disorders; about 300,000 cases occur each year.

Despite these numbers, many Americans with mental health concerns do not seek professional assistance. With more understanding of their conditions, they may develop a better understanding of what type of health professional to seek out, feel comfortable consulting and working with a professional and be able to realize their potential toward a better quality of life while enjoying a better sense of mental health.

Today many scientists agree that some mental health disorders can be caused by a variety of factors, such as outside stresses, genetic defects, organic diseases or by degrees of imbalances among neurotransmitters, the brain chemicals that carry messages between nerve cells. Such imbalances may be linked with depression and schizophrenia. Because of the great strides in understanding the physiological as well as chemical processes leading to good mental health in the past three decades, more accurate diagnosis and better treatment of many mental health disorders are now possible.

A very high percentage of our population suffering from some condition affecting their emotions and behavior can be helped by professional assistance. In response to these needs, those in the "helping" professions have developed a wide menu of therapies in an attempt to educate, counsel and assist struggling people to cope better. Help is available through psychiatrists, behaviorists, counselors, therapists, psychologists and social workers. All of these developments have resulted in an extensive and confusing array of terms describing symptoms, theories, belief systems and therapies, ranging from names of medications prescribed by physicians to tested self-help techniques.

Additionally, as each contemporary problem arises in our society—such as the scourge of AIDS in the last decade, environmentally caused illnesses and an aging population within a youth-oriented society—even more language evolves to describe attempts to deal with situations as individuals face them.

We have prepared the *Encyclopedia of Mental Health* as a place for lay readers to go for help in understanding terms, theories and beliefs. We have worked to provide the most factual and accurate definitions of terms relating to many emotional, mental and behavioral situations existing today. While this is not intended as a self-help book, it may help readers understand more and sort through the vast language explosion in this area. Curious readers who have heard terms can use this volume as a reference to orient themselves, perhaps explore certain areas further and, even more important, perhaps dismiss a term as not relevant to them. The first step in dealing with any problem is to obtain and understand accurate information about it. We hope this volume will provide readers with a good, solid first step on the path toward understanding what they and their loved ones face. In the interest of producing a book of manageable size, we have intentionally omitted many medical and psychiatric terms because they have been well described in other reference books and texts. We invite readers to make use of sources listed and the extensive bibliography at the back of the volume for further information on mental health in contemporary life.

Ada P. Kahn, M.P.H., Evanston, IL   Jan Fawcett, M.D., Chicago, IL

A

aberration Any behavior considered a deviation from the normal or typical in a particular culture. Aberrations are defined differently in different cultures. In some societies, for example, any sexual practice that is not related to reproduction (including any act from autoeroticism to voyeurism) is considered an aberration. In a sexually restricted culture, the strict "nonreproductive behavior" norm could apply. In a more liberal, sexually free culture, any type of sexual behavior occurring between or among consenting adults might be considered quite acceptable; in such a culture, the term "aberrant" might apply only to behavior in which there is victimization (for example, child abuse or the threat of violence) or adverse social consequences.

abnormal Applied to behavior, the term relates to any deviation from what is considered normal in the culture. Abnormal behavior is usually considered evidence of a mental disturbance that could range from a minor adjustment problem to a severe mental disorder. Abnormal psychology is the branch of psychology that studies mental and emotional disorders. Applied to statistics, the term indicates scores that are outside the expected range or normal range.

abortion Interruption or loss of any pregnancy before the fetus is capable of living. The term "abortion" usually refers to induced or intentional termination of a pregnancy, whereas spontaneous abortion, the natural loss of a pregnancy, is usually referred to as a miscarriage.

Abortion is so controversial because there is lack of agreement concerning what constitutes a human life. Some viewpoints hold that life begins at conception, while others believe life begins when a baby is capable of survival outside the womb. In 1973 the United States Supreme Court declared that under the Constitution, a woman was entitled to an abortion at any time during the first trimester (three months) of pregnancy; during the second trimester the individual states retained the right to regulate for health reasons where and by whom abortions could be performed. Since then, opponents of abortion have fought on moral and religious grounds to reverse and limit this decision.

There are mental health consequences for women who have undergone abortions. For example, some mourn the loss of their fetus; others, years later, fantasize about how old the child would have been and so on. All women who undergo abortion should seek mental health counseling before and after an abortion so that they may place the event in appropriate perspective within their life-style and expectations.

Laws regarding abortion vary in other countries, with Scandinavian countries historically more liberal than others. In Japan, nations of the former Soviet Union and eastern European countries, abortion performed by qualified doctors is unrestricted when performed during the first trimester.

Historically, many women have sought self-abortion and tried innumerable "abortifacients" without success. Indeed, in many cases these women have required emergency medical care and incurred permanent injury. They used such items as concentrated soap solutions, or they ingested quinine pills, castor oil or other strong laxatives. These methods can be dangerous to a woman's physical health and are not necessarily effective as abortifacients.

Women who find themselves with an unwanted pregnancy should seek counseling to determine their options.

Techniques In the United States, procedures used for elective termination of pregnancy depend on the length of the pregnancy. For pregnancies of 12 weeks or less, menstrual extraction or vacuum aspiration are commonly performed; the older procedure of surgical dilation and curettage (D &

1

C) is also used. The suction procedure consists of a gentle vacuuming of the lining of the uterus with a soft plastic tube, causing the lining to slough off. Early abortion, done between the seventh and 12th week, will probably be performed with a larger tube, or cannula, and may be followed by curettage, a procedure in which the uterine lining is scooped with a spoonlike surgical instrument (curette). These procedures take about 15 minutes and may involve some discomfort and cramping.

Surgical dilation and curettage (D & C), a procedure in which instruments are used to scrape the uterine lining (endometrium), may be performed legally (in the United States) at any stage of pregnancy up to the 24th week but is most commonly limited to the first 16 weeks from the last menstrual period. In a D & C, performed under anesthesia, the cervix is dilated by instruments, and then the curette is used; suction may also be used to remove the contents of the uterus. For some individuals, the D & C may require an overnight hospital stay.

For pregnancies of 13 to 18 weeks, a procedure known as dilation and evacuation (D & E) is used. In the D & E, when the uterus is enlarged, the cervix must be carefully dilated. Some surgeons insert laminaria tents (small sterilized sticks of absorbent seaweed material that swell gradually) to cause the cervix to dilate gently and painlessly. The surgeon will then use instruments to evacuate the contents of the uterus.

For pregnancies of 16 to 24 weeks, physicians occasionally use hysterotomy, a procedure performed through an abdominal incision, in which the uterine wall is opened and the contents are removed with instruments. The uterus remains intact; because scar tissue can form, however, future pregnancies after a hysterotomy may require a cesarean delivery.

Another technique for terminating a pregnancy of 16 to 24 weeks is instillation (also known as amnioinfusion), in which a solution is injected into the amniotic sac to induce labor contractions and delivery of the fetus and placenta. Fluids used may be a saline, or salt, solution or a solution containing prostaglandin, a body chemical that affects blood vessels and muscles. Alternatively, prostaglandins may be applied to the cervix in the form of suppositories, or pitocin (oxytocin)—a pituitary hormone that causes uterine contractions—may be used to induce labor.

Abortifacients Chemical agents, drugs or herbs that dilate the cervix, cause the uterus to contract and result in terminating a pregnancy before the fetus can survive outside the uterus are referred to as abortifacients. Saline (salt) solutions and prostaglandins are abortifacients. Prostaglandins, used as vaginal suppositories, cause uterine contractions to begin a few hours after insertion and are used both to induce abortion and to treat postpartum hemorrhage.

An abortifacient used historically in the southern part of the United States is cotton bark, which induces uterine contractions when chewed. Ergot, a parasitic fungus that grows on the cotton tree, is used to cause uterine contractions (though not in current use to trigger abortions). Pitocin (oxytocin), a synthetic form of a chemical produced in the pituitary gland, is most commonly used to stimulate labor, but it can also be used to help induce contractions for abortions.

During the early 1990s, a hormone called RU-486, an antiprogestin, was licensed in France. Given orally during the first few weeks of pregnancy, RU-486 will induce an abortion. Large doses of estrogen given after unprotected intercourse can prevent implantation—the so-called morning-after pill.

Selecting the Safest Method Before performing an abortion, physicians usually advise women to seek counseling and information. Women should have a medical examination before undergoing an abortion to become aware of a possible cardiac condition or bleeding disorder. In the United States, Planned Parenthood, with offices in many large cities, can provide information on clinics and services. Local health departments can provide names of services that meet acceptable health standards. Women may feel more confident if they have a recommendation from a trusted physician or from a member of a local hospital gynecology staff.

Women who have abortions are usually given information on means of birth control at the time of the abortion or during a follow-up visit.

"Abortion," *The World Book Encyclopedia,* vol. 1. Chicago: World Book, 1989.

Holt, Linda Hughey, and Weber, Melva. *AMA Book of Womancare.* New York: Random House, 1982.

Kahn, Ada P., and Holt, Linda Hughey. *The A to Z of Women's Sexuality.* Alameda, Calif.: Hunter House, 1992.

abstract thought An ability to appreciate ideas from multiple frames of reference. It is often associated with high intelligence. Abstract thinking is usually part of a mental status examination given by mental health professionals. An individual's capacity to think abstractly can be assessed in various ways, including interpreting proverbs or identifying commonalities between two items. Some answers may indicate a disturbance in the form of thinking, such as loose associations (no logical connection discernible), incoherence, illogicality, clanging (repeating words with similar sound and different meanings) or flight of thought (jumping from one somewhat related thought to another with no conclusion of the main idea).

abuse According to the American Nurses Association, abuse is an instance or pattern of conduct that exceeds a given norm determined by variables such as age, personality, culture and health conditions.

See also BATTERED WOMEN; DOMESTIC VIOLENCE; FAMILY VIOLENCE; SUBSTANCE ABUSE.

acceptance An attitude on the part of a psychotherapist toward the individual under treatment for a mental health concern. A nonjudgmental attitude is considered a necessary aspect in therapy.

The therapist conveys respect and regard for the individual, without implying approval of specific behaviors or an emotional attachment toward the client. Acceptance was defined by Carl Rogers (1902–1987), an American psychologist, as 'valuing or prizing all aspects of the client including the parts that are hateful to himself or appear wrong in the eyes of society." The term "acceptance" is used interchangeably with unconditional positive regard by client-centered therapists ascribing to the ideas of Carl Rogers.

See also BEHAVIORAL THERAPY; CLIENT-CENTERED THERAPY.

access to care A term that refers to the health care system in terms of both geographic accessibility of physicians and facilities and financial accessibility. Many individuals who are uninsured or underinsured do not have access to good mental health care because they cannot pay the costs themselves. Co-payments for individuals who are insured for health care also have an effect of reducing access to health care. In general, people in rural areas in the United States have less access to mental health care than those in metropolitan areas in which major teaching institutions are located.

Recent decisions to exclude insurance coverage or drastically reduce coverage for "mental disorders" in order to save money greatly remove patients' access to care.

See also SOCIAL SECURITY DISABILITY; SOCIOECONOMIC FACTORS AND CARDIOVASCULAR DISEASE; SOCIOECONOMIC TRENDS IN MENTAL HEALTH CARE.

accommodation Adaptation of language and specific therapeutic techniques to meet needs of each individual under treatment. With accommodation, the therapist enhances trust and rapport and helps promote change for the individual or family.

See also FAMILY THERAPY; PSYCHOTHER-
APY.

acetylcholine A naturally occurring substance in many body tissues that functions
as a neurotransmitter to facilitate transfer of
nerve impulses between nerve cells. Acetylcholine plays an important role in memory
storage and retrieval. Individuals who have
Alzheimer's disease show losses of acetylcholine. Dysregulation in the acetylcholine
system has been suggested as a possible
neurochemical mechanism for the symptoms
of depression. Many medications such as
antihistamines (antiallergy) and antidepressant medications can temporarily block acetylcholine function, resulting in dry mouth,
constipation and sometimes short-term
memory loss and blurred near vision.

See also ALZHEIMER'S DISEASE; DEPRES-
SION.

acquaintance rape See RAPE.

**acquired immunodeficiency syndrome
(AIDS)** Considered by many the "plague"
of the 20th century, AIDS has had more of
an impact on the civilized world than any
other disease in modern times. By the end
of 1989, reported cases of AIDS had reached
115,000 in the United States, with between
1 million and 2 million more believed to be
infected with the causative agent, the human
immunodeficiency virus (HIV). In equatorial
Africa, millions of people are already infected.

The projection for the end of 1993 is that
390,000 to 480,000 cases of AIDS will have
been diagnosed in the United States and
285,000 to 340,000 people will have died
from the disease. Annual costs of AIDS are
projected to climb as high as $5 billion to
$13 billion by 1992.

Approximately 60 percent of AIDS patients are white, 25 percent are black and 15
percent are Hispanic.

Individuals at high risk for developing the
disease live in fear, and the "worried well"

have concerns about acquiring the disease
through casual contact. Deaths from AIDS
have touched many families in the United
States. Dealing with death in people in their
twenties and thirties is difficult at best, but
for many families, dealing with AIDS has
meant recognizing their children's homosexual behaviors and drug addictions as well as
facing illness and death.

The virus is transmitted through body
fluids—usually semen or blood, but theoretically also saliva and tears. AIDS is also
transmitted from mother to infant in utero or
via passage through the birth canal or via
infected breast milk. Rare causes of AIDS
transmission include surgical exposure of
doctors or nurses to infected patients. There
have been isolated case reports of infection
through organ donations and artificial insem-
inations and from dentist to patient. In the
early 1980s, when AIDS was recognized as
a syndrome and its rising incidence acknowl-
edged, most of the patients were homosexual
males, intravenous (IV) drug users or their
partners. As recently as early 1992, there
was increasing recognition that the disease
is also spreading into the heterosexual population. Women and children are also dying
of AIDS.

In many developed countries, public health
measures have helped to stabilize the rate of
AIDS. For example, donated blood and semen samples are screened for AIDS. "Safe
sex" implies avoidance of any exchange of
body fluids by using condoms, avoiding oral
intercourse and limiting partners to a single
steady partner. Western medical centers exercise "universal precautions," which means
carefully covering any body surfaces that
might be exposed to a patient's body fluids.

For children with AIDS, there are special
problems for the infected child, the family,
the physicians involved in caring for the
child and for society in general. Many infected children require foster care because
of parental inability to provide the needed
care. At the end of 1989, estimates were
that nearly 2,000 children under age 13 rep-

resented about 2 percent of all reported AIDS cases. About 1 percent of all reported cases of AIDS are among adolescents, or children age 13 through 18.

One group of young people at high risk for acquiring HIV infection consists of runaway adolescents, many of whom subsist by engaging in prostitution. These teenagers have few support systems; usually they are school dropouts and have severed family connections. Society needs an approach to reach these youngsters before they are added to AIDS statistics.

Most communities have accepted the controversial opinion of the Centers for Disease Control that children in a normal classroom would not pose a hazard to their classmates. However, the reality is that few infants or young children with AIDS live long enough to be in school for very long. Meanwhile, any child with AIDS lives with a feeling of being different and, in many cases, being somewhat isolated by teachers and other students, leading to frustration, despair and depression, in addition to having to cope with a life-threatening illness.

Mental Health and HIV   Mark Etkin, M.D., of the University of Manitoba, Canada, described mental health needs of patients as well as caregivers during a seminar in 1991. According to Dr. Etkin, to properly coordinate the care of HIV patients, family physicians must be prepared to deal with an array of psychiatric and neurological syndromes, including depression and dementia.

There is a high suicide rate among HIV patients. According to Dr. Etkin, people with HIV are much more likely to commit suicide than cancer patients as a result of stress and the age of those afflicted. They are at an age and time in life at which they are not nearly ready to accept death. Cancer patients, in general, are older, and most do not develop dementia, which gives rise to more suicidal thoughts.

Psychosocial changes in an HIV patient involve changes in life-style and sexuality,

work, financial status, self-esteem, body image and expectations about the future. The incubation period is characterized by anxiety, stemming from isolation, rejection, family reaction, denial, insurance, homophobia and employment concerns. Dealing with the homophobia of friends and family is a high source of stress.

In addition to an awareness of psychosocial problems and neuropsychiatric disorders, sensitivity is essential in dealing with a group of patients "isolated and stigmatized by society, distrustful of the medical profession, and particularly psychiatry, which diagnosed homosexuality as a mental illness for a long time," according to Dr. Etkin.

Patients require nonjudgmental, forward-looking support, including strategies involving listening carefully, letting patients ventilate their fears, deal with the physical aspects and focus on the psychological aspects of being infected.

Dr. Etkin emphasized the power of just being there, helping the person maintain as much control as possible, helping in legal decisions before dementia sets in and in identifying referral programs.

Women and AIDS   According to a fall 1991 report from the Centers for Disease Control, women account for an increasing percentage of AIDS cases in the United States. The numbers nearly doubled between 1985 and 1990, from 6.6 percent to 11.5 percent. While heterosexual men with AIDS continue to outnumber women by slightly more than two to one, that is not because women are less vulnerable to contracting the virus through sex but rather because men are likelier to engage in IV drug use. Among women, the proportion of AIDS cases linked to drug use seems to be dropping, while sex-related cases are on the rise.

During a speech to a student-sponsored conference on AIDS at Stanford University, Stanford, California, in January 1991, then U.S. Surgeon General Antonia Novello emphasized that women must increasingly be seen as victims of AIDS, not just caretakers of men suffering from the deadly disease.

The following are excerpts from her address:

> Women have almost totally been forgotten in the AIDS questions . . . If there ever was a day when we thought women would serve only as caretakers for AIDS patients, that day has long passed. In the past, there has been attention given to the social and economic impact of this pandemic [AIDS] on women, particularly mothers and children. Now women should be seen as victims of the disease itself.
>
> Over the next decade, the heterosexual mode of transmission of HIV will become the primary means of spreading HIV infection in most industrialized countries, and by the year 2,000, according to Dr. Novello, the number of worldwide AIDS cases of women will begin to equal those of men. Our government must have a formal commitment to the idea that women are entitled to an equitable share of the resources. The fight against AIDS requires coordinated action among a wide spectrum of private and public sector groups, including women who must in many cultures have the courage to stand up to a society, and perhaps a family, that may condemn them for assuming a non-traditional role.
>
> Men and women are unequal in terms of their abilities to protect themselves against AIDS. In general it is safe to say that it is easier for the man to protect himself from AIDS than for the woman, and probably this is because the woman's protection is much more problematic. Although the condom is seen as the most effective method of preventing the spread of AIDS from an infected partner, to many women this safeguard is denied because of cultural restraints. In some societies, suggesting to a husband or partner that he use a condom may be a social taboo, because it is perceived as a communication of insolence or defiance against the man. In many societies, the price of challenging authority to protect oneself against AIDS is too high a price. We must understand that for many women, economic pressure and social pressures are more certain than the possibilities of contracting AIDS.

In a study reported in early 1992, results indicated that unprotected sex with an infected partner appears to be many times riskier for women than for men. The finding came from an ongoing six-year study of 379 couples in which one partner carried the virus. Epidemiologists from the University of California at San Francisco (UCSF) found that in only 1 percent of those cases did a woman infect her male partner, while 20 percent of the infected men passed the virus to their female partners. One reason for the difference, researchers pointed out, may be that the men in the study had more severe AIDS symptoms. Previous research has shown that sicker patients are more likely to transmit the virus.

AIDS and Pregnancy Starting in the late 1990s, the Centers for Disease Control recommended that doctors advise pregnant women to be tested for HIV infection if they acknowledge having engaged in high-risk behavior. However, a study reported in the fall of 1990 indicated that nearly half of all pregnant, infected women may be missed if doctors follow these guidelines. Between February 1987 and August 1988, women attending the obstetrics clinic at the Johns Hopkins Hospital were offered a test for HIV infection if they cited risk factors for infections; others were tested only if they requested it. Researchers checked results against the real infection rate among the pregnant patients, which they knew through anonymous testing of a sampling of blood routinely drawn from all clinic attendees for other purposes. The result was that the targeted testing picked up only 53 percent of all infected women. Then the clinic began routinely offering HIV testing to all women, and between November 1988 and May 1990, researchers identified 87 percent of those who were infected.

Researchers say HIV screening should be routinely offered to all pregnant women so that those testing positive can make decisions about continuing their pregnancies, about future pregnancies and about early medical treatment for their newborns.

Identification of Sex Partners At the UCSF's Center for AIDS Prevention Studies, researchers interviewed 150 clients of a methadone detoxification clinic and found that 33 percent of those who admitted to regularly sharing needles or to having multiple sex partners said they would not seek drug treatment if they were required to name names. In explaining their reasoning, the drug users cited fear of social stigma and of sexual rejection more than three times as often as a concern over a lost drug connection.

Testing for AIDS Virus During 1988, Illinois became the first and only state to require people applying for a marriage license to take an AIDS test. (The law has since been repealed.) Federal statistics show that the policy backfired because, rather than confront their HIV status, thousands of couples crossed state lines to get married. The number of Illinois marriages dropped by 18 percent in 1988, while the number of Illinois couples getting married in neighboring states doubled and even tripled.

AIDS in the Blood Supply A UCSF study reported in 1991 suggested that even in cities where AIDS is prevalent, the risk of transmitting the virus through transfusions is only about one in every 61,000, which is 50 percent lower than an estimate published a year previously. However, the threat of AIDS in the U.S. blood supply cannot be eliminated with good screening tests because, typically, there is at least a several-week time lag between infection and the production of blood markers.

Research on AIDS Vaccines Since the late 1980s, researchers have been working on vaccines to prevent infection. Emphasis in some centers has been placed on developing a vaccine aimed at the fetuses of pregnant women infected with the AIDS virus.

Reports during 1990 indicated that researchers working separately at three different centers were able to prevent infection in 30 to 100 percent of the rhesus monkeys exposed to the virus. In a number of studies along different lines, scientists have protected chimpanzees from infection using a vaccine based on a portion of the human AIDS virus. (Although chimpanzees do not develop AIDS, they are vulnerable to infection by the virus.) Some of this work suggests which parts of the virus may be crucial in spurring the body to make effective antibodies. In 1990, research on humans revealed indications that the immune systems of already infected people can be boosted by vaccination with inactivated AIDS virus.

In 1991, a study sponsored by the National Institutes of Health (NIH) indicated that a combination of two experimental vaccines given months apart to a small group of uninfected volunteers provoked a better immune response than any substance tested so far. Although the researchers at five universities who conducted the test said they could not predict whether the boost in immunity would be strong enough to protect against an actual infection, the approach of using vaccines in tandem looked promising. Both vaccines were synthetic versions of protein components of the virus's outer coat; the first, called gp160, was embedded in live *vaccinia* virus, the organism once used to vaccinate against smallpox. The booster shot, given 11 to 27 months after the first, consisted of multiple copies of the purified protein known as gp120. In other preliminary vaccine trials, researchers at Walter Reed Army Institute of Research gave a different version of gp160 to 30 volunteers who were already in the early stages of HIV infection. After a series of injections over several months, 19 mounted an improved immune response, providing another encouraging sign that AIDS vaccines might eventually benefit the sick as well as the healthy.

Drugs for AIDS In late 1991 the Food and Drug Administration approved a new drug for AIDS patients who suffer from cytomegalovirus (CMV) retinitis, a viral infection that often causes blindness. Foscarnet was developed specifically for the 20 to 40 percent of patients who cannot tolerate ganciclovir, the only drug now available for CMV. Foscarnet has serious side effects, however, including possible kidney damage.

While some therapeutic agents may extend survival, there is currently no available treatment to prevent death among people with AIDS. The survival rate in the early 1980s was only about 15 percent, before the licensure of antiviral drugs, such as zidovudine (AZT). AZT has been shown to slow replication of the virus and improve survival prospects. Other agents are also under further study.

Health Care Workers and AIDS   There is enormous personal stress among many health care professionals who work with AIDS patients, owing to the medical complexity of the disease, the stigma of AIDS and AIDS risk behaviors. Some health care workers fear contracting the disease from patients, while some inwardly rebel against caring for people whose concepts of behavior differ so radically from theirs.

According to the National Center for Infectious Diseases, Centers for Disease Control (CDC), health care workers have consistently accounted for 5 percent or less of AIDS cases reported to the CDC each year and, as such, are not overrepresented among persons with AIDS when compared with the proportion of the U.S. labor force employed in health services (6 percent). As of June 30, 1990, there were 137,385 adults and adolescents older than 13 with AIDS who had been reported to the CDC. Of those, 5,424 (4.8 percent) were classified as health care workers.

Follow-up information was collected on 303 of the 539 cases with undetermined risks; 237 were found to have nonoccupational risk factors. For the other 66, no occupational or nonoccupational risks were conclusively documented. Of the 236 on whom follow-up was not collected, 187 were under investigation and 49 had either died, refused interview or were not available. Three health care workers reported they developed AIDS following well-documented occupational exposure to HIV-infected blood.

In addition to these three, the CDC is aware of at least 20 additional health care workers in the United States (as of late 1991) who have not developed AIDS but who are reported to have seroconverted to HIV after a documented percutaneous injury or mucous membrane or skin exposure to blood. One laboratory worker seroconverted following a mucocutaneous exposure to concentrated virus.

The increasing number of persons being treated for HIV-associated illnesses makes it likely that more health care workers will encounter persons infected with HIV. According to the CDC in December 1991, recommendations made by the CDC to use universal precautions when caring for all patients and the Occupational Safety and Health Administration's proposed standard can help reduce this risk.

In 1991, findings of a research project at Purdue University were presented at the Seventh International Conference on AIDS in Florence, Italy. A survey of 136 nurses suggested that, as the number of AIDS patients cared for by each nurse increases to over 15, nurses' attitudes become more negative. In addition, while most nurses feel they can meet patients' physical care needs, only 43 percent believed they can meet patients' psychological needs. When caring for terminally ill patients, it is not unusual to feel burned out and hopeless. According to clinical nurse specialist Joyce Fitzpatrick, M.S., R.N., at Rush-Presbyterian–Luke's Medical Center, Chicago, "We may have to work to change nurses' perspectives, to help them realize that though they cannot cure AIDS, they can improve patients' quality of life."

Financial Costs of AIDS   At the Sixth International Conference on AIDS (1990), Jonathan Mann, the former director of the AIDS program of the World Health Organization, noted that the average national budget for AIDS in developing countries is smaller than the amount spent annually to care for only 15 people with AIDS in the United States.

The National AIDS Hotline provides information and referrals to local counseling groups. Phone: (800) 342-AIDS.

See also ZIDOVUDINE.

AMA news release, Dec. 24, 1991.

Davis, Lisa. "The Aids File." *In Health* (October 1990).

Franklin, Deborah. "The Aids File." *In Health* (September/October 1991).

Goodkind, Mike. "Women Need Equitable Share of Resources to Fight Aids, Surgeon General Says." News release, Stanford University Medical Center, Stanford, California, January 1991.

Griffin, Katherine. "The Aids File." *In Health* (December/January 1992).

Kahn, Ada P., and Holt, Linda Hughey. *The A to Z of Women's Sexuality*. Alameda, Calif.: Hunter House, 1992.

"Mental Health and HIV." *Canadian Family Physician* 37 (November 1991).

Sande, Merle A., and Volberding, Paul A. *The Medical Management of AIDS*, 2d ed. Philadelphia: W. B. Saunders Co., 1990.

U.S. Department of Health and Human Services, Public Health Service. *Healthy People 2000*. DHHS Publication No. (PHS) 91-50212. Washington, D.C.: USGPO, 1990.

acrophobia Fear of heights, one of the most common phobias. Individuals who have acrophobia fear being on the tops of mountains or on high floors of buildings. They usually feel a high level of anxiety when approaching overlooks or rooftops. Some fear falling or being injured. Fears of elevators, escalators, being on a balcony or on the steps of a ladder are related to acrophobia.

See also ANXIETY DISORDERS; PHOBIA.

acting out An uncontrolled release of aggressive, violent or sexual impulses to relieve anxiety or tension through acting on impulses. The term is sometimes applied to antisocial or delinquent behavior. Acting out is often more common in individuals who cannot express feelings verbally (alexithymia) or cannot stop and fantasize or anticipate the outcome of acting on impulses. These behaviors are often seen in patients diagnosed as having antisocial personality disorder as adults or conduct disorders as children. For example, children who are abused and beaten at home by a parent may "act out" in school, bully others or show signs of extreme, uncontrolled aggressiveness.

Recent research findings have shown that men with low breakdown metabolites of serotonin (5H IAA) in their spinal fluid have a higher risk for violent, impulsive behavior, drug or alcohol abuse and violent suicide.

action therapy A method of group psychotherapy in which goals of openness, self-disclosure and the giving and receiving of mutual feedback are emphasized.

See also GROUP THERAPY; PSYCHOTHERAPY.

active analysis
See ACTIVE ANALYTIC PSYCHOTHERAPY.

active analytic psychotherapy An approach in which the analyst gives more attention to conflicts in the individual's present life than to early childhood experiences. With this approach, the therapeutic process is sometimes accomplished in six months or less. Developed by Wilhelm Stekel (1868–1940), an Austrian psychiatrist, this approach uses free association to discuss important issues, focuses directly on the individual's resistance, offers appropriate advice and helps the individual interpret dreams in the light of current attitudes and concerns.

actualization The process of bringing together an individual's potentialities and expressing them in concrete form. Actualization (also known as self-actualization) is the ability to transform one's potentials into accomplishments. In a world preoccupied with intellectual and artistic potential, it is common to see pressured young people fear failure, avoid hard work and thus fail to reach their potential. Actualization is also known as actualization therapy.

See also PSYCHOTHERAPY.

acute bronchitis See BRONCHITIS.

acute depression   An intense mood disorder marked by feelings of extreme pessimism, futility, unreality, isolation, guilt, retardation in general activity, thought and speech and attempts at suicide. "Acute" is used to connote either sudden onset, severity or both.

See also ANTIDEPRESSANT MEDICATIONS; DEPRESSION; MANIC-DEPRESSIVE ILLNESS; DEPRESSION AND AFFECTIVE DISORDERS in BIBLIOGRAPHY.

acute dystonia   See DYSTONIC REACTION.

adaptation   The process by which an individual combines personal changes with alterations of the external environment. For example, a newcomer to a country learns to alter patterns of socialization, based on the need to learn a new language. Individuals who are better able to adapt have fewer episodes of depression and anxiety.

Since we all face severe stress and adversity at times, the ability to adapt is important in regard to how life turns out. It has been shown that individuals who demonstrate the ability to adapt well have qualities of being able to suppress worry about ongoing stress while addressing immediate issues and being able to maintain a sense of humor or perspective under stress. Self-esteem also helps one to adapt.

See also SELF-ESTEEM; STRESS.

adaptational approach   An approach to psychotherapy developed by Sandor Rado (1890–1972), a Hungarian-born American psychoanalyst, that bypasses Freudian analytic emphasis on childhood experience and the role of the therapist as a substitute parent. Instead, the focus is on the nature of the individual's unwanted behavior and directions that can be taken toward more effective behavior patterns. This approach is also known as adaptational psychodynamics.

addiction   Psychological dependence on the use of a chemical substance or activity.

Some individuals develop addictions to alcohol, caffeine, tobacco, narcotics and some sedatives, many of which are prescribed by physicians. Other individuals develop addictions to gambling, stealing or sexual activity.

The term "substance abuse" or "substance dependence" has largely replaced the word "addiction" when referring to drug dependence.

Criteria for addiction are a compulsive craving leading to persistent use or repeated actions, a need to increase the dose or level of activity due to increasing tolerance, and possibly acute withdrawal symptoms if the drug is reduced or withdrawn abruptly, depending on the drug involved (e.g., alcohol, narcotics, barbiturates). Withdrawal symptoms alone do not necessarily imply addiction. However, physical dependence can develop with prolonged use of a drug (e.g., morphine for pain). Psychological dependence can involve a loss of control of the substance use and a tendency to orient behavior or life priorities toward obtaining the drug or pursuing the addictive behavior.

See also ALCOHOL DEPENDENCE; ANXIETY; NARCOTIC DRUGS; SEDATIVE DRUG; SUBSTANCE ABUSE.

Bugelski, B. Richard, and Graziano, Anthony M. *Handbook of Practical Psychology.* Englewood Cliffs, N.J.: Prentice-Hall, 1980.

addictive personality   A personality pattern characterized by strong tendencies to become psychologically and physically dependent on one or more substances, such as alcohol and tobacco, or activities, such as sexual encounters. The existence of this as a specific personality type or disorder has been questionable, and it is not an officially accepted diagnostic term in the *Diagnostic and Statistical Manual of Mental Disorders,* (3d ed., rev.).

See also DIAGNOSTIC AND STATISTICAL MANUAL OF MENTAL DISORDERS.

additive effect   A term used when two drugs are taken together and the result is equal to the sum of the two separate effects. Two drugs given for different purposes may have additive side effects, such as taking a tricyclic antidepressant from one doctor and an antihistamine drug for allergies from another. Both have additive anticholinergic side effects.

See also ACETYLCHOLINE.

Roesch, Roberta. *The Encyclopedia of Depression*. New York: Facts On File, 1991.

ADHD   See ATTENTION-DEFICIT HYPER-ACTIVITY DISORDER.

adjustment disorders   Conditions in which an individual develops psychological symptoms in reaction to stressful ongoing serious life stressors. The term describes maladaptive behaviors on a continuum from mild to psychotic. The category of adjustment disorders was introduced during the 1980s to replace the terms ''transient situational personality disorders'' and ''transient situational disturbances.''

The American Psychiatric Association divides adjustment disorders into eight classifications, depending on the predominant symptoms that develop in response to the stressor:

Adjustment disorder with depressed mood

Adjustment disorder with anxious mood

Adjustment disorder with mixed emotional features

Adjustment disorder with disturbance of conduct

Adjustment disorder with work (or academic) inhibition

Adjustment disorder with withdrawal

Adjustment disorder with physical complaints

Adjustment disorder not otherwise specified

Usually adjustment disorders last no longer than six months; if they do, they would meet criteria for another disorder, such as major depression, dysthymia or generalized anxiety.

adolescent depression   See DEPRESSION.

adolescent suicide   See SUICIDE.

adoption   A legal proceeding that permits individuals to take a child into their family and raise him or her as their own child. At one time parents tried to keep their adopted children's origins a secret, but this rarely happens now. Most parents first tell their children of their adoption when they begin to question where babies come from. As adopted children grow older, they usually begin to dwell on the fact that they are not like other children, not related by blood to their adoptive families, and they become curious about the fact that their birth parents did not want them. The turbulence of adolescence may be more difficult for adopted children, who have additional problems added to the almost inevitable conflicts with their parents.

It is usually in adulthood that an adoptee will take steps to contact birth parents. Although most states have sealed adoption records, adoptees can sometimes go through the courts or contact their birth parents with the assistance of agencies that often act as go-betweens to determine if birth parents wish to make contact with their children. Although there are exceptions, many adoptive parents are distressed and feel threatened when their grown children wish to make contact with their birth parents.

Open adoption, a practice that is not new but is becoming more common, is a system that gives the birth mother access to her child although the child is placed with an adoptive family. Open adoption is a solution for mothers who are unable to care for their child but are distressed by the idea of complete separation. The mother may participate in the process of selecting adoptive parents and visits the child, who is eventually spared the shock of being told that he is adopted and the lack of knowledge of his true origin. Open adoption is controversial and may create uncertainty for adoptive parents; but with a dwindling supply of adoptable children, a birth mother who wants this arrangement will be more likely to get her way.

In 1991 there were approximately 3 million adopted persons in the United States. The National Committee for Adoption estimates that there will be about 60,000 adoptions in the United States per year. Despite what appears to be a high number of adoptions, many prospective parents who want an infant with no known physical or mental defects may expect a long wait. Because of improved birth control methods and legal abortions and because it has become acceptable for an unwed mother to keep and raise her child, the supply of infants who will match the typical prospective adoptive parents (financially secure white couples) is low. Some couples turn to the gray or black market in babies, through which an infant may be literally sold through a doctor, lawyer or other intermediary.

Because of difficulties of adopting a child, many couples are turning to children from abroad, frequently Asian, who need homes. These couples encounter a unique set of concerns ranging from adapting a child's eating habits from a diet high in rice or beans to American meat and potatoes to responding to questions and dealing with double takes from strangers because of the child's different appearance. Ironically, while approximately 10,000 children are being adopted from abroad per year, a 1989 study showed that 34,000 children, 51 percent minority and others with physical or mental problems, were awaiting adoption in the United States. White prospective parents who are willing and eager to adopt a black infant frequently find it frustrating that many agencies have adopted the objections of the National Association of Black Social Workers to placing black children in white homes. Basing their opinions on the outcomes of freer black-white adoptions before 1972, the social workers objected that black children

were growing up in white communities where they were out of touch with their roots and might encounter racism for which their idealistic parents had not prepared them.

Still another difficult-to-place group of adoptive children are older children who have memories and scars from earlier experiences. These children are the most likely to be among the 20 to 25 percent of adopted children who develop mental health needs that require professional help.

An extremely difficult situation arises when adoptive parents feel that they must return a child to the adoption agency because of behavior or physical problems that manifest themselves after the adoption that they cannot handle. Approximately 1,000 children per year are returned to agencies for these reasons. Some parents have accused agencies of hiding factors from them that, if known, would have kept them from adopting.

Qualities that agencies look for in adoptive parents are stability, a positive attitude toward adoption and a good marital relationship. Adoption agencies try to guard against parents who are adopting to solve their own personal problems, have unrealistic attitudes about adoption or negative feelings about illegitimacy.

See also INFERTILITY.

adoption studies   Researchers interested in the nature versus nurture question like to study adoptive children's characteristics in relation to their adoptive and biological parents. One study, undertaken by a group of American and European scholars, compared criminal records from 14,000 adopted children with those of their adoptive and biological parents from 1927 to 1947. The study showed a stronger relation between criminal behavior of the children and that of their biological parents than between criminal behavior of the children and that of their adoptive parents. A study at the University of Colorado, which consisted of testing the intelligence of adoptive children and their biological parents over a period of years, showed a higher correlation with the biological than with the adoptive parents. Although such studies are controversial, this was considered to be particularly significant because the children were not matched to adoptive parents by educational or socioeconomic level.

Several adoptions studies of alcoholism were conducted during the 1970s in Denmark. Sons of alcoholics raised by unrelated, nonalcoholic adoptive parents were four times more likely to become alcoholic by an early age than were adopted-out sons of nonalcoholics, but were no more likely to have other forms of psychopathology and no more likely to be classified as heavy drinkers.

Daughters of alcoholics raised by nonalcoholic adoptive parents and daughters raised by their own alcoholic parents were also studied in Denmark. The adopted-out daughters had a higher rate of alcoholism than exists in the general population (4 percent versus 0.1 percent), but adopted-out controls also had a high rate of alcoholism and the findings were equivocal. Daughters raised by the alcoholic parent or parents also had an alcoholism rate of 4 percent, but this rate contrasted with no alcoholism in matched controls.

Later, two other adoption studies were performed in Sweden and in Iowa. Both produced the same results as the Danish studies. There was an increased prevalence of alcoholism in adopted-out children of alcoholics, with no evidence of an increased prevalence of other disorders. The Iowa study recently produced evidence that adopted-out daughters as well as sons of alcoholics have increased rates of alcoholism when compared with controls.

In adoption studies of schizophrenia, it has been found that congenital factors (genetic or intrauterine environmental) may play a role in the development of chronic schizophrenia.

See also ALCOHOLISM; SCHIZOPHRENIA.

adrenal cortex   The outer layer of the adrenal gland. The adrenal cortex is the source of several hormones, including androgens, glucocorticoids and mineral corticoids. Functions of the adrenal cortex are controlled by ACTH, a hormone secreted by the pituitary gland especially under conditions of physiological and extreme psychological stress. Excessive production of one or more of the hormones of the adrenal cortex is known as adrenal-cortical hyperfunction. Some types of severe depression, including those that may result in suicide if not treated, show evidence of adrenal hyperfunction.

Recently, animal studies have shown evidence that prolonged stress-related adrenal hyperfunction can be associated with cell death in an area of the brain called the hippocampus, which regulates adrenal stress response and is essential for recent memory and learning. There is suggestive evidence that this process might occur in humans under conditions of prolonged severe stress (e.g., torture and severe depression).

adrenal gland   A small organ above the kidney that secretes several hormones. The medulla and the cortex are the two important parts of the gland. The adrenal medulla secretes two hormones, epinephrine (or adrenaline) and norepinephrine (or noradrenaline). The adrenal gland is also known as suprarenal gland.

See also ADRENAL CORTEX.

adrenaline   A hormone (also known as epinephrine) secreted by the central, or medullary, portion of the adrenal gland that produces an increase in heart rate, a rise in blood pressure and a contraction of abdominal blood vessels. These sympathetic changes can be reversed by activation of the parasympathetic system.

See also ADRENAL GLAND; EPINEPHRINE; NEUROTRANSMITTERS.

adrenergic blocking agents   Agents that inhibit some responses to adrenergic, or adrenaline-like (energizing), nerve activity. The term "adrenergic blocking agent" (a.b.a.) also applies to drugs that block action of the neurotransmitters epinephrine and norepinephrine. A.b.a.s are selective in action and are classed as alpha a.b.a.s (alpha blockers or alpha-receptor blocking agents) and beta a.b.a.s (beta blockers or beta-receptor blocking agents), depending on which types of adrenergic receptors they affect. Medications for some mental disorders may involve both alpha blockers and beta blockers, although the beta blockers are used primarily for certain forms of anxieties, such as test taking, performance and public speaking. Some beta blockers may produce depression as a side effect.

See also ADRENERGIC DRUGS; ADRENERGIC SYSTEM.

adrenergic drugs   Substances that stimulate activity of adrenaline (epinephrine) or mimic its functions and produce stimulation of the central nervous system. Adrenergic agents are produced naturally in plants and animals but can also be developed synthetically. Adrenergic drugs (a.d.s) are part of a group of sympathomimetic amines that includes ephedrine, amphetamines and isoproterenol.

See also ADRENERGIC BLOCKING AGENTS; ADRENERGIC SYSTEM.

adrenergic system   Part of the autonomic nervous system, including receptor sites, that is influenced by adrenergic drugs, which stimulate the activity of epinephrine or mimic its functions.

See also ADRENERGIC BLOCKING AGENTS; ADRENERGIC DRUGS.

adultery   Sexual intercourse between a married individual and another person who is not the legal spouse; also known as extramarital sex. Historically, in many countries adultery has been considered a taboo and major (and sometimes the only) grounds for divorce. In the United States, adultery is a source of stress within marriages and, in many cases, contributes to the depression of one or both partners in the marriage. Adul-

tery carries with it the strong threat of acquiring a sexually transmitted disease.

See also MARRIAGE.

Kahn, Ada P., and Holt, Linda Hughey. *The A to Z of Women's Sexuality.* Alameda, Calif.: Hunter House, 1992.

affairs, extramarital   A sexual relationship outside marriage in which at least one of the participants is married. Even when the affair is kept secret, it can produce conflict and guilt feelings on the part of the one involved in the affair and emotions ranging from anger to depression in the other partner. Affairs are a source of stress to all concerned, as well as a danger to all parties concerned of contracting a sexually transmitted disease.

See also ADULTERY; STRESS.

affect   Mood, or inner feelings at a particular moment. The word "affect" is often used to the describe the mood as perceived by another person. One whose mood does not change, is not excited or angered by any stimuli, is said to have flattened affect (affective flattening).

See also AFFECTIVE DISORDERS.

affective disorders   Affective disorders (also known as mood disorders) involve changes in affect, a term that means mood or emotion. An affective disorder usually is a mood disturbance intense enough to warrant professional attention. One who has an affective disorder may have feelings of extreme sadness or intense, unrealistic elation with the disturbances in mood that are not due to any other physical or mental disorder.

A disorder of the thought processes is not commonly associated with affective disorders; however, if the affective disorder becomes intense, there may be changes in thought patterns that will be somewhat appropriate to the extremes of emotion the person perceives.

Affective disorders differ from thought disorders, as schizophrenic and paranoid disorders are primarily disturbances of thought, although individuals who have those disorders may also have some distortion of affect.

Death rates for depressed individuals seem to be about 30 times as high as in the general population because of the higher incidence of suicide. Manic individuals also have a high risk of death, because of physical exhaustion, neglect of proper precautions to safeguard health or accidents (with or without alcohol as a contributing factor).

Historically, there have been descriptions of mood disorders in the early writings of the Egyptians, Greeks, Hebrews and Chinese. Descriptions of mood disorders appear in the works of Shakespeare, Dostoevski, Poe and Hemingway. Many historical figures have suffered from recurrent depression, including Churchill, Freud, Dostoevski, Moses, Queen Victoria, Lincoln and Tchaikovsky.

Affective disorders, or mood disorders, can be subcategorized as major depression and bipolar disorders. These disorders can be acute or chronic, and both show symptoms by changes in the biologic, psychological and sociological functioning of the individual. In some individuals, bipolar disorders and depressive disorders occur according to a seasonal pattern, with a regular cyclic relationship between the onset of the mood episodes and particular seasons.

A mood syndrome (depressive or manic) is a group of associated symptoms that occur together over a short duration. For example, major depressive syndrome is defined as a depressed mood or loss of interest, of at least two weeks' duration, along with several associated symptoms, such as difficulty concentrating and sleeping, fatigue, hopelessness, loss of pleasure and weight loss or gain with suicidal thoughts sometimes present.

A mood episode (major depressive, manic or hypomanic) is a mood syndrome not due to a known organic factor and not part of a nonmood psychotic disorder such as schiz-

ophrenia, schizoaffective disorder or delusional disorder. Psychiatrists diagnose a mood disorder by the pattern of mood episodes. For example, the diagnosis of major depression, recurrent type, is made when an individual has had one or more major depressive episodes without a history of a manic or hypomanic episode.

Manic Episodes   Manic episodes are distinct periods during which the individual experiences a predominant mood that is either elevated, expansive or irritable. Such individuals may have inflated self-esteem, increased energy, accelerated and loud speech, flight of ideas, distractibility, grandiose delusions and decreased need for sleep. The disturbance may cause marked impairment in working, social activities or relationships; an episode may require hospitalization to prevent harm to themselves or others. There may be rapid shifts of mood, with sudden changes to depression or anger. The mean age for the onset of manic episodes is in the early twenties, but many new cases appear after age 50.

Hypomanic Episodes   These are mood disturbances less severe than mania but sometimes severe enough to cause marked impairment in judgment, financial, social or work activities. Such episodes may be associated with increased energy and activity, exaggerated self-confidence, hypertalkativeness, euphoria and increased sense of humor. Hypomanic episodes may be followed by depressions of moderate to great severity.

Major   Depressive   Episodes   Major depression affects approximately 10 percent of the adult population. A major depressive episode includes either depressed mood (in children or adolescents, irritable mood) or loss of interest or pleasure in all, or almost all, activities for at least two weeks. Symptoms persist in that they occur for most of the day, nearly every day, during at least a two-week period. Associated symptoms may include feelings of worthlessness or excessive or inappropriate guilt, difficulty concentrating, restlessness, inability to sit still, pacing, handwringing, appetite disturbance, change in weight, sleep disturbance, decreased energy and recurrent thoughts of death or of attempting suicide.

Depressive episodes are more common among females than among males. The average age of onset of depressive episodes is in the late twenties, but a major depressive episode may begin at any age. Studies of depression show an earlier age at onset of depression among younger people, suggesting the rate of depressive disorders may be rising in successively younger-aged groups.

Bipolar Disorders Bipolar disorders (episodes of mania and depression) are equally common in males and females. Bipolar disorder seems to occur at much higher rates in first-degree biologic relatives of people with bipolar disorder than in the general population.

Cyclothymia In this condition, there are numerous periods of hypomanic episodes and numerous periods of depressed mood or loss of interest or pleasure that are not severe enough to meet the criteria for a bipolar disorder or a major depressive episode.

Dysthymia In dysthymia, there is a history of a depressed mood for at least two years that is not severe enough to meet the criteria for a major depressive episode. This is a common form of depression, and one who has this condition may have periods of major depressive episodes as well.

Causes of Affective Disorders There are many explanations for affective disorders, including psychoanalytic theory, interpersonal theory, cognitive theory, behavioral theory, learned helplessness theory and genetic theory. These theories have common points of focus that can be roughly categorized as biologic, psychosocial and sociocultural.

Personality characteristics of some individuals predispose them to affective disorders, such as lack of self-esteem and negative views of themselves and of the future. A stressful life event for some individuals activates previously dormant negative thoughts.

Individuals who become manic are generally ambitious, outgoing and energetic, care what others think about them and are sociable before their episodes and after remission. However, depressive individuals appear to be more anxious, obsessive and self-deprecatory. They often are prone to feelings of self-blame and guilt. Depressed individuals tend to interact with others differently than manics do. For example, some manic individuals dislike relying on others and try to establish social roles in which they can dominate others. On the other hand, depressed individuals take on a role of dependency and look to others to provide support and care.

Feelings of a loss of hope and helplessness are central to most depressive reactions. In severe depression, "learned helplessness" may occur, in which the individual sees no hope and gives up trying to cope with his or her situation.

There seems to be a hereditary predisposition, because incidence of affective disorders is higher among relatives of individuals with clinically diagnosed affective disorders than in the general population. There has been considerable research during the 1970s and 1980s to explore the view that depression and manic episodes both may arise from disruptions in the balance of levels of brain chemicals called biogenic amines. Biogenic amines serve as neural transmitters or modulators to regulate the movement of nerve impulses across the synapses from one neuron to the next. Two such amines involved in affective disorders are norepinephrine and 5-hydroxytryptamine (serotonin). Some drugs are known to have antidepressant properties and biochemically increase concentrations of one or the other (or both) of these transmitters.

In many individuals, psychosocial and biochemical factors work together to cause affective disorders. For example, stress has been considered as a possible causative factor in many cases. Stress may also affect the biochemical balance in the brain, at least in some predisposed individuals. Some individuals experience mild depressions following significant life stresses, such as the death of a family member. Other major life events may precipitate changes in mood, such as those involving reduced self-esteem, physical disease or abnormality or deteriorating physical condition.

Treatment A variety of treatments, including behavioral therapy and drugs, are used to treat affective disorders. Some behavioral approaches, known as cognitive and cognitive-behavioral therapies, include efforts to improve the individual's thoughts and beliefs (implicit and explicit) that underly the depressed state. Therapy includes attention to unusual stressors and unfavorable life situations and observing recurrences of depression.

Drugs used to treat affective disorders include antidepressants, tranquilizers and antianxiety drugs. Lithium carbonate, a simple mineral salt, is used to control manic episodes and is also used in some cases of depression in which the underlying disorder is basically bipolar. For many individuals, lithium therapy is often effective in preventing cycling from depressive to manic episodes.

See also AGORAPHOBIA; ALCOHOLISM; ANTIDEPRESSANT MEDICATIONS; BIPOLAR DISORDER; DEPRESSION; ENDOGENOUS DEPRESSION; EXOGENOUS DEPRESSION; LEARNED HELPLESSNESS; LEARNED OPTIMISM; MANIC-DEPRESSIVE ILLNESS; PHOBIA; SEASONAL AFFECTIVE DISORDER; SUICIDE.

American Psychiatric Association. *Diagnostic and Statistical Manual of Mental Disorders,* 3d ed., rev. Washington, D.C.: APA, 1987.
McFarland, Gertrude K., and Thomas, Mary Durand. *Psychiatric Mental Health Nursing.* Philadelphia: J. B. Lippincott, 1991.

affective flattening (blunting) A behavior pattern involving a lack of emotional expression, reactivity and feeling. The individual may fail to smile or laugh when prompted, fails to show normal vocal emphasis patterns, acts "wooden" and does not use hand gestures or body position as an aid to expressing ideas. Such behavior is also seen in the neurologic disorder Parkinson's disease. It can also be a symptom of severe hypothyroidism (myxedema).

Affective flattening can be evaluated by a mental health professional by observation of the individual's behavior and responsiveness during a routine interview. Some aspects of behavior may be affected by drugs, because side effects of some neuroleptics may lead to a masklike facial expression and diminished movements (pseudo-Parkinsonism). However, other aspects of mood, such as responsivity and appropriateness, are usually not so affected. Affective flattening is sometimes referred to as blunting. Affective flattening may develop in the psychiatric disorder schizophrenia or major depression.

See also AFFECTIVE DISORDERS; DEPRESSION.

Andreasen, Nancy C., and Black, Donald. *Introductory Textbook of Psychiatry.* Washington, D.C.: American Psychiatric Association, 1991.

affirmation An affirmation (self-affirmation) is a positive self-statement. Affirmations help many individuals change negative feelings to more positive ones. They help the individual break the stress-tension cycle. Affirmations are stated in a positive framework, such as "I feel great after exercising" or "I have a lot to offer" rather than "I won't just sit around so much." These are stated in the present tense, rather than future tense, and are repeated three to five times during daily relaxation practice sessions or other times frequently throughout the day. Individuals who benefit from affirmations imagine doing what they say in as much detail and with as much pleasure as possible. Affirmation statements often include the words "I can" or "I am" and are used by individuals to improve self-esteem and self-confidence, break the cycle of co-dependency and overcome addictions.

See also SELF-ESTEEM.

McFarland, Gertrude K., and Thomas, Mary Durand. *Psychiatric Mental Health Nursing.* Philadelphia: J. B. Lippincott, 1991.

agape (agapism)   In psychoanalytic terms, agape involves the practice of erotic love of the body and also feelings of tenderness and protectiveness for the traits, gestures or speech of another person.

The term is derived from the Greek word *agape,* referring to unselfish, spiritual love of one person for another with no sexual implications. In Christian tradition, agape also encompasses the love of God for humankind, as well as the love of humankind for God.

See also EROS.

Kahn, Ada P., and Holt, Linda Hughey. *The A to Z of Women's Sexuality.* Alameda, Calif.: Hunter House, 1992.

age factors   There is a significant rise in the rate of depression among adolescents, teenagers and young people. In the 1970s, mental health facilities reported more cases of young individuals who were depressed than the textbook description of depressed persons as middle-aged.

Today depression appears to occur more in the 20-to-40 age range than in older persons. As depression affects more people under the age of 45 and fewer over age 65, 25 to 44 may be the most susceptible age range. Until the last decade, depression in children and infants was underidentified. Now it is estimated that from 3 million to more than 6 million American children suffer from depression, much of it unrecognized and untreated.

Under age 65, twice as many women as men are treated for depressive disorders, with the exception of bipolar disorder (manic-depression), which occurs equally in both sexes. Although fewer people over age 65 are affected by depression, it is still common among the elderly. In elderly people, depression may occur because of loneliness, physical deterioration, poor health, death of loved ones and friends and an awareness of their own mortality. By contrast, schizophrenia has an early onset, in the late teens and twenties, and tends to be chronic. Panic disorders, which may accompany depression or occur by themselves, may have onsets from the late teens to the forties and tend to be recurrent. Agoraphobia often occurs in people in their twenties, and social phobias often originate in the teen years.

See also AGORAPHOBIA; DEPRESSION; PANIC DISORDER; PHOBIA; SCHIZOPHRENIA.

Roesch, Roberta. *The Encyclopedia of Depression.* New York: Facts On File, 1991.

aggression   A general term for a variety of behaviors that appear outside the range of what is socially and culturally acceptable. Aggression includes extreme self-assertiveness, social dominance to the point of producing resentment in others and a tendency toward hostility. Individuals who show aggression may do so for many reasons, including frustration, as a compensatory mechanism for low self-esteem, lack of affection, hormonal changes or illness. Aggression may be motivated by anger, over competitiveness, or directed toward harming or defeating others.

An individual with aggressive personality may behave unpredictably at times. For example, such an individual may start arguments inappropriately with friends or members of the family and may harangue them angrily. The individual may write letters of an angry nature to government officials or others with whom he has some quarrel.

Hormonal differences account for some aggression because excessive androgens, the male sex hormones, seem to promote aggression (e.g., the use of androgenic steroids to promote development of muscle mass in athletes).

Some psychiatric conditions occasionally are associated with aggression. These include antisocial personality disorder, schizophrenia and mania. The abuse of amphetamines, alcohol, PCP ("Angel dust"), cocaine and androgenic steroids (such as weight lifters use) is even more frequently associated with violent behavior. Other medical causes include temporal lobe epilepsy, hypoglycemia and confusion due to illness.

Individuals who are continuously aggressive may show changes in brain-wave patterns in electroencephalograms (EEG).

The opposite of aggression is passivity. The term "passive aggression" relates to behavior that seems to be compliant but in which "errors, mistakes or accidents" for which no direct responsibility is assumed result in difficulties or harm to others. (A passive-aggressive person might say, "Gee, I'm sorry, I didn't mean to ruin all your work.") Patterns of behavior such as making "mistakes" that harm others are considered "passive aggressive."

See also PASSIVE-AGGRESSIVE PERSONAL-ITY DISORDER.

aggressive behavior   See AGGRESSION; PASSIVE-AGGRESSIVE PERSONALITY DISOR-DER.

aging   Growing older is a lifelong concern. The aging process begins the day one is born, but concern mounts as the years go by. Anxieties about health status, financial capabilities, standard of living and surviving loved ones mount as one grows older. In 1990, according to the National Council on the Aging, there were 36 million Americans (one out of every seven persons) over the age of 60.

People have always been preoccupied with longevity and have dreaded old age. There have been three major categories of theories on achieving old age. One is the biblical theory, which holds that the righteous are granted long life. Second is the theory that there are special places in the world where people live long. Third, the modern theory, is that to some extent, people have an influence on the length as well as the quality of their lives. One's genetic makeup also influ-

Successful Aging

Eat a proper diet with a reasonable amount of fiber

Reduce intake of salt and cholesterol

Do a reasonable amount of exercise

Avoid smoking and excessive alcohol intake

Wear a seat belt in cars

Protect skin from the sun

Keep physically and intellectually active

Make constructive use of time

Undergo periodic health examinations

Examine risk factors; determine necessary life-style changes

Maintain friendships and relationships with others

ences one's life, but that is a situation over which one has no control. The object of successful aging is to make the best use of what one has.

During the first half of the 20th century, life expectancy was increased by reducing neonatal, infant and maternal deaths. Since the 1980s, there has been an increase in life expectancy even after the age of 60 that is probably due in part to the decreasing incidence of cardiovascular risk factors. Now there seems to be consensus by geriatricians that certain life-style components can help one age successfully.

Characteristics of aging can be slowed down by regular exercise programs. Exercise strengthens the body, improves one's outlook and widens one's social contacts. Older adults are now jogging, walking, bicycling and swimming. These exercises improve the condition of the heart and lungs, aid in weight control and decrease many aspects of stress.

Many older adults skip meals or seem to have a reduced appetite. Eating well is important to keep up vitality in old age. Even people who come from families with a history of heart disease can lower their own risk of becoming ill by following a low-fat diet, eliminating smoking, controlling their weight and exercising regularly.

One of the sad effects of aging is the loss of loved ones and treasured relationships. A nine-year study of 7,000 Alameda County (California) residents indicated that people with few relationships died at rates two to five times higher than those with more friendships. Another study, done in England, of females who had suffered severe depression revealed that women who experienced severe stress and did not have a confidante were approximately 10 times more likely to be depressed than women who did. Even caring for pets has a beneficial effect on aging; being responsible for something other than oneself is a morale booster.

Planning for retirement helps one stay active. In a study by the American Association of Retired Persons, members ranked boredom as one of the most serious problems of retirement.

Many healthy people move into retirement communities or buildings during their later years so that they will have companionship as well as available health care nearby. Among the fears of the aging population are concerns over ability to continue to manage one's own affairs, remaining independent and not being a burden to children or society and the dread of living out one's last years in a nursing home.

See also ELDERLY PARENTS; RETIREMENT; AGING in BIBLIOGRAPHY.

agitation   Behavior that is tense and excited, with rapidly fluctuating levels of physical activity. It may be evidenced by pacing, loud and rapid speech, tense facial expression, cursing, wringing of hands, perspiration, short attention span and inability to concentrate or purposeless, potentially injurious movements.

Agitation may be a reaction to stressful events or relationships or an untoward response to psychotropic medications (akathisia). Agitation can occur in some mental disorders, such as schizophrenia, bipolar disorder, major depression, delirium and dementia. Agitation has been observed in otherwise normal individuals when exposed to a crisis situation, such as bereavement or natural disasters, in which they often experience extreme fear, isolation and sleep deprivation.

See also AKATHISIA; ANXIETY; FEAR.

agnosia   A failure or impairment of the ability to recognize objects, grasp the meaning of words and other symbols or interpret sensory stimuli. The condition may be due to organic brain damage (strokes, brain tumors, brain injury) or to emotional factors, seen rarely in schizophrenia. Visual agnosia refers to an inability to respond appropriately to visually presented material. Color agnosia refers to an impaired ability to select colors of the same hue, name colors or give the color of a specifically colored object, such as the sky. Prosopagnosia refers to the inability to recognize faces of people well known or newly introduced to the individual. Spatial agnosia includes disorders of spatial perception and loss of topographical memory. Auditory agnosia is an impairment in recognition of nonverbal sound stimuli in the presence of adequate hearing. Agnosia for music includes tone deafness, melody deafness and disorders in perception of rhythm. Tactile agnosia is apparent in the individual who is unable to recognize objects by handling the objects without seeing them. Verbal agnosia implies the recognition of a word or object but the inability to verbalize its name (often as a result of strokes).

See also STROKE.

agonist   A drug that affects a nerve receptor by binding to its surface and producing a physiological change. Such a change might involve stimulation of a neuron, causing a nerve impulse to be fired, or it could provide the mediation needed to inhibit a nerve-cell discharge. The term also refers to a contracting muscle whose action is opposed by another muscle. L-dopa is a dopamine-receptor agonist used to treat Parkinson's disease.

See also PHARMACOLOGIC THERAPY in BIBLIOGRAPHY.

agoraphobia A complex syndrome characterized by a fear of being in public places where escape may be blocked or help unavailable in the event that embarrassing or incapacitating symptoms develop. Agoraphobia involves a combination of fears, such as being without help in stores, public transportation and crowds. Agoraphobia involves fear of losing control of oneself, as in fainting or "going crazy." Agoraphobia usually occurs in adults; the ratio of women with agoraphobia versus men is three to one.

Agoraphobia frequently results from panic attacks or panic disorder. Panic attacks are either "out-of-the-blue attacks" or those that occur in a setting of anticipatory anxiety related to previous panic attacks. They are attacks of overwhelming anxiety, leading the victim to fear death from a heart attack, or loss of mental control. After repeated panic attacks, victims frequently develop a fear of crowds, enclosed places (e.g., tunnels, airplanes) and even leaving home,; they are afraid that a repeat panic attack might occur. Panic anxiety is the most severe form of anxiety, and individuals suffering from panic attacks may exhibit suicidal impulses as an escape from this torment. There are successful pharmacologic and psychotherapeutic treatments for panic attacks and agoraphobia, which develops after panic attacks.

Many agoraphobics are socially disabled because they cannot travel to visit friends, work or shop. Many refuse invitations and often make excuses for not going out. Thus adjustments are necessary to compensate for the agoraphobic's lack of participation in family life and activities outside the home.

Anxious, shy women are the group of individuals most prone to agoraphobia. Some agoraphobics tend to be indecisive, have little initiative, are guilty and self-demeaning and feel they should be able to get out of their situation themselves. They may be-

come increasingly withdrawn into their restricted life. There is some evidence that dependency and perfectionism are associated with a subgroup of people who develop agoraphobia. There is also substantial clinical evidence that emotional suppression is strongly associated with development of agoraphobia.

Most agoraphobics are married at the time they come for treatment. In most research projects involving agoraphobics, spouses seem well adjusted and integrated individuals. In some cases, therapists use the Maudsley Marital Questionnaire to assess the individual's perception of his or her marriage before and after treatment. Questions relate to categories of marital and sexual adjustment, orgasmic frequency, work and social adjustment and "warmth" items. When agoraphobia improves with treatment, marriages usually remain stable or improve.

Agoraphobia may strain a marriage because the agoraphobic person may ask the spouse to take over chores that require going out, such as shopping or picking up children; spouses often must fulfill social obligations without the companionship of their mates. Spouses are additionally stressed by having to be "on call" in case anxiety attacks occur that require communication or a trip home to soothe the agoraphobic. Thus a couple that may have been happy may be driven apart by the disorder, with each blaming the other for a lack of understanding. The husband may think that the wife is not trying to overcome her phobic feelings, and the agoraphobic wife may think that her husband does not understand her suffering. The wife may become so preoccupied with fighting her daily terrors that she focuses little attention on their marital relationship and her husband's needs. However, in cases in which the agoraphobic has an understanding, patient and loving spouse, this support can be an asset in overcoming the agoraphobic condition. The spouse can attend training sessions with the therapist and group therapy sessions and act as the "understanding companion'' when the agoraphobic is ready to venture out.

When agoraphobics seek treatment, they are often in a constant state of alertness and have a passive, dependent attitude and a tendency toward sexual inhibition. Typically, the agoraphobic admits to being generally anxious and often expresses feelings of helplessness and discouragement. However, many agoraphobics were formerly active, sociable, outgoing persons. Some agoraphobics abuse alcohol and drugs, and researchers are beginning to uncover the extent of such abuse. Some current estimates place 30 percent of alcoholics as having a primary anxiety disorder that leads to the chronic use of alcohol.

Symptoms Symptoms may include fear of dizziness or falling, loss of bladder or bowel control, vomiting, palpitations and chest pain. There may be a fear of having a heart attack because of the rapid heart action, of fainting if the anxiety becomes too intense and of being surrounded by unsympathetic onlookers. The individual then develops a fear of the fear that brings about anxiety in anticipation of a panic reaction, resulting in avoidance of the feared situation.

A common characteristic of agoraphobia is a history of panic attacks in which the individual experiences many symptoms including an overwhelming sense of imminent catastrophe and fear of loss of control or of public humiliation. However, agoraphobia may occur with or without a history of panic attacks. Many women report that generalized anxiety and panic in agoraphobia tend to be worse just prior to and during menstruation.

Broader symptoms include general anxiety, spontaneous panic attacks and occasional depersonalization—a change in the perception or experience of the self so that the feeling of one's own reality is temporarily lost. For some individuals, anxiety in agoraphobia may be aggravated by certain predictable situations, such as arguments between marital partners and general stress. For some, the anxiety is nearly always re-lieved somewhat in the presence of a trusted companion, a pet or an inanimate object such as an umbrella or shopping cart.

Some agoraphobics develop ways to live more comfortably with their disorder. For example, those who go to churches or movie theaters may be less frightened in an aisle seat so that they can make a fast exit if they experience a panic attack. Having a telephone nearby is another comfort.

Many agoraphobics have episodes of depression. The first episode may occur within weeks or months of the first panic attack. Individuals complain of feeling ''blue,'' have crying spells, feel hopeless and irritable, suffer from a lack of interest in work and have difficulty in sleeping. Agoraphobia is often aggravated during a depressive episode. The increased anxiety may make individuals less motivated to work hard at tasks (such as going out) that they previously did with difficulty.

Some agoraphobics are also claustrophobic. Claustrophobia is usually present before the agoraphobia develops. The common factor between the two phobias is that escape is blocked, at least temporarily. Symptoms of the phobic anxiety in agoraphobia may include many physical sensations that accompany other anxiety states, such as dry mouth, sweating, rapid heart beat, hyperventilation, faintness and dizziness.

Panic Attacks and Agoraphobia Panic attacks are defined, discrete episodes of unpredictable, intense fearfulness, terror or extreme apprehensiveness, along with feelings of impending doom. An individual may experience symptoms such as difficulty in breathing (hyperventilation), palpitations, chest pain or discomfort, choking or smothering sensations and fear of going crazy or losing control. Attacks may last from minutes to hours. Diagnosticians use three panic attacks within a two-week span of time to characterize the panic ''syndrome.'' Panic attacks often precede the agoraphobic state, although some individuals have agoraphobia without panic attacks.

In panic disorder with agoraphobia, the individual meets the criteria for panic disorder and additionally has a fear of public places from which escape might be difficult or embarrassing or where help might not be available.

Obsessions Many agoraphobics experience obsessions, which are persistent and recurrent ideas, thoughts, impulses or images that occur involuntarily as ideas that invade consciousness. Obsessional behavior is usually present before an individual develops agoraphobia. Individuals may develop obsessional thinking about certain places, situations or objects that might cause them to experience their fear reaction. Obsessional thinking is difficult to control, often distorts or exaggerates reality and causes much anticipatory anxiety. Individuals may develop compulsive behavior in an attempt to reduce obsessional thoughts and resultant anxiety. Some agoraphobics often have obsessive symptoms, such as ritual checking or thoughts of harming others or themselves.

Causes For some individuals, learned experiences condition them to regard the world as a dangerous place. Many agoraphobics have had at least one agoraphobic parent, and many have had at least one parent who is somewhat fearful. In some cases, they received mixed messages from their parents; while they were encouraged to achieve, they were not well prepared to deal with the world, either because they were overprotected—taught that home is the only safe place—or underprotected, having to take on too much responsibility at an early age.

Recent studies have suggested evidence for a genetic predisposition to panic disorder. Family history studies have found panic disorder to be as much as 10 times more frequent in the biologic relatives of those with panic disorder as among normal control subjects.

The biologic basis for panic attacks and resultant agoraphobia is being researched, and theories abound. Symptoms of panic attacks, such as palpitations, sweating and tremulousness, lead to a theory that they are the result of massive discharges from the adrenergic nervous system. (Some studies suggest that beta-blocking agents such as propranolol may ameliorate panic attacks.)

The triazolobenzodiazepine drug alprazolam (trade name: Xanax) has been approved by the Food and Drug Administration for the treatment of panic attacks or panic disorder. Imipramine or monoamine oxidase inhibitors (MAOIs) such as phenelzine (trade name: Nardil) are helpful in suppressing panic attacks.

Another hypothesis is that panic attacks result from increased discharge in the locus coeruleus and increased central noradrenergic turnover. While electrical stimulation of this structure in the brains of animals has been shown to produce fear and anxiety, relevance of these animal studies to anxiety disorders in humans is unclear.

Researchers have found that intravenous infusion of sodium lactate will provoke a panic attack in most panic disorder sufferers, but not in normal subjects. The mechanism by which this occurs is not clear; further study may lead to an understanding of the biochemical factors in the etiology of panic attacks.

Treatment Treatment is usually targeted toward several aspects of the agoraphobic syndrome: agoraphobia, panic attacks and anticipatory anxiety. A variety of treatments are used, sometimes in sequence or in combination. Treatment of agoraphobia is more complicated than treatment of simple phobias because panic attacks themselves seem to be the basis of the disorder.

Many treatments are based on exposure therapy. A major component of treatment involves exposing the agoraphobic to situations that are commonly avoided and frightening in order to demonstrate that there is no actual danger. Treatment may include direct exposure, such as having the individual walk or drive away from a safe place or a safe person or enter a crowded shopping center. Indirect exposure is also used; this may involve use of films with fear-arousing cues. Systematic desensitization is included in this category, as this procedure is characterized by exposure (either in imagination or in vivo) to the least reactive elements of a situation or object until the anxiety response no longer occurs. Then a slightly more reactive element or item is presented and so on until the individual can be exposed to the most critical aspect without a strong anxiety response. Another imaginal procedure for anxiety treatment includes flooding or continuous presentation of the most reactive elements of a situation until anxiety reduction occurs.

Behavior therapy is used to treat many agoraphobics. This includes educating individuals about their reactions to anxiety-producing situations, explaining the physiology and genetics involved (where applicable) and teaching breathing exercises to help overcome hyperventilation. In many cases, three to six months of behavior therapy is effective, and subsequent supportive and behavioral techniques reduce the anxiety level and help individuals master their fear of recurrent attacks in specific situations.

Also known as in vivo therapy, exposure therapy uses real-life exposure to the threat. Facing the fearful situation with appropriate reinforcement may help an individual undo the learned fear. Some therapists set specific goals for the sufferer for each week, such as walking one block from home, then two and three, taking a bus and progressing after each session. Particularly in the early stages of treatment, many therapists accompany agoraphobic individuals as they venture into public places. In some cases, spouses or family members are trained to accompany the agoraphobic individual; other therapists recommend structured group therapy with defined goals and social skill training for the agoraphobic and their families.

Psychotherapy With psychotherapy, agoraphobics learn to resolve past conflicts that may have contributed to their agoraphobic state. Psychotherapy is often used in conjunction with an attempt to relieve symptoms with behavioral therapies and possibly drug therapy.

Drug Therapy The treatment of choice today for agoraphobia involves the use of behavioral exposure therapy and careful use of medication, with the latter withdrawn as progress is made in behavioral therapy. Particularly for those who have panic attacks, drug therapy initially seems to enhance results of exposure-based treatments. In many cases, drugs are used for three to six months and then discontinued once the individual has some control over bodily sensations. Some individuals never experience recurrence of attacks, while attacks return months or years later for others. When attacks recur, a second course of drug therapy is often successful.

A variety of drugs are used in the treatment of panic attacks associated with agoraphobia. These include the tricyclic antidepressants and the MAOIs (which are also used to treat severe depression) and alprazolam, an antianxiety drug. For many individuals, panic attacks are successfully controlled with use of particular tricyclic antidepressants (imipramine, desipramine or clomipramine). MAOIs are often used as second-line medications when patients do not respond to a tricyclic.

Free-floating or anticipatory anxiety is often treated with selective use of a benzodiazepine (for example, oxazepam) or alprazolam (Xanax) alone, because it both reduces anticipatory anxiety and blocks panic attacks. Xanax has recently been approved by the Food and Drug Administration to treat symptoms of panic attacks. Clonazepam (trade name: Klonopin) is a newer benzodiazepine that is also thought to have antipanic properties, but it has not yet been well studied. Buspirone (trade name: Buspar), a nonbenzodiazepine antianxiety agent, is less sedating and less prone to be abused than the benzodiazepines, but its efficacy in panic disorder is still under study.

Involvement of spouses and family members usually produces more continuing improvement with better results than treatment involving the agoraphobic alone. Greater improvement occurs because of the motivation for continued "practice" in facing feared situations both between sessions and after treatment is completed. Home-based treatment, where individuals proceed at their own pace within a structured treatment program, produces fewer dropouts than the more intensive, prolonged exposure or pharmacologic treatments.

Self-help Self-help groups for agoraphobic people encourage participants to offer one another mutual support in going out. As recovery from agoraphobia is a long-term process, self-help groups can provide valuable support. Individuals share common experiences and coping tips and have an additional social outlet. Some agoraphobics get together for outings, help take children to and from school, arrange programs and retrain themselves out of their fears and anxieties.

Alcoholism and Agoraphobia Because alcohol is somewhat effective in relieving chronic anticipatory anxiety, some agoraphobics move toward alcoholism in an unsuccessful attempt to prevent panic. However, alcohol may even exacerbate panic by bringing about a feeling of loss of control and causing strange body sensations. Moreover, the use of alcohol may interfere with effective treatment of the agoraphobia, as central nervous system depressants reduce the efficacy of exposure treatment. However, some agoraphobic men avoid social situations in which alcohol is not served and believe that alcohol helps to calm them before they venture out into public.

Agoraphobics who abuse alcohol and nonalcoholic agoraphobics may both have histories of disturbed childhoods. Disturbed childhoods of alcoholic agoraphobics frequently include familial alcoholism and depression. In addition, children whose early attachments to caretakers are characterized by lack of consistent support as well as frightening and dangerous interactions may fail to develop a sense of trust and security. Such individuals may be particularly vulnerable to later psychopathology, such as panic attacks and agoraphobia; alcoholism may be one mode of coping for such individuals.

The clinical picture of both agoraphobia and alcoholism often involves depression. Agoraphobics who are alcohol abusers may also be more socially anxious than their nonalcoholic peers. High rates of social phobia have been noted among inpatient alcoholics, and major depression has been found to increase both the likelihood and intensity of agoraphobia and social anxieties.

See also ALCOHOLISM; ANTIDEPRESSANT MEDICATIONS; ANXIETY; BEHAVIORAL THERAPY; CLAUSTROPHOBIA; DEPRESSION; ANXIETIES AND ANXIETY DISORDERS in BIBLIOGRAPHY.

Doctor, Ronald M., and Kahn, Ada P. *Encyclopedia of Phobias, Fears, and Anxieties.* New York: Facts On File, 1989.

Barlow, D. H., and Waddell, Maria T. "Agoraphobia," in Barlow, David H., ed., *Clinical Handbook of Psychological Disorders.* New York: Guilford Press, 1985.

Frampton, Muriel. *Agoraphobia: Coping with the World Outside.* Wellingstorough, Northamptonshire, England: Turnstone Press, 1984.

Kahn, Ada P. "Panic Attacks." *Chicago Tribune,* June 23, 1991.

Marks, Isaac M. *Fears, Phobias and Rituals.* New York: Oxford University Press, 1987.

McFarland, Gertrude K., and Thomas, Mary Durand. *Psychiatric Mental Health Nursing.* Philadelphia: J. B. Lippincott, 1991.

Waldinger, Robert J. *Psychiatry for Medical Students.* Washington, D.C.: American Psychiatric Press, 1990.

AIDS-related complex (ARC) A condition affecting some persons with HIV infection. Common symptoms include fatigue, weight loss, diarrhea and oral candidiasis. Some symptoms become severe enough to cause disability. Some persons in this group will suffer further damage to their immune system and will ultimately be diagnosed as having AIDS (acquired immunodeficiency syndrome). Persons who have been diagnosed as having ARC have a high level of anxiety related to their health status and may have depression related to changes in their life-style and possible impending death, fears related to loss of control, pain and suffering, powerlessness related to feelings of stigmatization and possible guilt related to having caused HIV infection through behavior (for example, needle sharing or sexual practices).

See also ACQUIRED IMMUNODEFICIENCY SYNDROME; ACQUIRED IMMUNODEFICIENCY SYNDROME in BIBLIOGRAPHY.

akathisia   An inability to sit still, which sometimes occurs as a side effect of an antipsychotic drug used to treat mental disorders such as depression and schizophrenia. Akathisia also occurs as a rare complication of Parkinson's disease.

Al-Anon   An organization for the families of alcoholics who belong to Alcoholics Anonymous, formed as a support system for those who want to cope better with the problems of living with an alcoholic. Spouses, children and parents meet with others who have similar concerns.

See also ALATEEN; ALCOHOLICS ANONYMOUS; ALCOHOLISM.

Alateen   An organization for teenagers from 12 to 20 who have been affected by someone, usually a parent, with a drinking problem. Alateen was started in 1957 by a boy in California whose father was an alcoholic in Alcoholics Anonymous (AA) and whose mother was in Al-Anon. Alateen was patterned after Al-Anon and shares with it the same Twelve Steps and Twelve Traditions. Alateen meetings are conducted by teenagers with an adult member of Al-Anon as a sponsor.

See also AL-ANON; ALCOHOLICS ANONYMOUS; ALCOHOLISM.

alcohol amnestic disorder   See ALCOHOLISM.

alcohol dependence   An illness characterized by compulsive, habitual, long-term heavy consumption of alcohol and withdrawal symptoms when intake of alcohol suddenly ceases. Estimates indicate that there are approximately 5 million alcohol-dependent persons in the United States.

Factors that lead to alcohol dependence include personality, environment and the addictive nature of the drug alcohol. Insecure or immature personalities are more at risk than more emotionally mature individuals. Many individuals are led to dependence on alcohol during times of stress, such as bereavement, while undergoing divorce or while facing other major illnesses, either of self or a close family member.

In some cases genetic factors may play a role in causing dependence. Environmental factors are important because of the widespread social acceptance of alcohol in the individual's culture, ready availability and affordability. Dependence on alcohol is more common in certain countries and social groups than in others.

In the first phase of dependence on alcohol, the heavy social drinker feels no effects from alcohol. In the second phase, the drinker experiences memory lapses relating to events that happen during drinking episodes. In the third phase, there is lack of control over alcohol, and the drinker cannot be certain of discontinuing to drink by choice. The final phase begins with long binges of intoxication, and there are observable mental or physical complications.

Behavioral symptoms may include hiding bottles, aggressive or grandiose behavior, irritability, jealousy, uncontrolled anger, frequent change of jobs, repeated promises to self and others to give up drinking and neglect of proper eating habits and personal appearance. Physical symptoms may include unsteadiness, confusion, poor memory, nausea, vomiting, shaking, weakness in the legs and hands, irregular pulse and redness and enlarged capillaries in the face. Alcohol-dependent persons are more susceptible than others to a variety of physical and mental disorders.

Medical help for alcohol dependence includes detoxification, or assistance in overcoming withdrawal symptoms, and psychological, social and physical treatments. Psychotherapy is usually done in groups, using a variety of techniques. Therapists for alcoholic-dependent persons may be psychiatrists, psychologists or social workers. Social treatments involve family members in the treatment process. Alcoholic-dependent persons are advised to become involved in self-help groups such as Alcoholics Anonymous.

See also ALCOHOLICS ANONYMOUS.

Alcoholics Anonymous (AA) An international organization devoted to the maintenance of sobriety of its members and control over the compulsive urge to drink through self-help, mutual support, fellowship and understanding. The program includes the individual's admission that he or she cannot control his or her drinking, the sharing of experiences, problems and concerns at meetings, and helping others who are in need of support.

The ''desire to stop drinking'' is at the core of the program. Members follow a 12-step program, which stresses faith, disavowal of personal responsibility, passivity in the hands of God or a higher power, confession of wrongdoing and response to spiritual awakening by sharing with others.

See also AL-ANON; ALCOHOLISM.

O'Brien, Robert, and Chafetz, Morris. *The Encyclopedia of Alcoholism.* New York: Facts On File, 1982.

alcoholism A chronic disorder associated with excessive consumption of alcohol over a period of time. Most authorities recognize alcoholism as a disease, although some say that it is a self-inflicted condition and cannot properly be designated a disease. Nevertheless, it is a physiological and psychological dependence on alcohol and therefore an addiction. Alcohol exerts mental and physical effects and becomes a major part of the dependent person's life.

Many people become dependent on alcohol for relief of symptoms ranging from loneliness to anxiety and panic attacks. Some agoraphobics become alcoholics as a way of coping with their fears. Because agoraphobic individuals do not go out, it is fairly easy for them to conceal their habit.

The term ''alcoholism'' was coined by Magnus Huss, a Swedish scientist, in 1852, when he identified a condition involving abuse of alcohol and labeled it ''alkoholismus chronicus.'' However, references to alcoholism are found in earlier works of Benjamin Rush, an 18th-century American physician, Cauder and the Roman philosopher Seneca. In 1956 the American Medical Association and the American Bar Association officially recognized alcoholism as a disease with a landmark resolution that affected the legal status of alcoholics, alcoholism-related state and federal laws, program financing, insurance coverage and hospital admissions.

Alcohol Problems Missed by Physicians
A study published in the *Journal of the American Medical Association* (Feb. 4, 1992) indicated that physicians may not be catching their patients' alcohol use and abuse. According to Diana Chapman Walsh, Ph.D., Department of Health and Social Behavior, Harvard School of Public Health, Boston, the signal findings of this study underscore the need for greater vigilance on the part of practicing physicians to alert their patients to potential hazards associated with heavy or problem drinking.

Dr. Walsh and her colleagues reported on 200 problem drinkers at a large New England manufacturing plant. The study participants' drinking problems were identified by the company's Employee Assistance Program (EAP) between February 1, 1982 and June 20, 1987. Each subject was followed for two years. The mean age of the subjects was 32 years. Subjects were overwhelmingly male (96 percent) and white (90 percent).

About half (51 percent) graduated from high school but not college; 47 percent had annual family incomes under $25,000. "Of the 200 seriously impaired workers in the sample, only 15 percent recalled warning that their abuse of alcohol might be compromising their health during the year before being identified on the job. Fully 74 percent (148) of the workers identified on the job had seen physicians in that year, but only 22 percent of them recalled health warnings. That the manifestations of alcohol abuse are overt enough to bring these heavy drinkers to the attention of intervention programs at work during the course of the year in which they have visited physicians lends further weight to the argument that many physicians are not sufficiently alert to their patients' alcohol use and abuse."

In an editorial accompanying the study, Thomas L. Delbanco, M.D., of the Division of General Medicine and Primary Care, Beth Israel Hospital, Boston, wrote: "Walsh and colleagues bring us both good and bad news . . . Welcome is their suggestion that when doctors address alcoholism with their patients, the outcome may improve. Confirming earlier reports, however, the bad news is the continuing inference that doctors are often loathe to intervene with patients who abuse alcohol."

Delbanco noted that physicians' reticence may result from a desire not to stigmatize or insult their patients, from confusion over what to do once a diagnosis of alcoholism is made, from concern about the time demands treating an alcoholic requires or from discomfort addressing the issue given the physician's own drinking. Delbanco pointed to an increase in the number of teaching institutions with programs focusing on the diagnosis and treatment of alcoholism and a "growing public consciousness" of the toll alcoholism takes. He concluded by saying: "As we grapple increasingly with chronic diseases, we encounter few where our intervention can be pivotal in turning patients away from a progressive, debilitating, and often tragic illness toward a fully healthy life. Alcoholism provides both patient and doctor with that opportunity."

Abstinence May Improve Alcoholics' Life Span According to a study published in the *Journal of the American Medical Association* (Jan. 4, 1992), alcoholics who go dry may improve their life expectancy. Results of a study support the notion that the achievement of stable abstinence reduces the risk of premature death among alcoholics. Kim D. Bullock, Psychiatry and Research Services, Veterans Affairs Medical Center, San Diego, and colleagues reported on 199 men who had histories of at least five years of drinking at alcoholic levels. All were current or former patients of the V.A. Alcoholism Treatment Program and/or members of Alcoholics Anonymous. The men were recruited from 1976 to 1987. Followup on relapse and mortality was obtained; 101 men had relapsed and 98 were abstinent. A control group of 92 nonalcoholics equated for age, education and sex were also studied for mortality. There were 19 deaths among the relapsed alcoholics, compared with the expected number of 3.83. There were four deaths among abstinent alcoholics. Alcoholic men who achieved stable abstinence did not differ from nonalcoholic men in mortality experience. However, alcoholics who relapsed died at a rate 4.96 times that of an age-, sex- and race-matched representative sample.

Possible Association Between Genes and Alcoholism In late 1991, an article published in the *Journal of the American Medical Association* reported that a gene possibly associated with alcoholism may not cause the condition but may increase the expression of its symptoms, as well as those of a number of other behavioral, neurological and psychiatric disorders. According to David E. Comings, M.D., Department of Medical Genetics, City of Hope National Medical Center, Duarte, California, "Results suggest the A1 allele of the DRD2 gene is associated with a number of behavior disorders in which it may act as a modifying gene rather than as the primary etiologic agent. As such, the DRD2 gene would not be genetically linked to alcoholism, but the A1 allele could be more frequent in some groups of alcoholics than in controls.''

The gene in question, DRD2 (the dopamine D2 receptor gene), helps structure the brain's reward system, including drug (including alcohol)-seeking behavior. DRD2 comes in one of two versions, either A1 allele or A2 allele. At issue is whether the appearance of DRD2 in the A1 version, instead of A2, puts someone at a higher risk for alcoholism. The authors looked for the prevalence of A1 in 314 non-Hispanic whites across a number of disorders, including alcoholism, attention-deficit hyperactivity disorder (ADHD), autism, drug addiction, major depression, obesity, panic attacks, Parkinson's disease, post-traumatic stress disorder, schizophrenia and Tourette Syndrome. The homogeneous study population was used to minimize the effect of racial differences in gene frequencies.

Of the 314 total controls, they found 24.5 percent carried the A1 allele. Of the 69 controls known not to be alcoholics, 14.5 percent carried the A1 allele.

They found the prevalence of the A1 allele significantly increased in patients with Tourette syndrome (44.9 percent, $n = 147$); ADHD (46.2 percent, $n = 104$); autism (54.5 percent, $n = 33$); alcoholism (42.3 percent, $n = 104$) and post-traumatic stress disorder (45.7 percent, $n = 35$). The prevalence of the A1 allele was not significantly increased in patients with depression, panic attacks, Parkinson's disease or obesity. They reported that the prevalence of the A1 allele in drug addiction and schizophrenia was only significant when compared with that of controls who were not alcoholics, and no correction was made for multiple comparisons.

According to the authors, if A1 of DRD2 acts as a modifying gene, it does not itself cause a disorder. ''In individuals who have another disease gene, the presence of the A1

allele may result in a modest increase in the expression of symptoms, as compared with individuals who do not carry the A1 allele.'' However, the researchers cautioned that these results should be considered preliminary until large studies can be completed.

See also ADDICTION; AGORAPHOBIA; ALCOHOL DEPENDENCE; CODEPENDENCY; EMPLOYEE ASSISTANCE PROGRAMS; ENABLER; ALCOHOLISM in BIBLIOGRAPHY.

American Medical Association. News releases, Oct. 1, 1991, Jan. 4, 1992 and Feb. 4, 1992 (Paul Tarini).

O'Brien, Robert, and Chafetz, Morris. *The Encyclopedia of Alcoholism.* New York: Facts On File, 1982.

alexithymia   An inability to express emotion.

algolagnia   A psychiatric term for a disorder in which an individual derives sexual excitement by inflicting pain on his or her partner (sadism), experiencing pain (masochism) or both (sadomasochism).

See also MASOCHISM; SADISM; SADOMASOCHISM.

alienation   A term that relates to withdrawal or separation of one's affections from an object or position of former attachment or from the values of one's family and culture. The term also refers to estrangement from one's own feelings. Alienation causes an individual to feel powerless and isolated. Boredom and depression may follow.

Alienation is a characteristic of obsessive-compulsive disorder and also occurs in extreme forms of schizophrenia.

See also DEPERSONALIZATION; OBSESSIVE-COMPULSIVE DISORDER; SCHIZOPHRENIA.

alliance, therapeutic   An individual's active collaboration with the treatment process for a mental health problem. The concept arose out of psychoanalysis but now applies to relationships with individuals in other settings as well. Therapeutic alliance correlates highly with therapeutic outcomes. Some individuals in treatment for a mental health problem may have difficulty at first in establishing a good therapeutic alliance because of anxiety about changing behavior and continuation of defense mechanisms.

Therapeutic alliance is encouraged by all mental health practitioners through respect, empathy and hope and assessing the individual's specific reasons for low therapeutic alliance, such as acknowledging the client's need to set goals and help the client find behaviors that make those goals possible.

See also SELF-HELP GROUPS.

alogia   A general term referring to impoverished thought processes that often occur in individuals who have schizophrenia. Persons with alogia have thinking processes that seem slow or empty. Because thinking cannot be seen, it is inferred from the individual's speech.

alpha adrenergic blockers   See ADRENERGIC BLOCKING AGENTS; ADRENERGIC MEDICATIONS.

alpha adrenergic function   See ADRENERGIC SYSTEM.

alprazolam   An antianxiety drug (also referred to as an anxiolytic or sedative) marketed under the trade name Xanax. Alprazolam is a member of the drug group known as the benzodiazepines. It has been useful in treating some individuals for anticipatory anxiety and panic attacks and in some cases of depression, particularly in mixed states of depression and anxiety. Alprazolam causes sedation and lethargy, and the clinical reasons for its antidepressant effects are still unknown. Studies have shown that it has no effect on nerve cell receptors that are targets of some antidepressive drugs.

Alprazolam offers effects comparable to tricyclic antidepressants and is often used as an antidepressant for individuals who have a high degree of anxiety and agitation. Alprazolam seems to have no cardiac side effects and is therefore applicable in treatment of anxious or depressed cardiac patients. As with other drugs of this class, dependency develops and withdrawal effects can occur. These can be prevented by tapering off the dosage of the drug gradually or relying on other drugs.

Alprazolam has been approved by the Food and Drug Administration for the treatment of panic disorder.

See also ANTIDEPRESSANT MEDICATIONS, BENZODIAZEPINE MEDICATIONS.

Fawcett, Jan A., and Kravitz, Howard M. "Alprazolam: Pharmacokinetics, Clinical Efficacy and Mechanism of Action." *Pharmacotherapy* 2, no. 5 (Sept.–Oct. 1982).

alternative therapies   Medical treatments that may seem incompatible with the science of medicine as it is taught in established medical schools.

Many such therapies have a holistic emphasis, holding that mind and body are one and that the individual cannot be understood out of the context of the environment in which he or she functions. Usually alternative therapies do not involve pharmacologic therapy.

In the 17th century, disease was seen as a breakdown of the body that only health professionals could heal. Later it became evident that what people did for themselves could have healing as well as health-promoting effects. During several centuries, many forms of alternatives to traditional medical treatment have evolved to improve mental and physical health.

Alternative therapies for healing mind as well as body include emotional release therapies with or without body manipulation, emotional control or self-regulating therapies, religious or inspirational therapies, cognitive-emotional therapies and emotional expression through creative therapies. Some of these have been known by names including encounter groups, gestalt therapy, primal therapy, EST, bioenergetic psychotherapy, rolfing, Z-therapy, transcendental meditation and biofeedback. It is important to remember that alternative therapies are not subject to scientific scrutiny through controlled efficacy studies with placebo or comparisons of treatments. They are accepted and promoted as helping on the basis of "anecdotal evidence" stemming from individual reports of success. Some may be truly helpful but others useless or ineffectual, with their use based on enthusiasm and strong belief.

Many individuals find relief for mental health problems from one or more or combinations of alternative therapies either along with or after seeking traditional care. However, as with other medical conditions, seriously troubled individuals should not overlook traditional psychiatric or medical treatments in favor of alternative therapies because they may be robbing themselves of valuable time as their condition progresses.

See also ENCOUNTER GROUP; PRIMAL THERAPY; TRANSCENDENTAL MEDITATION.

Alzheimer's disease   A progressive, irreversible neurological disorder that is the most common cause of dementia, named in 1907 by Alois Alzheimer (1864–1915) after diagnosing a 51-year-old patient. Currently, there are more than 4 million Americans who have Alzheimer's disease (AD). As the population continues to age, an increase in the incidence of the disease is anticipated. Although there is no cure (in the early 1990s), there are many research projects under way worldwide, and researchers increasingly understand more about the disease. More than 100,000 Americans die from Alzheimer's disease each year.

In late 1991, Congress voted to increase the government's investment in battling Alzheimer's disease to $284 million, about twice the amount spent two years previously. Most of the funds were to be directed toward finding a cure or effective treatment, testing promising new drugs and helping reduce the burden the disease places on families. A portion of the funds was earmarked to launch a new $4 million program to help states coordinate services available to families, such as respite care, adult day care and counseling.

Symptoms   Symptoms of Alzheimer's disease vary in rate of change from person to person. However, they generally include gradual loss of memory (particularly for recent events); dwindling powers of judgment, reasoning and understanding; disorientation; personality changes; an inability to perform normal activities of daily living; difficulty in learning; loss of language skills and general intellectual deterioration. The dementia is progressive, degenerative and irreversible, and eventually patients become totally incapable of caring for themselves. For caregivers of Alzheimer's sufferers, it is a very frustrating and dehumanizing condition to witness. It has been referred to as "old timer's disease," although it may occur as early as age 40. More commonly, it occurs in those 65 years of age and older. It is the fourth leading cause of death for people over age 65. More women than men are affected, but that may be because women statistically outlive men. Alzheimer's disease is a major cause for admission to long-term care facilities and nursing homes.

Symptoms of Alzheimer's should not be confused with age-associated memory impairment (AAMI), a term health care professionals use to describe minor memory difficulties that come with age. According to the Alzheimer's Disease and Related Disorders Association, Inc., there are some differences between AAMI and Alzheimer's.

Causes   Although causes are unknown, there are several theoretical explanations. Suspected causes include a genetic predisposition, a slow virus or other infectious agent, environmental toxins such as aluminum and immunologic changes.

One theory suggests that there may be a diminished concentration of choline acetyltransferase in the brain of Alzheimer's sufferers, which is necessary for normal communication between nerve cells. Defects

Some Differences Between Age-Associated Memory Impairment and Alzheimer's Disease

Activity	Alzheimer's Patient	AAMI
Forgets	Whole experience	Part of an experience
Remembers later	Rarely	Often
Follows written or spoken directions	Gradually unable	Usually able
Able to use notes, reminders	Gradually unable	Usually able
Able to care for self	Gradually unable	Usually able

in this neurotransmitter result in impaired memory and impaired learning.

Another theory is that higher-than-normal levels of aluminum deposits in the brain act as a toxin. In addition, the theory regarding impairment of the immune system contends that abnormally high levels of antibodies cause the immune system to attack its own cells. Impaired immune function causes many Alzheimer's sufferers to die of infections, including pneumonia. The slow-acting virus theory contends that because similar central nervous system diseases have been detected in animals, there may be a linkage in humans.

Diagnosis Before diagnosis of Alzheimer's disease is made, the physician will want to rule out other conditions, such as potentially reversible depression, adverse drug reactions, metabolic changes, nutritional deficiencies, head injuries and stroke. Until the last decade, when more technologically sophisticated testing procedures became available, many sufferers were misdiagnosed and consequently mistreated. For example, screen star Rita Hayworth was misdiagnosed with alcoholic dementia in the 1970s and was later diagnosed as suffering from Alzheimer's disease, from which she died in 1987. Her film career had ended when she could not remember her lines.

Diagnosis usually begins with a search for treatable causes for memory loss and mental changes. Evaluation includes screening for depression, previous history of mental illness and assessment of the overall mental state. Many diagnostic procedures may be done. These include blood studies, computerized axial tomography (CAT scan) and electroencephalogram (EEG). In some cases a lumbar puncture is done to rule out neurosyphilis, which can cause inability to carry out purposeful movements (apraxia), inability to express thoughts (aphasia) and an inability to recognize items (agnosia). The CAT scan for an individual who has Alzheimer's disease typically shows brain shrinkage. The EEG is characteristically slow in an Alzheimer's sufferer.

Course of the Disease Many individuals who have Alzheimer's disease live an average of six to eight years, while others live as long as 20 years. There are three progressive stages to the disease. In Stage One, symptoms start to become noticeable and are mild. There may be memory loss, but often this is associated with the aging process. Recent memory is affected, and the ability to learn and retain new information is impaired. Individuals may resort to writing themselves notes and labeling drawers and cabinets to remind themselves of items used in everyday living. There may be difficulty in concentrating or engaging in conversation without losing train of thought, tiredness and an unkempt appearance. Individuals at this stage often blame others for what is happening to them. They feel out of control, and many become depressed. Personality changes include becoming easily angered, particularly at the inability to communicate thoughts clearly. This stage may last two to four years.

In Stage Two of the disease, symptoms become more severe, losses increase and there are more marked changes in behavior. There is less ability to comprehend what is being said. Words are used in wrong and senseless combination (paraphasia), and there is an inability to recognize objects (visual agnosia). Supervision of daily activities may become necessary. There is increasing disorientation regarding time and place. Some sufferers do not recognize themselves in the mirror, and others do not recognize their spouses or children. Confusion often increases in the late evening (sundown syndrome). Bladder or bowel incontinence may develop; the individual may forget where the bathroom is or be unable to undress and use the facilities. Impaired gait develops, and the body weakens.

In Stage Three, signs and symptoms continue to progress until there is a deterioration causing the person to become bedridden.

Research and Treatment Although there is no cure for Alzheimer's disease, research efforts have contributed significantly to the quality of life for patients. A cornerstone of therapy is a team approach, with medical, psychological, neurological, pharmacologic and physical rehabilitation specialists working closely with family members to encourage the patient and attempt to slow the rate of mental and physical deterioration. According to the Alzheimer's Disease and Related Disorders Association, Inc. (ADRDA), good planning and medical and social management can ease the burdens on the patient and family. Appropriate medication can lessen agitation, anxiety and unpredictable behavior, improve sleeping patterns and treat depression. Physical exercise and social activity are important, as are proper nutrition and health maintenance. A calm and well-structured environment may help the afflicted person to maintain as much comfort and dignity as possible. Local chapters of

the ADRDA may be able to refer concerned individuals to appropriate medical resources in their area.

Researchers are applying the latest research techniques in molecular genetics, histology, virology, immunology, toxicology, neurology, psychiatry, pharmacology, biochemistry and epidemiology to find the possible causes and better treatments for Alzheimer's disease and related dementias.

Reports on Alzheimer's disease suggest that some cases are inherited. In addition, some people with Down's syndrome who live to the age of 40 or older develop Alzheimer's disease.

There are many investigations under way regarding medications and other treatments. One relates to the use of acetylcholine-like drugs that block the breakdown of acetylcholine and of foods that enhance its production. Vasopressin, a hormone, has been used with some success to improve memory in some patients. Lecithin has been found to increase production of acetylcholine in the blood, but results are inconclusive. Aluminum buildup in the brain has been considered a contributing factor to memory loss, and to eliminate aluminum buildup, drugs that bond with the aluminum and eliminate it from the body (chelating agents) have been used.

Other research revolves around short-term use of very-low-dose neuroleptics in controlling agitation and behavioral disturbances that occur in later stages of the disease. Short-term use is emphasized because of the possibility of causing tardive dyskinesia, a side effect that may become permanent with long-term use of neuroleptics. Chlorpromazine (Thorazine) and thioridazine hydrochloride (Mellaril) are two drugs sometimes prescribed to control agitation. Haloperidol (Haldol) is sometimes prescribed for violent behavior. Chloral hydrate is sometimes prescribed for insomnia and night restlessness.

When Alzheimer's patients have symptoms of depression that appear to be worsening, tricyclic antidepressants may be prescribed.

Both the health care team and the family should be aware of side effects of medications as well as interactions of medications and possible adverse drug reactions. Effects of such interactions and reactions should not be confused with disease symptoms.

Alzheimer's patients often exhibit signs of sundown syndrome, which is an increase in restlessness and verbal behaviors late in the afternoon and early evening, observed by researchers in nursing home populations.

Caregivers of Alzheimer's Patients According to Jerome H. Stone, president of the National Alzheimer's Disease and Related Disorders Association, "It is the disease that robs the mind of the victim and breaks the heart of the family." Alzheimer's disease can be an extraordinarily demanding and frustrating experience, both for those afflicted with the disease and for their families. Caring for a parent, grandparent or spouse whose mind is deteriorating requires stamina and patience. Confronted with a disease that afflicts the mind of a loved one, care-giving family members often feel alone and helpless. However, support groups and friends can be helpful, as can senior day-care centers.

In addition to the emotional strain on the caregiver, there may be financial expenses, such as reconstructing living arrangements for the safety and convenience of the patient, giving up a job to devote full time to care, hiring people to provide part-time care or do household chores and possibly paying for nursing home care, which may or may not be covered by health insurance.

The following guidelines for caregivers were compiled by the Pennsylvania Hospital, Philadelphia:

- Take one day at a time, tackling each problem as it arises. One cannot know how an Alzheimer's patient will behave the next day.
- Try to put yourself in the patient's shoes. You will feel less annoyed the 10th time

you are asked what day it is if you imagine how unsettling it must be not to be oriented in time and space.
- Maintain a sense of humor. This is especially valuable in getting through potentially embarrassing situations.
- Arrange for time for yourself. Get another family member or friend to relieve you for an hour or two each day. Hire a part-time caretaker. Arrange for the patient to spend time at a senior day-care facility.
- Pay attention to your own needs. Be sure to maintain good nutrition and get regular exercise; develop hobbies and outside interests. Find people you can talk to such as family members, friends or, if needed, professional counselors.

Writing in *The Quill,* a publication of the Pennsylvania Hospital, Todd Iscovitz advised those who give care to AD patients to keep in mind that the elderly and afflicted never outgrow their need for love and affection. What is most important in caring for a loved one is being honest with oneself. Know your limitations and recognize when the burden of care giving is too much. If your own health starts to fail or if you are feeling overwhelmed, consider other care alternatives. These guidelines for caregivers apply to caregivers of patients with other disorders as well.

Toll-Free Information Line The Alzheimer's Association has a national, toll-free information and referral service telephone number. The 800 line offers callers the most current information available on Alzheimer's disease and support services through the association. The number is: (800) 272-3900.

Alzheimer's Disease and Related Disorders Association (ADRDA) A privately funded national voluntary health organization, founded in 1980, headquartered in Chicago. ADRDA has over 1,000 support groups and 160 chapters and affiliates nationwide. ADRDA's board of directors is composed of business leaders, health professionals and family members. A medical and scientific advisory board consults on and monitors related issues.

Goals of ADRDA include supporting research on causes, treatments, cures and prevention; stimulating education and public awareness of both lay people and professionals; encouraging chapter formation for nationwide family support networks; implementation of programs at the local level; advocacy for improved public policy and legislation at federal, state and local levels; and patient and family services to aid present and future sufferers and caregivers.

Alzheimer's Disease International was formed in 1984 to share program and research developments on Alzheimer's disease worldwide.

To contact ADRDA:

Alzheimer's Disease and Related Disorders Association
70 East Lake Street
Chicago, IL 60601
Phone: (312) 853-3060

The nationwide hot-line number is (800) 621-0379.

See also ACETYLCHOLINE; CREUTZFELDT-JAKOB DISEASE; DEMENTIA; DEPRESSION; HUNTINGTON'S DISEASE; NORMAL PRESSURE HYDROCEPHALUS; PARKINSON'S DISEASE; PICK'S DISEASE; SUNDOWNING; SUPPORT GROUPS.

The Quill, Pennsylvania Hospital, Philadelphia (Summer 1990).

ambisexuality   Sexual behavior related to erotic interest in both males and females. The term was introduced by Sandor Ferenczi (1873–1933), a Hungarian psychoanalyst and an associate and follower of Sigmund Freud, to identify the psychological aspects of bisexuality. Ambisexuality also refers to the possession of sexual characteristics that are both male and female, such as pubic hair.

See also TRANSSEXUALISM.

ambivalence   The existence of two sometimes contradictory feelings, attitudes, values or goals at the same time. For example, some individuals have feelings of ambivalence toward a mate whom they love but who abuses them. Other individuals are ambivalent about work and other major life issues. The term was introduced by Eugen Bleuler, a Swiss psychiatrist (1857–1939), to refer to the simultaneous feelings of antagonistic emotions, such as approach or avoidance of the same activity or goal. Ambivalence is a characteristic of some individuals who have schizophrenia.

See also AGORAPHOBIA; SCHIZOPHRENIA.

ambulatory mental health organizations   There are a group of these organizations, many of which were classified prior to 1981 as federally funded community mental health centers (CMHCs). The types of organizations under this label include: (1) freestanding psychiatric outpatient clinics (OPCs), organizations that only provide services on an outpatient basis; (2) freestanding partial care organizations (PCs), organizations that only provide partial care services; and (3) multiservice mental health organizations (multiservice MHOs), facilities that provide services in outpatient programs as well as in partial care programs and in inpatient/residential programs.

The number of ambulatory mental health organizations with outpatient services rose progressively from 228 in 1970 to 1,243 in 1986. The number providing partial care grew from 333 in 1970 to 1,161 in 1980 and then decreased to 952 in 1982 before increasing to a high of 1,317 organizations in 1986.

See also OUTPATIENT.

National Institute of Mental Health. *Mental Health, United States, 1990.* Manderscheid, R. W., and Sonnenschein, M. A., eds. DHHS Pub. No. (ADM) 90-1708. Washington, D.C.: USGPO, 1990.

American Association of Suicidology (AAS)

A not-for-profit, tax-exempt organization whose goal is to understand and prevent suicide and to help suicide prevention centers throughout the United States and Canada. The work of AAS includes promoting research, public awareness and training for professionals and volunteers. Membership includes mental health professionals, researchers, suicide prevention and crisis intervention centers, school districts, survivors of suicide and lay persons interested in suicide prevention. The AAS has developed standards for the certification of suicide prevention centers.

Contact:

Executive Director, American Association of Suicidology Central Office
2459 S. Ash St.
Denver, CO 80222
Phone: (303) 692-0985

American Board of Medical Psychotherapists (ABMP)

An organization that provides training and certification to professionals who practice psychotherapy. The purpose of the ABMP is to apply high standards to the professional credentialing procedure and to encourage interdisciplinary excellence in medical psychotherapy and related methods of behavioral assessment and change. The ABMP was founded in 1982.

For information:

American Board of Medical Psychotherapists
Physicians' Park B, Suite 11
300 Twenty-first Avenue North
Nashville, TN 37203
Phone: (615) 327-2984

See also PSYCHOTHERAPY.

American Council for Drug Education (CDE)

The purpose of the CDE is to educate the public about health hazards associated with use of psychoactive drugs and drug abuse, including persons suffering from serious underlying depression. The CDE promotes scientific findings, organizes conferences and seminars, provides media resources and publishes educational materials. The CDE was established in 1977 as the American Council on Marijuana and Other Psychoactive Drugs (ACM); the name was changed in 1983.

For information:

American Council for Drug Education
204 Monroe Street, Suite 110
Rockville, Maryland 20850
(310) 294-0600

American Medical Association (AMA)

An association of physicians and surgeons that keeps the medical profession abreast of progress in clinical medicine, pertinent research and developments. Its primary function is to promote the art and science of medicine, improve public health and provide advisory, interpretative and referral information on medicine and health care.

The association publishes the *Journal of the American Medical Association,* in which articles on mental health frequently appear. The AMA is a source for statistics on mental health as well as other aspects of health, including brochures, pamphlets and library searches. A publication list is available.

Contact:

American Medical Association
515 N. State Street
Chicago, IL 60610
Phone: (312) 464-5000

American Psychiatric Association (APA)

A medical organization whose members specialize in psychiatry in the United States and Canada. The purposes of the APA include: (1) improving treatment, rehabilitation and care of the mentally ill; (2) promoting research; (3) advancing standards of all psychiatric services and facilities; and (4) educating medical professionals, scientists and the general public.

Founded in 1844 as the Association of Medical Superintendents of American Institutions for the Insane, it became the American Medico-Psychological Association in 1891 and adopted its present name in 1921.

The APA provides many services, including advisory, analytic, bibliographic and historical services and referrals and technical information on psychiatric care, psychiatric insurance and mental illness. The APA holds an annual meeting and publishes advance and postconvention news releases and articles on the proceedings. The American Psychiatric Association also publishes a regular tabloid-size newspaper for its members and many books and other publications that can be purchased by the public.

Contact:

American Psychiatric Association
1400 K Street, N.W.
Washington, DC 20005
Phone: (202) 797-4900

See also PSYCHOTHERAPY.

American Psychological Association (APA) A professional organization to which psychologists belong. The purpose, functions and services of the APA correspond to those of the American Psychiatric Association. The APA is a source of information and referrals on mental health concerns for professionals as well as the general public.

Contact:

American Psychological Association
1200 17th Street, NW
Washington, DC 20036
Phone: (202) 833-7600

American Suicide Foundation A foundation established by its present executive director, Herbert Hendrix, M.D., to raise private contributions to support research on the prevention of suicide and to provide support for family members and loved ones surviving a suicide.

Contact:

American Suicide Foundation
1045 Park Avenue
New York, NY 10028.
Phone: (212) 410-1111

amine A chemical produced by the central nervous system involved in the functioning of the brain. Some researchers indicate that depression may result from decreased levels of amines. Amines are technically known as biogenic amines or neurotransmitters and are chemical transmitters that nerves use to send messages to each other. Amines include norepinephrine, dopamine and serotonin.

See also BRAIN; CENTRAL NERVOUS SYSTEM; DOPAMINE; SEROTONIN.

amineptine An antidepressant drug not used in the United States.

See also ANTIDEPRESSANT MEDICATIONS.

aminobutyric acid, gamma See GAMMA-AMINOBUTYRIC ACID.

Amitid Trade name for amitriptyline, an antidepressant medication.

See also AMITRIPTYLINE; ANTIDEPRESSANT MEDICATIONS.

amitriptyline (amitriptyline hydrochloride) One of the antidepressant drugs known as tricyclic antidepressants (one of two major classes of antidepressants). It is prescribed in the treatment of depressive episodes of major depression, bipolar disorder, dysthymic disorder and atypical depression. It has moderate to marked sedative action. However, because the sedative effect of amitriptyline interacts additively with the sedative effect of alcohol, alcohol consumption should be avoided by individuals taking amitriptyline, particularly if they drive a car or work in a hazardous occupation. Amitriptyline is sometimes prescribed for eating disorders in bulimic individuals and headaches associated with depression that are the result of nonorganic causes.

Amitriptyline is known by many trade names, such as: Endep, Elavil, Amitid, Domical, Lentizol, Triptafen and Triptizol.

See also ANTIDEPRESSANT MEDICATIONS; DEPRESSION; HEADACHES; TRICYCLIC ANTIDEPRESSANT MEDICATIONS.

American Medical Association. *AMA Drug Evaluations Annual, 1991.* Chicago: AMA, 1991.

amnesia   Loss of memory; an inability to recall past experience. Amnesia may be due to many factors, including organic factors, such as a head injury, alcoholic intoxication, epileptic seizure, stroke or senile dementia, or psychological factors, such as the unconscious repression of painful experiences, in which the memory loss serves as a defense against anxiety.

One type of amnesia is an inability to remember recent happenings since the onset of amnesia (anterograde amnesia); the individual does not consolidate what is perceived into permanent memory storage or cannot retrieve recent memories from storage. Another type is a loss of remembrances before the memory disturbance began (retrograde amnesia). Episodic amnesia refers to a particular event or period from the individual's life that is forgotten. Fear of having amnesia is known as amnesiophobia.

Amnesic confabulation is a term applied to imagined occurrences unconsciously made up to fill gaps in memory; this occurs in Korsakoff's syndrome and other organic psychoses. Amnesic-confabulatory syndrome is another name for Korsakoff's syndrome.

See also ALZHEIMER'S DISEASE; REPRESSION.

amorous paranoia   An obsolete psychoanalytic term referring to a type of jealousy or delusion of infidelity that, in some cases, may represent a denial of unconscious homosexuality.

See also DELUSIONAL JEALOUSY; HOMOSEXUALITY.

amoxapine   An antidepressant drug of the tricyclic class. It is generally more effective in major depression than in dysthymic or atypical depression. It has relatively weak sedative and anticholinergic activities compared with imipramine or amitriptyline. Amoxapine has a more rapid onset of action, but this finding has not been consistently observed in all patients. Amoxapine is known under the trade name Asendin.

See also AFFECTIVE DISORDERS; ANTIDEPRESSANT MEDICATIONS; DEPRESSION; HEADACHES.

amphetamine drugs   Amphetamines and several chemically related drugs are central nervous system (CNS) stimulants that in small doses may give the user a feeling of increased mental alertness and a sense of well-being. As doses are increased, however, decreased appetite, excitement and tremor may occur, and tolerance and psychological dependence can develop with large doses. Thus amphetamines and other stimulants should be prescribed for specific purposes and only for a limited time. Rarely, amphetamines are used to treat adult attention-deficit hyperactivity disorder or to potentiate antidepressant medications in conditions resistant to conventional treatment.

Amphetamines are sometimes associated with dependence that can produce one or more organic mental disorders, including intoxication, delirium, delusional syndrome or withdrawal syndrome. Because of the possibility of developing dependency on amphetamines, many physicians no longer prescribe them.

Some individuals may take amphetamines in combination with alcohol in an attempt to counteract the depressant effects of alcohol. Although there may be some possible antagonism of the depressant effects of alcohol on the CNS, there is no improvement of impaired motor coordination, and the combination may produce a dangerous sense of false security. High levels of amphetamines and alcohol may produce gastrointestinal upsets. If amphetamines are taken with foods or beverages containing tyramine, an excessive rise in blood pressure may occur.

Amphetamine psychosis occurs in a more chronic form after prolonged use of the drugs. The psychotic symptoms can be difficult to distinguish from schizophrenia. Symptoms may include talkativeness, hyperactivity, repetitive behavior, grinding the teeth, suspiciousness and, in more severe cases, paranoia, hallucinations and delusions.

Crashing is the term used to denote the symptoms that occur with sudden withdrawal of amphetamines, including drowsiness, fatigue, apathy and severe depression. Individuals who "crash" need sleep as well as physical and emotional support.

Amphetamines are popularly referred to as "speed." They include dextroamphetamines, methamphetamines and methylphenidates.

See also ADDICTION; DEPRESSION.

Waldinger, Robert J. *Psychiatry for Medical Students*. Washington, D.C.: American Psychiatric Press, 1990.

amphetamine psychosis See AMPHETAMINE DRUGS.

amygdala A small, almond-shaped organ within the brain located below the cerebral cortex. Part of the limbic system, the amygdala is thought to be involved in memory and a wide range of internal activities including digestion and excretion, heart rate, arterial blood pressure, muscle tone, sexual activity and aggression and may also be involved in reactions to fear and avoidance.

See also BRAIN; LIMBIC SYSTEM.

anabolic steroids Steroids are chemical derivatives of, or structurally similar to, testosterone, the major male hormone. Some steroids have legitimate purposes. For example, they are used to treat certain kinds of anemia and specific cancers. When used

for these purposes, doses are carefully controlled and administered by injection, often in three- to six-week intervals. However, anabolic steroids have been used illegally by athletes to build muscle mass. In these cases, the drug is administered orally and often on a daily basis, sometimes exceeding legitimate dosage levels by as much as 20 times.

Steroids can cause mental health problems. These drugs have been reported to cause changes in brain wave activity and to increase moodiness, depression, listlessness and the violent aggressive behavior sometimes known as "body builders' psychosis."

See also HORMONES; SUBSTANCE ABUSE; TESTOSTERONE.

Media Resource Guide on Common Drugs of Abuse. Public Relations Society of America, National Capital Chapter, Fairfax, Va., September 1990.

Anafranil Trade name of clomipramine, a tricyclic antidepressant that is also used to induce remission of symptoms in some individuals who have obsessive-compulsive disorder.

See also ANTIDEPRESSANT MEDICATIONS; ANTIPSYCHOTIC MEDICATIONS; CLOMIPRAMINE; OBSESSIVE-COMPULSIVE DISORDER; TRICYCLIC ANTIDEPRESSANT DRUGS.

anal-erotic traits A psychoanalytic term for personality traits characteristic of obsessive individuals, such as overcautiousness and overconcern. Such traits are thought to come from the anal stage of psychosexual development, when the individual receives a primary source of pleasure from defecation. The theory holds that a child who derives satisfaction from retention of feces tends to develop personality traits marked by orderliness, frugality and obstinacy. In adulthood, such an individual may tend to be overconscientious, meticulous, rigid and compulsive.

See also ANAL FANTASY.

anal fantasy   A fantasy of anal intercourse or anal pregnancy and childbirth, sometimes reported by children. Psychoanalytic theory suggests that such fantasies may manifest themselves as gastrointestinal symptoms in later years. Some adults also fantasize about anal sexually related activities.

anal stage   According to Sigmund Freud's psychosexual development theory, the anal stage is the second stage of development (the first is the oral stage). Maturation continues, with one area of the body maturing before the child is aware of the next. Around the first birthday, the anal zone becomes the source of interest to the infant and the parents. The infant becomes aware of a full rectum and later develops control over the innate urges. During this stage, the child may consider producing feces as a gift to the parents and social environment or as something to withhold with stubbornness. Thus the anal area and associated activities become a means of interacting with the child's environment. Subsequent stages of development are the phallic stage, latency stage, and genital stage.

See also FREUD, SIGMUND; GENITAL STAGE; LATENCY; PHALLIC STAGE.

analgesia   Absence of sensitivity to pain. This can be produced by medications given for the relief of pain and can also occur in some rare emotional and physical disorders such as conversion hysteria. In this disorder, part of the body may develop analgesia not related to known patterns of neurological pain perception. Analgesia can also sometimes be achieved with hypnosis, which was used to reduce pain of surgery before the discovery of other anesthesia.

An analgesic is a drug or other agent that relieves pain without causing loss of consciousness. Analgesic drugs act on the central nervous system to reduce the ability of the body to feel pain. The most widely used drugs are aspirin and related compounds that provide inexpensive and fast relief for many everyday aches and pain, such as minor headaches and cold symptoms. In addition to relieving pain, aspirin and related medications combat fever and reduce inflammation that leads to pain. These drugs are not addictive, but for some people they are irritating to the lining of the digestive tract. Some people are allergic to aspirin and must take aspirin substitutes for pain.

For severe pain, morphine and chemically related drugs provide relief. Such drugs also produce a mild sensation of freedom from anxiety, which somewhat reduces the psychological reaction to pain. However, drugs in this group have disadvantages of depressing breathing in high doses and creating drug dependence or addiction when used without close supervision.

In some disease conditions, such as tabes dorsalis, the pain pathways on the spinal cord become affected. In the nerves, the fibers for pain, pressure, touch and temperature are usually combined. When they reach the spinal cord, the fibers are separated. As pain and temperature are nearly always in the same pathway, both senses can be lost at the same time.

See also PAIN.

analysand   The individual undergoing psychoanalysis.

See also ANALYST; PSYCHOANALYSIS.

analysis   See PSYCHOANALYSIS.

analyst   The term usually refers to therapists who follow the teachings of psychoanalysis as outlined by Sigmund Freud (1856–1939) to help restore mental health. However, the term also applies to analysts who adhere to the ideas of Heinz Kohut (1913–1981) and also Adolf Meyer (1866–1950), who coined the term "psychobiologist" for psychiatrists who consider both psychological and biological (medical) factors. Other analysts who follow fundamentals of Carl Jung (1875–1961) are known as analytical psychologists; those who follow Alfred Adler (1870–1937) are individual psychologists.

See also FREUD, SIGMUND; KOHUT, HEINZ; PSYCHOANALYSIS; SELF PSYCHOLOGY.

androgens See HORMONES.

anger An intense emotional state in which one feels a high level of displeasure and frustration. The spectrum of anger may range from slight irritation to explosive hostility. Anger is a source of energy that is discharged on others, objects or oneself. Anger is sometimes related to and involved with agitation and aggression.

Physiological changes occur when one feels angry. Anger increases the heart rate, blood pressure and flow of adrenaline. Suppressed anger may result in hypertension, skin rashes and headaches.

Some typical characteristics of anger include frowning, gritting the teeth, pacing and clenching the hands. There may be changes in vocal tone. One may yell or shout, or the person may speak in short, clipped sentences. During anger, some people may attempt to gain control of a situation or clearly demonstrate that they have lost control themselves.

Most people at times are caught between two attitudes with regard to anger. According to psychological and medical opinion, suppressed anger is physically and psychologically damaging, yet there are social pressures that at different levels label angry behavior destructive, illegal or unsophisticated. Further limiting expression of anger is the feeling that such behavior may bring regrets later.

Anger seems to be most directly related to frustration and feelings of inferiority. Bigotry or generally negative thinking appears to be anger turned against specific groups or humanity as a whole. Some mental health professionals believe, as Sigmund Freud observed in "Mourning and Melancholia," that feelings of depression are actually anger turned inward, directed at the self. Adults who express anger directly with physical violence or verbal abuse usually do so because they model their behavior on others in their environment or because there seems to be a reward for violent behavior. In American frontier society, for example, violent behavior was common and usually considered admirable. Since it is unacceptable in most situations to express anger directly, many people react by becoming sulky or indifferent or by adopting a superior, patronizing attitude toward the person or situation that angered them.

A baby's first cries may be an expression of anger or simply a less focused reaction to the birth experience. Small children do react most directly to situations that make them angry, sometimes by simply screaming or pulling or striking the object or person who has angered them. As children mature, angry behavior becomes focused on retaliation. By the early teens, sulking and impertinence have replaced retaliation. In both children and adults, hunger and fatigue increase the potential for anger. Researchers believe that anger is a product of the most primitive part of the brain that is capable of operating and becomes more dominant when other mental powers are impaired by illness or alcohol.

Constructive Anger Anger may be constructive. The exercise that an individual chooses to use to work off anger will do him or her good in other ways. Releasing an angry feeling sometimes brings with it a sense of pleasure. Some mental health professionals equate ambition and attempts to improve society with a healthy expression of anger.

Among athletes, anger can have a harmful effect on athletic performance. Anger drains energy and diverts attention from what must be done at the moment. However, professional athletes are trained to recover quickly from events that arouse anger. In some cases, anger may make a player more forceful and positive.

Overcoming Anger An individual in psychotherapy who expresses extremely angry feelings might be given three goals: first, to identify the feelings of anger; second, to use constructive release of the energy of anger and third, to identify thought and thought processes that lead to anger. For example, to identify feelings of anger, one might keep a diary of angry feelings and learn to recognize anger before losing control. The individual will learn to take responsibility for his or her own emotions and stop blaming others for arousing the anger. In addition, with validation from a therapist, the individual will learn to accept that some anger is justified in certain situations. In learning to use constructive release of the energy of anger, the individual may benefit from assertiveness training and learn to express anger verbally to the appropriate source. Assertive techniques will help the individual increase his or her feelings of self-esteem, demonstrate internal control over behavior and harness energy generated by the anger in a nondestructive manner. One will also learn to use energy through physical activity that involves the large muscles, such as running, walking or playing a racket sport.

Anger and Grief After a loved one dies, it is common to feel angry. The anger may be directed toward the person who died, for leaving the other person alone. Or the anger may be directed toward the medical care system for not being able to cure a disease or mend a body after an accident. In cases of accidents, often there is anger at a drunk driver or a person who has taken drugs and committed a crime or at the drug dealer who sold the drugs taken by the perpetrator of the loved one's death. Anger is a normal part of the cycle of the grief reaction. However, prolonged anger that leads to depression may indicate a need to consult a mental health professional.

See also AGITATION; AGGRESSION; ANXIETY; DEPRESSION; GRIEF.

Callwood, June. *Love, Hate, Fear, Anger and Other Lively Emotions.* Van Nuys, Calif.: Newcastle Publishing Co., 1964.
Goldstein, A. P. "Aggression," in Corsini, Raymond J., ed., *Encyclopedia of Psychology,* vol. 1. New York: Wiley, 1984.
McFarland, Gertrude K., and Thomas, Mary Durand. *Psychiatric Mental Health Nursing.* Philadelphia: J. B. Lippincott, 1991.
Plutchik, Robert. "Anger," in Wolman, Benjamin B., ed., *International Encyclopedia of Psychiatry, Psychoanalysis and Neurology,* vol. 2. New York: Van Nostrand, 1977.

angina pectoris A type of chest pain and discomfort that may be a symptom related to heart problems. Angina pectoris is not a sharp pain but rather a sensation of pressure, squeezing or tightness. Usually it starts in the center of the chest under the breastbone (sternum) and radiates to the throat area. Typically, the pains are along the inside of the left arm, part of the wrist, a few fingers and the shoulder. Symptoms of angina are usually due to muscle fibers of the heart not getting enough blood through the coronary arteries to nourish them.

Chest pains cause some individuals great mental anguish because they fear that they are having a heart attack and they also fear hearing a diagnosis from a physician. However, all chest pains should be carefully diagnosed by a physician as soon as possible. Most chest pains are not angina but are caused by emotional tension, strain of the chest muscles, referred pain from a spinal disk, indigestion, ulcers, lung problems or other disease not directly related to the heart. Knowing the source of a chest pain can reassure an individual and put her mind at rest concerning the condition of her heart.

Typically, an angina symptom appears when a person exerts himself and disappears when he rests. Most attacks last for only two or three minutes, but if they are set off by anger or other emotional tension and the individual cannot relax, they may last 10 minutes or longer.

Individuals who have angina pectoris should become aware of what it is that precedes attacks and learn to avoid those situations. Typically, such individuals are advised to reduce fat in their diet, lose weight, possibly take antianxiety medications when they feel extremely anxious and stop smoking (if they are smokers), as tobacco may provide an angina attack by speeding up the heartbeat, constructing blood vessels and raising blood pressure.

Treatment for angina pectoris includes immediate rest and a nitroglycerin tablet dissolved under the tongue. Some people take this drug as a preventive measure if they are subject to attacks and are going through a period of unusual stress. Amyl nitrite is another drug that can be administered by inhalation. When neither drug is available, a sip of whisky or brandy may be helpful.

See also CHRONIC ILLNESS.

angry-woman syndrome   A personality disorder in which a woman shows excessive and obsessive perfectionism, punctuality, neatness and outbursts of unprovoked anger. Such women often have marital troubles, a critical attitude toward others and a tendency to alcohol or drug abuse and may make serious attempts at suicide.

See also ALCOHOLISM; SUICIDE.

angst   A feeling of anxiety. Angst is a central concept in the existentialist approach to psychology, which interprets the essence of human existence by emphasizing basic human values such as self-awareness, love and free will. The word "angst" is derived from the German term meaning "fear, anxiety, anguish."

See also ANXIETY; FEAR.

anhedonia   A diminished capacity to enjoy or experience pleasure in situations or acts that normally would be pleasurable. Anhedonia is a marker for classic depression states. Anhedonia, also known as dystychia, in extreme forms may be a symptom of schizophrenia or a depressive disorder. The word "anhedonia" was coined by Ribot, a French psychologist, to refer to "an insensibility relating to pleasure alone," in contrast to "analgesia," or the absence of pain. Anhedonia was described as a schizophrenic symptom by Kraepelin and Bleuler, although both psychopathologists viewed anhedonia as only one facet of the deterioration of the emotional life of the individual.

Freud associated loss of capacity for enjoyment with the repression that accompanies neurotic conflict. Behavioral clinicians have suggested that changes in a person's reinforcement schedule or a change of reinforcers may shape depressive behavior, also causing anhedonia.

See also DEPRESSION; SCHIZOPHRENIA.

Fawcett, Jan; Clark, David C.; Scheftner, William A.; and Gibbons, Robert D. "Assessing Anhedonia in Psychiatric Patients." *Archives of General Psychiatry* 40 (Jan. 1983).

anniversary reaction   Around the anniversary of a significant event, such as the death of a family member or close friend, some people will have dreams, behavior patterns or other symptoms that recall and relive the event. In some individuals, minor illness occurs at the same time each year, often on the anniversary of some unhappy event, such as a death, date of divorce or date of leaving something to which one was attached. The person who has these symptoms is often unaware of the source of his or her behavior. Some mental health professionals believe that these symptoms represent an attempt to control feelings by reliving the event rather than by consciously remembering it in the usual way. In any case, such reactions are considered normal and not unusual if not carried to excess.

Campbell, Robert Jean. *Psychiatric Dictionary*. New York: Oxford University Press, 1981.

anomaly Anything that is abnormal or irregular or a deviation from the natural order, such as a structure that varies significantly from the normal. For example, an individual who has an extra X or Y sex chromosome, a female without an external vaginal opening or a male with three testicles is said to be an anomaly. A person whose sexual practices are outside his or her society's usual habits is also referred to as an anomaly.

anorexia nervosa An eating disorder characterized by intense fear of being fat and by severe weight loss. The term was suggested by Sir William Gull in 1874 and has been used in medical literature since then. Individuals who have anorexia are known as anorectics or anorexics. Anorexia nervosa is a life-threatening condition; there have been many deaths from the syndrome, which requires medical as well as psychological treatment.

Anorexia nervosa occurs mostly among adolescent girls but has been known among all age groups in both sexes. Girls may "feel fat," deny their illness and develop an active disgust for food. There may be a persistent lack of appetite and refusal of food. Most anorexics have a low sense of self-esteem. Symptoms include severe weight loss, wasting (cachexia), vomiting, amenorrhea (cessation of the menstrual period) and hyperactivity (i.e., constant exercising to lose weight).

Some psychiatrists believe that girls who refrain from eating wish to remain "thin as a boy" in an effort to escape the burdens of growing up and assuming a female sexual and marital role. Another contribution to the increase in anorexia nervosa is contemporary society's emphasis on slimness as a sign of beauty. Most women diet at some time—particularly athletes and dancers, who seem more prone to the disorder than other women.

In some cases, anorexia nervosa is a symptom of depression, personality disorder or even schizophrenia. Researchers are studying the possibility that altered neurotransmitter function or hormonal function may be involved in this disorder. Frequent mild cases occur in young women who do not progress to the malignant and sometimes fatal outcome from self-starvation but go through years of bingeing and purging with heightened concern about food and their body image.

See also BODY IMAGE; DEPRESSION; EATING DISORDERS; ANOREXIA, BULIMIA, AND EATING DISORDERS in BIBLIOGRAPHY.

Kasvikis, Y. G., et al. "Past History of Anorexia Nervosa in Women with Obsessive-Compulsive Disorder." *International Journal of Eating Disorders* 5, no. 6 (1985).

anorgasmia (anorgasmy) Inability to achieve orgasm. This term has been replaced with psychosexual dysfunction and refers to lack of orgasm that may be caused by sociocultural attitudes of the partners, anatomical or neurophysiological problems or fear of painful intercourse. Sex therapy is helpful in many such cases.

See also FRIGIDITY; PSYCHOSEXUAL DYSFUNCTIONS; SEX THERAPY.

Antabuse Trade name of the generic drug disulfiram, used to deter consumption of alcohol by individuals being treated for alcoholism. When a person taking Antabuse consumes alcohol, a severe reaction usually follows, including vomiting, breathing difficulty, headache and, occasionally, collapse and coma. Reaction to Antabuse begins within five to 10 minutes after ingesting alcohol and may last from 30 minutes to several hours, depending on the amount of alcohol in the body.

Antabuse works by interfering with the metabolism of alcohol in the liver by causing a toxic buildup of acetaldehyde. Antabuse is prescribed with the individual's full knowledge and consent. It should not be taken by pregnant women.

See also ALCOHOLISM.

O'Brien, Robert, and Chafetz, Morris. *The Encyclopedia of Alcoholism.* New York: Facts On File, 1982.

antianxiety medications   Also known as anxiolytics, these are medications prescribed to reduce anxiety and tension. They are sometimes referred to as minor tranquilizers. Antianxiety drugs are prescribed for many individuals during times of stress and in treatment of stress-related physical disorders. Antianxiety drugs or anxiolytics include those in the benzodiazepine class, such as alprazolam (Xanax), lorazepam (Ativan), diazepam (Valium) and chlordiazepoxide (Librium). Some are shorter acting because of more rapid body metabolism. While relatively nontoxic when first taken, they can reduce alertness (making driving inadvisable) and cause potentiation of alcohol (multiplying its sedative effects), and individuals prone to abuse drugs and alcohol can become dependent on them. They should not be stopped suddenly if taken regularly over two weeks because of possible withdrawal symptoms (nausea, sweats, tremulous feelings, possibly seizures) but should be gradually tapered or reduced in dose over two to four weeks. These medications are used to treat anxiety disorders or adjustment disorders with anxiety. Alprazolam (Xanax) is approved by the Food and Drug Administration for the treatment of panic disorder. Non-benzodiazepine anxiolytics such as buspirone have been developed but do not have immediate effects. Meprobamate and phenobarbital were once used but have high toxicity if used in overdose and have more serious addictive properties.

Sedating antihistamine medications are sometimes used (e.g., Vistaril, Benadryl) but have limitations in the effects and anticholinergic side effects. In severe anxiety disorders such as panic attacks, certain antidepressant drugs are sometimes used, including tricyclics (Prozac) and monoamine oxidase inhibitors (MAOIs).

See also ANXIETY; ANXIOLYTIC MEDICATIONS; PHARMACOLOGIC THERAPY in BIBLIOGRAPHY.

anticholinergic medications   A group of drugs that block effects of acetylcholine, a chemical released from nerve endings in the parasympathetic division of the peripheral autonomic nervous system in the brain. (The parasympathetic nervous system produces relaxation, calmness, digestion and sleep.) Anticholinergic drugs are used in the treatment of irritable bowel syndrome, certain types of urinary incontinence and in nervous system disorders, such as Parkinson's disease.

Well-known natural substances with anticholinergic effects are atropine (used as a drug to dilate the eye) and scopalamine (a plant substance used with morphine to induce sleep). Some antidepressants and antipsychotic drugs have anticholinergic effects; these side effects sometimes include extreme dryness of the mouth, abnormal retention of urine, constipation, blurred near vision, short term memory loss and mental confusion in high doses. All are reversible by changing dosage or stopping the medications.

See also AGORAPHOBIA; ANTIDEPRESSANT MEDICATIONS; DEPRESSION.

anticipatory anxiety   The anxiety an individual feels when thinking about an anxiety-producing situation, such as an approaching examination, a visit to the dentist or a difficult interview. Individuals who have phobias experience anticipatory anxiety when the possibility of facing their feared stimulus occurs.

See also ANXIETY; PHOBIA; ANXIETIES AND ANXIETY in BIBLIOGRAPHY.

anticipatory grief   See GRIEF.

anticonvulsant medications   A group of prescription drugs that prevent convulsions or limit their frequency or severity; also known as antiepileptics. In high doses, minor tranquilizers and hypnotic drugs may act as anticonvulsants. Many anticonvulsants are central nervous system depressants and also reduce some symptoms of anxiety.

See also MINOR TRANQUILIZERS.

antidepressant medications Prescription drugs used to counteract depression. Antidepressants are available only by prescription, and because depressive symptoms are merely suppressed, not cured, by these drugs, they are usually prescribed for three to six months or more until the symptoms remit on their own. These medications are also frequently used in conjunction with some type of psychotherapy.

Commonly, antidepressant medications take up to two to three weeks before having a full effect (although side effects may begin immediately). The time elapsing before the drug becomes therapeutic varies with the drug. Antidepressants may have to be taken regularly for months, even years in the case of patients with prior depressive episodes, if their gains are to persist. Relapse often occurs upon stopping the drug.

Most drugs used to treat depression either mimic certain neurotransmitters (biochemicals that allow brain cells to communicate with each another) or alter their activity. Antidepressants are thought to reverse the depletion or decrease activity of these neurotransmitters that occurs during depression. Two of the major neurotransmitters involved appear to be norepinephrine and serotonin. The precise pharmacologic mechanisms of antidepressant drugs, as well as the balances of neurotransmitters in individuals who have depression, are still not entirely understood. As newer, more specific antidepressants are developed, understanding of antidepressants and depression evolves.

Antidepressant medications were developed during the 1950s after physicians noticed that tuberculosis patients treated with iproniazid sometimes became extremely cheerful. The notion that this elevated mood might be a side effect of the drug led to the development of a class of antidepressants known as monoamine oxidase inhibitors. They were followed by the tricyclic antidepressants and lithium.

There are five major categories of antidepressants: tricyclic antidepressants (TCAs), monoamine oxidase (MAO) inhibitors, lithium, serotonin specific reuptake inhibitors (SSRI) and novel antidepressants such as trazodone and bupropion.

Tricyclic Antidepressants Tricyclic antidepressants are referred to as "tricyclic" because the chemical diagrams for these drugs resemble three rings connected together. An example of a tricyclic antidepressant is imipramine, which was first synthesized in the 1940s.

Tricyclics elevate mood, alertness and mental and physical activity and improve appetite and sleep patterns in depressed individuals. When given to a nondepressed person, tricyclics do not elevate mood or stimulate the person; instead, the effects are likely to increase anxiety and arouse feelings of unhappiness.

Tricyclic antidepressants are generally well tolerated and relatively safe, with minimal side effects. Their antidepressant effects, however, often take several weeks to appear, for reasons not yet well understood. Because of this lag, tricyclics are not prescribed on an "as-needed" basis.

Some depressed individuals may respond well to one tricyclic but not at all to another. Because of the time lag of several weeks before any beneficial effects are apparent, the physician will first try one drug for that time and then, if results are not achieved, prescribe another tricyclic, again for several weeks. Such trials, with their waiting and uncertainty, may lead to some anxiety and frustration for both the individual and the physician.

Some of the more well known tricyclic antidepressants (and their trade names) are shown in the following sidebar.

Tricyclic Antidepressant Drugs

Amitriptyline hydrochloride (Trade names: Elavil; Endep; Sk-Amitriptyline; Amitid)

Amoxapine (Trade name: Asendin)

Desipramine hydrochloride (Trade name: Norpramin; Pertofrane)

Doxepin hydrochloride (Trade name: Adapin; Sinequan)

Imipramine hydrochloride (Trade name: Imavate; Janimine; SK-Pramine; Tofranil)

Nortriptyline hydrochloride (Trade name: Aventyl; Pamelor)

Protriptyline hydrochloride (Trade name: Vivactil)

Side Effects Side effects of tricyclic antidepressants include excessively dry mouth, sweating, blurred vision, headache, urinary hesitation and constipation. Drowsiness and dizziness, as well as vertigo, weakness, rapid heart rate and reduced blood pressure upon standing upright, are likely to occur early on but usually disappear within the first several weeks. Tricyclics should be used cautiously in persons with heart problems and in elderly patients who may not break them down as rapidly as other adults.

Drug Interactions and Cautions Tricyclic antidepressants and MAO inhibitors are not recommended to be combined except under unusual circumstances by a physician expert in their use. Although very rare, a severe interaction between the two drugs can occur; in extreme cases, convulsions, seizures and coma can occur. A more common drug interaction involves the combination of tricyclics and alcohol, and possibly other sedatives, as tricyclics increase effects of these substances. Use of other anticholinergic drugs will increase likelihood of anticholinergic side effects.

Monoamine Oxidase (MAO) Inhibitors MAO inhibitors (or MAOIs) are primarily used for individuals who have not responded adequately to tricyclic antidepressants or serotonin reuptake inhibitors. Because of a wider range of potential, often unpredictable complications, use is limited. However, MAO inhibitors may be prescribed for certain types of depressions, generalized anxiety and phobic disorders and are used to help individuals who have panic attacks.

When a tricyclic antidepressant is tried and discontinued because of ineffectiveness, a gap of ten days is recommended before the monoamine oxidase inhibitor is prescribed. Tricyclic antidepressants and MAO inhibitors may be cautiously combined by physicians experienced in the use of this combination. In the reverse case, where the MAO inhibitor is ineffective and is to be replaced by a tricyclic, a period of two weeks between medications is recommended.

Interactive Effects A drawback of the MAO inhibitors, as a group, is that they may lead to unpredictable and occasionally serious interactions with some foods and drugs. For example, combining MAO inhibitors with a class of drugs called sympathomimetic drugs may lead to serious complications. Common nasal decongestant sprays often include phenylpropanolamine or phenylephrine, both sympathomimetics. Cough and cold preparations or any preparation not specifically recommended by a physician should also be avoided. The pain drug Demerol should not be given with MAOIs, but other pain-relieving drugs, such as morphine, can safely be used.

Individuals taking MAO inhibitors must conform to a special diet that avoids the amino acid tyramine or they may experience a dangerous rise in blood pressure. Tyramine is present in many foods, including alcoholic beverages, aged cheese, liver, fava beans and chocolate.

A side effect of monoamine oxidase inhibitors is that they lower blood pressure, an effect not well understood by researchers.

Lithium Lithium is effective in individuals who have both depression and mania and in preventing future episodes. It acts without causing sedation but, like the tricyclics and MAO inhibitors, requires a period of use before its actions take effect.

Some Major MAO Inhibitors (and their trade names)

Isocarboxazid (Trade name: Marplan)
Phenelzine sulfate (Trade name: Nardil)
Tranylcypromine sulfate (Trade name: Parnate)
Deprenyl (Trade name: Eldepryl) (approved for treatment of Parkinson's disease)
Lithium salts
Lithium carbonate (Trade name: Eskalith; Lithane; Lithonate)

Side effects of lithium may rule it out for use as an antidepressant; there may be nausea and vomiting, muscular weakness and confusion.

Other Treatments Amphetamines and related psychostimulant drugs, such as methylphenidate (a mild central nervous system stimulant), are sometimes used as antidepressants. While they may bring on temporary mood elevation, their prescription for such purposes is controversial, as they are subject to abuse. Some physicians try amphetamines for short-term use in certain patients and may also prescribe amphetamines diagnostically to determine more rapidly the value of moving on to tricyclic antidepressants and rarely to potentiate antidepressant medications in treatment-resistant depression.

Alprazolam may lift moderately severe depression, although it is primarily a drug used to treat anxiety. In some individuals, alprazolam has shortened or interfered with panic attacks and also induced sleep. In depressed individuals with a high level of anxiety, alprazolam may be added to tricyclic antidepressants.

New Developments of Antidepressant Medications The development of innovative antidepressants combined with more precise research approaches holds great promise for the understanding and more effective treatment of affective disorders. In the last several decades, while conventional antidepressants have been helpful for many individuals, limitations of these antidepressants have been noted, namely their lack of specificity of action, delayed onset of action, side-effect profile and potential for lethality in overdose. Approximately 20 to 30 percent of depressed persons do not respond to traditional antidepressants.

Similarly, electroconvulsive therapy has drawbacks, such as the potential for short term cognitive deficits and problems associated with sustaining the antidepressant response. Over the last several years, newer antidepressants have emerged, such as sertraline, paroxetine, fluoxetine and bupropion, that offer the advantages of antidepressants with more favorable side-effect profiles and a decreased potential for lethality in overdose. However, research has shown that while these agents have unique side-effect profiles, their overall efficacy appears to be no greater than conventional antidepressant treatments and they also have a delayed onset of action.

The goal of recently developed antidepressants is to act faster and with more power than previously used antidepressants, with less frequent and less severe side effects and with more ability to target an individual's specific type of depression. Newer antidepressants are not tricyclic or the monoamine oxidase inhibitors. They are unicyclic, bicyclic or of other molecular configurations. Whereas tricyclics and MAO inhibitors are understood to influence chemicals known as neurotransmitters, the newer antidepressants are technically classified by their preferential influence over individual neurotransmitters—norepinephrine and serotonin.

Selective Serotonin Reuptake Inhibitors Fluoxetine, sertraline and paroxetine are compounds which are part of a new class of selective serotonin reuptake inhibitors (SSRI) with low toxicity and free of many side effects attributed to tricyclic antidepressants. They are not sedative, have no anticholinergic side effects and do not promote weight gain.

Like other antidepressant drugs, SSRI medications do not help everyone with depression. They have their own unique side effects, including possible nausea, weight loss—both usually time limited—insomnia and rarely anxious agitation that is dose related. Most people accommodate to these side effects. A recent topic of controversy arose because of claims by the Commission for Human Rights—an organization dominated by Scientology, a lay organization advocating cures for psychological problems and a sworn opponent of psychiatry—that fluoxetine can promote suicidal ideas of violence. These claims have not been substantiated scientifically.

See also ADVERSE DRUG REACTIONS; AGORAPHOBIA; ANXIOLYTIC MEDICATIONS; BENZODIAZEPINE DRUGS; DEPRESSION; MANIC-DEPRESSIVE ILLNESS; POSTPARTUM DEPRESSION; SEDATIVE DRUG.

Ballenger, James C. "Pharmacotherapy of the Panic Disorders." *Journal of Clinical Psychiatry* 47; no. 6, supplement (June 1986).

Doctor, Ronald M., and Kahn, Ada P. *Encyclopedia of Phobias, Fears, and Anxieties.* New York: Facts On File, 1989.

Fawcett, Jan; Zajecka, John M.; Kravitz, Howard M.; et al. "Fluoxetine Versus Amitriptyline in Adult Outpatients with Major Depression." *Current Therapeutic Research* 45, no. 5 (May 1989).

Hollister, Leo E., M.D. "Pharmacotherapeutic Considerations in Anxiety Disorders." *Journal of Clinical Psychiatry* 47, no. 6, supplement (June 1986).

McMahon, Terry C. "A Clinical Overview of Syndromes Following Withdrawal of Antidepressants." *Hospital and Community Psychiatry* 37, no. 9 (Sept. 1986).

Ostraw, David, M.D. "The New Generation of Antidepressants: Promising Innovations or Disappointments?" *Journal of Clinical Psychiatry* 46, no. 10, Sec. 2 (Oct. 1985).

Zajecka, John M., and Fawcett, Jan. "Recent Advances in the Treatment of Depression." *Current Opinion in Psychiatry* 4 (1991).

antimanic medications   A group of drugs that reduce symptoms of mania or manic episodes of manic-depressive illness. Antimanics are also used as neuroleptics (major tranquilizers or antipsychotics). The major types of antimanics are butyrophenones, lithium, phenothiazines and anticonvulsants.

Antimanic medications reduce the agitation and lack of control seen in mania but may cause sedation; lithium produces this effect somewhat more slowly (5–10 days) without sedation and is useful in preventing recurrences that are usual without prophylactic treatment.

Certain anticonvulsant medications will reduce mania more rapidly. These include clonazepam (trade name: Klonopin); lorazepam (Ativan), which may be given by injection like some neuroleptics; and carbamazepine (Tegretol) and divalproex sodium (Depakote), which act more rapidly and have long-term effects with sedation or the side effects of neuroleptics.

Each of the types of antimanic drugs produces somewhat different pharmacologic actions. Lithium is particularly effective in preventing relapses in manic-depressive illness. Other drugs with antimanic effects are haloperidol and chlorpromazine.

See also ANTIDEPRESSANT MEDICATIONS; BUTYROPHENONES; LITHIUM CARBONATE; MANIC-DEPRESSIVE ILLNESS; PHENOTHIAZINE DRUGS.

antipsychotic medications   Medications used to treat serious psychotic illness sometimes with the risk of homicide or suicide. Although they have side effects and certain serious risks, they are currently the best available treatments for acute and chronic psychoses. Monitored carefully by a physician experienced in their use, they can be beneficial and safely used and often represent the only available treatment in carefully selected patients.

These medications are used to relieve symptoms of psychotic illnesses including thought disorders, hallucinations, delusions, bizarre behavior and agitation. They are useful in chronic schizophrenia because they reduce the rate of exacerbation. While primarily prescribed for schizophrenia and related illnesses (schizophreniform disorder, schizoaffective disorder), antipsychotics are also prescribed to psychotic patients who have mood disorders and organic mental disorders. They are also prescribed usually in lower doses to control behavior in some mentally retarded individuals, as well as individuals with borderline personality disorder, organic disorders and Tourette Syndrome. Antipsychotics are also known as neuroleptics because of their capacity to block dopamine receptors.

How Antipsychotic Drugs Work Antipsychotic drugs work on receptors in the brain to influence emotional behavior. Although the exact mechanisms of action are not clearly understood, most antipsychotics are known to inhibit transmission of nerve impulses in the central nervous system (CNS) by blocking the action of dopamine, a neurotransmitter, at certain receptor sites.

Antipsychotics have a number of adverse drug reactions. For example, reserpine is no longer used as an antipsychotic because it has been known to produce depression and low blood pressure. Antipsychotic drugs are not usually appropriate for use with anxiety reactions in the absence of severe psychotic symptoms.

Side Effects/Adverse Effects Side effects occur with therapeutic doses; close and critical observation by a physician is essential for therapeutic effects. Side effects include sedation and extrapyramidal effects, such as acute dystonia (a state of abnormal muscle tension), akathisia (restlessness, agitation) and Parkinsonism (rigidity, shuffling gait, hypersalivation and masklike facial appearance), all of which are reversible by dose change or a medication to prevent these effects. Tardive dyskinesia (unwanted movements of the face, jaw, tongue, trunk and extremities and restless movements) can occur with greater likelihood over time (risk increases about 4 percent per year of exposure, and effects can be permanent, especially if medications are not stopped). Clozapine thus far has not been found to have a significant risk of tardive dyskinesia but can produce epileptic seizures and dangerous decrease of white blood cell levels, which can be fatal if not monitored by weekly blood tests.

Individuals taking antipsychotics usually participate in informed-consent procedures. A physician may also wish to inform relatives or other responsible persons of the risks and benefits of treatment as well as the early symptoms of tardive dyskinesia, which are often unnoticed by the patient. Neuroleptic malignant syndrome is a rare but major adverse effect.

See also ADVERSE DRUG REACTIONS; HALLUCINATION; SCHIZOPHRENIA; TARDIVE DYSKINESIA.

American Medical Association. *AMA Drug Evaluations Annual, 1991.* Chicago: AMA, 1991.

Andreason, Nancy D., and Black, Donald W. *Introductory Textbook of Psychiatry.* Washington, D.C.: American Psychiatric Association, 1991.

antisocial personality disorder Characteristics include a consistent pattern of behavior that is intolerant of the conventional behavioral limitations imposed by a society, an inability to sustain a job over a period of years, disregard for the rights of others (either through exploitiveness or criminal behavior), frequent physical fights and, quite commonly, child or spouse abuse without remorse and a tendency to blame others. There is often a facade of charm and even sophistication that masks disregard, lack of remorse for mistreatment of others and the need to control others.

Although characteristics of this disorder describe criminals, they also may befit some individuals who are prominent in business or politics whose habits of self-centeredness and disregard for the rights of others may be hidden prior to a public scandal.

During the 19th century, this type of personality disorder was referred to as moral insanity. The term described immoral, guiltless behavior that was not accompanied by impairments in reasoning.

According to the classification system used in the *Diagnostic and Statistical Manual of Mental Disorders* (3d ed., rev. 1987), antisocial personality disorder is one of the four "dramatic" personality disorders, the others being borderline, histrionic and narcissistic.

See also CONDUCT DISORDER; PERSONALITY; PERSONALITY DISORDERS.

Andreason, Nancy C., and Black, Donald W. *Introductory Textbook of Psychiatry*. Washington, D.C.: American Psychiatric Association, 1991.

Davis, Kenneth; Klar, Howard; and Coyle, Joseph T. *Foundations of Psychiatry*. Philadelphia: W. B. Saunders, 1991.

anxiety Uneasiness, apprehension and tension that stems from anticipating danger, which may be imagined or real. Some definitions of anxiety distinguish it from fear by limiting it to anticipation of a danger from a largely unknown source, whereas fear is a response to a consciously recognized and usually external threat or danger. Others can see or recognize external dangers but not the "internal" threats that an anxious individual experiences. Signs and symptoms of anxiety and fear may seem the same, as they include hyperactivity, apprehension, excitability, irritability and suffering from exaggerated and excessive worry and fearful anticipation. Many abused and psychologically traumatized individuals, such as victims of family violence, have lifelong symptoms of anxiety.

The National Institute of Mental Health Epidemiologic Catchment Area Study found anxiety disorders to have the highest rate (8–10 percent) of all mental disorders.

Most mentally healthy people experience anxiety in everyday life. For example, many may experience anxiety about getting to a job interview on time, going on a first date or looking just right at an important event. Others become anxious about being held up in traffic because of a bridge raising or a delayed train, while still others become anxious when they hear reports of imminent bad weather conditions. Most people learn to cope with such transient anxieties by taking more time, making additional preparations and facing the fact that the situations are temporary and are not really threatening.

Many individuals who face a threat or change in their health status may become anxious. These anxieties may relate to a fear of the unknown or a fear of unpleasant treatment and possible pain and disability.

Anxieties also occur relating to socioeconomic status. For example, threats of job layoffs cause many people anxieties, while others become anxious over changes in stock market prices and develop constant fears that their fortunes will be wiped out. These situations, if severe enough to interfere with function or sleep in an otherwise well-adjusted individual, would be categorized as adjustment disorder.

Anxious individuals focus on a situation, object or activity that they want to avoid; extreme anxieties and fears of these experiences can become phobias. If the anxiety seems unfocused, it is known as free-floating anxiety. This is a fear of social criticism, diagnosed as a social phobia if it interferes with normal social or occupational function. Other phobias may be more specific, such as fear of public speaking, riding in cars, snakes or mice.

Those who suffer from agoraphobia often experience panic attacks first. Recent studies have shown that about 25 percent of patients with major depression suffer panic attacks. The suicide-attempt rate in patients with panic attacks has been found to be just as high as in those with depressive disorders.

Anxieties may be experienced in specific periods of sudden onset and be accompanied by physical symptoms such as nausea or dizziness. Anxiety focused on physical symptoms that preoccupy individuals to the point that they believe they have a disease can lead to hypochondriasis.

Many people turn to smoking, alcohol or drug use to cope with anxieties. These habits are not considered healthy coping mechanisms, as they can lead to health hazards and dependencies. Physicians may prescribe antianxiety drugs, or anxiolytic drugs, for some individuals who experience temporary anxieties at certain times.

See also ALCOHOLISM: ANXIETY DISORDERS; ANXIETY DISORDERS OF CHILDHOOD AND ADOLESCENCE; ANXIOLYTIC MEDICATIONS; HYPOCHONDRIASIS; PANIC ATTACK; PANIC DISORDER; PHOBIA; ANXIETIES AND ANXIETY DISORDERS in bibliography.

anxiety and diabetes The uncomfortable feeling of uneasiness or fear in people who have diabetes can take on added dimensions. For example, anxiety can develop in diabetics who become overly watchful for symptoms. Diabetics might fear a leg cramp as the start of diabetic neuropathy. If one's eyes become tired from reading, one might think he or she is showing signs of diabetic retinopathy. Usually, the symptoms are just normal aches and pains, but fear of debilitating diabetic complications can make anxiety hard to control.

Common sense approaches, such as discussing these fears with one's physician, can calm growing anxieties. When a new symptom occurs, it should be investigated by a physician. Many physical states, such as hypoglycemia (low blood sugar), can produce anxiety symptoms.

When a symptom, such as frequent urination, is checked out by the physician and no apparent cause is found, one may reason that the doctor has overlooked something during the checkup. A cycle of nervousness and anxiety may begin all over again. Many diabetic individuals find participation in a support group or psychological counseling helpful.

See also SUPPORT GROUPS.

Schwartz, Lee S. "When Anxiety Strikes," *Diabetes Forecast* 40, no. 2 (Feb. 1988).

anxiety disorders Disorders in which symptoms of anxiety and avoidance behavior are characteristic features. Anxiety disorders is a categorical term encompassing a group of mental health disorders including generalized anxiety disorder, panic disorder with or without agoraphobia, simple and social phobias, obsessive-compulsive disorder and post-traumatic stress disorder.

Of all mental health problems, anxiety disorders are the most frequently occurring in the general population. Eight out of every 100 Americans suffer from anxiety disorders. A survey by the National Institute of Mental Health showed that the six-month prevalence rate of anxiety disorders among the adult population in the United States was 8.3 percent. Only 23 percent of these individuals had received any form of treatment. This survey showed that anxiety disorders, the most common mental health problem in the community, usually go untreated.

Anxiety disorders are sometimes detected when an individual seeks repeated treatment for a nonexistent medical condition or makes needless visits to emergency rooms. The physical symptoms of anxiety disorders are often so severe that many people are convinced they have serious medical problems. Many victims of anxiety disorders find themselves isolated from the course of daily activity. Some individuals have symptoms so severe that they are almost totally disabled. While simple phobia is the most common anxiety disorder, panic disorder is the most common among people seeking treatment. According to the American Psychiatric Association, panic disorder, phobias and obsessive-compulsive disorder seem to be more common among first-degree biologic relatives of people with each of these disorders than among the general population. People who experience anxiety disorders are usually apprehensive and frequent worriers and anticipate something unfortunate happening to themselves or others. Characteristics may include "edginess," irritability, easy distractibility and impatience. Some have a feeling of impending death or a desire to run and hide.

Causes of Anxiety Disorders   Because anxiety disorders are such an individual matter, causes cannot be generalized. Usually it is not a single situation or condition that causes anxiety disorders for most individuals but rather a combination of physical and environmental factors linked together. Researchers have pinpointed several general theories relating to causes of anxiety disorders that may be applicable to some cases. Theories involve the psychoanalytic approach, the learning approach and the biologic approach. Individual causes may be traced to one or more of these theories. For example, a person may develop or inherit a biologic susceptibility to anxiety disorders, and events in childhood may teach a person certain fears, which then develop over time into a diagnosable anxiety disorder.

According to the psychoanalytic theory, anxiety comes from an unconscious conflict that originated in the individual's past. Such conflicts may have developed during infancy or childhood. Sigmund Freud suggested that one may carry unconscious childhood conflicts regarding sexual desire for the parent of the opposite sex. A person may also have developed conflicts because of an illness or a scare or other emotionally charged event during childhood. According to this theory, anxiety can be resolved after identifying and resolving the unconscious conflict.

According to learning theory, anxiety is a learned behavior that can also be unlearned. People who feel uncomfortable in certain situations or involved in certain events will try to avoid them. However, some individuals, by persistently confronting the feared situation or object, can relearn their responses and relieve anxiety. Behavioral therapy is largely based on learning theory.

Research has also indicated that biochemical changes occur as a result of emotional, psychological or behavioral changes. According to biochemical theory, biochemical imbalances may be responsible for some anxiety disorders, and some anxiety disorders seem to run in families. According to

this theory, medical treatment of biochemical imbalances in the central nervous system may relieve symptoms of anxiety.

Changes in Terminology   The language relating to anxiety disorders has changed over the years. For example, anxiety disorder was once termed "anxiety neurosis" but is no longer referred to in that way in psychiatric literature. "Anxiety hysteria" was once used to refer to what is now generally called phobia, phobic disorder or somatoform disorder.

Therapy for Anxiety Disorders   Anxiety disorders are usually treated with a variety or combination of approaches individualized for each person. According to Eric Stake, M.D., Pennsylvania Hospital, Philadelphia, following a comprehensive assessment, treatment is generally administered on an outpatient basis, with most patients showing improvement within five to six sessions.

Techniques include behavioral therapy, psychotherapy, medication and education. For example, phobias, agoraphobia and obsessive-compulsive disorders are often treated with behavioral therapy. According to Victor Malatesta, Ph.D., Pennsylvania Hospital, Philadelphia, behavioral therapy is based on the belief that changing how we approach a given situation can help change how we react toward it. It is crucial that patients actively come to terms with their fears. As part of the behavioral approach, therapists use a step-by-step process of introducing patients to a series of situations progressing from the mildly anxiety-provoking to the highly anxiety-provoking. This continual but graduated exposure helps patients tackle their fears one step at a time, slowly learning to control their anxiety, gain self-confidence and finally master the situation. With this method, many phobic individuals have experienced long-term recovery.

Many who have recovered from anxiety disorders have lived with their disorder for years without being properly diagnosed or offered appropriate and effective therapy.

Individuals with anxiety disorders should seek therapists who are experienced in recognizing and treating mental health problems. Recommendations may be obtained by contacting major medical centers of the Anxiety Disorders Association of America:

16000 Executive Boulevard
Suite 200
Rockville, MD 20852-3801
Phone: (301) 231-9350

Medications by themselves are not considered adequate treatment for anxiety disorders. However, for many people, the use of antianxiety medications (also known as anxiolytic medications) helps reduce intense symptoms so that they can benefit from behavioral therapy or other psychotherapeutic techniques. Individuals who are continuously anxious and tense find it difficult to relax sufficiently during a therapy session or topractice relaxation exercises between therapy visits. The use of medications seems to help many individuals do this more efficiently.

Ongoing patient education can help prevent a recurrence of symptoms during or after treatment. People with anxiety disorders learn to understand how and why they developed these problems and learn ways to cope with them. They learn to recognize the signs of an attack, to keep track of their breathing, to use relaxation techniques and to make life-style changes. Support groups in which patients help one another overcome fears and learn to relax are also helpful.

Generalized Anxiety Disorder (GAD)
Characteristics of this disorder are a constant feeling of being nervous and on edge without any apparent reason. Or there may be unrealistic or excessive anxiety and worry (apprehensive expectation) about two or more life circumstances, such as needless financial worries and concerns about possible misfortune to one's spouse (who is in no danger) for six months or longer. There may be signs of nervousness, hyperactivity and excitability that interfere only mildly with work or social activities. Individuals may feel shaky,

experience trembling or twitching, have muscle aches and soreness and become tired easily. Age of onset is usually between 20 and 40, and the disorder is equally common in men and women. In some cases, generalized anxiety disorder follows a major depressive episode. Generalized anxiety disorder is not an anxiety about having a panic attack (as occurs in panic disorder) or feeling embarrassed in public (as occurs in social phobia) or a fear of being contaminated (as occurs in obsessive-compulsive disorder).

Phobias According to the American Psychiatric Association, phobias afflict between 6 and 11 percent of all Americans. Phobias are intense, unrealistic fears that usually lead to avoidance of the feared object, situation or event. Phobic individuals feel terror, dread or panic when confronted with their feared situation. Some avoid the source of their fear to the extent that it interferes with their work and social and family life.

Simple or single phobias are fears of specific objects or situations. Well-known examples are fears of flying, snakes or high places. Simple phobias can begin at any age. When exposed to the sight of the feared object, any one or more anxiety responses occur, including trembling, sweating and feeling faint, nauseated or dizzy. For some phobics, just the thought of, or seeing a picture of, the feared object brings on these responses.

Social phobias are persistent fears of one or more situations in which the person is exposed to possible scrutiny by others and fears that he or she may do something or act in a way that will be humiliating or embarrassing. Social phobias usually begin in late childhood or early adolescence, at a time when the individual normally is keenly aware of comparison with and evaluation by peers. Examples of social phobias range from fears of public speaking to fears of vomiting in a public place.

When faced with the socially phobic situation, such as standing up at a meeting and speaking, the individual will almost invariably have an anxiety response, such as having a fast heartbeat, sweating and having difficulty breathing. Usually a cycle occurs, in which the individual fears a situation, such as going into a room and meeting new people, and then avoids the situation. Social phobias are generally not as disabling as agoraphobia, but social phobias may interfere with one's choice of employment, professional advancement or social life.

Agoraphobia, a fear of fear, includes an extreme fear of any situation in which escape is difficult and help unavailable. It may involve a fear of going outside, being in a public place alone or being in a place with no escape, such as an airplane, train or center aisle in a theater or church. This is the most disabling because many sufferers become housebound. Agoraphobia begins in late childhood or early adolescence and, without appropriate therapy, gets worse as the individual ages.

Agoraphobia occurs with or without panic attacks. Authorities differ on whether the panic attacks come first, leading to agoraphobia, or agoraphobia leads to the panic attacks.

Panic Attacks and Panic Disorder   Panic disorder involves an impending sense of doom marked by a sudden onset of severe anxiety attacks that reach their peak in a matter of minutes and then subside. People who have panic disorders experience intensely overwhelming terror for no apparent reason. Some individuals experiencing a panic attack for the first time rush to the hospital, convinced they are having a heart attack and will die. Although sufferers cannot predict when the attacks will occur, they know that certain situations, such as being in a closed place, might cause them because they recall having experienced a panic attack in such a place.

During an attack, persons feel helpless, out of control and, in some instances, as if they are going crazy. Shortness of breath, dizziness and heart palpitations usually accompany an attack.

Obsessive-Compulsive Disorders   Obsessions are repeated, unwanted thoughts.

Compulsive behaviors are rituals that get out of control. For many people, obsessions begin as a coping mechanism for overcoming anxieties. People who experience obsessive disorders do not automatically have compulsive behaviors. However, most people who have compulsive, ritual behaviors also suffer from obsessions.

Obsessive-compulsive disorders often begin during the teens or early adulthood. Generally they are chronic and cause moderate to severe disability. People who have obsessive-compulsive disorders usually have involuntary, recurrent and persistent thoughts or impulses that are distasteful to them. Examples are fears of becoming infected by shaking hands with others or fears of committing a violent act. These thoughts can last for seconds or hours. The most common obsessions focus on hurting others or violating socially acceptable behavioral standards, such as swearing or making inappropriate sexual advances. For some individuals they are focused on religious or philosophical issues.

Compulsive individuals go through repeated, involuntary ritualistic behaviors in the belief that they are preventing an unwanted future event, as in the case of those who worry about infection and develop compulsive hand-washing habits. Hand washing affects more women than men. Compulsives also check and recheck that doors are locked or that electric switches and ovens are turned off. The checking compulsion seems to affect more men than women.

Post-traumatic Stress Disorder (PTSD)   PTSD is an avoidance of thoughts, feelings, situations or activities that are associated with a shocking or painful experience in the individual's past. This can affect anyone who has survived a severe physical or mental trauma. It is now known that it can affect children as well as adults. For example, children who have witnessed a shooting in a school or restaurant, or violence in the streets, suffer symptoms similar to those of adults who have been through wars, witnessed airplane collisions or been physically attacked. The severity of the disorder seems to increase when the trauma is unanticipated. For that reason, not all war veterans develop post-traumatic stress disorder—despite prolonged and brutal combat—because soldiers expect a certain amount of violence, whereas rape victims may be especially affected by the unexpectedness of the attack.

Individuals who suffer from post-traumatic stress disorder reexperience the traumatizing event through flashbacks of the event, dreams or nightmares. Rarely does the person get into a temporary dislocation from reality, in which the trauma is relived for a period of days. "Psychic numbing," or emotional anesthesia, may occur, in which victims have decreased interest in or involvement with people or activities they once enjoyed. They may experience excessive alertness and a highly sharpened startle reaction. They may have general anxiety, depression, panic attacks, inability to sleep, memory loss, difficulty concentrating or completing tasks and survivors' guilt. There is evidence that neglected and abused children experience PTSD. It is also likely that many anxiety disorders develop as PTSD phenomena.

See also AGORAPHOBIA; DIAGNOSTIC AND STATISTICAL MANUAL OF MENTAL DISORDERS; OBSESSIVE-COMPULSIVE DISORDER; PANIC DISORDER; POST-TRAUMATIC STRESS DISORDER; PHOBIA; ANXIETIES AND ANXIETY DISORDER in BIBLIOGRAPHY.

Amchin, Jess. *Psychiatric Diagnosis: A Biopsychosocial Approach Using DSM-III R.* Washington, D.C.: American Psychiatric Press, 1987.

American Psychiatric Press. *Diagnostic and Statistical Manual of Mental Disorders,* 3d ed., rev. Washington, D.C.: APA, 1987.

Canty, Georgia. "Paralyzed by Fear." *The Quill,* Pennsylvania Hospital, Philadelphia (Winter 1989).

Potts, Nicholas L. S., Ranga, K., and Krishnam, R. "Long Term Use of Benzodiazepines." *Canadian Family Physician* 38 (Jan. 1992).

anxiety disorders of childhood and adolescence

Disorders in which symptoms

Anxiety Disorders of Childhood or Adolescence

1. Separation anxiety disorder
2. Avoidance disorder of childhood or adolescence
3. Overanxious disorder

of anxiety are central characteristics. While major symptoms may seem similar to anxieties in adults, mental health professionals have divided disorders of childhood and adolescence into three major categories. The first two involve anxiety focused on a specific situation (separation anxiety disorder and avoidant disorder of childhood or adolescence), and the third involves generalized anxiety related to a variety of situations (overanxious disorder).

Separation Anxiety Disorder Diagnosis of excessive anxiety, for at least two weeks, concerning separation from those to whom the child is attached. A diagnosis requires at least three of nine items from the following:

- Unrealistic and persistent worry about possible harm occurring to major attachment figures or fear that they will leave or not return.
- Unrealistic and persistent worry that an untoward calamitous event will separate the child from a major attachment figure (e.g., that the child will be lost, kidnapped or killed or be the victim of an accident).
- Persistent reluctance or refusal to go to school in order to stay with major attachment figures or at home.
- Persistent reluctance or refusal to go to sleep without being near a major attachment figure or to go to sleep away from home.
- Persistent avoidance of being alone, including clinging to and "shadowing" major attachment figures.
- Repeated nightmares involving the theme of separating.
- Complaints of physical symptoms (e.g., headaches, stomachaches, nausea or vom-

iting) on many school days or on other occasions when anticipating separation from major attachment figures.

- Recurrent signs or complaints of excessive distress in anticipation of separation from home or major attachment figures (e.g., temper tantrums or crying, pleading with parents not to leave).
- Recurrent signs of complaints or excessive distress when separated from home or major attachment figures (e.g., wants to return home, needs to call parents when they are absent or when child is away from home).

Onset must be before age 18. The disturbance must not occur only during the course of a pervasive developmental disorder, schizophrenia or another psychotic disorder. In some cases, school phobia is considered a type of separation anxiety disorder.

Avoidant Disorder of Childhood or Adolescence Diagnosis of excessive avoidance of contact with unfamiliar people, for at least six months, severe enough to interfere with social functioning in peer relationships. Additionally, there must be a desire for social involvement with familiar people and generally warm and edifying relationships with family or familiar figures. The child must be at least age two and a half. The child may retreat from strangers and seem extremely shy with other children.

Overanxious Disorder A diagnosis of excessive or unrealistic anxiety or worry for at least six months. The diagnosis requires at least four of seven items from the following:

- Excessive or unrealistic worry about future events.
- Excessive or unrealistic concern about the appropriateness of past behavior.
- Excessive or unrealistic concern about competence in one or more areas (e.g., athletic, academic or social).
- Somatic complaints (such as headaches or stomachaches) for which no physical basis can be established.

- Marked self-consciousness.
- Excessive need for reassurance about a variety of concerns.
- Marked feelings of tension or inability to relax.

The individual must not meet criteria for generalized anxiety disorder if over age 18. The disturbance must not occur only during the course of a pervasive developmental disorder, schizophrenia or another psychotic disorder.

See also ANXIETY; ANXIETIES AND ANXIETY DISORDERS and CHILDHOOD in BIBLIOGRAPHY.

anxiogenic A term referring to activities, drugs or substances that may raise anxiety levels and arouse physical symptoms of anxiety. Examples of anxiogenic agents or activities include hyperventilation, caffeine, yohimbine, sodium lactate or isoproterenol infusion, carbon dioxide inhalation and exercise in some individuals. In phobic individuals, the thought or sight of the phobic object is usually anxiogenic; agoraphobics regard the idea of going outside or on a public bus alone as anxiogenic.

See also CAFFEINE; ANXIETIES AND ANXIETY DISORDERS in BIBLIOGRAPHY.

apathy A characteristic of mild boredom and lack of energy and drive. There may be little emotional response to stimuli. Most people become apathetic at some time, depending on their circumstances. However, the situation is usually temporary rather than chronic. Apathy occurs during depression and some types of schizophrenia. People who are apathetic are usually unable to mobilize themselves to get started or complete many different kinds of tasks. Apathy can result from lack of interest or stimulation. For example, a highly trained individual who, because of economic necessity, is forced to take a more menial job in which his training cannot be used may develop characteristics of apathy toward his employer's activities or the other workers around him.

aphasia A disturbance of the ability to read and write and/or the ability to comprehend and read, when these abilities previously existed. The term "aphasia" usually refers to a complete absence of these communication and comprehension skills, while dysphasia is a disturbance. Related disabilities that may occur as a characteristic of aphasia or, more rarely, by themselves are alexia (word blindness) and agraphia (writing difficulty).

Aphasia occurs as a result of brain damage following a stroke or head injury.

aphonia Total loss of the voice, usually suddenly, caused by emotional stress. The loss of voice occurs because the vocal cords do not meet as they normally do when the individual tries to speak. However, they do come together when the individual coughs. The voice usually returns as suddenly as it disappeared. Reassurance and psychotherapy are frequent treatments.

apraxia Loss of ability to perform purposeful movements such as getting dressed or lifting a simple item. Apraxia may occur when the parietal lobe of the brain is damaged, causing loss of memory for certain acts or series of skills. No paralysis or loss of sensation occurs.

art therapy Use of artistic activities during psychotherapy and rehabilitation to promote a healthier communication of feelings as well as a way to channel impulses. Activities such as clay modeling or painting offer individuals a nonthreatening emotional release, a means of restoring self-esteem and self-confidence, an opportunity for communicating in a nonverbal way and a means of reestablishing social relationships. In some cases, the therapist may watch for hidden sources of emotional problems. Art therapy with children is particularly useful when they tell their story by drawing a picture or express the feelings they experience when looking at artwork. In some cases, children are asked to draw themselves or their families or depict what they want to be when they grow up. These drawings can then be discussed in individual therapy sessions with the child or in family therapy sessions.

See also ALTERNATIVE THERAPIES.

asociality Behavior characteristics that indicate withdrawal from society, a lack of involvement with other people or lack of concern for social values and customs. Asociality is sometimes associated with recluses or hermits. Individuals with asocial characteristics may have few or no interests or hobbies and may show an inability to feel closeness and intimacy of a type appropriate for his or her age, sex and family status.

However, like many other psychological characteristics, asociality represents a continuum, and most individuals fall somewhere along the line between being socially well adjusted to their life circumstances and totally asocial. Social withdrawal is often associated with depression.

assertiveness training A process through which the individual learns to speak up whenever he or she believes an injustice is done. Assertiveness training helps raise self-esteem and is helpful in treating some anxiety disorders.

See also AGORAPHOBIA; BEHAVIORAL THERAPY.

assignment A way in which a psychiatrist, psychologist or other mental health professional is compensated for services covered by Medicare (in the United States) when the practitioner wishes to receive direct payment from Medicare and is willing to permit it to determine the amount of payment. Under this system, both the patient and the practitioner agree to accept Medicare's determination of a "reasonable charge" for the services involved. Medicare reimburses the practitioner directly, paying only 80 percent of what is considered the reasonable charge. The individual is usually asked to pay the remaining 20 percent. Alternatively, when a practitioner does not accept assignment, the individual is billed directly and then sends the bill to Medicare for reimbursement of 80 percent of Medicare's predetermined reasonable charge. Not all mental health practitioners accept assignment. Individuals concerned about this aspect of payment should inquire before beginning therapy with a new practitioner.

See also SOCIOECONOMIC TRENDS IN MENTAL HEALTH CARE.

"assisted" suicide   See SUICIDE.

association, free   A method used by Sigmund Freud that required the patient to speak freely of whatever might come to mind during a therapy visit. This method formed the basis of the therapeutic application of psychoanalysis and of continued study and research into the nature of mental processes.

See also FREUD, SIGMUND; PSYCHOANALYSIS.

assortative mating   The tendency of individuals with a specific mental illness or mental retardation to mate with, or marry, a person who has a similar condition. This may occur as a consequence of simple social convenience, because the partners often meet each other in therapy groups, group living situations or hospitals and may have few friends without mental health problems because of social handicaps produced by these problems. It may occur because people with similar problems (alcoholism, depression, etc.) have a propensity for one another. Assortative mating causes problems for researchers in family and genetic mental health studies, because it results in a double genetic loading, increasing the risk for illness in offspring.

astereognosis   A condition in which one does not recognize objects by touch when they are placed in one hand. Testing for astereognosis is part of an examination of the central nervous system. Astereognosis is either left-sided or right-sided. Astereognosis (and tactile agnosia) are due to a disease or malfunction of parts of the cerebrum (the main mass of the brain) concerned with recognition by touch. This term is not applicable if objects cannot be recognized by touch because of difficulty holding the object or defect of sensation in the fingers.

asthenic personality   A type of personality characteristically lacking energy, chronically fatigued and oversensitive to emotional or physical stress. This type lacks enthusiasm and capacity for enjoyment of life. The term comes from the word *asthenia,* which means a loss of strength and energy.

See also CHRONIC FATIGUE SYNDROME; PERSONALITY.

asthma, anxiety and depression   Asthma is characterized by recurrent attacks of breathlessness, accompanied by wheezing. Asthma attacks vary in severity from day to day. In many individuals, attacks begin in childhood and tend to become less severe in adulthood; however, asthma attacks can begin at any age. Asthma may be extrinsic—in which an allergy (usually to something inhaled) triggers an attack—or intrinsic, in which there is no apparent external cause. Intrinsic asthma tends to develop later in life than extrinsic asthma. Emotional factors, such as stress or anxiety, may bring on attacks.

During a severe attack, breathing becomes increasingly difficult, causing sweating, rapid heart beat and a high anxiety level. The individual may be unable to speak, cannot lie down or sleep, breathes rapidly and wheezes loudly. The individual may fear dying, and those watching and trying to help the sufferer may add to the overall anxiety level.

With current drug treatment, people who suffer repeated attacks can expect to live a normal life. Quality of life need not be impaired, as demonstrated by successes of athletes who have had asthma. Nevertheless, individuals who have asthma have particular mental health concerns, as many become depressed because of their chronically recurring condition and anxious during asthma attacks. With children who have asthma, family counseling is often helpful.

See also CHRONIC ILLNESS.

attentional impairment   A diagnostic term used by mental health professionals that applies to individuals who have trouble focusing attention or who are able to focus only sporadically and erratically. They may ignore attempts to be conversed with, wander away while in the middle of an activity or task or appear to be inattentive when engaged in formal testing or interviewing. Such individuals may not be aware of their difficulty in focusing attention. In social situations, such an individual seems inattentive, may look away during conversation and may seem to have poor concentration when playing games, reading or watching television. In popular terms, such an individual may seem ''out of it.''

attention-deficit hyperactivity disorder (ADHD)   A common chronic disorder of childhood affecting 3 to 7 percent of the school age population, and more common in boys. No precise definition or approach to treatment is universally accepted, although there is extensive literature on which rational approaches to management of individual cases are based. Symptomatic treatment with stimulant medication in selected patients is effective and safe but not curative. Successful outcome depends on multimodal therapy involving parents, teachers and mental health professionals.

Usually ADHD is noticed before age five; ADHD sufferers are often overactive, impulsive and easily distractible. When young people are untreated in childhood, they often develop very negative attitudes toward school and patterns of failure that can be avoided

with prompt diagnosis and treatment. Even with treatment, some develop behavioral and substance abuse problems in later life.

In recent years, diagnosis and management have created public and professional controversy. According to the *Diagnostic and Statistical Manual of Mental Disorders* (3d ed., rev.), the definition of ADHD emphasizes the attention deficit as the central feature, and the other symptoms to a variable extent. It also recognizes that ADHD exists as a separate entity from conduct disorder. The essential feature of conduct disorder is a persistent conduct pattern in which rights of others and age-appropriate societal norms or rules are violated. While the two conditions often occur in the same individual, it is not assumed that one is a necessary concomitant of the other. Making the distinction has important implications for outcome. Mental health professionals treating children with ADHD generally agree that individualized management, on a case-by-case method, is most effective.

Diagnosis of ADHD   Diagnosis is based on description of the child's behavior obtained from parents and teachers, as well as observation of behavior in the office. Questions for the child are directed toward features of hyperactivity, impulsiveness and lack of attention. Such children are often restless, particularly while the physician talks with parents.

In retrospect, many parents say their child was hyperactive from a very early age, even from one to two years of age. In those with a later onset, the disorder is more likely to be associated with social disruption or specific difficulties at school. However, many parents do not seek medical attention until the child presents difficulties in first or second grade.

Psychological tests are useful to determine whether the child has an associated disorder, such as a learning disorder or mild mental retardation. Biochemical studies have shown statistically significant differences in catecholamine excretion and peptide-containing urinary complexes. While these findings have not reached diagnostic significance, they represent a promising field for further study.

Treatment The physician usually explains the nature of ADHD to the child and family, with the objective to reduce feelings of guilt and blame in the family and at the same time improve self-esteem. When there are disorders of family dynamics or a learning disorder underlying the symptoms, these should be addressed. Often other health and educational professionals, such as psychologists, special education specialists or social workers, become involved in the total management of a case.

Physicians counseling families with an ADHD child usually give some general advice about behavior management and how to avoid confrontation with the active, restless child. Such a child should be encouraged to channel energy into productive activities, such as erasing the blackboard or doing errands.

Various therapies are used with ADHD children, including behavior modification and cognitive therapy. Other approaches include dietary restrictions of food additives or refined sugar (Feingold diet); supplementation with megavitamins, trace elements or amino acids; and compensating for vestibular dysfunction. However, the best results have been noted with multimodal therapy, including behavior management, special educational intervention and, in some cases, the use of stimulant drugs. Although this remains controversial, it is supported by double-blind studies.

The most widely used stimulant medication is methylphenidate (trade name: Ritalin). The drug is effective for three to four hours and is often prescribed for use in the morning and at noon. Individualizing dosage is important because high doses may help hyperactivity but have been found to impair learning. When the dose is too high, some children become excessively quiet, indecisive and cry easily. When symptoms occur only in school, the medication may be given only on school days. A child on stimulant medication should be evaluated by the prescribing physician with some regularity. Controversy continues regarding the use of medication for this disorder.

See also TOURETTE SYNDROME.

attitude A characteristic of personality that includes a fixed tendency to like or dislike classes of people or things based on one's beliefs and feelings. For example, employers who do not want to hire older workers may be said to have a prejudiced attitude.

Attitudes can also be characterized as positive or negative. A positive attitude can be helpful in performance in school, taking examinations or learning a new skill, whereas a negative attitude can get in one's way of moving ahead. The well-known phrase "power of positive thinking" is an example of positive attitude in play.

Attitude can also make a difference in recovering from disease. An example is the late Norman Cousins (1912–1990), former editor of the *Saturday Review of Literature* and writer, who used a happy mental attitude to overcome a severe, disabling joint disease (ankylosing spondylitis). He spent weeks watching old comedy movies; he believed that laughter and the positive attitudes it aroused in him were vital to his recovery.

See also CHRONIC ILLNESS; LAUGHTER.

aura Sensations that warn an individual that a migraine headache or epileptic attack is approaching. For example, before a migraine headache becomes full-blown, there may be perceptions of colored lights or flashing lights, numbness or stomach distress. Different individuals learn to recognize their own symptoms, sometimes in time to take a medication to ward off the attack. The word comes from the Greek word meaning "breeze."

See also EPILEPSY; HEADACHES.

autism A condition in which children withdraw from others, either by pretending or experiencing muteness, having a delayed onset of speech or developing strange speaking patterns. Also known as autistic disorder, this occurs in about two to four out of every 10,000 children, affects more boys than girls and is usually evident when the child is about two or two and a half years old. It may be caused by a subtle form of brain damage. Usually autistic infants appear normal for the first few months of life but then become increasingly unresponsive to their parents or caretakers. Autism may be linked to variations from normal patterns of speech control by the hemispheres of the brain. A majority of autistic children are left-handed. Often autistic children show considerable artistic or musical abilities. One in 50 autistic children becomes a fully normal adult, but almost half become moderately well adjusted.

Most autistic children require special schooling. Children and their parents can benefit from counseling. In some cases, medications are given to reduce hyperactivity.

autohypnosis   See   AUTOSUGGESTION; HYPNOSIS.

autonomic nervous system (ANS)   The part of the nervous system that controls the automatic activities of organs, blood vessels, glands and many other tissues in the body. The ANS is made up of a network of nerves categorized as the sympathetic nervous system and the parasympathetic nervous system.

The sympathetic nervous system heightens activity in the body, such as causing the breathing rate to increase and making the heart beat faster as though it were preparing the body for a "fight or flight" response. The parasympathetic system has the opposite effect. The two systems work together and usually balance each other, except at times of extreme stress or fear or during exercise, when the sympathetic nervous system takes over. During sleep, the parasympathetic nervous system (PNS) is in control. The PNS slows down heart rate, reduces blood pressure and aids in digestion. In individuals who are blood phobic, there is an intense PNS response, resulting in blood pressure reduction, dizziness and even fainting.

The autonomic nervous system is affected by certain drugs. For example, anticholinergic drugs, those that block the effect of acetylcholine, can reduce painful muscle spasms in the intestine. Beta-adrenergic-blocking drugs block action of epinephrine and norepinephrine on the heart, slowing down the heart rate and reducing situational anxiety.

ANS side effects may result from use of some antipsychotic and antidepressant drugs (tricyclic and monoamine oxidase inhibitors). Such disturbances may benefit ANS functions, such as lowering of blood pressure, but they also cause lightheadedness (dizziness), blurred vision, nasal congestion, dryness of the mouth and constipation.

See also BLOOD PRESSURE; DIZZINESS.

Ost, L.-G.; Sterner, U.; and Lindahl, L.I. "Physiological Responses in Blood Phobics." *Behavior Research and Therapy* 22 (1984).

autonomy   A feeling associated with attitudes of independence and freedom that may take many forms. Individuals may express autonomy by making simple decisions for themselves. When one loses a sense of autonomy, one may lose self-esteem and become frustrated.

Peer groups are important for the development of autonomy. Children with good peer relationships will generally acquire good feelings about themselves and develop confidence that others will still like them even if they are at times unconventional or critical. They will also develop the ability to realize what others expect of them and to make choices about meeting those expectations in a flexible way. Peer groups may also be destructive to autonomy for individuals, particularly teenagers whose experiences with peers have not enabled them to develop self-confidence. Under these circumstances, a desire for approval or acceptance may lead to drugs or other destructive behavior that makes the individual feel like part of the group.

Autonomy may take forms as extreme as dying for beliefs that conflict with those of church or state or as mundane as wearing clothes that are pleasing and comfortable but conflict with social standards. Autonomy may also take forms such as love of adventure, desire for isolation, willfulness, irresponsibility, rebellion or anger. Autonomy has fluctuated as a social standard in recent history. The rebellion and individualism of the 1960s exploded from the repression and conservatism of the 1950s. A different type of more personal, introspective individualism evolved in the 1970s, to be replaced by the more conventional materialism of the 1980s.

In studies of independent thinking, participants fell into two groups, the independents and the yielders. Both groups admitted to feeling uncomfortable when their thinking went against that of the group, but the independents were able to state opinions or observations that went against those of the group, while the yielders either consciously or unconsciously went along with the group, in some cases convincing themselves that observations that were actually correct were wrong because they would have conflicted with the group. Independents tended to have a constellation of personality traits that included self-reliance, persuasiveness, the ability to express themselves well and to think for themselves. The yielders tended to be submissive, conventional and easily affected by stress and to have less insight into themselves than the independents. On the other hand, further research into dependent as opposed to independent behavior showed that the more dependent personalities have better interpersonal skills. They were frequently able to handle their emotions more effectively, pick up on nuances of behavior and show interest and affection toward oth-

ers. Research has also shown that autonomy is very much a function of specific situation and that most individuals are not consistently dependent or independent. The same person might be critical and adventuresome in a work situation but dependent and willing to go along with the group when with her family.

See also AGING; ANGER: FRUSTRATION; SELF-ESTEEM.

Johnson, D. S., and Johnson, R. T. "Peer Influences," in Corsini, Raymond I., ed., *Encyclopedia of Psychology,* vol. 2. New York: Wiley, 1984.

May, Rollo. *Freedom and Destiny.* New York: W. W. Norton, 1981.

Vinack, W. E. "Independent Personalities," in Corsini, Raymond J., ed., *Encyclopedia of Psychology,* vol. 2.

autosome   Chromosomes other than sex chromosomes. Normal human beings normally have 22 pairs of autosomes, plus the sex chromosomes (XX for women and XY for men), which are responsible for determining male or female sexual characteristics.

See also CHROMOSOME.

autosuggestion   Adopting a mental attitude or putting oneself in a mood that makes one more receptive to therapy and improvement of a mental or physical condition. For example, if one suggests to oneself that self-improvement will occur, one will be more receptive to learning.

Autosuggestion is related to the "power of positive thinking." It is useful in controlling anxiety symptoms and phobic reactions. Learned relaxation techniques are a form of autosuggestion; biofeedback is based on autosuggestion, because the individual learns to control certain physical functions, such as muscular tensions, and even temperature and heart rate.

See also HYPNOSIS.

aversion   A term referring to a mild dislike for situations or things. This word is commonly misused in place of phobia, which is a more severe reaction.

See also AVERSION THERAPY; PHOBIA.

aversion (aversive) therapy   Therapy to help a person overcome habits and unwanted behaviors by associating those habits or behaviors with painful experiences or unpleasant feelings. Aversion therapy has been used to treat many conditions, including alcoholism, bedwetting, smoking, sex addiction, nail biting and many other problems. In some cases, it has been useful in treating obsessive-compulsive disorder.

Therapy is designed to help the person connect the habit with the unpleasant reaction, thus reducing the occurrence of the unwanted habit. New behaviors that are more acceptable to the individual have to be developed and reinforced. To create aversions, many techniques have been used. One is electrical therapy in which a trained therapist administers a mildly uncomfortable shock to the individual whenever the unwanted behavior, either real or imagined, is present. The electrical method has been used predominantly in the treatment of sexual disorders. This method of treatment is no longer deemed acceptable and is prohibited by mental health codes of several states. With chemical therapy, the patient receives a drug to induce nausea and is then exposed to smoking, nail biting or other habit that he or she is trying to overcome. The chemical method has been used most widely in the treatment of alcoholism.

A more modern form of aversion therapy is known as covert sensitization. In this form of therapy, the individual is asked to imagine the unwanted habit and then to envision some extremely undesirable consequence, such as nausea or pain.

See also ALCOHOLISM; BEHAVIORAL THERAPY; COGNITIVE THERAPY; SEX ADDICTION.

Blake, B. "The Application of Behavior Therapy to the Treatment of Alcoholism." *Behavioral Research Therapy* 5 (1967).

Cautela, J. "Covert Sensitization." *Psychological Reports* 20 (1967).

avoidant personality disorder   Individuals who have avoidant personality disorder may show a pattern of timidity, anxiety, low self-esteem, social discomfort and fear of rejection. Some individuals develop social phobias or agoraphobia, and others may have depression and feel angry at themselves for failing to adapt better in social ways. Avoidant personality traits may be thought of as a continuum, and many individuals have avoidant personality traits but not to the extreme that they may be categorized as having a personality disorder.

According to the American Psychiatric Association, diagnostic criteria for avoidant personality disorder include:

- Reticence in social situations out of fear of saying something inappropriate or seeming foolish, or of being unable to answer a question
- Fears being embarrassed by blushing, crying or showing signs of anxiety in front of others
- Exaggerates potential difficulties, physical dangers or risks involved in doing ordinary activities outside his or her usual routine.
- Easily hurt by disapproval or criticism
- No close friends or confidants (or only one) other than first-degree relatives
- Unwilling to become involved with people unless certain of being liked
- Avoids social or occupational activities involving significant interpersonal contact; for example, refuses a promotion that will increase social demands

See also AGORAPHOBIA; ANXIETY; PERSONALITY DISORDERS; PHOBIA.

American Psychiatric Association. *Diagnostic and Statistical Manual of Mental Disorders,* 3d ed., rev. Washington, D.C., 1987.

awareness (self-awareness)   In the language of psychotherapy, the consciousness of information and understanding about personal facts that the individual may have repressed or previously refused to acknowledge. Self-awareness is often the first step toward improving a mental health concern.

azidothymidine (AZT) See ZIDOVUDINE.

AZT The abbreviation for azidothymidine, the old name for the drug zidovudine, used to treat patients with AIDS (acquired immunodeficiency syndrome). This drug is one of a very few thus far discovered that will in some patients delay the development or progression of AIDS symptoms.

See also ACQUIRED IMMUNODEFICIENCY SYNDROME; ZIDOVUDINE.

B

"baby blues" A mild form of depression that many women experience after childbirth. It may be caused by a combination of factors, including hormonal changes, the realization that one's life is changed with the addition of another person to care for, and the tiredness that naturally occurs after childbirth. A supportive family can be helpful at this time. Usually the "blues" disappear within a few weeks; if a woman continues to experience depression for an ongoing period—and particularly if her ability to care for her baby is hindered by her moods—professional help should be sought.

See also CHILDBIRTH; DEPRESSION; POST-PARTUM DEPRESSION.

baby boomers A generation considered to be the population born from 1946 to the mid-1960s. The actual population explosion began during World War II, peaked following the war and lasted until the mid-1950s. The baby boom has been attributed to several causes, including wartime prosperity that ended the Great Depression; increased births as servicemen returned to family life following the war; a lower marriage age than in previous years; and a tendency to have two or three children in quick succession early in marriage rather than scattering childbearing over a period of years. The "boom" brought about many social changes, as it first created a scarcity of teachers to instruct the large population of children. Later, as the birthrate dropped, there was an excess of teachers.

The social pressure of a large group of young people, particularly students, in the population brought about an emphasis on changes that gave impetus to both the civil rights movement for racial minorities and the women's movement. Improved birth control, more permissive sexual standards and an emphasis on education for both sexes plunged women into a world of choices that included pursuing careers but still made marriage and children attractive. Women who were active in the social movements of the 1960s but kept in less powerful positions by males eventually became active in their own women's rights movement. The results have been beneficial but have led many women to feel torn by the need to be a "superwoman": a wife, mother and successful career woman.

The sheer numbers of the baby boom generation created a population bulge that increased competition for education and jobs and, in its wake, a dearth of young people to fill lower-level or part-time jobs. As baby boomers mature and vie for top positions in the various fields, their large numbers mean that more will be locked in lower-level positions or must strike out on their own in some area of self-employment; for many this leads to frustrations and additional stress.

The affluence and good job market of the 1960s and a social reaction to the conservatism of the 1950s produced a generation that has been variously characterized as hedonistic, rebellious and undisciplined. Most parents of baby boomers carried with them memories of the depression and the war that made them value security and a stable family life. In reaction, baby boomers tended to question belonging to a corporate or bureaucratic structure to become entrepreneurial and to see a job as something that should be fulfilling and stimulating rather than simply a means to the end of supporting themselves and their families. Even the concept of family has not been totally attractive to baby boomers, who have frequently substituted networks of friends or live-in or communal arrangements for the traditional marriage and family. When marriages took place among baby boomers, they were generally at a later age than previous generations and frequently ended in divorce. Some couples experimented with the idea of open marriage to alleviate what they considered to be the frustrations and boredom of traditional marriage.

The concentration of so many young adults in the population in the late 1960s also produced a new cultural phenomenon: the "flower child." Rock and folk music, long hair and offbeat clothing styles dominated the youth of this era. Many young people experimented with drugs and "dropped out" of mainstream society.

See also SEXUAL REVOLUTION; WOMEN'S LIBERATION MOVEMENT.

Giesel, James T. "Population," in the *Encyclopedia Americana,* vol. 22. Danbury, Conn.: Grolier Incorporated, 1984.

Mills, D. Quinn. *Not Like Our Parents: How the Baby Boom Generation Is Changing America.* New York: William Morrow, 1987.

back pain   While back pain has many causes, there are also many psychological implications, especially when one is diagnosed with "nonspecific back pain" and continues to suffer with pain. Stress may be a factor, as tension can contribute to a tightening of muscles and improper posture that lead to back pain and muscle spasms in the back.

Back pain is sometimes called a psychosomatic illness because is it hard to prove or disprove, is a lingering complaint and is often an "excuse" for avoiding work, social or family obligations.

Many workdays are lost because of back pain. People who do heavy lifting, carrying or sitting in one place or are overweight often develop backaches that may be due to a ligament strain, a muscle tear, damage to a spinal facet joint or a disk prolapse. Understanding one's work habits can be a step toward alleviating chronic discomfort.

When back pain persists over time, many individuals experience mild depression and withdrawal. Persistent pain without relief makes one feel out of control of one's body; taking a positive attitude and pursing avenues of relief can give one more of a feeling of control over the situation. Self-helps for back pain include resting in bed on a firm mattress or bedboard; taking analgesics (pain-killing medications); applying heat to the back; and doing specific exercises under the guidance of a trained exercise therapist. When pain persists or is severe, a physician should be consulted. A physician may prescribe aspirinlike medications, anti-inflammatory drugs or muscle-relaxant drugs. In some cases, acupuncture, massage, spinal manipulation, physical therapy, wearing a back brace or spinal surgery is recommended. Consultation with a mental health worker or participation in a support group helps many people alleviate some of the stress of dealing with surgical treatments when necessary.

See also PSYCHOSOMATIC.

baldness   Because some individuals view baldness as a blemish on their self-image and self-esteem, baldness has created an industry for our society that advertises hair-restoring preparations, treatments and hairpieces. In many people's minds, baldness is associated with aging, and when an individual—male or female—loses hair, it is often interpreted as a sign of old age and an indicator of one's mortality.

Baldness, or extreme hair loss, often follows a course of chemotherapy. Thus the psychological stress of baldness is compounded by fears of recurrence of the disease. Hair loss and temporary baldness may also be produced by heredity, infections, systemic diseases, some scalp disorders, pregnancy and as a side effect of certain drugs.

Male pattern baldness accounts for about 95 percent of all cases of baldness in men. It often begins at the temples with a receding hairline or at the crown, forming a bald area sometimes referred to as a "monk's spot." Male pattern baldness may begin in the early twenties but is more often a condition of middle age.

In women, hair usually thins with age. "Female pattern baldness" involves receding hairline, with a diffuse thinning over the crown and the front of the scalp. Many individuals who are concerned about their body image and appearance because of balding use wigs, hairpieces or hair implants temporary or permanent aids to building their self-esteem.

See also BODY IMAGE; SELF-ESTEEM.

barbiturate drugs Medications used to induce sleep and provide sedation for tension and anxiety that act as central nervous system depressants. These medications are legitimately sold by prescription only. Barbiturates slow down the activity of nerves that control many mental and physical functions, such as emotions, heart rate and breathing. The first barbiturate drug, a derivative of barbituric acid, was manufactured and used in medicine in 1882 as barbital and sold under the trade name Veronal. Since then many bartituric acid derivatives have become available as tablets, capsules, suppositories and injectable liquids. Some sleeping pills are "short-acting" barbiturates; their effects last only five or six hours and produce little or no aftereffects if used properly. When abused, barbiturates can cause

addiction and the sleeping problem can worsen.

Barbiturates have many serious disadvantages that have led to a sharp decline in their use by physicians. They are very toxic, and thus death through overdose—accidental or intended—is a significant danger, particularly if they are combined with alcohol. Regular use can produce physical and psychological dependency and mood changes. Chronic use at high dosage can produce damage to brain cells.

In recent years, physicians have been prescribing drugs in a class known as benzodiazepines for many anxiety situations in which barbiturates were once prescribed. Benzodiazepines can produce dependency but have not been shown to cause the degree of overdose toxicity, dependency or evidence of cell death associated with barbiturates.

See also BENZODIAZEPINE MEDICATIONS.

Bardet-Biedl syndrome One of many genetic conditions that can cause moderate to severe mental retardation. Characteristics of an infant born with this syndrome include obesity, retinal abnormalities, small genitals and extra digits on hands and feet (polydactyly).

See also MENTAL RETARDATION.

Barr-Harris Center for the Study of Separation and Loss During Childhood Part of the Chicago Institute for Psychoanalysis, this nonprofit program established in 1976 specializes in the treatment and study of children who have experienced the loss of a parent by death. It is one of the few places in the United States that focuses on the treatment of the bereaved child and his or her family. The center also studies the effect of loss and separation on children as they mature and disseminates information for lay persons and professionals on ways to prevent lasting damage to children from traumatic events such as loss of parents or siblings.

For information, contact:

Barr-Harris Center
Institute for Psychoanalysis
180 N. Michigan Avenue
Chicago, IL 60601
Phone: (312) 726-6300.

battered child syndrome   Rough physical handling by adults that results in injuries to the baby or child, failure to grow, disability and sometimes death. Studies have shown that parents who repeatedly injure or beat their babies and children have poor control of their own aggressive feelings or may have been abused or psychologically rejected as children. The syndrome is found among people with stable social and financial backgrounds as well as in parents who are mentally unstable, alcoholic or drug-dependent. In most states, laws require physicians to report instances of suspected willfully inflicted injury among young patients. When it appears that the children will continue to be battered, steps are taken to remove the child from the home.

See also ABUSE; ALCOHOLISM; BATTERED WOMEN; DOMESTIC VIOLENCE; FAMILY VIOLENCE.

battered women   Battered women are victims of physical assault by husbands, boyfriend or lovers. Battering may include physical abuse sometimes for purposes of sexual gratification—breaking bones, burning, whipping, mutilation and other sadistic acts. Generally, however, battering is considered part of a syndrome of abusive behavior that has very little to do with sexual issues. Batterers were often abused themselves as children; drug- and alcohol-related problems are more common among families with battering behavior. Women who select and stay in abusive relationships were also often abused as children. Many women choose to stay in such relationships without reporting the abuse and without seeking counseling.

Treatment for battered wife syndrome must occur on many different levels. First, physical protection (often provided by women's shelters) must be assured for the woman and her children. Second, social support services must provide economic protection, since women often stay in abusive relationships because of lack of practical economic alternatives. Finally, psychotherapeutic intervention must be aimed at both batterer and victim to trace antecedents of violent behavior, correct substance abuse problems and substitute positive coping mechanisms for violent behavior patterns.

During early 1992 a study at the University of California at San Francisco revealed many details about the living conditions and circumstances surrounding battered women. According to the study of 218 women, many did not depend on their violent partner for the bulk of their financial support. Almost 30 percent had jobs, and many had income from families, welfare, social security and other sources.

Among other findings, fully 40 percent of the women needed to be hospitalized for their injuries. One in three of the women had been attacked with a weapon, most often a knife or a club. Four had been shot. One in 10 was pregnant when beaten, and 30 percent of the group said they had been abused previously while they were pregnant. In about half the cases, the husbands or boyfriends drank heavily or abused drugs; 86 percent of the women had been beaten at least once before.

See also ABUSE; ALCOHOLISM; FAMILY VIOLENCE.

Kahn, Ada P., and Holt, Linda H. *The A to Z of Women's Sexuality*. Alameda, Calif.: Hunter House, 1992.

Beckwith-Wiedeman   syndrome   A form of mild to moderate mental retardation that probably has a genetic cause. Features of the syndrome include hypoglycemia in early infancy, large stature with large muscle mass, large tongue and unusual ear creases.

See also MENTAL RETARDATION.

bedwetting Unconscious or unintentional wetting by a person over the age of three during sleep, medically known as enuresis. When the child or adult urinates involuntarily during waking hours, the condition is known as incontinence. In both cases, the problem may have emotional as well as physical causes and consequences.

Some children fear having a urinary accident or may have reacted severely to punishment or embarrassment for such an accident in the past. As a result, he or she may have nightmares about the accident or about going to the bathroom, and during the dream urinates in the bed. Punishment and shaming may increase and perpetuate this type of problem. A better solution is to reassure the child and relieve his or her fears. A skilled counselor may be able to help locate and explain the habits and reactions of the child, parents or other caretakers. All concerned should try to reinforce a child's successes and reward good behavior by compliments and possible special privileges.

Some children sleep so heavily that they cannot awaken to normal urinary impulses. This problem may be due to a new schedule, such as a child who is used to napping early and has just begun kindergarten. The new schedule means that the daily nap is postponed until after school. In cases of repeated bedwetting, physical causes such as infection or illness can be ruled out by a physician. If the cause of bedwetting is emotional, try to identify contributing factors and start taking positive steps to correct the situation. Whether the causes are physical or emotional, a child can be retrained regarding toilet habits to help restore coordination of mental, neurological and physical impulses involved. Figure out the approximate times when bedwetting occurs and list contributing factors before bedtime. Give the child less

liquid in the few hours before bedtime. Plan on awakening the child a few hours after he has gone to sleep and have him go to the bathroom. Help him train reflexes during waking hours by having him visit the bathroom immediately on feeling the first impulse. Since bedwetting may lead to further shame and problems, other symptomatic treatments have been used. The use of appropriate doses of imipramine, a tricyclic antidepressant, may be appropriate in some cases. This decision should be made by a pediatrician.

behavioral therapy (behavior modification)   A type of psychotherapy used to treat some mental health problems that emphasizes learned responses. It is often used in conjunction with other types of therapies, including psychopharmacotherapy. Behaviorial therapy is used to treat people who have a wide variety of mental health concerns, including anxieties, phobias, agoraphobia, obsessions, compulsions and alcoholism.

Behaviorial therapy is also widely used in the treatment of sexual dysfunction. At one time, sex therapists were criticized for using a behavioral approach, as psychoanalytic thinking viewed sexual dysfunctions as originating during childhood. However, as the success rates for behaviorial therapy are often quite high in sexual dysfunction, behavioral approaches have gained credibility.

Therapists strive to modify or alter the undesirable or self-defeating behaviors of an individual, such as anxiety and avoidance, instead of working toward changing the "personality" by probing into the individual's "unconscious." Behavioral therapists work on the theory that behavior has a learned component (as well as a biologic component) and thus many unwanted behaviors and reactions can be replaced with more desirable behaviors and reactions.

The focus of behaviorial therapy is on observable aspects of specific behaviors, such as the frequency or intensity of a physiological response (e.g., sweating as a reaction to anxiety) or of obsessive hand washing. Reports by the patient and self-rating scales are also often used to describe details of behavior. Specific treatment techniques are tailored by each therapist to the particular needs of each individual.

Goals of treatment are determined by the therapist and the patient and often the patient's family as well. The patient in behaviorial therapy views the therapist as a coach and usually makes choices about trying to learn new behaviors and responses. Usually the goal is for the patient to learn self-control of her bad behaviors and increase her number of revised, more acceptable, behaviors.

A variety of learning techniques are used by behavioral therapists. These include classical conditioning, desensitization, flooding, operant conditioning and modeling. In cases of social phobias, for example, therapists may use techniques in which the individual is gradually exposed to the fear-producing situations. The exposure may take place in the patient's imagination first and then in reality. Sometimes the reality never occurs (some situations are easy to imagine but difficult to simulate). However, the key to effective treatment is the gradualness of the exposure combined with the simultaneous use of relaxation training and new physiological and behavioral responses.

Exposure   Therapy   (Desensitization)
Exposure therapy refers to many behavioral techniques that involve the use of gradual exposure to an anxiety-producing situation. These techniques include systematic desensitization and exposure at full intensity (flooding and implosive therapy).

In systematic desensitization, a technique used by behavioral therapists, patients learn to rank situations that cause anxiety and distress, as well as a variety of deep-muscle–relaxing techniques. For example, an individual who fears the sexual act might place coitus at the top of the list of activities that make him or her anxious; thinking about

sitting with a date in a restaurant might rank at the bottom of the list.

The individual is trained in relaxation, both mental and physical. When these techniques are mastered, the person is asked to imagine, in as much detail as possible, the least fear-producing item from the list; when a comfort level is reached in imagining this item, the patient can move up the hierarchy with success. However, when the individual has completed treatment and goes out in the real world to face anxieties and fears, there may be slight regression down the list. For example, an individual who has learned to remain calm while walking into a party and meeting new people may not be comfortable alone with a date. However, the individual will eventually be able to move from non-threatening group social events to more intimate settings and progress to a desired level of sexual behavior.

Systematic desensitization was explained in 1958 by John Wolpe, an American psychiatrist (1914–   ). His first reports were on adults who had many mental health problems, including obsessive-compulsive disorder, reactive depressions and phobias. He adapted his technique from experiences gained in the 1920s when he worked with children in overcoming phobias of animals.

Flooding   and   Implosive   Therapy
Flooding is another technique used by behavioral therapists. The individual is asked to experience an anxiety-producing situation by imagination or in actuality (in vivo) while experiencing the supportiveness of the therapist. Then the individual is directly exposed to a high-intensity, peak level of the anxiety-producing situation without benefit of a graduated approach, as is the case in the systematic desensitization technique. The therapist controls the content of scenes to be imagined and experiences that reoccur. The therapist describes scenes with great vividness, deliberately making them as disturbing as possible to the anxious individual, who has not been instructed to relax. Prolonged

experience with these situations is planned to help the individual to experience "extinction" of the anxiety responses and thus overcome them.

Implosive therapy is another technique used by therapists. The individual is repeatedly encouraged to imagine anxiety-producing situations at maximum intensity and experience an intense anxiety reaction. The anxiety response is not reinforced and thus becomes gradually reduced.

Like desensitization, the techniques of flooding and implosion reduce anxieties and unwanted behaviors in some persons (such as those with simple fears), but desensitization seems to be more effective and to have more permanent results.

Modeling As a form of behavioral therapy, the individual watches another person—often of the same sex and age as the troubled person—successfully perform a particular feared action, such as entering a room full of strangers or being introduced to members of the opposite sex. The fearful person experiences extinction of the feared responses in a vicarious way. This technique is really social learning or observational learning.

Modeling has another aspect; in "covert modeling" the anxious patient simply imagines that another person faces the same anxieties or concerns without unwanted physiological responses.

Operant Conditioning This is a theory applied in behavioral therapy work. Because people will either maintain or reduce frequency of certain behaviors because of responses they get from their environment, behaviors that produce reinforcing consequences can be strengthened and behaviors producing unpleasant consequences reduced. Behaviors of avoidance in certain situations are considered under "operant" control and are thus changeable.

Hypnosis and Biofeedback Hypnosis is considered a behavioral technique and is often used in conjunction with other techniques. Hypnosis can help the individual reach a trancelike state in which he or she becomes extremely receptive to suggestion. Then, through posthypnotic suggestions, the individual may learn to change patterns of behavior, such as having fearful reactions to entering a room full of strangers at a party. By itself, hypnosis is not considered an appropriate treatment for most mental health disorders. It is often used to modify specific, unwanted behaviors, such as smoking cigarettes.

Biofeedback is often used in conjunction with relaxation training and to enhance possibilities for a person's response to treatments. In biofeedback, physiological reactions can be monitored electrically. An anxious person can learn to regulate certain processes, such as breathing or heart rate.

Family Therapy Behavioral techniques are often used in modifying ways in which an individual interacts with other members of his or her family. It is useful in some cases of childhood behavior problems, school phobia and agoraphobia, in which other members of the family "enable" the agoraphobic to persist in fearful habits.

See also AGORAPHOBIA; FAMILY THERAPY; PSYCHOTHERAPY; SEX THERAPY; BEHAVIORAL THERAPY in BIBLIOGRAPHY.

behaviorism A school of thought that holds that learning comes from conditioning, the most important factor in shaping who we are. Behaviorists believe that environment—not heredity—counts and that behavior, rather than experience, is all that can be observed in others. This school of thought was founded by James Broadus Watson (1878–1958), an American psychologist, early in the 20th century. Behavioral therapy techniques are generally based on these tenets.

benzodiazepine medications A class of drugs now widely used as antianxiety agents, sedatives, muscle relaxants and anticonvulsants. There are subtle differences between the drugs within the class; different ones are approved by the Food and Drug Administration for different indications. For example, alprazolam (Xanax) is approved for use in panic disorder, diazepam is approved for treatment of muscle spasms or musculoskeletal disorders and clonazepam is used to treat certain seizure disorders. As a class, they have a higher therapeutic index, less toxicity and fewer drug interactions than barbiturates and nonbarbiturate sedative-hypnotics. Because benzodiazepines carry a low risk of cardiovascular and respiratory depression compared with barbiturates, they are often used as induction agents before general anesthesia.

Benzodiazepines work by binding to specific benzodiazepine receptors in the brain; these receptors are linked to receptors for gamma-aminobutyric acid (GABA), a major inhibitory neurotransmitter. The drugs bind to benzodiazepine receptors, activate GABA and lead to an anxiolytic effect on the limbic system.

Individuals taking benzodiazepine drugs should be advised to avoid alcohol, because interaction may result in depression of the central nervous system. Benzodiazepines seem to be safe during pregnancy after the first trimester; because they are secreted in breast milk, however, mothers taking these drugs should not breast-feed.

See also PHARMACOLOGIC THERAPY in BIBLIOGRAPHY.

bereavement   A feeling of grief, numbness, emptiness and deprivation, particularly following the death of a loved one. Bereavement may also follow the loss of a pet, a material item or a relationship. In most cases, bereavement is diagnosed as a ''normal'' response to a situation. However, when signs and symptoms of bereavement become excessive, the condition may be considered a disorder and require professional treatment. In the course of the grieving process, each person progresses at an individual pace. While some people are ready, after a certain period of time, to socialize and resume many former activities, others take longer to feel comfortable in conversation with strangers, in crowds or attending any type of social events.

Many individuals find self-help groups for widowed people helpful after the loss of a spouse. There are also self-help groups for individuals who have lost a child or miscarried a pregnancy.

See also BARR-HARRIS CENTER FOR THE STUDY OF SEPARATION AND LOSS DURING CHILDHOOD; BEREAVEMENT AND LOSS CENTER.

Bereavement and Loss Center   An organization that provides professional counseling services for individuals who have suffered loss—or who anticipate a loss—of a spouse, child, relative or friend. The center is nonsectarian and provides psychiatric social workers and psychiatrists with an advisory staff including other medical specialists, financial advisers and attorneys.

For information, contact:

Bereavement and Loss Center of New
    York
170 East 83rd Street
New York, NY 10028
Phone: (212) 879-5655

See also BEREAVEMENT; GRIEF.

beta adrenergic-receptor blockers   A group of drugs, also called beta blockers, some of which are used to relieve symptoms of anxiety. While beta blockers have been considered effective in treating generalized anxiety disorder (GAD), they are not considered as effective as benzodiazepines, since they seem more effective at blocking peripheral or somatic anxiety symptoms.

Examples of some uses for these drugs are to reduce rapid heart rate, palpitations, sweats and hand or voice tremors rather than to relieve feelings of fear or anxiety.

There is some evidence that beta blockers may increase depressive feelings in some individuals, but they do not characteristically produce drowsiness. They are typically used by people who react to anxiety-producing situations in which somatic anxiety symptoms may impair function, such as addressing a large group. Beta blockers are also used in general medicine to prevent heart arrhythmias, treat high blood pressure and prevent migraine headaches. Examples of beta blocking drugs are propranolol (Inderal) and atenolol (Tenormin). They are not generally associated with the development of physical dependency but should not be discontinued suddenly in patients with atherosclerotic heart disease.

See also HEADACHES.

binge eating Eating excessive amounts of food, often part of the binge-purge syndrome (bulimia), which is characterized by consuming large quantities of food and then inducing vomiting or abusing laxatives. Not all binge eating is related to this disorder, however. Many individuals with apparently normal habits use binge eating occasionally as a comfort for disappointment in love, setbacks at work or as a relaxant after stressful events. Some individuals have their favorite bingeing foods, such as ice cream, cakes, cookies or other items. For many, however, periods of binge eating are followed by periods of remorseful feelings as they realize that their mental concerns are still there as well as additional pounds. For others, all that holds them back from binge eating is a stronger desire to maintain what they perceive as an attractive body image.

See also ANOREXIA NERVOSA; BODY IMAGE; BULIMIA; EATING DISORDERS; ANOREXIA, BULIMIA AND EATING DISORDERS in BIBLIOGRAPHY.

binge-purge syndrome See BINGE EATING; BULIMIA; EATING DISORDERS.

bioavailability A means by which the effectiveness of various types of drugs or methods of administration can be compared. Preparations with the same bioavailability are said to be bioequivalent. This term is often used with regard to generic forms of drugs. Bioavailability refers to the amount of a drug that enters the bloodstream and reaches tissues and organs around the body. It is usually expressed as a percentage of the dose given. For example, intravenous administration (injection) produces 100 percent bioavailability as the drug is injected directly into the bloodstream, whereas only a proportion of the drug can be absorbed through the digestive system with drugs taken by mouth. Some drugs are broken down in the liver before getting into the circulatory system. When prescribing antidepressants and tranquilizers, physicians take into account the bioavailability of various preparations and the needs of the individual.

See also ANTIDEPRESSANT MEDICATIONS.

biochemical disturbances See BRAIN CHEMISTRY.

biofeedback See ALTERNATIVE THERAPIES; BEHAVIORAL THERAPY.

biogenic amines Chemicals produced by the central nervous system that are involved in the functioning of the brain. Their role is to assist in the transmission of the electrochemical impulses from one nerve cell to another. Examples of biogenic amines include norepinephrine, dopamine and serotonin.

See also AMINE; NEUROTRANSMITTERS; NOREPINEPHRINE; SEROTONIN.

biological clock A term in contemporary usage referring to the limit on the period of time a woman has in which to bear children. Women in their mid- to late thirties say their "biological clock is running out." For many who desire to become mothers, this is a source of stress and anxiety.

Actually, the central nervous system has been found to have several "biological clocks" such as circadian rhythms and diurnal rhythms, which affect levels of brain chemicals or neurotransmitters and affect preparation of the individual for physical and intellectual response during varying times of the day. This is being increasingly recognized as an important factor in shift workers, especially those who must change shifts and maintain alertness, productivity and a sense of well-being.

biological markers Genes or genetic characteristics that can be identified and followed from generation to generation. Theories about the causes of affective disorders suggest that a disruption of neurotransmitters occurs, either by blockage of receptors or changes in receptors associated with the hypothalamus. The hypothalamus receives input from almost all regions of the brain. Changes in neurotransmitter patterns in a variety of brain areas alter neurotransmitter patterns in the hypothalamus. The hypothalamus exerts direct control on the anterior pituitary by a process known as neuroendocrine transduction. In this process, electrical signals determine the secretion patterns of hypothalamic neurotransmitters that stimulate specialized hypothalamic cells to secrete certain hormones. The hormones travel throughout the bloodstream to determine the release patterns of anterior pituitary hormones. Thus, changes in the neurotransmitters in the hypothalamus, as evident in an individual with affective disorders, may exhibit changes in the hormonal secretion patterns from the pituitary.

The first disrupted hormonal pattern to be studied was alteration in cortisol production. It was known that acutely depressed individuals showed extremely elevated levels of circulating cortisol. Cortisol (a glucocorticoid) is secreted by the adrenal cortex and regulated by the hypothalamic-pituitary-adrenal axis. Adrenocorticotrophic hormone (ACTH), released from the pituitary, is the major regulator of cortisol production. Release of ACTH is controlled by corticotrophin-releasing factor (CRF) from specialized cells in the hypothalamus. Secretion of CRF is stimulated by serotonin and acetylcholine and inhibited by norepinephrine.

The pituitary gland secretes ACTH in bursts, with the lowest levels secreted in late evening and highest levels in early morning, just after awakening. There are eight to nine secretory bursts during the day, for a total of approximately 16 mg. of cortisol released per day. Feedback loops, to the pituitary and hypothalamus, exist to regulate the release of ACTH and, subsequently, cortisol.

Some individuals who have affective disorders have increased levels of cortisol as measured in the plasma, CSF and urine. The elevated levels of cortisol secretion have been shown in individuals with unipolar depression and bipolar disorder. The secretion pattern is shifted, with the largest increase occurring from six to eight in the morning. In addition to elevated cortisol levels, individuals also have a flattened curve with loss of its normal circadian pattern.

There are two basic tests relating to biological markers. One is the dexamethasone suppression test; the other is the thyroid-releasing hormone challenge test.

Dexamethasone Suppression Test (DST) The dexamethasone suppression test was the first biological marker for affective disorder. Dexamethasone is a synthetic glucocorticoid that has the effect of turning off the secretion of ACTH and, subsequently, cortisol. In normal persons, a dose of dexamethasone given at 11:00 P.M. reduces cortisol levels for the next 24 hours. In depressed individuals, however, the suppression effect of dexamethasone does not occur. The nonsuppression of cortisol is called a positive dexamethasone suppression test. A positive DST result suggests depression but other illnesses such as alcoholism may show nonsuppression. However, a negative DST result does not rule out the diagnosis of major depression. In addition, studies suggest a positive correlation between the severity of depression and the rate of DST nonsuppression. There is also a correlation between the DST nonsuppression index and risk of suicide.

Individuals identified as nonsuppressors upon testing before antidepressive medication return to a normal suppression pattern when the treatment is successful. Individuals who show no reversal effect after treatment are at increased risk of relapse. The DST test is not considered specific enough for routine clinical use but may be of value in special circumstances.

While DST is considered a biological marker for mood disorders, it identifies only about 30–50 percent of clinically depressed individuals.

Thyroid-releasing Hormone (TRH) Challenge Test Indications for clinical use of the TRH challenge test are similar to those for DST. It is sometimes used as an aid in diagnosing depression and assessing thyroid status. A positive test result suggests the diagnosis of major depression, but a negative test result does not eliminate the diagnosis. When the two tests are used together, the increased sensitivity rate has been reported as high as 84 percent.

The hypothalamic-pituitary-thyroid (HPT) axis is the thyroid gland link to the central nervous system. The hypothalamus releases thyroid-releasing hormone (TRH) from neurons that stimulate pituitary cells to release thyroid-stimulating hormone (TSH) into the blood. TSH then stimulates release of other chemicals from the thyroid gland. Release of TRH is facilitated by dopamine and norepinephrine and is inhibited by serotonin. Levels of TSH have a circadian rhythm, with the highest levels of secretion from 4:00 A.M. to 8:00 A.M. Some individuals who are depressed have symptoms of hypothyroidism. A TRH test is used to determine if the HPT axis is functioning normally.

See also ANTIDEPRESSANT MEDICATIONS; DOPAMINE; NOREPINEPHRINE; SEROTONIN.

McFarland, Gertrude K., and Thomas, Mary Durand. *Psychiatric Mental Health Nursing.* Philadelphia: J. B. Lippincott, 1991.

biorhythms A term that describes all of the body's physiological functions that vary in certain predictable rhythmic ways. An example is the menstrual cycle in women, which is usually about 28 days. On a day-to-day basis, human bodies and their periods of sleepiness and wakefulness are governed by an internal clock regulated by hormones. When the internal clock is upset by long-distance jet travel, a syndrome known as jet lag occurs. This involves becoming sleepy at unusual times of the day, a groggy feeling, becoming hungry at odd hours and waking up during the middle of the night.

See also CIRCADIAN RHYTHMS; HORMONES.

bipolar disorder A mental disorder in which the individual experiences alternating mood swings of mania and severe depression. During the manic phase, the individual may have an enormous amount of energy and may feel strong, agitated, excited and capable of any undertaking. There may be constant talking, inappropriate degrees of self-confidence, little need for sleep, irritability, aggressiveness and impulsive behavior, such as excessive shopping and spending.

During the depressive phase, the individual will feel "down" and suffer from any of the symptoms associated with major depression. They may feel sad, helpless and hopeless. About 50 to 70 percent of such individuals are helped by taking the mood-stabilizing drug lithium. Others have been helped by taking anticonvulsant medications (e.g., carbamazepine or valproate). The disorder runs in families, and evidence from family and twin studies supports genetic transmission of the vulnerability. Evidence from both biochemical and imaging studies using PET scanning, MRI and CAT studies also offers further support for the biologic nature of this illness.

See also ANTIDEPRESSANT MEDICATIONS; DEPRESSION; LITHIUM CARBONATE; DEPRESSION AND AFFECTIVE DISORDERS in BIBLIOGRAPHY.

birth defects Also known as congenital anomalies. The birth defects most likely to be lethal include malformations of the brain and spine, heart defects and combinations of several malformations. Defects may be obvious at birth or detectable early in infancy. Infant mortality from congenital anomalies has been declining, although the last decade has seen slight increases in the incidence of some birth defects. In 1985, about 11,000 babies were born with moderate to severe impairments. Congenital anomalies, when they do not result in death, may cause disability. One-fourth of all congenital anomalies are caused by genetic factors, suggesting a need for preconception genetic counseling for both men and women. Environmental hazards and alcohol use during pregnancy are other important factors. Fetal alcohol syndrome (FAS) affects as many as one to three infants per 1,000 live births. In some populations, the incidence is higher. A similar syndrome has been observed in babies born to drug-addicted mothers.

Parents of children born with congenital anomalies can benefit from special counseling.

See also MENTAL RETARDATION.

birth order   Researchers in the area of birth order study personality development and mental health in relation to position in the family constellation. Alfred Adler, a student of Sigmund Freud, began the study of birth order in the early 1900s. Many studies of birth order have been undertaken as data were compiled for other projects. Birth order has been studied in relation to characteristics ranging from alcoholism to affiliation with religious orders. Most researchers believe that it is not a dominant force in personality development but one of the many determining factors in shaping a child's personality.

Studies of birth order have led to some generalizations about how a child's position in relation to his parents and siblings may affect his personality and view of the world.

The older child shares many of the qualities of the only child, as he or she is alone until the birth of a brother or sister. He has the attention and resources of the family for a certain length of time. As a result, older children tend to be more adult in behavior, are more interested in goals and personal achievement and are strongly represented in the ranks of the successful and powerful. Older children tend to score highest on intelligence tests. The arrival of a sibling, even though happily anticipated by the first child, has the ultimate effect of making him feel, in Adler's term, "dethroned." The older child often assumes a certain amount of responsibility for younger children in the family. He may be held responsible for setting a good example, showing younger children how to do things and baby-sitting. Older children are frequently more aware of family difficulties and problems and their own parents' insecurities. As a result, they tend to be more anxious, conservative and responsible than younger brothers and sisters.

The middle child position in the family has more variables attached to it, since the ages and sex of siblings may have a profound effect on the middle child. Middle children usually become good at sharing but also guard their privacy. Because of what they may perceive as a chaotic situation at home in which they are too young for the privileges of the oldest and too old for the coddling of the youngest, the middle child may show off to get attention and may also seek rewarding relationships outside the family. Middle children are team players and are frequently quite popular. The need to belong to a peer group is strong in middle children. To compete with an older sibling, a middle child develops her abilities in an area quite different from the talents of her older brother or sister. Middle children are frequently mavericks and are sensitive to inequities and injustices.

The youngest child of a family never has the experience of having his position usurped by a younger sibling. Younger children tend to preserve and use childish characteristics such as crying, acting cute or emphasizing their dependence and inadequacy to get what they want. Younger children frequently have very positive feelings about themselves because of their position in the family and tend to be charming and popular. They often have the best sense of humor in the family. Younger children are at a disadvantage in that they tend to obtain information and opinions from other children rather than adults and therefore lack the wisdom and realism they might gain from adult contact.

A very specific type of younger child is the "little caboose," often a "change of life" baby who arrives several years after the other siblings. This younger child is really more in the position of being the only child, but with several parents, since usually one or more of his siblings acts as a parent. These children grow up with a great deal of attention and support but may also have a confused sense of themselves, as they get a variety of images and ideas from siblings who are perceived as adult but are, in fact, children.

See also ONLY CHILDREN.

bisexuality Sexual attraction to members of the opposite sex as well as to members of the same sex. Sexual preferences are probably influenced by environment, early childhood experiences, possibly genetic makeup and intrauterine hormonal exposure effects on early central nervous system development.

See also HETEROSEXUALITY; HOMOSEXUALITY; LESBIANISM.

blocking An interruption in thought or speech that is abrupt and involuntary, when the individual cannot remember what it was he or she was about to say. This is also referred to as thought deprivation, thought obstruction and emotional blocking. This happens to most people at some time, especially if they are in a state of severe anxiety, grief or anger. In such circumstances it is normal to experience blocking at intermittent times. By itself, blocking is not a symptom of poor mental health. However, some individuals who are mentally disturbed may use blocking to keep distasteful ideas out of their consciousness. In some forms of schizophrenia, thoughts and speech may be blocked for prolonged periods of time.

Blocking should not be confused with "word finding" difficulties or recent memory loss seen in patients with multi-infarct dementia or with medication side effects.

See also MULTI-INFARCT DEMENTIA; SCHIZOPHRENIA.

blood brain barrier A physiological metabolic system that limits entry into the brain, protecting it from a number of potentially brain-damaging substances throughout the body, as well as from fluctuations in chemicals it needs to function normally.

It is a physiological "barrier" that regulates certain substances' rate of entry or egress in or out of the brain to or from its blood circulation. This is one reason why specific blood tests for mental disorders have not been developed beyond the stage of research findings.

Because of the blood brain barrier, chemicals composed of large molecules generally cannot pass from the blood into the brain as they do into other organs. This is so because in most parts of the body the smallest blood vessels are porous, whereas cells in the brain are tightly joined and adjacent cells are almost fused together. However, substances with small molecules, including oxygen, alcohol and medications that are highly fat soluble—anesthetics, for example—can cross the barrier.

Some substances, such as amino acids, require energy provided by glucose metabolism to cross the blood brain barrier.

See also BRAIN.

blood pressure The force of the blood against the walls of the arteries, created by the heart as it pumps blood through the body. As the heart pumps or beats, the pressure increases. The pressure decreases as the heart relaxes between beats. High blood pressure, known as hypertension, is the condition in which blood pressure rises too high and stays there. One cannot feel blood circulating through the body; thus one usually does not feel symptoms of high blood pressure. The only effective way to measure blood pressure is to have it checked with specially designed equipment.

Many individuals who are told that they have high blood pressure are advised to change their diet (lower cholesterol, lose weight) and exercise more. For some, medications that lower blood pressure are prescribed. Many individuals have difficulty complying because they cannot "see" or "feel" their disease. For these reasons high blood pressure has been referred to as "the silent killer."

blood tests Many individuals who are taking medication as part of their treatment for a mental health condition will be asked to have frequent and repeated blood tests. The reason is to determine how much of the medication remains in their bloodstream over a prolonged period of time. Blood tests help the prescriber determine an effective dose for each individual.

One such test is the lithium blood level test that individuals who have manic-depressive disorder undergo. With these measurements, the physician can choose and maintain the most effective dose for the individual and avoid a toxic dose. When a patient stops taking lithium, the blood level drops and symptoms may reappear.

Other tests are used to monitor the function of various organs (e.g., kidneys, liver) or thyroid gland function to ascertain that no medical illness is causing a mental disturbance or that medications are not causing any toxic effects.

Currently, there are no blood tests considered clinically reliable enough to diagnose mental disorders not related to medical illnesses (hypothyroidism, vitamin deficiencies) because the metabolism of the brain is not reliably reflected in blood or urine samples.

See also ANTIDEPRESSANT MEDICATIONS; BLOOD BRAIN BARRIER; DEPRESSION; LITHIUM; MANIC-DEPRESSIVE ILLNESS.

"blues" When people feel down, they are often referred to as suffering from the "blues." A "blue" mood is considered a sad mood. Most people experience these mood changes from time to time, but this does not necessarily indicate depression. Changes in mood are normal with the ups and downs of daily life, and individuals are able to function normally. It is only when mood characteristics meet the criteria for depression and interfere with daily living that professional help should be sought. The "baby blues" is the feeling of being overwhelmed or helpless after the birth of a baby. If the feeling continues and interferes with function or relationships, this is known as POSTPARTUM DEPRESSION.

See also DEPRESSION; POSTPARTUM DEPRESSION; SEASONAL AFFECTIVE DISORDER.

boarder babies A term denoting babies born with HIV infections (human immunodeficiency virus) who remain in the hospital because their mothers are too ill to care for them and they are difficult to place in foster homes. The 1988 Report of the Presidential Commission on the Human Immunodeficiency Virus Epidemic had predicted 10,000 to 20,000 HIV-infected births by 1991. These babies live their entire brief and tragic lives in hospital wards, with only doctors and nurses as family, unless they are taken into foster homes.

See also ACQUIRED IMMUNODEFICIENCY SYNDROME.

Report of the Presidential Commission on the Human Immunodeficiency Virus Epidemic, June 24, 1988.

body builder's psychosis See ANA-BOLIC STEROIDS.

body dysmorphic disorder A disorder in which the person is usually preoccupied with a specific organ or body part rather than having various complaints involving multiple organ systems. The condition is also known as dysmorphophobia. The individual may believe that he or she suffers from a serious disease because of a minor lesion such as a freckle. Some patients who focus on perceived defects on their faces often seek plastic surgery.

The disorder is considered a somatoform disorder because is it characterized by a physical complaint occurring in the absence of an identifiable physical disease.

See also SOMATOFORM DISORDERS.

body image The mental picture an individual has of his or her body at any moment. Perception of one's own body often determines one's level of self-esteem and self-confidence. Body image is derived from internal sensations, postural changes, emotional experiences, fantasies and feedback from others. A misperception of one's body image can lead to avoidance of social or sexual activities and eating disorders such as anorexia nervosa or bulimia.

Fear of deformity of one's own body is known as dysmorphophobia.

See also ANOREXIA NERVOSA; BODY DYS-MORPHIC DISORDER; BULIMIA; EATING DIS-ORDERS; SEX APPEAL.

body language Expression of impulses, feelings, desires, conflicts and attitudes through facial expression, posture, gestures or movement. In situations between women and men, or individuals in a business relationship, body language plays an important role. For example, a smile or a look can be sexually provocative. How one moves one's body and places oneself near another person can also convey messages regarding sexual interest or messages of aggression or passivity.

body narcissism Excessive interest in one's body and especially the erotic zones, such as the genitals or breasts. Psychoanalytic theory holds that this interest is particularly noticeable in young children when boys and girls begin to explore their bodies. Signs of narcissism might be evident in preoccupation with elimination activities, sexual response to masturbation and fear of injury to parts of the body. When the excessive interest in one's body continues throughout adulthood, the condition may be reason for psychological counseling.

See also BODY IMAGE; NARCISSISM.

bondage A form of sexual activity in which one person pretends to enslave the other to arouse sexual pleasure in one or both partners. Bondage may involve heterosexual or homosexual participants and may include threats or acts of humiliation and danger, with the enslaved person restrained by chains, ropes or other devices. Discipline is a variation of bondage that involves sadomasochistic activities such as whipping. Partners usually have a signal to use when the activity exceeds pleasurable limits.

See also PERVERSION, SEXUAL.

bonding The psychological process through which a mother forms a loving relationship with her child (also known as maternal bonding and paternal bonding). This may begin when a woman feels her baby move in her uterus for the first time, when she hears the first fetal heartbeat or during or after childbirth. Bonding develops further as she and her husband care for their newborn baby. According to M. H. Klaus and J. H. Kennel, authors of *Maternal-Infant Bonding* (1976), the first hour after birth is an especially critical time for bonding and is the "early sensitive period" when mother and child are particularly receptive to each other. When childbirth occurred mainly at home, mothers and infants were together after childbirth and there was little concern about bonding. Today many hospitals encourage parents to spend the first hours after delivery with their newborn and have arranged rooms so that the baby can remain with the mother after delivery.

Bonding is indicated by behaviors such as smiling, following, clinging, calling or crying when the mother leaves the child. This kind of behavior is the basis for later emotional attachments and is part of a series of normal developmental stages.

borderline mental retardation See MENTAL RETARDATION.

borderline personality disorder According to the *Diagnostic and Statistical Manual of Mental Disorders* (3d ed., rev.), essential features of this disorder include a pervasive pattern of instability of self-image, interpersonal relationships and mood, beginning by early adulthood and present in a variety of contexts. There may be impulsiveness regarding spending, sex, substance use, shoplifting, reckless driving or binge eating; chronic feelings of boredom and emptiness are also common. There is often social contrariness and a generally pessimistic outlook. Alternation between dependency and self-assertion is common, and there may be some impairment of social functioning at times. The individual may make frantic efforts to avoid real or imagined abandonment.

Possible complications include major depression, dysthymia, psychoactive substance abuse; premature death may result from suicide. The disorder is more common in females than males.

See also PERSONALITY DISORDERS.

brain The center and largest and most complex portion of the central nervous system. The brain includes all of the higher nervous centers that receive stimuli from the sense organs, interprets and correlates information and is the source of motor impulses.

Located within the skull, it is also the best protected part of the central nervous system.

The cerebrum is in the upper portion of the skull. It is the largest part of the brain and consists of the right and left cerebral hemispheres, which handle some of the more advanced processes of the nervous system. Some of these areas have been charted, and it is possible to determine the corresponding changes in certain areas of the body when certain parts of the brain are damaged. Separate parts of the cerebrum have certain functions. For example, sensory portions receive and interpret sensations of vision, hearing, touch, heat, pressure and others. Motor portions control muscles and movement, and association areas handle higher mental processes, such as memory, reasoning and analysis.

Below the cerebrum and toward the back part of the skull is the cerebellum, which controls many activities of the body below conscious level. For example, it automatically deals with reflexes of posture and balance, coordination of muscles and maintenance of muscle tone. Damage to the cerebellum, or inherited defects in it, make it difficult for an individual to move parts of the body properly. When there is a disturbance of a portion of the cerebellum, only the parts of the body on the same side as the disturbance are affected.

The midbrain, in front of the cerebellum, connects various divisions of the brain, including the brain stem and the medulla oblongata (spinal bulb), a control center for functions such as blood circulation and breathing. The spinal cord, which sends nervous system messages to and from the lower portions of the body, merges into the brain stem.

The thalamus is above the midbrain; it is an important center for processing and interpreting various sensations in the body (including pain) and is closely coordinated with the sensory parts of the cerebrum. The thalamus is thought to play a role in one's general mood or affect.

The hypothalamus is in the brain stem and takes on part of the brain's tasks of maintaining fluid balance in the body, sensing hunger, regulating body temperature and signaling a need for sleep or wakefulness. The hypothalamus secretes a hormone and other substances that aid in regulating water in the system and converting food and blood substances to energy (metabolism). Improper functioning of the hypothalamus may contribute to obesity, and when anxiety or excitement makes a person sweat and the heart beat faster, it is the hypothalamus that sends out messages for these reactions throughout the nervous system. Emotional tone may be affected by the chemical functions of neurons in the hypothalamus (depression, mania, anxiety and panic attacks).

Meninges surround the brain structures and extend down to enclose the spinal cord. These are membranes in three layers known as the dura mater (outer layer), arachnoid (middle layer) and the pia mater (inner layer). The meninges form spaces for the cerebrospinal fluid, which helps to cushion the brain and spinal cord against injury and to keep nerve tissues moist and lubricated. This fluid becomes altered with various diseases; samples of spinal fluid are sometimes taken with a lumbar (lower back) puncture, also known as a spinal tap. This is done by insertion of a needle between the lumbar vertebrae. Examination of the spinal fluid can help diagnose infectious meningitis (inflammation of the meninges), as well as some types of brain hemorrhage or tumors. Spinal fluid defects are sometimes detected at birth. When this occurs, the pressure may enlarge a child's head (hydrocephalus). Treatment for hydrocephalus includes tapping the fluid to reduce the pressure and draining the fluid through a plastic tube inserted in the child's stomach.

Brain Disorders Some brain disorders are characterized by symptoms rather than causes. These include migraine, narcolepsy (excessive episodic sleepiness) and idiopathic epilepsy (epilepsy of unknown cause), although epileptic seizures can also have specific causes, such as a tumor or infection.

Thought, emotion and behavioral disorders are generally described as emotional, mental or psychiatric illness. In some cases there is no obvious physical brain defect or disorder, although with many illnesses, such as depression and schizophrenia, there is often an underlying disturbance of brain chemistry.

See also ALCOHOLISM; AMYGDALA; BLOOD BRAIN BARRIER; BRAIN CHEMISTRY; BRAIN DAMAGE; BRAIN DEATH; BRAIN ELECTRICAL ACTIVITY MAPPING; BRAIN IMAGING; BRAIN SYNDROME, ORGANIC; BRAIN TUMORS.

brain abnormalities See BRAIN SYNDROME, ORGANIC.

brain chemistry Since the 1950s, researchers have learned an increasing amount of knowledge regarding brain chemistry. At first they noted that certain medications had mood-altering qualities. For example, some patients taking reserpine, a drug used to control blood pressure, became depressed. Some patients taking iproniazid to treat tuberculosis became euphoric. These and other observations led researchers and clinicians to studies indicating that mood disorders can be a function of a biochemical disturbance and can be stabilized with antidepressant drugs.

In animal brain tissue studies, biogenic amines—a group of chemical compounds—have been shown to regulate mood. Two of the amines, serotonin and norepinephrine, seem to be particularly important and are concentrated in areas of the brain that also control drives for hunger, thirst and sex.

Although there has been considerable progress in understanding the role of brain chemistry in depression and other mental health disorders, much is still unknown about the role of brain chemistry and mental health. There is evidence that in some types of depression there are abnormalities in brain function and that some individuals with major depressive disorders have too little or too much of certain neurochemicals the antidepressant drugs relieve. Imbalances in a neurotransmitter set up a chemical imbalance in the hypothalamus, leading to an imbalance of a hormone in the pituitary and causing the adrenal glands to produce too much cortisol, which in turn has widespread physiological effects.

Tricyclic antidepressant drugs seem to enhance certain neurotransmitters. Monoamine oxidase inhibitors (MAOIs) lead to an elevation of the levels of amine messengers in certain regions of the brain; as the brain becomes filled with extra amounts of chemical transmitters, the presumed chemical amine deficiency is corrected.

Effects of lithium are less clearly understood, but some researchers theorize that lithium stabilizes the chemical-messenger levels, so that cycling in amine concentrations is less likely to occur.

See also ANTIDEPRESSANT MEDICATIONS; BRAIN; DEPRESSION; LITHIUM; NEUROTRANS- MITTERS.

Roesch, Roberta. *The Encyclopedia of Depression.* New York: Facts On File, 1991.

brain damage   Death or degeneration of nerve cells and areas within the brain. There may be damage to particular areas of the brain, resulting in specific defects of brain function, such as loss of coordination, or more diffuse effects, causing mental retardation or severe physical disabilities.

Hypoxia, not enough oxygen reaching the brain, may occur during birth. A baby's brain cannot tolerate a lack of oxygen for more than about five minutes. At any age, hypoxia may occur as a result of cardiac arrest (stoppage of the heart) or respiratory arrest (cessation of breathing), as well as from other causes such as drowning, electric shock or prolonged convulsions.

Diffuse damage may also result from an accumulation of substances poisonous to nerve cells in the brain, such as phenylketonuria

or galactosemia; damage may also result from inhaling or ingesting pollutants such as mercury compounds or lead. Brain damage may also be caused by infections of the brain and, in rare cases, may occur following immunizations.

Localized brain damage sometimes happens following head injury, especially penetrating injuries. In later life, it occurs as a result of stroke, brain abscess or brain tumor. At birth, local brain damage caused by a variety of factors can lead to kernicterus, a condition characterized by disorders of movement and sometimes mental deficiency.

Cerebral palsy may result from brain damage that occurs before, during or after birth. It is characterized by paralysis and abnormal movements; it is often associated with mental retardation and, in some cases, deafness. Disturbances of movement, speech or sensation or epileptic seizures may result from head injury, stroke or other causes of localized or diffuse brain damage.

Treatment to improve some physical and mental functions following brain damage include physical therapy, speech therapy and occupational therapy. Some improvement may be expected in many cases after brain damage, as the individual learns to use other parts of the brain and other muscle groups.

Congenital Defects   Infants are sometimes born with damage due to genetic or chromosomal disorders, such as Down's syndrome and cri du chat syndrome. Structural defects arising during fetal development may be untreatable, such as microcephaly (small head), or fatal, such as anencephaly (congenital absence of the brain). Other defects can be corrected even while the fetus is in the uterus.

See also BRAIN TUMORS; CEREBRAL PALSY; CRI DU CHAT SYNDROME; DOWN'S SYN- DROME.

brain death   A concept meaning that a person is dead if the brain is dead; this is not a point on which all theologians, doctors and lawyers agree. Although still controversial, a widely accepted definition of the term with four criteria was proposed in 1968 by a Harvard Medical School committee: unresponsiveness to touch, sound and all other external stimuli; no movements and no spontaneous breathing; no reflexes; and a flat EEG, or the absence of all electrical activity in the brain as measured by the electroencephalogram.

There are various attitudes about brain death. One holds that the brain is dead only when the cerebral cortex—or the part of the brain humans use for thinking—stops functioning. Another attitude is that before the brain can be declared dead, the brain stem, which regulates lower processes, must also stop functioning.

The Harvard criteria are used by some, but not all, American states; other countries have differing definitions. Recognition of brain death permits physicians to certify death even when the heart and lungs continue activity with connections to life-sustaining equipment but when there is no brain function.

brain disorders   See BRAIN.

brain electrical activity mapping (BEAM)   A technique using a computer to perform spectral analysis of data from an electroencephalogram (EEG). The BEAM technique calculates the relative quantity of each brain-wave frequency as detected by each recording electrode location, showing patterns that may be too subtle to detect on a routine EEG. BEAM or brain mapping has been used in psychiatric research to study schizophrenia.

See also SCHIZOPHRENIA.

brain imaging   Computer-assisted methods to permit physicians and researchers to see detailed anatomical structures, abnormalities and actions within the brain; it is also known as brain scan or scanning. With imaging or scanning techniques, determinations can be made about the neurobiologic bases of mental disorders. For example, the size, shape and position of tumors or a specific area in the brain responsible for epileptic seizures or other conditions can be pinpointed. Images can indicate to physicians brain functions based on differences in metabolism or biochemical differences among different anatomical areas. Brain imaging or scanning techniques use X-ray, radioactivity and radio waves to produce detailed visualizations of the brain.

X ray   An X ray produces pictures of the bony structures of the skull but not the brain itself. However, with an X-ray image, a physician can sometimes detect erosion in the inner side of the skull, possibly indicating a brain tumor, as a growth can wear away bone. In some cases, bleeding inside the brain can also be detected with an X ray.

Angiography   This technique involves injecting a dye into an artery leading to the brain and then taking X rays, which show blood vessels in the brain. It is sometimes used to help diagnose some brain hemorrhages, aneurysms, abnormalities of blood vessels and other circulation disorders.

Computerized Axial Tomography (CAT)   Scanners that X-ray the brain in cross section, allowing the computer screens to display views of "slices" of the brain from various angles. In use since the early 1970s, CAT scanning reveals images of the brain substance itself, including pictures of the fluid-filled cavities of the brain (ventricles) that may indicate blood clots, aneurysms, abscesses, tumors or evidence of strokes. To help differentiate normal from abnormal brain tissue, contrast dye is often used.

Magnetic Resonance Imaging (MRI)   A technique that does not involve use of radiation and is particularly useful in showing tumors of the back of the skull. CAT and MRI have replaced previously used techniques of radionuclide scanning, which involved the use of radioactive isotopes to detect abnormalities of the blood vessels, tumors and other lesions.

Positron Emission Tomography (PET)   This technique combines use of radionuclides with CAT scanning and may reveal activities in various parts of the brain. Metabolic activity and the effects of specific drugs can be studied in humans with mental disorders yielding evidence of biochemical changes with this noninvasive procedure.

Ultrasound Scanning Ultrasound waves cannot penetrate bones of a mature skull but are useful in premature or very young infants. It can be used to detect hydrocephalus and ventricular hemorrhage in premature babies.

With ultrasonography, sound waves above the range of human hearing are sent into the head and bounce back, with echoes varying according to the tissue reached, helping to locate any displacement of the midline of the brain because of the pressure of a tumor. Repeated scans can be performed, as no radiation is involved.

brain scan See BRAIN IMAGING.

brain stem See BRAIN.

brainstorming Interchange of a free flow of creative ideas without regard for criticism or evaluation. Many creative individuals, such as those in advertising agencies, use brainstorming sessions to develop new concepts and ideas. Typically, there will be a leader, or facilitator, to stimulate ideas. One idea builds on another, and after a short period of time a list of ideas, topics or concepts will evolve. Individuals who are self-conscious and usually withdrawn often find themselves caught up in the spirit of generating and express ideas freely in this environment.

After a brainstorming session, ideas are organized categorically, and choices are made from which later plans will evolve.

brain syndrome, organic Disruptions of mental functioning and consciousness resulting from physical (organic) causes rather than psychological origins. Causes include degenerative diseases, such as Alzheimer's disease, imbalances of metabolism, reac-

tions to medications, infections, vitamin deficiencies and effects of tumors, strokes or trauma.

Symptoms may range from slight confusion to coma or may include memory impairment, hallucinations, delusions and disorientation. A chronic form of organic brain syndrome results in a progressive decline in intellectual functions. Treatment includes dealing with underlying causes wherever possible; treatment is most likely to be helpful in the acute stages of the illness.

See also ALZHEIMER'S DISEASE; BRAIN TUMORS; DEMENTIA.

brain tumors Any growth in the brain, more commonly a term referring to a cancerous growth within the brain substance. Brain tumors can be benign or malignant. Intrinsic tumors are those that arise from brain tissue or grow within the brain. Metastatic tumors are those that grow within the brain after having spread to the brain from another region of the body.

Brain tumors occur at all ages and reach peak incidence in individuals in their fifties and sixties. Classification of brain tumors is based on the cell type from which the tumor originated and can be determined by removing the tumor surgically and analyzing it microscopically.

Diagnosis of brain tumor is often difficult because tumors may cause very generalized symptoms. As tumors grow and occupy more space within the cavity of the skull, pressure on the brain increases. When the tumor presses on specific regions of the brain, there may be more specific complaints, such as headache, nausea, vomiting, partial blindness, double vision, seizures or weakness. There may be changes in personality, changes in speech and impaired memory and judgment. However, individuals with one or more of these symptoms should not rush to the conclusion that they have a brain tumor.

Physicians use brain imaging or brain scanning techniques to help diagnose brain tumors. Forms of treatment include surgery, radiation and chemotherapy.

brainwashing A form of mind control related to propaganda or political indoctrination. In its most extreme form, it was practiced by Communist governments, particularly during warfare. Some American prisoners of war who were incarcerated in China during the Korean War returned with their personalities and attitudes changed. They had been conditioned to the point that they made no attempt to escape their captors. Some came home with feelings that rejected America and accepted Communist propaganda. They also showed no interest in returning to their families. The same techniques—characterized by isolating individuals from friends and families and keeping them socially deprived, exhausted and overworked—are employed by cults professing a wide range of beliefs that promise to "save" the subject. People with low self-esteem and severe identity problems who are socially isolated or reject their own family values are particularly susceptible.

Although situations and techniques of brainwashing vary, there are common elements that are used to change thought patterns and deeply held values. For example, the subject is made to feel totally out of control, that his needs and actions are subject to an authority before which he is powerless. He may be subjected to mental or physical harassment and his deeply held beliefs ridiculed. As much as possible, he is made to feel that his future is uncertain and he must rely on the person who is controlling him. As his body weakens from the treatment, his thought processes become disorganized and he will agree to almost anything. His suggestibility increases as his self-esteem decreases. He begins to feel guilty about past behavior that is at odds with his captors' standards. As he becomes more agreeable to his captors' wishes, he is rewarded and his living conditions improve, only to deteriorate again if he regresses.

While true brainwashing is rare outside the realms of warfare and totalitarian governments, members of religious cults that flourished in the years following the 1960s showed evidence of techniques similar to brainwashing, such as changed speech and behavior patterns, obedience to an authoritarian leader and a rejection of friends and family outside the cult.

Johnson, Joan. *The Cult Movement.* New York: Franklin Watts, 1984.
Somit, Alters. "Brainwashing," in Sills, David, ed., *International Encyclopedia of the Social Sciences,* vol. 1. New York: Macmillan, 1968.

brain waves Electrical currents pulsing through brain cells. Although weaker than those in the heart, they can be detected by an electroencephalograph (EEG), a machine that records changes in electrical pressure and frequency on a moving graph. Physicians use the EEG as well as brain electrical activity mapping (BEAM) to study the brain and diagnose brain disorders. There are differing patterns of brain waves. Alpha waves occur when an individual is in a state of relaxed awareness. In a state of alertness, the brain gives off beta waves. When one is sleeping deeply, lying anesthetized during surgery or is suffering from severe brain damage, delta waves occur. Theta waves are a combination of mixed waves. In 1932, Edgar Adrian (1889–1977), a British electrophysiologist, won a Nobel prize for demonstration of brain waves.

Studies of sleep using EEG have shown specific abnormalities in the delayed onset of rapid-eye-movement (REM) sleep in many depressed patients.

See also BRAIN; BRAIN DAMAGE; BRAIN ELECTRICAL ACTIVITY MAPPING (BEAM); BRAIN IMAGING.

breath-holding spells Childhood breath-holding spells are a common and frightening phenomenon occurring in healthy, otherwise normal children.

Treatment of children with breath-holding spells has largely been to provide reassurance to families after a diagnosis has been made.

Some children use breath-holding as an act of rebellion or demonstration of autonomy. When children know that they can terrify their parents with this behavior, the behavior becomes somewhat reinforced. According to Francis DiMario, Jr., M.D., Department of Pediatrics, University of Connecticut Health Center, Farmington, "It is neither feasible nor helpful for parents to attempt to avoid circumstances that may provide emotional upset in their child. Even though pain and fear may serve as provocatives, simple frustration and the expression of autonomy are both normal and expected in young children."

If parental anxiety leads to continuous attempts at appeasement, the child may soon learn to manipulate the parent with the threat of crying. This does not imply a willful attempt at breath-holding, since in some cases it is reflexive and unpredictable. There is, nonetheless, the potential for parents to reinforce behavioral outbursts if appropriate calm firmness is not displayed at times of customary disciplining.

Should a breath-holding spell occur, have the child lie on his or her back, face upward, to protect the child's head from inadvertent injury and aspiration.

Earliest written descriptions of breath-holding spells are credited to Nicholas Culpeper, an English herbalist practicing in the early 1600s.

See also PARENTING; CHILDHOOD in BIBLIOGRAPHY.

DiMario, Francis J. "Breath-Holding Spells in Childhood." *American Journal of Diseases of Children* 146, no. 1 (Jan. 15, 1992).

breathing   Although breathing seems very easy and very normal, relearning breathing techniques can help many individuals who suffer from stress, anxieties and phobias. Deep, diaphragmatic breathing is a cornerstone for many relaxation therapies. In breathing exercises, individuals are taught to be very aware of their breathing rate and learn to control it and, at the same time, reduce their increasing heartbeat and some of the symptoms of anxiety. Some exercises, such as closing the eyes and breathing deeply, affect the hypothalamus and decrease the activity of the sympathetic nervous system. This brings on relaxation and enables a person to regain control of his or her emotions. Some performers and athletes learn this technique and use it to combat stage fright or performance anxiety.

See also BREATH-HOLDING SPELLS; STRESS; SYMPATHETIC NERVOUS SYSTEM.

brief psychotherapy   A form of therapy, often effective in "crisis management" situations, limited to 10 to 15 sessions. Active and goal directive techniques and procedures are used by the therapist. Brief psychotherapy is useful for some individuals and in some group settings to treat a variety of mild disorders. Recent studies have found brief therapy effective in certain forms of depression and anxiety disorders.

See also ANXIETY DISORDERS; BEHAVIORAL THERAPY; PSYCHOTHERAPY; SEX THERAPY.

bronchial asthma   See ASTHMA, ANXIETY AND DEPRESSION.

bronchitis   A disease marked by inflammation of the bronchial tubes of the lungs, coughing, spitting up of phlegm and mucus and breathing difficulty. Because of the breathing difficulty, the disease causes sufferers and their families great anxieties. At times the sufferer may fear that he or she will never regain breath and suffocate.

Acute bronchitis is a complication of a respiratory or other viral infection. Chronic bronchitis occurs in many people who have been lifelong smokers and is more common in areas of high air pollution. Sometimes attacks are seasonally related. Chronic bronchitis may also be a symptom of other diseases, such as emphysema or cor pulmonale.

To relieve distress, a person with chronic bronchitis should avoid smoking and being in a place where others are smoking. There are specific medications for bronchitis. In some cases, physicians also prescribe medications to help the patient relax and sleep more soundly.

See also CHRONIC ILLNESS.

bruxism Grinding or clenching of the teeth. This habit usually occurs during sleep, but some individuals unconsciously do it during the day. In some cases it is caused by unresolved stress; in other cases, it may be related to the occlusion of the teeth when they are brought together.

Some individuals who seek treatment for bruxism are given low doses of anxiolytic drugs to help them relax, particularly before bedtime. Ongoing bruxism may result in wearing away and loosening of the teeth and jaw stiffness. When causative problems cannot be easily resolved, dentists devise bite plates (similar to those worn by athletes during high-contact sports) to be worn at night.

See also STRESS.

bulimarexia A term relating to the combination of eating disorders commonly known as bingeing, purging and anorexia (starvation). An individual with this disorder alternates overeating and vomiting through self-induced methods, and avoidance of eating. This disorder is more common in young women than in older women or men. The disorder may result from the woman's misperception of her body as being unattractive to men, too heavy or otherwise disproportioned. Treatment for this disorder involves psychotherapy and group therapy to enhance the woman's self-esteem and self-respect.

See also ANOREXIA NERVOSA; BODY IMAGE; BULIMIA; EATING DISORDERS.

bulimia An eating disorder marked by periods of binge eating alternated with purging episodes, either self-induced vomiting, ingestion of laxatives or fasting. The term "bulimia" is derived from a combination of the Greek words *bous,* meaning "ox," and *limos,* meaning "hunger." Bulimia is more prevalent in women than in men and usually begins during adolescence or young adulthood.

Anxieties about their body shape, their eating habits or their lives in general cause some people to become bulimic. Low self-esteem, lack of impulse control and emotional instability are usually characteristics of bulimic women. Bulimia can be a dangerous condition, however, as it often leads to secondary problems requiring immediate treatment such as intestinal inadequacies, excessive dental cavities and esophageal lesions (sores or holes).

See also ANOREXIA NERVOSA; BODY IMAGE; BULIMAREXIA; EATING DISORDERS.

bullies People who take on a type of intimidating, aggressive behavior that may take place at any time of life but is of great concern among children and teenagers. Research has shown that of a group of 20 school children, one is a bully and one a victim. Male bullies are more likely to use physical size and power to intimidate; female bullies are more likely to use verbal harassment.

Bullies have been thought to be compensating for anxieties or failure, but in actual fact they have been found to be self-confident people who look down on their victims and see violence as a positive way to solve problems. Some bullies tend to have parents who show them little warmth, give them a great deal of freedom but also punish them harshly.

Bullies tend to be drawn to children who are smaller, physically weaker and less secure than the average child. Children who are being bullied may show it by a changed attitude toward going to school, school phobia, lowered performance in school, behavior on weekends that differs from school days, taking detours coming home from school to avoid the bully and odd requests for money that is actually used to satisfy the bully's demands.

Parents may find it difficult to handle a situation that involves their child and a bully, in part because children are frequently ashamed of being bullied. Parents must also tread a fine line between avoiding violence or revenge and teaching their children to stick up for themselves. Parents must also try to determine whether their own intervention will improve or exacerbate the situation.

See also SCHOOL PHOBIA.

Kesler, Jay; Beers, Ron; and Neff, LaVonne. *Parents and Children.* Wheaton, Ill.: Victor Books, 1987.

bupropion hydrochloride   An antidepressant (trade name: Wellbutrin) that is chemically unrelated to tricyclic or other known antidepressant agents and is not a monoamine oxidase (MAO) inhibitor. Compared with tricyclic antidepressants, it is a weaker block of the neuronal uptake of serotonin and norepinephrine and, to some extent, also inhibits the neuronal reuptake of dopamine. According to the 1990 *Physicians' Desk Reference,* effectiveness of the drug in long-term use, that is, for more than six weeks, has not been systematically evaluated in controlled trials. Physicians prescribing the drug for extended periods should periodically reevaluate its long-term usefulness for the individual patient.

This drug is contraindicated in individuals who have a seizure disorder, as the incidence of seizures with this drug may exceed that of other marketed antidepressants by as much as fourfold; but this is only an approximation, since no direct comparative studies have been conducted. It is also contraindicated in individuals who have a current or prior diagnosis of bulimia or anorexia nervosa because of higher incidence of seizures noted in such persons treated by the drug. Additionally, taking bupropion hydrochloride and an MAO inhibitor at the same time is contraindicated. At least 14 days should elapse between discontinuing an MAO inhibitor and starting bupropion. Adverse reactions commonly encountered with this drug may include difficulty sleeping, dry mouth, headache, constipation, nausea, vomiting and tremor.

See also ANTIDEPRESSANT MEDICATIONS; DEPRESSION; MONOAMINE OXIDASE INHIBITORS; TRICYCLIC ANTIDEPRESSANT MEDICATIONS.

Roesch, Roberta. *The Encyclopedia of Depression.* New York: Facts On File, 1991.

burnout   The progressive loss of energy, purpose and idealism leading to stagnation, frustration and apathy. It strikes anyone in any job, from top executive to mother with small children to singles "with everything going for them." It has nothing to do with intelligence, money or social position. Victims are usually high achievers, workaholics, idealists, romantics, competent self-sufficients and overly conscientious souls. Their common denominator is the assumption that the real world will be in harmony with their dreams. They hold unrealistic expectations of themselves, their employers and society and often have a vague definition of personal accomplishment. In their attempt to gain some distance from the source of anguish, they contract their world down to the smallest possible dimension and/or take on more and more work.

Physical symptoms of burnout include excessive sleeping, eating or drinking, physical exhaustion, loss of libido, frequent colds, headaches, backaches, neckaches and bowel disorders. The burnout victim desires to be alone, is irritable, impatient and withdrawn and complains of boredom, difficulty concentrating and burdensome work. Fellow workers may notice indecisiveness, indifference, impaired performance and high absenteeism. Intellectual curiosity declines, identity diffuses and interpersonal relationships deteriorate. "Overloaded," "tired of thinking" and "I don't know what I'm doing any more" express the inner agony.

Burnout begins slowly and progresses gradually over weeks, months and years to become cumulative and pervasive. It runs the gamut from initial enthusiasm to stagnation to frustration to apathy in an ever downward spiral.

Recovery from burnout is possible through rediscovery of self and the formation of new attitudes about living.

The following is a series of guidelines suggested by Dorothy Young Riess, M.D., Pasadena, California:

• Recognize that no one job (or personal relationship) is a total solution for life. Variety is the spice of life.
• Learn how to put priorities where they belong, and stop trying to be "all things to all people."
• Set aside personal time (no phone, no TV, no eating or reading) and answer the vital questions "Where am I going?" "What do I want to achieve?" and "How am I going to do it?"
• Develop competence in simple tasks to enhance optimism and lift depression.
• Learn how to accept reality and assume responsibility for self.
• Differentiate between authentic personal goals and those foisted on you by someone else.
• Create an "outside life" of family, friends, interest and activities unrelated to work.
• Strive for variety in work; avoid routine.
• Develop a support system that emphasizes problem solving, for example, "How can I improve on this situation?"
• Learn how to manage personal time.
• Establish an exercise program at least three times a week.
• Take minivacations.

See also CHRONIC FATIGUE SYNDROME; DEPRESSION.

Reprinted with permission of Dorothy Young Riess, from *Better Health Newsletter*, Pasadena, Calif., vol. 3, no. 1 (Feb. 1987).

BuSpar   Trade name for buspirone hcl.
See also BUSPIRONE HYDROCHLORIDE.

buspirone hydrochloride   A drug (trade name: BuSpar) approved for use by the Food and Drug Administration in 1986, used primarily in treating generalized anxiety disorder. Research shows that buspirone's effect on chronic anxiety is equal to that of diazepam, although its effects are not apparent for one or two weeks. In clinical trials, the drug was considered as effective for treating anxiety as benzodiazepines, and some clinicians considered it an advance because it lacked some side effects of other tranquilizers. For example, it may cause less drowsiness than other tranquilizers and does not produce physical dependency in individuals after prolonged use. It is considered safer to take in conjunction with alcohol because it does not exacerbate effects of alcohol as the benzodiazepines do, and it is less likely to be overused because it does not give users a euphoric high. However, side effects include headache, lightheadedness, dizziness and nausea.
See BENZODIAZEPINE MEDICATIONS.

butyrophenones   A class of antipsychotic drugs, including haloperidol.
See also ANTIPSYCHOTIC MEDICATIONS; HALOPERIDOL.

C

cacolalia   An impulse to use obscene words.
See also PERVERSION, SEXUAL.

caffeine   A stimulant of the central nervous system primarily consumed in coffee and tea but also present in cola drinks, cocoa, certain headache pills, diet pills and over-the-counter medications such as Nodoz and Vivarin. Regular use of over 600 mg. a day (approximately eight cups of percolated coffee) may cause chronic insomnia, anxiety, depression and stomach upset.

Caffeine is a naturally occurring alkaloid found in many plants throughout the world. It was first isolated from coffee in 1820 and from tea leaves in 1827. Both "coffee" and "caffeine" are derived from the Arabic word *gahweh* (pronounced "kehveh" in Turkish).

In beverage form, caffeine begins to reach all body tissues within five minutes; peak blood levels are reached in about 30 minutes. Normally, caffeine is rapidly and completely absorbed from the gastrointestinal tract. Little can be recovered unchanged in urine, and there is no day-to-day accumulation in the body.

Caffeine increases the heart rate and rhythm, affects the circulatory system and acts as a diuretic. It also stimulates gastric acid secretion. There may be an elevation in blood pressure, especially during stress. Caffeine inhibits glucose metabolism and may thereby raise blood sugar levels.

Caffeine is a mild behavioral stimulant. It may interfere with sleep and may postpone fatigue. It appears to interact with stress, improving intellectual performance in extroverts and impairing it in introverts. When taken before bedtime, caffeine may delay the onset of sleep for some individuals, may shorten sleep time and may reduce the average "depth of sleep." It also may increase the amount of dream sleep (REM) early in the night while reducing it overall.

While caffeine in moderate doses may, for some individuals, increase alertness and decrease fatigue, regular use of 350 mg. or more a day may result in a form of physical dependence. (Coffee contains 100 to 150 milligrams of caffeine per cup; tea contains about half, and cola about one-third, that amount.) Interruption of such use can result in withdrawal symptoms, the most prominent of which is sometimes severe headache, which can be relieved by taking caffeine. Irritability and fatigue are other symptoms. Regular use of caffeine produces partial tolerance to some or all of its effects.

Caffeine and Panic Attacks Individuals who have panic attacks should avoid caffeine, as it has been known to produce panic attacks in susceptible individuals. About half of panic disorder sufferers have panic experiences after consuming caffeine found in four to five cups of coffee. Research may determine whether caffeine has a direct or causative effect on panic or simply alters the body state, which triggers a panic cycle as perceived by the individual. Caffeine may produce its effects by blocking the action of a brain chemical known an adenosine, a naturally occurring sedative.

Caffeine Intoxication (caffeinism) Caffeine intoxication is an organic disorder caused by recent consumption of over 250 mg. of caffeine and involving at least five of the following symptoms: restlessness, increased anxiety, nervousness, excitement, insomnia, frequent and increased urination, gastrointestinal complaints, rambling thought and speech, cardiac arrhythmia, periods of inexhaustibility, psychomotor agitation and increases in phobic reactions in phobic individuals.

See also CAFFEINE; PANIC ATTACK; PANIC DISORDER; SLEEP.

Doctor, Ronald M., and Kahn, Ada P. *Encyclopedia of Phobias, Fears, and Anxieties*. New York: Facts On File, 1989.

O'Brien, Robert, and Cohen, Sidney. *Encyclopedia of Drug Abuse*. New York: Facts On File, 1984.

"calling cards" The presenting complaints of individuals as they seek help for a mental health concern.

cannabis A plant *(Cannabis sativa)* commonly known by many names, including marijuana, maconha and hashish. Cannabis has been known to humans since 2500 B.C., when it was listed in a Chinese book of pharmacology. Cannabis has been used in times past for treatment of headaches, arthritis, malaria, stomach ailments and constipation. Its euphoria-producing properties are well known throughout the world. It is abused because of its effects, and its possession is illegal in the United States and many other countries. It is widely believed that cannabis abuse leads to other, more dangerous forms of substance abuse.

carbamazepine   An anticonvulsant (trade name: Tegretol) used to treat depression, though not approved as of the early 1990s by the U.S. Food and Drug Administration for this use. Some manic-depressives who cannot tolerate lithium do well on carbamazepine. Some individuals who have many cycles (up to four) during a year appear to do less well on lithium and better on carbamazepine. Valproate is another anticonvulsive, marketed under the trade name of Depakote.

See also ANTIDEPRESSANT MEDICATIONS; LITHIUM; MANIC-DEPRESSIVE ILLNESS; PHARMACOLOGIC THERAPY in BIBLIOGRAPHY.

Kravitz, Howard, and Fawcett, Jan. "Carbamazepine in the Treatment of Affective Disorders." *Medical Science Research* 15, no. 1 (Jan. 1987).

Zajecka, J. M.; Fawcett, J.; and Easton, M. S. "Treatment of Psychotic Affective Disorders." *Current Opinion in Psychiatry* 3 (1990).

carbon dioxide sensitivity   An abnormal sensitivity to inhaling small amounts of carbon dioxide, which causes symptoms of hyperventilation, trembling, facial flushing, blurring of vision and dizziness. Individuals prone to panic attacks have occurrences of their disorder upon inhaling carbon dioxide because of increased activity in the locus coeruleus (a small area of the brain rich in neurotransmitters). Such panic attacks occur in nearly all predisposed individuals but rarely in non–panic attack individuals.

See also ANXIETY DISORDERS; LACTATE-INDUCED ANXIETY; NEUROTRANSMITTERS; PANIC ATTACK.

caregivers   Individuals who are health care professionals, social workers, friends or family members of a child, elderly, ill or disabled person who cannot completely care for himself.

Within families, the responsibility of the caregiver has usually fallen heavily on women. This tendency has not changed even though other institutional options are available; 75 percent of care of the elderly is still provided by a family member. Now other social forces are making the responsibility particularly difficult. Social mobility and shrinking family size may make some women the sole relative responsible for care of both their own and their husbands' aging parents. At the same time, women are moving into highly responsible professional positions at about the time in life that their parents need care. The Older Women's League in Washington, D.C. has determined that at least a third of all women over age 18 can expect to be continuously in the caregiver role from the birth of their first child to the death of their parents. According to the American Association of Retired Persons, some women are pressured to turn down promotions, avoid traveling and even take early retirement to care for aging parents.

The caregiver role can be extremely draining of both physical and mental energy. Caregivers may feel powerless and depressed in the face of the suffering of a loved one and may somehow feel that they should be able to give their own youth and health. Professional caregivers must be on guard against both the tendency to build a wall around themselves or allowing the constant pain and suffering they see to dwarf their own needs.

As caregivers have a considerable amount of power and work in a close, personal relationship with their charges, frequently with little or no supervision, the position is vulnerable to abusive behavior. Recently more attention has been focused on this problem by government and the media. Children are more frequently victims of sexual abuse by their caregivers. The elderly are more often subjected to neglect or emotional and financial abuse.

See also ABUSE; AGING; ALZHEIMER'S DISEASE; ELDERLY PARENTS; ALZHEIMER'S DISEASE, ELDERLY, ILLNESS AND DISABILITY IN THE FAMILY in BIBLIOGRAPHY.

Boyd, Malcolm. "Finding Strength in Peace." *Modern Maturity* 34 (June–July 1991).
"The Daughter Track: Are You Prepared to Be a Lifetime Caregiver?" *Glamour* (May 1990).
Yovanovich, Linda. "A Caregiver's Guide to Self-care." *Nursing* 21 (Oct. 1991).

castration   Removal of the ovaries or the male testes by surgery, or inactivation of these glands by radiation, drugs or infections. In males and females, castration changes the hormonal balance of the individual, with the possible result of reducing libido. However, with appropriate counseling, behavioral changes need not result from castration.

Women whose ovaries are removed (oophorectomy) are put into a state of premature menopause and may experience menopausal symptoms, such as hot flashes. Estrogen replacement therapy is helpful for many women.

Removal of the male sex glands has been practiced historically in many cultures and was probably first performed in ancient Egypt and other Near Eastern cultures. Hundred of young boys were castrated in one religious ceremony and their genitals offered sacrificially to the gods. Castrated males were used as eunuchs to guard women in harems. If the operation was performed after puberty, the penis would be of adult size and capable of erection, because the adrenal glands continue to produce androgen even after the testes have been removed.

The term "castrating" is also used to refer to a psychological threat to the masculinity or femininity of an individual. The term "castrating woman" usually refers to a wife or mother who emasculates a man or men in the psychological sense through domination and derogatory remarks and behavior.

The term "castration complex" is used by psychoanalysts to refer to the unconscious feelings and fantasies associated with loss of the sex organs; in males, this relates to loss of the penis, while in females, the belief that the penis has already been removed. In boys, fear of losing the penis is associated with punishment for sexual interest in the mother (the Oedipus complex). It is also associated with threats of castration as punishment for masturbation and the discovery that girls do not have a penis. In girls, the castration complex takes the form of a fantasy that the penis has already been removed as a punishment, for which they blame their mother (Electra complex).

See also ELECTRA COMPLEX; MENOPAUSE; OEDIPUS COMPLEX.

Goldenson, Robert M., ed. *Longman Dictionary of Psychology and Psychiatry*. New York: Longman, 1984.
Kahn, Ada P., and Holt, Linda Hughey. *The A to Z of Women's Sexuality*. Alameda, Calif: Hunter House, 1992.
Katchadourian, Herant A., and Lunde, Donald T. *Fundamentals of Human Sexuality*. New York: Holt, Rinehart and Winston, 1972.

castration complex   See CASTRATION.

Catapres   See CLONIDINE.

catatonia   A physical state marked by an apparent lack of responsiveness to the point of near stupor and either muscular rigidity or the "waxy flexibility" of the muscles in which, if placed in one position, the individual will stay that way until moved to another. Catatonia is a clinical syndrome seen in association with affective disorders, organic mental syndromes, schizophrenia and some neurological diseases. Since the availability of modern antipsychotic medications, catatonia has been diagnosed less frequently, owing to the masking of symptoms or the aborting of a catatonic state by the medications.

The term was first used by Karl Kahlbaum in 1887 to name a state of lowered tension. The term was later absorbed by Emil Kraepelin into his subtypes of dementia praecox and later still became the 20th-century diagnostic category of catatonic schizophrenia.

In catatonic stupor, the individual may be immobile, mute and unresponsive and yet fully conscious. In catatonic excitement, the individual may exhibit uncontrolled and aimless motor activity. Such patients may assume bizarre or uncomfortable postures, such as squatting, and maintain them for long periods. With prolonged catatonic excitement and resultant restraint, hyperthermia that may cause death or residual nervous system damage may result. This condition is called lethal catatonia.

Catatonic schizophrenia is a subtype of schizophrenia dominated by stupor or mutism, negativism, rigidity, purposeless excitement and bizarre posturing. This subtype of schizophrenia is reported to be less common than in the past, possibly because of modern medications.

See also SCHIZOPHRENIA.

catatonic excitement See CATATONIA; SCHIZOPHRENIA.

catatonic schizophrenia See CATATONIA; SCHIZOPHRENIA.

catharsis Therapeutic release of anxiety by talking about disturbing feelings and impulses. It also means bringing to the surface and reliving events and experiences stored in the unconscious mind that produced the anxiety symptoms. Catharsis occurs during psychotherapy and group therapy.

cathexis An investment of mental energy in an object of any kind, such as a person, a goal or a social group. When one attaches emotional significance to them, such objects are said to be cathected.

central nervous system (CNS) Part of the nervous system consisting of the brain and spinal cord; the CNS is primarily involved in the control of mental activities and in coordinating incoming and outgoing messages. All sensory impulses are transmitted from the CNS, and all motor impulses originate there. The CNS coordinates activities of the entire nervous system; the CNS is affected by many psychotropic drugs, anxiolytic drugs and antidepressant drugs.

See also ANTIDEPRESSANT MEDICATIONS; DEPRESSION.

cerebellum See BRAIN.

cerebral cortex See BRAIN.

cerebral palsy The word "cerebral" refers to the brain; palsy refers to a lack of muscle control. Cerebral palsy involves muscular coordination problems related to the brain. Almost all cerebral palsy cases begin before or during birth. Brain cells may be damaged in various ways. For example, there may be insufficient oxygen reaching the brain during labor if pressure squeezes off the umbilical cord's blood supply. There may be brain damage to a child born of a mother who had rubella during her pregnancy (vaccines now can reduce this cause to a minimum). There may be blood incompatibility between the mother and father; this can be detected before conception to reduce the number of cases of cerebral palsy from this cause.

There is no cure for cerebral palsy, but corrective exercises, braces and surgery help many children born with the disease. The condition can be complicated by parents and friends creating emotional problems for the child as well as the family. As with any other chronic disease, empathy, understanding and moral support from those around the patient will be helpful to all.

See also CHRONIC ILLNESS; ILLNESS AND DISABILITY IN THE FAMILY in BIBLIOGRAPHY.

cerebrospinal fluid (CSF)   The fluid within the central canal of the spinal cord, four ventricles of the brain and the subarachnoid space of the brain. The CSF protects vital tissues from damage by shock pressure.
See also BRAIN.

cerebrum   See BRAIN.

certification   The process of preparing the legal documents necessary for the procedure of commitment to a mental institute for detention and treatment. The term is also used to refer to the formal signing of a statement of cause of death issued by a medical practitioner. Additionally, the term is used to indicate that a medical specialty board has approved a physician as a specialist (board certification).

change of life   A term referring to menopause.
See also CLIMACTERIC; MENOPAUSE.

checking   A symptom of obsessive-compulsive disorder (OCD). Checking is the repetitious act of looking to see that one's door is locked or one's stove has been turned off. As a common sense precaution, most people do check for these and other important matters. However, when the checking becomes a ritual and takes up most of one's time, it is a symptom of an obsession. About one-third of all sufferers of OCD have checking as a symptom. Checking seems to be more common in men than women.
See also OBSESSIVE-COMPULSIVE DISORDER; OBSESSIVE-COMPULSIVE DISORDER in BIBLIOGRAPHY.

chemical imbalance   See ANTIDEPRESSANT MEDICATIONS; BRAIN CHEMISTRY.

CHEST PAINS   See ANGINA PECTORIS.

child abuse   See FAMILY VIOLENCE; MULTIPLE PERSONALITY DISORDER.

childbirth   The birth of a child, usually by passage through the birth canal. Many women view childbearing as a transition to adult female sexuality. In many cultures, the figure obtained during pregnancy—wider hips, extra body fat, more rounded contours—is equated with the sexuality of fertility. Other cultures try to separate childbirth from female sexuality and may equate a feminine ideal with slimness and a less rounded image. For most women, childbearing is viewed as an important sexual rite of passage, owing both to the pride of bearing a child and to the often sexually satisfying process of nursing and snuggling an infant. Some male partners find the process of pregnancy and childbirth appealing sexually, and a close bonding of partners occurs; other men have great difficulty in relating to a woman as a mother and a sexual object at the same time.

Natural and Prepared Childbirth   In the latter half of the 20th century, many women became concerned about using pharmacologic methods to relieve pain and render them literally unconscious during the birthing procedure. Indeed, many older mothers believe that they "missed out" on the entire process of giving birth to their children because of pharmacologic interventions. The term "natural childbirth" generally refers to childbirth without drugs or medical intervention. The term is specifically used to refer to a movement toward unmedicated deliveries started by Fernand LaMaze (1891–1957), a French obstetrician.

Interest in natural childbirth began developing during the 1940s and 1950s when the use of drugs for pain relief and medical procedures such as routine episiotomies, shaves, enemas and sterile technique during hospital deliveries removed the woman and her family from a sense of participation in the childbirth process. While the specific methods for childbirth put forward by LaMaze, Dick-Reed and Leboyer vary, they all incorporate nonmedical relaxation techniques as a "natural" method of pain control during labor. In addition, they question the need for routine medical procedures and advocate a more active participation in labor by the woman and lay labor coach, often meaning the father of the baby. The movement has expanded to include the use of birthing rooms (rooms in which labor and delivery take place in a homelike setting) and the inclusion of extended family and friends in the delivery process. Some women choose to have their babies delivered at home to assure being surrounded by their family members. Some women opt for delivery by specially trained nurse-midwives rather than physicians. Nurse-midwives, however, have the backup of physicians in case of medical emergencies.

The term "prepared childbirth" became popular in the early 1990s; it includes prenatal exercise classes and a wide variety of breathing and relaxation techniques.

Special Mental Health Concerns Relating to Childbirth Some women approach childbirth with many concerns because of reports from friends and relatives. First-time mothers, in particular, are anxious about the unknown aspects related to childbirth. Some first-time fathers who attend the birthing event have anxieties as well. Some men and women have a fear of the entire birthing process, which is known as maieusophobia. While some fear pain, others fear blood, doctors and the uncertainties of facing parenthood. Women often become anxious about many of the practical details surrounding the birthing experience, such as wondering if they will recognize the start of labor and getting to the hospital on time.

Women whose babies are delivered by cesarean section have concerns that the procedure denies them what they believe should be a natural experience. Women who have cesarean sections wonder if they will be able to have subsequent children by vaginal delivery. This depends on whether or not the reason for the cesarean section was a one-time occurrence (such as a breach presentation), if the cesarean scar is strong and if the physician is agreeable to a subsequent normal labor, assuming that the woman's pelvis is wide enough for a baby's head.

See also BONDING; PARENTING; POSTPARTUM DEPRESSION.

Beauvoir, Simone De. *The Second Sex.* New York: Modern Library, 1968.
Eisenberg, Arlene; Murkoff, Heidi Eisenberg; and Hathaway, Sandee Eisenberg. *What to Expect When You're Expecting.* New York: Workman Publishing, 1984.
Kahn, Ada P., and Holt, Linda Hughey. *The A to Z of Women's Sexuality.* Alameda, Calif.: Hunter House, 1992.

chlordiazepoxide An antianxiety drug (trade name: Librium); one of a group of drugs known as benzodiazepines. It is effective in the management of generalized anxiety disorder and is also used to ameliorate the symptoms of alcohol withdrawal and as a preanesthetic medication. It is considered more useful in relieving anxiety than most nonbenzodiazepines.

See also ANXIETY; ANXIOLYTIC MEDICATIONS; BENZODIAZEPINE MEDICATIONS; CENTRAL NERVOUS SYSTEM.

chlorpromazine A tranquilizer (trade name: Thorazine). The first antipsychotic drug marketed, it is used primarily to treat schizophrenia, other psychoses or mania. It is used less commonly in schizoaffective disorder or major depression with psychotic features, paranoia, intractable hiccups, disturbed behavior associated with mental retardation, nausea and vomiting. The drug has a relatively low potency; it is one of the most sedative antipsychotic drugs, but tolerance to this effect usually develops. It is probably best tolerated by patients under 40 years of age. In older patients, the incidence of dizziness, hypotension, ocular changes and dyskinesia increases, although the latter is more commonly associated with the more potent antipsychotic agents.

See also TRANQUILIZER MEDICATIONS.

American Medical Association. *AMA Drug Evaluations Annual, 1991*. Chicago: AMA, 1991.

cholinergic medications The word "cholinergic" pertains to nerve cells and organs that are activated by the neurotransmitter acetylcholine. Cholinergic drugs are agents that increase the activity of acetylcholine or have effects similar to those of acetylcholine, such as facilitating the transfer of nerve impulses between cells. These drugs are used as substitutes for acetylcholine in therapy and research, as they resist destruction by enzymes that usually deactivate acetylcholine. Cholinergic drugs are also known as parasympathetic drugs. Cholinergic drugs are frequently used to reverse the anticholinergic effects of many therapeutic agents to promote normal bowel and bladder function (for example, postsurgery).

See also ANTICHOLINERGIC MEDICATIONS.

choosing a psychotherapist See PSYCHOTHERAPY.

chromosome All members of a species normally have the same number of chromosomes. The normal number for humans is 46 chromosomes, or 23 pairs, which contain the genes for specific hereditary traits. Chromosomes are usually invisible strands or filaments of DNA, RNA, or other molecules carrying the genetic or hereditary traits of an individual. Chromosomes are located in the cell nucleus and are visible through a microscope only during cell division. Defects in chromosomes can result in birth defects or hereditary disorders. For example, mental retardation is caused by absence of part of a chromosome, a defective chromosome or an extra chromosome. A condition known as trisomy 21 is one that is associated with 85 percent of Down's syndrome cases. There are three number 21 chromosomes in

the body cells instead of the normal pair. The extra chromosome may come from either the father or the mother. Some writers use trisomy 21 as a synonym for Down's syndrome.

See DOWN'S SYNDROME; GENETIC COUNSELING; MENTAL RETARDATION.

chromosome 21 See CHROMOSOME; DOWN'S SYNDROME.

CHRONIC BRONCHITIS See BRONCHITIS.

chronic fatigue immune dysfunction syndrome (CFIDS) Another name for chronic fatigue syndrome. Some physicians and patients prefer this name because it suggests an immunological component to the disorder.

See also CHRONIC FATIGUE SYNDROME.

chronic fatigue syndrome (CFS) An illness characterized by fatigue that starts suddenly, improves and relapses, bringing on debilitating tiredness or easy fatigability in an individual who has no apparent reason for feeling this way. The profound weakness of CFS does not go away with a few good nights of sleep but instead steals a person's vigor over months and years. Because many individuals with CFS experience frustration before being diagnosed, many develop depression.

In 1988, the Centers for Disease Control (CDC) published an official definition of chronic fatigue syndrome. The move was widely hailed as an acknowledgment of the legitimacy of CFS and as an important step toward better scientific understanding of CFS. According to the CDC, a case of CFS must fulfill these two major criteria:

1. New onset of persistent or relapsing debilitating fatigue or easy fatigability in a person who has no previous history of similar symptoms. The fatigue does not resolve with bed rest and is severe enough to reduce or impair average daily activity

below 50 percent of the patient's customary level for at least six months.

2. Other clinical conditions that may produce similar symptoms must be excluded by thorough evaluation, based on a medical history, physical examination and appropriate laboratory tests. Conditions specifically mentioned by the CDC include malignancy; autoimmune diseases; localized infection; chronic or subacute bacterial, fungal or parasite disease (such as Lyme disease, tuberculosis, toxoplasmosis, amebas or giardia); AIDS, AIDS-related condition (ARC) or any other HIV-related infection; chronic psychiatric disease (such as depression, neurosis, schizophrenia); chronic use of tranquilizers, drug dependency or abuse; side effects of medication or a toxic agent (such as a chemical solvent or a pesticide); chronic inflammatory disease; neuromuscular disease, such as multiple sclerosis or myasthenia gravis; endocrine disease, such as hypothyroidism or diabetes; any other known chronic pulmonary, renal, cardiac, hepatic (relating to the liver) or hematologic (relating to the blood or blood-forming tissues) disease.

According to the National Institutes of Health, CFS leaves many people bedridden, or with headaches, muscular and joint pain, sore throat, balance disorders, sensitivity to light, an inability to concentrate and inexplicable body aches. Symptoms wax and wane in severity and linger for months and sometimes years, causing the individual to retreat from professional and social obligations. Some individuals have been helped with various treatments. Some individuals do recover, while others must function at a reduced level for years.

CFS can affect virtually all of the body's major systems: neurological, immunological, hormonal, gastrointestinal and musculoskeletal. As a syndrome, it has a constellation of signs and symptoms—and possibly multiple causes—rather than one specific cause. The course of CFS from onset to recovery varies greatly from one individual to another. However, for all sufferers the cumulative effect is the same, namely, transforming ordinary activities into tremendous challenges. Sufferers cannot tolerate the least bit of exercise, and often their cognitive functions become impaired. Memory, verbal fluency, response time and the ability to perform calculations and to reason abstractly suffer.

Chronic fatigue syndrome came into the public consciousness during the 1980s. It is difficult to diagnose because many of its symptoms are like those of other disorders. For example, it is not infectious mononucleosis, although profound fatigue is common in both disorders. It is not Alzheimer's disease, although there is memory loss and periodic confusion associated with both disorders. While there are immune system abnormalities, just as there are in AIDS, it is not AIDS. It has also been confused with rheumatoid arthritis, Hodgkin's disease, multiple sclerosis and lupus.

Clinicians say there is a clear distinction between ordinary fatigue and the exhaustion that characterizes CFS. Physicians generally regard fatigue as a "soft" finding because it cannot be measured with a laboratory test or observed during a physical examination. As it is nonspecific, no precise diagnosis can be arrived at based on the symptom of fatigue. However, to the sufferer the effects of fatigue are real and devastating.

Until the mid-1980s, many patients were misdiagnosed as suffering from depression, accused of malingering, encouraged to undergo costly and inappropriate laboratory tests or simply pushed aside by the medical community because of lack of understanding of the disease. In the early 1990s many researchers are engaged in studies, and the scientific knowledge accumulated in recent years about the immune system, viruses and the physiological effects of stress has contributed to a better understanding of CFS. Individuals with CFS no longer need to feel abandoned by their physicians or fear that they are "going crazy" because they feel so badly and no one really takes them seriously.

Although the illness strikes children, teenagers and people in their fifties, sixties and seventies, it is most likely to strike adults from their mid-twenties to their late forties. Women are afflicted about two or three times as often as men; the vast majority of patients are white.

Because of the age group most afflicted, the name "yuppie flu" was attached to CFS. However, individuals afflicted regarded the new name as tending to trivialize their illness.

CFS and Depression   There are some commonalties between CFS and depression. However, the symptoms of CFS do not fit the description of exogenous depression, which is depression precipitated by external factors. Additionally, in CFS, there is usually no evidence in the recent personal or family history to support a diagnosis of primary depression. Instead, the CFS-related depression seems to be endogenous, meaning that it has physiological origins within the body. Secondary depression, which follows from disease rather than causes it, is just as disabling. However, knowing that there is a chemical basis for mood swings and that they are directly related to illness can be reassuring to many individuals.

CFS and Sleep Patterns   Typically, sleep patterns of CFS sufferers are markedly disturbed. Despite constant exhaustion and the desire for sleep, sufferers rarely sleep uninterruptedly and awake feeling refreshed. Some have severe insomnia, while others have difficulty maintaining sleep once they have gone to sleep. There is often not enough rapid-eye-movement (REM), sleep, which is considered necessary for a good night's rest; REM usually takes up about one-fifth of the average night's sleep.

There is a cyclical relationship between CFS symptoms of pain, depression and anxiety and difficulty sleeping soundly. All symptoms seem to be exacerbated by the others.

CFS and Vestibular Disorders   Many CFS sufferers experience disorders of balance, or of the vestibular system, which is modulated by the inner ear. Any event that causes chemical changes in the brain, such as emotional stress or trauma, can influence the vestibular system. Those with balance disorders sometimes feel dizzy, lightheaded or nauseated. According to the Dizziness and Balance Disorders Association of America, severe balance problems are "periods of violent, whirling sensations where the world is spinning out of control" (vertigo). Sometimes even walking is difficult, with sufferers tilting off balance or stumbling for no apparent reason. Some individuals who have balance disorders develop phobias, such as the fear of falling. Some who have this fear even become housebound.

Therapies for CFS   Many therapies have been tried on CFS sufferers. Usually a plan is devised for each patient, depending on symptoms. Pharmacologic therapies include use of antidepressant drugs, pain-relieving drugs and muscle-relaxing drugs.

Other therapies that have been tried include deep relaxation, yoga, biofeedback and visualization therapy to relieve stress and chronic pain. Nutritional therapies that have been tried include emphasizing certain vitamins, such as vitamins A, B6, B12, C and E, as well as zinc, folic acid and selenium, all of which are said to have immune-boosting potential. Oil extract from the seeds of the evening primrose plant is another medicine with which some CFS patients have experimented and found helpful. The theoretical basis (although not scientifically proven in known double-blind studies) for its use is that evening primrose oil contains gamma-linolenic acid (GLA), which converts in the body to prostaglandin, a vital substance in the regulation of cellular function.

CFS and Social Relationships   CFS causes stress on family and social relationships. Sufferers of CFS are likely to feel estranged from their friends because they believe that no one really understands their constant feelings of emotional and physical tiredness and exhaustion. Because CFS has been plagued with credibility problems, many sufferers have felt that others do not take their suffering seriously. Some friends and family members may fear that CFS is contagious and may try to maintain a distance from the sufferer. (Medical opinion seems to indicate that CFS is not contagious.) The issue of sexual activity comes up between spouses; engaging in sexual activity during peak periods of energy helps many satisfy needs of both partners.

Supportive family and friends can contribute to the individual's mental well-being by being helpful, understanding and available to listen to the complaints.

Role of Self-help Several nationwide organizations encourage research and political advocacy and can provide lists of local support groups that may help with practical and emotional support for CFS sufferers. These include:

Chronic Fatigue Immune Dysfunction
    Syndrome Society
P.O. Box 230108
Portland, OR 97223
Phone: (503) 684-5261

Chronic Fatigue and Immune Dysfunction
    Syndrome Association
P.O. Box 220398
Charlotte, NC 28222
Phone: (704) 362-CFID

National Chronic Fatigue Syndrome
    Association
919 Scott Avenue
Kansas City, KS 66105
Phone: (913) 321-2278

See also CHRONIC ILLNESS; DEPRESSION; SOCIAL SECURITY DISABILITY; SUPPORT GROUPS; and DEPRESSION AND AFFECTIVE DISORDERS.

Feiden, Karyn. *Hope and Help for Chronic Fatigue Syndrome.* New York: Prentice-Hall Press, 1990.

chronic illness Chronic illness often brings with it physical symptoms, such as

pain, and emotional consequences that can be more far reaching than the disease itself. Emotional consequences affect not only the patient but the immediate caregivers and family as well. Many families let anxieties take over their lives; in other cases, depression arises while coping with illness and the threat of possible loss of physical functioning or life itself.

Many ill persons turn to substance abuse to escape their pain and fears about disability and death. Anger, denial or perceived helplessness leads others to abandon treatment or assume a "why me" attitude that gives them a pessimistic view of their world.

According to Lloyd D. Rudley, M.D., an attending psychiatrist at the Institute of Pennsylvania Hospital, Philadelphia, the crucial issue is "whether you can get past the stage of rage, sadness and overwhelming anxiety. Will you resume the initiative for living or become psychologically paralyzed?" Dr. Rudley says that many people become trapped by emotions that do not serve them well.

Reactions to illness are similar to the stages of grief. First there is shock and a feeling of many losses, including a sense of control, autonomy and the way things used to be. Those who suffer from chronic illness might suffer losses ranging from having to give up a cherished sport or favorite food to impaired speech or the inability to bear children. Stress and symptoms of depression may follow, including hopelessness, self-blame, shattered self-esteem or withdrawal. The ill person may develop many fears, including one of being active again, while others may deny the realities of their condition and overdo activities too soon.

Many chronically ill people do not comply with instructions from their physicians. This may take the form of not showing up for physical therapy, refusing medication or driving a car against the physician's advice. Individuals with emphysema may continue to smoke. According to Dr. Rudley, "People want to think everything will be normal again if they follow the doctor's orders.

When things don't work this way and there is no magic formula, a patient may give up on treatment.''

Some individuals neglect medical advice as a means of getting more attention. Others who harbor shame or guilt about their condition may punish themselves, in effect, by not complying with prescribed treatment. Forces of denial may be at work, too, in whose who try to ''bargain with illness'' by following some recommendations but not others.

An individual's prior coping abilities will determine how well he or she responds when illness occurs. However, even when symptoms of illness go into remission or the person adjusts successfully, a whole new set of external problems may discriminate against him or her, or family dynamics can change dramatically.

''Patients need to accept that illness changes them permanently, that a change in lifestyle is necessary,'' advises Dr. Rudley. Healthy acceptance is achieved when people come to terms with their illness as a part of who they are, ''forming a sort of coexistence with it.''

Some individuals feel certain ''benefits'' from being chronically ill. Such motivations are referred to as secondary gains and increase the likelihood of the individual continuing to be ill or to have symptoms. Common benefits of illness include receiving permission to get out of dealing with a troublesome problem, situation or responsibilities of life, getting attention, care or nurturing from people around them and not having to meet their own or others' expectations.

Ill health affects every area of a person's life, including marriage, family, work, financial affairs and future plans. Professional counseling can help individuals and their families adapt to changes brought on by chronic illness. Counseling may help individuals who have insomnia or disrupted sleep, feel a need to hide their illness, observe an increased use of drugs or alcohol, fail to follow treatment recommendations or have prolonged depression, marked negative personality changes, feelings that they are ''victims,'' undue fears about resuming activities, obsessive anxiety or preoccupation with death.

See also CAREGIVERS; ELDERLY PARENTS; ILLNESS AND DISABILITY IN THE FAMILY in BIBLIOGRAPHY.

''Conquering the Psychological Hurdles of Chronic Illness.'' *The Quill*, Pennsylvania Hospital, Philadelphia (Fall 1991).

chronic pain   See PAIN.

circadian rhythms   Circadian rhythms are cyclical biological activities that repeat at approximately 24-hour intervals. They are coordinated by an inherent timing mechanism known as a biological clock. Alertness and mental capability seem to be most available to us when we follow our internal clocks. Most people's ''clocks'' are synchronized to the sun's 24-hour cycle. For example, sunrise means waking and working, and sundown means dinner and sleep. However, individuals who are shift workers find that their ''day'' is reversed. Most shift workers go home to sleep during the day when their bodies want to be awake and then have to work at night when their bodies want to sleep.

The circadian rhythm of body temperature is a marker for internal clocks. Body temperature rises and falls in cycles parallel to alertness and performance efficiency. When body temperature is high, which it usually is during the day, alertness and performance peak, but sleep is difficult. A lower temperature (generally during the night) promotes sleep but hinders alertness and performance.

See also BIOLOGICAL CLOCK; SHIFT WORK; BIORHYTHMS.

Insights into Clinical and Scientific Progress in Medicine, Rush-Presbyterian–St. Luke's Medical Center, vol. 14, no. 3 (1991).

circumstantiality   See THOUGHT DISORDERS.

civil rights The concept of civil rights gives legal expression to the desire for equal treatment in regard to participation in government, employment, housing and education. Civil rights were once thought to be only the rights of the individual in relation to government, but through legislation and practice the civil rights concept has now extended to many other social institutions.

Racial discrimination has been the most significant target of civil rights activities and legislation. Following the Civil War, the 13th Amendment to the Constitution abolished slavery, the 14th Amendment made people born or naturalized in the United States citizens and the 15th Amendment gave blacks the right to vote. Discriminatory practices against blacks continued until the 1950s, when a variety of civil rights actions and legislation gave blacks equal access to education and seating on public transportation. The Civil Rights Act of 1964 gave blacks equal access to public accommodations and ended such contradictory and insulting situations as those encountered by black entertainers who could perform—but not be served—in a restaurant or club. Racial discrimination in housing was attacked by the Civil Rights Act of 1968, which prohibited discriminatory practices in financing, advertising, showing, selling and renting property. Affirmative action legislation has also attempted to give blacks equal access to education and employment. The latter movement has given rise to actions based on feelings of reverse discrimination involving white men who feel that hiring quotas give blacks and women an unfair advantage in being accepted for employment or for educational opportunities.

The social changes of the 1960s also made the civil rights of women an important issue. Although some individual states had given women the right to vote, it was not until 1920 that the federal government guaranteed women's suffrage with the 19th Amendment. The Civil Rights Act of 1964 included the prohibition of employment discrimination based on sex as well as race and established the Equal Employment Opportunity Commission to investigate charges of unequal treatment or harassment. Pregnancy or the possibility thereof is no longer an acceptable reason for dismissing or refusing to hire a woman, although her employment may be terminated if pregnancy actually interferes with her work. An important recent issue has been the exposure of women of childbearing age to radiation, which might affect a developing fetus. The unsuccessful attempts to pass the Equal Rights Amendment were the product of feelings that other constitutional amendments and antidiscriminatory legislation were not strong enough to guarantee women equal opportunities.

Other issues that have been considered sources of discrimination and freedom of expression are grooming and appearance codes. For example, young men who prefer long hair have pointed to perfectly acceptable longer hairstyles on women as proof that a school or employer who insists on haircuts for men is being discriminatory. With the aging population, age discrimination has also become an important issue and a target of federal legislation.

On some occasions, one set of civil liberties seems to be in conflict with another. For example, a person's right to choose personal associates or to express himself freely may be in conflict with civil rights principles; such rights are generally upheld if they do not conflict with the interests of society as a whole.

Civil Rights and the Mentally Ill Rights of hospitalized psychiatric patients are defined by states. The only right an involuntarily committed person loses is the right to liberty.

Some examples of civil rights are guaranteed. These include the right to dispose of property; to execute instruments such as wills and deeds to property; to make purchases; to enter into contracts; to vote; and to retain a driver's license and a professional license. However, under certain circumstances, a license can be revoked if the holder suffers from a mental condition that makes him or her incapable of practicing that profession. In such a situation, due process rights would be afforded the individual before the license would be suspended or revoked. In addition, a court procedure, often depending on expert testimony, can appoint a conservator in the case where a person can no longer manage her money and personal affairs because of illness.

See also AGING; WOMEN'S LIBERATION MOVEMENT.

"Civil Rights," in *The Guide to American Law*, vol. 2. St. Paul: West Publishing Co., 1983.
McFarland, Gertrude K., and Thomas, Mary Durand. *Psychiatric Mental Health Nursing*. Philadelphia: J. B. Lippincott, 1991.
Sigler, Jay. "Civil Rights," in *Academic American Encyclopedia*, vol. 5. Danbury, Conn.: Grolier Incorporated, 1986.

clanging   See THOUGHT DISORDERS.

claustrophobia   An intense fear of being in closed places, such as elevators, phone booths, small rooms, crowded areas or other confined spaces. The word comes from the Latin word *claustrum,* meaning "lock" or "bolt." Claustrophobia is one of the most common fears. Most people feel slightly uncomfortable in a closed space, but true phobics may have a panic attack and will tend to avoid such places. Some fear they will suffocate, while others have specific fears relating to the enclosure, such as an elevator or airplane that may suddenly fall. For some individuals, claustrophobia begins after a bad experience involving an enclosed space, such as being locked in a closet or room. With behavioral therapy techniques, many people overcome this phobia.

See also AGORAPHOBIA; PANIC DISORDER; PHOBIA.

client-centered therapy   A form of therapy developed by Carl Rogers (1902–), an American psychologist. Also known as Rogerian therapy, the technique is a nondirective approach that aims to encourage the individual's personal growth. Emphasis is placed on the individual's uniqueness of personality. This type of therapy led to many other developments in the field of psychology during the middle of the 20th century.

See also BEHAVIORAL THERAPY.

client's rights   See LEGAL ISSUES.

climacteric   The medical term for an approximately 10- to 15-year span of life—usually falling any time between 35 and 55—when a woman changes from a reproductive to a nonreproductive stage. Historically, many women experienced reduced self-esteem as they completed this stage of life. In more recent years, however, most women no longer base their sexual appeal on the capability of bearing children. In the absence of physical symptoms, the climacteric does not reduce a woman's feeling of mental and physical well-being or a woman's interest in sexual activity or responsiveness.

Some women at mid-life have many psychological symptoms, ranging from irritability to depression. Climacteric melancholia is a term that has been applied to a form of depression that develops during the climacteric.

Women at mid-life face many psychological stresses, such as facing retirement, their husband's retirement, divorce, widowhood, caring for aging parents, coping with grown children and their problems and economic concerns. These concerns are often misinterpreted as depression and irritability, and such irritability should not be attributed to physiological changes.

There is no specific time for the climacteric to occur. Some women complete this phase of life during their forties, while other women continue to have regular menstrual periods into and throughout their fifties. For some women, the climacteric span is shorter than 10 years; for others it is longer. The average is about 10 years.

During the climacteric, the body's hormonal production decreases, the ovaries gradually stop producing and releasing eggs, the menstrual cycle changes and monthly flow ceases. After age 35–40, hormonal levels gradually decrease, and in the late forties levels decline sharply.

To evaluate a woman's hormonal status, a physician may take blood samples to determine levels of two pituitary hormones called LH (luteinizing hormone) and FSH (follicle-stimulating hormone). Levels of these hormones are elevated after menopause but tend to be low in women whose periods have temporarily stopped because of stress or weight loss. Physicians also may use vaginal cytology (a microscopic study of the cells from the vagina) to estimate a woman's estrogen level. However, interpretations of estrogen production from such a smear are not conclusive because factors such as vaginal infections, tissue sensitivity and the effects of certain medications and disease may influence the findings.

Physicians generally divide the climacteric into several clinical phases: premenopause, perimenopause, menopause and postmenopause.

Premenopause   For most women, this stage begins some time after age 40. Menstrual periods may or may not become irregular. Ovulation may cease. A woman may have a span of months or even years in this stage.

Perimenopause   The period of time closest to the last menstrual period. Omission of menstrual periods for several months is common. Some women may think that they had their last period because they have not had one in many months or even a year. However, pregnancy is still possible during this time, and women concerned about pregnancy should use contraceptive measures during sexual intercourse.

Menopause   The date of a woman's final menstrual period is the "formal date" of menopause. While the age at which women begin to menstruate has become earlier

throughout generations, the age of menopause has changed only slightly over hundred of years. In ancient times, menopause occurred at age 40; in the years 1500 to 1830, at age 45; and in 1948, 48. In 1986 in the United States the usual age of menopause was between 48 and 55 years, with the median age of 51.4

If menopause occurs before age 35, it is termed "premature." Early menopause may also occur as a result of surgical removal of the ovaries or excessive irradiation of the ovaries (for example, in therapy for Hodgkin's disease or kidney cancer). Diagnostic X rays do not induce early menopause.

Delayed menopause (long after age 55) may occur for many reasons, including taking hormones—because of the presence of a type of cell tumor that secretes estrogen—and because of a uterine growth that results in bleeding.

Certain diseases are associated with either early or late menopause. Diseases associated with early menopause are "vulvar dystrophy," a group of vulvar conditions often characterized by delicate or raw, itchy vaginal tissues and osteoporosis. Diseases associated with late menopause include diabetes, cancer of the uterus, cancer of the breast, cancer of the cervix, fibroids and polyps. Obesity and high estrogen levels are common in women who have late menopause.

Postmenopause.   The period after at least one year without having a menstrual period. Women in the postmenopausal stage may enjoy the freedom of sexual intercourse without the concern about pregnancy.

Changes in hormonal levels may lead to hot flashes for some women; women whose hot flashes are severe may experience sleeplessness and fatigue. In some women, vaginal atrophy and dryness may contribute to discomfort during sexual intercourse and diminution of enjoyment of sexual activity. Many of these concerns, however, can be overcome with appropriate counseling, medical intervention and, for some women in whom their use is not contraindicated, the use of hormonal replacement therapy.

See also HOT FLASHES; MENOPAUSE.

Hacker, Neville F., and Moore, J. George. *Essentials of Obstetrics and Gynecology.* Philadelphia: W. B. Saunders, 1986.

Kahn, Ada P., and Holt, Linda Hughey. *Midlife Health: A Woman's Practical Guide to Feeling Good.* New York: Avon Books, 1989.

climate and mental health   Effects of climate on mental health is an ongoing subject for research, even though the subject has been studied and analyzed since Aristotle and Hippocrates wrote on the subject. Climate has an effect on housing, sports and leisure activities, transportation, work and the types of products and businesses that are necessary to satisfy basic human needs.

Cool climates have generally been considered easier to live in than areas that are consistently too hot for human comfort. It has only been recently that air conditioning has been perfected and become widespread in industrialized countries. Greater control over the environment has been thought to give greater impetus to creativity and change. Inhabitants of cool climates have generally been thought to be more industrious and goal-oriented than those who live in warm climates. Cooler climates require that the body burn and produce energy more quickly and therefore stimulate activity. On the other hand, cold weather raises blood pressure, is generally hard on the circulatory system and tends to make even people who spend most of their time in sedentary activities indoors crave foods high in fat and starch. Warmer climates slow the body's metabolism and, if humidity is added to the heat, produce a more languid life-style. Stormy and changeable weather, which is usually accompanied by sudden barometric changes, may produce irritability and mood changes because the rising and falling pressure affects body fluids.

Some authors and researchers have attempted to connect a population's religious and philosophical outlook to its environment. For example, inhabitants of a forest civilization may develop beliefs about spirits or other metaphysical phenomena from their observations of trees and animals. An open desert atmosphere might give a completely different outlook.

Relationship of Weather and Violence
One correlation between weather and human activity that is supported by statistics is the relationship between hot weather and violence. Figures show that crimes and riots are far more likely to occur in hot weather than in cool or rainy weather.

Palmer, Bruce. *Body Weather.* Harrisburg, Pa.: Stackpole Books, 1976.

Sherrets, S. D. "Climate and Personality," in Corsini, Raymond J., ed., *Encyclopedia of Psychology.* Vol. 1. New York: Wiley, 1984.

clinical depression   This term applies to depression that lasts for more than a few weeks or has severe symptoms that last long enough to require professional treatment. A person with a clinical depression may experience changes in feelings, behavior, physical health and appearance. In severe cases, delusions may occur. Clinical depression may interfere with job performance and the ability to handle everyday decisions and stresses. Clinical depression is a term that overlaps with the terms "major depression," "dysthymia," "unipolar depression" and "exogenous depression."

Some individuals may have only one episode of clinical depression during their lifetime. More commonly, it is a recurrent disorder that may require maintenance on medication to prevent additional episodes. The National Institute of Mental Health Epidemiological Catchment Area Study has found that the six-month prevalence of clinical depression is 6 percent in the United States. Antidepressant medications are effective in treating clinical depression.

See also AFFECTIVE DISORDERS; ANTIDEPRESSANT MEDICATIONS; DEPRESSION; MANIC-DEPRESSIVE ILLNESS.

Roesch, Roberta. *The Encyclopedia of Depression.* New York: Facts On File, 1991.

clinical psychology A branch of psychology specializing in the study, diagnosis and treatment of behavior disorders. Clinical psychology became popular in the United States during the late 1940s and 1950s. Much of the research in clinical methods, diagnosis and therapy has taken place within departments of clinical psychology. In most states, clinical psychologists must be licensed to treat clients and have a Ph.D. degree. Training for a Ph.D in clinical psychology includes course work, development of research skills and clinical practice.

See also PSYCHOLOGY.

clitoris An erectile organ of the female external genitalia that is the center of sexual feeling and stimulation. It is located at the top of the folds where the labia majora and labia minora (larger and smaller lips) meet. The term is derived from the Greek word *kleiein,* meaning "to shut or close." Because it contains many nerve endings, the clitoris is sensitive to tactile stimulation during sexual activity. Many women enjoy stimulation of the clitoris as a means of increasing sexual excitement and reaching orgasm.

The clitoris is composed of tissue that becomes engorged with blood during sexual arousal, causing the clitoris to become erect. The clitoris has a sensitive tip called the glans, which has many nerve receptors, making it extremely sensitive to touch. The size of the clitoris and the degree it projects from under the clitoral hood varies from woman to woman.

The clitoris originates from the same embryonic tissue as the penis. The prepuce, or clitoral hood, covers the clitoris from the external folds of the labia minora, and stimulation of the labia minora may have the same effect as direct stimulation of the clitoris.

The term "clitoral orgasm" refers to an orgasm induced by direct stimulation of the clitoris, manually by the woman herself (masturbation), by contact with and motion of the penis, by the partner's mouth or tongue or by a sexual aid such as a vibrator.

Clitorism and Clitoridotomy Clitorism is prolonged clitoral erection, a painful and dangerous condition similar to priapism in the male. Clitoridotomy is the surgical excision of the prepuce of the clitoris, a procedure somewhat equivalent to circumcision of the male.

Surgical Removal of the Clitoris Clitoridectomy, the surgical removal of the clitoris, was performed during the 19th century in Europe as a means of controlling masturbation and nymphomania. Clitoridectomy was first performed in the United States in the late 1860s and was practiced until the first two decades of the 20th century. Today, clitoral amputation is rarely performed except in cases of severe enlargement, to relieve a disorder of continuous clitoral erection or as a result of a neoplasm or other serious medical problem. However, among many African societies, Islamic groups and the Pano Indians of Ecuador, removal of the clitoris is practiced ritualistically, in the belief that the absence of the clitoris will prevent a woman from experiencing orgasm and enjoying sexual intercourse.

See also MASTURBATION; ORGASM.

Goldenson, Robert, and Anderson, Kenneth. *Sex A–Z.* London: Bloomsbury Publishing Limited, 1987.

Hite, Shere. *The Hite Report.* New York: Macmillan, 1976.

Kahn, Ada P., and Holt, Linda Hughey. *The A to Z of Women's Sexuality.* Alameda, Calif.: Hunter House, 1992.

clomipramine A tricyclic antidepressant drug (trade name: Anafranil). It has been widely used as an antidepressant drug in Europe for many years. In the 1980s, open and controlled studies demonstrated that clomipramine had an antiobsessional action as well. The drug is now used in the treatment of depressive disorders, panic disorder with and without agoraphobia, and phobic disorders and is approved in the United States for obsessive-compulsive disorder (OCD). Research indicates that approximately 50 to 75 percent of patients (children and adults) with OCD respond favorably but seldom completely. Most commonly, six to eight weeks of treatment is required, although patients will occasionally respond in only two weeks. Continued behavioral therapy as well as drug therapy for six months to a year in responsive patients is recommended to minimize relapse.

See also ANTIDEPRESSANT MEDICATIONS; MONOAMINE OXIDASE INHIBITORS; OBSESSIVE-COMPULSIVE DISORDER; PANIC DISORDER.

American Medical Association. *AMA Drug Evaluations Annual, 1991*. Chicago: AMA, 1991.

clonazepam   A drug (trade name: Klonopin) with anticonvulsant effects, which has been demonstrated to have potential benefits in the acute treatment of mania. It is a member of the benzodiazepine class of drugs. For certain individuals, it has been helpful in treating anxiety disorders and tardive dyskinesia (a drug-induced movement disorder). Both psychological and physiological dependence have been reported; withdrawal symptoms similar to those observed with barbiturates have occurred following sudden withdrawal of clonazepam.

See ANTICONVULSANT MEDICATIONS; BENZODIAZEPINE DRUGS; TARDIVE DYSKINESIA.

Fawcett, Jan, and Zajecka, J. M. "Treatment of Psychotic Affective Disorders." *Current Opinion in Psychiatry 3* (1990).

clonidine   A drug used to treat high blood pressure (trade name: Catapres). It is also rarely used as an anxiolytic drug for some individuals. It has antimanic properties, and alone or in combination with lithium it may

have advantages over neuroleptics in the acute stages of mania. Side effects include drowsiness, sedation and, in some cases, depression. Clinical studies are under way to determine additional uses and efficacy in a variety of disorders.

Clonidine is considered an adrenergic autoreceptor agonist; it acts on the central nervous system, reducing the action of the sympathetic nervous system by altering the brain-chemical balance. The brain then slows the heart rate and decreases action in some nerves that control blood vessel constriction. It is also prescribed for some symptoms during menopause.

The trend is toward using carbamazepine (an anticonvulsant drug) much more than clonidine, especially in mania.

See ANTICONVULSANT MEDICATIONS; BLOOD PRESSURE; CARBAMAZEPINE; MENOPAUSE.

clozapine   An antipsychotic drug used to treat schizophrenia (trade name: Clozaril). It was approved for use in the United States in 1989 and appears to be an effective treatment for some schizophrenic patients who do not respond to other drugs. It is not a cure but seems to improve symptoms of some schizophrenia patients so that they can function in the community and benefit from rehabilitative services and therapy. One advantage of clozapine over other antipsychotic drugs is that its use does not seem to cause severe movement disorders known as tardive dyskinesia. Patients taking this drug should be closely monitored by a physician to guard against a fatal decrease in the promotion of white blood cells, a weakening of the immune system in response to the drug.

See also SCHIZOPHRENIA.

Clozaril   See CLOZAPINE.

cluster headaches   See HEADACHES.

Clytemnestra complex   A woman's obsessive impulse to kill her husband in order to possess one of his male relatives. The term is derived from the classical myth in which Clytemnestra, wife of Agamemnon, fell in love with her husband's cousin, then killed Agamemnon and was herself later killed by her son, Orestes.

See also OBSESSIVE-COMPULSIVE DISORDER.

cocaine   An addictive drug that stimulates the central nervous system and induces feelings of euphoria. Cocaine is most often found in the form of white powder and is typically ingested by inhaling or "snorting," usually through a straw or other tube, into the nose. It can also be injected into the veins. After conversion back to its base form, cocaine can be smoked, which is known as "free-basing."

Cocaine use can lead to severe psychological and physical dependence. It can increase the pulse, blood pressure, body temperature and respiratory rate. Paranoid psychosis, hallucinations and other mental health problems can result from cocaine use. Cocaine use also causes bleeding and other damage to nasal passages. Cocaine-related heart and respiratory failure can lead to death.

In pregnancy, cocaine use endangers the unborn child, who may be born prematurely, with low birth weight, a variety of serious birth defects and later learning and behavioral problems.

Crack is a form of cocaine base that is smoked and is most highly addictive. Cocaine is sometimes used with other drugs. The cocaine-heroin combination is called a "speedball," and the cocaine-PCP mixture is known as "space base."

Different users react to the drug in different ways. However, many experience an instant feeling of enormous pleasure known as a "rush." Initially it may also make the user feel energetic and self-confident. However, the pleasurable feelings produced by cocaine are followed by depression and fatigue, known as a "crash." To avoid the "crash," users take more cocaine, establish-

ing a cycle of use and dependency that is extremely difficult to end and often requires lengthy treatment.

Cocaine is produced from the coca leaf in two stages to yield coca paste and then cocaine base. The coca leaf is grown primarily in Peru, Bolivia and, to a lesser extent, Colombia. The conversion to the white crystalline powder form, cocaine HCl, is done primarily in Colombia but occurs elsewhere in the Andean region.

See also SUBSTANCE ABUSE; SUBSTANCE ABUSE in BIBLIOGRAPHY.

Media Resource Guide on Common Drugs of Abuse. Public Relations Society of America, National Capital Chapter, Fairfax, Va., September 1990.
O'Brien, Robert, and Cohen, Sidney. *Encyclopedia of Drug Abuse.* New York: Facts On File, 1984.

codeine   A drug obtained from the juice of an unripe white poppy. It is chemically similar to morphine, also an opium derivative, but milder. It is commonly used as a painkiller in tablet form and in cough medications. Codeine has a mild sedative reaction. Use of codeine causes the body to build up a tolerance that stimulates the user to need an increasing amount of the drug to achieve a desired result.

See also ADDICTION; SUBSTANCE ABUSE; SUBSTANCE ABUSE in BIBLIOGRAPHY.

codependency   A relationship is which the participants have a strong need to be needed but also continue to create their mutual needs in a detrimental, weakening manner in order to preserve the dependent relationship. One example of a codependent relationship is one in which a husband covers up for his wife's alcoholism. He does the household chores, drives the children to their activities and explains her problem as an "illness." He is an enabler, because he makes it possible for her to continue with her addiction.

Another example of a codependent relationship is one in which a parent continues to compensate for or cover up a child's difficulties in school or with the law, thinking that he is protecting the child. It is often interpreted that this behavior persists because preserving the child's flaws and immature behavior will keep her forever dependent on the parent. Since codependency is viewed as a type of addiction, the advocates of the codependent theory feel that these tendencies can be overcome with a process similar to the recovery process used by Alcoholics Anonymous.

Codependence has been loosely defined and overgeneralized, attempting to include almost every problem as an addiction when other possible causes are not identified.

Codependency has been criticized for promoting tendencies to blame the parent-child or other relationships for individual problems and failures rather than accepting responsibility for one's own actions. The codependent philosophy has also been called yet another symptom of self-absorption and narcissism.

See also AGORAPHOBIA; ALCOHOLISM.

Becnel, Barbara. *The Co-dependent Parent*. San Francisco: Harper, 1991.
Rieff, David. "Victims All?" *Harper's* (Oct. 1991).

cofactors   Factors that do not cause a disorder alone but that can intensify effects of other causative factors. For example, stress can be a cofactor in a viral disease, and burnout or grief can be cofactors in depression.

See BURNOUT; DEPRESSION; STRESS.

coffee   Many people rely on coffee to relieve stress. Having a cup of coffee is also considered a social experience, as it is an opportunity for individuals to sit together and relax for a few moments of conversation. Coffee is primarily a stimulant, as it contains caffeine. Some individuals believe that coffee gives them a feeling of instant energy and use coffee to help wake themselves up or recharge themselves throughout the day. This is so because it affects the central nervous system, increasing the heart action in rate and strength. There is also increased activity of the kidneys, and brain centers are aroused. Different individuals can tolerate different levels of caffeine in coffee. Those who have cardiac conditions or hyperthyroidism, in which the heart is already overstimulated, should reduce their coffee intake. Some people are overly sensitive to caffeine, while others overdose themselves, developing anxiety, insomnia and irritability, all symptoms of "caffeinism." Individuals complaining of anxiety symptoms or insomnia should be evaluated for excessive caffeine use or hypersensitivity.

See also CAFFEINE; CENTRAL NERVOUS SYSTEM; STRESS.

cognitive dysfunction   Problems with retention or use of information, judgment or the ability to learn and think. For example, in Alzheimer's disease, cognitive dysfunction begins early on in the course of the disorder. There may be elements of cognitive dysfunction in depression as well as many other disorders.

Certain medications may cause dose-related, reversible cognitive dysfunction as side effects. For example, tricyclic antidepressants and antihistamines, because of their anticholinergic side effects, may reduce short-term memory and word-finding ability at high doses; the newer selective serotonin reuptake inhibiting (SSRI) drugs, such as Prozac and Zoloft, do not. Benzodiazepine tranquilizers, such as alprazolam (Xanax), may also reduce short-term memory at higher doses. Reduction of dose will reverse these temporary effects, unless the problem is related to another underlying cause, such as depression.

Cognitive dysfunction is used in another psychotherapeutic context to refer to dysfunctional attitudes (heightened self-criticism, low self-esteem) that lead to depression and anxiety.

See also COGNITIVE THERAPY.

cognitive therapy An approach sometimes used to treat individuals who have depression or anxiety disorders. Treatment centers follow the concept that in some people unwanted behaviors and moods can result from distorted patterns of thinking and attitudes and that individuals can change their behaviors or moods by alterations in thinking. This approach was introduced in the 1970s by Aaron T. Beck (1921–), an American psychiatrist.

See also BEHAVIORAL THERAPY; DEPRESSION.

Beck, A. T., et al. *Cognitive Therapy of Depression.* New York: Wiley, 1979.
Beck, A. T. *Cognitive Therapy and the Emotional Disorders.* New York: International Universities Press, 1976.
Wolpe, J. "Cognition and Causation in Human Behavior and Its Therapy." *American Psychologist* 33 (1978).

cohabitation A term for unmarried individuals who live together. Living together has shown a dramatic increase during the last decades of the 20th century. Cohabitation implies the performance of sexual intercourse. At one time cohabitation was referred to as "living in sin." Greater approval and societal acceptance of living together have resulted from general attitudinal changes regarding doubts about marriage, fears of permanent commitment and effectiveness of contraception during a long-term sexual relationship, as well as convenience and financial reasons.

Cohabitation Contract A legal document in which unmarried partners living together agree to specified arrangements, such as how much each partner pays toward specified expense.

See also MARRIAGE.

coital death Death resulting from a heart attack or respiratory failure during sexual intercourse, which occurs rarely among coronary patients engaging in prolonged and highly active intercourse and coital positions that excessively raise the heartbeat and blood pressure. This is a common fear of many men after heart surgery or after a heart attack. Women also fear that their mates might die during sexual intercourse as a result of vigorous activity. With appropriate counseling, couples learn to overcome this fear.

coitus Sexual intercourse; also known as copulation or coition. The term is derived from the Latin word *coire,* meaning "to go together." It usually implies insertion and penetration of the penis in the vagina. Coitus can take many different forms regarding positions, duration and speed.

Coital Positions Couples use many positions, called coital postures or intercourse positions, during coitus to enhance or maintain excitement and pleasure, as well as for comfort, or to improve or reduce the likelihood of conception. Different couples find their own unique advantages in certain positions and also discover what pleases them. The man-above position (commonly known as the "missionary position") is most common. Other erotic postures include face to face; woman above; side by side; sitting; standing; kneeling; and rear entry.

Coital movements by a male and female during intercourse vary, but in general, intercourse begins with slow, gentle penetration by the penis into the vagina; movements of the penis become progressively deeper and faster and may involve temporary withdrawal or interruption. The woman can move her pelvis in the same general pattern until both reach orgasm or the point of satisfaction.

Coitus à la vache, meaning "in cow fashion," is a French term for heterosexual intercourse in which the woman is in the knee-chest position with the man kneeling behind her and entering the vagina from the rear.

Coitus analis is a Latin term for anal intercourse.

Coitus ante portas (Latin for "coitus before the door") is a sexual activity with the penis between the woman's thighs instead of penetrating the vagina. This practice is common among adolescents as a contraceptive technique (not adequate) or as a way to prevent rupturing the hymen. It is also known as interfemoral intercourse, *coitus inter femora,* intracrural intercourse.

Coitus a tergo ("coitus from behind") is heterosexual intercourse with the man's penis entering the woman's vagina from the rear, as in *coitus à la vache.* It is also called *coitus a posteriori.*

Coitus in ano ("coitus in the anus") is anal intercourse between heterosexual or homosexual couples. It is also called *coitus per anum, coitus in anum* and *coitus analis.*

Coitus in axilla ("coitus in the armpit") is intercourse between heterosexual or homosexual couples in which the penis is inserted in the armpit of the partner.

Coitus in os (mouth coitus) is a term for fellatio.

Coitus intra mammas ("coitus between breasts") refers to sexual intercourse in which the penis is inserted between the woman's breasts, which she may press together with her hands. It is also called *coitus intermammarius.*

Coitus more ferarum is an obsolete term for intercourse from the rear; it is derived from the Latin words meaning "coitus in the manner of beasts."

Coital Techniques *Coitus incompletus* is an alternative term for coitus interruptus or withdrawal, a contraceptive technique in which the penis is withdrawn from the vagina before ejaculation. Although this may be the oldest form of contraception, mentioned in the Book of Genesis, it is an unreliable technique because semen may be emitted before orgasm.

Coitus reservatus is a deliberate suppression of orgasm in the male, as ejaculation

approaches. It is also called *coitus prolongatus.*

Kahn, Ada P., and Holt, Linda Hughey. *The A to Z of Women's Sexuality.* Alameda, Calif.: Hunter House, 1992.

coitus condomatus   Use of a condom during sexual intercourse.

See also SAFE SEX.

coitus interruptus   A contraceptive technique involving the man's withdrawal of the penis from the vagina before ejaculation; it is also known as the withdrawal method. Its main advantage is that no supplies are needed. The disadvantages are that it requires a high level of motivation, self-control and practice by the male. It also interferes somewhat with the sexual response cycle and satisfaction of both the man and the woman. It is not an effective contraceptive method, since failures can occur due to either failure to withdraw before ejaculation or due to leakage of small amounts of semen prior to ejaculation.

See also SEXUAL RESPONSE CYCLE; SEXUALITY in BIBLIOGRAPHY.

color   Color carries with it psychological associations that are expressed in language. For example, we are "green with envy," "see red" and have the "blues." Many people associate certain musical tones or other sounds with colors. Certain clear shades of red, orange and yellow are associated with food and are very appetizing. Tinting food with blue, violet or other mixtures of colors has been found to make it unappetizing.

Attraction to colors changes somewhat with age. Babies tend to be attracted to yellow, white, pink and red. Older children are less attracted to yellow and tend to like colors in the order of red, blue, green, violet, orange and yellow. As adults mature, blue tends to become a favorite color, possibly because of changes in the eye itself and the way it sees color. Differences in light perception between dark and light eyes may account for the fact that brunettes tend to prefer red and blondes blue.

Studies have determined that colors have certain psychological and physical effects. For example, red is the strongest and most stimulating of colors. It has been shown to increase hormonal activity and to raise blood pressure. Red stimulates creative thought and is a good mood elevator but is not conducive to work. Orange shares many of the qualities of red but, especially in its combined forms, is considered more mellow and easy to live with. Yellow's characteristic of being the most visible color makes it useful for signs or other purposes that promote safety. It also seems to have a good effect on metabolism. Green and blue green have been found to be relaxing colors that promote work requiring concentration and a meditative atmosphere. Blue has the opposite effect of red. It lowers bodily functions and promotes a restful atmosphere; however, it may be depressing if used too extensively. Being surrounded with blue has caused participants in psychological tests to underestimate time periods and the weight of objects. Purple, a combination of red and blue, has a neutral effect. In large amounts, it is disturbing because the eye does not focus on it easily. Monotonous use of the same color has been found to be more disturbing than a variety of colors.

Healing and mystical properties have been ascribed to color throughout history. Ancient peoples associated colors with the houses of the zodiac and with the elements. Color was highly important in the practice of magic. The superstitious feel that blue and green divert the power of the evil eye. Color has been important in religious symbolism and ritual. For example, in Judaism red, blue, purple and white have been considered divine colors. In Chasidic sects, women are forbidden to wear red or other bright colors

that draw attention to themselves. Green, the color of life and rebirth, is important in Christianity. In many cultures even close to modern times, red was considered to have healing properties to the extent that it was thought beneficial to actually surround a patient with red clothing, red furnishing and covers and give him or her red food and red medicine.

Fear of colors is known as chrematophobia, chromophobia and chromatophobia.

See also BLOOD PRESSURE; CREATIVITY.

Birren, Faber. *Color Psychology and Color Therapy.* Secaucus, N.J.: Citadel Press, 1961.

coma   When the cortex of the brain cannot be aroused, an individual is said to be in a coma. Many syndromes can produce coma, including cerebral hemorrhage; large cerebral infarction; blood clots in the brain; tumors; failure of oxygen supply; nutritional deficiency; poisonings; concussion and other trauma; and electrolyte disorder.

Metabolic problems impair function in the brain, and when nerve impulses are abnormal, a state of coma ensues. Diabetic coma is one of the metabolic coma-producing diseases. Treatment of diabetic coma is specific, usually beginning with massive doses of insulin. On the other hand, excessive insulin can cause coma in diabetics from hypoglycemia (low blood sugar), requiring immediate administration of sugar (glucose). In other types of coma, measures are taken to ensure that no further damage will be done to the brain. This means being sure that breathing is normal and that the heart is functioning properly. Glucose is given intravenously to assure sufficient nutrition to the brain. Careful diagnosis and special therapy are essential. Medication may be necessary to combat an infection in another organ that led to the coma.

See also BRAIN; DIABETES.

Andelman, Samuel. *Home Medical Encyclopedia.* Chicago: Quadrangle Books, 1973.

combat fatigue   A term relating to anxieties occurring after stresses in war or battles, replaced in contemporary usage with post-traumatic stress disorder (PTSD). Veterans of World War I were said to have "combat fatigue," while Vietnam veterans with the same symptoms have PTSD.

combat neurosis   See COMBAT FATIGUE.

commitment   People requiring psychiatric care are hospitalized through either a voluntary or an involuntary admission. A voluntary admission involves the individual signing into a treatment source of his own free will. An individual who enters a facility voluntarily may reject any type of treatment prescribed and may sign himself out of the facility at any time. Involuntary admission, or involuntary commitment, is the process by which an individual suffering from a severe mental disorder is legally deprived of her freedom. An individual may be committed legally in most states if she is likely to physically harm herself or other people or is unable to physically care for herself. Physicians who have examined the person explain to the court, usually in writing, why they believe the person should be placed in a mental institution.

Commitment is unpopular, as it forces a physician to make a decision that deprives a person of his liberty against his wishes. Yet physicians are held responsible for making the decision to avoid harm (death from suicide) to the patient or others (homicide). Patients may also be so severely ill that they are unable to care for themselves physically (maintain nutrition, protection from the elements) or exhibit lack of judgment that physically endangers the patient. The certified patient is entitled to a defense attorney, and the decision to exact the commitment must be made by a judge based on the evidence. The procedure is set up to protect people who are mentally ill while at the same time protecting individual rights.

See also LEGAL ISSUES.

community mental health services   See AMBULATORY MENTAL HEALTH ORGANIZATIONS.

competency (to stand trial)   See LEGAL ISSUES.

complex   Ideas that are linked together and related to feelings that affect an individual's behavior and personality. For example, a person may have suffered an early experience that made him feel inferior; he may have an inferiority complex as an adult. He may react by being timid or do just the opposite and act aggressively to compensate for his true feelings. Individuals who act like bullies often have superiority complexes and believe (or at least act as though they do) that they are superior to those around them.

Well-known complexes are the Oedipus complex and Electra complex, in which, according to Freudian thought, the individual is attracted to the parent of the opposite sex.

See also ELECTRA COMPLEX; OEDIPUS COMPLEX.

compliance   The agreement by an individual in following treatment outlined by a physician or therapist. In some cases, compliance may mean changing life-style habits, such as stopping smoking or eating less. Compliance also refers to following a prescribed drug regimen, taking pills on time as prescribed or omitting certain foods because they cause adverse drug reactions. An example of the last is omitting foods that contain tyramine if one is taking a monoamine oxidase inhibitor (MAOI) for depression. Various studies show a strong relationship between recovery, health and compliance with treatment recommendations.

See also ANTIDEPRESSANT MEDICATIONS; NON-COMPLIANCE.

compulsion   See OBSESSIVE-COMPULSIVE DISORDER.

compulsive disorder See OBSESSIVE-COMPULSIVE DISORDER.

computerized axial tomography (CAT) See BRAIN IMAGING.

concurrent therapy Simultaneous treatment of husband and wife and possibly other family members in marital therapy or psychotherapy, either by the same or different therapists.

See also SEX THERAPY.

condom A cylindrical sheath of rubber placed on the penis prior to coitus (sexual intercourse) that catches seminal fluid and prevents sperm from entering the vagina and impregnating the woman. Condoms are also known commonly as "rubbers" or "sheaths."

Condoms also act as barriers to bacteria, helping to prevent sexually transmitted diseases (STDs) from passing between partners. The condom should be put on the penis before any contact and should be properly removed after ejaculation, so that no sperm makes contact with the vagina. However, condoms are not 100 percent effective in preventing the spread of certain sexually transmitted diseases, because the male scrotum, if infected, may spread the infection to a partner.

In the 1980s, during the escalation of the AIDS (acquired immunodeficiency syndrome) epidemic, the use of condoms was promoted as a safe sex measure and means of reducing the risk of the spread of AIDS and STDs.

Advantages of using a condom as a contraceptive include relatively low cost, availability without a physical examination or prescription and protection against STDs. Disadvantages include the care in user behavior required to make it effective and its reputation for dulling sensation in the penis.

The condom may have been invented by Dr. Condom, a physician in the court of Charles II (1650–1685). However, the first published report of condom use to prevent venereal disease was in the work of the Italian anatomist Fallopius in 1564.

Historically, the French have referred to the condom as the "English cape," and the English have referred to it as the "French letter."

See also ACQUIRED IMMUNODEFICIENCY SYNDROME; COITUS; SAFE SEX; SEXUALLY TRANSMITTED DISEASES.

conduct disorder Also known as juvenile delinquency; the largest single group of mental health disorders during adolescence. The rate is approximately 20 percent in adolescent boys and 2 percent in adolescent girls. Adolescents are responsible for a substantial proportion of violent crimes, accounting for over 18 percent of all arrests for violence. The escalation of such deviant behavior in adolescents is twice that of the adult rate.

The adolescent prone to violence often has low self-esteem, is easily frustrated, has difficulty controlling impulses and has repressed rage. About 50 percent of adolescent delinquents progress to serious antisocial behavior as adults. Adolescent delinquency also predicts a high rate of alcohol abuse in adulthood.

Factors that lead to conduct disorder seem to be both social and biologic. Social factors include poverty, overcrowding, parental unemployment, broken homes and parental rejection. The youth may have had poor parenting techniques and received harsh, punitive discipline. Many boys with conduct disorders had fathers who also engaged in delinquent behaviors as adolescents but who also later developed antisocial disorders and alcohol abuse as adults. Some adolescent delinquents have a history of serious medical and neurological illness. Many are more accident-prone than their peers and have been victims of birth injury and physical abuse as young children. Another factor is the presence of a depressive disorder; aggressiveness and antisocial behaviors are the externalized expression of the disorder. Research studies are beginning to show that treatment of underlying depression may reduce aggressive and antisocial behaviors.

In younger children as well as adolescents, conduct disorder may include some of the following behaviors:

Steals without confrontation of a victim on more than one occasion (including forgery); steals with confrontation of a victim (e.g., mugging, purse snatching, extortion, armed robbery)

Runs away from home overnight at least twice while living in parental or parental surrogate home (or once without returning)

Often lies (other than to avoid physical or sexual abuse)

Deliberately engages in arson

Often truant from school (for older person, absent from work)

Breaks into someone else's house, building or car

Deliberately destroys others' property (other than by fire setting)

Is physically cruel to animals or people

Forces someone into sexual activity

Uses a weapon in more than one fight

See AGGRESSION; PERSONALITY DISORDERS; ADOLESCENCE, AGGRESSIVE BEHAVIOR in BIBLIOGRAPHY.

Davis, Kenneth; Klar, Howard; and Coyle, Joseph T. *Foundations of Psychiatry.* Philadelphia: W. B. Saunders, 1991.

confabulation   See KORSAKOFF'S SYNDROME.

confidentiality   See LEGAL ISSUES.

congenital defects   Malformations or other bodily disorders that are present at birth; also known as birth defects. Some birth defects manifest themselves years later. Some birth defects can be prevented with genetic counseling before pregnancy.

See also CHROMOSOME; DOWN'S SYNDROME; GENETIC COUNSELING; GENETIC DISORDERS.

conscience   The part of the mind that provides judgment of one's own values and actions. Conscience plays an important role in developing a positive self-image and avoiding feelings of guilt and shame.

See also BODY IMAGE; SELF-ESTEEM.

consent, informed   Agreement to a plan for medical care, surgery or other type of therapy. In some cases, informed consent must be obtained from the individual to prescribe certain drugs that are used for research purposes only. In all cases, individuals who enter therapy for a mental health condition should be informed about choices of therapy, possible side effects of medications if a medication is prescribed for them and desired outcome, before going ahead with the therapy plan. In a legal sense, informed consent also refers to the right of a health professional such as a therapist to release information learned in therapy sessions only upon the consent of the patient involved.

See also LEGAL ISSUES.

constipation   Inability to have a bowel movement. Many people cause themselves stress and worry because they do not have a bowel movement every day. However, many healthy people may not have a movement for several days and suffer no ill effects. Advertising for laxatives seems to have created an "illness" called "irregularity," which laxatives are said to cure. A better approach to solving the problem is through diet and exercise. A diet rich in fiber, including fresh fruits and vegetables as well as whole grains, will help establish patterns of regularity.

Emotional factors, such as tension, frustration and resentment, may result in constipation. Tensions may cause the muscles of the intestines to tighten, or contract, in what is called spastic constipation. This is often a part of the syndrome known as irritable bowel syndrome.

Elderly people often suffer from constipation, in some cases because of diminishing tone of intestinal and other muscles, as well as the slowing down of body signals from reduced efficiency of the nervous system.

See also IRRITABLE BOWEL SYNDROME.

content, latent   See DREAMING.

contract (therapeutic contract)   A mutually agreed upon statement of the changes an individual desires to accomplish through psychotherapy; it is also known as a therapeutic contract. Some therapists ask the individuals to put their goals in writing. In many cases, the contract is revised several times as therapy progresses.

See also PSYCHOTHERAPY.

contraindication   Circumstances in which a drug should not be prescribed for a particular person. For example, the stimulant dextroamphetamine would not ordinarily be prescribed for an individual who has high blood pressure.

Contraindications may be considered absolute, that is, never considered justified, or relative, implying that a procedure may entail significant risk or adverse effects. Use of a treatment in the face of the relative contraindications should be weighed against the risks of not giving treatment.

control   Having a feeling of control over one's life—including everyday events and their outcomes—is a factor in maintaining good mental health. Although people do not always consciously think about their level of control while things are going well for them, they are aware of losing control when their sense of control is threatened. For example, agoraphobics fear having a panic attack while they are away from a safe place because they fear losing control of themselves in ways such as fainting or becoming ill. Individuals who are fearful of flying

remain that way because they feel totally out of control while in the hands of the pilot. While individuals cannot always control the event, such as fly the airplane, they can learn to control their own responses to stressful situations. For example, a phobic person can learn relaxation techniques to control the rapid breathing that occurs when he faces a feared situation. In that sense, he then takes control of the situation.

control group   This group is involved during many drug tests and other experiments in which one factor is being tested. In the control group, the specific factor is deliberately left out. An example is a drug test for a new high blood pressure drug, in which the control group may be given a placebo instead of the new drug.

conversion reaction   An emotional conflict transformed into a physical symptom. Often the emotional problem is too painful for the person to face consciously, so the conflict is converted into a sensory or motor disability. For example, a person may have what appears to be a real paralysis of an arm or leg when there is no organic cause for the disability.

convulsions   Involuntary spasmodic contractions of muscles. This can be accompanied by loss of consciousness that occurs with certain neurological disorders as well as during withdrawal of central nervous system depressants or following an overdose of a stimulant.

See also EPILEPSY; SEIZURES.

coping   A way of dealing with everyday situations, some of which may be more stressful than others. Different individuals develop different ways of coping and learn to adapt their responses to stress to reduce anxieties. To some, "coping" means just getting along. To others, it is consciously using skills they have learned to help them face fearful or extreme anxiety-producing situations. Many individuals learn new coping skills during therapy sessions. For example, they may learn how to use relaxation and deep-breathing techniques to overcome their fear of a very rapid heartbeat that occurs when they are faced with a difficult situation.

Coping also refers to the practical solutions that individuals must find for many distressing problems, such as dealing with cancer in the family, making a decision about having an aging parent in the home, readjusting after a death in the family or facing unemployment.

See also BEHAVIORAL THERAPY.

copulation   See COITUS.

cortisol   A hormone secreted by the adrenal cortex, also known as hydrocortisone. Cortisol is released in response to stress. Depressed individuals show consistently increased concentrations of plasma cortisol. In contrast to normal patients, depressed patients also do not consistently suppress their plasma cortisol levels in response to dexamethasone. Dexamethasone suppresses cortisol secretion by acting on receptors at the hypothalamopituitary level to "turn off" adrenocorticotropic hormone (ACTH) and, in turn, cortisol; in depressed individuals this feedback mechanism is deficient.

See also AUTONOMIC NERVOUS SYSTEM; BIOLOGICAL MARKERS.

cotherapy   A form of psychotherapy in which more than one therapist works with an individual or group. Cotherapy is also known as combined therapy, cooperative therapy, dual leadership, multiple therapy and three-cornered therapy. Cotherapists work in various areas. For example, in sex therapy, one therapist is a male and the other is female, which encourages both viewpoints in sexuality problems affecting a married couple.

See also MARRIAGE; SEX THERAPY.

counseling   A term used to cover a variety of professional services available to an individual with a mental health concern. Such services may range from a trained social worker to a psychiatrist. Services may be provided in a school or employment setting or in a health center.

Counseling may be available for an individual, a couple or a family. When one is seeking counseling, help can be obtained by calling a local hospital or looking in the yellow pages of the telephone directory under psychologists or psychiatrists. Some listings have the heading "counselors." There are also many self-help and support groups in which members who have similar situations share experiences. A sense of improvement takes place for many participants in the group because they realize that they are not alone with their problems and concerns.

As anyone can claim to be a "professional counselor," it is wise to learn what training the counselor has had and whether he or she is certified by any state agency or professional board.

See also PSYCHOTHERAPY; SUPPORT GROUPS; PSYCHOLOGY AND PSYCHIATRY in BIBLIOGRAPHY.

countertransference   A term first identified in the psychiatrist-patient relationship. Countertransference in a general sense is any strong emotional reaction by a therapist to a patient. As the converse of transference, it is the displacement onto the client of the helping person's feelings that arise from the helping person's early childhood experiences with significant persons. Such distortions can interfere with the therapist-patient relationship. Indications of this process at work may be the therapist having sexual or aggressive fantasies toward the patient, dreaming about the patient, having extreme feelings of liking or disliking the patient, preoccupation with the patient in nonclinical situations and defensiveness with others about interventions with the patient.

Therapists in training who experience these

feelings discuss them with their supervisors, who help them decrease these distortions.

While it is not uncommon for expert therapists to encounter countertransference feelings, they are by virtue of their training and self-understanding expected to be able to identify these feelings and use them to enhance therapy rather than distort and block therapeutic progress.

See also PSYCHOANALYSIS; PSYCHOTHERAPY; TRANSFERENCE.

couvade A custom followed in some non-Western societies in which the father feels ill and stays in bed before and during delivery of the child. He may even show some symptoms of pregnancy and pangs of childbirth. The custom may be a sympathetic reaction or a means of drawing evil influence away from the wife and baby.

There are references in medical literature to severe behavioral or mental problems associated with paternity: episodes of delirium; psychotic decompensation generally of a paranoid nature; panic attacks; and even cases of false pregnancy. Expectant fathers may become hyperactive, sometimes resulting in increased incidence of sports injuries. There may also be an increase in aggressive behavior leading to fights and alcohol abuse. Fathers have been known to engage in avoidance behavior, disappearing during the delivery. There is also a significant increase in the number of divorces and suicides during the postpartum period and a decrease in libido and frequency of sexual relations.

Today psychosomatic symptoms are the main characteristic of the couvade syndrome. Some men have reported digestive problems, nausea, vomiting, abdominal pain or bloating or a change in appetite or weight. Toothache is reported with surprising frequency.

During a study reported in *Canadian Family Physician,** interviews were found to have reassuring effects on fathers. Most seemed happy to be participating in the study and to have an opportunity to verbalize their ex-periences. The researchers said that interviews with fathers during pregnancy are an excellent means of helping them express fears and of reassuring them about any possible minor symptoms that they might feel. An interview is also an excellent opportunity to assess the father's general anxiety level and, possibly, to bring to light any personality problems.

The Headache Study Group of the University of Western Ontario found that there was a relationship between the patients' sense that they had been able to fully discuss their problem and some improvement of their headaches.

In contemporary American society, pregnancy has an impact on the expectant father, frequently in the form of physical symptoms, as well as in the form of anxiety, difficulty sleeping and changes in family and professional relationships. Pregnancy can also affect sexual activity, as well as the use of alcohol and tobacco. An increasing number of fathers-to-be are reducing their intake of alcohol and tobacco prior to conception because research has suggested that alcohol and nicotine in sperm may influence fetal development.

Since the 1960s in the United States an increasing number of young fathers have attended prepared childbirth classes with their wives, in which they learn and practice breathing techniques during pregnancy so that they can be birthing "coaches" later on. Doing so gives them a sense of participating in the event and probably contributes to a reduction of their own psychosomatic symptoms.

See also CHILDBIRTH; PREGNANCY.

*Adapted from LaPlante, Patrice. "The Couvade Syndrome." *Canadian Family Physician* 37 (July 1991).

crack The street name given to tiny chunks or "rocks" of freebase cocaine, a smokable form of the drug extracted from cocaine hydrochloride powder in a simple chemical procedure using baking soda, heat and water. Crack is even more rapidly physically and psychologically addictive than powdered cocaine. Cocaine powder breaks down with heat and so cannot be effectively self-administered by smoking. In contrast, base cocaine or "freebase," which has been chemically "freed" from its hydrochloride salt, readily vaporizes into smoke by heat. Inhalation of the smoke gets the cocaine rapidly into the bloodstream through the lungs, faster than if powder cocaine is snorted. Extremely high blood levels of cocaine produced and delivered to the brain by smoking crack increase the likelihood of serious toxic reactions, including potentially fatal brain seizures, irregular heartbeat and high blood pressure. Congestion in the chest, wheezing, black phlegm and hoarseness may also result from smoking crack.

Use of crack by pregnant women can cause fetal loss or damage and babies with low birth weights, who are extremely sensitive to noise, touch and other stimuli and cry frequently. Anyone who uses it is vulnerable to developing an addiction.

See also COCAINE; SUBSTANCE ABUSE.

Media Resource Guide on Common Drugs of Abuse. Public Relations Society of America, National Capital Chapter, Fairfax, Va., September 1990.

cranial nerves Twelve pairs of nerves that emerge directly from the brain and mediate several of our senses. All but two of the nerve pairs connect with the brain stem, the lowest section of the brain. The other two, the olfactory and optic nerves, link directly with parts of the cerebrum, the main mass of the brain. Studies suggest that visual and olfactory stimuli may affect mood and motivation in significant ways without the awareness of the person affected.

All the nerves emerge through various openings in the skull, and many then divide into major branches.

See also BRAIN.

crank The name for illegal methamphetamine, a potent stimulant that attracted attention during the 1960s and early 1970s when it was popularly known as speed, meth and crystal. At low doses, crank effects include insomnia, dizziness, confusion, a sense of increased energy and alertness, suppressed appetite and feelings of well-being followed by depression. At higher doses, crank may produce severe anxiety, hallucinations, paranoid thinking and extremely aggressive behavior. Very high doses may result in convulsions, coma, cerebral hemorrhage and death.

Crank is easily manufactured in illicit "basement" laboratories and is sold as yellow or off-white powder, chunks or crystals wrapped in foil or plastic bags or in capsule form. When first used, crank is frequently inhaled. Users learn to inject the drug, to obtain a brief but powerful euphoria or "rush," similar to that produced by crack cocaine. Crank users describe the feeling as an intense pleasure jolt or shock that pushes them to use the drug repeatedly.

See also COCAINE; SUBSTANCE ABUSE.

Media Resource Guide on Common Drugs of Abuse. Public Relations Society of America, National Capital Chapter, Fairfax, Va., September 1990.

creativity An unusual association of words or ideas and ingenious methods of problem solving, which may involve using everyday objects or processes in original ways. A free and voluminous flow of ideas is also part of the creative process even though most of the ideas may not be truly creative. The technique of brainstorming is related to this aspect of creativity.

Although some aspects of the creative process have been defined and identified, creativity is a difficult mental activity to study or even to define because of its inherent subjectivity and various forms of manifesting itself in different areas of life. Behaviorists even adopt the position that there is no such thing as a creative act; what appears to be new is, in fact, "old wine in new bottles" or arrived at by luck and random experimentation. However, most discussions of creativity contain the concepts of the new, novel or unique or whether an idea is actually a combination of existing and known elements and ideas in a new way. For example, Shakespeare created dramatic masterpieces without using original plots. Another element of creativity is its relation to reality, to something others can relate to or use. A unique solution to a problem is not, in the end, creative if it does not work. A work of art may be original but not truly creative unless it relates somehow to experiences, feelings or thoughts—even though previously undefined—of the observer. Some creative ideas, however, are ahead of their time and may not be understood or appreciated until after the creator's lifetime.

The Creative Process   Researchers and biographers of creative individuals have identified certain stages in the creative process. Often the scientist or artist will identify an area of work that he wishes to attack, but after approaching it in a rational manner, he leaves it feeling dissatisfied and returns to less creative endeavors for a period that has been called incubation. A frequent experience is that after this period a solution or artistic concept may come rather suddenly, which then must be fleshed out, elaborated or tested. The ability to let go of proven reasonable concepts, to reach out beyond ordinary thought and then to return to test and rework the fruits of these irrational explorations is thought by many experts to be central to the creative process.

Certain personality and intellectual characteristics have been found to correlate with creativity. Although intelligence and creativity are thought to be separate mental gifts, and not all intelligent people are creative, intelligence does seem to be necessary to creativity. Creative people have been found to be leaders and independent thinkers. They are self-assured and unconventional and have a wide range of interests. Since they are frequently involved in their own thoughts and inner life, they tend to be introverted and uninterested in social life or group activities. Passion for their field of work and a sense that what they do will eventually be recognized and make a difference are also qualities that support creativity.

There is a somewhat prevalent attitude that creative people have a reputation of being mentally unstable. Some experts say that creativity is actually limited or impossible in the presence of severe neurosis. Both tests and observations indicate that while creative individuals may have unusual personality structures and the potential for extreme behavior, they also possess extremely strong mechanisms for keeping these tendencies under control. On the other hand, studies of creative individuals have shown that a common element is a severe childhood trauma or loss, such as the death of a parent, and that many have a period of mental disturbance. Depression seems to be common among the creative. A common pattern is a period of depression followed by an explosion of creative thought and work.

Measuring creativity has challenged mental health professionals. For example, J. P. Guilford (1897–1987), who explored this area in the 1960s, described two areas of thinking: convergent or narrow, focused thinking and divergent thinking, which allows the individual to let her mind roam and explore a broad spectrum of ideas. Guilford felt that the latter type of thinking was most creatively productive. Under Guilford's direction, the Torrance Tests of Creative Thinking were developed at the University of Southern California.

Researchers have also taken an interest in stimulating and increasing creativity. It has been found that an individual's creativity may increase or decrease according to her environment and work habits. For example, changing the atmosphere, time of day and even clothing for work may make certain people more or less productive. Techniques, such as brainstorming and other group techniques, encourage the flow of ideas. Certain techniques of thought may allow the distancing that gives a fresh view of the project or problem.

Although creativity is strongly associated with the arts, it is equally important to fields such as science, business and manufacturing.

See also BRAINSTORMING.

Benson, P. G. "Creativity Measures," in Corsini, Raymond J., ed., *Encyclopedia of Psychology,* vol. 1. New York: Wiley, 1984.

Flach, Frederic. "Creativity, An Overview," in Wolman, Benjamin B., ed., *International Encyclopedia of Psychiatry, Psychoanalysis and Neurology,* vol. 3. New York: Van Nostrand, 1977.

Levy, Norman, and Kelman, Harold. "Creativity: Horney's View," in Wolman, Benjamin B., ed., *International Encyclopedia of Psychiatry, Psychoanalysis and Neurology,* vol. 3. New York: Van Nostrand, 1977.

Skolnik, Yitzchok, and Fried, Ahron H. "Creativity," in Wolman, Benjamin B., ed., *International Encyclopedia of Psychiatry, Psychoanalysis and Neurology,* vol 3. New York: Van Nostrand, 1977.

Spruiell, Vann. "Creativity: Psychoanalytic Studies," in Wolman, Benjamin B., ed., *International Encyclopedia of Psychiatry, Psychoanalysis and Neurology,* vol. 3. New York: Van Nostrand, 1977.

Weisberg, Robert. *Creativity, Genius and Other Myths.* New York: W. H. Freeman and Company, 1986.

Creutzfeldt-Jakob disease (CJD)   A rare fatal brain disease caused by a transmissible infectious agent, possibly a virus. Failing memory, changes in behavior and a lack of coordination are some of the symptoms observed in the early stages of the disease. The disease progresses rapidly, usually causing death within one year of diagnosis. According to the Alzheimer's Disease and Related Diseases Association, examination of brain tissue reveals distinct changes unlike those seen in Alzheimer's disease.

No treatment is available to stop the progression of the disease.

See also ALZHEIMER'S DISEASE.

crime, witnessing   Witnesses to crimes must quickly decide if they wish to become involved in assisting the victim and then how to intervene. Many simply decide not to get involved, particularly in urban situations. In a well-known case in 1964 in New York, Kitty Genovese was brutally murdered after an hour-long attack while 38 neighbors watched from their windows. Researchers now believe that a person's response to such a situation depends on how much responsibility he feels. For example, if he thinks that there are others present who might assist, he will be less likely to help and will thereby avoid a difficult and personally dangerous situation.

A witness to a crime who intervenes or offers information and assistance to law enforcement officials faces many of the same problems as the victim of the crime. A witness, who is very likely to be distressed by what he has seen, may have to deal with police who have developed attitudes that block out the horror and violence of crime and who therefore may treat the witness in a cold, businesslike way. Witnesses must also face the possibility of threats or harassment from family or other associates of the criminal. Postponement and rescheduling of trials is also discouraging to witnesses, who must adapt their work schedule and other responsibilities to these changes and delays. When the trial actually does take place, witnesses may be placed close to the offender and his friends or family.

In response to the difficulties that witnesses face, which may lessen their willingness to become involved in the judicial process, some areas have developed Victim/Witness Assistance Programs. These programs offer psychological counseling, assist witnesses with arrangements to get in and out of court buildings without contact with the offender's supporters and may help with difficulties caused by the witness having to be away from work for the trial. They may also intervene to speed up a trial for which a witness is suffering threats or intimidation.

See also POST-TRAUMATIC STRESS DISORDER.

Greenberg, M. D. "Bystander Involvement," in Corsini, Raymond J., ed., *Encyclopedia of Psychology,* vol. 1. New York: Wiley, 1984.

Saltzman, Alan. "Victim and Witness Assistance Programs," in Kadish, Sanford, ed., *Encyclopedia of Crime and Justice,* vol. 4. New York: Free Press, 1983.

crisis   A turning point, usually dangerous, because it threatens to overwhelm the individual and family members. For example, a crisis is a situation in which an individual is in an extreme state of anxiety, agitation and stress, such as threatening suicide or threatening to kill someone. There may be feelings of extreme depression, helplessness, guilt and fear. The crisis may result from a combination of the individual's perception of an event as well as an inability to cope with it. The term has also been used to refer to the turning point in the course of a disease, such as the onset of either recovery or deterioration.

crisis intervention   Provision of immediate help, advice or therapy for individuals with acute psychological or medical problems, known as "crises," which are turning points as well as opportunities for changing one's life patterns into more acceptable or productive ways. The goal of crisis intervention is to avoid catastrophe, such as suicide or homicide, and restore the individual's equilibrium to the same level of functioning as before the crisis or to improve it. Such help may last from a few days to a few weeks. A wide variety of therapists and self-help groups provide crisis intervention. Therapy may include talking to the individual and appropriate family members or short-term use of appropriate prescription drugs. Crisis intervention is not a substitute for longer-term therapy. The individual may learn to immediately modify certain environmental factors as well as interpersonal aspects of the situation causing the crisis. There is emphasis on reducing anxiety, promoting self-reliance and focusing on the present. In many cases of crisis intervention, longer-term therapy is recommended after the individual has regained some degree of composure and coping skills.

Crisis intervention centers for suicide prevention often utilize telephone counseling. In some cases, a rape victim's first step toward seeking professional assistance is a call to a rape crisis hot line. In a case of a mass shooting in a restaurant or school, crisis intervention services are provided to survivors who witnessed the event. In many cases, crisis intervention may prevent the onset or ameliorate post-traumatic stress disorder (PTSD).

See also CRIME, WITNESSING; POST-TRAUMATIC STRESS DISORDER; RAPE, RAPE PREVENTION AND RAPE TRAUMA SYNDROME; SUICIDE; SUPPORT GROUPS.

criticism   Comments directed to another regarding behavior, appearance, performance, quality of work or other personal characteristics. Criticism may be favorable but is usually regarded as the opposite of praise.

Receiving criticism may lower one's self-esteem and even make one reluctant to do or try certain activities. For example, when a child receives negative criticism regarding his singing ability from a teacher, the child may become reluctant to sing out loud again. Some individuals who have social phobias have them because of a fear of criticism. Examples are fears of public speaking, eating in public or writing in public.

Normal self-esteem is required to self-correct ineffective behavior that is continued. The capacity to accept criticism that is appropriate and modify behavior is often associated with self-improvement and success. Narcissistic individuals or others with very low self-esteem cannot accept even appropriate criticism.

Some depressed people take criticism very harshly and sink even deeper into their feelings of worthlessness and helplessness.

Children as well as others who are in the position of being students or followers thrive on encouragement rather than criticism, since they are actually in an inferior position to a parent, teacher or supervisor. Parents may be tempted to coax children out from bad to good behavior with rewards, but the end result is really rewarding objectionable behavior, rather than providing constructive solutions. Criticism should genuinely define what is desirable and undesirable. Directions that are positive, clear and specific are more likely to produce results than short, general commands, such as "behave yourself." When criticism is essential, the child's attempt should be viewed as important. It is more productive to focus criticism on the task or skill than on the person and to avoid comparison with other students or siblings.

Criticism is usually not pleasant for the one being criticized and is often also unpleasant for the critic. In work situations, some supervisors find it difficult to offer criticism to employees. In some situations, supervisors avoid direct criticism, which may actually make problems worse. Putting criticism in writing is a way to avoid direct confrontation but may seem harsher than intended and gives the employee no immediate opportunity to respond. Writing a memo to a group criticizing acts that only a few have committed is another way of avoiding confrontation, but this usually offends the innocent and makes the guilty feel that what they are doing is a common practice. Employers may also have a tendency to mix praise and blame in such a way that the employee takes neither seriously.

Some supervisors may have a tendency to scrutinize the employee too closely and make general comments about his behavior in addition to what is needed to resolve the situation. Any criticism of an employee that fails to get to the heart of the problem and to deal with elements of the problem that may recur is counterproductive. A supervisor should expect that her criticism of an employee should be a learning experience for him as well.

See also ANXIETY DISORDERS; INFERIORITY COMPLEX; PHOBIA.

Leach, Penelope. *The Child Care Encyclopedia.* New York: Knopf, 1984.
Platt, J. M. "Encouragement," in Corsini, Raymond J., ed., *Encyclopedia of Psychology,* vol. 1. New York: Wiley 1984.
Quick, Thomas. *Person to Person Management; An Executive's Guide to Working Effectively with People.* New York: St. Martin's, 1977.

crying A characteristic vocal expression of emotion, accompanied by tears. Crying is a normal response to grief as well as extreme happiness. People cry when they are very sad or very happy. Additionally, crying may occur during certain emotional disorders. For example, during depression, an individual may cry easily and without appropriate cause. In severe depression, an individual may lose the capacity to cry or weep, despite profound sadness.

A newborn baby's crying serves to inflate the lungs, clear secretions from the lungs and clear the eyes. In an infant, hunger and pain stimulate crying.

See also DEPRESSION; GRIEF.

CAT scan See BRAIN IMAGING.

cults The original concept of the cult was religious. Groups known as cults, which grew out of the thoughts and attitudes of the 1960s, frequently had a religious philosophy and were often started by religious leaders. These groups may also have social or political reform as their goal, possibly even including terrorism.

The cult experience varies. One new recruit to the "Moonies," or members of the

Reverend Sun Myung Moon's Unification Church, recalled being awakened on his first morning in the cult by a guitarist singing "You Are My Sunshine." Jim Jones, a former Disciples of Christ minister, led his followers, members of the People's Temple, into isolation and mass suicide in Guyana.

Despite their differences, cults do share certain similarities. They seem to have arisen from a time period when social values were questioned and thought to be inadequate. New recruits are frequently young people who, although they may be emotionally stable, lack family and close friends and are searching for relief from confusion or emotional distress. Cults welcome new members with an attitude of caring and acceptance that creates a strong emotional experience for the new member. Once in the cult, the new members behavior and attitudes are dictated by strong pressure in a very close-knit atmosphere. Members are made to feel that there are continually higher levels of commitment or sanctity that they can attain in relationship to the group often involving considerable psychological or physical stress. Questioning the values of the group is looked upon as evil or sinful. Members who were experiencing problems before their entrance into the group are reminded that to return to the outside would be to return to those difficulties. Cult leaders tend to be charismatic individuals who may be considered to be divine by group members. Their whims, desires and opinions are obeyed without question.

Family and friends of recruits are usually distressed by their affiliation, which sometimes seems to occur with no warning. They observe strange speech and behavior patterns if the recruit maintains contact at all. Some new cult members sever all close ties and disappear. In response to cult movements, certain groups and individuals have undertaken deprogramming efforts that attempt to extricate group members, usually at the request of their families. Deprogrammers may

use force or coercion to remove members and have been accused of using brainwashing techniques similar to those used by the cults to hold their members.

See also BRAINWASHING.

Galanter, Marc. *Cults, Faith, Healing and Coercion.* New York: Oxford University Press, 1989.
Johnson, Joan. *The Cult Movement.* New York: Franklin Watts, 1984.

culture shock   See MIGRATION.

Cushing's syndrome   Excessive production of glucocorticoids (cortisol) by the adrenal cortex. The term is also applied to a benign tumor of the pituitary gland. There is a continuous loss of protein from the body, indicated by skin changes and weakened bones. Blood glucose is increased, and there may be glucose in the urine despite increased insulin secretion. In women there may be loss of menses. Diagnosis is made on the basis of puffiness of skin, masculinizing effects, increased blood pressure, higher-than-normal glucose levels in the blood and high amounts of excreted corticoid steroids in the urine. The disease is treated by partial removal of the cortex portion of the adrenal glands.

Patients with Cushing's syndrome may suffer from depression, confusion, organic psychosis and suicidal tendencies. Cushing-like syndrome can be induced by taking corticoid-like steroids (for example, prednisolone, cortisone) for various medical conditions such as lupus erythematosus, Crohn's disease and severe asthma.

See also ADRENAL CORTEX; ADRENAL GLAND; CORTISOL.

cyclothymia   A mood disturbance in which one has moods of elation and depression. Cyclothymia is now categorized as a mild type of bipolar (manic-depressive) disorder. To be diagnosed as having cyclothymia, a person must have at least two years of this disorder (one year for children and adolescents) and many periods of depressed mood or loss of interest or pleasure usually unrelated to external sources. With cyclothymia, the person is not as socially or occupationally impaired as with severe depression or manic episodes, but anxieties develop because of rapid mood changes. Cyclothymia usually begins in adolescence or early adult life. It is equally common in males and females.

See also AFFECTIVE DISORDERS; BIPOLAR DISORDER; DEPRESSION; MANIC-DEPRESSIVE ILLNESS; DEPRESSION AND AFFECTIVE DISORDERS in BIBLIOGRAPHY.

American Psychiatric Association. *Diagnostic and Statistical Manual of Mental Disorders,* 3d ed., rev. Washington, D.C., 1987.

cyproterone acetate   An antiandrogenic drug (trade name: Cyproteron/Androcure) used in some women to counteract effects of excess male hormones. Some women develop facial hair and other masculine features as a result of a disorder of the adrenal gland or after use of hormonal therapy for cancer. Cyproterone acetate also has been used to control precocious puberty in boys and in sexual offenders to reduce sex drive.

D

dance therapy   A form of creative therapy that permits expression of emotion through movement. It can be used with a wide variety of patients, from those who have no serious disorders to those who do. Many individuals who will not speak about their mental health concerns will indicate something about them with movement. Therapists who use this technique are usually trained in dance and body movement as well as psychology. Dance therapy alone does not relieve symptoms of ill mental health

but may be used in conjunction with other therapies.

See also ALTERNATIVE THERAPIES.

Darvon   Trade name for dextropropoxyphene hydrochloride, a synthetic derivative of opium. This drug is a moderately strong painkiller and has sedative effects. It also has the potential for the development of tolerance as well as psychological and physiological dependence.

See also OPIOID SUBSTANCE ABUSE; SUBSTANCE ABUSE.

date rape   See RAPE, RAPE PREVENTION AND RAPE TRAUMA SYNDROME.

day care   Although certain types of day care have been available for many years, recent changes in the economy, employment and family patterns have made day care an important and emotionally charged issue. The women (and men) who want a family and career (''having it all'') are faced with the dilemma of day care versus staying at home with the child. Many parents feel some degree of guilt about seeking day care for their children. However, as a practical matter, it has become economically more difficult to support a family on one income. Additionally, wives and mothers who are not forced to work for financial reasons are encouraged by modern thinking to feel that the position of being a housewife and mother is not rewarding. Still, others faced with the specter of a high divorce rate may want to keep up their skills and have their own employment benefits ''just in case.'' For the single-parent family with small children, some type of child care is a necessity. Social mobility has also increased the need for some type of daytime child care. At one time, mothers could frequently depend on grandmothers for daytime child care. Now a grandmother may be hundreds of miles away and working herself.

Many children today are still taken care of by a sitter in either their own or the sitter's home. However, the day-care situation does offer certain benefits. Children learn to socialize with their peers before entering school. Day-care centers are licensed and run by professionals. They may offer educational programs, toys and equipment that would not be available through a sitter. On the other hand, children sometimes object to being in a situation that is not homelike. Lack of concentration of children in a given geographic area may mean that day care is distant or unavailable. Day care may be more costly than care at home. However, credentials of day-care operators must be carefully checked. During the 1980s, several cases of child abuse were alleged.

Today some day-care centers have a separate area for sick children. Day-care centers specifically for sick children have been set up either independently or in pediatric wards of hospitals. Studies of the effects of day care on children have not shown that children suffer any real difficulties from participation in day care. In some cases, children from deprived backgrounds benefit from day care; however, putting children in the hands of caregivers may lessen the extent to which mothers can influence their child with their own values and standards.

A more recent trend in day care is the establishment of facilities for daytime care of elderly persons, whose condition does not necessitate institutional care but who have difficulty performing certain daytime activities alone. A recent study by Northwestern University showed that while this service is used, there is not the potential demand that was anticipated.

With the increasing number of women in the work force and their advance to positions of increasing responsibility, day care has, to a certain extent, become a corporate responsibility. A day-care center in the mother's place of employment solves transportation problems and allows the parent to visit with the child during the daytime. The Stride Rite Corporation in Cambridge, Massachusetts is an example of a company that has started a program combining care of both small children and elderly dependents of employees in the same facility.

See also CAREGIVERS; WOMEN'S LIBERATION MOVEMENT.

Deutsch, F. "Day Care Centers," in Corsini, Raymond J., ed., *Encyclopedia of Psychology,* vol. 1. New York; Wiley, 1984.

Edmundson, Brad. "Where's the Day Care?" *American Demographics* 12 (July 1990).

Gallo, Nick. "Too Sick for School?" *Better Homes and Gardens* (Sept. 1990).

Kantrowitz, Barbara. "Day Care: Bridging the Generation Gap." *Newsweek* (July 16, 1990).

Maynard, Firedelle. *The Child Care Crisis.* New York: Viking, 1985.

daydreaming Letting one's thoughts wander with specific direction. People of all ages daydream. Office workers may be seen staring out the window, seemingly at nothing. Children may be seen watching birds or flowers, sometimes in a trancelike state. For many people daydreaming may be the forerunner for creativity and developing great ideas or inventions or for taking new directions in life. In daydreaming, one's mind is free to roam without inhibition and self-censorship or criticism from others. Different ways of looking at work, play and family situations are often developed during moments of daydreaming. When workers or children are looking out the window instead of doing homework, they may be daydreaming; to an observer, however, it is difficult to tell if the child is developing an idea for the future or is simply bored.

When daydreaming is filled with impossible fantasies and one lives in the daydreams instead of reality, one's mental health may be considered impaired.

deafness and hearing loss Loss of hearing, either complete or partial. Hearing is related to many things, including problems within the ears themselves, overall body health, the emotions and the external environment. Estimates are that about a quarter of a million people in the United States are completely deaf, and about 3 million have major hearing problems. Many individuals who begin to lose their hearing try to draw attention away from their loss or cover up for it. Hearing aids help many individuals, but some are embarrassed to wear one or fear that others will think less of them if they do. Some people associate loss of hearing with aging and hence postpone getting a hearing aid to preserve their image of youthfulness.

A number of factors can contribute to deafness, including heredity, subjection to noise exposure, damage to the eardrum (by insertion of a foreign object into the ear canal) and certain illnesses (encephalitis). Often hearing loss is rooted to a buildup of cerumen (ear wax) in the ear canal. This can be removed through a simple procedure by an audiologist or ENT (ear, nose, throat) specialist. (Patients should never do this themselves.)

People tend to shut off certain sounds at certain times and admit only what is interesting and significant. For example, in some nursing homes, it has been observed that individuals say they cannot hear but suddenly perk up when ice cream or something they like is mentioned.

The term ''psychogenic deafness'' pertains to such mental shutting off of hearing carried to an extreme. Some patients with mental illnesses may have such a strong subconscious desire not to hear that they become completely deaf even though they have physically normal ears.

The term ''psychosomatic deafness'' pertains to a situation in which actual physical deterioration occurs in the ear in response to a mental or emotional problem. There also may be combinations of both physical and mental hearing difficulties.

One who suspects he has a hearing loss should consult an audiologist to undergo a hearing test.

See also PSYCHOSOMATIC (PSYCHOSOMATIC ILLNESS).

death Death and dying are major emotionally charged issues. Many people fear death as well as the process of dying. Although death is something everyone will eventually face, it is one of the least talked about topics in Western society. However, as medical science has created ways to prolong life even in those with terminal illness, an increasing number of people are beginning to ''take charge'' of their own deaths by preparing legal documents such as living wills and giving others durable power of attorney so that they will not be kept artificially alive on respirators or other machines. On these legal documents, people can specify the types of life support systems they do and do not want. For example, one person may say that he will not tolerate being tube-fed when he can no longer keep food down in the normal way; another might want nutrition provided but not assistance in breathing. This permits a physician to omit more heroic treatment efforts without civil or criminal liability.

Legal definitions of death vary. At one time it was simply when the heartbeat and breathing stopped. Now it is recognized that the brain is the basis for life, and ''brain death'' has supplanted the breath and heart tests for death. People whose hearts and lungs have stopped working can be maintained for years on machines, but no one is really ''alive'' when they are brain dead. Brain death means an unconscious state in which the person has no reflexes, cannot breathe or maintain a heartbeat. The electroencephalogram (EEG) of the person would be flat, without any regular oscillations indicating function of the brain. Brain death occurs naturally within a few minutes after the heart stops, because oxygen necessary for life would not be carried through the blood to the brain.

In most states a physician must certify death and indicate the time, place and cause. In some cases, circumstances of death play a major role in insurance payments. When there are suppositions of homicide or suicide, the situation takes on additional dimensions.

Death is an ethical issue for physicians and health care professionals. Some patients who are near death ask for a death-inducing potion or instrument. Physicians are faced with the ethical and legal dilemma of providing assistance in such cases. There have been instances in which loved ones provide such assistance, sometimes incriminating themselves in subsequent unpleasant legal situations. The question of assisted suicide is both a moral and legal issue. It is also a mental health issue, since severely depressed individuals may feel hopeless as a symptom of the depression. It is possible for them to develop the conviction that they have a terminal illness and ask for assistance in committing suicide, when successful antidepressant treatment would change their outlook.

In the latter part of the 20th century, many people choose the place for their death. Some who have terminal illnesses opt to go home rather than stay in the hospital with its impersonal surroundings, despite its high-technology equipment. Others opt for hospice care, where all of the patients are facing death very soon.

Religious beliefs console many people as their own death approaches or after the death of a loved one.

See also BRAIN DEATH; CAREGIVERS; GRIEF; LEGAL ISSUES; NEAR-DEATH EXPERIENCES; STRESS; SUICIDE; TERMINAL ILLNESS.

decompensation A breakdown in the psychological defense mechanisms that help individuals maintain good mental functioning. Decompensation may occur under stress or in mental disorders such as anxiety, depression or psychoses with hallucinations or delusions.

See also ANXIETY; DEFENSE MECHANISMS; DELUSION; DEPRESSION; HALLUCINATION.

deconditioning A technique used in behavioral therapy; also known as desensiti-zation. Under a therapist's guidance, individuals are gradually exposed to the situation or event that causes them anxiety responses. In time, they are exposed to the situation at its maximum. Instead of responding with their former, unwanted response to which they had become conditioned, they are desensitized to the event and no longer respond with their unwanted behavior, which might have been extreme anxiety or a panic attack.

See also BEHAVIORAL THERAPY; DESENSITIZATION.

defense mechanisms Techniques that individuals use to preserve and protect their self-esteem as well as to control their reactions to situations and life circumstances. Individuals may or may not be aware that they are putting their own defense mechanisms into play. Defensive behaviors are a way in which people cope with daily life, including ordinary as well as extraordinary circumstances. People have a wide variety of defense mechanisms, ranging from projection (blaming someone else for one's situation), rationalization (justifying questionable behavior by defending its propriety) and sublimation (rechanneling sexual energy into creative projects). Denial is another defense mechanism. The presence of pathological denial (of a drinking problem) is often seen in people with alcoholism or substance abuse problems. In cases of extreme child abuse, dissociation—a splitting of one's mind from the physical circumstance—becomes a defense mechanism. While defense mechanisms can be helpful in coping with daily life, excessive use of such devices and dependence on them can be a threat to good mental health.

In follow-up studies of the Harvard University class of 1934, Dr. George Vaillant found that though virtually all of his subjects had significant life crises, those who overcame them tended to have "mature" defenses such as suppression (the capacity to focus on only the most important issue at the time) and a good sense of humor. Those who were overwhelmed by life crises tended to employ "less mature/more primitive" defenses (blaming others) and denial (not admitting the presence of a problem to oneself).

See also DISSOCIATION; DISSOCIATIVE DISORDERS; MULTIPLE PERSONALITY DISORDER.

deja vu The French term for "already seen," this refers to a sensation that an event seemingly happening for the first time has been experienced before. The feeling is sometimes accompanied by a sense of what is going to happen next. The sensation may cause a sense of disorientation because of the gap between rational, objective knowledge and feelings.

Deja vu experiences may be profound and may last several days in epileptic patients. In normal individuals the experience is usually brief.

The deja vu experience has been explained by the possibility that there may be a link between the current situation and a past situation that cannot be remembered. Another possibility is that the feelings experienced in the new situation may be so similar to a previous situation or experience that there is a sense of repetition. Still, another explanation of deja vu is that the situation was experienced before in a dream or imagined situation.

See also EPILEPSY; MEMORY.

Harre, Ron, and Lamb, Roger, eds. *The Encyclopedic Dictionary of Psychology.* Cambridge: MIT Press, 1983.
Nicholi, Armand M., Jr., ed. *The New Harvard Guide to Psychiatry.* Cambridge: Belknap Press of Harvard University, 1988.

delibidinization A term used in psychoanalysis to refer to elimination or neutralization of a sexual aim, also known as desexualization. An example is diverting an impulse toward voyeurism (scopophilia) to curiosity about an intellectual matter.

delinquency See ANTISOCIAL PERSONALITY DISORDER; CONDUCT DISORDER.

delirium A deranged state of mind characterized by a clouding of consciousness, disorientation regarding time and place, memory disturbances, severely impaired concentration and slowing of the EEG (brain waves). There may be hallucinations, and delirious people may believe that they see and hear things that are not there. Delirium may be associated with high fevers in diseases such as pneumonia, meningitis and encephalitis. Alcohol and morphine or a head injury can induce delirium. Treatment requires constant medical and nutritional supervision.

See also DELIRIUM TREMENS.

delirium tremens An acute mental disturbance characterized by delirium, trembling and excitement (abbreviated as "DTs") that occurs after periods of chronic alcoholism. It can also occur during withdrawal from alcohol. It is rare in individuals under age 30 or after less than three or four years of chronic alcoholism. A person with the DTs has rapid pulse and often a high temperature, perspires copiously, has terrifying visual hallucinations (dogs, rats) and paranoid delusions and may have convulsions similar to those in epilepsy. Often a patient will not remember anything that occurred during her bout with DTs. If not treated, DTs may be fatal.

See also ALCOHOLISM; DELIRIUM; ALCOHOLISM in BIBLIOGRAPHY.

delusion A strong but false mental conception of an event or image. Delusions are classified as nonbizarre (events that could happen but did not, such as being followed) and bizarre (totally impossible, such as visits from Martians). Most people at some time think small lies to themselves or indulge in a moment of wishful thinking to protect themselves against anxiety. However, when a person can no longer distinguish between fact and fiction, he is having a delusion. To the delusion sufferer, his fantasy is real, and no amount of information will change his attitude.

One common delusion seen by mental health professionals is the delusion of grandeur, which arises from feelings of insecurity or inferiority. A person who believes that he is Elvis Presley or Winston Churchill is escaping from negative feelings he has about himself. Another common delusion is that of persecution. A person who is hostile to others may not admit to this feeling but instead believes that other people (such as the FBI) are harassing her, bugging her telephone or following her. A delusion of illness (often terminal cancer) is fairly common in persons suffering from severe psychotic depression.

Delusions are one of the characteristics of delusional disorder (nonbizarre delusions) or schizophrenia, especially paranoid schizophrenia.

See also DELUSIONAL JEALOUSY; SCHIZOPHRENIA.

delusional jealousy A term for a paranoid jealousy reaction marked by a delusion that one's spouse or lover is unfaithful; an obsolete term for this habit is amorous paranoia. Such individuals constantly watch for indications of infidelity and justification of their suspicion and may make up evidence if no evidence is available. In males, this type of behavior is known as the Othello syndrome.

Case reports suggest successful treatments with newer medications such as fluoxetine (Prozac).

See also AMOROUS PARANOIA.

dementia A loss of functions such as thinking, remembering and reasoning severe enough to interfere with one's daily functioning. Symptoms may also include personality changes and changes in behavior and mood. While not a disease, dementia is a group of symptoms that may accompany certain conditions or diseases.

The most common cause of dementia is Alzheimer's disease. Other diseases that produce dementia include Parkinson's disease, Pick's disease, Creutzfeldt-Jakob disease, amyotrophic lateral sclerosis (Lou Gehrig's disease) and multiple sclerosis. Other conditions that can cause or mimic dementia include hydrocephalus, depression, brain tumors, thyroid disorders, nutritional deficiencies, alcoholism, infections (for example, meningitis, syphilis, AIDS), head injuries and drug reactions. Some of these conditions may be treatable and reversible.

Individuals suspected of having dementia should be examined by a physician experienced in the diagnosis of such disorders, as well as evaluated by a psychologist, and have a thorough laboratory testing. A competent diagnosis will help the individual obtain treatment for reversible conditions and help both the individual and the family plan future care.

Persons with dementia have symptoms that require specialized care. Individualized planning is necessary, based on the symptoms and degree of impairment. Treatment should be aimed at helping patients make the most of their remaining abilities and helping family members cope with the burden of the patient's increasing care needs.

Multi-infarct dementia (MID) Multi-infarct dementia, also known as vascular dementia, is mental deterioration caused by multiple strokes (infarcts) in the brain. MID may appear suddenly, as many strokes can occur before symptoms are apparent. Such strokes may damage areas of the brain responsible for specific functions, such as calculating or remembering. There may also be generalized symptoms, such as confusion, disorientation and changes in behavior. MID may appear similar to Alzheimer's disease. According to the Alzheimer's Disease and Related Disorders Association, Inc., MID and Alzheimer's disease coexist in 15 to 20 percent of dementia patients.

Risk factors for MID include a history of high blood pressure, vascular disease, diabetes or previous stroke. While MID is not reversible or curable, recognition of an underlying condition, such as high blood pressure, may help lead to a specific treatment that may slow the progression of the disorder.

To help identify strokes in the brain, brain scanning techniques such as computerized axial tomography (CAT) and magnetic resonance imaging (MRI) are used.

For information on dementia and related disorders, contact:

Alzheimer's Disease and Related Disorders Association, Inc.
70 East Lake Street
Chicago, IL 60601–5997
Phone: (800) 621–0379
in Illinois, (800) 572–6037
or (312) 853–3060

See also ALZHEIMER'S DISEASE; BRAIN IMAGING; CREUTZFELDT-JAKOB DISEASE (CJD); DEPRESSION; HUNTINGTON'S DISEASE (HUNTINGTON'S CHOREA); PICK'S DISEASE.

dementia praecox   An earlier term for schizophrenia. When the disease was first defined more than 100 years ago by Kraepelin, the word *praecox,* Latin for "early ripening," was used because it was believed that the onset of the disease came in early life, or adolescence.

See also SCHIZOPHRENIA; SCHIZOPHRENIA in BIBLIOGRAPHY.

Demerol   The trade name for the drug meperidine hydrochloride. Many of its pharmacologic properties and indications are similar to those of morphine. The drug is considered a synthetic derivative of opium; it is useful in medical situations but also subject to abuse.

As a pain reliever, Demerol is widely used in anesthetic premedication, in balanced anesthesia and in obstetric analgesia (pain relief). It is preferred to morphine for ob-

stetric use because its rapid onset of action and shorter duration usually permit greater flexibility, possibly with less effect on neonatal respiration. However, it can produce significant respiratory depression in the newborn infant proportional to the fetal blood concentration. This can be minimized by giving small incremental doses intravenously during labor.

In individuals who are taking antipsychotic drugs, sedative drugs or other drugs that depress the central nervous system, the dose of Demerol should be carefully adjusted and reduced. Severe toxic reactions and even death have followed the use of Demerol in patients receiving monoamine oxidase inhibitors (MAOIs).

See also OPIOID SUBSTANCE ABUSE; PAIN; SUBSTANCE ABUSE.

American Medical Association. *AMA Drug Evaluations Annual, 1991*. Chicago: AMA, 1991.

denial   A mechanism for coping with everyday life as well as crises; also known as a defense mechanism. Using denial, an individual can filter out anxiety-producing thoughts and ideas. Denial is largely an unconscious mechanism, although at times it seems to be at a conscious level. For example, individuals who are terminally ill and fear death will deny the severity of their illness. Children who are abused by their parents will deny the abuse, yet some— because of the severity of their abuse— develop a dissociative disorder, such as multiple personality disorder. The antidote for extreme denial is facing reality and coping with it in the present.

Denial should be distinguished from the defense of suppression, a diverting of attention from minor threats or problems in order to focus all attention on dealing with a major current threat or problem. Suppression is a mature defense that allows individuals to cope with stressful events by focusing attention.

See also DEFENSE MECHANISMS; MULTIPLE PERSONALITY DISORDER.

deoxyribonucleic acid (DNA) The primary determinant of hereditary traits passed on from generation to generation through the genes and chromosomes. This substance is the most important part of the nucleus of the cell.

See also CHROMOSOME; HEREDITY.

dependency Psychological or physical reliance on other people or on drugs. In the case of dependence on people, it is a feeling that assistance from others is necessary for emotional or financial security or other reasons and is expected and actively sought. The person who is dependent looks to others for nurturance, guidance and decision making. It is not uncommon for a highly dependent person to feel resentment toward the depended-upon person or feel ''controlled by him.'' This can be illustrated by the observation that in a relationship ''anger equals dependency,'' a problem seen between adolescents and their parents, sometimes in marriages or in elderly people who have become dependent on their children. The solution, when possible, is to attain emotional and economic independence.

A dependency on drugs (or alcohol) means that one uses the drugs as a means of coping with everyday life and cannot get along without them. A codependent person is one who enables another to be dependent on a drug habit or to continue with a mental disorder such as agoraphobia.

See also AGORAPHOBIA; ALCOHOLISM; CO-DEPENDENCY; SUBSTANCE ABUSE.

dependent personality disorder A personality disorder characterized by a pattern of dependent and submissive behavior. Such individuals usually lack self-esteem and frequently belittle their capabilities; they fear criticism and are easily hurt by others' comments. At times they actually bring about dominance by others through a quest for overprotection.

Dependent personality disorder usually begins in early adulthood. Individuals who have this disorder may be unable to make everyday decisions without advice or reassurance from others, may allow others to make most of their important decisions (such as where to live), tend to agree with people even when they believe they are wrong, have difficulty starting projects or doing things on their own, volunteer to do things that are demeaning in order to get approval from other people, feel uncomfortable or helpless when alone and are often preoccupied with fears of being abandoned.

See also DEPENDENCY; PERSONALITY DISORDERS; SELF-ESTEEM.

American Psychiatric Association. *Diagnostic and Statistical Manual of Mental Disorders,* 3d ed., rev. Washington, D.C., 1987.

depersonalization A state of feeling unreal. The sensation usually comes on suddenly and may be momentary or last for hours. People in this state may feel that they are elsewhere looking down on themselves, watching themselves. Depersonalization is sometimes accompanied by derealization, a feeling that the world is unreal. An otherwise healthy person may experience depersonalization, especially during a time of extreme fatigue or sorrow. It is a frightening experience because it makes the individual feel out of control during the episode. People who have agoraphobia and panic attacks sometimes experience depersonalization, particularly if they hyperventilate (rapid, shallow breathing). Depersonalization also occurs in some drug users, as an adverse effect to some antidepressant drugs, during a migraine headache attack and in some forms of epilepsy.

When episodes of depersonalization that are severe enough to impair an individual's social and occupational functioning occur frequently, the disorder is known as depersonalization disorder. Frequent episodes of depersonalization may also occur in schizotypal personality disorder and schizophrenia.

See also SCHIZOPHRENIA; SCHIZOTYPAL PERSONALITY DISORDER.

American Psychiatric Association. *Diagnostic and Statistical Manual of Mental Disorders,* 3d ed., rev. Washington, D.C., 1987.

Deprenyl Trade name for selegiline, a drug that in some research projects has been shown to slow the progress of Parkinson's disease. It was approved for use in the United States in 1989. Additional research is under way concerning the drug and its use in neurological disorders.

See also PARKINSON'S DISEASE.

depressants Agents, such as drugs, that reduce or slow down functions (metabolism) or activities of the central nervous system or brain. Examples of depressants are alcohol, barbiturates and tranquilizers. These agents must be differentiated from drugs that may cause depression.

See also ALCOHOLISM; BARBITURATE DRUGS; TRANQUILIZER DRUGS.

depression A mood or affective disorder characterized by sadness, dysphoria, hopelessness, despair, personal devaluation and helplessness. (An affective disorder refers to a condition involving the external expression of an internal state [mood or emotion]). Some depressions are marked by anxiety, withdrawal from others, loss of sleep or excessive need for sleep, constant fatigue, loss of appetite or compulsive eating, loss of sexual desire, lethargy or agitation, an inability to concentrate and make decisions and possibly exaggerated guilt feelings or thoughts.

The term ''depression'' applies to a condition on a continuum of severity. It can be a temporary mood fluctuation, a symptom associated with a number of mental and physical disorders, and a clinical syndrome encompassing many symptoms, such as major depression or dysthymic disorder. When psychological, physical or interpersonal functioning is affected for over two weeks because of depression, it can be considered a mental health problem. Depression is the most common and most treatable of all mental health problems. On the other hand, it has been shown to be second only to severe heart disease in days of work lost, and in its more severe forms carries a 15 percent lifetime risk of suicide.

Depression can appear at any age, although major depressive episodes peak at age 55 to 70 in men and 20 to 45 in women. Recent studies have shown a trend for earlier onset of depression, especially in females. About 20 percent of major depressions last two years or more, with an average duration of eight months. About half of those experiencing a major depression will have a recurrence within two years.

Some victims of depression have episodes that are separated by several years, and others suffer clusters of episodes over a short time span. Between episodes, such individuals function normally. However, 20 to 35 percent of sufferers have chronic depression that prevents them from functioning totally normally.

Estimates are that 2 to 3 percent of men and 4 to 9 percent of women suffer a major depression at any given time in the United States. The lifetime risk may be as high as 10 percent for men and 25 percent for women. About 66 percent of those who suffer from depression fail to recognize the illness and do not get treatment for it.

Symptoms Depressed individuals usually have pervasive feelings of sadness, hopelessness, helplessness and irritability. Often they withdraw from human contact but do not admit to symptoms. They may also experience noticeable change of appetite, either significant weight loss when not dieting or weight gain; change in sleeping patterns, such as fitful sleep, inability to fall asleep or sleeping too much; loss of interest in activities formerly enjoyed; feelings of worthlessness; fatigue; an inability to concentrate; feelings of inappropriate guilt; indecisiveness; recurring thoughts of death or suicide or even attempting suicide.

Many depressed individuals have chronic mental and physical feelings that appear to have no end in sight and cannot be alleviated by happy events or good news. Some depressed people are so disabled by their condition that they cannot build up enough energy to call a friend or relative or seek medical help. If another person calls for them, these people may refuse to go because of hopelessness that they can be helped. Many depressed persons will not follow advice and may refuse help and comfort. Persistence on the part of family and friends is essential because in many cases depression is the illness that underlies suicides. On the other hand, it is common for those patients to see general physicians with ''medical'' complaints.

Causes There is no single cause for depression. It is related to many factors, including a family history of depression, psychosocial stressors, diseases, alcohol, drugs, gender and age. Depression occurs in mood disorders, anxiety disorders, psychotic disorders, adjustment disorders and psychoactive substance use disorders, including alcoholism. Individuals who have personality disorders, especially obsessive-compulsive, dependent, avoidant and borderline personality disorders, are susceptible to depression.

Psychosocial Factors An individual's lack of confidence in her interpersonal skills and personality traits such as overdependency on others as a source of support and self-esteem, perfectionism and unrealistic expectations work together with psychosocial stressors to cause depression. Such psychosocial events include death of a spouse, loss of a job and, for some, urban living.

Social Learning Theory Some psychologists say that stress disrupts involvement with others, resulting in a reduction in degree and quality of positive reinforcement. This leads to more negative self-evaluation and a poor outlook of the future. Depressed people view themselves and the world negatively, which leads to a further sense of low self-worth, feelings of rejection, alienation, dependency, helplessness and hopelessness.

Cognitive Theory Often unrecognized negative attitudes toward the self, the future and the world result in feelings of failure, helplessness and depression. These distorted attitudes may activate a prolonged and deepening depressive state, especially under stress. Learning what they are, understanding their negative distortions and challenging those hopeless and negative thoughts in real life can reverse both depression and a tendency for future depression.

Psychoanalytic Theory A psychoanalytic position regarding depression is that a loss, or a real or perceived withdrawal of affection, in childhood may be a predeterminant of depression in later life. Sigmund Freud and Karl Abraham mentioned the role of ambivalence toward the lost love object, identification with the lost object and subsequent anger turned inward.

Later theories suggested an unrealistic expectation of self and others and loss of self-esteem as essential components leading to depression. Depression arising after a saddened reaction in experiencing loss may result from a failure to work through the loss.

Interpersonal Theory This theory emphasizes the importance of social connections for effective functioning. An individual develops adaptive responses to the psychosocial environment during early developmental experiences. When early attachment bonds are disrupted or impaired, the individual may be vulnerable later on to more interpersonal and social problems that lead to depression.

Genetic Factors Some individuals may be biologically predisposed to develop depression, based on genetic factors that researchers do not yet fully understand. There are genetic markers that indicate susceptibility to manic-depressive illness, and considerable research has been under way in the last 25 years toward understanding the biochemical reactions controlled by these genes.

There is considerable evidence that depression runs in families. For example, if one identical twin suffers from depression or manic-depression, the other twin has a 70 percent chance of also having the illness. Research studies looking at the rate of depression among adopted children have supported this finding. Depressive illnesses among children's adoptive family had little effect on their risk for the disorder; however, among adopted children whose biologic relatives suffered depression, the disorder was three times more common than the norm. Among more severe depressives, family history is more often a significant factor.

Neurotransmitter Theory Recent research indicates that people suffering from depression have imbalances of neurotransmitters, natural biochemicals that enable brain cells to communicate with each another. Three biochemicals that are often out of balance in depressed people are serotonin, norepinephrine and dopamine. An imbalance of serotonin may cause the anxiety, sleep problems and irritability that many depressed people experience. An inadequate supply of norepinephrine, which regulates alertness and arousal, may contribute to the fatigue, depressed mood and lack of motivation. Dopamine imbalances may relate to a loss of sexual interest and an inability to experience pleasure. Several neurotransmitter imbalances may be involved, and research is finding other neurotransmitters that may be important in clinical depression.

Cortisol Another body chemical that may be out of balance in depressed people is cortisol, a hormone produced by the body in response to extreme cold, fear or anger. In normal people, cortisol levels in the blood peak in the morning and decrease later in the day. In depressed people, however, cortisol peaks early in the morning and does not level off or decrease in the afternoon or evening. Recent research in animals suggests that abnormal elevations of cortisol sustained over three months may cause changes in brain structure.

Environmental Influences Environment plays an important role, although researchers view depression as the result of interaction of environmental as well as biologic factors. Historically, depression has been viewed as either internally caused (endogenous depression) or externally related to environmental events (exogenous or reactive depression). Major changes in one's environment (such as a move or job change) or any major loss (such as a divorce or death of a loved one) can bring on depression. Feeling depressed in response to these changes is normal, but when it becomes a severe long-term condition (over one month) and interferes with effective functioning, it requires treatment.

Some environmental factors related to depression include being unemployed, elderly and alone, poor, single and a working mother of young children. However, depression changes an individual's way of looking at ordinary life stresses so as to exaggerate the negative aspects, leading to feelings of being hopeless, helpless and overwhelmed.

Illness Psychological stressors caused by physiological dysfunctions can lead to depression. For example, a debilitating disease can severely restrict usual life-style, resulting in depression. Any illness that impinges on cerebral functioning and impairs blood flow to the brain can produce depression. Such illnesses may include adrenal cortex, thyroid, and parathyroid dysfunctions and many neurological, metabolic and nutritional disorders, as well as infectious diseases.

Medications as a Cause Some medications have been known to cause depression. For example, during the 1950s, doctors learned that some people taking reserpine, a medication for high blood pressure, suffered from depression. Since then, depression has been noted as a side effect of some tranquilizers, hormones and a number of medications. However, alcohol is more likely to cause depression than any medication.

Adolescent Depression Recognizing depression in oneself or in one's children or students is important. Depression is an illness and should be treated as such with available help. Adolescence is a period of demanding and complicated conflicts that lead many young people to develop anxieties, negative self-esteem and fears about their future. Some develop depression when overwhelmed by peer pressure, feelings of loneliness, powerlessness and isolation. Low performance in school can also lead to a feeling of rejection.

The lack of ability to embrace what life has to offer often results in boredom, which may be an indicator of vulnerability to depression.

Contributing factors to adolescent depression may include exaggerated concerns, misperceptions and continual self-criticism. Cognitive behavior therapies focus on these processes.

Symptoms related to adolescent depression include:

Sadness; feelings of helplessness or hopelessness

Poor self-esteem and loss of confidence

Overreaction to criticism

Extreme fluctuations between boredom and talkativeness

Sleep disturbances

Anger, rage and verbal sarcasm; guilt

Intensive ambivalence between dependence and independence

Feelings of emptiness in life

Restlessness and agitation

Pessimism about the future

Refusal to work in school or cooperate in general

Increased or decreased appetite; severe weight gain or loss

Death wishes, suicidal thoughts, suicide attempts

Depression in a young person may be somewhat different from that in an adult because adolescents do not always understand or express feelings well. Some of their symptoms may be overlooked as part of growing up. There is a strong cycle of "getting into trouble" and feeling depressed. A teenager may be depressed because of being in trouble, or in trouble because of being depressed. Depression in adolescents is sometimes linked to poor school performance, truancy, delinquency, alcohol and drug abuse, disobedience, self-destructive behavior, sexual promiscuity, rebelliousness, grief and running away. The young person may have felt a lack of support from family and other significant people and a decrease in the ability to cope effectively. In many instances where depression is attributed to adolescent conflicts, it turns out that depressive episodes are the beginning of mood cycles related to recurrent major depression, bipolar disorders or dysthymia, which require expert diagnosis and psychiatric treatment.

Melancholia Melancholia is a severe form of depression that may originate without any precipitating factors, such as stress. This is in contrast to a reactive depression, which occurs after some stressful life event such as loss of a job or divorce.

Seasonal Mood Disorder (Seasonal Affective Disorder) Some individuals have mood symptoms related to changes of season, with depression often occurring most frequently during winter months and improvement in the spring. Many of these individuals experience periods of increased energy, productivity and even euphoria in the spring and summer months. Also called seasonal affective disorder, this type of depression has often been found responsive to light therapy.

Treatments A variety of therapies and medications help people of all ages who have depression. Estimates are that between 80 and 90 percent of all depressed people can be effectively treated. Many types of therapists provide help. In general, therapists use "talk" treatment to try to understand the individual's disturbed personal and social relationships that may have caused or contributed to the depression. Depression, in turn, may make these relationships more difficult. A therapist can help an individual understand his or her illness and the relationship of depression and particular interpersonal conflicts. If psychotherapy is not helpful or the depression is of such a severe level that there is a loss of work, function or persistent and increasing suicidal ideation over one to three months, medications may be needed to lift the depression in conjunction with therapy.

Psychoanalysis   Treatment of depression with psychoanalysis is based on the theory that depression results from past conflicts pushed into the unconscious. Psychoanalysts work to identify and resolve the individual's past conflicts that have led to depression in later years.

Short-Term Psychotherapy   In the mid-1980s, researchers reported effective results of short-term psychotherapy in treating depression. They noted that cognitive/behavioral therapy and interpersonal therapy were as effective as medications for some depressed patients. Medications relieved patients' symptoms more quickly, but patients who received psychotherapy instead of medication had as much relief from symptoms after 16 weeks and their gains may last longer. Data from this and other studies may help researchers better identify which depressed patients will do best with psychotherapy alone and which may require medications.

Cognitive/Behavioral Therapy   This therapy is based on the understanding that people's emotions are controlled by their views and opinions of the themselves and their world. Depression results when individuals constantly berate themselves, expect to fail, make inaccurate assessments of what others think of them, overvalue situations, catastrophize and have negative attitudes toward the world and their futures. Therapists use techniques of talk therapy to help the individual replace negative beliefs and thought patterns.

Electroconvulsive Therapy (ECT)   Use of ECT to treat depression has declined in the last two decades as more effective medications have been developed. However, ECT is still used for some individuals who cannot take medications because of their physical conditions or who do not respond to antidepressant medication. ECT is considered as a treatment when all other therapies have failed or when a person is suicidal.

Medications   Effectiveness of medication depends on overall health, metabolism and other individual characteristics. It may be necessary for an individual to try several medications or a combination of medications to determine which work best. Results are not usually evident right away. Antidepressant medications usually become fully effective in about 10 to 20 days after an individual begins taking them. Approximately 70 percent of patients will improve or recover while taking antidepressant medications, but some may need to continue medication over a six-month or year-long period to prevent relapse or recurrence.

There are four major types of medication used to treat depressive disorders. They are tricyclic antidepressants, MAO inhibitors (MAOIs), lithium and novel antidepressants.

Tricyclic antidepressants: These are often prescribed for individuals whose depressions are marked by feelings of hopelessness, helplessness, fatigue, inability to experience pleasure, loss of appetite and resulting weight loss.

Monoamine oxidase inhibitors (MAOIs): These are often prescribed for individuals whose depressions are characterized by anxiety, phobic and obsessive-compulsive symptoms, increased appetite and excessive sleepiness or "rejection sensitivity" or those who fail to improve on other antidepressant medications.

Lithium: Lithium is sometimes prescribed for people who have manic-depressive illness (a severe affective disorder characterized by a predominant mood of elation or depression and in some cases an alternation between the two states). Sometimes it is prescribed for people who suffer from depression without mania, especially to potentiate other antidepressant medications. Those most likely to respond to treatment with lithium are depressed individuals whose family members have manic-depression or whose depression is recurrent rather than constant.

Novel antidepressants: Recently more specifically active antidepressant drugs with less propensity for side effects such as sedation, dry mouth and weight gain have been developed. Selective serotonin reuptake inhibitors (SSRIs), such as fluoxetine (Prozac) and sertraline, are one class; bupropion (Wellbutrin) is another. Many other new medications are being developed to treat depression and will be available in the next several years.

Anticonvulsants as antidepressants: For patients with manic-depressive illness (bipolar disorder) where lithium is not effective, drugs used to prevent temporal lobe seizures are now often used successfully.

Side effects of antidepressant medications: Some people experience side effects from antidepressant medications, including dry mouth, constipation, drowsiness and weight gain. These effects usually diminish somewhat or disappear as the body makes adjustments.

Self-help Many depressed individuals in self-help groups share ideas for effective coping and self-care for depression. These include regular exercise, more contact with other people (for example, in special interest groups) and coping with exaggerated thoughts (such as self-deprecation) and catastrophizing by introducing more realistic thoughts and supporting them.

The National Depressive and Manic-Depressive Association is a national self-help organization, formed in the early 1980s. Chapters throughout the country meet locally to help members cope effectively with depression. For more information, contact:

National Depressive and Manic-Depressive Association
730 North Franklin Street, Suite 510
Chicago, IL 60610
Phone: (312) 642-0049

National Alliance for the Mentally Ill
1901 North Ft. Meyer Drive, Suite 500
Arlington, VA 22209-1604
Phone: (703) 524-7600

National Institute of Mental Health
Public Information Branch
5600 Fishers Lane
Rockville, MD 20857
Phone: (301) 443-3673

National Mental Health Association
1020 Prince Street
Alexandria, VA 22314
Phone: (703) 684-7722

See also AFFECTIVE DISORDERS; AGORAPHOBIA; ANTIDEPRESSANT MEDICATIONS; ANXIETY; CORTISOL; ELECTROCONVULSIVE THERAPY; MONOAMINE OXIDASE INHIBITORS; NEUROTRANSMITTERS; NOREPINEPHRINE; PSYCHOTHERAPY; SEASONAL AFFECTIVE DISORDER; SEROTONIN; SUICIDE; TRICYCLIC ANTIDEPRESSANT MEDICATIONS; DEPRESSION AND AFFECTIVE DISORDERS in BIBLIOGRAPHY.

Depression and Related Affective Disorders Association (DRADA) DRADA is a nonprofit organization focusing on manic-depressive illness and depression. DRADA distributes information, conducts educational meetings and runs an outreach program for high school counselors and nurses. DRADA helps organize support groups and provides leadership training programs and consultation for those groups.

For information:

DRADA
Meyer 4-181
The Johns Hopkins School of Medicine,
    Dept. of Psychiatry
600 N. Wolfe Street
Baltimore, MD 21205
Phone: (410) 955-4647

Depression Awareness, Recognition and Treatment Project (D/ART) A national public education campaign on depressive illness that began in 1988. It was launched by the National Institute of Mental Health (NIMH), a part of the Alcohol, Drug Abuse and Mental Health Administration. The D/ART program disseminates information about symptoms and treatments of depressive illnesses. Its slogan is "Depression, Define it, Defeat it."

For information, contact:

D/ART
National Institute of Mental Health
Room 15-C-05
5600 Fishers Lane
Rockville, MD 20857
Phone: (301) 443-3673

depth psychology An approach to therapy that emphasizes unconscious mental processes as the source of emotional symptoms such as depression, anxieties and personality disorders. An example of depth psychology is Freudian psychoanalysis. Historically, other noted therapists have also used a depth approach, including Karen Horney, Carl Jung and Harry Stack Sullivan. Included in the category of depth psychology are other techniques that investigate the unconscious, such as hypnoanalysis, narcosynthesis and psychodrama.

derangement An obsolete term for severe mental disorder, first used during the 19th century to describe an orderly man who suddenly became "disarranged."

dermatitis An inflammation of the skin sometimes occurring for no known reason. Dermatitis is a very individual condition. In some people it happens because of allergies and as a result of taking prescription medications. Dermatitis can cause painful itching and extreme discomfort, leading to feelings of helplessness and depression if the irritation persists without relief.

The term "dermatitis" also refers to any self-induced skin condition that may range from a mild scratch to extensive mutilation by a psychologically disturbed individual. The skin damage usually has a symmetrical or bizarre pattern and does not resemble any pattern seen in any skin disease.

desensitization A behavioral therapy procedure sometimes used in treating anxiety disorders; it is also known as systematic desensitization. In this procedure, individuals learn relaxation techniques, to imagine their responses in difficult situations, ultimately face their feared or highly emotionally charged situations and practice new, more acceptable responses. An example is learning to travel by airplane and not experience a panic attack.

See also BEHAVIORAL THERAPY.

"designer drugs" A term applied to synthetically manufactured drugs that mimic the appearance and/or effects of other drugs. Many have been falsely depicted as synthetic heroin. One such drug is China White, also known as fentanyl. Hundreds of times more powerful than heroin, fentanyl has been responsible for deaths and overdoses. Ecstasy (XTC, or more properly named 3,4-methylenedioxyamphetamine) is also considered a designer drug. Several "designer drug" users have developed symptoms similar to those produced by Parkinson's disease, characterized by uncontrollable tremors, drooling, impaired speech and muscular paralysis. Designer drugs are sometimes chemically synthesized to utilize novel chemical structures to produce enhanced effects and to avoid the structure of outlawed drugs of abuse.

Designer drugs are usually taken orally. Although tolerance levels are unknown, this class of drugs has a stormy history of compulsive use. The long-term effects are also unknown. They may be particularly dangerous when used in combination with alcohol and other drugs.

Designer drugs affect developing fetuses in ways similar to those of the drugs they mimic. For example, fentanyl acts like heroin, Ecstasy like amphetamines.

See also AMPHETAMINE DRUGS; HALLUCINOGENS; HEROIN; METHAMPHETAMINES; SUBSTANCE ABUSE.

Media Resource Guide on Common Drugs of Abuse. Public Relations Society of America, National Capital Chapter, Fairfax, Va., September 1990.

desipramine   A tricyclic antidepressant (trade names: Norpramine and Pertofrane) that is as effective as imipramine in the treatment of depression. Side effects are similar to those produced by imipramine, but anticholinergic and sedative actions are less pronounced. Thus desipramine may be especially useful in patients who are particularly sensitive to these effects, such as the elderly. These drugs are also sometimes used to treat headaches due to nonorganic causes and to treat attention-deficit hyperactivity disorder in some selected cases.

See also ANTIDEPRESSANT MEDICATIONS; HEADACHES; TRICYCLIC ANTIDEPRESSANT MEDICATIONS.

American Medical Association. *AMA Drug Evaluations Annual, 1991.* Chicago: AMA, 1991.

despair   See DEPRESSION; HOPELESSNESS.

Desyrel   Trade name for trazodone hydrochloride, an antidepressant drug that is not related to the tricyclic antidepressant drugs or the monoamine oxidase inhibitors (MAOIs). Controlled studies have demonstrated that trazodone is as effective as amitriptyline and imipramine in patients with major depressive disorders and other types of depressive disorders. Because of its sedative effect, trazodone is generally more useful in depressive disorders associated with anxiety. It does not aggravate psychotic symptoms in patients with schizophrenia or schizoaffective disorders.

In therapeutic doses, trazodone inhibits the neuronal uptake of serotonin. Experimentally, prolonged administration decreases the number of serotonin receptors.

See also ANTIDEPRESSANT MEDICATIONS; DEPRESSION; SEROTONIN.

detoxification   The removal of poisons from the body, either by the body itself or with medical treatment. In current usage, the term usually applies to the process by which a person overcomes alcoholism or other addictive drugs. During the 1970s, hemodialysis was used in the United States to remove a polypeptide believed to cause schizophrenia. Initial research findings were not replicated, and dialysis units in the United States are no longer used to treat mental illness. However, dialysis is used in the detoxification of patients after potentially lethal overdose ingestions.

See also ALCOHOLISM.

dexamethasone suppression test (DST)
See BIOLOGICAL MARKERS.

dextroamphetamine   A drug that is a stimulant for the central nervous system. It is prescribed for narcolepsy (a rare condition characterized by excessive sleepiness) and also in some cases to treat children with hyperactivity. It is no longer recommended as an appetite suppressant for people who want to lose weight.

Dextroamphetamine is one of a group of drugs commonly known on the street as "uppers." However, some individuals may actually feel sedated when taking a test dose of dextroamphetamine. When the drug is used on a prolonged basis, its stimulant effects lessen and a higher dose must be taken to produce the desired effect. Seizures and high blood pressure may result from overdoses.

See also SUBSTANCE ABUSE.

diabetes (diabetes mellitus)   A disorder in which the pancreas produces too little or no insulin, the hormone responsible for absorption of glucose into cells for energy and into the liver and fat cells for storage. With insufficient insulin, the glucose level in the blood becomes abnormally high, leading to excessive urination and constant thirst and hunger. When the body cannot store or use glucose, there is weight loss and fatigue and accelerated degeneration of small blood vessels. Diabetes is a chronic disease and brings with it many mental health concerns for the individual as well as the family.

Diabetes is not contagious, although it tends to run in families. While there is no cure for it, the disease can be kept under control with appropriate medical care and patient compliance. Individuals who have diabetes can enjoy good mental health and an active life-style.

Diabetes is a major public health problem. Approximately 6 million people in the United States have diabetes, and an additional 5 million have the disease but have not yet been diagnosed. Each year, more than 500,000 new cases of diabetes are identified. In terms of human suffering, individuals afflicted with diabetes face not only a shortened life span but also the probability of incurring acute and chronic complications.

As soon as diabetes is diagnosed by a physician, the individual will have many questions about the disease and how to live to the fullest while coping with a chronic disease. The individual may at first have a "why me" reaction and then get down to the basics of how to cope. Diabetes is a very individual disease, and within the types of disease there are many variations.

Diabetes is a disease in which one's mental attitude and personal role in treatment has an important effect on the quality of life.

Diabetic individuals need to devote more attention to some personal care than may have been done before, such as specific attention to skin, feet and teeth, and promptly treating minor injuries such as burns, cuts and bruises. Proper control of diabetes can help one avoid other problems such as vascular system difficulties, kidney disease and eye difficulties.

Types of Diabetes   Type I is insulin-dependent diabetes, and though it can occur at any age, it most commonly develops during youth. This type of diabetes used to be called juvenile-onset diabetes and is still called that by some physicians and health care professionals. About one of every 2,500 children has this disease. Because the pancreas produces little or no insulin, such patients become dependent on outside sources of insulin. The disease can be controlled with insulin, proper diet and exercise and careful monitoring.

Type II is non–insulin-dependent diabetes. It is estimated that between 60 and 90 percent of those with non–insulin-dependent diabetes in Western societies are obese and must lose weight as part of treatment. This type of diabetes used to be called maturity-onset diabetes and may still be called that by some health care professionals. Type II is much more common than Type I, with more than 5 million Americans suffering from the disease. This type is less severe than insulin-dependent diabetes and starts more slowly. Most often it can be controlled by diet alone or by a combination of diet, exercise and oral medication.

Mental Health and Causes of Diabetes   Heredity, obesity and stresses such as emotional shocks or surgery can lead to the development of diabetes. Pregnancy also places extra stresses on the body, and diabetes is often diagnosed in pregnant women or women who have repeated miscarriages. People who have diabetes, especially Type II, often also have high blood pressure. People of middle or old age are more likely to develop diabetes than younger people, and women are more likely to have diabetes than men.

Coping with diabetes will be an ongoing challenge for the individual as well as for members of the family. Many feelings will enter into acceptance of the diagnosis. There may be some anger, guilt or anxieties, both expressed and unexpressed. It is important for the diabetic to discuss these feelings with loved ones. In the case of a diabetic child, it is important to encourage discussion of these factors so that the child understands that having such feelings is part of the coping procedure.

Stable mental health is important for proper control of diabetes. Emotional stresses affect secretions of hormones that may counteract or interfere with the helpful effects of insulin. However, stresses cannot always be avoided easily. It is part of the human condition to react in different ways to different situations. More stress results at some times than at others. Situations that one meets calmly at one time may plunge the same individual into turmoil at another. The diabetic's health care team discusses with each individual emotional needs and problems along with a menu plan, an exercise plan and therapy by insulin and other medications. Health professionals have had experience in helping diabetic patients cope with emotional responses to their illness, and their background can help most individuals with their concerns and those of their families.

Problems such as consistently mishandling the food plan, refusing to take insulin injections, consciously overeating and suffering from depression occur in some diabetics. Health care professionals know that these situations can be handled well with the support of parents, spouses or significant others. As one becomes acquainted with the health care team and how they can help, individuals begin to feel freer to discuss details about the disease.

Diabetic health care teams have many constructive ideas for diabetic individuals. For example, they may encourage partici-

pation in a family therapy session to learn about family coping mechanisms along with other families with diabetes. Such groups foster exchanges of helpful ideas concerning the practical aspects of diabetes. They may suggest that one use the "buddy system," working with another diabetic to reinforce support and provide a model for adjustment to life with diabetes. There are groups run by local affiliates of the American Diabetes Association, hospital or community health department. Most social workers are trained in diabetes counseling. Being aware of existing services is the first step toward obtaining assistance and maintaining a good mental attitude about the disease.

See also CHRONIC ILLNESS; SUPPORT GROUPS.

Adapted with permission of the author, Kahn, Ada P. *Diabetes*. Chicago: Contemporary Books, 1983.
Schade, David S. "The Stress Factor." *Diabetes Forecast* (March–April 1982).

Diagnostic and Statistical Manual of Mental Disorders (DSM-III-R) A publication of the American Psychiatric Association that contains general descriptions of diagnostic categories of mental health concerns. It is considered the standard manual for the classification of mental disorders throughout North America and has been translated into many languages. A demand for a standardized diagnostic language developed during World War II and after. The first edition of this handbook appeared in 1952, a second edition in 1968, the third in 1974 and a revised third edition in 1987. A further revision (DSM-IV) is expected in the mid-1990s.

The manual outlines symptoms that must be present to make a specific diagnosis and organizes these diagnoses together into a complex system of classification. Although there is not complete agreement with criteria for diagnosis in all cases—and classification of mental disorders is not rigidly fixed or all-inclusive—many psychiatrists refer to

DSM-III-R when making diagnoses. It is important for the layperson to understand that the criteria listed in the book are considered simply guidelines for clinical diagnosis; special training in the field is necessary for appropriate use of the manual. It is available in most public libraries in the reference sections.

DSM-III-R continues to be important to the mental health profession as diagnosis-related groups (DRGs) are involved in fees paid by insurance payers. To help avoid controversies regarding its content, the development of the revision has been closely monitored by mental health professionals from all fields who have contributed their influence and expertise.

Diana complex A psychiatric term for a woman's repressed desire to be a man. The name comes from the Roman deity Diana, who filled a masculine role as goddess of hunting and protectress of women.

See also COMPLEX.

diazepam An antianxiety drug (trade name: Valium), effective in the management of generalized anxiety disorder and panic disorder in appropriately selected patients. It is also used for skeletal muscle relaxation, for seizure disorders, for preanesthetic medication or intravenous anesthetic induction and for alleviating abstinence symptoms during alcohol withdrawal. Diazepam is one of a group of benzodiazepine drugs.

Psychological and/or physical dependence can result from overuse or inappropriate use.

See also ANTIANXIETY MEDICATIONS; ANTIDEPRESSANT MEDICATIONS; BENZODIAZEPINE MEDICATIONS.

disorientation Confusion about time, place and personal identity. Disorientation on a very temporary and sometimes fleeting basis occurs in many mental health disorders, including psychoses, schizophrenia, dissociative disorders, panic attacks and agoraphobia. Disorientation can also result from head injuries or intoxication. A disoriented person's speech may be unclear and behavior confused, and the person may be unable to answer clear questions about name, address and present whereabouts. Disorientation is most common in organic mental disorders causing dementia or stroke or after epileptic seizures.

See also AGORAPHOBIA; PANIC ATTACK.

disruptive behavior disorders. See ANTISOCIAL PERSONALITY DISORDER; CONDUCT DISORDER.

dissociation A nonconscious defense mechanism during which thoughts and attitudes unconsciously lose their normal relationships to each other or to the rest of the personality. Dissociation may prevent conflict between logically incompatible thoughts, feelings and attitudes, such as love for a parent and the realization that one is being abused by the parent. In addition, some individuals experience dissociation during periods of panic attacks. Dissociation is the end of a continuum from normal awareness to suppression, denial, repression and then to dissociation.

See also DISSOCIATIVE DISORDERS; MULTIPLE PERSONALITY DISORDER; PANIC DISORDER.

Braun, Bennett G. "The BASK Model of Dissociation." *Dissociation* 1, no. 1 (Mar. 1988).

dissociative disorders A group of disorders characterized by a sudden, temporary alteration in normal functions of consciousness. These include multiple personality disorder (MPD), psychogenic fugue, psychogenic amnesia and depersonalization disorder. Most commonly, dissociative disorders and dissociative disorder (not otherwise specified) are often misdiagnosed as multiple personality disorders. These are cases in which there is more than one personality state capable of assuming executive control of the individual, but no more than one personality state is sufficiently distinct to meet the full criteria for multiple personality disorder (MPD).

Additionally, there are several other disorders categorized as dissociative disorders, because the predominant feature is a dissociative symptom, such as a disturbance or alteration in the normally integrative functions of identity, memory or consciousness, but that do not meet specific criteria for dissociative disorders in the *Diagnostic and Statistical Manual of Mental Disorders* (3d ed., rev.) of the American Psychiatric Association. These include Ganser's syndrome, in which an individual gives "approximate answers" to questions, commonly associated with other symptoms such as amnesia, disorientation, perceptual disturbances, fugue and conversion symptoms. Trance states are altered states of consciousness with markedly diminished or selectively focused responsiveness to environmental stimuli. In children this may occur after physical abuse or trauma. Dissociative states may also occur in people who have been subjected to periods of prolonged and intense coercive persuasion, such as those subjected to brainwashing or taken hostage by a terrorist government or cult. There are also cases in which sudden unexpected travel and organized, purposeful behavior with inability to recall one's past are accompanied by a new identity, partial or complete. This is called a fugue state.

An obsolete term for dissociative disorders is "hysterical neuroses, dissociative type."

See also DEPERSONALIZATION; MULTIPLE PERSONALITY DISORDER; PSYCHOGENIC AMNESIA; PSYCHOGENIC FUGUE.

disulfuram   A drug used in overcoming alcoholism (trade name: Antabuse). When taken with alcohol, this drug interacts with body chemistry to produce uncomfortable and sometimes dangerous or fatal reactions. The unpleasantness of this interaction is the basis for its adjunctive use to help a motivated individual to stop the consumption of alcohol. The drug should be used with supportive counseling or psychotherapy.

See also ALCOHOLISM; ALCOHOLISM in BIBLIOGRAPHY.

divorce   The legal ending of a marriage. During the 1980s, about half of all marriages ended in divorce. Women and men who seek divorce do so because they have any one of a wide range of problems in their marriage, which may include a poor sexual relationship, differences in goals or financial problems. Divorce differs from annulment, in which a court declares that a marriage has been invalid from its beginning; reasons for annulment vary among states and countries.

Many divorced individuals marry again. According to researcher Judith Wallerstein, Center for the Family in Transition, Corte Madera, California, 60 percent of second marriages fail, particularly if one or more of the mates bring children into the marriage.

Meeting new people and dating after divorce brings anxieties and concerns about acquiring a sexually transmitted disease, such as AIDS (acquired immunodeficiency syndrome).

Many divorced people remember being treated poorly, perhaps exploited, suspecting infidelities and feeling angry. Depending on what triggered the anger, it may not be easy to forget. However, if appropriately contained, one's anger will not interfere with adjusting to a new life.

Feelings of failure are common when a marriage breaks up. Usually what individuals do is what they thought best under the circumstances; lack of success in the marriage should not reflect on their sense of self-worth in other areas. Most divorced individuals learn from their experiences and bring new insights to new relationships.

According to Ada P. Kahn, in "Divorce: For Better Not For Worse," a brochure published by the Mental Health Association of Greater Chicago, recent studies show that when parents are wretched, children do not feel that keeping the marriage together on their behalf is a gift. There is no advantage for children when parents stay in a marriage in which they cannot resolve basic issues.

Kahn advised that parents should explain divorce to their children, that it was a rational decision, deliberately and carefully undertaken with full recognition of how difficult it would be. Children have the right to know why, with the explanation given in language suited to their age and understanding. Parents should try to communicate what divorce will mean for them, very specifically how it will affect their visiting and living arrangements. Children should be assured that they will not be forced to take sides, they have permission to love both parents and both will continue to love them. More complex explanations are in order in the case of desertion or abuse. In every instance children must be assured that they are not responsible for the rupture and that they are not responsible for healing it.

As a consequence of divorce, many children feel a diminished sense of being parented, because their parents are less available, emotionally, physically or both. The child feels that he or she is losing both parents. This is a common but usually temporary part of the divorce experience.

The most serious long-range effect is that children feel less protected in their growing-up years and, having seen a failed man-woman relationship, become concerned that they will repeat their parents' mistakes. Parents should address this issue by talking about it or being ready to talk when children ask questions. Parents should not continue to fight the battles that persisted during the marriage. Parents should not criticize their former mate in front of the children. Doing so will encourage the child to grow into adulthood with fears about man-woman relationships. Divorced parents must realize that they are role models in the divorce just as they were in the marriage.

Rebuilding life after divorce may be complicated and difficult. Most experts offer the following advice; take one step at a time; start by choosing one step you really need or would like to take; seek out resources for your particular needs in the community; churches, synagogues and community mental health agencies may be able to help.

See also MARRIAGE; SEXUALLY TRANSMITTED DISEASES.

Kahn, Ada P., and Holt, Linda Hughey. *The A to Z of Women's Sexuality*. Alameda, Calif.: Hunter House Publications, 1992.
Wallerstein, Judith S. *Second Chances: Men, Women, and Children a Decade after Divorce*. New York: Ticknor & Fields, 1989.

dizziness   A feeling of being unsteady, lightheaded or faint. Most people describe dizziness as a feeling of spinning, turning or falling in space or of standing still while the objects around them are moving. (Medically, this is termed vertigo.) Dizziness is often a symptom of a phobic reaction. People who come into contact with their feared object may react with weak knees, sweaty palms and dizziness, which may intensify their physical sensations, making them fear that they will faint, have a heart attack on the spot or die.

During a phobic reaction or a panic attack, an individual may hyperventilate (breathe more than they need to). This results in a drop in the carbon dioxide in the blood, which causes constriction of blood vessels in the brain. Dizziness as a result of an emotional feeling usually disappears when the phobic object is removed or when the person gets to a place of safety.

For many people, dizziness also accompanies seasickness. Some sailors advise keeping one's eyes on the horizon to give one a steady spot to watch. In most cases, dizziness disappears when the individual sets foot on land. Dizziness as a result of intoxication with alcohol usually subsides after a period of sleep.

See also AGORAPHOBIA; PANIC ATTACK.

DNA See DEOXYRIBONUCLEIC ACID.

domestic violence Abuse of spouses, children or parents in the home. This may take the form of wife battering, child abuse, incest or abusing elders. According to Kevin J. Fullin, M.D., cardiologist and medical director of the domestic violence project at St. Catherine's Hospital in Kenosha, Wisconsin, as many as one in two women has suffered from an episode of domestic violence sometime in her life. Because of such a high rate, physicians and health care workers are developing new responses to domestic violence in order to increase its detection. The goal is to properly identify anyone who comes to a hospital with domestic abuse problems. This can be done by asking the woman or the elderly, who are suspected of being abused, questions in a confidential way. These should be asked in a nonthreatening, nonjudgmental manner without the husband or family members present in order to find the real cause of the problem and do something to stop the abuse.

Often there is a poor medical response to battered women during pregnancy, during visits to the emergency room and in cases of elder abuse. According to the Kenosha facility, 35 percent of the women who come to the emergency room are victims of domestic violence. Only 5 percent of that group are asked questions to determine if they are victims of such abuse.

Women are more likely to present themselves as victims of domestic violence to health care professionals than to shelters or law enforcement officials. Inadequate detection of this violence and lack of appropriate referrals may lead to further abuse and even death.

Legal Rights In the past, police and the legal system often viewed domestic violence as a private matter and not a crime. Now, in many states, the police may arrest a batterer if there is evidence of abuse.

Civil actions might include legal separation, child custody, child support and divorce. One common civil action is the temporary restraining order, which involves making a complaint and going to a hearing to obtain a legal document that limits how close a person may come to a woman and her children.

A criminal complaint can be filed in addition to or instead of civil actions. A criminal complaint involves a police investigation and, if enough evidence is found, may lead to an arrest and involvement of the judicial system.

See also BATTERED CHILD SYNDROME; BATTERED WOMEN; FAMILY VIOLENCE.

Shannon, Kari. "Domestic Violence Detection at St. Catherine's." *Chicago HealthCare* (Dec. 1991).

dopamine A precursor of the neurotransmitter norepinephrine. A deficiency of dopamine in the brain is a diagnostic sign of Parkinson's disease. The dopamine hypothesis is a concept holding that schizophrenia is caused by an excess of dopamine in the brain, owing either to an overproduction of dopamine or a deficiency of the enzyme necessary to convert dopamine to norepinephrine. Neurons that release dopamine also control the so-called pleasure system in humans and animals. The addicting effects of cocaine and amphetamine stimulants have been attributed to their effect on hyperstimulation of the dopamine-pleasure system, thus producing feelings of artificially induced euphoria, excitement and pleasure beyond that of everyday life. It also causes changes in brain chemistry to promote a need for the substance in order to achieve a state of well-being, thus producing addiction. Recent research has suggested that other addictions such as alcoholism and narcotic addiction may also be based on the function of the dopamine-pleasure system. Dopamine also controls the release of certain hormones from the anterior pituitary gland (for example, prolactin).

Dopaminergic drugs are those that affect the production or utilization of dopamine.

Drugs that enhance the maintenance of adequate levels of dopamine have therapeutic value in the treatment of Parkinson's disease. A commonly used dopaminergic drug is levodopa (L-dopa).

See also BRAIN; NEUROTRANSMITTERS; NOREPINEPHRINE; PARKINSON'S DISEASE; SCHIZOPHRENIA.

double depression See DEPRESSION; DYSTHYMIA.

downers A popular street term for a class of drugs that subjectively cause sedation or relaxation, including barbiturates and synthetic derivatives, other non-barbiturate sleeping pills, benzodiazepine drugs and even dextromethorphan, a synthetic narcotic in cough syrup and antihistamine drugs that cause sedation as a side effect. They are prescription drugs (and sometimes over-the-counter medications used legitimately as tranquilizers and sleeping pills. The most common depressant, usually classified by itself, is alcohol. Barbiturates have very similar effects, while tranquilizers are less sedating. These are highly addictive, both psychologically and physically, and are associated with intense withdrawal problems. The state of intoxication associated with true depressants is similar to that of alcohol: a weak and rapid pulse, slow or rapid shallow breathing, cold and clammy skin, drowsiness and impaired motor function.

These drugs are usually in tablet or capsule forms, which are swallowed. Some abused barbiturates include Amytal, Fiorinal, Seconal and Phenobarbital. Other well-known depressants that are abused include tranquilizers such as Equanil and Miltown and sleeping pills such as Doriden and Placidyl. The use of sedative hypnotics with alcohol is particularly dangerous and can lead to death.

The terms ''downer'' and ''upper'' are frequently used incorrectly. Alcohol, sometimes considered an ''upper'' or euphoriant for the first hour or two after ingestion (depending on amount ingested), later becomes a ''downer'' as it produces intoxication and central nervous system depression. Even small doses of barbiturates will make some individuals ''high'' or ''up'' depending on environmental stimulation. The terms ''downer'' and ''upper'' therefore have misleading meanings that ignore dosage and time-related drug effects.

See also BARBITURATE DRUGS; BENZODIAZEPINE MEDICATIONS; SUBSTANCE ABUSE.

Down's syndrome A chromosomal abnormality that results in mental handicap and a characteristic physical appearance. People with Down's syndrome have 47 instead of the normal 46 chromosomes. In most cases the extra chromosome is number 21; the disorder is also called trisomy 21.

About one in 650 babies born is affected with Down's syndrome. The incidence of affected fetuses rises with increased maternal age to about one in 40 among mothers over age 40. Pregnant women over age 35 and those with a family history of Down's syndrome are usually offered chromosome analysis of the fetus's cells after they have been obtained by amniocentesis or chorionic villus sampling. If the fetus is found to be affected, termination of the pregnancy may be one of the options.

While there is no cure for Down's syndrome, such children can make the most of their capabilities through appropriate educational opportunities. In some cases, institutional care is necessary. For some children, improvement of facial appearance can be made with plastic surgery.

Until the second half of the 20th century, many Down's syndrome children did not live beyond their teen years because of birth defects and their susceptibility to infection. Now advances in medical and surgery techniques and improved long-term care facilities have extended their life expectancy; however, most do not live beyond early middle age.

Caring for a child with Down's syndrome presents particular parenting problems and an exceptional degree of patience. The degree of mental handicap varies; the child's IQ may be anywhere from 30 to 80. Almost all affected children are capable of a limited amount of learning and, in some cases, reading. Usually affected children are cheerful and affectionate and get along well with people.

See also MENTAL RETARDATION; MENTAL RETARDATION in BIBLIOGRAPHY.

doxepin hydrochloride   A tricyclic antidepressant medication also used as an antianxiety medication; sold under the trade names of Adapin and Sinequan. When prescribed for adult patients of all ages, it is safe and well tolerated, even in elderly patients. For many individuals, doxepin helps relieve symptoms of depression, insomnia, anxiety, fear and worry.

The usefulness of doxepin is comparable to that of imipramine in the treatment of depressive episodes of major depression and bipolar disorder. It also may be effective in the depressive periods of dysthymic disorder and in atypical depression. Therapeutic doses produce more anticholinergic effects than some other tricyclic medications and pronounced sedation. Other untoward effects are typical of tricyclic antidepressants.

See also ANTIANXIETY MEDICATIONS; ANTIDEPRESSANT MEDICATIONS; TRICYCLIC ANTIDEPRESSANT MEDICATIONS.

dream analysis   Interpretation of a person's dreams as part of psychotherapy or psychoanalysis. However, many people try to self-analyze their dreams or talk to their families about their dreams. Dream analysis is based on the concept developed by Sigmund Freud that an individual's repressed feelings and thoughts are revealed in a disguised way in dreams. The therapist analyzes the dreams, based on an understanding of the individual's personality, character traits, family ties and background. Patient and therapist make associations and try to determine the meaning of the dream.

See also DREAMING; SLEEP.

dreaming   Mental activity that occurs when one is asleep. Dreaming usually involves many vivid sensory images, such as sights, sounds, motion, touch and even smell or taste. For many people, dreaming is a continuation of activities and thoughts from the previous day, and there are no deeply hidden meanings. They may be sorting out events from the day in a distorted way because of the lack of the conscious, awake mind. For others, images in dreams may be symbols of unconscious thoughts. Symbols in dreams may mean nothing or may refer to death, family members and sexual functions. For example, water may symbolize birth. Through interpretations of symbols, a therapist may assist an individual in dream analysis and a better understanding of the causes of anxieties or other mental health problems.

According to Sigmund Freud, most people have dreams about fire and water, being naked, the death of loved ones or fear of flying and falling, of facing school examinations or of missing a train.

Dreaming occurs during periods of rapid-eye-movement (REM) sleep, which last about 20 minutes and occur four or five times a night. Disruptions of schedule or sleep deprivation, depression, stress and drug use often interfere with REM time. Necessary biochemical changes occur at REM and non-REM times that are essential for normal daytime functioning. People who are awakened during periods of REM sleep usually can report their dreams clearly. Those who awaken normally may not remember dreams at all or only in a fragmentary way. Fear of dreams is known as oneirophobia.

More recently, dreaming has been thought to be a form of unconscious problem solving during sleep. Attempts have been made to help people use dreams positively to solve problems that emerge in dreaming.

See also DREAM ANALYSIS; FREUD, SIGMUND; SLEEP.

drug abuse See ALCOHOLISM; SUBSTANCE ABUSE.

drug addiction See SUBSTANCE ABUSE.

DSM-III-R See DIAGNOSTIC AND STATISTICAL MANUAL OF MENTAL DISORDERS.

dual-orgasm theory Sigmund Freud's theory that contended that there are two types of female orgasm, vaginal and clitoral. According to Freud, normal female development involved transferring the center of sexual pleasure from the clitoris to the vagina, and he labeled the clitoral orgasm as immature. He believed that a vaginal orgasm was the orgasm of maturity. This theory went largely unchallenged until the 1960s when sex researchers determined that clitoral stimulation is helpful to many women in reaching climax during sexual intercourse.

See also CLITORIS; FREUD, SIGMUND; SEXUAL DYSFUNCTION; SEX THERAPY.

dual sex therapy The team approach to sex therapy developed by William H. Masters (1915–   ), an American physician, and Virginia Johnson (1925–   ), an American psychologist. Dual sex therapy is based on the theory that two therapists are needed—one male and one female—because male therapists acting alone cannot be expected to fully understand the feelings and reactions of a woman, and a female therapist acting alone cannot be expected to fully understand male sexuality. However, when they collaborate in the process, therapy will be more effective.

See also SEX THERAPY.

durable power of attorney See DYING WITH DIGNITY.

dying with dignity A term that gained popularity during the 1980s and 1990s as high-technology equipment enabled health care practitioners to maintain a terminally ill individual or person who has suffered a life-threatening accident on a life-support system. Individuals who want to ''die with dignity'' can plan ahead by executing a document known as an advance directive, in which one makes treatment wishes known while still healthy. In 1991, a federal law was enacted (Patient Self-Determination Act) under which health care providers must give patients information about advance directives, including living wills and durable power of attorney for health care.

Living Will This allows one to specify when and under what conditions one wants treatment to be withheld should a terminal illness be suffered. One can spell out, for example, that if an irreversible coma occurs, one does not want heroic lifesaving measures to be carried out. In some states, the living will must be signed by the person executing it, as well as two witnesses who are at least 18 years old.

When the physician determines and notes in the medical record that the patient has met four specific conditions, a living will goes into effect. The four criteria are that the patient has a condition that is terminal, incurable and irreversible and death is imminent. Additionally, some state laws regarding living wills do not recognize the withdrawal of hydration and nutrition. Individuals who do not wish fluids and nutrition to be administered when they meet the four conditions will either cross those items off the living will document or execute a durable power of attorney for health care spelling out this wish.

Durable Power of Attorney for Health Care This is a document that allows one, as the principal, to appoint another person, known as the agent, to make medical care decisions in case one becomes mentally or physically incompetent. The document permits one to determine at what point the power of attorney becomes effective and the scope of the agent's decision-making powers. Durable powers of attorney enable people to give very specific directions about what treatment they want and do not want.

Advance directives may be revoked at any time while one is still competent. If it is necessary to revoke a durable power of attorney after one becomes incapacitated, legal action may be necessary.

Advance directives become part of the individual's permanent medical record. However, health care providers are not bound to carry out an advance directive that conflicts with state legislation, and it is important for concerned individuals to check the laws of each state involved for optimal peace of mind.

See also DEATH; LEGAL ISSUES.

Today's Chicago Woman, December 1991.

dysfunctional family A term indicating that the developmental needs of one or more members of a family are not being met. Often, the basic problem is poor communication between family members, even though they live in the same household. An example of a dysfunctional family is one in which there is marital conflict and a young child who is showing signs of aggressive behavior in school. The parents may be unaware that their behavior is causing a great deal of stress for the child, which he expresses in aggressive behavior instead of talking about it with his parents.

In a dysfunctional family, there is little emphasis on encouraging each child to develop autonomy. An example is a family that expects its adolescent child to obey curfew rules appropriate for a younger child.

Dysfunctional families do not deal constructively with difficult times. For example, when a child becomes seriously ill, there may be little communication about the illness between family members, or there may be unexpressed feelings of guilt. Alcoholism and substance abuse tends to lead to dysfunctional families, as the substance abuser cannot be depended on or to fulfill expec-

tations. Families in which there is domestic violence, child abuse or spouse abuse are dysfunctional.

Family therapy is helpful in improving life situations for members of dysfunctional families. In therapy, family members learn to improve their communication skills and learn new coping skills to deal with everyday problems as well as major life stressors.

See also COPING; STRESS.

dyskinesia Abnormal muscular movements usually caused by a brain disorder. These may include uncontrolled twitching, jerking or writhing movements that interfere with the individual's willful movements. Such movements may involve the whole body or only a group of muscles, such as those around the eye. Dyskinesias may be caused by brain damage at birth or may be side effects of certain drugs, such as some drugs used to treat psychiatric illnesses. When dyskinesias are caused by drugs, the problem often ceases when use of the drug is stopped. However, prolonged use of some antipsychotic drugs can result in a permanent or chronic condition known as tardive dyskinesia.

See also TARDIVE DYSKINESIA.

dyslexia A reading disability characterized by difficulty in recognizing written symbols. Those with the disorder tend to reverse letters and words. Writing from dictation is difficult for such children. Those with the disability feel frustrated and often develop reduced self-esteem because they feel different from their peers. Specific remedial teaching can help such children learn to overcome their deficit. It is important that parents avoid pressuring the child and offer praise for the child's accomplishments. Many individuals who were dyslexic as children are successful at completing educational programs and entering highly professional and public careers.

dysmenorrhea Painful menstruation. Many women experience pain and cramps in their back and lower abdomen during menstruation. Dysmenorrhea may occur for many reasons and can cause stress, frustration, absenteeism from work, withdrawal from social and family obligations and a sense of "missing out" on several days a month. An understanding of the physiology involved as well as medical intervention can help women cope with this aspect of life.

Primary dysmenorrhea is menstrual pain that occurs in the absence of any observable pelvic lesion. Mechanical dysmenorrhea is a form of the disorder resulting from an obstruction, such as narrowing of the cervix (stenosis), that prevents the normal flow of menstruation from the uterus. Primary dysmenorrhea is often associated with the beginning of menstrual flow and may occur in the presence of an underdeveloped uterus or the presence of clots in the cervix or both. Spasmodic dysmenorrhea pain usually increases over a period of several hours and then subsides. Some women experience a diminution of dysmenorrhea after their first pregnancy.

Functional or congestive dysmenorrhea, also known as psychogenic dysmenorrhea, may increase during periods of anxiety or stress. However, most dysmenorrhea is due to the production of chemicals, called prostaglandins, in the uterine lining that cause powerful contractions. These cramps are effectively treated with drugs (such as ibuprofen) that inhibit prostaglandin formation. When these agents do not work, other disorders such as endometriosis may be found.

See also MENSTRUATION.

dysmorphic disorder A disorder in which a normal-appearing individual is preoccupied with some imagined defect in appearance. If there is a slight anomaly, the individual's concern is grossly excessive. This is associated with anorexia nervosa and other eating disorders in which the person perceives herself as obese.

This disorder has been related to a number of single-symptom disorders and severe obsessional disorders. The delusional disorders, which include morbid jealousy, have been reported to respond to treatment with selective serotonin-uptake inhibiting medications such as fluoxetine (Prozac) and Pimozide.

See also ANOREXIA NERVOSA.

dyspareunia Sexual intercourse that is painful for the woman. Pain may occur for many reasons, including dryness of the vagina, tightness of the vaginal muscles, a vaginal infection, an infection of the urethra or urinary tract or a local irritation, such as from a spermicide or the material of a condom or diaphragm. The first step in reducing discomfort during sexual intercourse is a discussion with one's partner.

For some women, psychological factors play a part. If they have experienced pain in the past, they may fear its recurrence. This happens to some women who have been abused as children or raped. Some women may fear pregnancy or acquiring a sexually transmitted disease and are not able to relax during intercourse. Tension and anxiety or a lack of adequate stimulation before actual penetration may contribute to pain during intercourse. During foreplay (stimulation before intercourse), the vaginal walls secrete lubricating fluid that makes intercourse more comfortable. However, after menopause and during breast feeding, many women find that secretions are not sufficient; a water-soluble jelly may be helpful as a lubricant. Hormone replacement therapy postmenopausally also helps to increase lubrication and thicken the skin of the vaginal wall.

A change in position during intercourse can help relieve pain for some women. They may feel a discomfort when the penis contacts their cervix (the neck of the uterus) and can avoid discomfort by less deep penetration. A pain felt deep in the pelvis may be caused by endometriosis, ovarian tumors or cysts or some other condition that should be investigated and treated by a physician as soon as possible.

Medical treatments, psychological counseling and sex therapy are available to help these conditions.

See also COITUS; SEXUALITY in BIBLIOGRAPHY.

Kahn, Ada P., and Holt, Linda Hughey. *The A to Z of Women's Sexuality*. Alameda, Calif.: Hunter House, 1992.

dysphoric mood A mood in which one feels sad, despondent and discouraged with anxiety and tension. A dysphoric mood may be a symptom of depression.

See also AFFECTIVE DISORDERS; DEPRESSION.

dyssomnia A category of sleep disorders. Dyssomnias include disorders of initiating or maintaining sleep, such as insomnia or hypersomnia. These differ from other sleep disorders, such as nightmares and sleepwalking.

See also SLEEP.

dysthymia A chronic and persistent disturbance in mood that has been present for at least two years and is characterized by relatively typical symptoms of depression, such as low self-esteem, difficulty concentrating, feelings of hopelessness, loss of appetite and difficulty sleeping. Individuals who have dysthymia are usually chronically unhappy. Some develop major depression, improve and then return to the milder state of dysthymia. The coexistence of these mild and severe forms of depression is referred to as double depression.

See also AFFECTIVE DISORDERS; DEPRESSION.

American Psychiatric Association. *Diagnostic and Statistical Manual of Mental Disorders* 3d ed., rev. Washington, D.C. 1987.

dystonic reaction A state of abnormal muscle tension that sometimes occurs as a side effect of antipsychotic medications. There may be spasms of the eyes, eyelids, face, neck and back muscles. In rare instances, spasms of the larynx and pharynx can cause asphyxia. The side effect is alleviated by changing to a lower dose of medication or to another, less potent antipsychotic or by using anti-Parkinsonian medications prophylactically in conjunction with the antipsychotic.

See also ANTIPSYCHOTIC MEDICATIONS.

E

eating disorders Compulsive misuse of food to achieve some desired mental equilibrium. Eating disorders share common addictive features with alcohol and drug abuse, but unlike alcohol and drugs, food is essential to human life and proper habits are a central element of recovery.

The two most well known syndromes are anorexia nervosa and bulimia. Anorexia nervosa is a syndrome of self-starvation in which the person willfully restricts intake of food out of fear of becoming fat. Anorexic individuals are 95 percent female. Bulimia is characterized by recurrent episodes of binge eating followed by self-induced vomiting, vigorous exercise and/or laxative and diuretic abuse to prevent weight gain.

Another disorder is bulimarexia, which is characterized by features of both anorexia nervosa and bulimia. Eating disorders sometimes accompany other mental health disorders, such as depression. Eating disorders can be serious conditions; deaths from anorexia nervosa are higher than from any other psychiatric illness.

See also ANOREXIA NERVOSA; BODY IMAGE; BULIMAREXIA; BULIMIA.

ECG See ELECTROCARDIOGRAM.

echolalia   Compulsive repetition of what is said by another person. The accent, tone and words of the speaker are mimicked. This occurs in some people with autism and some forms of mental retardation; it is an unusual symptom of catatonic schizophrenia.

See also CATATONIA.

echopraxia   Compulsive imitation of the movements and gestures of another person. Echopraxia often accompanies echolalia.

See also ECHOLALIA.

ECT   See ELECTROCONVULSIVE THERAPY.

EEG   See ELECTROENCEPHALOGRAM.

ego   A region of the mind believed to contain both conscious and unconscious parts, which serves a mediating role between bodily needs, (id) and the external world. People acquire certain moral and ethical demands as they mature, and these are taken into account by the ego in this mediating function. The ego is also responsible for planning and thinking.

Most ego functions are automatic. A basic ego function is adaptation to reality, which is accomplished by delaying drives and calling up defense mechanisms as safeguards against unacceptable impulses.

Individuals use defense mechanisms to protect the ego from conflicts; such defense mechanisms include projection, repression and sublimation.

Sigmund Freud said the ego was one of three aspects of mental functioning, along with the id and superego. The ego lets one reason, test reality and solve problems, while the id modifies instinctual impulses following wishes of the person's conscience (superego).

See also DEFENSE MECHANISMS; FREUD, SIGMUND; ID; SUPEREGO.

ejaculation   A phase of the male orgasm during which semen is ejected from the glans penis. Sex researchers Masters and Johnson reported that ejaculation is the second stage of a physiological action in which emission is the first stage. Ejaculation is a subjective response to emission, marked by contractions of the ductus deferens, prostate and seminal vesicles. Men vary greatly in their ability to withhold ejaculation.

Early ejaculation, also known as premature ejaculation, is one that occurs within 10 to 60 seconds after penile penetration of the vagina.

See also MALE SEXUAL DYSFUNCTION.

Elavil   Trade name for amitriptyline hydrochloride, a tricyclic antidepressant drug. It is as effective as imipramine in the treatment of depressive episodes of major depression, bipolar disorder, dysthymic disorder and atypical depression. Concomitant administration of amitriptyline with an antipsychotic drug can be beneficial in schizoaffective disorder and depression with psychotic features. It is used to help control abnormal eating behavior in bulimic patients and may also be useful in the prevention of migraine headaches and in some patients with chronic pain, including tension-type headache that is unresponsive to analgesic therapy.

Though effective, amitriptyline has a high rate of such side effects as sedation, dry mouth, constipation and weight gain associated with its use.

See also ANTIDEPRESSANT MEDICATIONS; HEADACHES.

elderly parents   Caring for elderly parents is an increasingly common and complicated issue in today's society. There are many emotional and practical challenges involved when middle-aged adults begin to assume a bigger role in their parents' affairs and cope with their own feelings about this "role reversal."

Knowing when to take a more active role in parents' lives as they get older is a question many middle-aged adults face. They should be attentive for changes in the parents' judgment and ability to take care of themselves and their affairs. Elderly parents may present a variety of needs. Some may need physical assistance and others emotional assistance. Some may need financial help. As their behaviors change, one should try to determine to what extent those changes are part of a lifelong personality style. The adult child should also ask others who know the parent if they see changes, too. One may want to seek professional help in making this evaluation.

Many middle-aged children feel awkward about being responsive to their parents' needs without being overprotective. To overcome this awkwardness, children should talk to their parents, find out how they perceive their circumstances and discuss mutual concerns. They can agree to explore the situation further and work together toward a mutually agreeable approach. If the parent does not acknowledge problems, one can keep the dialogue going by asking how they would advise a friend in similar circumstances. This technique may help everyone focus more clearly on immediate needs and solutions.

Most older people want to live independently as long as possible. There are many noninstitutional arrangements for those who become increasingly dependent. Many participate in adult day-care programs, some have meals delivered to their homes, others live semi-independently with daily outside help and some live in ''retirement projects'' with a nurse on duty. One should encourage one's parents to stay involved with friends and to enjoy as many activities as they can.

As parents age, they may decide that it is in their own best interests to discuss and review their options. Some, despite increased physical or mental frailty, may want to keep things as they are. Social workers usually advise not rushing things, unless needs are immediate and obvious. When difficult questions arise, all people—the elderly included—may not be ready to make decisions. They may want more time before

talking about the problem again. One should consider involving others, such as grandchildren, trusted friends or a family doctor, in discussions. Everyone responds in different ways to different individuals. It may be useful to determine which individuals one's parents are most likely to listen to and involve those people in discussions.

As elderly parents become more dependent, interpersonal role relationships change. The adult child may experience a range of emotions and possibly the reappearance of long-forgotten feelings. For example, in some families, adult children may have always felt grateful to their parents and now feel able to finally repay their parents in financial, emotional and physical ways. In other families, however, adult children who already have other heavy responsibilities may find additional dependency too much to accept and feel overburdened, resentful or guilty about their inability to help.

Parents may feel resentful about losing their independence and direct their hostility toward the grown-up child. In such cases, one must keep in mind that their hostility is really directed at the situation and not necessarily at the child.

Taking on more responsibility for one's parents is an evolving process. At first one may feel uneasy and uncertain in taking control from parents. There are likely to be conflicts as different people perceive problems in different ways. Some people resist recognizing problems. Sometimes one sibling does not want to accept the fact that the parent is becoming dependent. In time, children and parents become more comfortable with the role reversal and move toward new patterns of meeting everyday situations.

As parents age, many begin thinking more about death and will offer their wishes regarding life-prolonging interventions. Increasingly common living will arrangements help ease the ethical dilemma of decision making when facing a parent's major illness or prolonged disability. A living will is a legal document that can allow a child to do what the parent desires when the time comes.

Recognizing signs of mental health problems in the elderly is important. In general, the elderly as a group are as mentally healthy as the general population. Nevertheless, there are some illnesses specific to this age group that can affect their behavior, judgment and memory. For example, elderly parents may be overly fearful of losing control of what is going on around them. Symptoms may be mild, such as sadness, loneliness, irritability or confusion, or they may be severe, such as depression, agitation or delusions. One should watch for such symptoms and get appropriate help. There are specialists in geriatric mental health who can be consulted.

Many adult children find that they cannot cope alone with elderly parents. In many cases it is too much for one individual, or one couple, to care for aging parents. There may be reasons why others cannot be involved in the responsibility; one may have few or no other family members, or they may live far away or already have heavy demands on themselves.

The idea of sharing responsibilities is important for the major caregiver and also to increase the number of people to whom parents continue to relate. One can consult the local Office on Aging to get some ideas about available services in the community, such as day care, meals, recreation, living arrangements and respite help. Many such programs feature sliding-scale fees. Additionally, community mental health programs have specialists in the care of older adults who can provide counsel and suggest support groups to help share concerns and practical approaches.

For adult children whose parents live in distant places, local social workers are affiliated with networks that can help arrange for long-distance care of elderly parents.

See also AGING; SUPPORT GROUPS; ELDERLY in BIBLIOGRAPHY.

Excerpted with permission, Kahn, Ada P. *Becoming a Parent to Your Parents*. Mental Health Association of Greater Chicago, 1988.

Electra complex   According to Sigmund Freud, a term relating to a relationship of a daughter to her father during an early stage of psychosocial development. The presumed desire of a young girl to sexually possess her father is a parallel to the Oedipus complex boys presumably develop toward mothers. In mentally healthy individuals, these unconscious feelings are resolved as the individual moves into a more mature stage of development.

The name of this complex comes from Electra, a mythical figure, daughter of Agamemnon, king of Mycenae. While Agamemnon was at war, his wife Clytemnestra, and her lover conspired to kill her husband upon his return to usurp his kingdom. To avenge her father's death, Electra planned to murder her mother and the lover.

See also COMPLEX; MYTH; OEDIPUS COMPLEX.

electrocardiogram (ECG, EKG)   A record of the electrical impulses that precede contraction of the heart muscle. Wave patterns are known as P, Q, R, S and T. The ECG is a useful means of diagnosing disorders of the heart, many of which produce deviations from normal electrical patterns. Individuals who have anxieties and panic disorder may suffer from heart palpitations or a very fast heartbeat; a physician may request an ECG for them to rule out heart problems. In the ECG, electrodes are placed on the individual's chest and amplified by the electronic machine that creates the electrocardiogram, or the printed tracing of the patterns of the heartbeat.

An abnormal ECG may help to diagnose a myocardial infarction (heart attack), tissue damage, arrhythmia (abnormal heart rhythm), coronary insufficiency (coronary artery sclerosis) or other cardiac condition. The ECG is often used along with increasingly vigorous levels of exercise on a treadmill or in a battery-operated recorder (Holter monitor) worn for 24 hours to diagnose heart disease more accurately.

electroconvulsive therapy (ECT) A treatment involving the use of anesthesia and administration of muscle relaxants and oxygen that produces a convulsion by passing an electrical current through the brain; it is also known as electroshock therapy. Historically, this treatment was used for a variety of serious symptoms of mental illness. Under close medical monitoring, it is given to carefully selected patients with psychosis or severe depression who are unresponsive to treatment, especially patients with high levels of suicide risk. ECT has been shown to affect a variety of neurotransmitters in the brain, including GABA, norepinephrine, serotonin and dopamine. It is also sometimes used to treat acute mania and acute schizophrenia when other treatments have failed. The number of ECT treatments needed for each person is determined according to the therapeutic response. Individuals with depression usually require an average of six to 12 treatments; commonly, treatments are given three or four times a week, usually every other day. After a course of ECT treatments, such patients are usually maintained on an antidepressant drug or lithium to reduce the risk of relapse of the condition. ECT has a high rate of therapeutic response (80 to 90 percent) but may have a relapse rate of 50 percent in one year, which can be reduced to 20 percent with maintenance medication.

The treatment can be lifesaving in people who are too medically ill to tolerate medication or who are not eating or drinking (catatonic). Side effects, including memory loss, are not uncommon. Patients must give informed consent to ECT, similar to any operative procedure.

See also DEPRESSION; SCHIZOPHRENIA.

electroencephalogram (EEG) An instrument that measures small electrical discharges from cortical areas of the brain through electrodes placed at standardized locations on the scalp. Irregularities are identified by examining patterns produced on a graph. EEG is used to study sleep and dreaming and in diagnosing brain tumors and epilepsy. It is also often one of many tests a physician will recommend for an individual who suffers from severe headaches, chronic insomnia and other disorders.

See also HEADACHES; INSOMNIA.

electroshock treatments See ELECTROCONVULSIVE THERAPY.

ELISA test (enzyme-linked immunosorbent assay) A laboratory test commonly used in the diagnosis of infectious diseases, and a highly sensitive screening test for evidence of the presence of HIV antibodies, considered a causative agent of AIDS (acquired immunodeficiency syndrome).

Tests found positive by this procedure are usually followed with another confirmatory assay (in the late 1980s, the Western blot confirmatory assay). Learning about a positive test result causes considerable stress and increasing dilemmas for many individuals. Therefore, appropriate counseling and expert interpretation should be done before and after test results are known.

See also ACQUIRED IMMUNODEFICIENCY SYNDROME.

emotional charge The buildup of anger, rage and hurt feelings, stored in the body and mind. An emotionally charged discussion is one in which one or more of the participants have built up a store of emotions and often "let loose," sometimes speaking without thinking first. An example of emotional charge is often shown at a support group for individuals who care for aging parents and feel overwhelmed by their circumstances. When they finally talk about their feelings to others with many of the same concerns, they "let loose."

Emotional Health Anonymous   A national self-help program to offer support to men and women who have experienced emotional problems and illnesses. The self-help groups of this program use a modified version of the 12 steps to recovery of Alcoholics Anonymous to help participants during and after their crisis periods. Founded in 1970, the program has support groups throughout the United States as well as in other countries.

For information, contact:

Emotional Health Anonymous
General Service Office
2430 San Gabriel Blvd.
San Gabriel, CA 91779
Phone: (818) 573-5482

See also SUPPORT GROUPS.

emotions   A range of feelings humans experience. These may include anger, joy, happiness, sadness, gladness, despair, love, disgust, fear or surprise. How an individual feels is unique to that individual, and it is impossible to describe feelings, although people try through psychotherapy and creative release (song, poetry, etc.).

Emotions are also expressed at times with sweaty palms, weak knees or rapid heartbeat, such as when the individual is feeling fear or anxiety.

Researchers say that experiencing emotional feelings begins before the age of two months when a baby first smiles, and emotions continue to develop as the infant realizes how separation from the mother feels. As we grow older, our emotional reactions are influenced by experiences. For example, before a job interview we may feel nervous; before a happy occasion we will probably feel joy or gladness.

Emotion is important to an infant's development of good mental health in later life. Researchers have found that lack of loving attention and a trusting relationship during infancy may result in later difficulty with normal emotional development. A child may be emotionally deprived if there is frequent separation from parents during the first few years of life and bonding does not occur. Children who are emotionally deprived often crave attention and have difficulty coping with frustration.

The term "emotional problems" or "emotional disorders" is used to apply to many mental health difficulties. How people express their emotions is an important aspect of mental health. Many emotional responses are considered within the range of normal. When responses are out of the range of normal, such as pervasive sadness in depression, mental health is threatened.

empathy   An ability to mentally feel and understand what someone else is feeling. People who have been in the same situation as another can empathize. For example, a widow can have empathy with another individual who recently lost a spouse.

Employee Assistance Programs (EAP)
Programs to identify employed persons whose personal problems adversely affect their job performance and to provide them and their immediate families with confidential, professional assistance. Types of problems that influence job performance may include alcoholism, drug abuse, depression or other mental health concerns, marriage and family difficulties and legal and financial problems. Most EAPs offer assessment of problems and referrals to appropriate professional services as necessary. Confidentiality is assured, as employees do not want their employers to know about their personal problems and most would not use an EAP if they thought that their problems would be revealed.

Employers implement EAPs for many reasons, including hoping to retain the services of valuable employees and avoiding costs of turnover and replacement, removing from supervisors their responsibility to counsel employees who have alcohol or other personal problems, providing a policy-based "due process" for employees who have problems, providing a benefit to enhance employees' morale and commitment to the organization and promoting health care cost containment.

Incentives for employers to provide an EAP for employees include the cost saving from rehabilitating valued and useful employees. A four-year study of mental health care received by employees of the McDonnell Douglas Corporation, concluded that assessing each case individually and providing quality care at the outset is the most cost-effective approach. The study compared employees who sought mental health care (including chemical dependency treatment) on their own with those who sought help through the company's EAP. The study, based on medical claims and absentee rates of more than 20,000 of McDonnell Douglas's 125,000 employees, estimated that the company would save $5.1 million over three years based on the employees who sought treatment through the EAP compared with those who sought treatment outside the EAP. Employees who used the EAP for chemical dependency treatment lost 44 percent fewer work days. They also had an 81 percent lower rate of turnover and filed fewer medical claims than employees who did not use the EAP .

There are two basic types of EAPs: internal and external. The majority of EAPs are external, that is, independent companies that provide EAP services under contract to an employer. Beginning in the 1970s, a few large employers had programs to deal with personal problems such as alcohol and drug abuse. In the early 1990s, about one-third of American workers were covered by some form of EAP, and about 75 percent of the "Fortune 500" companies have EAPs, according to the Employee Assistance Professional Association (Arlington, VA).

See also ALCOHOLISM; BURNOUT; STRESS.

empty nest syndrome   A mild form of depression that occurs in middle-aged people when their children grow up and leave home. Typically, the syndrome seems to affect women more than men, and particularly women whose lives have focused on their children at the expense of engaging in activities for their own fulfillment. Such individuals no longer feel needed and feel a void in their life. However, many middle-aged people view children leaving home with a sense of relief and of accomplishing a major life task.

enabler   A participant in a codependent relationship. The enabler promotes the codependent relationship by compensating for or covering difficulties or flaws in the behavior of the other out of an addictive need to be needed and to keep the relationship going. For example, a parent who continues to support an adult child who should be responsible for herself because the parent enjoys the feeling of the child's dependence would be considered an enabler. Another example is a husband who does all the household chores—shopping, driving children to activities, etc.—and explains that his wife is not feeling well in order to cover for an agoraphobic wife. It is difficult for an individual to live with agoraphobia without an enabler. Many alcoholics and drug addicts also have enablers.

See also AGORAPHOBIA; ALCOHOLISM; CODEPENDENCY; COURTSHIP, LOVE, ROMANCE, RELATIONSHIPS in BIBLIOGRAPHY.

Becnel, Barbara. *The Co-Dependent Parent.* San Francisco: Harper, 1991.

encephalitis   An inflammation of the brain that may result from many causes, including viruses, bacterial infection or lead poisoning. Symptoms may be mild or serious, with fever, convulsions, delirium and coma.

See also BRAIN.

encounter group   A form of small-group therapy in which personal growth is encouraged through sensitivity to others and interactions on an emotional level. A leader functions as a facilitator rather than a therapist and encourages participants to focus on "here and now" feelings and interactions. The term was coined by J. L. Moreno in 1914. In the 1990s, such groups are often referred to as "rap" groups, and individuals with similar concerns come together to discuss mutual concerns, such as depressions, parenting children who abuse drugs, or women who are abused by their husbands.

See also SUPPORT GROUPS.

enculturation   The process of modifying attitudes, behavior and language while adjusting to a different culture. Many immigrants from other countries have mental health concerns when adjusting to a new place. Such concerns may relate to their feeling "different," not being able to keep up with the pace of the new society and a sense of longing for their former familiar surroundings and traditions. Many community mental health centers in American urban areas treat individuals who have enculturation problems, for example, minority patients (Hispanics and Asians).

See also MIGRATION; NOSTALGIA.

Endep   Trade name for amitriptyline, an antidepressant drug.

See also AMITRIPTYLINE.

endocrine disorders   In disorders of the endocrine system, there is either not enough or too much production of a hormone by a gland. Endocrine disorders may cause many symptoms in body functions and behavior related to mental health, such as growth, metabolism, response to stress and sexual activity. Too much hormone production may be a result of a tumor, an autoimmune disease affecting a gland or a disorder of the pituitary or the hypothalamus, which control many other glands. When there is unusual hormone production, there may be a feedback effect on the secretion of hormones by the pituitary and the hypothalamus. To diagnose endocrine disorders, many laboratory and diagnostic tests are used, including tests that measure levels of hormones in the blood and urine.

Examples of endocrine disorders include Addison's disease, thyrotoxicosis and Cushing's syndrome. In Addison's disease, a defective adrenal cortex results in reduced hormone production. In thyrotoxicosis, there is an excess of hormone production. In Cushing's syndrome, there is an excess of adrenocorticotropic hormone (ACTH) secretion by a pituitary tumor.

The most common endocrine disease is hypothyroidism, in which the thyroid gland, for a number of possible reasons, fails to produce enough thyroid hormone to convert food (glucose) into energy. Hypothyroidism may cause fatigue, apathy, a tendency toward weight gain and mental dullness. Decreases in thyroid function can cause depression. Some medications such as lithium can bring out a tendency toward hypothyroidism. Endocrine disorders can rarely cause mental disorders such as depression or even psychosis.

See also ENDOCRINE SYSTEM; ENDOCRINOLOGY.

endocrine system   A series of ductless glands that secrete hormones directly into the bloodstream. Examples include the thyroid gland, which secretes thyroxine; ovaries (in females), which secrete estrogen; testes (in males), which secrete testosterone; and the adrenals, which secrete hydrocortisone. These glands and their secretions regulate the body's rate of metabolism, growth, sexual development and functioning. Some endocrine glands increase their activity during stress and emotional arousal. In research, these hormones appear to have very significant affects on fetal development and even on the central nervous system (brain) in adults.

Recent research is showing that even the supportive cells (glial cells) of the brain may produce hormones, though their function beyond this is not yet known.

See also ADRENAL GLAND; HORMONES.

endocrinology The study of the body's endocrine system and the hormones they secrete. A physician who specializes in diseases of the endocrine system is known as an endocrinologist.

endogenous Arising from causes within the body. The term is often linked with depression (endogenous depression), which refers to a type of depression not due to an identifiable external cause as opposed to an exogenous depression, which may be linked to a death in the family, job loss or other identifiable causes. Such depression may be treated with psychotherapy and/or antidepressant drugs.

See also ANTIDEPRESSANT MEDICATIONS; DEPRESSION.

endogenous depression A type of depression that originates from within the body, as when there is a chemical imbalance, contrasted with a type of depression known as exogenous depression, which is not physiological in origin.

See also ANTIDEPRESSANT MEDICATIONS; DEPRESSION; ENDOGENOUS.

endorphins A group of substances formed within the body that relieve pain and may improve mood. Endorphins have a chemical structure similar to that of morphine. Since the early 1970s, researchers have understood that morphine acts at specific sites called opiate receptors in the brain, spinal cord and at other nerve endings. From this knowledge, they identified small peptide molecules produced by cells in the body that also act at opiate receptors. These morphinelike substances were named endorphins, short for endogenous morphines. Effects of endorphins are noted, for example, in accident victims, who feel no initial pain after a traumatic injury, or in marathon runners, who do not feel muscle soreness until they complete their race.

In addition to their effect on pain, endorphins are considered to be involved in controlling the body's response to stress, regulating contractions of the intestinal wall and determining mood. Addiction and tolerance to narcotic analgesics, such as morphine, are thought to be due or to cause suppression of the body's production of endorphins; withdrawal symptoms that occur when effects of morphine wear off may be due to a lack of these natural analgesics. Conversely, acupuncture is thought to produce pain relief partly by stimulating release of endorphins.

See also MEDITATION; RUNNER'S HIGH.

enkephalins A small group of peptide molecules that are secreted within the brain and by nerve endings such as in the digestive system and adrenal glands. Enkephalins have an analgesic (pain relieving) effect and are thought to affect mood and produce sedation.

See also ENDORPHINS.

enuresis See BEDWETTING.

envy An emotional feeling that most people experience at one time or another in which they have a sense that something is lacking in their lives that others may have. For example, they may desire the status or possessions of another person. Usually envious people are unwilling to admit to these feelings. Envy can spring from many types of relationships, but the situations close at hand involving friends, relatives, neighbors or colleagues are generally most intense. It is easier to compare ourselves with people close at hand and to think that their good fortune might have been ours. Because feelings of envy imply that someone is in a superior position and is often considered to be a sinful feeling, people develop various ways of masking or suppressing it. To avoid expressing envy, some people develop snobbish attitudes, gossip, criticize or imply that the person envied is the envious one.

This ability to imagine or mentally project into or identify with an admired person's strengths is an intellectual asset that may enable people to progress and better themselves. However, it becomes negative when it becomes fixated on another person's life without spurring the envious person to better his or her life through effort in a constructive way.

Modern American life is full of elements that create envy. For example, the mobile quality of society deemphasizes social class and creates feelings that all things are possible for all people. This can also create feelings of frustration, failure and envy when expectations are thwarted. Mass media, especially television, allows us to view "lifestyles of the rich and famous." Advertising plays on feelings of envy. The "Me Decade" of the 1980s, with its narcissism and the "yuppie" life-style, created a climate in which it has been easy for envy to flourish. As one is faced with a wide array of consumer products made available by high technology, it is always possible to feel that someone else has more.

Low self-esteem produces envy that often does not improve by the attainment of material things, status symbols or fame. Normal self-esteem makes envy unlikely but allows creative identification with admired traits in others.

The reverse side of feelings of envy is the fear of being envied. This may be the reason that many people are less willing to talk about their salaries or general financial situation than other topics that might seem far more personal. Members of other societies carry this fear even further by sharing food and other possessions or by avoiding direct compliments, which are seen as a sign of envy and which may bring the power of the "evil eye" to bear on the fortunate person. Even people who find compliments pleasant still quite frequently experience an awkward feeling in accepting them.

See also FRUSTRATION; SELF-ESTEEM.

enzyme-linked immunosorbent assay (ELISA)   See ELISA TESTS.

enzymes   Proteins that regulate rates of chemical reactions in the body. Thousands of enzymes in the human body are produced by cells and tissues. Activities of enzymes are influenced by factors including certain drugs, such as barbiturates, that affect the rate at which other drugs are metabolized. This effect (enzyme induction) causes some drug interactions. Other drugs block action of enzymes. An example is antibiotics, which destroy bacteria by blocking bacterial enzymes.

Enzymes that break down medications in the body are sometimes induced (or increased) by concomitant use of other drugs such as nicotine (as in smoking) or large amounts of alcohol or sedatives. People with induced enzymes may break down and excrete antidepressants or anxiolytic drugs more rapidly, requiring higher than usual doses to achieve effects. If a smoker ceases smoking while taking other medications, the enzymes may no longer be induced and the usual dose may now be too high, causing side effects.

epidemic   The sudden and rapidly spreading outbreak of a disease that affects a significant number of people in one location at the same time. An example is influenza, which seems to recur every year. Another is food poisoning, which might affect many individuals who eat the same food at a picnic and become ill. There have been and still are, in parts of the world, epidemics of some diseases, such as measles and chicken pox.

Epidemics cause mental health consequences because the ill people temporarily cannot function with their normal capacity, and the well people become worried about others who are ill and concerned that they will also contract the disorder. There are usually many anxieties and stresses associated with any epidemic.

The increase in the number of AIDS (acquired immunodeficiency syndrome) has been referred to as an epidemic by the public and has aroused many fears in the general population, including fears of any kind of casual contact with homosexuals and fears among health practitioners of caring for AIDS patients.

See also EPIDEMIOLOGIC CATCHMENT AREA (ECA) STUDY: EPIDEMIOLOGY.

epidemiologic catchment area (ECA) study   A landmark study conducted in the early 1980s by the National Institute of Mental Health involving 18,000 adults aged 18 years or older from five U.S. communities: New Haven, Connecticut; Baltimore, Maryland; St. Louis, Missouri; Piedmont County, North Carolina; and Los Angeles, California. Findings from the study indicated that prevalence rates and age of onset of major depression, bipolar depression and dysthymia are fairly consistent across geographic areas in the United States. There was some suggestion that rates of depression are lower in rural than in the urban and suburban areas. Findings also suggested a separation between bipolar disorder and major depression and that the onset and highest risk periods for these disorders are in young adulthood.

See also NATIONAL INSTITUTE OF MENTAL HEALTH.

epidemiology   The science that studies prevalence in the distribution of diseases in populations. Unlike single clinicians who deal with one patient at a time, epidemiologists study large numbers of people in a community, country or area of the world. Although epidemiology originally dealt mainly with infectious diseases such as plague and cholera, epidemiologists now study many mental health disorders as well as contemporary physical problems such as AIDS. For example, the epidemiology of bipolar disorder, dysthymia and major depression was studied in the National Institute of Mental

Health's Epidemiologic Catchment Area (ECA) study.

See also EPIDEMIC; EPIDEMIOLOGIC CATCHMENT AREA STUDY.

epilepsy   A disorder in which there is a tendency to have recurrent seizures or temporary alterations in one or more brain functions. Seizures are neurological abnormalities that come and go that are caused by unusual electrical activity in the brain. Seizures usually happen spontaneously, with no apparent cause, but are a symptom of brain dysfunction; they can result from a variety of diseases or injuries. For example, head injuries, brain infection (encephalitis or meningitis), drug intoxication and alcohol withdrawal states may at times be causes of seizures.

Many epileptics lead normal lives and are healthy individuals between seizures. However, some may be limited in their choice of jobs because of their disorder. Many epileptics wear a tag bracelet or carry a special card indicating that they are epileptic; they should advise people with whom they work about what to do if a seizure occurs.

Historically, epileptic people have often been the subject of fear, avoidance and lack of understanding. Although epilepsy is considered a brain disorder, these people are not ''crazy'' and should be helped, not shunned, as has happened to some epileptic individuals. Family members, friends and bystanders need to be educated to show understanding and compassion rather than criticism and ridicule. Epileptics remain mentally healthier individuals with a supportive system around them.

Epilepsy occurs in about one in 200 persons, with about 1 million epileptics in the United States. Epilepsy usually begins in childhood or adolescence; when epilepsy develops during childhood and there is a family history of the disease, there is a strong likelihood that symptoms will decrease after adolescence. Many people outgrow it and recover without medication, while others control their disease with anticonvulsant drugs.

In some epileptics, seizures occur at times of extreme stress or fatigue or during an infectious illness. Epileptics can reduce the frequency of seizures by taking appropriate medication and avoiding certain situations known to bring on their seizures. Some epileptics can anticipate an attack when they experience an aura, which is a vaguely uncomfortable feeling of restlessness and irritability.

Symptoms and Types   The occurrence and progression of a seizure depends on the part of the brain in which it arises and how it fans out. For example, generalized seizures may arise over a wide area of the brain and cause loss of consciousness, while partial seizures are usually caused by damage to a more limited area of the brain (temporary lobe epilepsy). Generalized seizures are divided into two main types, grand mal and petit mal (absence) seizures. During a grand mal seizure, the individual becomes unconscious and falls down, and the entire body stiffens, jerks and twitches uncontrollably; breathing is irregular or absent. After the seizure, bladder and bowel control may be lost; the person may feel disoriented and confused and may feel a need to sleep. When the effects are over, in several hours, the individual may have no recollection of the seizure.

During a petit mal, or ''absence'' seizure, there is a momentary loss of consciousness, without abnormal movements. The individual may lose memory for only a few seconds or up to half a minute. As the attack happens, the individual may appear to be inattentive or daydreaming. In children, these seizures may occur hundreds of times a day and can hinder school achievements.

During simple partial seizures there will be an abnormal twitching movement, tingling sensation or even visual or other hallucinations without warning that last several minutes. With this type of seizure, the individual recalls details of the occurrence.

When seizures cause twitching movements on the same side of the body, the term applied is Jacksonian epilepsy.

During complex partial seizures the individual may not respond if spoken to and looks dazed. There may be involuntary actions, such as lip smacking, that usually are not remembered by the sufferer.

Diagnosis   The physician will take a complete history from the individual as well as other family members and do a complete neurological examination and a sleep electroencephalogram (EEG); however, even the sleep EEG cannot always confirm or refute the diagnosis of seizure. Tests of heart function (such as an ECG or Holter monitor) are also used to test for cardiac irregularities as a cause of loss of consciousness. Additionally, CAT scanning of the brain and MRI scanning can give additional information, as can specific blood tests.

Treatment   In most cases, anticonvulsant drugs lessen the frequency of seizures. However, these drugs may have side effects such as drowsiness and impaired concentration. Medications are tailored to the needs of each individual patient and the severity of the disease. In rare cases, brain surgery is recommended when seizure disorders are severe, do not respond to medication and emanate from a single operable area or ''focus'' in the brain.

Helping During an Epileptic Seizure   Those standing by and witnessing an epileptic attack should watch to see that the individual can breathe while unconscious and is not in any physical danger from the surroundings. The person should not be restrained or held down but permitted to move freely; something soft should be placed beneath the head. Tight clothing, particularly around the neck, should be loosened. The mouth should not be forced open. Reasons to call an ambulance include consciousness not being regained after the seizure, a seizure lasting for five minutes or longer or a second seizure occurring immediately after the first one. Bystanders can be most helpful by remaining calm and reassuring to the sufferer.

See also ANTICONVULSANT MEDICATIONS.

epinephrine   A hormone secreted by the adrenal gland; also called adrenaline. Epinephrine (or adrenaline) is sometimes referred to as the "emergency" hormone, as it affects the entire body and is responsible for reactions to fear and anger, such as rapid heartbeat and feelings of nervousness and agitation. Release of epinephrine throughout the body is part of the human body's "fight or flight" readiness response to danger or a threat of danger. Epinephrine is a powerful stimulant; in cases of cardiac arrest, it is injected as a last resort into the heart to start it beating again.

See also ADRENALINE; NEUROTRANSMITTERS.

Epstein-Barr virus   A virus that causes infectious mononucleosis and several rare forms of cancer. It is one of the herpes family of viruses. The activated virus is often a sign of chronic fatigue syndrome. A characteristic of an infection with EB virus is extreme tiredness and easy fatigability on exercising.

See also CHRONIC FATIGUE SYNDROME.

Equanil   Trade name for the antianxiety drug meprobamate.

See also ANXIETY; MEPROBAMATE.

ethical drug   A drug that requires a physician's prescription. (An "over-the-counter drug" does not require a prescription.) Psychotropic medications, including antidepressant drugs, are examples of ethical drugs.

ethics   There are many aspects to defining ethics; one that fits most circumstances is the biblical one: "Do unto others as you would have others do unto you." Ethics is involved in everyday behavior. People learn to "do the right thing" according to the unstated or stated rules of each culture.

In health and medicine, many ethical issues are involved. Usually, four basic principles are considered: (1) autonomy: respecting the wishes of the patient; (2) independence: maintaining independence from overbearing technology; (3) beneficence: doing what is best for the patient; and (4) justice: balancing individual needs with the social good. At times these values may conflict, causing additional dilemmas.

Medical science has developed to the point at which it can prolong physiological life. Aspects of ethics are involved, because technologically people can be kept alive after they are physiologically dead. During the mid-1990s, bioethicists, scientists concerned with ethics, still struggle with decisions regarding artificial life-support machines as well as other issues. Bioethicists have techniques for looking at questions about life-prolonging technology, genetic research and testing, organ transplantation, reproduction, AIDS and rationing medical care.

Legal issues as well as ethical issues arise when wishes of the family differ from the scientific pursuit of knowledge possibly derived from watching the progress of a terminally ill patient on life support. Many hospitals now have ethics committees that help make difficult decisions.

In December 1991, a federal Patient Self-Determination Act was enacted, which requires hospitals to tell all patients they have the right to refuse treatment. Some states also have laws. One example is Illinois, which has a Health Care Surrogate Act (September 1991) allowing people to decline such treatment as intravenous feeding or respirators for terminally ill relatives.

Physicians are faced with ethical decisions when terminally ill patients ask for assisted suicide. Legally, a physician cannot assist in inducing death.

Another dimension of ethics in medicine involves drug testing. For example, when a promising new drug is tested, some people are involved in trials. An ethical dilemma arises in random tests in which new drugs are compared with inactive placebos to determine the safety and effectiveness of the new drugs.

At one time mentally retarded persons and prisoners were used in medical and psychological tests. This is no longer the case, because they are not in a position to give informed consent.

Many U.S. medical schools are including courses in ethics for physicians. Lawyers take written examinations regarding ethics as part of their licensure procedure.

See also DYING WITH DIGNITY; EUTHANASIA; LEGAL ISSUES; SUICIDE.

euphoria A state of mind in which one feels extremely exalted, elated and jubilant (euphoric mood). Such a reaction is appropriate after hearing extremely good news, such as passing a major examination, or after a long climb to the top of a mountain. However, when this state occurs inappropriately or is too intense, the individual might be in a manic or hypomanic state or may have manic-depressive illness or bipolar disorder.

See BIPOLAR DISORDER; MANIC-DEPRESSIVE ILLNESS.

euthanasia A term relating to inducing the death of another person as a ''mercy killing.'' Some spouses of terminally ill persons wish to help their loved one out of misery by giving them death-inducing potions. Some individuals ask physicians for such drugs, and there have been instances in which physicians have cooperated. However, euthanasia is an illegal procedure, and offenders can be prosecuted. Euthanasia has been referred to as ''assisted suicide.'' The question of whether or not euthanasia should be considered legal is a matter of ethics.

See also ETHICS; SUICIDE.

exercise Exercise can have positive mental health benefits and serve as a way to raise self-image and increase creativity. According to Jeff Zwiefel, M.S., Director, The National Exercise for Life Institute, physical strength and stamina and a confident attitude are the main by-products of exercise. A study at Baruch College, New York, found that people who are stronger and more muscularly fit have a significantly better self-image than their peers. Psychological tests have discovered that those who exercise are more confident, emotionally stable and outgoing than those who are sedentary.

Joan C. Gondola, associate professor of physical education at Baruch College, found the same positive results of exercise on creativity levels when she administered a test on female college students. One group had exercised 20 minutes before the tests and the other group had not; the exercise group had more imaginative responses than those that had not.

The boost in creativity may be attributed to the release of adrenaline and endorphins during exercise. The right side of the brain is stimulated by these chemicals, which control creative and intuitive processes.

Exercise is an excellent way to relieve stress, whether caused by pressures at work, family tensions or grief. However, exercise may also become a compulsion, when the individual drops other responsibilities in favor of improving body image or losing weight. Because of our society's emphasis on a thin, slender body shape, many individuals have become exercise addicts. For some individuals, such addiction interferes with their mental well-being. An example is compulsive exercise that accompanies eating disorders.

See BODY IMAGE.

exogenous depression A type of reactive depression that originates outside the body and is often caused by emotional factors, such as burnout, grief or stress. This type of depression is contrasted with endogenous depression, which may be caused by a chemical imbalance in the body.

See also ANTIDEPRESSANT MEDICATIONS; DEPRESSION; ENDOGNOUS DEPRESSION;

DEPRESSION AND AFFECTIVE DISORDERS in BIBLIOGRAPHY.

experiential family therapy A type of family therapy emphasizing experiences between family members and between family members and therapist during therapy. The therapy is based on humanistic approaches that focus on helping family members learn to use symptoms and anxieties constructively. It is also known as symbolic-experiential family therapy.

See also FAMILY THERAPY.

De'Ath, E. "Experiential Family Therapy," in Walrond-Skinner, S., ed., *Developments in Family Therapy*. London: Routledge & Kegan Paul, 1981.

exposure therapy Behavioral therapies that emphasize changing an individual's responses to phobic situations while gradually increasing exposure to the feared situation. Exposure therapy may be effective for some phobias and for agoraphobia; to be effective, appropriate drug therapy is also used in many cases.

See also AGORAPHOBIA; BEHAVIORAL THERAPY; PHOBIA; PSYCHOTHERAPY.

Isaac M. Marks. *Living with Fear*. New York: McGraw-Hill, 1978.

extrapyramidal side effects See EXTRAPYRAMIDAL SYSTEM.

extrapyramidal system A system that influences and modifies electrical impulses sent from the brain to the skeletal muscles. The system consists of nerve pathways linking nerve nuclei in the surface of the cerebrum (the main mass of the brain), the basal ganglia deep within the brain and parts of the brain stem. Degeneration of or damage to parts of the system can cause disturbances in execution of voluntary (willful) movements and in muscle tone and can cause the appearance of involuntary (unwanted) movements such as tremors or writhing motions.

Disturbances of this type occur in Huntington's disease, Parkinson's disease and some types of cerebral palsy.

Extrapyramidal side effects can also occur as a result of taking some phenothiazine drugs, used for treating some mental disorders.

See also PHENOTHIAZINE DRUGS.

extroversion A personality trait that involves characteristics of outgoingness, friendliness, openness and general optimism. Extroverts like to be with people, work well in groups and are often leaders. How and why personality traits develop is unknown. Some say that family background may influence personality traits, but others believe that the basis for the difference between the extroverted and introverted personality lie in the cerebral cortex, the part of the brain involved in learning, reasoning and planning. In brain scans, activity of this area can be visualized. In the extrovert, the cortex is quiet and seems to welcome noisy, exciting situations that arouse it. The introvert's level of cortical arousal is already high, and the introverted personality does not need much outside stimulation and seems to prefer quiet and peace.

Extroverts seems to fall asleep faster than introverts, and extroverts may be less sensitive to pain. The theory about the cerebral cortex was suggested by British psychologist Hans Eysenck. The concept of extroversion was first proposed by C. G. Jung.

See also INTROVERSION.

F

factitious disorder See MUNCHAUSEN'S SYNDROME.

familial A characteristic or disorder that runs in families. Depression seems to run in families, as does panic disorder.

See also DEPRESSION; PANIC DISORDER.

family history When a mental health professional begins treating a new client, the individual will be asked many questions about the physical as well as mental health of parents and siblings. If any first-degree relatives had a history of any mental illness, it is important that the specific illness be discussed, along with information about treatment and long-term course and outcome. The mental health professional may run through a series of specific disorders, because many individuals will not recognize alcoholism or shoplifting in their parents or siblings as emotional problems. Any relevant information about the family background may be included in the family history part of the interview because it will help the mental health professional diagnose and treat the individual.

Honesty and forthrightness on the part of the individual can help in her own diagnosis and treatment.

See also FAMILY THERAPY; PSYCHOTHERAPY.

family therapy A form of psychotherapy that tends to focus on the family unit or at least the parent and child (in single-parent families). Family therapy, begun in the 1950s, is geared to help individual family members become aware of their reactions and defensive habits and encourages them to communicate more openly with one another.

Typically, the therapy group will consist of both parents, or a parent and stepparent, two separated parents or other parental pairings depending on the environment in which the child lives.

In many cases, the child is brought to a mental health professional because of difficulties in school, such as aggressive behavior, or school phobia. When it becomes clear to the therapist that the child's problems appear to arise from the home situation, the family will be invited to join one or more sessions. Often such families are not dysfunctional families but, because of changing circumstances and demands, may not be providing the understanding and open communication that the child needs at the time.

Family therapy usually focuses on present problems and their practical solutions. Family therapy can be helpful when at least one member has a relatively serious mental illness, such as recurrent depression or schizophrenia. In these situations, family members need reassurance that neither the individual nor members of the family are responsible for the illness. The approach minimizes guilt and permits the patient and family members to find coping methods that may be more consoling and constructive to the patient. For example, a young schizophrenic individual who lives with his parents may need ongoing assistance in developing social skills, while the parents need ongoing assistance in coping with outbursts or anger and emotional withdrawal.

See also PSYCHOTHERAPY; SEX THERAPY.

family violence Violence against first-degree relatives or those living in the home. In American society, family violence involves acts of incest, physical child abuse, neglect, sexual child abuse, battered women, spouse abuse and marital rape. Family violence happens in all strata of society, and there are many more cases than official records indicate because it is a subject often covered up out of fear and shame.

Characteristics of persons who are victims of family violence include anxiety, powerlessness, guilt and lack of self-esteem.

According to Paulette Trumm, M.D., Director, Women's Program, Forest Hospital, Des Plaines, Illinois, women who are abused by their husbands or boyfriends not only sustain injuries from physical beatings, but they also suffer from many mental and emotional scars, including post-traumatic stress disorder, depression and anxiety. In most cases, the women suffer from low self-esteem; the healing process takes a long time.

Mental health professionals who treat victims of family violence are concerned with getting the women or children away from the abuser and into therapy before the beatings become too severe or other problems arise. Some victims of family violence compound their difficulties with use of alcohol or drugs.

Most abused women do not seek help until beatings become severe and have occurred over a period of time, often two to three years. Some women are too embarrassed or believe that if they report the beating to police, they will not be taken seriously. The majority of women who seek help from family violence are between age 20 and 60. In 75 percent of households in which abuse takes place, the husband or boyfriend is an alcoholic or on drugs.

Many women do not report family violence because they do not have the courage or financial resources to report the attacks and leave. For women who want to break the cycle of violence and abuse, Suzette Rush at Forest Hospital, Des Plaines, Illinois, suggests:

- Leave the abuser; stay with a friend or family member who will be supportive emotionally and provide a safe haven.
- Leave the home when the abuser is absent to eliminate any confrontations.
- Take bank records, children's birth certificates, cash and other important documents along with clothing and personal items.
- If possible, photograph or videotape any consequences of abuse, such as injuries or damage to the home. These could be important for possible later court proceedings.
- Call the police and file a police report. Obtain an order of protection as soon as possible.
- Seek counseling for yourself and your children; join a support group along with others who have been victims of family violence.

Family violence also includes acts of violence against a defenseless, elderly person in the home.

See also ABUSE; BATTERED WOMEN; DYSFUNCTIONAL FAMILY; INCEST; SUPPORT GROUPS.

McFarland, Gertrude K., and Thomas, Mary Durand. *Psychiatric Mental Health Nursing.* Philadelphia: J. B. Lippincott, 1992.
''Women Can Get Help, Support and Healing for Physical and Mental Abuse.'' *Branching Out,* Forest Health System, Inc., Des Plaines, Illinois (Fall/Winter 1991).

fantasy   Imagining events or objects that are not present. Many people indulge in fantasy, and, in fact, fantasy may lead to creativity. However, when fantasy takes the place of realistic thinking, the individual may have a thought disorder. Fantasies give one the temporary illusion that wishes are being met or desires satisfied.

Many people have fleeting sexual fantasies, sometimes involving people other than their mates or involving acts with their mates. Individuals may fantasize about sexual acts that they have heard about, read about or have seen in pictures. Having sexual fantasies is a normal habit for most individuals, but if carried to an extreme, and if the individual finds satisfaction and fulfillment from a fantasy life, the habit may be considered out of bounds of normalcy and require psychotherapy.

See also PRIMAL FANTASIES; PROCREATION FANTASY.

farming, stress in   Farming is a stressful occupation because farmers have little control over their lives; weather affects yield, international trade wars dictate price and government subsidies affect income. According to Lynda Haverstock, a Canadian psychologist, farming is a life, not an occupation, and it comes with a whole set of values, standards, mores and characteristics. Currently, as a life-style, it is threatened by disrespect. People no longer respect farmers because they see farmers as having to rely on the government rather than being self-reliant. According to Haverstock, the farmer's private stress and the public's negative view of farming can lead to family violence. Experts view it as a major problem but one that they cannot address because of the private, independent nature of farmers. With greater isolation and fewer options, there are more pressures, conflicts and frustrations, which can result in physical violence, first focused on the spouse and then on the children.

According to an article in *Canadian Family Physician,* farmers are disadvantaged by teachings of rural society traits, such as the inability to express emotion, and feelings of independence and pride that are barriers to seeking help. "Their independent nature and the taboo attached to psychiatry make it difficult for them to look for help."*

See also FAMILY VIOLENCE.

*"Stress in Farming." *Canadian Family Physician* 38 (Feb. 1992).

fatigue See CHRONIC FATIGUE SYNDROME; DEPRESSION.

fear An emotion resulting in intense and unpleasant tension that comes about because of a real threat or the imagination of a threatening situation, as in a phobia. There may be an intense feeling of wanting to escape, together with physiological reactions, which might include weakness, dizziness, rapid breathing, rapid heartbeat, nausea, muscle tension or weakness in the knees. Different individuals have different physiological responses to fear.

The general public often misuses the term "fear" for phobia, and vice versa. Fear is a real and knowable danger and can usually be recognized by others. On the other hand, phobia is an inappropriately fearful response to a situation and out of proportion to the real danger; the danger in a situation perceived by one as phobic cannot be seen or realized by another. Real fear is normal. Chronic phobias that cause avoidance behavior are considered anxiety disorders.

Fear can be a helpful emotion. For example, the fear reaction enables people to get out of the way when they hear the whistle of a train. The fear reaction sets off a signal in the hypothalamus that triggers a release of adrenaline into the body. Adrenaline acts immediately to prepare the body for fight or flight. The heart beats more strongly, breathing deepens, perspiration increases to cool the body, pupils dilate to sharpen vision and the face may turn pale.

See also ANXIETY DISORDERS; FIGHT OR FLIGHT RESPONSE; PHOBIA.

feedback The sharing of feelings or thoughts without evaluating them or demanding changes. Feedback involves objective information given by a therapist, teacher or parent or by others in a support group. Feedback may help an individual make changes or reinforce certain behaviors. For example, the individual who is fearful of public speaking may develop confidence when he gets very favorable feedback after his first public speech.

See also BEHAVIORAL THERAPY; PSYCHOTHERAPY.

feminism See WOMEN'S LIBERATION MOVEMENT.

fertility See INFERTILITY.

fetal alcohol syndrome A condition in which the growth of the fetus is retarded, resulting in possible cranial, facial and limb anomalies as well as mental retardation. This is caused by a woman's heavy alcohol consumption during pregnancy. Even moderate drinking can produce less severe but undesirable effects on the fetus. The National Institute on Alcohol Abuse and Alcoholism advises total abstention from alcohol during pregnancy. It is only in the latter half of the 20th century that the effects of alcohol on a fetus have become better understood. Many deformities and problems in newborns have been eliminated because of this knowledge.

See also ALCOHOLISM.

Alcohol, Drug Abuse and Mental Health Administration News, May 2, 1980

fight or flight response A reaction to a threatening or stressful situation in which the sympathetic nervous system (SNS) mobilizes the body for maximum use of energy. When a person faces a threatening situation, the SNS causes many physiological reactions, including faster heartbeat, deeper breathing, slower digestion and rising blood pressure.

See also AGORAPHOBIA; ANXIETY DISORDERS; FEAR; PHOBIA.

5-Hydroxytroptophan See NEUROTRANSMITTERS; SEROTONIN.

flashbacks Images of events that occurred in the past that recur in the mind. This happens to people who have post-traumatic stress disorder (PTSD) as well as victims of violent crimes or witnesses to violent crimes. Flashbacks can be distressing, make individuals fearful, cause insomnia or seriously disrupt sleep. Flashbacks of psychedelic experiences induced in the past by psychedelic drugs such as LSD have been reported.

See also POST-TRAUMATIC STRESS DISORDER.

flight of ideas See THOUGHT DISORDERS.

flooding A behavioral therapy technique in which the individual is repeatedly exposed to the precipitating factor for a phobia, panic attack or ritualistic behavior, in combination with a relaxation technique until the individual no longer responds to the situation with anxiety or subsequent ritualistic behavior.

See also BEHAVIORAL THERAPY; DESENSITIZATION.

fluoxetine hydrochloride An antidepressant drug (trade name: Prozac). It is a relatively new drug, not in the categories of tricyclic antidepressants or monoamine oxidase inhibitors. The efficacy of fluoxetine in treatment of major depression is comparable to that of the tricyclic antidepressant drugs. Most studies have been of moderately depressed outpatients; its efficacy in severely depressed hospitalized patients has not been established. In limited studies in those with bipolar disorder, fluoxetine was useful in treating the depressed component of this illness. The selection of fluoxetine appears to be most appropriate for patients who are at special risk for sedative, hypotensive and anticholinergic side effects caused by other antidepressants. Fluoxetine has a much lower overdose toxicity than other antidepressant medications.

See also ANTIDEPRESSANT MEDICATIONS; DEPRESSION.

American Medical Association. *AMA Drug Evaluations Annual, 1991.* Chicago: AMA, 1991.

folie a deux A rare psychotic disorder, also known as ''shared paranoid disorder.'' It occurs when the delusions of one individual develop in another person who is in a close relationship with the first individual. In such a situation, the second person did not have a delusional disorder before the onset of the disorder in the other person. Once this disorder was known as paranoid disorder; when it was originally described in the late 19th century, it was given the French name *folie a deux,* or folly between two.

Specifically how this disorder develops is not clearly understood. However, it seems to involve the presence of a dominant person with an established delusional system and a more submissive person who develops the induced disorder, thereby gaining acceptance of the more dominant individual.

See also DELUSION.

forgetfulness See FORGETTING; MEMORY.

forgetting   An inability to retrieve stored memories. This is a common occurrence; mentally healthy people forget short-term as well as long-term memories. They may forget recently made appointments, forget what their boss told them earlier in the day or forget occurrences that happened in childhood. Forgetting is a common experience, just as is the experience of suddenly remembering something that was previously forgotten.

How memory changes over time has been the subject for many scientific studies and has concentrated primarily on two factors, inhibition and loss of retrieval clues. Inhibition refers to how similar kinds of learning, either before or after the event to be remembered, interferes with later recall of that event. Theories about retrieval cues involve the knowledge that recall is easier regarding familiar people, things and situations.

Other theories hold that individuals have "selective" memories and may forget events or situations previously encountered that were unpleasant or even traumatic. This concept is related to repression, which suggests forgetting as a coping mechanism.

Forgetting may be a symptoms of some disorders, such as Parkinson's disease, multiple-infarct dementia, or Alzheimer's disease.

See also MEMORY; PARKINSON'S DISEASE; REPRESSION.

formication   A sensation that ants or other insects are crawling on the skin, sometimes resulting from abuse of cocaine or other drugs. This unpleasant sensation should be distinguished from a delusion in which the individual may believe they have ants, insects or worms on or in them. Scratching of the skin may result in redness or rash and a misdiagnosis of a skin disease.

See also COCAINE; DELUSION.

foster homes   Homes in which children are placed on a temporary or permanent basis. The concept of removing children from abusive or absent parents developed during the latter half of the 20th century. Usually such children are placed by court order or at least at the recommendation of a social service agency. Children of criminals or of known drug abusers or child abusers are sometimes placed in foster homes. Foster homes are usually those of "intact" families, and new residents are incorporated into the family structure as "members." Psychiatric mental health support is provided for the residents as well as for members of the foster family. Usually a formal arrangement with a court or community mental health center is mandatory. Foster homes are regularly monitored by a placement agency.

Children who have grown up in orphanages or mentally retarded children are sometimes placed in foster homes. In some cases, children return to their original families; in other cases, they may continue to live in the same or other foster homes or return to an institution.

See also COMMUNITY MENTAL HEALTH in BIBLIOGRAPHY.

fragile X syndrome   A cause of mental retardation resulting from an inherited defect of the X chromosome. After Down's syndrome it is the most common cause of mental retardation in males. Approximately one in 1,500 men is affected; one in 1,000 women is a carrier. The disorder happens in families, and while males are mainly affected, women may carry the genetic defect responsible for the disorder and pass it on to some of their sons or their daughters, who may become carriers of the defect. About one-third of female carriers have some degree of mental impairment.

When a young couple knows that there is a history of the syndrome on either side of the family, genetic counseling should be sought before planning a family.

See also DOWN'S SYNDROME; GENETIC COUNSELING; MENTAL RETARDATION; MENTAL RETARDATION in BIBLIOGRAPHY.

free association   See ASSOCIATION, FREE.

free love   A term meaning sexual permissiveness as advocated by such individuals as George Bernard Shaw, Bertrand Russell, H. G. Wells and, at one time, by the Oneida, New York community. The permissiveness includes making love with anyone without any restrictions. During the 1950s and 1960s, in the era of "hippies," many young people believed in and engaged in free love as a protest against established values and institutions in the United States. At that time free love was also one of the characteristics of communal living.

Disillusionment on the part of many women and disappointment with the lack of long-term committed relationships have since put limitations on the movements popularity. The increase of sexually transmitted diseases such as herpes simplex, papilloma virus and AIDS virus infections have severely limited the free love movement in most Western cultures. However, much freer sexual mores exist in certain subcultures, such as central Africa.

See also MARRIAGE; COURTSHIP, LOVE, ROMANCE, RELATIONSHIPS in BIBLIOGRAPHY.

Freud, Sigmund   (1856–1939) Austrian neurologist and psychiatrist and the originator of psychoanalysis (the "talking cure") as a therapeutic process. Freud's contributions to the study of mental health influenced later thoughts on psychology, child development and personal interactions. His writings provided possibilities for major advances in the scientific understanding of human behavior, particularly in bringing the topic of sex to the attention of the general public and as an appropriate topic for scientific research. Although controversial during his time and continuing to be so, Freud's theories affected subsequent approaches to psychology and psychiatry.

His many writing have influenced literature, history and social sciences. Among his books are *The Interpretation of Dreams* (1900), *Three Essays on the Theory of Sexuality* (1905), *Totem and Taboo* (1913), *Beyond the Pleasure Principle* (1920) and *The Ego and the Id* (1923).

Freud based his treatment on helping the patient bring back to consciousness repressed emotions, reviving and reliving painful experiences buried in the unconscious, thereby releasing painful emotions. Freud replaced the early use of hypnosis with interpretation of dreams, free association and analysis of behavioral and speech lapses now known as "Freudian slips."

The "Freudian view" (Freudianism) holds that people are driven by unconscious and particularly psychosexual impulses. In his method of free association, unconscious sexual conflicts and their repression are viewed as factors in neuroses. These concepts became the keystones of the new discipline he called psychoanalysis, which focused on procedures including interpretation of dreams, analysis of resistance, the transference relationship between the therapist and the patient and a study of the patient's current symptoms in terms of his psychosexual development and early experiences. Freud's theory of personality holds that personality and character traits come from experiences based on early stages of psychosexual development. In psychoanalysis over a period of years, he sought to reconstruct the patient's psychic life from early childhood to the present.

According to Freud's writings, personality has three parts, or forces: the id, representing the instincts one is born with and still harbors in the unconscious, the superego, the voice of civilization and restraint, and the ego, which tries to reconcile the two with each other and with the outside world. There are, of course, inevitable conflicts among these forces.

According to Freud, once the needs of hunger and thirst are met, the id is driven by sexual desire and aggression. In his view, a young child has sexual feelings toward the opposite-sex parent and hates and fears the same-sex parent. Thus a boy who does not rechannel such urges may develop an Oedipus complex and girls may develop an Electra complex.

Freud termed the sex drive or sex energy "libido." He viewed libido as one of two major human instincts, the other being thanatos, or the death instinct. Freud believed that much nonsexual behavior is actually motivated by a redirection of the libido in a process called sublimation, through which sexual motivations are expressed in other ways, such as painting or other creative forms of expression.

Psychosocial Development Freud believed that psychosocial development included a series of phases. The oral stage comes first, lasting from birth to about one year of age, in which the child derives pleasure from sucking and stimulating the lips and mouth. The second, or anal stage, occurs during the child's second year, during which interest is focused on elimination. The third stage, lasting from about age three to about five or six, is the phallic stage, in which a boy focuses his interest on his penis and derives pleasure from masturbation. During this stage, a girl realizes that she has no penis, envies boys and feels cheated or believes that she once had a penis and that it was cut off. She may even hate her mother for this defect. The latency stage comes next and lasts into adolescence. During this stage, sexual impulses are repressed, but in the genital stage, which begins with adolescence, young women's and young men's interests become more specifically genital. This stage is less self-directed and increasingly directed toward other people as appropriate sexual objects.

According to Freud, people do not always mature from one stage to the next and might remain fixated at one or more stages, so that most adults have some traces of earlier stages in their adult personalities.

Attitudes About Women Freud believed that "anatomy is destiny" and that women's lack of a penis was a major factor in per-

sonality development, leading to lifelong feelings of imperfection, inferiority and jealousy. He believed that women were inherently passive and had masochistic feelings about sexual intercourse.

Freud suggested that women experienced two kinds of orgasm, a clitoral orgasm and a vaginal orgasm (dual-orgasm theory). He believed that the vaginal orgasm was better and more mature than the clitoral orgasm. Later researchers, including Masters and Johnson, disagreed with any distinction between clitoral and vaginal orgasms, as their research indicated that physiologically, female orgasms are the same, regardless of the source of stimulation. Additionally, they found that some clitoral stimulation is almost always involved in reaching orgasm.

In his psychiatric practice, Freud heard reports from women of sexual abuse from their fathers and regarded this as fantasy and an innate need to compensate for their lack of a penis. Followers of Freud, such as Helene Deutsch, accepted Freud's view and argued that a degree of paternal seductiveness was essential to normal feminine development.

Some of Freud's contemporaries as well as later psychiatrists differed with Freudian views, many of which were offensive to the patriarchal Victorian culture that found shocking the notion that innocent children and well-bred women had sexual desires. The first expressions of controversy, in about 1911–1912, by Carl Jung and Alfred Adler, included views that Freud overestimated the role of sexual conflict in developing neuroses. Later, in the early 1920s, Karen Horney initiated and led an effort to indicate flaws in Freud's viewpoints centered around penis envy; her work influenced many subsequent practitioners and writers.

Feminists have objected to much of Freud's theory, including the notion that women are inferior to men and that they are sexually masochistic and passive. Feminists argue that psychoanalytic theory is a male-centered theory. Regarding the dual-orgasm theory, feminists state that Freud's notion includes the necessity of the presence of a penis for sexual satisfaction. Contemporary feminists have denounced Freud as a male chauvinist.

See also ELECTRA COMPLEX; OEDIPUS COMPLEX; PSYCHOANALYSIS; PSYCHOTHERAPY; SEXUALITY in BIBLIOGRAPHY.

Abraham, K. "The Experiencing of Sexual Trauma as a Form of Sexual Activity," in Jones, E., ed., *Selected Papers on Psychoanalysis*. London: Hogarth Press, 1973.

Deutsch, Helene. *The Psychology of Women*, vol. 1. New York: Grune & Stratton, 1944.

Freud, Sigmund. "Female Sexuality," In Strachey, J. ed. and trans., *The Standard Edition of the Complete Psychological Works of Sigmund Freud*, vol. 21. London: Hogarth Press, 1961. (Original work published in 1931.)

Freud, Sigmund. "Femininity," in Strachey, J., ed. and trans., *The Standard Edition of the Complete Psychological Works of Sigmund Freud*, vol. 22. London: Hogarth Press, 1964. (Original work published in 1933.)

Gillespie, William H. "Woman and Her Discontents: A Reassessment of Freud's Views on Female Sexuality." *International Review of Psycho-Analysis* 2 (1975).

Kahn, Ada P., and Holt, Linda Hughey. *The A to Z of Women's Sexuality*. Alameda, Calif.: Hunter House, 1992.

Mahoney, E. R. *Human Sexuality*. New York: McGraw-Hill, 1983.

Moulton, Ruth. "Early Papers on Women: Horney to Thompson." *American Journal of Psychoanalysis* 35 (1975).

Westerlund, Elaine. "Freud on Sexual Trauma: An Historical Review of Seduction and Betrayal." *Psychology of Women Quarterly* 10 (1986).

Freudian slips   See FREUD, SIGMUND; SLIPS OF THE TONGUE.

friends (friendship)   Friendship is unique among human relationships in the degree of freedom it allows. Individuals have little or no choice in blood relations or neighbors; marriage and employment ties are made cautiously and severed with difficulty. Friendships flow along more easily and casually, developing, changing and dissolving sometimes with little effort or even awareness. Friendships are more flexible and variable than other relationships. Some friendships evolve from shared interests, some simply from a shared history and compatible personalities. Qualities most appreciated in friends include loyalty, trust and an ability to keep a confidence. People want to feel that they can rely on their friends and that their friends will be open and honest with them.

Friendships are involved in maintaining good mental health. Friendships can be supportive in our daily lives as well as during periods of turmoil or crisis. Individuals who experience depression often report a lack of friends, although having a wide circle of friends is not a preventive factor for depression. Some reports have indicated that individuals who have many social contacts may be healthier and actually live longer than those who do not.

Friendships also affect mental health because they may challenge or be challenged by other relationships in contemporary life. For example, an employer, supervisor or teacher, particularly one with an authoritarian personality, may feel that friendships among students or employees give them too much power as a group. In the workplace, a friendship may dissolve when one is promoted and the other stays behind. A friendship may be broken or changed when one friend marries, and disruptive friendships can weaken a marriage. A friend of the opposite sex is frequently unsettling to a spouse or lover. Friends who do not meet with parents' approval can also be a source of family conflict. Friends who decide to share housing or enter into a business partnership sometimes learn about undesirable qualities of the other that could be ignored when the relationship was less formal.

The freedom inherent in friendship has its negative as well as positive aspects. There are fewer social rules about friendship than other relationships, and two people may have entirely different expectations from each other until those expectations clash. The lack of structure for friendships may also allow one friend to take the other for granted until the friendship disintegrates.

Among early humans, friendship was a banding together to avoid danger. In contemporary life, friendship may again play a role in combating the physical and psychological dangers of high crime and anonymity of modern urban life.

The nuclear family of modern life puts increasing pressures on family members to be one another's friends. Parents and children, husbands and wives who, in the past, may have had a network of relatives and longtime friends now turn to their immediate family for friendship, not always with satisfactory results.

A Gallup poll reported in 1990 showed that the typical American places much importance on friendship and indicates some frustrations that people have in forming friendships. Friendship requires time and a certain degree of flexibility. Twenty-five percent of the total surveyed said that they did not have enough time to spend with friends, and 46 percent of those who said they would like to have more friends indicated, almost in contradiction, that they did not have enough time to spend with the friends they had. Working women and couples with children at home were most likely to feel that they had insufficient time to spend with friends.

The survey showed that women and men approach friendship quite differently. Women tended to form more intimate relationships with other women than men with men. One to one activities that promote conversation are more popular with women, whereas men are more likely to get together in groups for activities such as sports or cards. Men rely on their wives for emotional support rather than other men; but many women, even those who are married, often rely on other women. Women are more likely than men to have a best friend of the same sex. Almost

a third of the men surveyed said a woman was their best friend.

When participants were asked about arguments with friends, those under age 30 reported more disagreements. Friendship evidently becomes more tranquil with age, possibly because friends settle their differences and learn to recognize sore spots and perhaps because age enables people to recognize and discard difficult relationships.

The survey also measured longevity of friendship. Half of those surveyed keep in touch with a friend they made when they were younger than age 17, and half also keep in touch with friends who live miles away.

People make friends in many ways. In the Gallup report, 51 percent of the 18- to 29-year-olds made most of their friends at school. Of the 30- to 49-year-olds, 51 percent said they made most of their friends through work. From the age of 50 and up, friends came from a greater variety of sources, including church, work, clubs or other organizations.

Despite the emphasis that the participants in the Gallup survey placed on friendship, 71 percent said they did not try particularly hard to make new friends. This may be a reflection of the fact that 75 percent of those surveyed were satisfied with their current friendships; but this may also be a product of conventional wisdom that to give the appearance of eagerly and actively searching for friends in a programmed manner is usually counterproductive.

DeStefano, Linda. "Pressures of Modern Life Bring Increased Importance to Friendship." *Gallup Poll Monthly* (Mar. 1990).

Marty, Martin. *Friendship*. Allen, Tex Argus Communications, 1980.

frigidity A term for the inability of a woman to obtain satisfaction (usually orgasm) during sexual intercourse. Sex researchers and Johnson coined the term "female orgasmic dysfunction" to replace this term. A woman's lack of satisfaction during sexual intercourse may result from a combination of many factors, including a lack of desirability of the partner, lack of adequate stimulation, lack of communication between the partners concerning sexual behaviors and desires and cultural rejection of certain practices. In addition, the fear of desertion or pregnancy may interfere with satisfaction. The amount of time necessary for a woman's arousal and satisfaction varies widely between individuals.

In some cases lack of interest in sexual activity and lack of satisfaction may result from depression, stress, fatigue or alcohol. Narcotics and some tranquilizers may also reduce interest in sexual activity.

Counseling, therapy and prescribed sexual exercises help many women who have orgasmic dysfunction to become more physically responsive and emotionally free to enjoy sexual pleasures.

See also DUAL-ORGASM THEORY; FEAR; FREUD, SIGMUND; ORGASM; SEXUAL DYSFUNCTION.

frontal lobe   Part of the cerebral hemispheres at the frontal or anterior side of the brain, associated with personality factors in humans. Ability for foresight, initiative, judgment (especially regarding consequences of behavior) and tact is affected by frontal lobe defects; but intelligence is apparently not affected.

Frontal Lobe Syndrome   A mental disorder due to lesions in the frontal lobe; it is also known as organic personality syndrome. Symptoms may include impaired social judgment and impulse control, marked apathy and impairment of purposeful behavior.

Frontal Perceptual Disorders   Difficulties in performing certain problem-solving tasks, such as matching numbers, letters or other symbols, seen in individuals with tumors or other lesions of the frontal lobes.

Leukotomy   A surgical procedure, also called frontal lobotomy, involving severing certain nerve fibers connecting the frontal lobes with the rest of the brain. It was

performed as therapy for individuals suffering from certain forms of chronic psychosis resulting in undesirable behaviors or for certain forms of pain. This procedure is no longer used. Cingulotomy is used in certain cases of severe, treatment-resistant depression and obsessive-compulsive disorder.

See also BRAIN.

frontal lobe syndrome   See FRONTAL LOBE.

frottage   A form of sexual disorder in which the individual persistently seeks sexual excitement and enjoyment by rubbing against other people. The term is derived from the French, meaning "rubbing," and the individual who displays this type of behavior is known as a *frotteur*. Such an individual may be fearful of engaging in a mature sexual relationship.

See also SEXUAL DYSFUNCTION.

frustration   Interference with impulses or desired actions by internal or external forces. For example, internal forces are inhibitions and mental conflicts, and external forces may be from parents, teachers and friends, as well as the rules of society. A mentally healthy person is usually able to cope with a good degree of frustration despite obstacles.

People who are repeatedly and constantly frustrated respond in many ways, some with anger, hostility, aggression or depression; others become withdrawn and passive. Some children and adults who are constantly frustrated show regressive behavior and may become unable to cope with problems on their own.

Modern life is filled with frustrations, from childhood through old age. Some children are frustrated by their parents' high expectations, and many parents are frustrated by their inability to provide material goods for their children. Many individuals are frustrated by lack of job opportunities, layoffs and lack of advancement on their jobs. Other individuals are frustrated in their marriages, while some single individuals feel frustrated by their lack of a partner. Many who are not satisfied in sexual relationships experience ongoing frustration. As people age, many become frustrated by their increasing inability to do things they did at earlier ages. Frustration sets in when retired individuals cannot function independently and must live with their children or in nursing homes.

fugue A psychiatric term for a state of altered consciousness that causes individuals to suddenly flee from home or work, forget their entire past and start a new life with a new name. After recovery, such individuals will recall their earlier lives but not events that occurred during the fugue. This state is also referred to as amnesia and may last hours or days. During a fugue of a few hours, individuals may show symptoms of agitation and confusion. During dissociative or fugue states, people "allow" themselves to behave in a manner that their normal consciousness and good judgment would not permit.

Among many possible causes of fugues are head injuries, epilepsy and dementia. In other cases, fugue states that become extended may be due to an unconscious wish to avoid unpleasant or threatening situations.

Treatment for fugue episodes (when the individuals are brought to treatment) may include hypnotic suggestions or use of amobarbital sodium. Such episodes have been the focus of plots for movies and novels, because the public seems fascinated by others' experiences of amnesia, perhaps out of a secret wish to escape from their own life situations.

See also AMNESIA; DISSOCIATIVE DISORDERS.

funding for mental health care Historically, expenditures for mental health care have been dominated by publicly financed state psychiatric hospitals. In the 1950s, 80 to 90 percent of expenditures for mental health illness were for care in this setting, and 80 to 90 percent of those expenditures were funded by state governments. In 1986, while the funding base had broadened for state psychiatric hospitals, they were still predominantly funded by the state and dominated most states' expenditures for mental illness.

While health insurance coverage grew to cover the majority of the U.S. population in the 1950s and 1960s, coverage for mental illness was restricted, emphasizing inpatient care in acute general hospital settings. Less coverage was available for outpatient care, and when such coverage was offered, it had more copayments and limits. In the 1980s, coverage for mental illness remained at a disadvantage relative to health insurance. Almost 30 percent of the U.S. population had no coverage for outpatient care of mental illness, and 20 percent had no coverage for inpatient care in 1986, compared with a much lower percentage of the population without coverage for medical illness.

Medicare and Medicaid, as introduced in the mid-1960s, incorporated the principles and coverage package typical of health insurance of the day. Medicare covered acute psychiatric inpatient care in general hospitals the same as medical conditions, but placed a 190-day lifetime limit on care in any public or private psychiatric hospitals. Outpatient coverage was severely restricted. Medicaid followed suit and provided care in general with no limit, but only on an optional basis for those under 22 and over 65 years of age in psychiatric hospitals. Minimal outpatient benefits were provided patients under Medicaid on a mandatory basis, while the major outpatient benefits were made optional. In 1983, almost 80 percent of Medicaid expenditures for mental illness were for nursing home and state psychiatric hospital care rather than outpatient care. Medicare expenditures also remained predominantly inpatient, with 82 percent devoted to inpatient care.

Total expenditures by mental health organizations increased from $3.3 billion in

1969 to $18.5 billion in 1986; per capita expenditures ranged from $16.53 1969 to $77.10 in 1986. Of the $19 billion in revenues generated by mental health organizations in 1986, 36 percent was from state mental health agencies; 26 percent from Medicare, Medicaid (including federal and state shares) and other federal sources; 21 percent from client fees; 8 percent from local sources; and 10 percent from all other sources.

Excluding general hospital psychiatric services, the distribution of funds was similar in 1983 and 1986. State mental health agency funds accounted for the overwhelming majority of total funds (42 percent in 1986, 41 percent in 1983). The major differences in the two years were in client fees, which constituted a larger proportion of total funds in 1986, and other federal funds, with a smaller proportion compared with 1983.

See also SOCIOECONOMIC TRENDS IN MENTAL HEALTH CARE.

National Institute of Mental Health, *Mental Health, United States, 1990*, Manderscheid, R. W., and Sonnenschein, M. A., eds. DHHS Pub. No. (ADM) 90-1708. Washington, D.C.: USGPO, 1990.

G

GABA   See GAMMA-AMINOBUTYRIC ACID.

GAD (generalized anxiety disorders) See ANXIETY DISORDERS.

galvanic skin response (GSR) Measurement of changes in resistance in the skin to emotional or psychological stimulation as measured by an electronic device. Electrical resistance is reduced by sweating activity induced by emotional arousal. As sweat glands are activated by activity, the GSR measures reflect changes in the sympathetic nervous system.

Skin responses are measured by pairing an imperceptibly small electrical current between two electrodes on the skin. Increases in conductance (lowered resistance) are considered reflective of increased autonomic (emotional) activity.

See also SYMPATHETIC NERVOUS SYSTEM.

gambling   Gambling is considered to be a compulsion or addiction when it becomes the only important thing in one's life and all of one's efforts are aimed toward obtaining money to gamble. Although gambling does not involve ingesting a substance, many of the characteristics of compulsive gambling are similar to alcoholism. The National Council on Compulsive Gambling and Gamblers Anonymous have estimated that there are 6 million compulsive gamblers in the United States. The typical compulsive gambler is a married man in his early to mid-thirties who is employed in a field that involves money and possibly high risk such as investment, business or law. Compulsive gamblers are usually outgoing, generous and gregarious but are prone to sudden negative mood swings. Even in serious stages of compulsive gambling, the addict will express concern about his health but not about his addiction. Gamblers Anonymous offers a recovery program similar to Alcoholics Anonymous. The Council on Compulsive Gambling offers a crisis intervention hot line for compulsive gamblers and their families.

The well-publicized problems of ex-baseball star Pete Rose in the late 1980s focused attention on the problem of compulsive gambling. A 1989 Gallup poll taken shortly after Rose's difficulties became public showed a somewhat ambivalent public attitude toward gambling. It revealed that while gambling activity—both legal and illegal—is on the upsurge and extremely popular and that public sentiment runs toward increasing legalized gambling, 61 percent of those surveyed said that they thought that legal gambling encouraged excessive gambling.

People gamble for many reasons. Some simply enjoy the sociability and atmosphere of events surrounding the activity. Some people begin gambling because it helps to relieve a stressful situation. The fascination with the game and the prospect of winning make certain individuals forget their problems. Others find the risk and unpredictability of the game exciting and stimulating. In addition to wanting the actual winnings, some derive a sense of power and importance from winning. They have a sense that when they win, people are watching and admiring them. Some may gamble out of rebellion, since gambling is thought to be sinful by some religious groups. Despite its sometimes seedy, underworld aspects, gambling may also appear to be glamorous to some people. Films frequently depict expensively dressed, sophisticated characters gambling in casinos in exotic locations.

Gambling may be experienced at different levels. The lowest level of consistent gambling is probably as part of participation in a club or other group. With an increasing number of states establishing lotteries, this has become the most common type of gambling. More serious gamblers tend to gamble or bet several times a week and to take vacations in resorts that offer gambling.

Young men are attracted to card games, racetrack wagering and sports betting. Older people, particularly women, patronize casinos. Professional gamblers and those with underworld connections who use illegal techniques make up only a small percentage of gamblers. Frequent gamblers and those who use gambling to relieve psychological stress are usually able to control their gambling by setting a dollar amount for themselves on occasions when they gamble.

For information, contact:

Gamblers Anonymous
3255 Wilshire Blvd., Suite 610
Los Angeles, CA 90010
Phone: (211) 386-8789

National Council on Problem Gambling
John Jay College of Criminal Justice
445 W. 59th St.
New York, NY 10019
Phone: (212) 765-3833

Custer, Robert, and Milt, Harry. *When Luck Runs Out*. New York: Facts On File, 1985.
Hugick, Larry. "Gambling on the Rise; Lotteries Lead the Way." *Gallup Poll* (June 1989).

gamma-aminobutyric acid (GABA) A neurotransmitter in the brain that tends to result in an inhibition of the release of activating neurotransmitters, such as norepinephrine. Some medications bind to the GABA receptors; these include alprazolam, a benzodiazepine (popularly known as Xanax). (A drug "binds" to chemical receptors that are shaped to receive and use it rather than other chemicals.) When taken in therapeutic doses, both diazepam and alprazolam change the shape of the receptor molecule (GABA) they share. Chemical interactions between alprazolam and the diazepam receptor alter metabolism of GABA, which in turn produces a change in cell biochemistry. As this occurs, anxiety is reduced.

See also ALPRAZOLAM; ANXIETY; BENZO-DIAZEPINE MEDICATIONS; NEUROTRANSMIT-TERS; PANIC DISORDER; PHARMACOLOGIC THERAPY in BIBLIOGRAPHY.

Ganser's syndrome   See DISSOCIATIVE DISORDERS.

gay   A word that in the latter part of the 20th century refers to male or female homosexuals, but more often to males. Female homosexuals are known as lesbians.

See also GAY LIBERATION; HOMOSEXUAL-ITY; LESBIANISM; SEXUALITY.

gay liberation   A social movement during the mid-20th century in which homosexuals asserted their rights to their individual sexual orientations, sought recognition of their behavior as normal and encouraged reduction of societal prejudices. Many gay organizations were formed to promote homosexual causes and interests.

See also HOMOSEXUALITY; LESBIANISM.

gender dysphoria Unhappiness with one's gender role. In extreme cases gender dysphoria may lead an individual to seek a sex change operation. Some psychoanalysts attribute gender dysphoria in girls to maternal deprivation, claiming girls deprived of a maternal bond develop a competitive relationship with the father and then become dissatisfied with their own gender role.

See also GENDER IDENTITY; GENDER ROLE.

gender identity An individual's inner feeling of "maleness" or "femaleness," as well as an acceptance and awareness of one's biologic makeup. Gender identity problems occur when one has persistent feelings of discomfort about his or her sexuality. Transsexualism is the most common example of this problem. When one has internal conflicts regarding gender identity and does not accept his or her biologic designation, anxieties may develop, leading the individual into practices such as "cross dressing" and adopting the role of the other sex.

Gender identity is fixed within the first two to three years of life and is reinforced during puberty. Once established, it usually cannot be changed.

Gender identity disorder is a type of psychosexual disorder in which an individual's gender identity is incongruent with his or her anatomical sex. Many individuals who believe that they are men or women in the body of the other sex experience anxieties, and some individuals have surgical sex change operations.

See also SEXUAL FEARS; GENDER IDENTITY in BIBLIOGRAPHY.

gender role Attitudes and behaviors that are culturally and socially associated with maleness or femaleness, which are expressed to varying degrees by individuals. For example, in Western cultures, the gender role for many women was historically passive and submissive, until the "women's liberation" movement and "sexual revolution" during the latter half of the 20th century. Along with many societal changes, gender roles have also changed significantly. An example is child care, which is no longer exclusively the woman's role, and earning the larger part of the family income is no longer exclusively the man's role. However, changes in gender roles have led to many contemporary mental health problems, such as women's conflicts between motherhood and career and men's fears of inferiority when wives advance more rapidly in their career than they do in theirs.

gene The part of the chromosome containing a code for a specific functional molecule of an organism.

generalized anxiety disorders (GAD) See ANXIETY DISORDERS.

generic drug A prescription drug sold under its chemical (generic) name rather than under a patented trade name. Names for generic drugs are chosen and approved by government agencies.

See also ETHICAL DRUGS.

genetic counseling Advising a family about the risk of occurrence of mental retardation or other inherited conditions and the problems that may arise from their occurrence. Genetic counseling requires considerable training and sensitivity. It is often preferable for a mental health professional to refer appropriate couples to specialized centers for this purpose.

In many cases, the need for counseling is recognized by a pediatrician, an obstetrician or another primary care physician after the delivery of a defective child. Such an urgent and unexpected situation may arouse feelings of guilt, anxiety or anger in both parents and physician. While counseling before pregnancy is preferred, and many advances in antenatal diagnosis are aimed at early detection, occasional unanticipated genetic defects appear after delivery. Unfortunately, some of these (e.g., Huntington's disease) cannot be recognized until middle age.

Identification of high-risk couples is one method of prevention of birth defects and mental retardation. Concerned potential parents can be advised of the medical facts regarding the severity and prognosis of the genetic disorder, the risk of its recurrence if they already have a retarded child and options available for managing the affected child and for avoiding recurrence.

Individuals interested in receiving professional advice now have numerous resources. The number of genetic counseling centers has increased rapidly in recent years; there are now more than 200 major university-based centers with many satellites.

The March of Dimes Foundation directs its efforts toward prevention of birth defects and improving the outcome of pregnancies. This organization also publishes an international directory of resources relevant to genetic disorders and can refer parents to appropriate genetic clinics.

See also MENTAL RETARDATION; GENETICS in BIBLIOGRAPHY.

Grossman, Herbert J., ed. *AMA Handbook on Mental Retardation.* Chicago: American Medical Association, 1987.

genetic disorders   Disorders caused totally or partially by faults in inherited genes and chromosomes of an individual's cells. Some genetic disorders, known as congenital, are present at birth. However, many genetic defects do not become apparent until many years later, and many congenital abnormalities are not genetically caused. Most

Indications for Genetic Counseling

Family history of an inherited disorder
Genetic or congenital anomaly in a family member
Parent who is a known carrier of a chromosomal translocation
Woman who has previously given birth to a child(children) with chromosomal aberrations
Parent who is a known carrier of an autosomal recessive disorder in which in utero diagnosis is possible
Abnormal somatic or behavioral development in a previous child
Mental retardation of unknown etiology in a previous child
Pregnancy in a woman over age 35
Specific ethnic background that may suggest a high rate of genetic abnormality (e.g., Tay-Sachs disease)
Three or more spontaneous abortions and/or early infant deaths
Infertility

genetic disorders are familial, which means that one has one or more relatives affected by the same disorder. However, there are times when a child is born with a genetic disorder and no family history of a disorder.

There are three general categories of genetic disorders: chromosome abnormalities, unifactorial defects and multifactorial disorders.

Chromosome Abnormalities   When a child is born with an abnormal number of whole chromosomes, or extra or missing bits of chromosomes in the cells, this can lead to multiple disturbances and disorders. Down's syndrome and Klinefelter syndrome, forms of mental retardation, are in this category.

Unifactorial Defects   Unifactorial disorders are caused by a single defective gene or pair of genes. These disorders are distributed among members of an affected family according to simple laws of inheritance.

Multifactorial Disorders   These are caused by the additive effects of several genes, along with environmental factors. The pattern of inheritance is less straightforward. Many disorders fall into this category, including asthma, insulin-dependent diabetes and some conditions present at birth, such as cleft lip and palate, schizophrenia and manic-depressive (bipolar) disorder. According to a study reported in the early 1980s, the risk for full siblings of a schizophrenic person to develop schizophrenia is 7 to 8 percent, the children of one schizophrenic parent have a 9 to 12 percent risk and the children of two schizophrenic parents have a 35 to 45 percent risk.

In recent years, studies have revealed a possible link between genetic makeup and alcoholism. Scientists also suspect that genetic factors may underlie personality types and particularly disorders such as manic-depression. Genetic disorders are only a partial explanation, however; as with other mental health disorders, environment may also influence the expression of these conditions. Genetic defects in hearing and vision may lead to a misdiagnosis of mental retardation, and children born with Marfan's syndrome (a genetic disorder with symptoms including a gangly, uncoordinated look) may develop depression because they feel "different" than their peers.

See also ALCOHOLISM; DEPRESSION; GENETIC COUNSELING; GENETICS in BIBLIOGRAPHY.

genital stage In Freudian theory, the final or mature stage of psychosexual development. The genital stage or phase follows the oral and anal stages and occurs during adolescence, when sexual interest focuses on a relationship with another. When appropriate transitions from other developmental stages did not occur, one may have difficulty adjusting to sexual relationships and/or marriage.

See also FREUD, SIGMUND.

geriatric depression The most common mental health disorder among the elderly. According to the National Institute of Mental Health (NIMH), estimates of depression among elderly people ranges from 10 to 65 percent. Other estimates and epidemiologic studies report that 20 percent of geriatric outpatients are clinically depressed and that up to 75 percent of nursing home patients have some type of mental health disorder. Depression in the elderly takes on much the same form as it does in younger people. For example, the depressed person will have a pervasive feeling of hopelessness and helplessness with regard to improving his or her outlook, not show interest in previously enjoyed activities, may experience insomnia and may become easily distracted and bored.

See also AGING; DEPRESSION; ELDERLY PARENTS; GERIATRIC DEPRESSION RATING SCALE; DEPRESSION AND AFFECTIVE DISORDERS, ELDERLY in BIBLIOGRAPHY.

Geriatric Depression Rating Scale (GDRS) A specific screening device to measure depression in the elderly. The GDRS is a 30-item tool with a simple yes/no format that takes only about five to 10 minutes. It has well-established reliability and validity when used with the elderly. The GDRS differs from the Hamilton Depression Inventory (HAM-D) in that it does not have physical symptoms included on the Ham-D.

See also AGING; DEPRESSION; ELDERLY PARENTS; GERIATRIC DEPRESSION ANXIETY SCALE.

Yesavage, J. A.; Brink, T. L.; Rose, L.; and Adey, M. "The Geriatric Depression Rating Scale: Comparison with Other Self-Report and Psychiatric Rating Scales," in Crook, T.; Ferris, S.; and Bartus, R., eds. *Assessment in Geriatric Psychopharmacology.* New Canaan, Conn.: Mark Powley and Associates, 1983.

geropsychiatry A specialized form of mental health care that addresses the complexities involved between mental and physical illness in the elderly. For example, an elderly patient who might appear to have psychotic symptoms may be experiencing symptoms of toxicity resulting from taking two or more incompatible drugs. Many psychosomatic disorders and chronic conditions manifest themselves with symptoms of depression.

Many physicians specializing in geropsychiatry are located in community hospitals where they can provide a safe and secure environment and offer psychological evaluation in conjunction with medical testing and liaison services for elderly patients being treated for medical or surgical conditions.

An increasing number of hospitals are adding this component to their mental health programs. Some hospitals contract with various organizations who provide these services on a contract basis.

See also AGING; DEPRESSION; ELDERLY PARENTS; GERIATRIC DEPRESSION.

gestalt psychology   A type of therapy based on the concept that the whole is more important than the sum of its parts, or that "wholeness" is more important than individual components of behavior and perception. It aims to increase self-awareness by looking at all aspects of an individual within his or her environment. It achieved a good degree of popularity as a means of coping with personal problems and is still practiced by some therapists.

The movement toward this type of psychology was founded in Germany in the early 1900s by a group that adopted the name *gestalt,* meaning "form, pattern, or configuration."

See also PSYCHOTHERAPY.

Gilles de la Tourette syndrome   See TOURETTE SYNDROME.

glass ceiling   An impenetrable but almost invisible barrier perceived by working women that they believe keeps many of them from rising to the top of their field despite their good qualifications, experience and hard work. This frustration leads to anxiety, depression and less than optimal mental health.

Estimates of women in top management positions in the mid-1980s range from 2 to 4 percent despite the fact that college enrollment is more than 50 percent women and women make up about one-quarter of the enrollment in master of business administration (MBA) programs.

The glass ceiling may take many forms. Qualified women already in the organization may be passed over as men are brought into high-level positions in the organization from the outside for the sake of providing a fresh outlook and new blood. In organizations involving teamwork and negotiations, discussions may be held in such a way that women are kept on the periphery. Teasing and harassment of women may discourage them and make it difficult for some of them to perform. Women who have a "mannish" style may be hired over women who are more feminine and then thought to be strange and unacceptable because they have masculine characteristics. Women in lower-level positions are sometimes given responsible, demanding work that is reflected in neither their title nor salary. As women attempt to progress in an organization, they may be frustrated by performance standards that are higher for them than for men. Women may also be limited by assumptions that there is a feminine management style that is more passive and nurturing toward fellow workers and less goal-oriented and driven than the masculine style.

Women who do make it past the glass ceiling frequently credit the influence of a mentor, spouse or parent. Some women have decided to avoid the glass ceiling by striking out on their own. In the late 1980s, the number of self-employed women was growing faster than that of men.

See also MENTOR; WOMEN'S LIBERATION MOVEMENT.

Mills, D. Quinn. *Not Like Our Parents: How the Baby Boom Generation Is Changing America.* New York: William Morrow, 1987.

"granny dumping"   The term applied to the elderly and often confused Americans who are being abandoned on hospital emergency room doorsteps. According to a report in the *Bulletin* of the American Association of Retired Persons (AARP) (Sept. 1991), anecdotal reports indicate that the number of abandoned elderly is increasing. As of the end of 1991, congressional committees were looking into the problem. Many caregivers feel overwhelmed and unable to continue. According to AARP legislative director John Rother, this is a symptom of the inadequacies of the long-term care policies in the United States. Emergency room physicians say families are so stressed in part because Medicare does not pay for custodial nursing home care or at-home long-term care, because little respite care is available and because families in crisis are often unaware of community resources.

See also AGING; RETIREMENT; AGING in BIBLIOGRAPHY.

" 'Granny Dumping': New Pain for U.S. Elders." *Bulletin,* American Association of Retired Persons, vol. 32, no. 8 (Sept. 1991).

grief   An intensely painful emotional reaction caused by the loss of a loved one. Although the expression of grief is unique to each individual, there are recognized stages of grief (bereavement) that have some common characteristics for most people.

At first there may be numbness and an unwillingness to recognize the death (denial). These are defense mechanisms that help the individual cope with the pain of the loss. Numbness is a pervasive feeling that enables the mourner to get through the experience of the funeral and the first few days following the death of the loved one; this may last from a few days to a few months. Hallucinations are also common among the recently bereaved; in some cases, they believe they see the deceased person walk into the room. In the case of a deceased infant or child, the parent may think they see the child in their crib or bed or hear his or her cry or voice.

When the initial feeling of numbness wears off, the individual may feel anger, despair and overwhelmed by the circumstances; these feelings can lead to depression. Many people feel angry that the deceased person deserted them; these are natural feelings that will pass in time. Other physical symptoms are fairly common; some have headaches, and others have insomnia or gastrointestinal complaints. Attempted suicide is an abnormal expression of grief but is not uncommon. There may be an increase in alcohol intake at this time.

The individual may experience intense feelings of helplessness. One may think, "Could I have prevented this from happening? Why wasn't I powerful enough to do something more?" Such thoughts are part of the human condition. People like to feel that they are in control at all times. Death often leaves those behind feeling helpless.

Many people who have experienced loss say that within two years a bereaved person adjusts to the loss and gets on with his or her life. However, overwhelming feelings of loss do recur, and such moods continue to alternate with those of enthusiasm. In the long run, a positive attitude should overcome the depressed feelings.

How well an individual adjusts after a period of grief depends to some degree on his or her immediate support system. If friends and family are nearby, it may accelerate the recovery process. Widowed persons with no relatives and few friends seem to have the most difficult time adjusting to their losses. Some parents who have lost an infant try to have another baby within a few years; however, the feeling of loss of the first one never really goes away.

Anniversaries of birthdays, weddings and other events come up every year. Individuals who have suffered a loss should recognize and accept that they will feel sad at certain times. What one does to observe treasured memories is a very individual matter, depending on one's tradition. With time, each person learns to do what feels right. Remembering a loved one with joy, instead of sorrow, is an honor to his or her life.

For individuals who continue to suffer in their grief reaction without relief or help from other sources of support, mental health counseling may help. Getting help when one needs it is sign of strength and wisdom. Appropriate referrals for mental health care can be made by a social worker or physician. Support groups for widows and widowers help many people. Knowing that others had the same emotional reactions may help one cope better with getting on with one's life. Those grieving for the loss of a child may also find help in appropriate support groups.

Many organizations offer telephone information and referral services that also suggest sources of help. Crisis telephone lines and centers and hospital emergency rooms are sometimes a fast way of getting help; these numbers should be listed in a special section of local telephone books.

For information on obtaining brochures on grief, contact:

Mental Health Association of Greater
  Chicago
104 South Michigan Avenue
Chicago, IL 60603-5901
Phone: (312) 781-7780

Other resources:

Afterloss (monthly newsletter)
P.O. Box 2545
Rancho Mirage, CA 92270
Phone: (800) 423-8811

Pregnancy and Infant Loss Center
1415 Wayzata Blvd., Suite 105
Wayzata, MN 55391
Phone: (612) 473-9372

Parents of Murdered Children
100 E. Eighth St., Suite B41
Cincinnati, OH 45202
Phone: (513) 721-LOVE

Elisabeth Kubler-Ross Center (workshops, regional groups)

So. Rte. 616
Head Waters, VA 24442
Phone: (703) 396-3441

Theos (groups in the United States and
  Canada for widowed people)
1301 Clark Bldg.
717 Liberty Ave
Pittsburgh, PA 15222
Phone: (412) 471-7779

See also BEREAVEMENT; DEATH; DEPRESSION; INSOMNIA; STILLBIRTH; STRESS; SUDDEN INFANT DEATH SYNDROME.

Kahn, Ada P. "Living with the Death of a Loved One" (brochure). Mental Health Association of Greater Chicago, Chicago, 1989.
Kubler-Ross, E. *On Death and Dying*. New York: Macmillan, 1971.
Ramsay, R. W., and Noorbergen, R. *Living with Loss*. New York: William Morrow, 1981.

See also OEDIPUS COMPLEX.

group residential treatment centers
See HALFWAY HOUSE.

group therapy   A term applying to a wide range of types of therapies and groups. They may be self-help support groups, without a trained professional leader, or they may be led by a mental health professional.

A group organized for group therapy attracts individuals with similar concerns. For example, such groups may be for recently widowed persons (grief), for parents who have lost a child to sudden infant death syndrome, for individuals who are suffering from depression or for those wishing to lose weight. Within the group, individuals find that others share their feelings and experiences; this helps them feel less alone and less helpless. Problems in interpersonal relationships are sometimes benefited by a group therapy experience. Individuals may re-create typical problems in their relationships in the therapy group.

See also PSYCHOTHERAPY; SUPPORT GROUPS.

GSR   See GALVANIC SKIN RESPONSE.

guardianship   Legal appointment of another person to make decisions for one who is not able or not legally competent to do so. An individual is considered legally competent if he or she possesses the requisite natural or legal qualifications, is capable and is legally fit according to appropriate statutes. However, a mentally ill individual may not necessarily need a guardian, as not all mental illnesses interfere with an individual's decision-making ability.

For all medical and psychiatric procedures, informed consent must be given. If the individual cannot be educated appropriately to give informed consent, a court will appoint a guardian. Substituted consent is the authorization that is given by a court-appointed guardian on behalf of the incompetent individual.

See also INFORMED CONSENT; LEGAL ISSUES.

McFarland, Gertrude K., and Thomas, Mary Durand. *Psychiatric Mental Health Nursing.* Philadelphia: J. B. Lippincott, 1991.

guilt   An emotional response to a perceived or actual failure to meet expectations of self or others. Guilt feelings can be destructive if carried to an extreme. They can be devastating to one's self-esteem and feeling of capability. However, they can also be constructive when the individual begins to understand his or her sources of guilt and learns to cope with this aspect of the human condition.

People experience feelings of guilt throughout life. For example, a young child may be aware of not pleasing his parents with certain behaviors. Later, the individual may experience guilt feelings for not remembering the birthday of a parent or spouse. Depending on differences in conscience, some individuals can steal or commit crimes against others and society and not feel any guilt, while others will suffer from guilt feelings over minor matters. Middle-aged adults experience guilt feeling when dealing with aging parents. Those who find it necessary to admit a parent to a nursing home for care often suffer guilt feelings; in these cases, guilt feelings are often related to previous relationships. Individuals who are in bereavement over a loved one often feel some guilt about not having done enough for the person when he or she was alive. Some parents of infants who die of sudden infant death syndrome have feelings of guilt over not having been able to prevent the death of their child. Such feelings are unfounded but can be troublesome to the sufferer. Mental health counseling can help relieve many of these uncomfortable feelings of guilt.

Some people feel a sense of guilt over certain circumstances because of their religious upbringing. Talking with a member of the clergy or mental health professional may be helpful. Otherwise, parents or spouses of a person who commits suicide, for example, may struggle with guilt feelings for many years, wondering if they could have prevented the death.

There are also legal implications to the concept of guilt, according to cultural mores and statutes.

See also DEPRESSION; GUILTY BUT MENTALLY ILL VERDICT.

guilty but mentally ill verdict   Some states have a plea "guilty but mentally ill"; it is recognized in about one-third of the states and is still the subject of constitutional controversy. The disposition of a case in which there is a "guilty but mentally ill verdict" usually results in treatment of mentally ill individuals in a correctional setting instead of putting them in prison.

See also LEGAL ISSUES.

H

Haldol   See HALOPERIDOL.

half-life   See SYNERGY.

halfway house A facility that provides temporary living quarters and assistance in daily living to people who require some degree of professional supervision away from home. The halfway house can help the patient make the transition from the hospital to the community. Some individuals who have been hospitalized for a mental health disorder live in halfway houses for periods of time.

hallucination A perception without a stimulus. Hallucinations may include seeing, hearing, smelling, tasting or feeling something that is not there. Hallucinations occur in some severe mental disorders, such as schizophrenia; they can also occur during high fever or serious illness or as a reaction to some medications.

See also HALLUCINOGENS; SCHIZOPHRENIA.

hallucinogens Drugs and agents that produce profound distortions to the senses, sight, sound, smell and touch, as well as sense of direction, time and distance. Hallucinogens do not have an accepted medical use.

Hallucinogens occur naturally but are primarily created synthetically. The most common hallucinogens are LSD (d-lysergic acid diethylamide, lysergide, LSD-25), mescaline, peyote, psilocybin mushrooms, 3,4-methylenedioxymethamphetamine) and phencyclidine PCP.

The high associated with hallucinogens usually lasts about eight hours; acute anxiety, restlessness and sleeplessness are common effects. Long after the hallucinogen is eliminated from the body, the user may experience "flashbacks," which are fragmentary recurrences of effects.

See also SUBSTANCE ABUSE; HALLUCINATION.

Media Resource Guide on Common Drugs of Abuse. Public Relations Society of America, National Capital Chapter, Fairfax, Va., September 1990.

haloperidol A drug (trade name: Haldol) used primarily to treat schizophrenia and other psychoses. It is also used in schizoaffective disorder and Tourette syndrome and occasionally as adjunctive therapy in mental retardation and the chorea of Huntington's disease. It is a potent antiemetic and is effective in the treatment of intractable hiccups.

Haloperidol can cause significant side effects and toxic effects such as neuroleptic malignant syndrome and tardive dyskinesia.

See also SCHIZOPHRENIA.

hashish A refined form of cannabis (marijuana) that is found in brown or black sheets, "cakes" or "balls." Hashish (or "hash") generally comes from the Middle East, is more potent than marijuana and is smoked in a pipe. The active ingredient is delta-9-tetrahydrocannabinol, which is metabolized in the liver to a related substance that produces intoxicating effects. Hashish oil is extracted from cannabis plant materials to produce a dark, viscous liquid that averages around 20 percent THC.

See also SUBSTANCE ABUSE; MARIJUANA.

Media Resource Guide on Common Drugs of Abuse. Public Relations Society of America, National Capital Chapter, Fairfax, Va., September 1990.

"having it all" An expression that became popular during the 1980s when career women discovered that they could follow their chosen business or profession, get married and raise a family. For many this has become a satisfying way of life, but for others it has involved many frustrations, anxieties and, in some cases, feelings of guilt. Some women feel that they are not giving adequate attention to the marriage and children, are constantly tired and feel some guilt over having their children in day-care centers. Nevertheless, an increasing number of women opt to enter business and professions. Those who are most successful say it is because of the helpfulness and understanding of their spouse.

See also MARRIAGE; WOMEN'S LIBERATION MOVEMENT.

headaches One of the most frequent complaints that people make during visits to mental health care professionals as well as other physicians. Most people have had a headache at some time. Headaches are fairly normal reactions to certain situations, such as overindulgence in alcohol, extreme fatigue and certain infections. Headaches are fairly common in depression, sleep disorders and in individuals who have many anxieties and in those suffering from boredom. Other headaches may be indicative of a more serious underlying disease.

Headaches cannot be seen by others and are sometimes used by malingerers to avoid responsibilities and family activities. However, headaches are a serious mental as well as physical concern. Estimates are that more than 45 million Americans develop headaches each year that are serious enough to warrant treatment by a physician; approximately 16 million to 18 million of them suffer from migraine headaches. More than 64 million workdays are lost as a result of headache pain. Thus there is a high cost of headaches to society in terms of medical bills, lower productivity and absenteeism.

In a study reported during 1990, of 35 women and five men who sought treatment for headaches, two-thirds of them scored at least "mildly depressed" on one psychological test. Of those who reported daily headaches, 74 percent were depressed. While headache patients have long reported depression, many researchers thought the chronic pain was caused by patients' low moods. However, the 1990 study strongly suggested that headaches may be the major symptom of an underlying disorder. It is also possible that chemical changes in the hormonal system might cause both headaches and depression.

Causes of Headaches While causes of headaches are not well understood, some suspected causes include poor posture, irregular meals, too much alcohol consumption, heredity, anxiety, stress, sleeplessness, environmental pollutants (including cigarette smoke), food additives, illness, toothache and earache. More than three-fourths of migraine sufferers come from families in which other members have the same disorder.

According to the late Harold G. Wolff, M.D., Professor of Neurology, Cornell, New York Hospital, one or more of six basic causes of headache may be applicable to individual cases. They are:

1. traction on the veins that pass to the venous sinuses from the surface of the brain and displacement of the great venous sinuses;
2. traction on the middle meningeal arteries;
3. traction on the arteries at the base of the brain and their main branches;
4. distention and dilation of intracranial arteries;
5. inflammation in or about any of the pain-sensitive structures of the head; and
6. direct pressure on the cranial and cervical nerves that contain pain-afferent fibers from the head.

For many individuals, certain foods (such as cheese, chocolate and red wine) containing a substance known as tyramine trigger migraine attacks. Another food additive that may cause headache sufferers a problem is sodium nitrite, a preservative used in ham, hot dogs and many other sausages. Monosodium glutamate (MSG) is a natural salt used in Chinese and Japanese food; it has also been known to cause headaches in those susceptible. Although some migraine researchers have recommended that all migraine sufferers avoid these foods, only about 30 percent of people who have migraine headaches experience this reaction because of consuming them.

Headaches are caused by brain tumors, high blood pressure, inflammation of the arteries of the brain and scalp (temporal arteritis), localized swelling of a blood vessel (aneurysm) and increased pressure within the skull in rare cases.

Some headaches have biologic causes. Migraine headaches, in particular, may begin by the way the arteries leading to the brain react to triggering factors. Arteries become narrowed and then swollen; this change in the caliber of the arteries may produce pain. Narrowing of the arteries also reduces the blood supply to parts of the brain, which may also explain some of the other symptoms of migraine, such as disturbed vision.

Some migraines may be caused or worsened by hormones. Although migraine headaches are more common in young boys than in young girls, the number of girls affected increases sharply after the onset of menstruation. Certain hormonal changes that occur during puberty in girls and remain throughout adulthood may be implicated in the triggering and frequency of migraine attacks in women.

The notion of a link between female endocrine changes and migraine headaches is reinforced by the finding that 60 percent of women sufferers involved in a clinical study related attacks to their menstrual cycle. Differences among individuals exist: attacks may occur several days before, during or immediately after the woman's menses; women may get the headache at the time of ovulation or at the time between ovulation and menstruation.

The treatment of choice is the nonsteroidal, anti-inflammatory agents, which are medications used to treat arthritis and pain but also work selectively well with migraines that are related to hormonal fluctuations. Other methods of treatment can be the use of small dosages of the beta adrenergic blocking agents or ergotamine tartrate given specifically around the menstrual time. If one is unresponsive to intermittent therapy, certain daily preventative treatment may be necessary.

One or more genetic factors may be involved in an individual's susceptibility to migraine, as some women seem predisposed to it. Compared with normal individuals, the blood vessels of migrainous patients are less sensitive to the effect of cooling and their platelet membranes retain serotonin less efficiently. This observation is significant because it substantiates a current theory that a migraine headache may be triggered by a rapid drop in blood serotonin.

Migraine is also influenced by pregnancy. In female patients with migraine, about 77 percent find their attacks disappear completely, occur less often or are milder during pregnancy. Attacks either worsen or remain unchanged in others.

Oral contraceptives also affect the incidence of migraine attacks. Some migraine sufferers find their attacks are worsened while they are on the Pill. Others find that they are not affected, and a small percentage report improvement. Yet even some women without any predisposition to migraine develop it while on the Pill, and nearly three-quarters find their headaches disappearing after stopping the Pill. In addition, women using estrogen replacement therapy after hysterectomy or menopause developed frequent migraine headaches, and reduction or discontinuation of estrogen therapy improved the headaches in 58 percent of these cases.

Women with migraine are usually advised not to take oral contraceptives or other female hormone preparations. The restriction becomes even more emphatic if the migraine is of the complicated type, for these may give rise to stroke or a strokelike condition if the hormone is continued. Hormone replacement therapy used postmenopausally for migraine sufferers should be given at the lowest possible dosage and, unless medically contraindicated, on a daily uninterrupted basis.

Link with Limbic System Dysfunction
According to Alan R. Hirsch, M.D., director of Chicago's Smell and Taste Treatment and

Research Foundation, a study reported that 18 percent of migraine sufferers have a decreased ability to smell certain odors, a known sign of limbic system dysfunction. The olfactory loss seen among migraine sufferers is further evidence of limbic system involvement in migraine. According to Dr. Hirsch, knowing this may improve scientists' ability to diagnose, treat and ultimately prevent migraines.

Link with Sexual Activity   Some headache sufferers report discomfort before, during or after sexual intercourse. Their headaches may then become involved in a cycle of stress and anxiety. Headaches related to sexual activity may be muscle contraction (tension) headaches and benign orgasmic headaches. Muscle contraction headaches cause dull, aching pains on both sides of the head and are relatively short in duration. More men than women experience these, possibly because many couples use positions during intercourse in which the man takes a more active role, often above his partner, with his head and neck unsupported.

Rises in blood pressure during sexual arousal and orgasm may lead to benign orgasmic headaches; these are intense headaches of short duration and usually occur in people who also have occasional migraine headaches.

Diagnosing Headaches   When a headache does not respond to rest, sleeping or simple self-medication (aspirin, nonsteroidal anti-inflammatory drugs available over the counter, cold compresses on the head, relaxation in a dark room), medical assistance should be sought. During a complete physical and neurological examination, the physician will ask about the history of the headaches, for what period of time they have been occurring, when they occur, the circumstances at the time and how long they last. Diagnostic techniques may include use of computerized axial tomography scanning (CAT scanning) or magnetic resonance imaging (MRI) to determine if there is any physiological reason for the headaches.

Headaches can be divided into general categories: tension/migraine headaches and cluster headaches.

Migraine and Tension Headaches   Also known as vascular headaches, these may occur because blood vessels in the scalp expand and contract to produce a throbbing pain. Tension headaches are the most common type of headache, often characterized by pain around the entire head. According to Thomas Bosley, M.D., Chair, Department of Neurology, Pennsylvania Hospital, Philadelphia, the difference between migraine and tension headaches is mainly a matter of degree. Migraine symptoms can include severe pain, nausea, dizziness and visual impairment. Attacks may last for several hours, a day or even longer.

Men and women between the ages of 35 and 45 years of age suffer most from migraine headaches, according to a study reported in the *Journal of the American Medical Association* (Dec. 31, 1991). In a mail survey of 20,468 people in the United States, it was also found that migraine prevalence was strongly associated with household income. Study respondents were between the ages of 12 and 80. "Prevalence in the lowest income group (under $12,000) was more than 60 percent higher than in the two highest income groups (over $30,000)," reported Walter Stewart, Ph.D., and colleagues at the Department of Epidemiology, The Johns Hopkins School of Hygiene and Public Health, Baltimore.

The researchers speculated that this may be due to diet, stress and other factors associated with low income, which may precipitate migraine attacks. Alternatively, they said, access to good health care may decrease the duration of the illness and therefore the prevalence among higher-income groups. In some individuals, migraine may cause low income, as headache-related disability may seriously disrupt function at work or school.

The researchers reported that according to their study, 8.7 million females and 2.6 million males suffer from migraine headache with moderate to severe disability. Of these, 3.4 million females and 1.1 million males experience one or more attacks per month. Females between the ages of 30 and 49 from lower-income households are at especially high risk of having migraines and are more likely than other groups to use emergency care services for their acute condition. Study results found that 17.6 percent of females and 5.7 percent of males were found to have one or more migraine headaches per year.

Some individuals experience migraine pain just on one side of the head. For others, it may shift from side to side or ache on both sides. Migraine headaches usually recur; sufferers become anxious because they know that attacks occur with unpredictability and are concerned that an attack will happen at an unfortuitous time, such as on the day of a graduation, wedding or other important appointment.

Migraine headaches often begin during times filled with anxieties, such as during adolescence or menopause, or around the time of a divorce or death of a mate. When a physician diagnoses headaches, anxieties in the individual's life and coping styles will be considered.

Migraine headaches result from distension and dilation of blood vessels of the scalp. Some individuals who have migraines report nausea and vomiting during a migraine attack. Generally, an attack begins with a warning, known as an aura. This may include some kind of visual disturbance, such as blurring or wavy lines resembling heat waves, or a hearing disturbance. This disturbance may persist for 10 to 15 minutes. Sometimes hands, face, arms or legs feel numb or may twitch; there may be extreme sensitivity to light and sound. When the headache pain begins, sudden movement of the head, vomiting, sneezing or coughing may aggravate it; there may be chills or sweating. Sleep usually provides relief, and many migraine sufferers become sleepy during an attack and go to sleep. The entire attack, including the warning period, pain and sleep, may last from several hours to several days.

Migraine headaches, which often occur in members of the same family, may result from a predisposing genetic biochemical abnormality. Moreover, personality traits may play a role in determining who gets migraine headaches. Although there is no typical personality associated with migraines, some migraine sufferers have characteristics of compulsivity and perfection.

Emotional tension and stress may lead to migraine attacks, because under extreme stress, the arteries of the head and those reaching the brain draw tightly together and restrict the flow of blood. This in turn may result in a shortage of oxygen to the brain. When blood vessels dilate or stretch, a greater amount of blood passes through, putting more pressure on the pain-sensitive nerves in and close to the walls of the arteries.

Cluster Headaches The term "cluster headaches" refers to the characteristic grouping of attacks. The headaches occur in groups or clusters, and the cause is unknown. Cluster is one of the least common types of headache. It is vascular in nature and is caused by swelling of the blood vessels of the head. Although rare, it is possible for someone with a cluster headache to also suffer from migraine headache. The pain of cluster headache is generally very intense and severe and is often described as having a burning or piercing quality. It may be throbbing or constant. The scalp may be tender, and the arteries often can be felt increasing their pulsation. The pain is so intense that most sufferers cannot sit still and will often pace during an acute attack. Cluster headaches generally reach their full force within five or 10 minutes after onset. The attacks are usually very similar, varying only slightly from one attack to another.

Although the pain of a cluster headache starts suddenly, a minimal type of warning of the oncoming headache may occur, including a feeling of discomfort or a mild one-sided burning sensation. The pain is of short duration, generally 30 to 45 minutes. It may, however, last anywhere from a few minutes to several hours. The headache will disappear only to recur later that day. Most sufferers get one to four headaches per day during a cluster period. They occur very regularly, generally at the same time each day, and have been called "alarm clock headaches." Cluster headaches often awaken the sufferer in the early morning or during the night. Periods of headaches can last weeks or months and then disappear completely for months or years. The cluster headache sufferer has considerable amounts of pain-free intervals between series. The cluster headache often occurs in the spring or autumn. Because of their seasonal nature, cluster headaches are often mistakenly associated with allergies or business stress. In about 20 percent of cluster sufferers, attacks may be chronic. They are present throughout the year and do not occur in groups, thus making the control of headaches more difficult.

In a cluster headache, the pain is almost always one-sided, and during a series, the pain remains on the same side. When a new series starts, it can occur on the opposite side. The pain is localized behind the eye or in the eye region. It may radiate to the forehead, temple, nose, cheek or upper gum on the affected side. The affected eye may become swollen or droop. The pupil of the eye may contract, and the nostril on the affected side of the headache is often congested. Excessive sweating may also occur, and the face may become flushed on the affected side. Cluster headaches are not associated with the gastrointestinal disturbances or sensitivity to light that are found in other vascular headaches, such as migraine.

In many patients, minimal amounts of alcohol can bring on attacks. Other substances that cause blood vessel swelling, such as nitroglycerin or histamine, can also provoke an acute attack during a series. Smoking can also increase the severity of cluster headaches during a cluster period. During these series, the sufferer's blood vessels seem to change and become susceptible to the action of these substances. The blood vessels are not sensitive to these substances during headache-free periods. Hormonal influences (see above) in women do not appear to be a factor in cluster headaches.

Tension headaches are often associated with contraction of the head and neck muscles. In many cases, such headaches are not severe and do not last long, but in other cases, scalp muscle contraction headaches may be incapacitating. Individuals who have these headaches describe them as tight, pressing, squeezing or aching sensations.

Some individuals have chronic muscle contraction headaches in which the pain is constant for weeks or longer, and at times there may be feelings of jabbing, stabbing or piercing. Some sufferers of muscle contraction headaches also have an associated vascular headache, which is aggravated by jarring of the head due to coughing, sneezing or bending over.

More women than men have tension headaches, and these often run in families.

Other Forms of Headache

Sinus Headaches   These are caused by an infection or allergic reaction; the headache may worsen as the day goes on. A fever usually accompanies the headache. Common approaches to relieve sinus headaches include decongestants and antibiotics or draining of the affected sinus. Sinus headaches are fairly rare, and people who think they have sinus headaches may actually be suffering from muscle contraction headaches or migraines.

Temporomandibular Joint (TMJ) Headaches   These cause a dull ache in and around ear that gets worse when one chews, talks or yawns. Sufferers may hear a clicking sound on opening the mouth and feel soreness in the jaw muscles. Stress, a poor bite or grinding of the teeth (or a combination of the three) may bring on the headache. Treatment includes the use of heat, massage, pain-reducing medications and, in some cases, an individually made bite plate. Several relaxation techniques, including biofeedback, can also be effective.

Traction Headaches   These apply to a variety of nonspecific headaches that occur as a result of several of diseases, including brain tumors and strokes. The cause may actually be an inflammation of the pain-sensitive structures inside and outside the skull.

Mixed Headaches   These are a combination of tension-vascular headaches that have characteristics of both vascular head pain and muscle contraction head and neck pain. There may be some discomforts of vascular headaches, such as throbbing pain on one side of the head, nausea and vomiting, along with features of tension headache, including a dull, constant aching pain or tightness around the head and neck and tenderness of the scalp or neck.

Caffeine Headaches   These occur in some individuals who drink too much caffeine in coffee, tea and soft drinks. Along with caffeine-induced headaches there may be sleeping problems, upset stomach, shortness of breath and shaky hands. Some people can relieve their symptoms by eliminating coffee from their diet. Others, however, who drink large quantities of coffee and stop abruptly may suffer caffeine withdrawal symptoms, including headache, irritability, depression and sometimes nausea.

Hangover Headaches   These are symptomatic of excessive consumption of alcohol. The headache from a hangover occurs because alcohol causes blood vessels to swell, brings on nausea by irritating the digestive system and leads to dehydration by causing excessive urination.

Mountain Sickness   These headaches are the most frequent complaint of climbers who ascend to high altitudes without support of additional oxygen. This type of headache commonly affects both sides of the head, but in about one-quarter of the cases it is limited to only one side of the head. These headaches resemble migraine headaches. In some cases they may be prevented by taking medications that alter salt and fluid balance.

Depression-caused Headaches   When suffering from depression, certain individuals may have headaches. Some antidepressant drugs provide relief from headaches for some individuals. An example is a monoamine oxidase inhibitor (MAOI) such as phenelzine sulfate.

Childhood Headaches   These often have their own unique set of causes. Some children's headaches are symptomatic of anxiety conditions, but many headaches have other causes and are just as distressing. By age 15, 5.3 percent of youngsters have migraine headaches, and 5.4 percent have infrequent headaches.

Children seem to have four basic types of headaches: acute, acute recurrent, chronic progressive and chronic nonprogressive. An acute headache is one single severe headache and may be caused by general infections or infection of the central nervous system, sinuses or teeth, high blood pressure or a blow to the head. An acute recurrent headache returns after months of pain-free days. Migraine headaches fall into this pattern. Some youngsters who have classic migraine headaches report accompanying visual phenomena, such as shimmery lights or halos around objects, and sometimes nausea and vomiting. Chronic progressive headaches increase in severity and frequency over time and may be caused by a physical problem.

Headaches that come and go are referred to as chronic nonprogressive headaches. Called ''functional'' headaches because they may have no physical cause, they may be brought on by muscle contractions or worries about schoolwork. A chronic sinus infection, dental infection or jaw condition may also be a physical cause for this type of headache.

Treatment Treatments for headache include self-help, prescription medications and nonpharmacologic treatments, such as biofeedback, meditation and other relaxation techniques.

Diagnosis is important before an individual takes any medication for headaches. Medications that help tension headaches will not help severe migraine headaches, and drugs targeted to relieve migraine headaches may not help any other type. It is also important that one does not overmedicate for headaches and bring on other side effects.

Medication For migraine or vascular headaches, medication is targeted at altering responses of the vascular system to stress, hormonal changes, noise and other stimuli. Such medications affect the dilation reaction of the blood vessels. Ergot, a naturally occurring substance that constricts blood vessels and reduces the dilation of arteries, is the most popular medication. Ergot may be given by inhalation, injection, orally or rectally. Some people find that if they take the ergot medication early enough in prepain stages of an attack, they can abort their headaches or at least reduce their intensity. Individuals who are nauseated and vomiting usually take the drug by some means other than orally. In some cases, a sedative, such as a barbiturate, is given along with the ergot to help relax the individual and make him or her more receptive to the ergot's action.

Some vascular headaches are helped with prophylactic (preventive) measures. The drug of choice for prevention of migraine in carefully selected patients is propranolol. Propranolol is a vasoconstrictor that can be taken daily for as long as six months. This drug may slow down the vascular changes that occur during the migraine attack; it is frequently prescribed for some individuals who have headaches more than once each week. Propranolol is helpful for migraine sufferers who also have severe high blood pressure, angina pectoris or conditions for which ergot preparations are contraindicated. For those individuals, propranolol relieves the headache as well as the coexisting disorder. Propranolol has an advantage over ergot medications in that rebound headaches are not brought on by discontinuance of propranolol.

Medication for sufferers of tension or muscle contraction headaches are directed toward relieving muscular activity and spasm. Some individuals find injection with anesthetics and corticosteroids helpful. Commonly used analgesics (pain relievers) include aspirin, dextropropoxyphene and ethoheptazine.

Research under way: A preliminary study suggests that fluoxetine, an antidepressant drug, soothes some chronic headache pain that does not respond to conventional over-the-counter and prescription medications. Of 52 chronic headache patients treated with fluoxetine, 34 said the drug significantly reduced pain severity. Other antidepressants are used to treat chronic pain, but side effects, such as weight gain, sedation and blurred vision limit their use. A study presented by Alan R. Hirsch, M.D., researcher at Rush Presbyterian–St. Luke's Medical Center in Chicago, at the American Academy of Pain Medicine's 1992 annual conference in January 1992 suggests that fluoxetine appears to minimize pain with fewer side effects.

Medications for cluster headaches: The selection of medications depends on the frequency and severity of the headache, as well as response to previous treatments. Some of the drugs include ergotamine, methysergide, cyproheptadine, lithium and steroids. Oxygen inhalation and histamine desensitization may be used. These treatments should only be used under the careful guidance of a physician who is familiar with their use. Consultations with other medical specialists such as neurologists, ophthalmologists (eye specialists) and otolaryngologists (eye, ear, nose and throat specialists) may be necessary before medications for traction or inflammatory headaches are prescribed. Depending on the specific cause, treatment may range from surgery to anticonvulsants.

Biofeedback This method of treating tension headaches involves teaching a person to control certain body functions through thought and willpower with the use of machines that indicate how a part of the body responds to stress. Sensors are attached to the patient's forehead (frontalus muscle) to measure muscle tension; responses are relayed to an amplifier that produces sounds. When the person is tense, the sounds are loud and harsh. As the person concentrates on relaxing, the sounds begin to purr quietly or cease altogether. The headache subsides as the tension is relieved.

Meditation Also known as transcendental meditation, this is a relaxation technique of inward contemplation that helps some people alleviate anxieties and in turn relieve some headaches. During meditation, the mind as well as other organs in the body slow down. For example, heart rate decreases, breathing becomes slower and muscle tensions diminish.

Although some people can relieve their headache pain by meditation, for others it works as an adjunct to pharmacologic therapy, making the sufferer more receptive to the pharmacologic effects.

Other Relaxation Techniques

Hypnosis This is rarely used today to treat headaches, but it may be used during adjunctive psychotherapy on an individual or group basis.

Acupuncture While controversial, acupuncture has been successfully used to treat some headache sufferers. Acupuncture probably works because the needle insertions somehow stimulate the body to secrete endorphins, naturally occurring hormonelike substances that kill pain. Acupressure involves pressing acupuncture points with hands and can be done by a professional as well as a lay person who is properly trained.

See also BIOFEEDBACK; CAFFEINE; DEPRESSION; MENOPAUSE; MENSTRUATION; PREMENSTRUAL SYNDROME; TEMPOROMANDIBULAR JOINT (TMJ) SYNDROME

Kahn, Ada P. *Headaches*. Chicago: Contemporary Books, 1983.

Kahn, Ada P., and Holt, Linda Hughey. *The A to Z of Women's Sexuality*. Alameda, Calif.: Hunter House, 1992.

Wolff, Harold G. "Personality Features and Reactions of Subjects with Migraine." *Archives of Neurology and Psychiatry* 37 (1937).

———. *Headache and Other Head Pain*, 2d ed. New York: Oxford University Press, 1963.

health maintenance organization (HMO) An organized system of health care that, for a set monthly fee, individuals join to receive a comprehensive array of basic and supplemental health services, including some mental health services. In most cases, the member may only see the physicians who work for the particular HMO, or the member must pay the fee for services received from other doctors. In most cases, only employed individuals join HMOs.

heart attack See ANGINA PECTORIS.

helplessness A feeling that one cannot do anything by oneself or for oneself; a common symptom of depression. Helplessness often goes along with hopelessness. It is a feeling of being "stuck" and that there is "no way out." Individuals who feel this symptom severely should seek mental health counseling.

See also DEPRESSION; LEARNED HELPLESSNESS; LEARNED OPTIMISM

heredity Transmission of traits as well as disorders through genetic mechanisms. Some mental disorders are hereditary; researchers have found that depression, particularly bipolar disorder, obsessive-compulsive disorder, alcoholism and panic disorder occur more frequently in some families than others, as well as in identical as opposed to fraternal twins, suggesting a hereditary vulnerability for the illness.

See also PANIC DISORDER.

heroin   A controlled narcotic that has no legitimate medical use in the United States. Because tolerance to heroin develops rapidly, it is one of the most addictive drugs known. Heroin addiction is a strong physiological and psychological dependence characterized by tolerance and, when discontinued, withdrawal syndrome. Heroin abuse is a major health problem in many countries. It is a major sociological and economic problem as well as a personal danger for the user. A major danger to heroin users is an overdose from an unexpectedly pure sample, which, if untreated, can cause depressed breathing, possible convulsions, coma or death.

Sharing of contaminated needles for injection also poses a risk of transmitting diseases such as AIDS and hepatitis. Children of pregnant addicts are born addicted and suffer acute withdrawal upon birth, including irritability, tremors and anxieties.

Heroin is synthesized from morphine, which originates from opium poppies cultivated in Southeast Asia, Southwest Asia and Latin America. Most illicit heroin is in the form of a powder, which may vary in color from white to dark brown. Another form called "black tar" or "tootsie roll" is of substantially higher purity and is thus more potent.

Heroin is usually sold on the street in small bags, cellophane envelopes or foil packages. These are called "nickel" or "dime" bags. Pure heroin is rarely sold on the street. Usually it is "cut" with diluents such as sugar, starch and powdered milk, making it between 4 and 6 percent pure. Street heroin has been known to be cut with toxic substances.

Heroin can be combined with water, "cooked" down and injected. It can also be sniffed or smoked, both of which are becoming increasingly more common methods of administration.

Adapted from *Media Resource Guide on Common Drugs of Abuse.* Public Relations Society of America, National Capital Chapter, Fairfax, Va., September 1990.

heterophobia   Fear of the opposite sex. Some learning theorists consider this fear a contributing factor to some homosexual behavior.

See also HOMOSEXUALITY.

Heterosexual-Homosexual   Behavior Rating Scale   A scale developed by Alfred Kinsey and his researchers to measure the degree of heterosexuality and homosexuality by placing an individual in one of seven categories based on sexual interest and behavior: exclusively heterosexual; predominantly heterosexual with incidental homosexuality; predominantly heterosexual with more than incidental homosexuality; equally heterosexual and homosexual; predominantly homosexual with more than incidental heterosexuality; predominantly homosexual with incidental heterosexuality; and exclusively homosexual.

heterosexuality   A term referring to sexual activity between a woman and a man. A heterosexual is a person who chooses to relate sexually to the opposite sex.

Heterosexual bias is an assumption that someone is heterosexual, usually based on the judgment that heterosexuality is the only normal and desirable sexual orientation.

See also BISEXUALITY; HOMOSEXUALITY; LESBIANISM; SEXUALITY.

high blood pressure   See BLOOD PRESSURE.

hippocampus   See ADRENAL CORTEX.

HIV   See ACQUIRED IMMUNODEFICIENCY SYNDROME; HUMAN IMMUNODEFICIENCY VIRUS.

HMO See HEALTH MAINTENANCE ORGA-
NIZATION.

holiday depression A low mood swing
experienced during a period of the year in
which holidays occur or on the holidays
themselves. Some single and widowed individuals experience holiday depression because they feel alone and lonely on holidays
and see the rest of their society in a celebra-
tory mood with families around them. This
type of depression often occurs when an
individual has been uprooted from his or her
family and moved elsewhere for employment or other reasons. Some individuals in
family settings experience mood shifts out
of nostalgia for lost loved ones or for circumstances that existed earlier in their lives.
Some people who know that they will be
alone on holidays avoid their holiday depressive episodes by planning ahead to take
a trip to an interesting place, engage in some
enjoyable activity with a group, or invite
other people without families to share holiday activities together. Some individuals who
know they will be alone on holidays volunteer their services to hospitals or shelters for
the homeless so that others may be with
their families. Feeling that one is helpful to
others is a way of combating the low mood.

The depressed mood is usually brought
about by holidays under such circumstances
and disappears after the holiday season.
However, when the depressive mood does
not improve as the calendar rolls on, the
individual should seek counseling from a
mental health professional.

See also DEPRESSION; SEASONAL AFFEC-
TIVE DISORDER.

homelessness Mental health concerns of
homeless people range from solving practical everyday problems such as finding enough
food to serious disorders such as substance
abuse, depression and schizophrenia. Physical as well as mental health problems are
intensified by homelessness; conversely,
homelessness precipitates health problems.
Because of the nature of the population, it

is difficult to assess the numbers of homeless
people and their characteristic mental health
problems and for society to provide care for
them.

Problems in providing mental health care
for the homeless are related in part to reluctance of the people to present themselves for
care as well as the poor funding of community mental health centers. Since the psychiatrically impaired homeless often avoid
contact with the health care system, mobile
outreach services in some communities are
an important way to help these individuals
obtain food, clothing and medical and psychiatric care.

Many emergency department physicians
are the primary care physicians for the poor
and homeless population. These physicians
often provide care for poor children and
adolescents, the elderly, victims of rape and
domestic violence and drug abusers.

A survey of homeless adults living in
beach areas near Los Angeles revealed a
high rate of prior psychiatric hospitalization.
The survey covered 529 people who had
spent the previous night outdoors, in a shelter, in a hotel or in the home of a relative
with whom they did not expect to stay very
long. Sixty-four percent of the people interviewed were white; 73 percent were men.
They had been homeless for an average of
two years. Altogether, 44 percent had been
in hospitals for psychiatric reasons, including alcoholism and drug dependence. Twenty-
one percent had made an outpatient visit for
a mental or emotional problem within the
past year. Forty-one percent had never used
mental health services.

The worst symptoms were noted in the
hospitalized group. There were more suicide
attempts, daily drinking and delirium tremens. Seventy-six percent of the hospitalized group and 48 percent of the others had
been arrested. People who had been hospitalized were more likely to be living in
shelters. The 41 percent who had never used
mental health services had been homeless
about half as long as the rest and were least
likely to be sleeping outdoors. Surprisingly,

they scored at the same level as the general population on a questionnaire estimating well-being.

Mental health professionals agree that to address the complex needs of those categorized as homeless persons requires a multidisciplinary approach. Social services are needed for the short-term and long-term provision food, housing and entitlement services. Networks must be developed to enable access for those people to specialty medical services, emergency food pantries, transportation, overnight shelter and respite care for children while the parent negotiates the systems. Churches often provide for emergency needs and long-term support. Legal services are needed to advocate for the rights and entitlements. Children who are homeless require interaction with school systems, health care providers, day-care centers and often child protective services to promote health and prevent further illness or trauma.

See also SOCIOECONOMIC TRENDS IN MENTAL HEALTH CARE; COMMUNITY MENTAL HEALTH in BIBLIOGRAPHY.

Gelberg, Lillian; Linn, Lawrence S.; and Leake, Barbara D. "Mental Health, Alcohol and Drug Use and Criminal History among Homeless Adults." *American Journal of Psychiatry* 145 (Feb. 1988).

McFarland, Gertrude K., and Thomas, Mary Durand. *Psychiatric Mental Health Nursing.* Philadelphia: J. B. Lippinott, 1991.

Council on Large Range Planning and Development. "The Future of Psychiatry." *Journal of the American Medical Association* 265, no. 19 (Nov. 21, 1990).

homesickness   See MIGRATION; NOSTALGIA.

homosexuality   Sexual activity between members of the same sex, ranging from sexual fantasies and feelings through kissing and mutual masturbation, to genital, oral or anal contact. A male individual who practices homosexuality is termed a homosexual; a female homosexual is referred to as a lesbian. Both male and female homosexuals are sometimes referred to as gay.

Homosexuals in the United States have faced much social discrimination. In 1979, the surgeon general ordered that homosexuality not be classified as a mental disease and defect. The "gay liberation" movement of the 1970s brought about open discussions of homosexuality and human rights. During the 1980s, homosexual activists increased public acceptance of homosexuality as a lifestyle.

It seems that the term "homosexuality" was coined in 1969 in a pamphlet by Karoly Maria Bankert. During the 19th century, other terms were proposed, including "homoerotic" (aroused by the same sex) and "homophile" (lover of the same sex). Cunnilingus between two women was called sapphism after the ancient Greek poet Sappho; lesbianism came from the Greek island of Lesbos where she lived.

Fear of or prejudice against homosexuals is known as homophobia.

See also BISEXUALITY; SEXUALITY.

homosexual panic   Homosexual panic (Kempf's disease) is a panic attack that develops from a fear or delusion that one will be sexually assaulted by an individual of the same sex. The term, coined by Edward Kempf, an American psychiatrist (1885–1971), in 1920, also applies to the fear that one is thought to be homosexual. This feeling occurs more often in males than females. There may be depression, conscious guilt over homosexual activity, agitation, hallucinations and ideas of suicide. This type of panic attack may develop after many varied life circumstances, such as a loss of or separation from an individual of the same sex to whom one is emotionally attached, or after failures in sexual performance, illness or extreme fatigue.

See also BISEXUALITY; GAY LIBERATION; HETEROSEXUAL-HOMOSEXUAL BEHAVIOR RATING SCALE; LESBIANISM; SEXUAL FEARS; SEXUALITY.

Campbell, Robert J. *Psychiatric Dictionary.* New York: Oxford University Press, 1981.

Kite, Mary E., and Deaux, Kay. "Gender Belief Systems: Homosexuality and the Implicit Inversion Theory." *Psychology of Women Quarterly* 11 (1987).

Mahoney, E. R. *Human Sexuality*. New York: McGraw-Hill, 1983.

Owen, William F., Jr. "Medical Problems of the Homosexual Adolescent." *Journal of Adolescent Health Care* 6 (1985).

Wyers, Norman L. "Homosexuality in the Family: Lesbian and Gay Spouses." *Social Work* (Mar.–Apr. 1987).

hope   A feeling about the uncertainty of the future in a positive, optimistic and, in some cases, unrealistic way. Imagination, seeing alternatives and the ability to create wishes are important in maintaining a hopeful attitude. Scientists have long recognized the power of hopeful feelings in physical health. In controlled experiments, patients who received placebos frequently reported feeling better and, at times, have unaccountably improved. A hopeful attitude is helpful in maintaining good mental health, because the opposite of hope is hopelessness, a characteristic of depression that correlates to the development of heart disease as well as earlier death in cardiac patients.

In a Gallup poll published in 1990, Americans were hopeful and optimistic about their own futures but pessimistic about the future of society. Participants in the survey looked forward to improvement in their finances, career and general quality of life to the extent that the hopeful outnumbered the pessimistic eight to one. Adults over age 50 were less hopeful about their personal futures. The greatest optimism was among the young, the educated and those who were financially secure. In seeming contradiction, the survey showed attitudes of pessimism in regard to society as a whole. Many said that inflation and unemployment would increase and that there will be little progress with regard to such problems as homelessness and drug addiction.

There are elements of fear and prayer in a hopeful attitude. For example, one World War II veteran said: "I flew 30 missions in a bomber. As the going got rougher, I would just hope all the harder that we would get out of harm's way. Fear motivated the hoping and where hoping ends and prayer begins, I don't know." From his concentration camp experiences of the 1930s and 1940s, Victor Frankl developed the philosophy that where there is life there is hope and that hope is essential to continue living.

In Christianity and other religious thought, hope is considered to be a virtue. Religious groups encourage hopeful feelings through concepts such as the coming of the Messiah or the second coming of Christ, life after death and the forgiveness of sins.

See also DEPRESSION; HOPELESSNESS.

hopelessness   A state of mind in which one feels that it is impossible to deal with life, that situations have no solutions. The person may see only limited or no available desirable personal alternatives. There may be feelings of emptiness, pessimism and being overwhelmed. Nothing matters to the person who feels hopeless, and the individual "gives up."

Hopelessness is a characteristic of depression. A hopeless person is passive and lacks initiative. Such an individual may not be able to reach a desired goal, accept the futility of planning to meet goals, have negative expectations of the future, perceive a personal loss of control and see "no way out." Successful treatment of depression with medication and certain types of psychotherapy can reverse this profound state of hopelessness.

Feelings of hopelessness may lead to addiction or suicide. Hopelessness sometimes results from false or unrealistic expectations. For example, the hopeless person may feel that he or she should be able to accomplish anything and everything and descends into despair upon failure. Some individuals with depression feel that nothing they do will work out and that they are powerless.

Hopeless feelings sometimes result from magnifying events to the extent that everything and everyone seem to be insurmountable obstacles in relation to the self. Still, another type of magnification results in despair when people and events are idealized. For example, a new friend may be thought to be perfect, or an upcoming vacation is planned to run a smooth course. When the friend proves to have perceived personality flaws or when bad weather spoils the vacation, the individual who is the most unrealistically idealistic may begin to lose hope about any friends or any vacation.

Hopelessness may also result from a sense of being trapped in a negative set of circumstances from which there is no escape. When presented with a task that must be performed but seems to be impossible, a sense of frustration and futility leads to hopelessness. Prisoners and members of social and ethnic groups that suffer discrimination frequently feel so limited that their lives become hopeless. In societies that practice hexing and voodoo, victims sometimes become ill and die because they see themselves as literally having no future. In some of these situations—when victims are convinced that the hexing was a mistake and that the curse is lifted—health is recovered.

Confusion also leads to a sense of hopelessness, as it contributes to an individual's feeling of loss of control. What is important to understand is that hopelessness is a subjective state, related to the way an individual perceives his or her prospects. It is potentially reversible even though the hopeless person always has "reasons" to justify the hopelessness.

See also DEPRESSION; LEARNED OPTIMISM.

hormones   Chemical messengers produced by various organs and tissues that regulate or modulate effects elsewhere throughout the body. Hormones produced by the brain are known as neurohormones; they are produced by neurons known as neuroendocrine transducers, which release a hormone in response to activation at the synapses of neurotransmitters.

Examples of hormones are cortisol, estrogen, insulin and epinephrine. Hormones control many body functions, including growth, sexual development and the body's response to illness.

See also CORTISOL; ENDOCRINE SYSTEM; EPINEPHRINE.

hospice   An organization that provides care and assistance through several mental and physical health disciplines for the terminally ill and their families. The hospice movement started in the middle of the 19th century in Ireland but did not attract attention in the United States until the 1960s. Hospices may be part of a hospital complex or separate institutions. They may supply both inpatient and home care. Hospice care usually involves the joint efforts of physicians, mental health professionals, nurses, social workers, chaplains and volunteers. Many hospice patients suffer from cancer and AIDS. Hospice treatment only begins when the patient's chances of survival are nonexistent and life expectancy is short. Long-term degenerative neurological illnesses are not usually treated in a hospice setting. Hospice treatment concentrates on relieving the symptoms of the patient and providing psychological comfort and support rather than further attempts at curing the disease, which, particularly in cancer cases, may actually increase the patient's discomfort. Hospice programs also assist families with practical and psychological concerns during the terminal illness and may provide continuing service for a time following the patient's death.

See also ACQUIRED IMMUNODEFICIENCY SYNDROME; DEATH; TERMINAL ILLNESS.

Kitch, D. L. "Hospice," in Corsini, Raymond J., ed., *Encyclopedia of Psychology*, vol. 2. New York: Wiley, 1984.

Zimmerman, Jack. *Hospice*. Baltimore: Urban and Schwarzenberg, 1986.

hostages   Hostages are usually victims who are subjected to isolation, confinement and sometimes mental and physical torture. They may be blindfolded, kept in darkness and have their ears covered. The sensory deprivation experience may produce hallucinations. Their captors frequently keep them in a state of uncertainty about their fate. Some hostages have become paranoid and depressed and have developed feelings that their country and families have forgotten them. An odd familiarity occasionally develops between terrorist and hostage, especially given that both are in dangerous situations. Some hostages have even developed hostile feelings toward the government and agencies who are attempting to rescue them. Patty Hearst, the heiress who was kidnapped in February 1974 by the Symbionese Liberation Army, became interested in their cause and joined the group in bank robberies and other illegal activities until the leaders were killed and she was captured and imprisoned.

Readjustment to normal life after their release, though welcome, is sometimes difficult for hostages. Many experience nightmares, insomnia, bouts with abnormal fears, depression and feelings of rage and helplessness for some time. There have been cases of suicide. Mental health professionals are gaining understanding of the state of mind of former hostages through experience. Current thinking is that a regulated "decompression period" helps former hostages adjust to normal life and to being back with their families.

Following the Persian Gulf War during 1991, several hostages were released after long years of captivity. Interviewed in *Psychiatric News,* Richard Rahe, M.D., director of the Nevada Stress Center at the University of Nevada School of Medicine and a former Navy psychiatrist with extensive experience working with hostages and disaster victims, said, "People who do well have done well in the past with stress. They have had adequate-to-good childhoods. They did well in captivity. They passed through depression, past themselves, to helping others. They turned the experience into a positive one, by

reviewing their lives, making positive changes."

Dr. Rahe also said that survivor guilt is common, as are recriminations about the way they might have behaved in captivity, and many are angry toward their families or the government for not doing enough to help them. At greatest risk of developing full-blown post-traumatic stress disorder (PTSD) are those people already having symptoms and those without a good support system.

In advising therapists regarding hostages, Dr. Rahe suggested dealing with the PTSD only if it becomes chronic. Rather, he suggested they deal with the day-to-day issues.

Elmore Rigamer, M.D., chief psychiatrist at the U.S. State Department, was quoted in *Psychiatric News* (Jan. 4, 1991) regarding the "keys to staving off deterioration" in a hostage situation. "Mastery" and "connectedness" are the keys to overcoming psychological hurdles associated with having been a hostage. Mastery (a sense of control) and connectedness (feeling accurately informed) are both important for hostages and their families. As Dr. Rigamer said, "The ones who were able to take control of themselves will do wonderfully. The more feeling of loss of control, the worse. In therapy we go over and over what happened, and imagine what they would like to have done that gives them a post-facto mastery and catharsis."

Dr. Rigamer emphasized the psychological value of relaying information to hostages and families during and after the crisis. He said that during the crisis he spent as much time as he could on the telephone with State Department hostages in Baghdad and Kuwait and their families back home, clearing up rumors and giving out information. Being in communication increases one's sense of mastery, which helps prevent PTSD in both the hostages and their families.

In *Psychiatric News* (Jan. 4, 1991), Thomas M. Haizlip, M.D., director of the Child Psychiatry Division at the University of North Carolina at Chapel Hill, outlined seven stages of mastery that he believes are applicable to both the hostages and their families:

1. Discriminating between good and bad forces
2. Coping by knowing what to do if it ever happens again
3. Putting your life back in order
4. Dealing with survivor guilt (having left some people and worldly goods behind)
5. Realizing that healthy people are willing to ''seal it over'' and taking advantage of a two- to three-week ''window'' after the experience, when willingness to talk is greatest.
6. Hooking up any symptoms with the event, rather than further repressing
7. Recognizing that many people do not want help because they feel they themselves are important dispensers of help

Many of these stages are also applicable after other life traumas, such as witnessing or being a victim of a crime or family violence.

See also BRAINWASHING; DEPRESSION; POST-TRAUMATIC STRESS DISORDER; TERRORISM; POST-TRAUMATIC STRESS DISORDER in BIBLIOGRAPHY.

Psychiatric News (Jan. 4, 1991).

hot flashes A common symptom of MENOPAUSE experienced by many women before menstrual periods stop and after cessation of menses. Hot flashes are disturbing to a woman's sense of well-being because they are unpredictable. A hot flash is a sudden feeling of warmth occurring on the face, chest or entire body. The woman's body may become flushed, and patches of redness may appear on her chest, back, shoulders and upper arms. As her body temperature readjusts, she may perspire profusely and have a cold, clammy sensation. Episodes may last from seconds to minutes. As sweat evaporates, the body temperature decreases, which sometimes causes chills or the cold, clammy sensation. Many women say that the worst aspect of hot flashes is

that it makes them feel out of control of their bodies and interferes with their sense of mental well-being. Previous generations of women were sometimes told that hot flashes were ''all in their head'' and that menopause was expected to be a time filled with bizarre behavior and delusions.

Modern women know that hot flashes are not a threat to health; however, they may make a woman uncomfortable and even anxious about having one in social or professional situations. Because hot flashes may occur during the night and disrupt sleep, women experiencing hot flashes may become irritable, tired and depressed. In a 1986 survey (Kahn and Holt), typical complaints about hot flashes included waking up at night drenched in sweat, ruining clothes from perspiration, feeling embarrassed at flushing and shivering with no control and being intolerant of heat or cold. Many women find their bodies unable to deal comfortably with even slight variations in temperature.

Some women have hot flashes several times a day, once a week or less frequently. For most women, hot flashes are self-limiting symptoms and disappear without any treatment. However, there is some disagreement concerning when hot flashes stop. According to a report in the *Journal of the American Geriatric Society* (Sept. 1982), they usually stop within one to five years, yet some women report that they had hot flashes over a 10-year period.

Causes Understanding why hot flashes happen helps women cope with the anxieties produced by the anticipation of flashes. A hormone known as luteinizing hormone (LH) rises after menopause. Before menopause, it is the substance that helps trigger ovulation. LH ''surges'' seem to set off hot flashes by dilating surface blood vessels. Hormonal changes associated with the hot flash may also be due to nerve activity in the hypothalamic area that controls temperature and anterior pituitary function.

Medical and Mental Health Help When hot flashes occur so often that a woman frequently cannot get a good night's sleep, if they interfere with sexual activity or work or if they make her chronically exhausted and depressed, medical assistance should be sought. Hot flashes are often treated with hormone replacement therapy and alternatives including sedatives and anticholinergic agents (substances that block or interfere with transmission of certain impulses in the parasympathetic nervous system).

Self-helps Many women overcome their fears of being out of control of their bodies and their hot flashes by developing a series of self-help techniques. The following are some recommendations regarding hot flashes based on a survey of 967 women in 1987:

- Air stuffy rooms, keep a window open if one is too warm. Layer clothing. A suit with a lightweight blouse gives the wearer more flexibility than a wool dress.
- Wear a cotton (or other absorbent material) blouse under a sweater. Avoid wearing a sweater next to the skin.
- For desk workers, use a small desktop fan.
- During a hot flash, do not overreact. By keeping calm, others will not pay attention.
- Learn relaxation techniques to feel in control of the situation.
- Regular exercise will tone the vascular system and may help a woman feel better.
- Keep weight down. Slender women seem to have less erratic estrogen production and hence less erratic experiences with hot flashes.

See also AGING; CLIMACTERIC; MENOPAUSE.

Kahn, Ada P., and Holt, Linda Hughey. *The A to Z of Women's Sexuality*. Alameda, Calif.: Hunter House, 1992.

Kahn, Ada P., and Holt, Linda Hughey. *Midlife Health: A Woman's Practical Guide to Feeling Good*. New York: Avon Books, 1989.

hot lines　Throughout the United States, hot lines cover many mental health and related concerns. The numbers available for information and help are often toll-free and usually operate on a 24-hour basis. Most city telephone directories include a list of some of the available hot lines.

A listing of national self-help groups can be obtained by writing to:

St. Clares–Riverside Medical Center
Dept. P
1 Indian Road
Denville, NJ 07834
Phone: (201) 625–6000

See also SUPPORT GROUPS.

human immunodeficiency virus (HIV)
The virus responsible for causing the infection that leads to acquired immunodeficiency syndrome (AIDS). When the virus was first isolated in the early 1980s, it was known as HLTV-III. The virus is transmitted by direct exchange of body fluids, such as blood or semen, or by using contaminated needles for illicit drug use. Many individuals have anxieties about contracting the virus by eating in restaurants in which infected individuals work or by sending their children to a school that an infected child is known to attend. In most cases, these anxieties are unfounded, as, according to research reports, the virus does not survive outside the body. As of the early 1990s, casual contact through sharing utensils or towels or even kissing has not been shown to transmit the virus.

The virus is found in semen; the most common form of semen transmission in the United States is anal intercourse, during which tears of and bleeding from the delicate rectal lining can occur. The vaginal wall is tougher and less prone to tear and bleed, but sperm does travel through the uterus into the abdomen as a result of sexual intercourse. It has been reported that women have a seven to 10 times greater likelihood of infection from vaginal intercourse than men.

Individuals who suspect their partners of having outside, high-risk sexual contacts, such as homosexual men or prostitutes, should seek medical advice about screening for and preventing transmission of the HIV virus. Use of condoms during sexual intercourse is promoted as a way to prevent the transmission, yet it is known that they are not 100 percent safe. Distribution of condoms in schools to young people in areas of high prevalence of the infection in the 1990s caused controversy among parents and educators but was viewed as one step toward slowing down the rapid rise of the infection among young people.

See also ACQUIRED IMMUNODEFICIENCY SYNDROME (AIDS); HOMOSEXUALITY.

Kahn, Ada P., and Holt, Linda Hughey. *Midlife Health: A Woman's Practical Guide to Feeling Good.* New York: Avon Books, 1989.

humanistic psychology A approach to understanding human nature, behavior and mental health that focuses on an individual's personal experience. The American Association for Humanistic Psychology was founded in 1962 by Carl Rogers, Abraham Maslow, Kurt Goldstein, Rollo May and others. Humanistic psychology emphasizes individual choice, creativity, valuation, self-realization and the development of the each person's potential.

Humanistic psychologists believe that people have a hierarchy of many needs, beginning with physiological needs, as well as those for safety, love, "belongingness," self-esteem, to know and understand and, finally, self-actualization.

Humanistic psychology differs from the Freudian approach, which suggested that sexual drive is the motivating force, and behavioral psychology, which explains behavior as a result of various environmental relationships.

See also SELF-ESTEEM.

humor A balanced sense of humor is an aspect of good mental health. Ancient scholars understood the role of humor in good health. The Book of Proverbs says: "A merry heart doeth good like a medicine." Conversely, many individuals who suffer from depression lose their sense of humor, and few things make them smile or laugh. Studies in the late 20th century suggested that an ability to enjoy humor and to laugh has effects on mental as well as physical health.

For most people, humor and laughter usually provide a helpful release of tension and anxieties. Laughter may actually ease pain and may help the respiratory system by exercising the lungs. Laughter and other positive emotions may influence the immune system, possibly by stimulating production of certain hormones.

Shared humor relieves anxiety in stressful group situations, such as delayed airplanes or trains, and also relieves stress that results from boredom. At times when it seems that nothing is left to talk about, familiar topics can be renewed by employing humor

Some therapists employ humor to momentarily relieve depression during therapy sessions. One technique is known as paradoxical therapy, in which the therapist gives the individual new perspectives on his or her problems by exaggerating them to the point of making them seem funny. The therapist assigns the individual to be depressed or anxious at a certain time of day. Sometimes the silliness of such situations helps alleviate the individual's depressed or anxious feelings.

Humor is a universal language and has universal appeal. The basis for much humor is that we are prepared for one thing and something else happens. Although we are startled, we know there is no danger and we release our surprise in laughter. Thus a story with an unexpected ending or a game of peek-a-boo for an infant can bring about a laughter response.

See also LAUGHTER.

Fry, William F., and Salameh, Waleed A., eds. *Handbook of Humor and Psychotherapy.* Sarasota, Fla.: Professional Resources Exchange, 1987.
Morreall, John. *Taking Laughter Seriously.* Albany: State University of New York, 1983.
Ziv, Avner. *Personality and Sense of Humor.* New York: Springer Publishing Co., 1984.

Hunter's syndrome A form of mental retardation caused by the X-linked recessive gene. There may be moderate to severe developmental delay.

See also MENTAL RETARDATION.

Huntington's disease (Huntington's chorea)   A hereditary progressive brain disease that causes involuntary movements and dementia. Due to a single autosomal dominant gene, the disease was first described by George Huntington (1815–1916), an American neurologist, in 1972.

The average age of onset is 35. In early stages, the individual may have symptoms that appear to be anxiety and depression. There is moodiness, irritability and a poor ability to concentrate or remember.

According to the Alzheimer's Disease and Related Diseases Association, a family history of the disease, recognition of typical movement disorders and CAT brain scanning provide evidence for a diagnosis of Huntington's disease (HD). A genetic marker liked to the Huntington gene has been identified and further research is under way.

Sedative drugs help some individuals. The movement disorders and psychiatric symptoms seen in HD can be controlled by drugs, but there is no treatment available to stop the progression of the disease. Developments in understanding of human genetics in the early 1990s continue to give researchers more information on this somewhat rare disease.

See also ALZHEIMER'S DISEASE.

Hurler syndrome   A form of mental retardation that causes severe and progressive developmental delay, caused by a genetic deficiency.

See also MENTAL RETARDATION.

hyperactivity   Mental and physical restlessness. Hyperactive children have unlimited energy and short attention spans, are prone to temper tantrums and seem to require little sleep. The condition is more common in male children. Until their disorder is understood, many are considered unmanageable or troublemakers by teachers and parents. There is a difference of opinion regarding causes of hyperactivity. Some physicians say hyperactive behavior may be due to minimal brain damage that cannot be detected by any diagnostic tests or due to birth trauma. Others attribute hyperactivity to food allergies. Diagnosis requires careful evaluation and is usually made before the child is seven years old; children so diagnosed exhibit at least six months of disruptive behavior.

Some physicians prescribe a stimulant medication called Ritalin (methylphenidate hydrochloride) or Dexedrine (dextroamphetamine sulfate) for hyperactivity, which makes hyperactive children more manageable and able to concentrate better. The drugs may work by diminishing the brain's excess of natural stimulants and replacing them with milder, synthetic ones. Stimulant medications should be used cautiously because they can be addictive in young adults.

Therapy may include psychotherapeutic counseling, meeting with parents and teachers and participating in support groups for parents and children. Coping with a hyperactive child requires a great degree of understanding and patience.

Hyperactivity in children is also known as attention-deficit hyperactivity disorder (ADHD).

See also ATTENTION-DEFICIT HYPERACTIVITY DISORDER.

hypersomnia   Excessive daytime sleepiness and an inability to wake up quickly. This can be seen in one form of depression, which also may manifest in increased eating and weight gain, as opposed to another form associated with insomnia, weight loss and agitation-anxiety. Patients with sleep apnea syndrome or narcolepsy may also show excessive daytime sleepiness.

See also DEPRESSION; NARCOLEPSY; SLEEP APNEA.

hypertension   See BLOOD PRESSURE.

hyperthyroidism   Overactivity of the thyroid gland, which causes an increase of all chemical reactions within the body, affecting mental as well as physical processes. It is more common in women than men.

Because some of the symptoms of hyperthyroidism seem similar to those of anxiety and depression, an evaluation by a physician is essential to make a careful diagnosis.

Normally, thyroid gland activity is controlled by a hormone produced in the pituitary gland. Even when normal levels of hormone are produced, the thyroid gland itself continuously produces quantities of its own hormone, thyroxin.

Symptoms of hyperthyroidism include anxiety, tiredness with an inability to sleep, shakiness, trembling and insensitivity to cold and perspiration when others are comfortable. There may be irregular and fast heartbeat, palpitations, a fluttering feeling in the chest and breathlessness after mild exertion.

Individuals who have hyperthyroidism may eat more and lose weight, muscles may waste away, and women may have absent or scant menstrual periods. The thyroid gland in the neck may enlarge (goiter). In severe cases, eyes may look wide open and protrude, leading to blurred or double vision.

Hyperthyroidism is treated with medications containing antithyroid drugs, with surgery to remove a lump in the thyroid gland or, in some cases, most of the gland. More commonly, sufferers take a drinkable form of radioactive iodine, which acts on the glandular tissue in the thyroid gland to control the overactivity of the cells.

Underactivity of the thyroid gland is known as myxedema. Individuals with underactive thyroid glands feel tired much of the time. This condition, too, can mimic or mask depression and needs careful diagnosis.

Recent research has shown the presence of subtle abnormalities of thyroid function in clinical depression.

See also HYPOTHYROIDISM.

hyperventilation   Deep and fast breathing, sometimes referred to as overbreathing. Some individuals who have panic attacks and phobias react with hyperventilation, which in turn makes them fear that they are dying or having a heart attack. While individuals who overbreathe feel short of breath and breathe deeply and faster to get more air into their lungs, they are really taking in too much air. This breathing pattern makes them feel worse, as it removes too much carbon dioxide from the blood; some is needed in the body to perform efficiently.

Overbreathing leads to rapid heartbeat, lightheadedness, dizziness, sweating and numbness or tingling in the hands and feet. Fainting sometimes occurs; hyperventilation may be mistaken for a heart attack. At the least, it exacerbates the individual's anxiety level.

When an individual has a dizzy spell or feels the effects of hyperventilation, breathing into a paper bag for a few minutes can help restore the balance of oxygen and carbon dioxide in the blood. When some of the exhaled carbon dioxide from the bag returns to the lungs, the individual will begin to breathe more normally again.

Relaxation therapy, including breathing instruction, helps some individuals who suffer from panic attacks and other anxiety disorders.

According to sex researchers William Howell Masters and Virginia Johnson, hyperventilation is a reaction of women and men during the late plateau phase of sexual intercourse. The physiological intensity and duration of the reaction indicate the degree of developing sexual tension.

See also RELAXATION TRAINING.

hypnosis   A type of attentive, receptive and focused concentration accompanied by a diminished awareness of environmental stimuli. In a therapy situation utilizing hypnosis, the patient cooperates with the therapist to utilize this form of intense concentration to facilitate and accelerate reaching particular therapeutic goals. Individuals cannot be hypnotized against their will, but some individuals are more or less capable of achieving a hypnotic trance. Hypnosis has been described in detail in the writings of Sigmund Freud.

Hypnosis is sometimes used to relieve specific symptoms such as insomnia, anxiety, conversion reactions, phobias and pain and well as to control habits, such as smoking, nail biting and overeating. While hypnosis has limitations as a therapy, many clinicians believe that hypnosis can be helpful when used selectively.

Therapy with hypnosis involves teaching the individual self-hypnosis techniques so they can induce a trancelike state in themselves and use suggestions that help them restructure their thinking regarding the condition for which they are seeking help. For example, in management of pain, hypnosis helps to block the perception of pain by drawing the individual's attention away from it.

Self-hypnosis is sometimes used with anxiety reactions to promote relaxation on cue in fearful situations. In general, autohypnosis by itself will not significantly relieve anxiety responses. It can, however, be used as a supplement to behavioral therapy to make images more vivid and to heighten one's ability to concentrate.

hypnotic drugs   Short-acting drugs that induce sleep by depressing the central nervous system. An example of a hypnotic drug is sodium secobarbital (Seconal). In the past, hypnotics were sometimes prescribed for individuals who were anxious and could not sleep soundly. Because of possibilities for abuse of drugs in the category of hypnotics, they are no longer widely prescribed. Tranquilizers or benzodiazepine drugs are now more commonly prescribed as sleep-inducing medications in individuals with anxieties.

See also ANXIETY; ANTIANXIETY MEDICATIONS; TRANQUILIZER DRUGS.

hypochondriasis   An overconcern or preoccupation with one's health problems that may be real or imaginary. Some individuals (hypochondriacs) become extraordinarily concerned with their heartbeat, digestion or minor physical abnormalities, such as a skin blemish. People who are hypochondriacs often have symptoms of anxiety, depression and obsessive-compulsive personality traits.

American Psychiatric Association. *Diagnostic and Statistical Manual of Mental Disorders,* 3d ed., rev. Washington, D.C., 1987.

hypoglycemia   A reduced amount of glucose in the blood, which can produce nervousness, trembling and some symptoms mimicking anxiety disorders.

hypomanic episode   An episode in which symptoms are similar to those in a manic episode but less severe. In a manic episode, the individual has a period in which the predominant mood is elevated, expansive or irritable to such an extent that functioning and social activities are impaired. The individual with a manic episode may need hospitalization to avoid harm to self and others, while those with hypomanic episodes may exhibit poor judgment but usually do not require hospitalization, unless it is necessary for the depression that almost inevitably follows the manic or hypomanic episode.

See also BIPOLAR DISORDER; MANIC-DEPRESSIVE ILLNESS.

hypothalamus   The coordinating center of the brain. It is a small area located above the pituitary gland, with nerve connections to most other areas of the nervous system. It controls the sympathetic nervous system (which in turn controls the inner body organs). During excitement or fear, the brain sends signals to the hypothalamus, which initiates a chain of activity, including faster heartbeat, faster breathing rate and increased blood flow to the muscles (the fight or flight response). The hypothalamus also controls reactions that cause sweating or shivering, stimulates appetite and thirst, regulates sleep, motivates sexual behavior and determines emotions and moods; it also indirectly controls many of the endocrine organs, which secrete hormones.

See also BRAIN; BRAIN CHEMISTRY.

hypothyroidism Underactivity of the thyroid gland and below-normal production of thyroid hormones, which stimulate energy production from sugar. Symptoms of lack of the hormone may include muscle weakness, a slow heart rate, dry, flaky skin, hair loss and a deep and husky voice. The disorder is diagnosed by tests to measure the level of thyroid hormone in the blood. Treatment consists of replacement therapy with the thyroid hormone thyroxin. Depression may be associated with thyroid hypofunction.

See also HYPERTHYROIDISM.

hysterectomy Surgical removal of the uterus. It is an operation that causes many women emotional upheaval and, for some, physiological concerns. The word "hysterectomy" comes from the Greek work *hystera,* meaning "woman."

The first successful hysterectomy in the United States was performed in 1853. More than 650,000 American women undergo hysterectomies each year, nearly one-quarter of which are over age 50.

There is a great deal of confusion among the public over the precise meaning of hysterectomy. A better understanding contributes to better psychological acceptance of the event. A "total" hysterectomy refers to removal of the uterus and cervix. "Partial" refers to removal only of the body of the uterus. If the fallopian tubes and ovaries are removed, the procedure is called a "total hysterectomy bilateral salpingoophorectomy." A hysterectomy can be done vaginally or via an abdominal incision.

Some women experience sexual dysfunction following hysterectomy. Women who had preexisting sexuality problems are more likely to develop postoperative problems than are women who enjoyed a healthy sex life prior to surgery. Sexual problems can result from underlying poor self-concept; a woman who equates sexuality with fertility may feel like "less of a woman" without a uterus; a woman who has been raised to think sex is evil unless aimed at procreation may feel guilty about sexual activities following hysterectomy. Some women experience painful intercourse after a hysterectomy; this can be due to vaginal dryness if the ovaries were removed or due to loss of some of the lubricating glands.

Part of female orgasm consists of rhythmic uterine contractions; while women still experience orgasm, some women are aware of a difference in internal sensations with orgasm.

However, many women experience an improvement in sexual relations if the hysterectomy successfully treated a painful condition such as endometriosis or if a bleeding problem made sexual activity messy or distasteful.

Evaluation for depression and psychotherapy may be helpful for women following hysterectomy.

See also ANTIDEPRESSANT MEDICATIONS; DEPRESSION.

Kahn, Ada P., and Holt, Linda Hughey. *The A to Z of Women's Sexuality.* Alameda, Calif.: Hunter House, 1992.

hysteria A medical diagnostic term for illnesses characterized by emotional outbursts and transformation of unconscious conflicts into physical symptoms, such as pain, paralysis or blindness. The term encompasses a wide range of symptoms that are usually attributed to mental stress. Derived from the ancient Greek word *hysteron,* meaning "uterus," the term was first used to refer only to diseases of women that ancients explained arose from problems in the uterus. Until the late 1800s, when Sigmund Freud presented a case of male hysteria, the illness was considered solely a female problem.

Psychiatrists say that the term is no longer helpful in diagnosis, and symptoms formerly grouped under this term are now included in more specific diagnostic categories such as conversion disorder, dissociative disorders, somatization disorder and factitious disorder.

Mass hysteria refers to the psychological spread of symptoms (for example, itching, nausea or fainting) from person to person. This situation occurs in schools or institutions in response to group tensions or worries, such as worries about the threat of toxins in the water supply.

See also FREUD, SIGMUND.

I

iatrogenic psychiatric disorder

Symptoms that mimic psychiatric disorders induced by prescribed medications. This seems to happen more in elderly individuals than in younger people. For example, patients treated with diuretics for hypertension may have a potassium deficiency that produces fatigue, appearing to be depression; propranolol may have a similar effect. Digitalis toxicity and phenytoin (Dilantin) toxicity can induce fatigue and mental confusion that may mimic depression, psychosis or dementia. Anxiolytic drugs and hypnotic drugs can also produce symptoms that appear to be a psychiatric disorder, such as confusion, lethargy or withdrawal. Sometimes the diagnosis of a psychiatric condition due to prescribed drugs can be made from the individual's history. In other cases, laboratory tests are needed.

See also PHARMACOLOGIC THERAPY in BIBLIOGRAPHY.

Andreason, Nancy C., and Black, Donald W. *Introductory Textbook of Psychiatry.* Washington, D.C.: American Psychiatric Association, 1991.

id According to Sigmund Freud, the id consists of human instincts and the energy associated with them. He believed that there were no conflicts within the id and that all functions existed side by side to fulfill the id's aims. When the newborn has to obtain substances from the environment to survive, aims are met by initiating activity such as breathing, crying or sucking. When conflicts occur between the internal and external realities, one portion of the id was modified to become the ego, which would deal with the conflicts between the internal and external worlds and mediate between what the individual needed and what was possible.

See also EGO; FREUD, SIGMUND; PSYCHOLOGY AND PSYCHIATRY in BIBLIOGRAPHY.

ideas of influence Ideas that a source, such as a radio or television broadcast, speaker, animal or voice is telling one what to do or is influencing behavior. The individual takes these messages seriously and does not question the fact that no one else hears them. This symptom is often a characteristic of schizophrenia.

See also DELUSION; IDEAS OF REFERENCE; PARANOID; SCHIZOPHRENIA.

ideas of reference Insignificant remarks, statements or events interpreted by the individual to have some special meaning to him or her. For example, one who walks into a room and sees people laughing may think they are laughing at her or him. For another individual, items read in the newspaper or heard over the news on television are thought to have some special meaning for that person. The individual may be suspicious but recognizes that the ideas may be erroneous. When the individual truly believes that the statements or events refer to him or her, this is considered a delusion of reference. Ideas of reference are a characteristic of paranoid schizophrenia.

See also PARANOID; SCHIZOPHRENIA.

idiot savant An individual who shows general low mental ability but exhibits high ability in the areas of music, art, mathematics, geography, the calendar, motor coordination or extrasensory perception. Idiot savants are also called "autistic savants" by some authorities. Others feel that their behavior stems from retardation rather than autism.

Holmes, D. L. "Idiot Savant," in Corsini, Raymond J., ed., *Encyclopedia of Psychology*, vol. 2. New York: Wiley, 1984.

illiteracy Illiteracy is a social problem in the United States and a personal problem for many individuals. Those who cannot read have a poor self-image and have difficulty obtaining employment with which to support themselves and their families. Illiterates or those who read very poorly feel inferior and frequently develop techniques to hide or compensate for their lack of reading ability. Embarrassment may also keep them from seeking help for their problem.

It is estimated that 75 percent of unemployed Americans are illiterate. Recently the New York Telephone Company had to test 60,000 people on an entry level exam to hire 3,000 employees. One major corporation had to use graphics on its assembly line to compensate for workers' inability to read simple phrases. As jobs become more technical and the economy shifts from an industrial to service base, more jobs will require skills beyond the ninth grade level, compared with the fourth grade level skills typical after World War II. In 1986, a National Advisory Council on Adult Education survey showed that 40 percent of all armed service enlistees read below a ninth grade level. Illiteracy is strongly related to poverty, crime and drug use. About 75 percent of adult prison inmates are functionally illiterate.

A large segment of the illiterate population is afflicted with learning disabilities. According to a study undertaken in 1987 by the Federal Interagency Task Force, 12 million to 24 million Americans have learning disabilities that make it difficult for them to learn to read. Complicating this problem is the issue of whether illiteracy in itself constitutes a learning disability.

illusion A distorted sensation, perception or memory, based on misinterpretation of a reality. For example, one may interpret seeing a pen or pencil as a dangerous knife. Optical illusions occur in daily life. An example is a narrow road that appears to come together ahead; or, when one is anxious and waiting, one may think that an hour has passed when only a few minutes have gone by. Illusions are usually brief and can be understood upon explanation. They may occur with anxiety or tiredness, as a reaction to drugs, as a result of certain forms of brain damage or in delirium tremens.

See also DELIRIUM TREMENS.

imagery Imagination to change a mental or physiological condition. It is a self-regulation skill that can be learned and can be used alone or together with other relaxation techniques. Imagery helps some people because it creates a positive mental picture and can help reduce stress and promote healing processes. The individual selects an image, such as looking at a calm, serene lake with sailboats slowing moving along, breathes in a relaxed manner and becomes more relaxed. Self-talk is involved; the individual gradually learns to notice every detail of the imagined scene and notices how the sense of relaxation deepens. The individual learns that he or she can create a sense of calm at any time by breathing and creating the positive, calming vision.

In terms of combating disease, imagery techniques have been used to help individuals imagine themselves in a healthier state, with their good cells fighting off the diseased cells. Athletes more often use imagery to enhance their athletic performance.

imaging techniques See BRAIN IMAG-ING.

imipramine hydrochloride The origi-nal tricyclic antidepressant drug (trade name: Tofranil), which is effective in treating de-pressive episodes of major depression and bipolar, dysthymic, panic and phobic dis-orders. Like other drugs in its class, imipra-mine may take up to three to four weeks to become effective. It is quite toxic in an overdose and may produce seizures or seri-ous cardiac arrhythmias.

See also ANTIDEPRESSANT MEDICATIONS, DEPRESSION.

immune system Cells and proteins that work to protect the body from possibly harmful microorganisms such as viruses, bacteria and fungi. The immune system is involved in problems of allergies and hyper-sensitivity, rejection of tissues after grafts and transplants and probably cancer.

Defects in the immune system cause the body's own proteins to be misidentified as antigens, and the body then attacks them, resulting in autoimmune disorders.

Suppression of the immune system can occur as an inherited disorder or after infec-tion with certain viruses, including HIV (the virus that causes AIDS), resulting in lowered resistance to infections that are usually re-sisted and to the development of malignan-cies. There is evidence that severe stress and depression may inhibit normal immune func-tion, but it has not yet been proven that the reduced function measured is of clinical sig-nificance. This research continues and may show that pathological stress responses and moods affect physical health.

Many people believe that a positive men-tal attitude can influence the immune system in a positive way.

See also HUMAN IMMUNODEFICIENCY VI-RUS; IMAGERY.

implosive therapy (implosion) A tech-nique used in behavioral therapy in which the individual imagines an intense anxiety-producing situation for long periods of time without escaping. Developed by Thomas G. Stampfl, an American psychologist at the University of Wisconsin, this procedure is designed to eradicate the avoidance response that feeds the anxiety.

See also BEHAVIORAL THERAPY; CATHAR-SIS; PSYCHOTHERAPY; BEHAVIORAL THERAPY in BIBLIOGRAPHY.

impotence The inability of a male to complete sexual intercourse due to partial or complete inability to achieve or maintain an erection. Short episodes of erectile impo-tence are common and should not be a cause for undue concern by the man or his partner. In certain situations, such as times of stress or after drinking too much alcohol, many men experience temporary erectile impo-tence. Chronically impotent men, however, are continually unable to have an erection.

It is estimated that 10 million American men have erectile impotence and consequent mental health problems of frustration, em-barrassment and irritability.

Scientific and medical views vary regard-ing the numbers of those afflicted with psy-chological and physiological impotence. Recent research, according to Surgitek/Med-ical Engineering Corporation, indicates that nearly 50 percent of impotent men suffer from physiological problems, with a large number afflicted with irreversible organic impotence.

The penis contains two cylindrical cham-bers filled with tiny, spongelike compart-ments. When a man becomes sexually aroused, his nervous and circulatory systems cause microscopic valves in the penis to open, filling the spongy erectile tissues with eight times the normal amount of blood, resulting in erection.

Impotence may take the form of low in-terest in sexual activity, premature ejacula-tion, coitus without ejaculation or erectile capacity only with prostitutes. Impotence differs from sterility, which means that a person is not capable of producing a child.

Although some men believe that liquor and drugs make them more potent, two of the most common causes of impotence are heavy cigarette smoking and excessive consumption of alcohol. Nicotine constricts blood vessels and can impair sexual function.

Sex researchers Masters and Johnson have given the label primary impotence to the condition of never having had an erection, and secondary impotence to the condition of having had an ability in the past to have an erection but no longer being able to do so. There are multiple causes of impotence. Some of the most common causes include illnesses such as diabetes, which affects the nervous and vascular supply to the penis; circulatory problems, such as arteriosclerosis; neurological disorders resulting from diabetes; Parkinson's disease; multiple sclerosis; prostate surgery; injury to the nerves, spinal cord or brain; hormonal abnormalities, such as thyroid disease or decreased testosterone; and medications, such as antihypertension drugs, which affect nerve function. Emotional factors, such as marital stress or depression, also affect impotence. It was once thought that psychological factors caused most impotence, but with increasing medical knowledge, the proportion that can be explained on physiological grounds is increasing.

It is important for a man suffering from impotence to have a thorough checkup for physical as well as emotional causes of impotence by a knowledgeable physician and/ or sex therapist. Treatment may be as simple as treatment of the disease or elimination of the drug causing it, or as complicated as surgical implantation of a prosthesis.

Sex therapy is helpful to many men. It can often be as simple as helping him relax during sexual activity.

Diagnosing the causes of impotence involves a battery of sophisticated physical and psychological tests conducted with the impotent man and, in some cases, his partner. The physical examination includes blood, hormone and circulation tests, neurological studies and tests on penile blood pressure and temperature, among others.

An important test to distinguish organic from psychological impotence is the Nocturnal Penile Tumescence (NPT) Test, in which erections that occur during sleep are measured. A normal man has between two and five erections while asleep, each lasting from five minutes to half an hour. In the test, which can be conducted in sleep laboratories or the home, an electronic device is used to record changes in penile size. An insufficient number of nocturnal erections may indicate a physical problem.

See also MASTERS, WILLIAM H.; SEX THERAPY.

impulse control disorders Several mental health disorders in which individuals are unable to resist an impulse or temptation that is harmful to themselves or to others. These disorders include kleptomania (shoplifting, stealing), pathological gambling and pyromania (setting fires). Some people are arrested for stealing and setting fires before a mental diagnosis is made. Individuals with these disorders should seek psychotherapy before their compulsions interfere with the rest of their lives in a personal or legal sense.

Other impulse disorders may involve violent suicidal or self-mutilatory behavior. Evidence is developing that impulse disorders may be related to decreased serotonin levels in the brain.

See also GAMBLING; SEROTONIN.

incest Sexual intercourse between closely related individuals, within degrees wherein marriage is prohibited by law or custom. Almost all societies have some incest taboos. In some societies sexual intercourse between cousins or between uncles and nieces, aunts and nephews, is prohibited. In the United States, father-daughter, mother-son and brother-sister seem to be the most heinous infraction of mores. When sexual relations occur against a person's will, even with a family member, the situation is considered sexual abuse. Many family members do not report such abuse to authorities out of fear of reprisal from the family member, fear of being abandoned or other reasons.

See also SEXUAL ABUSE AND SEXUAL ASSAULT in BIBLIOGRAPHY.

Vidmar, Lou Ann Lalani. "A Multidimensional Psychotherapy for Women Incest Victims." Thesis, Rosemead School of Psychology, 1985.

infectious mononucleosis A disease thought to be caused by the Epstein-Barr virus and transmitted via saliva; it is also referred to as simply mononucleosis. It is commonly called the "kissing disease" because it can be spread by kissing. It occurs most frequently during adolescence and in the twenties, often among college students who are already tired from late nights of studying and become susceptible to viruses. Because of the prolonged chronic fatigue brought on by the disease, many sufferers also become depressed and concerned about getting back to school or work. Symptoms include chronic fatigue, malaise and excessive sleeping.

See also CHRONIC FATIGUE SYNDROME; EPSTEIN-BARR VIRUS.

inferiority complex First described by Carl Jung, an inferiority complex is a feeling of very low self-esteem and that other people are better looking, better achievers or more successful than oneself. Some children develop an inferiority complex because they are the victims of bullies as they are growing up. Other children do so because their parents have not encouraged them or belittle or overcriticize all their efforts. In some families one child may be compared unfavorably with another; this can lead to an inferiority complex. Some people have inferiority complexes because of their body image. Many people learn to raise their self-image during psychotherapy.

See also COMPLEX; SELF-ESTEEM.

infertility An inability to become pregnant and give birth to a child. Usually the diagnosis of infertility is made when a couple fails to conceive after at least one year of sexual intercourse without contraception; some reproductive endocrinologists make this diagnosis after six months. Infertility is often a cause of anxiety and stress for many couples, particularly those who have delayed marriage and childbearing until their late thirties. This frustrating and often anguishing problem affects about 15 percent of all couples of childbearing age.

According to William W. Hurd, assistant professor of obstetrics and gynecology, University of Michigan Medical Center, Ann Arbor, about one in 10 couples are considered "subfertile," which means that their chances of having a baby without professional intervention are slim. The infertility rate increases dramatically with age; couples between ages 30 and 35 have a 33 percent chance of being subfertile, and the odds jump to 50 percent by the time they reach 40. The probability of becoming pregnant the "old-fashioned" way is less than 10 percent among couples age 40 and older.

Reasons why subfertility increases with time are largely based on changes that take place in a woman's body as she ages. For example, older ovaries produce less fertility-enhancing hormones. Additionally, middle-aged ova are not as receptive to sperm penetration, and they tend to be spontaneously aborted once fertilized. During the 1980s, the number of American married couples unable to conceive diagnosed with an infertility problem rose from 15 percent to 20 percent. Infertility is touching an increasing number of young people whose reproductive systems have been damaged by chronic infections and sexually transmitted diseases such as gonorrhea and chlamydia.

According to Dana A. Ohl, M.D., assistant professor of surgery, Section of Urology, University of Michigan Medical Center, Ann Arbor, anabolic steroids, which can lower sperm count drastically and sometimes irreversibly, will also leave an indelible mark on infertility statistics in the years to come; young men in high school who use steroids will find difficulty in impregnating their wives five to 10 years from now.

Infertility does not always mean that conception is impossible. Many people with reproductive problems eventually have babies. According to the Center for Assisted Reproduction (CFAR), Northwestern University, Chicago, medicine has made great strides in the area of infertility in the last generation. Forty years ago, physicians had neither the knowledge base nor the technology to offer infertile couples a lengthy list of options. Adoption was the principal and many times painful alternative. Doctors knew little then about the value of fertility drugs to stimulate ovulation or laparoscopy to view the pelvis and correct problems of the reproductive organs. They had not yet imagined the diagnostic and therapeutic value of in vitro fertilization (IVF), which moves the actual fertilization of the egg from the fallopian tubes inside the woman to a glass petri dish inside the laboratory.

Today there are advances in at least seven areas that might affect fertility: ovulation, cervical, uterine and endometrial, tubal, pelvic and sperm. In diagnosing infertility, CFAR physicians look at the seven medical factors that, alone or in tandem, could prevent pregnancy. They want to know, for example, if the ovaries release an egg each month and, along with it, the necessary amount of hormones to allow for implantation. They also want to know if the male partner's sperm is of sufficient volume, motility and quality to fertilize an egg.

In approximately 40 percent of infertility cases, the problem is solely female; in another 40 percent it is solely male; in 17.5 percent of the cases, it involved both partners. In the remaining 3.5 percent of cases, infertility is never explained.

While infertility problems were once considered the woman's domain, today sperm production and motility, hormonal imbalances, anatomical factors, infections and inflammatory diseases are known to affect a man's ability to father a child. Some men perceive their condition as a threat to their masculine identity, which they may associate with their sexual prowess. One of the best ways to get men to accept infertility is to encourage them to talk about their condition, both with their partners and with supports groups. For women, the inability to have a child can attack the depths of femininity.

According to Ann Colston Wentz, M.D., CFAR, research has never established that stress causes infertility but rather that the reverse is true. When a couple is infertile, however, the partners become frustrated, anxious, hostile and angry. They question their own sexuality, and their infertility becomes one of the greatest stressors of their lives.

However, according to Dr. Hurd, some researchers have reported a correlation between stress reduction and increased fertility. When couples consciously stop trying for a while and replace their anxiety with relaxation, pregnancy rates have actually been shown to increase. A study compared the effects of relaxation therapy on infertility. Researchers took 100 people with unexplained infertility and did relaxation therapy on half of them. That half had a higher pregnancy rate than the half that did not have such therapy.

The stress of infertility can also result in sexual problems, such as low or nonexistent sexual desire. Fortunately, for most couples, this is usually a situational problem; when the infertility is resolved, the desire problem goes away.

According to Sally A. Kope, M.S.W., a senior clinical social worker in the Department of Obstetrics and Gynecology, University of Michigan Medical Center, in couples facing ongoing infertility, symptoms of overt depression can occur, including frequent crying, poor concentration and difficulty completing tasks. Such symptoms often resolve, however, as soon as the couple starts taking control of their future, even if it is the decision to stop trying so hard to have a baby.

Couples interested in exploring how medical technology can help them conceive should contact a local medical center for names of physicians who specialize in infertility or reproductive endocrinology.

See also PREGNANCY.

Corson, Stephen L. *Conquering Infertility: A Guide for Couples.* New York: Prentice-Hall Press, 1990.

Daya, Salim. "Investigation of the Infertile Couple." *Canadian Family Physician* 35 (June 1989).

Finn, Kristen Lidke. "Beating the Biological Clock: The Fertile Territory of Assisted Reproductive Technology." *Health Feature Service,* University of Michigan Medical Center Health News Service, Ann Arbor (Aug. 1991).

Hintz, Christine A. ". . . And Baby Makes Three." *Northwestern Perspective,* Chicago (Fall 1991).

Iscovitz, Todd N. "Male Infertility: Problems and Treatments." *The Quill,* Pennsylvania Hospital, Philadelphia (Fall 1990).

informed consent   Agreement to a treatment plan for physical or emotional disorders. For example, one must give informed consent before undergoing electroshock treatment. If one is incompetent to sign a form indicating consent, another individual may do so. Elements of informed consent include:

- Adequate and accurate knowledge and information must be given to the patient.
- The patient has the legal capacity to consent.
- Consent is voluntarily given without coercion.

The term also refers to the right of the health care professional to release information learned during visits only with the consent of the patient.

See also GUARDIANSHIP; LEGAL ISSUES.

inhalants   Substances that can be inhaled through the nose or "huffed" by mouth. Like anesthetics, inhalants slow down the mind and body. Common inhalants include paint thinner, gasoline, spray paint, glue, kerosene and other solvents, amyl and butyl nitrate, aerosol sprays and nail polish remover.

Amyl nitrate and butyl nitrate, respectively nicknamed "snappers" or "poppers" and "locker room" or "rush," are liquids that produce highs that last up to several minutes after they are inhaled. Other than amyl nitrate, which has a legitimate use for heart patients, inhalants do not have an approved medical use.

Among the effects of inhalants are "sudden sniffing death" (a form of acute cardiac arrest) and breathing difficulties, headaches, vomiting, diarrhea and impaired reflexes. Some inhaled materials coat the lung tissue and may cause severe or even fatal pneumonia. Solvent use has been linked to kidney failure and other problems. Users can become dependent on inhalants and suffer painful symptoms of withdrawal if they stop using them. Inhalant users may appear to be alcohol intoxicated and may black out, have panic attacks or become disoriented or aggressive.

See also SUBSTANCE ABUSE.

Adapted from *Media Resource Guide on Common Drugs of Abuse.* Public Relations Society of America, National Capital Chapter, Fairfax, Va., September 1990.

inhibition   The inner restraint that prevents individuals from carrying out any mental or physical activity. As a psychoanalytic term, inhibition means unconsciously restraining instinctual impulses. People who have many inhibitions are often shy and withdrawn, whereas extroverted personalities are usually less inhibited. Some individuals who are extremely inhibited about certain areas of their life and activities may develop social phobias. These can be overcome with a variety of therapies, including behavioral therapy. Some people have inhibitions related to sexual activity; sex therapy helps some people in this area of life.

See also PHOBIA; SEX THERAPY.

inkblot test   See RORSCHACH TEST.

insanity   The legal term for a severe mental illness that renders the person incapable of managing his or her own affairs in a competent manner. The definition of insanity and its legal aspects vary among states in the United States. Aspects of the definition may include guardianship, lack of responsibility for contracts or crimes and inability to distinguish between right and wrong.

A person can be mentally ill or have an addiction problem but not be found legally insane as a defense for a felony. Most states require that it be proved that as a result of a mental disease (for example, schizophrenia, organic psychosis) or defect (mental retardation) an individual did not recognize the wrongfulness of the act or was unable to conform his or her behavior to the requirements of the law.

See also GUARDIANSHIP; LEGAL ISSUES.

insanity defense   See LEGAL ISSUES.

insomnia   Insomnia, the inability to sleep or stay asleep, is usually a symptom of other disorders. Among the most prevalent of the causes is a history of stress, recent grief or mental disorders such as anxiety or depression. According to a study reported in *Canadian Family Physician* (Feb. 1992), insomnia occurs in up to 35 percent of those patients who have depression, anxiety and mania. Certain prescription drugs (antihypertensives, antiasthmatics) along with caffeine, nicotine and alcohol are believed to account for another 12 percent of cases of insomnia. While alcohol helps some people fall asleep more easily, they awaken in about four hours with rebound insomnia. Other causes of insomnia include tolerance to, or

withdrawal from, sedative-hypnotics, restless leg syndrome and sleep apnea.

See also ANTIDEPRESSANT MEDICATIONS; ANXIETIES; DEPRESSION; SLEEP.

Harrison, Pam. "Insomnia Not a Diagnosis but a Complaint." *Canadian Family Physician* 38 (Feb. 1992).

instinct   An innate urge. Humans have needs for food, warmth, love and sex, but the instinct for survival is probably the strongest. An instinct is different from a reflex, which is an involuntary response to a stimulus, such as slowing down at the sound of a railroad train whistle. Sigmund Freud saw life as a contest between the two most important instincts, Eros—the life instinct, a positive creative force—and Thanatos—the death instinct, which is negative and destructive.

See also FREUD, SIGMUND.

insulin-shock therapy (insulin-coma therapy)   A treatment for severe mental disorder, such as schizophrenia, consisting of intramuscular administration of insulin, which results in a short-term hypoglycemia coma. The treatment is rarely used now because it has been replaced by electroconvulsive (electroshock) therapy and psychoactive drugs, which are less dangerous and more effective.

See also ELECTROCONVULSIVE THERAPY.

integration   A psychiatric term referring to the developmental process in which separate personality characteristics, experiences, abilities and values are brought together. A "well-integrated person" is one who functions well in various relationships and at various levels. In the layperson's language, such a person is "all together."

intelligence   An ability to understand concepts and reason them out. Intelligence involves many factors, including speed of thought, learning and problem solving. It also includes the meaning of words, fluency with words, working with numbers, visualizing things in space, memory and speed of perception.

Intelligence can be rated on a continuum, from highly gifted (IQ over 140) people on one end to mentally retarded people on the other.

See also INTELLIGENCE TESTS.

intelligence tests   Tests planned to provide an estimation of a person's mental capabilities. The result of standard tests is known as intelligence quotient (IQ). In recent years, there has been criticism of the use of intelligence tests as the basis for predicting whether a person can cope with certain jobs or pass certain examinations. Some say standardized tests are biased regarding gender and race. In any event, intelligence tests are useful in assessing effects of brain disease and in assessing the nature of a child's problem so that effective remedial instruction can be initiated.

There are many different tests; the most widely used is the Wechsler Adult Intelligence Scale (WAIS) and the Wechsler Intelligence Scale for Children (WISC). These are divided into sections relating to words and actions. Another test is the Stanford-Binet Test, the original of which was devised in 1905 by Alfred Binet (1857–1911), a French psychologist. Other tests focus on testing one particular aspect of intelligence. For example, the Goodenough-Harris test assesses performance by asking a child to draw a picture of a man. In scoring, details such as proportion of the body and details of clothing are counted.

Scoring of intelligence tests is usually based on mental age (MA) in relationship to actual chronological age (CA), as intelligence usually increases with maturity.

See also MENTAL RETARDATION.

introversion   A personality characteristic marked by self-reliance and a preference for working or doing recreational activities alone. This is in contrast to extroversion, a characteristic of a more outgoing character. Introverts may be preoccupied with their own inner thoughts and feelings rather than with other people. Introverts tend to be rather contemplative and sensitive people and may seem aloof to others.

involutional melancholia   An obsolete term referring to a depressive disorder that was commonly believed to affect people, particularly women, at mid-life and after. Today it is diagnosed as major depression.

See also CLIMACTERIC; MENOPAUSE.

iproniazid   Known by the trade name Marsalid, this drug was one of the first in the monoamine oxidase (MAO) inhibitor class. It is no longer used in the United States.

See also ANTIDEPRESSANT MEDICATIONS; DEPRESSION; MONOAMINE OXIDASE INHIBITORS.

irrational beliefs   Ideas that are unreasonable and unrealistic; such ideas are characteristic of some mental illnesses. For example, mentally ill persons frequently have unrealistic concepts such as a feeling that everyone is or should be paying attention to them or that they are being persecuted (paranoia). They may feel that they are being poisoned or that the government or other powerful organizations are eavesdropping or tapping their telephone. Some people who are not mentally well may develop fixations and feel that they have personal relationships with movie stars, political figures or other celebrities. These fixed beliefs are considered delusions.

Experiences and ideas that cannot be proved rationally are also present in the population that does not have mental disorders. According to a recent Gallup poll, one out of four Americans believes in ghosts, and 55 percent of Americans believe in the devil. One in four Americans feels that he or she has had a telepathic experience, and 17 percent believe that they have been in touch with someone who has died. While only 18 percent of the population admits to being very or somewhat superstitious, another 16 percent admits to a slight level of superstition. Black cats crossing the path leads the list of experiences to be avoided, followed by walking under a ladder.

See also DELUSION; EXTRASENSORY PERCEPTION.

Gallup, George, Jr., and Newport, Frank. "Belief in Psychic and Paranormal Phenomena Widespread among Americans." *Gallup Poll Monthly* (Aug. 1990).

irritable bowel syndrome (IBS) A chronic disorder of the colon. Most IBS symptoms are related to an abnormal movement pattern of the colon. In people who have IBS, the muscle of the lower portion of the colon contracts abnormally. An abnormal contraction, or spasm, may be related to episodes of crampy pain. Sometimes the spasm delays the passage of stool, leading to constipation. At other times, the spasm leads to more rapid passage of feces, or diarrhea.

Though IBS can cause a great deal of discomfort, it is not serious and does not lead to any serious disease. However, for some people it can be disabling. Some people may be afraid to go to dinner parties, seek employment or travel on public transportation. However, with attention to proper diet, stress management and sometimes medication prescribed by a physician, most people with IBS can keep their symptoms under control.

Because doctors have been unable to pinpoint its organic cause, IBS has often been considered to be caused by emotional conflict or stress. Many individuals who suffer from anxiety disorders, panic attacks or panic disorder also suffer from IBS.

In addition to stress, there are other contributing factors. For example, eating causes contractions of the colon. Normally, this response may cause an urge to have a bowel movement within 30 to 60 minutes after a meal. In people with IBS, the exaggerated reflex can lead to cramps and sometimes diarrhea.

Stress also stimulates colonic spasm in people with IBS. This process is not clearly understood, but scientists point out that the colon is partially controlled by the nervous system. Mental health counseling is sometimes helpful for alleviating the symptoms due to IBS. However, according to the American College of Gastroenterology, this does not mean that IBS results from a personality disorder.

Self-help Relief from IBS For many people, eating the proper diet helps lessen IBS symptoms. Before considering a change in diet, one should note whether any particular foods seem to cause distress; these facts should be discussed with a physician. If dairy products cause symptoms to flare up, one can try decreasing the amount consumed at any one time. Yogurt can be a satisfactory substitute.

Dietary fiber, present in whole grain breads and cereals and in fruits and vegetables, also has been shown to be helpful in lessening IBS symptoms. High-fiber diets keep the colon mildly distended, which helps to prevent spasms from developing. Some forms of fiber also keep water in the stools, thereby preventing hard, difficult-to-pass stools from forming. High-fiber diets may cause gas and bloating; however, over time, these symptoms may dissipate as the digestive tract becomes used to the increased fiber intake.

Large meals may also cause cramping and diarrhea in some people. Eating smaller meals more frequently, or eating smaller portions of foods at mealtimes (especially foods that are low in fat and rich in carbohydrates and protein), may also help alleviate symptoms.

Pharmacologic Therapy Some doctors prescribe a combination of antispasmodic drugs and tranquilizers to help relieve symptoms. The major concerns in drug therapy of IBS are dependency on the medication and the effects the disorder can have on life-style. In an effort to regulate colonic activity or minimize stress, some patients become dependent on laxatives or tranquilizers. If this becomes the case, the physician should try to withdraw the drugs slowly.

See also ANXIETY; PANIC DISORDER.

Current Topics in Gastroenterology. American College of Gastroenterology. Winter 1991.

isocarboxazid An antidepressant drug in the monoamine oxidase inhibitor (MAOI) class (trade name: Marplan). It is effective in the treatment of major depression, dysthymic disorder and atypical depression. It is also useful in the treatment of panic disorder and the phobic disorders. All MAOIs can produce serious adverse reactions; patients should be supervised closely and must follow a special diet and avoid certain foods and medications that can cause a reaction.

See also ANTIDEPRESSANT MEDICATIONS; DEPRESSION; MONOAMINE OXIDASE INHIBITORS; TYRAMINE.

J

Janimine Trade name for imipramine hydrochloride, a tricyclic antidepressant drug. Imipramine is the prototype of the tricyclic antidepressants and is effective in the treatment of depressive episodes of major depression and bipolar, dysthymic, panic and phobic disorders.

See also ANTIDEPRESSANT MEDICATIONS; IMIPRAMINE HYDROCHLORIDE.

jealousy An emotion that encompasses a continuum of envy, reduction in self-esteem and hostility toward another. Jealousy is a feeling that some infants experience when a new sibling arrives. In adults, jealousy occurs when one's mate has a relationship with another individual, or in a divorce situation when one partner feels abandoned because his or her partner has been attracted to an-

other individual. Sexual jealousy, real or imagined, can trigger abuse of a spouse. Sexual jealousy is also referred to as the "Othello syndrome," which may be a type of delusional disorder, and has been reported to respond to medication therapy.

Homosexual jealousy may be more common among males than among female homosexuals, possibly because they are in a fairly closed community with some degree of social prejudice against it.

See also EMOTIONS.

Buunk, Bram, and Hupka, Ralph B. "Cross Cultural Differences in the Elicitation of Sexual Jealousy." *Journal of Sex Research* 23, no. 1 (Feb. 1987).

jet lag A disruption of one's body rhythms (circadian rhythms) resulting from traveling through several time zones within a short span of time. It takes many individuals several days to readjust their sleep schedule, appetite and ability to concentrate well while recovering from jet lag.

See also CIRCADIAN RHYTHMS.

journal keeping Writing things is practical advice for dealing with confusion and problems. Writing can put the individual close to or further from his concerns. Writing and reading what has been written sometimes exposes one's subconscious, suppressed feelings that can be dealt with more constructively when they are recognized. In this sense a diarist may get closer to himself and better understand self-motivations.

Some mental health professionals say that symptoms such as anxiety, depression and apathy are actually masks for envy, jealousy and rage turned inward at the self. Writing may help to get to the core of such feelings by bringing some of the repressed thoughts and attitudes into the open and eliminating some of the restrictions that sap energy and limit productivity. Some diarists have found it useful to write a portrait of a person whom they envy or who has angered them. The portrait sometimes reveals qualities of their own (which they see in the other person) that they wish to either develop or change.

The cathartic effect of writing involves a distancing from negative feelings and experiences. Once the feelings or experiences are described on paper, the writer frequently has a sense of being rid of them, of being ready to go on to something else. Simply the act of writing may also give a sense of control, a way of giving some order and manageability to problems. List making in a diary has also been found to be a good way of setting goals and giving order to what may seem to be an enormous or chaotic task. Keeping a journal has also been useful for the person who is attempting to control addictive or obsessive behavior. The diary not only improves self-understanding and serves as a way to record progress, but it also gives the individual something she can refer to when she wants a drink or a cigarette or is about to give in to a desire to overeat.

Journal keeping is used by many support groups for overeaters, as well as those who wish to stop smoking or drinking. Writing in a journal or diary also serves the obvious purposes of recording the events and impressions of the day and of improving writing style.

See also CONTROL; EATING DISORDERS; SUPPORT GROUPS.

Baldwin, Christina. *One to One: Self-understanding Through Journal Writing.* New York: M. Evans, 1977.
Rainer, Tristine. *The New Diary.* Los Angeles: J. P. Tarcher, 1978.

juvenile delinquency See CONDUCT DISORDER.

K

kinesics The study of communication as expressed through facial expression and other body movements. Theories and techniques of studying this type of nonverbal communication were developed by Ray L. Birdwhistell (1918–), who found that certain gestures and expressions were specifically male or female and also related to regional and national groups. Body language also changes with mood, health, age and degree of tension or relaxation. Birdwhistell developed his theories with the use of photography and with a notation system of symbols called kinegraphs to describe gestures and expressions.

See also BODY LANGUAGE.

Birdwhistell, Ray L. *Kinesics and Context.* Philadelphia: University of Pennsylvania Press, 1970.

kleptomania An overwhelming desire to steal or to pick up things that do not belong to oneself. An example is shoplifting, which accounts for countless lost millions of dollars' worth of merchandise from retail businesses around the world. Kleptomania may be a form of compulsion, similar to compulsive gambling in some cases. Some kleptomaniacs are highly professional people and, when apprehended, have no explanation for their behavior. Some kleptomaniacs perform their compulsion frequently; others are very selective and only do it when they believe that they will not be caught. Many famous and highly respected people are arrested in the United States every year for petty thievery, some of which may be compulsive.

See also OBSESSIVE-COMPULSIVE DISORDER.

Kohut, Heinz (1913–1981) Austrian-born American psychoanalyst. His work combined an interest in neurology, neuropathology and literature that led him to psychoanalysis. He developed a "self psychology" theory that challenged many of the theories of Sigmund Freud. Although Freudian in his training, Kohut differed with Freud's concept of sex and aggression as the basis of human emotion and personality structure. Instead he explored his interest in the narcissistic personality, which he felt was caused by social and family pressures rather than Oedipus conflict. Those who have followed his teachings and applied his theories in working with patients are known as Kohutians. His major works include *The Analysis of the Self* (1971), *The Restoration of the Self* (1977) and *The Search for the Self* (1978).

Kohut also differed from contemporary mental health practitioners and aroused criticism by being supportive to his patients rather than using the usual confrontational, challenging methods common in the field. Kohut was born in Vienna; in the United States he worked at the University of Chicago hospitals and the Institute for Psychoanalysis of Chicago.

The Heinz Kohut Archives were established in 1991 at the Institute for Psychoanalysis. For details on the archives, contact:

Kohut Archives
Institute for Psychoanalysis
180 North Michigan Avenue
Chicago, IL 60601
Phone: (312) 726-6300

See also FREUD, SIGMUND; NARCISSISM; PSYCHOANALYSIS; PSYCHOTHERAPY.

"Heinz Kohut, Whose 'Self' Theory Challenged Freud's, Is Dead at 68." *New York Times Biographical Service,* Oct. 1981.

Korsakoff's syndrome (psychosis)   An

organic syndrome that occurs in some chronic alcoholics, in some individuals who have severe head trauma and in several other conditions, such as prolonged infections, metallic poisoning or brain tumor. It was described in 1898 by Sergei Korsakoff (1854–1900), a Russian neurologist. Major symptoms include amnesia, confusion, confabulation (made-up stories) and disorientation.

L

labile   A term used in medical reports and records meaning likely to undergo change, or unstable. In mental health, the term is sometimes used to refer to emotional instability. Blood pressure that has a tendency to fluctuate is sometimes described as labile.

laboratory tests   A variety of different tests are available to determine medical conditions (such as thyroid hormone) that may contribute to depression, anxiety and other conditions that may detract from good mental health. Tests involve analyzing chemicals in the blood and/or urine or measuring brain waves.

The metabolism of the brain is separate from body metabolism to a great extent because of the existence of a physiological blood brain barrier that selectively allows chemicals to pass from the blood to the brain and back. There are presently no reliable tests for clinical use. Many tests used for research in mental illness have been advocated as useful, but none has been established as clinically useful to diagnose mental illness.

Tests of certain chemicals in cerebrospinal fluid, blood or urine, in response to the administration of challenges by single doses of hormones or chemicals that react in the brain, are producing new knowledge about some of the biochemical factors in some mental illnesses.

Neurological tests such as electroencephalograms, CAT (computerized axial tomography) scans and MRI (magnetic resonance imaging) are used to rule out neurological causes. "High-tech" research instruments, such as PET (positron emission tomography) scanning, allow for measurement of chemical changes in the human brain, while magnetic resonance spectroscopy (MRS) is able to measure chemical changes in certain brain regions.

Illness such as manic-depression, major depression, panic disorder and obsessive-compulsive disorder have shown changes from normal function in PET scans.

See also BLOOD TESTS; COMPUTERIZED AXIAL TOMOGRAPHY (CAT); ELECTROEN-CEPHALOGRAM.

lactate-induced anxiety See SODIUM LACTATE INFUSIONS.

latency (latency stage) A term relating to the stage of psychosexual development when sexual interest is repressed and sublimated. During this period, the child controls his or her energies and drives in socially acceptable ways, such as school work and group activities. For example, the child focuses attention on peer activities with members of his or her own sex. During this period, the child learns basic patterns of relating to people and the environment that will carry over when adult relationships are established. This stage lasts approximately from the fourth or fifth year until the onset of puberty.

latent content See DREAM ANALYSIS; DREAMING.

laughter A reaction of amusement and joy. Laughter is an involuntary sign indicating instant pleasure. As we laugh at a comic situation or funny story, we retreat temporarily from the reality of the seriousness of the adult world. A good laugh can help individuals relieve worries and stress. An ability to laugh easily is related to one's sense of humor. Often, a good sense of humor can help individuals deal with difficult situations in a sensible, more relaxed manner. Being able to maintain one's sense of humor can help one cope better with a chronic disease, for example. Some individuals suffering from depression lose their ability to laugh and see any humor in their lives or around them.

At times, laughter may also be a sign of defense against feelings of self-consciousness or embarrassment. An ability to laugh at oneself can be helpful, if not overdone. Some individuals find it difficult to laugh at themselves because they cannot acknowledge that they have either made a mistake or have done something "stupid."

There may be some physiological benefits from laughter. A good hearty laugh increases heartbeat, respiratory activity and oxygen exchange and may enhance the body's ability to fight inflammation. Laughter, like exercise, may also stimulate the brain to produce endorphins, which may increase one's sense of physical and mental well-being.

The late Norman Cousins (1912–1990), former editor of the *Saturday Review* and later a member of the faculty of the medical school at the University of California at Los Angeles, used laughter's curative power to help himself recover from a degenerative disease of the body's connective tissue.

The following are a few excerpts from Cousins's *Anatomy of an Illness,* in which he described the benefits of laughter:

> I made the joyous discovery that ten minutes of genuine belly laughter had an anesthetic effect and would give me at least two hours of pain-free sleep . . . Exactly what happens inside the human mind and body as the result of humor is difficult to say. But the evidence that it works has stimulated the speculations not just of physicians but of philosophers and scholars over the centuries.

While fighting ankylosing spondylitis, Cousins checked out of the hospital and spent weeks watching Marx Brothers movies and other comedies. He attributed his recovery to the positive feelings that laughter aroused in him.

Excessive giggling or totally inappropriate laughter or smiling may be symptoms of a form of schizophrenia (hebephrenic).

See also HUMOR; SCHIZOPHRENIA.

lay analyst Any nonmedical individual who performs psychoanalysis; such a person is trained in the theory and practice of psychoanalysis but does not have a medical degree.

See also PSYCHOANALYSIS.

L-dopa See LEVODOPA.

lead poisoning Lead poisoning is very harmful to young children. If they accidentally eat paint chips containing lead, they may develop severe learning disabilities. However, if detected early enough, lead poisoning can be treated. Lead encephalopathy is a brain disorder seen in children who eat lead-containing paint. Symptoms include convulsions, mania, delirium and coma. (Lead encephalopathy can also occur in adults who inhale tetraethyl lead in gasoline fumes.)

learned helplessness A term developed during the 1970s by Martin Seligman (1942–) to refer to a feeling of helplessness and stifling of motivation caused by exposure to aversive events over which the individual has no control, sometimes leading to depression.

When individuals believe they have no control over their situation, they feel powerless and helpless. Having no ability to gain praise or positive reinforcements, they become passive and nonassertive. Under these circumstances, tendencies toward depression increase. The situation develops sooner or later in individuals who experience their efforts having no positive effect on a negative or painful situation.

This researcher said that self-initiated behavior is learned and that hindrance to initiation contributes to the helpless feeling the individual develops over time. However, there is emerging evidence that the development of learned helplessness or resistance to this development in experimental animals may be controlled by a genetic trait and modified by drugs used to treat depression.

See also LEARNED OPTIMISM.

learned optimism An attempt to identify habits of thinking that lead to negative feelings and giving up (learned helplessness), coined by Martin Seligman (1942–) and reverse them so that when under stress or facing a failure, an individual may persist or fight back and not "give up." Examples of such negative beliefs are: (1) If I fail, it is always my fault. (2) If I fail in one area, I will fail in others. (3) If I fail now, I will continue to fail. Seligman attempts to show how reversal of these responses can produce learned optimism. Seligman expounded on this theory in his book *Helplessness: On Depression, Development, and Death* (San Francisco: W. H. Freeman, 1975).

See also LEARNED HELPLESSNESS.

learning disabilities A group of psychological and neurological disorders that interfere with learning or make learning impossible. Children with learning disabilities are often taunted by their peers, which further reduces their sense of self-esteem and motivation. Learning disorders are generally difficult to diagnose; after diagnosis, children should be observed and taught by specialists in their education. Such disabilities include problems in learning caused by defects in speech, hearing and memory but do not include disabilities due to emotional or environmental deprivation or to poor teaching.

There are some specific learning disabilities. For example, dyslexia is difficulty reading; dyscalculia is an inability to perform mathematical problems; and dysgraphia refers to writing disorders. Specific learning difficulties in children of normal intelligence may be caused by forms of minimal brain dysfunction, which may be inherited.

Children with minimal or borderline mental retardation generally have difficulty learning.

See also ATTENTION-DEFICIT HYPERACTIVITY DISORDER (ADHD); HYPERACTIVITY; MENTAL RETARDATION.

least restrictive care See THERAPEUTIC FOSTER CARE.

legal issues Many legal issues are involved in mental health care. As consumers become more aware of the standard of care required for mental health disorders, increasing attention is focused on issues including clients' rights, confidentiality between therapist and patient, competency of the mentally ill, the insanity defense, competency to stand trial, malpractice by health care practitioners and sexual misconduct by a therapist. Dying with dignity is also considered a legal issue, as a living will and a durable power of attorney are legal documents that can be enforced by courts of law.

Clients Rights and Civil Rights In 1986 the Protection and Advocacy Bill for Mentally Ill Individuals was enacted in the United States, which covers areas such as access to records and protection from abuse and neglect. Many states have laws stating rights of patients while hospitalized for psychiatric illnesses. The only right one loses under such circumstances is the right to liberty.

Confidentiality Confidentiality is the duty of a mental health practitioner to keep certain information from disclosure. This duty is usually governed by state laws but is also covered under many codes of ethics followed by health care workers. Confidentiality assures that client information is not used for personal gain or curiosity and that it is shared only among other individuals involved in the care of that client.

The concept of privileged communication involves statements between certain individuals, such as husband-wife, priest-penitent or psychiatrist-client, whom the law protects from disclosure. Some states have strict confidentiality laws relating to psychiatric hospitalizations; some states recognize nurse-client privilege.

Exceptions to confidentiality and professional privilege include allegations of child abuse, threats voiced to a therapist by a client toward himself or against a third person and a client's waiver of confidentiality and privileges by filing of a lawsuit or for medical insurance reimbursement. In most

Tests for Insanity (M'Naughten Rule)

The individual suffered from a mental condition that affected his reason, and he was unaware of the nature and quality of his act or that his act was wrong.

Irresistible impulse rule
The individual either met the M'Naughten test or in response to an irresistible impulse also lacked criminal responsibility even though he or she knew the wrongfulness of the act.

Durham rule
The acts were the product of a mental disease or defect.

American Law Institute
The individual was suffering from a mental illness at the time of the act and was unable to appreciate the wrongfulness of the act or was unable to conform behavior to requirements of law.

states, information regarding child abuse must be disclosed to proper authorities. In some cases, nonreporting of such information may be a criminal offense.

Mental health practitioners have a duty to use reasonable care to protect possible victims if they believe that their patients have intentions to kill or otherwise harm themselves or others. This protection may take the form of notifying police or other authorities.

Clinical information must be disclosed if an individual is in a court of law for a hearing on involuntary commitment or a guardianship proceeding. In addition, when a client brings a lawsuit in which his or her own mental status is an issue, medical information from a health care practitioner may be brought before the court. In such an event, the individual waives the right to confidentiality.

Insanity Defense In some cases, a pretrial order may require that the defendant's mental condition at the time the crime was committed be assessed. Several tests are used to determine "sanity."

Competency to Stand Trial Competency to stand trial refers to the mental condition of a defendant at the time of a criminal trial. If an individual is judged not competent to stand trial, he or she will be given immediate mental health treatment, with the main goal to restore competency. Such treatment may include medication, individual and group therapy and education about courtroom proceedings.

The rules for competency vary from state to state; however, a widely used assessment includes whether the client has an ability to assist the attorney with the defense, an ability to understand the nature and consequences of the charge and an ability to understand courtroom procedures.

Sexual Misconduct of Mental Health Practitioners Sexual relationships in a therapist-client relationship are unethical behavior and a criminal offense on the part of the therapist, who is presumed to be "taking advantage" of the patient. In some cases, sexual relations have been considered rape. In the early 1990s, cases have come to light in which the therapist included "sexual therapy" as part of psychotherapy and the client has brought charges against the therapist.

Least Restrictive Alternative Least restrictive alternative is a concept emphasized during the 1960s which says that less treatment rather than more is the most desirable objective, with the minimum level of restrictions on the patient's freedom.

This concept led to housing mentally retarded individuals within communities rather than segregating them in institutions.

McFarland, Gertrude K., and Thomas, Mary Durand. *Psychiatric Mental Health Nursing.* Philadelphia: J. B. Lippincott, 1991.

lesbianism   Female homosexuality. The term is derived from the name of the Greek island of Lesbos, home of the poetess Sappho. Women who practice lesbianism (lesbians) prefer women as sexual partners, although some lesbians also have or have had heterosexual partners. Lesbians as well

as homosexual men are referred to as part of the "gay community."

Lesbian sexual expression includes caressing, kissing, mutual masturbation and oral-genital contacts. Tribadism is the term for a practice in which one woman lies above the other, simulating coitus while the genitals are mutually stimulated. Masters and Johnson were among the first to write about sexual dysfunctions in homosexuals and included some lesbians in their study of anorgasmia.

Many lesbians have taken an active role in the "gay liberation" movement during the 1970s and 1980s, encouraging homosexuals to meet and discuss important issues and provide a political organization to work toward legal change and fight job discrimination. The National Gay Task Force is the clearinghouse for these groups and provides information on local organizations. The most well known lesbian organization is the Daughters of Bilitis (founded in 1956).

Lesbian couples have become parents (comothers) through artificial insemination and adoption. Lesbian relationships have been depicted in art, for example, in Rubens's *Jupiter and Callisto,* and in films, such as Bergman's *Persona* (1967).

For information, contact:

The National Gay Task Force
80 Fifth Avenue
New York, NY 10011
Phone: (212) 741-1010
See also HOMOSEXUALITY.

Furnell, Peter J. "Lesbian and Gay Psychology: A Neglected Area of British Research." *Bulletin of the British Psychological Society* 39 (1986).

Golombok, Susan; Spencer, Ann; and Rutter, Michael. "Children in Lesbian and Single-Parent Households: Psychosexual and Psychiatric Appraisal." *Journal of Child Psychology and Psychiatry* 24, no. 4 (1983).

Groves, Patricia, and Ventura, Lois A. "The Lesbian Coming Out Process: Therapeutic

Considerations." *Personnel and Guidance Journal* (Nov. 1983).

Harris, Mary B., and Turner, Pauline H. "Gay and Lesbian Parents." *Journal of Homosexuality* 12, no. 2 (Winter 1985/86).

Owen, William F., Jr. "Medical Problems of the Homosexual Adolescent." *Journal of Adolescent Health Care* 6 (1985).

Polikoff, Nancy. "Lesbian Mothers, Lesbian Families: Legal Obstacles, Legal Challenges." *Review of Law and Special Change* 14 (1986).

leukotomy, leucotomy (prefrontal lobotomy)   A surgical procedure on the brain in which certain nerve pathways in the prefrontal lobes are severed from the rest of the brain as therapy to reduce violent behavior and treat severe resistant forms of depression, psychosis and obsessive-compulsive disorder. However, since the advent of better methods of psychotherapy and improved pharmacologic means, this treatment is rarely used.

More specific procedures involving less brain tissue destruction and side effects have been developed in a neurosurgical procedure called cingulotomy.

See also TRANQUILIZER MEDICATIONS.

levodopa   (trade names: Dopar, Larodopa) Levodopa is beneficial in both Parkinson's disease and postencephalitic parkinsonism. All major Parkinson's symptoms may be ameliorated, particularly bradykinesia, rigidity and, to a lesser extent, tremor. Balance, posture, gait and handwriting improve promptly; mood may be elevated. Although all intellectual functions may improve initially, this effect is often transient. Mental deterioration and dementia may develop during long-term therapy. It has not been established whether mental changes reflect progression of degenerative disease or are a direct effect of levodopa.

See also PARKINSON'S DISEASE.

American Medical Association. *Drug Evaluations Annual, 1991*. Chicago: AMA, 1991.

libido   A term derived from the Latin words for "desire, lust" commonly used for sexual desire or "love energy." An active libido is generally considered a sign of good mental health, particularly in younger, healthy individuals. In some individuals, libido wanes with age but not necessarily so in every case.

Sigmund Freud used the term to relate to human drives including the sexual instinct, love-object seeking and pleasure. To Freud, libido was one of two vital human instincts, the drive toward self-preservation and the drive toward sexual gratification. According to Freud, when an individual represses libido because of social pressures, ongoing repression leads to personality changes and to anxieties.

Freud's original concept was expanded by Carl Jung to relate the term to the general life force that provides energy for all types of activities, including sexual, social, cultural and creative.

Loss of libido is one of the most frequent problems sex therapists encounter. It is one of the more difficult problems to treat, as the cause is often an underlying physical, emotional or psychological problem and not correctable by simple behavioral approaches.

Loss of libido occurs in men and women during many illnesses, including depression, alcoholism and drug addiction. Stress and overwork can cause loss of libido, as can certain medications or loss of an appropriate partner.

See also DEPRESSION; FREUD, SIGMUND; SEX THERAPY.

Librium   Trade name for chlordiazepoxide hydrochloride, a widely prescribed sedative-tranquilizer containing a benzodiazepine derivative. It is used to reduce anxieties and tension and to treat or prevent withdrawal symptoms during alcoholic withdrawal and detoxification treatment. It should not be taken with alcohol or other central nervous system depressants. Physical and psychological additive effects and dependency can develop. Overdoses can result in drowsiness, confusion, reduced reflexes and possibly coma.

See also ANTIANXIETY MEDICATIONS; BENZODIAZEPINE MEDICATIONS; CHLORDI-AZEPOXIDE; DELIRIUM TREMENS.

limbic system The part of the parasympathetic nervous system that controls expression of emotional behavior, including sweating, trembling, breathing, alterations in facial expression, drives such as attack (fight or flight), defense, thirst, hunger and sexual motivation.

See also BRAIN.

listening A skill necessary for good communication between an individual and any type of mental health professional or psychotherapist. Listening on the part of the therapist requires more than just not speaking. It is an active process in which the therapist gives complete attention to what the client is saying and how he is saying it. The therapist looks for nonverbal behavior, such as body posture and eye contact or lack of it. The therapist stops thinking of personal experiences as well as personal judgments of the client. During the listening process, the therapist conveys concern and respect and can reinforce or encourage client verbalizations. The therapist can also influence the client to verbalize by nonverbal gestures such as a nod of the head or a smile.

See also BODY LANGUAGE.

McFarland, Gertrude K., and Thomas, Mary Durand. *Psychiatric Mental Health Nursing.* Philadelphia: J. B. Lippincott, 1991.

literacy See ILLITERACY.

lithium carbonate (trade names: Eskalith, Lithane, Lithonate, Lithotabs) A therapeutic agent that counteracts mood changes and is considered to be the only specific antimanic drug for the prophylaxis (prevention) and treatment of bipolar disorder. Acute hypomanic and manic episodes respond to lithium, but combined therapy with an antipsychotic agent may be preferred to control behavior initially. Lithium may be effective in maintenance therapy for major depression, although antidepressants are preferred. Lithium carbonate is also used in preventing cluster headache in some people.

The antimanic action of lithium is not fully understood, but it seems to act by altering the metabolism of norepinephrine in the brain, thus altering the chemical balance within certain nerve cells. Synthesis and release of acetylcholine are depressed. Because lithium interferes with calcium, the release of many neurotransmitters, including monoamines, is diminished.

Lithium has little effect on otherwise healthy patients except for mild sedation, and it has an antiadrenergic or anticholinergic action. In normal individuals, lithium produces mild subjective feelings of lethargy, inability to concentrate and possibly a decrease in memory function; slow waves in the electrocardiogram increase.

Lithium salts were used during the 1940s as a sodium chloride substitute for cardiac patients on salt-free diets, but its use was stopped when severe side effects and deaths were reported. Then, in the late 1940s, Australian researchers noted that lithium had certain tranquilizing properties; lithium safely quieted manic patients to whom it was administered. However, because of known toxic effects of lithium, interest in it dropped for almost a decade. In the 1950s and 1960s, some European studies led to increased acceptance of lithium in European psychiatric practices as safe and effective therapy for manic-depressive illness. In the 1970s, lithium began to be used in American practice after the need for careful monitoring of blood levels to overcome side effects was understood.

See also ANTIDEPRESSANT MEDICATIONS; BIPOLAR DISORDER; HEADACHES; MANIC-DE-

Checklist for Patients Taking Lithium

- Take medication regularly as prescribed.
- Obtain regular blood tests for lithium levels.
- Have the physician take blood tests for lithium levels 12 hours after the last dose.
- Inform the physician if other medications are being taken, as they can change lithium levels.
- Notify the physician whenever there is a change in diet, since it may cause the lithium level in the body to change.
- Advise the physician about any changes in frequency of urination, diarrhea, vomiting, excessive sweating or illness; further adjustments in dosage may be necessary.
- If planning to become pregnant, advise the physician.
- It takes time for mood swings to be completely controlled by lithium; be patient and continue taking the medication until advised otherwise by the psycisian.

SOURCE: Roesch, Roberta. *Encyclopedia of Depression*. New York: Facts On File, 1990.

PRESSIVE ILLNESS; NOREPINEPHRINE; TRICYCLIC ANTIDEPRESSANT.

American Medical Association. *AMA Drug Evaluations Annual, 1991*. Chicago: AMA, 1991.

live-in   A common term for a member of the opposite sex who lives with one and to whom one is not married. The term evolved during the last two decades of the 20th century when this practice became fairly common in the United States among men and women of all ages. The demographic term for this situation, used by the U.S. Census department, is POSSLQ (person of the opposite sex sharing living quarters). It is also known as cohabitation.

living alone   See SOCIOECONOMIC FACTORS AND CARDIOVASCULAR DISEASE.

living together   See COHABITATION; LIVE-IN.

living will   See DYING WITH DIGNITY; LEGAL ISSUES.

lobotomy   A surgical procedure on the brain in which certain nerve pathways from the frontal lobes are cut in an attempt to change behavior.

See also LEUKOTOMY.

logotherapy   An approach to the spiritual and existential aspects of mental disorders, developed by Victor Frankl, a German-born American psychiatrist (1905–).

See PSYCHOTHERAPY.

loneliness   A state of mind and a unique set of circumstances, not to be confused with being alone. An element in loneliness is the lack of control or choice in being alone. For example, a happily married woman who moves to a new city because of her husband's career may feel lonely. She will be cut off from her previous network of acquaintances and very much on her own while he is welcomed by his new colleagues and absorbed in his new position. On the other hand, those who have chosen life-styles and careers that require isolation and independence sometimes profit from, rather than resent, solitude. Lifelong conditioning may also make solitude attractive and even essential to some people. For example, only children, who have had to rely on their inner resources since childhood, are disproportionately present among astronauts and writers.

The potential for loneliness is strong in adolescence, when teenagers long to be part of their peer group and are deeply wounded by slights and rejections. Conditions such as mental or physical handicaps and language or ethnic barriers sometimes produce isolation that results in loneliness.

Loneliness sometimes results from a sense of loss, a feeling that the past was better than the present. A 1990 Gallup poll showed that loneliness is most common among the widowed, separated and divorced. Over half of this group felt lonely "frequently" or "sometimes," compared with 29 percent of the married participants. Adults who had never married fell in between. According to the survey, women are more likely to be lonely than men, possibly not because they genuinely have less companionship but because they place more importance on friendship and are more willing to confess to being lonely.

Money played a role in the Gallup survey as a preventive for loneliness. The survey showed 27 percent of adults with incomes over $50,000 are "frequently" or "sometimes" lonely, compared with 46 percent of those whose incomes were under $20,000.

Lonely people behave in different ways. Some fit the shy, retiring stereotype often assigned to the lonely. Others compensate for their feelings by trying to become the life of the party, throwing themselves into frenetic activity or by accumulating possessions.

Loneliness is often a factor in depression, drug addiction and alcoholism.

See also DEPRESSION.

longitudinal study A study in which the same group of individuals are observed and characteristics are noted at two or more different points in time. For example, in a longitudinal study of a group of depressed patients taking the same drug, their responses to the drug therapy will be measured at two or usually more points in time. Much research on pharmacologic treatment of mental health disorders is based on longitudinal studies. They are often submitted as evidence of drug efficacy when applications for approval of drug products are submitted to the U.S. Food and Drug Administration.

lorazepam A drug (trade name: Ativan) effective as an antianxiety and hypnotic agent.

See also BENZODIAZEPINE MEDICATIONS.

love object The person in whom one invests affection, devotion and usually sexual interest.

LSD See LYSERGIC ACID DIETHYLAMIDE.

L-tryptophan An essential amino acid found in eggs, turkey, milk, beans and wheat that human bodies use to manufacture proteins. The human brain uses L-tryptophan to manufacture serotonin, an amine transmitter. When the diet does not include an adequate amount of L-tryptophan, brain serotonin levels fall; some have speculated that this may contribute to depression and some anxieties. During the 1970s and 1980s, many individuals obtained L-tryptophan as an over-the-counter medication in tablet, capsule and powder form as a sleep aid and relaxant. The product was withdrawn from the market in 1989 when the Food and Drug Administration found that there may be a link between consumption of L-tryptophan supplements and an outbreak of a rare blood disorder (eosinophilamyalgia syndrome).

See also ANTIDEPRESSANT MEDICATIONS.

Kahn, Rene S., and Westenberg, Herman G. M. "L-5-Hydroxytryptophan in the Treatment of Anxiety Disorders." *Journal of Affective Disorders* 8 (1985).

Ludiomil Trade name for an antidepressant drug (generic name: maprotiline). Its pharmacologic and clinical profiles, as well as efficacy, resemble those of imipramine.

See also ANTIDEPRESSANT MEDICATIONS; IMIPRAMINE HYDROCHLORIDE.

lumbar puncture See BRAIN.

lump in the throat Many individuals have experienced this unpleasant sensation at some time as part of an anxiety reaction. It feels like there is something to swallow, but the sensation does not go away upon swallowing. It may often feel difficult to swallow. Some individuals have this feeling before a stressful event, such as a public appearance, and are concerned that they not be able to speak appropriately. Relaxation and breathing techniques can help overcome this feeling. The medical term for lump in the throat is globus hystericus.

See also ANXIETY; STRESS.

lunacy An obsolete term meaning insanity. The term "lunacy" derives from the word *luna,* meaning "moon" in Latin. Ancients believed that phases of the moon could bring on mental illness and that as the moon waxed and waned, mental illnesses came and went. Until the 20th century, individuals with mental problems were referred to as lunatics, and mental hospitals were referred to as lunatic asylums.

See also INSANITY.

lysergic acid diethylamide (LSD) LSD is a very potent, odorless and colorless chemical hallucinogen that was first synthesized in the late 1930s. Effects of LSD can last from two to 12 hours and may include impaired judgment of time, distorted visual perceptions and hallucinations. LSD causes dilated pupils, elevated body temperatures and high blood pressure. Psychological reactions include suspicious behavior, fear, confusion, anxiety, loss of control and flashbacks. Flashbacks are common over a period of several years after the drug was consumed.

LSD is also known as acid and microdot and is usually found in liquid form, which is placed on a sugar cube or on blotter paper and then digested.

See also FLASHBACKS; HALLUCINATION; HALLUCINOGENS.

Media Resource Guide on Common Drugs of Abuse. Public Relations Society of America, National Capital Chapter, Fairfax, Va., September 1990.

M

magic An ability to exert control over human affairs and the forces of nature. Practitioners of magic may be known as witch doctors, wizards, diviners, wise women, witches, sorcerers or magicians. Magic may also fall within the bounds of religious practice and may include contact with supernatural forces. Historically, the mental health of those who practice magic, as well as those who believe in it, has been challenged or questioned by less believing individuals.

The ability to practice magic has often been thought to be inborn or hereditary. Magical arts are often acquired secretly in an individual manner with the aspiring magician progressing ever higher in his art in his own way rather than being taught in the usual manner. The ability to practice magic is thought by some to be amoral. Magical spells may be used to create or destroy; they may also have a preventive, protective nature. An evil spell may be cast without the victim's knowledge to keep her from hiring a more powerful sorcerer. For victims of magic who are aware of the spell, it may become a self-fulfilling prophecy, since in civilizations in which magical beliefs are strong, simply the knowledge of being bewitched is enough to make the victim weaken and, sometimes, die. In such cases it is the power of suggestion that is the strong force at work.

Early humans and the classical civilizations believed in and practiced magic. Christianity has both used and rejected magical beliefs and practices. Early Christians gained power by claims that their mystical ceremonies and rituals were superior to those of pagans. Later Christianity rejected magic as a vestige of paganism and an attempt to interfere with God's will. During the Middle Ages various temples and secret societies preserved magical beliefs and practices. The scientific, rational philosophies of the 17th and 18th centuries caused magic to fall into disrepute. In the 19th century, Aleister Crowley and a fraternal group, the Hermetic Order of the Golden Dawn, revived interest in magic. An interest in magic resurged again with the religion of neo-pagan witchcraft, which forbids the use of magic for other than beneficial purposes.

Throughout history, magic has been used as an explanation for things that cannot be seen or answered logically. Individuals seeking answers become believers.

"Magic," in Guiley, Rosemary Ellen, *Harper's Encyclopedia of Mystical and Paranormal Experience*. San Francisco: Harper, 1991.

magnetic resonance imaging (MRI)
See BRAIN IMAGING.

maieusiophobia   A morbid fear of childbirth. Women who suffer from maieusiophobia may fear that the child will die during childbirth or be born with a birth defect. Such women may also fear they will be physically deformed themselves and may have an aversion to blood, surgical procedures, doctors or hospitals. Women who have this fear may view adoption as a more comfortable option than childbirth.

See also PHOBIA.

mainstreaming   An educational technique that involves placing students who are handicapped or exceptional in other ways as much as possible with normal students in an environment that offers as few restrictions as possible. Mainstreaming programs allow for a flexible assessment of each child's needs with the consultation of a variety of support personnel, such as school psychologists, to give each child an individual program that will suit his needs and specific disabilities and talents. This concept also calls for frequent assessment of a child's progress in consultation with his parents.

See also MENTAL RETARDATION.

"Least Restrictive Environment," "Mainstreaming," In Dejnozka, Edward L., *American Educator's Encyclopedia*. Westport, Conn.: Greenwood Press, 1982.

major affective disorders   A term referring to disorders characterized by noticeable and persistent mood disturbances, such as depression, mania or bipolar disorder. These disorders may be episodic or chronic.

See also AFFECTIVE DISORDERS; BIPOLAR DISORDER; BRAIN CHEMISTRY; DEPRESSION; MANIC-DEPRESSIVE ILLNESS.

major depression   The term used to indicate a clinical depression that meets specific diagnostic criteria regarding duration, functional impairment and involvement of several physical and mental symptoms.

See also ANTIDEPRESSANT MEDICATION; BRAIN CHEMISTRY; DEPRESSION.

male sexual dysfunction   Any condition that interferes with a man's sexual performance and gratification owing to psychological or physiological factors or both. These include low sexual drive, erectile dysfunctions, premature ejaculation and inhibited ejaculation.

See also IMPOTENCE; SEX THERAPY; SEXUAL DYSFUNCTION.

LoPiccoli, Joseph, and Stock, Wendy E. "Treatment of Sexual Dysfunction." *Journal of Consulting and Clinical Psychology* 54, no. 2 (1986).

malingering   Purposeful pretense of physical or psychological symptoms for a particular reason, such as to obtain time off from work or to avoid a family affair. This differs from factitious disorders, in which one pretends illness for no reason other than to gain attention. This also differs from hypochondriasm, in which the person is obsessed with her own physical condition and believes that she has symptoms.

See also MUNCHAUSEN'S SYNDROME.

mania   A mental disorder characterized by periods of elation, overactivity or irritability. Mania usually occurs in conjunction with moods of depression, and when the two occur at intervals in the same individual, the disorder is known as manic-depressive illness.

A manic individual will show an abnormal increase in activity and believe that he is capable of achieving any goal. There may be a grandiose sense of knowing more than others around, extravagant spending of money, little need for sleep, increased appetite for food, alcohol and sex or inappropriate bursts of laughter or anger. Severe mania may result in violence, and hospital admission is often required. Relatively mild symptoms are known as hypomania.

The first appearance of manic attacks is usually before age 30 and may last for a few days or several months. When attacks begin after age 40, they may be more prolonged. Mania often runs in families and may be genetically transmitted.

Treatment of mania includes the use of antipsychotic drugs; relapses are prevented with the use of lithium.

See also ANTIDEPRESSANT MEDICATIONS; ANTIPSYCHOTIC MEDICATIONS; LITHIUM CARBONATE.

manic-depressive illness   A mental disorder characterized by disturbances of moods, including depression, mania (unipolar) or a swing between the two states (bipolar disorder). In the manic state, the individual is excessively elated, agitated and hyperactive and has accelerated thinking and speaking.

In the manic phase, overactivity may be due largely to extra amounts of the neurochemical dopamine in parts of the brain.

Depression is more common than mania, affecting about one in 10 men and one in five women at some time in their lives. Mania (unipolar or bipolar) affects only about eight per 1,000 people, men and women equally. More than 80 percent of patients recover from this disorder.

Severe manic-depressive illness often requires hospitalization. Antidepressant drugs or electroconvulsive therapy are sometimes used in treating depression. Antipsychotic drugs are used to control the symptoms of mania. To prevent relapse, lithium is often used. When taking lithium as advised by their physician, many people who have manic-depressive illness can lead healthy, well-balanced lives.

See also AFFECTIVE DISORDERS; ANTIDEPRESSANT MEDICATIONS; ANTIPSYCHOTIC MEDICATIONS; BIPOLAR DISORDER; LITHIUM CARBONATE; MANIA.

manic episode   See MANIA; MANIC-DEPRESSIVE ILLNESS.

MAOI   See MONOAMINE OXIDASE INHIBITORS.

MAO Inhibitors   See MONOAMINE OXIDASE INHIBITORS.

maprotiline   An antidepressant drug (trade name: Ludiomil). The pharmacologic and clinical profiles, as well as efficacy, resemble those of imipramine. This drug principally blocks the neuronal uptake of norepinephrine; it has relatively weak serotonergic activity.

See also ANTIDEPRESSANT MEDICATIONS; DEPRESSION; TRICYCLIC ANTIDEPRESSANT MEDICATIONS.

marijuana   Marijuana is a drug derived from the plant *Cannabis sativa*. Marijuana's effects vary considerably, depending on the personality and health of the user, frequency and circumstance of use, potency and other factors. The larger the dose, the greater the hypnotic effects and the loss of psychomotor functions. Marijuana use intensifies sensory experiences, including seeing, hearing, tasting and touching. The user may feel relaxed or, less commonly, anxious, fearful and distrustful. Sustained mental effort may be difficult for marijuana users; they are easily distracted and often cannot complete a thought. There is no accepted medical use for smoking marijuana, though THC (delta-9 tetrahydrocannabinol) in capsule form is used in certain medical cases.

Problems associated with chronic marijuana use include decreased blood supply to the heart; damage to the lungs and pulmonary system; impaired sexual development and fertility; damage to the immune system;

and "amotivational" syndrome, which includes low motivation, loss of attention, impaired communication skill, lethargy and impaired learning ability. Marijuana impairs motor ability and judgment, increasing the likelihood of accidents. Marijuana adversely affects the user's ability to drive because of impaired perception and reaction time. Marijuana smoke contains more cancer-causing agents than tobacco smoke.

Marijuana use during pregnancy is associated with low birth weight and body length, prematurity and a range of other problems. Marijuana is also transmitted in breast milk.

Marijuana is an ongoing problem for law enforcement officials as well as mental health workers who treat drug abusers. Most of the marijuana consumed in the United States comes from Colombia, Mexico, Jamaica and Thailand. It is also cultivated domestically. Marijuana consists of crumbled dried leaves, stems, seeds and flowering tops of the plant. It is composed of over 400 chemicals; when smoked, it produces more than 2,000 separate chemicals. THC is the principal psychoactive ingredient that causes the marijuana "high." THC is also available in capsules.

The THC content of marijuana averages about 6 percent. A form of marijuana, sinsemilla (in Spanish, meaning "without seeds"), is prepared from the unpollinated female cannabis plant and is generally more potent (up to 20 percent THC) than other forms of marijuana.

Marijuana is smoked in hand-rolled cigarettes, called "joints," or in pipes or water pipes called "bongs." Marijuana can be smoked alone or in mixture with other drugs. It can also be eaten in foods such as brownies or spaghetti sauce.

See also SUBSTANCE ABUSE.

Media Resource Guide on Common Drugs of Abuse. Public Relations Society of America, National Capital Chapter, Fairfax, Va., September 1990.

marital rape   See RAPE, RAPE PREVENTION AND RAPE TRAUMA SYNDROME.

marital therapy   Therapy for individuals in a troubled marriage. This may involve couples therapy or therapy for the individuals alone. The therapy may be aimed at overcoming specific problems, such as coping with the other's depression, or at saving a marriage that might end in divorce. Marital therapy may involve only psychological counseling or sexual therapy or a combination of both.

See also BEHAVIORAL THERAPY; DIVORCE; FAMILY THERAPY; MARRIAGE; SEX THERAPY.

Marplan   See ISOCARBOXAZID.

marriage   Lifelong emotional and legal commitment to another individual. Some form of marriage has been present in all cultures, and most societies have considered marriage necessary for a satisfying adult life. Romance, mutual selection and compatibility are generally considered less important in other cultures than in the modern Western world. In some societies, couples are promised to each other as children or even before birth. Family or tribal relationships and economic considerations quite often take precedence over individual wishes. Some arranged marriages result in lifelong loving relationships, while others lapse into marriages of convenience and for procreation, with one or more of the spouses acquiring other romantic and sexual partners.

Marriage ceremonies may be lengthy and complex or very simple. Most marriage ceremonies involve, or are followed by, a meal or the ceremonial consumption of food. Ceremonies are frequently a blend of religious observance and superstition or folk culture.

Monogamy, the marriage of one man with one woman, is the common form of marriage in the Western world. Polygyny, the union of one man and several wives, is practiced in some African tribes and Islamic cultures. In Tibet, one woman may have several husbands who are brothers. The Catholic church and other religious groups consider members of religious orders married to their divine being. Many religious groups have prohibitions against marrying outside the group. Most cultures prohibit incest to some degree.

In her early 1980 work, *Outrageous Acts and Everyday Rebellions,* feminist Gloria Steinem issued a veiled warning that the reason that women are not attracted to gambling is that the uncertainties and precariousness of marriage satisfy most women's gambling instincts. However, in the face of recent reports showing the statistical difficulty of acquiring a husband and of career possibilities opened up by the women's movement, women still seem to favor marriage as a way of life. A Gallup poll in 1987 showed that only 8 percent of the women surveyed thought that being a single career woman was an ideal way of life, approximately the same percentage as when the question was asked in 1975. Another Gallup poll indicated what may be a return to a more conservative approach to marriage and sexual relationships. Whether a product of a heightened national interest in religion, an overall conservative trend or fears about sexually transmitted disease, the segment of the population who believe that premarital sex is wrong rose from 39 percent in 1985 to 46 percent in 1987.

Opposites may attract, but they probably will not marry or stay married, according to researchers. People do tend to marry within their own social and educational groups, although tendencies to marry within religious groups are crumbling. This may be due in part to the fact that modern American life brings people of differing religions together but somewhat segregates by social and educational status. People who "marry down" in social, financial or educational terms quite often acquire a more physically attractive or personable spouse than if they married at their level.

Dissolution of Marriage Rising A 1980s statistical projection predicted that four out of 10 marriages of the 1970s would end in divorce. Marriage has undergone great stress and strain in the last 30 years. From a romantic commitment that was entered into for life and was almost a social requirement

in the 1950s, traditional marriage became a subject that aroused feelings of rebellion and disdain in the late 1960s and 1970s as divorce became more common and socially acceptable and premarital sex became more common. Young people experimented with communal arrangements or simply lived together without benefit of marriage vows.

Because so many traditional monogamous marriages have resulted in divorce, many individuals have experimented with alternative marital-sexual relationships. Recently the possibility of marriages between homosexual couples has become an issue.

Open Marriage This emphasizes equality and flexibility in female roles in the marriage and includes an agreement not to be emotionally, socially or sexually exclusive. The concept was espoused by Nena and George O'Neil in their book *Open Marriage* (1972). Disadvantages of this system include possibilities for jealousy and fear of losing one's spouse. Although this system attracted attention, it was largely discarded as generally unworkable for most couples.

Group Marriage A term for "multilateral" marriage. This involves a group of individuals with some type of marriage ties to one another. For example, each person may be married to at least two others in the group. Sexual activities with each of one's spouses occur on a rotation schedule. Group sex is uncommon.

Swinging A married couple's sharing sexual activities with another couple or couples. A pair may switch partners with another married couple, or a married couple may engage in sexual activities with a single female, single male or an unmarried couple. Recreational swingers are primarily interested in sexual activities without close friendships or involvement with their sexual partners. "Utopian" swingers seek sex activity as well as close interpersonal relationships.

Swinging first gained public attention during the 1950s (then known as "wife swapping"). There have been magazines and clubs devoted to swinging. Major reasons for dropping out of swinging is jealousy, the threat to marriage and the threat of sexually transmitted diseases and even acquiring the HIV virus or AIDS.

Child Marriage   A marriage between an adult (usually male) and a minor female is known as child marriage. Historically, some parents permitted daughters to marry older men in order to provide support.

Fear of marriage is known as gamophobia or gametophobia. In the late 1980s and early 1990s, many young people developed a fear of commitment and have thus avoided marriage until their late thirties. Marriage later in life brings with it the stress of the "biological clock" for women and increased anxieties about becoming mothers before they are too old.

See also COHABITATION; DIVORCE; LIVE-IN; MOTHERS; REMARRIAGE; STEPFAMILIES; COURTSHIP, LOVE, ROMANCE, RELATIONSHIPS in BIBLIOGRAPHY.

Filsinger, E. E. "Marital Adjustment," in Corsini, Raymond J., ed., *Encyclopedia of Psychology,* vol. 2. New York: Wiley: 1984.

Kahn, Ada P., and Holt, Linda Hughey. *The A to Z of Women's Sexuality.* Alameda, Calif.: Hunter House, 1992.

Steinem, Gloria. "Late Night Thoughts of a Media Watcher," in *Outrageous Acts and Everyday Rebellions.* New York: New American Library, 1983.

Stuart, R. B. "Spouse Selection," in Corsini, Raymond J., ed., *Encyclopedia of Psychology,* vol. 3. New York: Wiley, 1984.

Turner, Edith, and Frese, Pamela R. "Marriage," in Eliade, Mircea, ed., *The Encyclopedia of Religion,* vol. 9. New York: Macmillan, 1987.

"U.S. Women Endorse Jobs, Marriage and Children" *Gallup Report* (Dec. 1987).

Marsalid   See IPRONIAZID.

masked depression   A depression that a person hides behind a facade of appearing to be well. These individuals outwardly do what they think is expected of them while inwardly feeling hopeless and even suicidal. They may have little facial animation and appear to have a fixed expression, showing little emotion. The terms "depressive equivalents" "affective equivalents," "hidden depression" and "missed depression" are also used for this situation. Many health care professionals feel that "borderline depression" may be categorized as masked depression.

See also DEPRESSION; MANIC-DEPRESSIVE ILLNESS.

masochism   A desire to be abused either physically or emotionally. It is often used to refer to achievement of sexual excitement by means of one's own suffering. The condition can be life threatening if individuals increase the degree of their masochistic acts. The term was derived from the name of the 19th-century Austrian novelist Leopold von Sacher-Masoch.

See also SADISM; SADOMASOCHISM.

massage   Massage is an effective way of relieving stress and body aches caused by tension for many people. Massage increases blood flow and relaxes muscles.

As a prelude to lovemaking, massage is enjoyed by many couples. Advantages include relaxing one's partner and learning the partner's preferences for areas to be touched and caressed.

mastectomy   Surgical removal of a breast or breast tissue. This is usually done to remove malignant tumors and to prevent metastasis of tumor cells to other areas. A simple mastectomy involves removal of a whole breast. A radical mastectomy involves removal of the entire breast, lymph nodes, fat and underlying muscles to the chest wall. A lumpectomy is limited to the area of the tumor. There are many psychological consequences of mastectomy. Many women fear a loss of sexual attractiveness and a lack of femininity following surgery. Many opt for reconstructive surgery either at the time of the mastectomy or at a later date.

It is helpful to women to consult a psychological counselor at the same time as consulting a surgeon, oncologist and plastic surgeon. Several major medical centers across the country include mental health counseling as part of a comprehensive breast center.

A national support group for women who have had mastectomies is Y-ME.

For information, contact:

Y-ME Breast Cancer Support Program
1757 Ridge Road
Homewood, IL 60430
Phone: (708) 799-8338

See also BODY IMAGE.

masturbation Sexual self-stimulation for gratification and pleasure and usually to orgasm. The usually method is massaging the penis or clitoris with the hand. In previous generations, parents warned young people against masturbation, suggesting that doing so would lead to acne, impotence, insanity or worse consequences. Thus, many people who believed that they were going against cultural mores developed anxieties and guilt about the practice. Now it is considered normal behavior, particularly among teenagers and those without sexual partners. Masturbation can be done on oneself and can also be performed on another person.

In the 1960s, Alfred Kinsey said that more than 90 percent of men reported masturbatory experiences in their adolescence. In the early 1980s, Shere Hite, an American researcher on female sexuality, reported that about 82 percent of American women masturbate.

Sex therapists during the latter part of the 20th century use masturbation as a technique to instruct clients in learning to know what pleases them so that they can later instruct a partner.

Compulsive masturbation is an obsessive urge to masturbate without sexual feeling or satisfaction. Such an individual may substitute masturbation for lack of social satisfaction, to compensate for shyness or an inability to establish relationships with the opposite sex or to relieve anxieties.

See also SAFE SEX; SEX THERAPY; SEXUAL DYSFUNCTION.

Kahn, Ada P., and Holt, Linda Hughey. *The A to Z of Women's Sexuality*. Alameda, Calif.: Hunter House, 1992.

Medicaid A federal-state medical assistance program authorized in 1965 to pay for health care services used by people defined as medically needy or categorically needy. The latter type of persons are low-income aged, blind, disabled, first-time pregnant women or families with dependent children. Medically needy persons are any of the above whose incomes are above eligibility limits for the categorically needy but who have high medical expenses that reduce their resources below established limits.

See also MEDICARE.

Medicare A nationwide, federally administered health insurance program authorized in 1965 to cover the cost of hospitalization, medical and mental health care and other related services. Eligible persons must be over age 65, receive Social Security Disability Insurance payments for two years or suffer from end-stage renal disease. Medicare consists of two separate but coordinated programs: hospital insurance (Part A) and supplementary medical insurance (Part B). Health insurance protection is available to insured persons without regard to income.

Medicare intermediaries or carriers are fiscal agents (typically Blue Cross plans or commercial insurance firms) under contract to the Health Care Financing Administration for administration of specific Medicare tasks. These tasks include determining reasonable costs for covered items and services, making payments and guarding against unnecessary use of covered services for Medicare Part A payments. Intermediaries also make payments for home health and outpatient hospital services covered under Part B.

See also MEDICAID.

U.S. Congress, Office of Technology Assessment. *Health Care in Rural America*. OTA-H-434. Washington, D.C.: USGPO, 1990.

meditation   A technique for focusing attention so that one becomes wholly involved with a single focus. Meditation is a very self-disciplined routine and a way to learn more about one's own thoughts and feelings. Modern techniques of meditation have developed from centuries-old Eastern cultures. People who have learned to meditate find that they can control their heart rate, blood pressure and oxygen consumption. Meditation can help control some symptoms of stress. For meditation, it is necessary to have a quiet atmosphere and 20-minute periods of time once or more daily. In addition, there is often a focus on either a special word or "mantra"—which the individual repeats over and over again—or steadily watching an object, such as a candle flame.

See also STRESS; TRANSCENDENTAL MEDITATION.

medulla oblongata   See BRAIN.

megalomania   Exaggeration of one's own abilities or importance. Megalomania may become a delusion that one is someone famous. It may also take the form of becoming involved in some grandiose activity, such as renting an amusement park for a party. Although megalomania is not considered a mental disorder by itself, it may be an aspect of mania or manic behavior in manic-depressive illness.

See DELUSION; MANIA; MANIC-DEPRESSIVE ILLNESS.

melancholia   An old term meaning depression. It is derived from the Greek word meaning "black bile." Ancients believed that an excess of black bile caused low moods. The term "melancholia" is used currently to refer to certain symptoms that occur during severe depression, such as loss of pleasure in most activities and lack of reaction to pleasurable stimuli.

See also AFFECTIVE DISORDERS; DEPRESSION.

memory   An ability to retain, remember and call up information presented through the senses. For example, memories of smell, touch and taste are placed in several places in the brain, awaiting a similar stimulus, such as the smell of a familiar food, to reactive the memory.

Verbalizing the memory involves finding the right words, which then calls into play the entire left side of the brain, where words are stored. All parts of the brain are required for comprehension and storage of memory.

Minor memory difficulties may be caused by depression, grief, fatigue, stress, illness, medication, alcohol or just simply trying to remember too much at once. Minor memory difficulties do not mean that the person is not mentally well.

Individuals have recall in various steps. Immediate recall involves remembering from a few seconds to a few minutes; an example is remembering a phone number long enough to write it down. Short-term recall involves memory from a few minutes to a few days. Long-term memory refers to memory from a few days to a few years.

According to Sid Gilman, M.D., professor and chairman of the Department of Neurology at the University of Michigan Medical Center, Ann Arbor, memory is a cell-to-cell transmission of information across a synapse that has both electrical and chemical properties. This interaction and transmitting across cell walls takes place in a split second.

Many individuals are less able to remember certain types of information as they get older. The term "age-associated memory impairment" (AAMI) is used to describe minor memory difficulties that come with age. When the person is relaxed, he or she will be able to remember the forgotten material with no difficulty. There is no treatment for AAMI, but written reminders, lists, using association to remember names and allowing more time to remember may be helpful.

According to Stanley Berent, Ph.D., neuropsychologist at the University of Michigan, Ann Arbor, individuals should seek professional help for memory difficulties if they feel uncomfortable, anxious or fearful because of the loss, if they feel out of touch with reality because they cannot remember what day of the week it is or where they are or if they feel that forgetting things is upsetting their role as a parent or grandparent.

See also ALZHEIMER'S DISEASE; DEMENTIA.

"Memory and Aging" (brochure). Alzheimer's Disease and Related Disorders Association, Inc.

"The Power to Remember." Ann Arbor: University of Michigan Medical Center Health News Service (Oct. 1987).

menarche The first menstruation, usually occurring when a girl is between 11 and 17, which marks the onset of female puberty. It is a time characterized by changes in body shape and increased interest in young men and sexual matters. Many young women do become sexually active during these years, and many pregnancies result in unwed mothers.

See also MENSTRUATION; UNWED MOTHERS.

meninges See BRAIN.

menopause Cessation of menses (menstrual periods). Because menopause occurs at mid-life, when women have many psychosocial concerns as well as those of their bodies, it is often a time filled with stress, conflict and challenges. In past generations, the "change of life" was considered to be a time when women would be naturally irritable and even irrational. Many of women's complaints around the time of meno-

pause were written off by doctors as being "all in their head." Now, however, it is recognized that other issues in a woman's life at this time contribute to her mental health in addition to changes in hormonal levels.

Menopause occurs in the United States between age 50 and 51; in the United Kingdom, about a year earlier. Menopause is brought on when a woman's ovaries stop producing eggs (ovulating) and monthly bleeding from the uterus ceases. During the climacteric, a time period when gradual hormonal changes occur before and after menopause itself, the ovaries gradually produce less estrogen and progesterone. Women face many health care controversies around the time of menopause. A major one is the issue of hormone replacement therapy, which, at the beginning of the 1990s, is still controversial. While some authorities say that hormone replacement therapy can be a preventive for osteoporosis and heart disease, others caution that there may be cancer-related risks. However, advances in hormone replacement therapy have made them safer to use with fewer side effects. Hormone replacement therapy helps many women who have hot flashes and vaginal dryness. However, differences of opinion regarding hormone replacement therapy by experts leave many women feeling confused and in search of additional opinions. The number of educational programs featuring speakers on the topic of menopause and hormone replacement therapy is testimonial to the interests and confusion pertaining to the subject.

Women develop many mental health concerns around the time of menopause. One is a feeling that they are no longer attractive to men; another is a feeling of loss because they are no longer able to bear children. They may be divorced, widowed, facing a husband's (or their own) retirement, dealing with grown children who have returned home or anticipating financial difficulties due to an inflationary economy. All of these factors contribute to a woman's mental outlook; when irritability and depression occur, they should not be confused with effects of hormonal changes.

Physiological problems interfere with women's feeling of mental well being, too. Hot flashes plague many women, and they feel embarrassment when they occur. Vaginal dryness that occurs along with diminishing estrogen levels contributes to painful sexual intercourse and hence reduced interest in sexual activity. What a husband or lover may interpret as lack of interest may actually be physical discomfort and fear of painful intercourse.

See also CLIMACTERIC.

Kahn, Ada P., and Holt, Linda Hughey. *Midlife Health: A Woman's Practical Guide to Feeling Good.* New York: Avon Books, 1989.

Kahn, Ada P., and Holt, Linda Hughey. *Menopause: The Best Years of Your Life.* London: Bloomsbury Publishing, 1987.

menstruation (menstrual period)
Uterine bleeding that commonly occurs approximately once a month between puberty and menopause. Historically, for many women the onset of menstruation (menarche) has been filled with anticipation, wonder, awe and sometimes fear. Menstruation marks the beginning of physical adulthood for women, as bearing children becomes possible after menarche. Many young women become pregnant shortly after the onset of menstruation, with, in many cases, unwanted children.

Menstruation consists of periods of bleeding (menstrual periods) that occur in most (but not all) women every 28 days. Although the blood flow usually lasts about four to five days, it can last fewer or more and still be considered within the range of normal.

Menstruation is the removal of products from the uterus that are prepared each month as a uterine lining to provide for a potential pregnancy. At the same time, the ovary ripens an egg (ovum) each month and releases it (ovulation) so that it can be fertilized and implanted in the uterus. If fertilization does not occur, the uterus empties and these cyclical preparations begin again. Blood loss during each period averages about 25 cc (about one ounce) but can vary from a third of an ounce to almost two ounces.

Menstruation usually begins two weeks after ovulation if the egg is not fertilized. Duration between two menstrual periods can vary from three to five weeks. When a woman experiences irregular ovulation, irregular menstruation may be the only symptom she notices.

Menstruation is caused by cyclic fluctuation of the hormones estrogen and progesterone. During a "typical" menstrual cycle, ovarian estrogen is produced in response to stimulation from the pituitary hormones FSH (follicle stimulating hormone) and LH (luteinizing hormone). Estrogen builds up the uterine lining. At midcycle, ovulation occurs in response to an "LH surge," and the ovary forms a small cyst called a corpus luteum in the area of cells (called a follicle) that had surrounded the egg or ovum. These cells produce progesterone, which causes structural changes in the uterine lining.

If the ovum is fertilized and implants in the uterine lining, menstruation does not occur; hence, a missed menstrual period is a common signal of pregnancy. If the ovum is not fertilized, the uterine lining is sloughed off approximately two weeks after ovulation, resulting in a few days of vaginal bleeding. An artificial menstrual flow can be induced by giving a woman estrogen and progesterone; this is commonly done in the form of birth control pills or hormone replacement therapy.

First Menstruation The first menstruation is known as menarche and usually indicates the beginning of the years during which a young woman can become a mother. However, the female anatomy does not mature until several years after the onset of menstruation. Some young women in the United States begin menstruating as early as age nine and as late as age 16. Many have an irregular pattern of menstruation varying from one-to three-month intervals for several years until their organs mature. Periodic flow may vary from extremely light to moderate or very heavy during these years.

Menstrual Disorders Most women experience a few days of predictable flow every month (on average, every 28 days), but variations in this pattern are common.

Irregular Periods In women who have just begun menstruation, irregular periods may be due to the immaturity of their female organs. Periods will regulate normally within a few years without medical intervention. Throughout the childbearing years, lack of ovulation (anovulation) may cause menstrual irregularities. A woman may not ovulate, particularly as she gets near her climacteric, when menstruation will cease. Without ovulation, predictable menstrual cycles do not occur. However, unpredictable bleeding can occur owing to stimulation of the uterine lining from irregular hormone production. In some cases, physicians will prescribe progesterone, the "ovulation" hormone, to correct irregular bleeding due to anovulation.

Menstrual Stoppage Even though a woman is not pregnant, menstruation may stop at any time between the teen years and the climacteric. When women's periods stop for an unexplained reason, some fear pregnancy or disease. Infrequent or very scanty menstrual bleeding is called oligomenorrhea. Absence of menstruation is called amenorrhea. Amenorrhea is normal prior to puberty or after menopause; it occurs frequently as a response to extreme stress, weight loss or a wide range of hormonal, physical or emotional causes. There may be diseases or tumors of female organs or of the organs secreting hormones that control menstrual functions. Anorexia nervosa, an eating disorder, usually results in amenorrhea, although it is not clear whether the loss of menses results from low body weight or underlying psychological or endocrinological disturbances. Runner's or athlete's amenorrhea is a commonly observed syndrome in which women undergoing rigorous physical training temporarily cease having periods.

Lack of menses resulting from anovulation probably evolved as a protective mechanism for women to suggest that it is to a woman's advantage not to conceive under severe physical or emotional stress or after childbirth. However, lack of menses can have many causes and requires medical evaluation.

Painful Menstruation In medical terms this is known as dysmenorrhea. In past generations women were told that they were imagining menstrual cramps; physicians now, however, take such complaints seriously and can prescribe medications to relieve many discomforts. Cramplike pain may be associated with the passage of uterine clots. It may start just before or during menstruation and may last only while the mass is passing out of the uterus or may continue for hours or days. Menstrual cramps also occur because of large amounts of prostaglandins (hormonelike substances), which induce severe contractions and cause cramping in the uterus as the uterine lining is sloughed off. Many women feel cramps in their lower abdomen, lower back and thighs. Many women learn to prevent normal menstrual discomforts by general good health measures, such as exercising, eating properly, getting adequate rest and improving and maintaining good posture.

Medications that inhibit prostaglandins and decrease uterine contractions are prescribed for many women. Medications include mefenamic acid (tradename: Ponstel), ibuprofen (trade name: Motrin) and naproxen and sodium salts (trade name: Anaprox).

Abnormal Bleeding Many women become concerned about variations in their menstrual periods. There are many normal variations in menstrual bleeding. In an individual woman, whenever menstrual bleeding is different from her normal pattern, it may be considered abnormal. It may be a heavier flow, lighter flow or shorter or longer cycle. Such variations call for a medical examination.

Abnormal bleeding during the teen years may be related to the maturation and function of the sexual and endocrine organs, such as the thyroid.

Some women have bleeding around the time of ovulation, halfway between monthly periods. This may be related to ovulation and related hormones; it is usually no cause for alarm but should be brought to the attention of a physician. Infections and tumors of various female organs can be a cause for abnormal bleeding, and choice of treatment depends on the cause as well as the woman's age.

Women who use intrauterine devices (IUDs) for contraception may notice irregular bleeding at some time. This should be brought to the attention of a physician right away.

Excessively heavy bleeding is common in obese women, women who have polycystic ovarian disease and women in the climacteric; it is termed menorrhagia or dysfunctional uterine bleeding.

Women who have harmless fibroid tumors (leiomas) of the uterus may notice heavy bleeding during menstrual periods. Fibroids are hard, circular whorls or fibrous tissue in the uterus muscles. While they do occur in younger women, they are more common in women in their forties who have high estrogen levels. Fibroids grow under the influence of estrogens; obese women are more prone to fibroids than slimmer women. Usually, the uterus contracts during a menstrual period, sometimes causing cramps. Fibroids may prevent this "clamping down" process, perhaps by increasing the surface area of the lining and preventing the muscle from contracting sufficiently.

Vaginal bleeding before the onset of menstruation in a young woman, or after menopause in an older woman, is often an alarming symptom to a woman and a particular signal for medical attention because normally there is no bleeding at all at these times. However, menopausal and postmenopausal women who take hormone replacement therapy may notice some periodic bleeding; this may be considered normal under some circumstances but should be discussed with a physician.

Premenstrual Syndrome (PMS). Many women are more irritable or depressed just before and during a menstrual period. Some notice annoying bloating, fluid retention, breast tenderness and headaches. Most women cope successfully with these symptoms by getting a little extra rest, limiting or decreasing salt intake and recognizing the temporary nature of these annoyances. Women who have excessive premenstrual symptoms should bring them to the attention of a physician. Therapy used may involve vitamin supplements, progesterone injections, the drug bromocriptine, antidepressants or tranquilizers and oral contraceptives.

Some women who have migraine headaches find that their onset is associated with their menstrual periods. Newer prophylactic (preventive) therapies for migraine headaches can help many women with this problem.

Treatment for Menstrual Irregularities
Women with menstrual irregularities should discuss them with their physicians, as there are many individual variations contributing to irregularities. In some cases, menstrual dysfunction is accompanied or caused by failure of the ovaries to ovulate, and the menstrual dysfunction may be associated with infertility. Treatment may consist of various female sex hormones, such as estrogen, progesterone or thyroid. Unusual bleeding as well as pain during sexual intercourse (dyspareunia) may result from endometriosis, a disorder in which tissue from the uterus migrates throughout the abdominal cavity. In some cases, menstrual difficulties are cleared up by a dilation and curettage (D & C), a surgical scraping of the lining of the uterus.

Mental Health Concerns About Menstruation   Fear of menstruation is known as menophobia. Some uninformed young women may become anxious about menstruation because they have not learned about their bodies. Because blood flow is usually a signal of physical injury, and a common fear among young children, adolescent girls may become alarmed at the first sight of monthly bleeding with the onset of menstruation. Some women who fear menstruation reflect anxiety felt by their mothers and generations of women before them; they feel shame if men around them are aware that they are menstruating.

In some cultures, menstruating women are excluded from society during their periods. Over centuries, concerns regarding menstruation have included the notions that sexual intercourse during menstruation is harmful to both men and women's health and that deformed children may result from intercourse during this time. Anxieties surrounding menstruation can be overcome with education, information and reassurance that monthly periods are a normal part of the female life cycle.

Protecting one's clothing and hiding the fact that a woman is having her menstrual period have been concerns among women for generations. At one time ''sanitary supplies'' were sold only in drug stores and wrapped in plain wrapping paper. Women were embarrassed to ask their husbands, fathers or brothers to buy these supplies for them. The most common ways of disposing of menstrual fluid is the use of externally worn sanitary napkins (in Britain, known as sanitary towels) or internally worn tampons. Commercially prepared sanitary napkins developed during the early 20th century after generations used cloth bandages, towels, and absorbent rags, washed and reused. Today sanitary napkins are available in many sizes and styles, to accommodate all body sizes and types of menstrual flow.

Internally worn tampons can be used by young women from the start of menstruation. Many mothers of young daughters are concerned that use of a tampon interferes with ''virginity.'' Physicians say that virginity is intact until one's first act of sexual intercourse. The hymeneal ring, a tissue be-

tween the internal and external genital organs, is usually large enough to admit a tampon, which has been slightly lubricated for easier insertion. Many young women find tampons a neater way to deal with menstruation and a way to avoid external irritation of the genital area with a napkin or pad. Many women of all ages use tampons or napkins for different rates of menstrual flow at different times. In fact, some women, during period of heavy flow, use a tampon and a napkin at the same time.

During the 1980s, concern about a condition called toxic shock syndrome—a serious infectious disease—caused many women to stop using tampons. However, with proper attention to hygiene and frequent replacement of tampons, women need not fear toxic shock syndrome. In addition, some of the materials used in tampons have been changed by the manufacturers, making them safer for use.

Sexual Intercourse During Menstruation
For aesthetic reasons, many couples abstain from sexual intercourse during a woman's menstrual period. Some men and women find sexual activity distasteful during this time, while some women enjoy the closeness and support of their mate. There is no medical reason to avoid intercourse; the woman will not be injured by the thrusting of the penis, and the man will not ''catch'' anything from the woman. If a couple desires to have sexual intercourse during menstrual bleeding, preparations, such as putting a heavy towel under her buttocks, will prevent soiling the bedclothes with blood. Some women report that sexual activity during menstruation—particularly leading to orgasm—actually relieves cramps and menstrual discomforts.

See also HEADACHES; MENSTRUATION AND PSYCHOTROPIC DRUGS; PREMENSTRUAL SYNDROME; PREMENSTRUAL TENSION.

Beauvoir, Simone de. *The Second Sex.* New York: Modern Library, 1968.
Delaney, Janice, et al. *The Curse, a Cultural History of Menstruation.* New York: E. P. Dutton, 1976.

Douglas, Mary. "Menstruation," in Deutch, Yvonne C., ed., *Man, Myth and Magic,* vol. 7. New York: Marshall Cavendish, 1983.

Holt, Linda Hughey, and Weber, Melva. *Guide to Woman Care.* New York: The American Medical Association and Random House, 1984.

Kahn, Ada P., and Holt, Linda Hughey. *Midlife Health: A Woman's Practical Guide to Feeling Good.* New York: Avon Books, 1989.

Sarafino, Edward P. *The Fears of Childhood.* New York: Human Sciences Press, 1986.

Weideger, Paula, ed. *Menstruation and Menopause: The Physiology and Psychology, the Myth and the Reality.* New York: Knopf, 1976.

menstruation and psychotropic drugs

In many women the menstrual cycle influences the pharmacokinetics of psychotropic medications. According to Margaret F. Jensvold, director of the Institute for Research on Women's Health, Washington, D.C., physicians should select medication doses with regard for the menstrual cycle. In an article in *Psychiatric News* (Oct. 4, 1991), Jensvold advised that premenstrual or menstrual symptoms should not be confused with drug effects, and she suggested that the issue of constant or periodic dosage is understudied. Jensvold referred to some case reports of women with bipolar disorder whose symptoms recurred relative to their menstrual cycles. One woman on a constant lithium dosage had premenstrual recurrence of bipolar symptoms and a premenstrual serum level drop premenstrually. With an increased dose for a week premenstrually, her serum levels remained constant and prevented the premenstrual recurrence of bipolar symptoms, giving her good control of the symptoms.

Another case was reported of a woman with bipolar disorder who became hypomanic early in each menstrual cycle and depressed in the latter part of the cycle, with relief at onset of menses. Her serum lithium levels were lowest while she was hypomanic, highest when she was depressed and intermediate when she was feeling well and calm (euthymic).

There may be a subgroup of women who have bipolar disorder whose mood and lithium levels vary with the menstrual cycle. However, it raises the question of whether lithium levels varied with the menstrual cycle or with the pathological state. To address that question, a study in 1990 looked at six women taking birth control pills and six women not taking birth control pills; all were asymptomatic. Lithium levels after a single dose were the same through all phases of the menstrual cycle on or off birth control pills.

Bipolar disorder is equally common in women and men, but rapid cycling bipolar disorder (more than three mood switches per year) is much more common in women. In a study of 52 people with rapid cycling bipolar disorder, 92 percent were women. There was not one woman whose rapid cycling was related to her menstrual cycle. In another case, in 1983, moods of women with bipolar illness cycled with their menstrual cycles but sometimes became out of synchronization with their cycles.

These reports suggest that for a subgroup of women with bipolar disorder, their illness may cycle relative to the menstrual cycle and they may show changes in lithium levels relative to their menstrual cycle. Once such a pattern is identified, a clinician can adjust treatment across the menstrual cycle to give a woman better control. However, this does not apply to all women with bipolar disorder. Changes in bipolar disorder do not always occur in relation to the normal menstrual cycle. It is still unclear why the mood cycle goes out of synchronization with the menstrual cycle at times. Clinicians should consider each woman an individual case and determine how individual differences in the menstrual cycle affect medications.

See also ANTIDEPRESSANT MEDICATIONS; LITHIUM CARBONATE; PSYCHOTROPIC MEDICATIONS.

Psychiatric News (Oct. 4, 1991).

mental health   Mental health refers to an individual's ability to negotiate the daily challenges and social interactions of life without experiencing undue emotional or behavioral incapacity; mental health is more than just the absence of mental disorders. It can be affected by many factors, ranging from exogenous stresses that are difficult to manage to biologic defects or organic diseases that impair brain function.

Often initially disguised as physical problems, some mental disorders are widespread among the U.S. population. An estimated 23 million noninstitutionalized adults in the United States have cognitive, emotional or behavioral disorders, not including alcohol and other substance abuse. Schizophrenic disorders affect about 1 percent of the adult population. Schizophrenic disorders most often result in functional disabilities, but depression is the most common of the major disorders, affecting about 5 percent of the population at any one time.

In 1980, mental disorders were conservatively estimated to cost the American public $73 billion annually, about half of which reflected lost productivity.

Areas of biologic research are advancing and providing encouraging results. For example, imaging technology, such as positron emission tomography (PET) and magnetic resonance imaging (MRI), has been applied to help diagnose many mental health disorders including schizophrenia and panic disorder and has begun to give clues about structural and functional brain abnormalities. Advances have also been made in discerning the roles of various neurotransmitter systems in the etiologies of mental disorders. Psychoneuroendocrinology is investigating the relationships between the endocrine system and central nervous system and behavior. Molecular genetics and genetic linkage studies are examining the inheritance of mental disorders and associated biochemical abnormalities. The rapid advance in understanding the biologic correlates and causes of mental disorders is a positive sign for the development of prevention strategies in the future.

Psychopharmacologic interventions have proved to be highly effective in the treatment of mental disorders and are in widespread use. Psychotherapeutic agents accounted for one-quarter of all outpatient prescriptions in 1984. There is increasing evidence, however, that the effectiveness of pharmacologic interventions is enhanced by psychosocial interventions.

Suicide is the most serious of the potential outcomes of mental health disorders; it claims more than 30,000 lives each year. Injuries from firearms are directly responsible for a majority of suicidal deaths since the 1950s. There has been a steady increase in deaths from suicide among youth age 15–19, and by the mid-1980s suicide was the second leading cause of death in this age group.

Many approaches have been proposed to reduce the impact of mental health problems. Stress, whether stemming from life events, chronic strain or environmental pressures, is associated with biologic changes linked to cognitive, emotional and behavioral dysfunctions. Healthful habits, such as good nutrition and adequate amounts of exercise and relaxation techniques, may be useful in helping to relieve stress. Because people with low levels of control over their environment (actual or perceived) appear to be at greater risk, interventions have also been directed at increasing individuals' resources and coping skills through education and social support. For those needing more aggressive attention, medical interventions are available that include use of psychotherapies, antidepressant drugs and a variety of other techniques such as biofeedback and meditation.

Developmental delays in childhood and specific skill disorders have also been linked to learning and adjustment problems in adolescence and early adulthood. Early interventions with parents and children that address prenatal care, parental skills and remedial help in early school programs may help prevent developmental problems and their progression to mental health problems.

Use of mental health services is increasing as the stigma for getting treatment diminishes. To improve mental health and prevent mental disorders by the year 2000, the federal government has recommended increasing utilization of community support programs as well as increasing use of broad social support mechanisms for those with trouble coping: more attention by employers to services related to managing employee stress; better access to mutual-help clearinghouses; and more attention by primary care providers to the cognitive, emotional and behavioral needs of their patients.

See also BRAIN CHEMISTRY; DEPRESSION; EMPLOYEE ASSISTANCE PROGRAMS; STRESS; PHARMACOLOGIC THERAPY in BIBLIOGRAPHY.

Adapted from U.S. Department of Health and Human Services, Public Health Service. *Healthy People 2000*. DHHS Publication No. (PHS) 91-50212. Washington, D.C.: USGPO, 1990.

mental hospital   A hospital specializing in treating psychiatric illnesses. Admissions to mental hospitals are usually for acute psychiatric illnesses. Individuals are admitted to obtain treatment possible only in the hospital or to protect them and others from harm. Most admissions are voluntary, but some are committed through legal processes. During the 19th and 20th centuries, mental hospitals were referred to as ''asylums'' and often ''lunatic asylums.'' During the second half of the 20th century, large mental institutions have been closed, and patients have been returned to the community for treatment. Availability of better therapy as well as more pharmacologic treatments contributed toward this trend.

See also HALFWAY HOUSE; PARTIAL HOSPITALIZATION; PHARMACOLOGIC THERAPY in BIBLIOGRAPHY.

mental illness   Any form of psychiatric disorder, commonly divided into two categories: psychoses, which are more severely disturbing; and neuroses, which are less disturbing. Psychoses are largely caused by complex biochemical dysfunctions, and neuroses are considered more the result of personality and background. Personality disorders may or may not be classified as mental illness. A diagnosis of mental illness is important in determining whether or not people can be held responsible for their actions.

See also BRAIN CHEMISTRY; INSANITY; LEGAL ISSUES; MENTAL HEALTH; NEUROSIS; PSYCHOSIS.

mental retardation   Impaired intellectual function that results in an inability to cope with the normal responsibilities of life. Mental retardation involves significantly subaverage general intellectual functioning, significant deficits or impairments in adaptive functioning and onset before age 18. About 1 percent of the U.S. population is so affected. According to the American Psychiatric Association, a person must have an IQ (intelligence quotient) below 70 on standardized general intelligence tests. (Many states, schools and other entities may give additional dimensions to defining mental retardation.)

There are degrees of severity and different levels of handicap. Mild retardation is the most common form, affecting about 80 percent of the retarded population. The other 20 percent have moderate, severe or profound retardation. Mild mental retardation seems to be concentrated in the lowest economic classes; malnutrition may contribute to it along with inheritance.

Specific physical causes account for the more severe grade of retardation (IQ below 50). About a quarter are due to Down's syndrome, another quarter to other inherited or congenital conditions (such as phenylketonuria) or brain damage due to hemolytic disease of the newborn and about a third from trauma or infection around birth or early childhood. The cause is unknown in about 15 percent of cases. Fragile X syndrome may account for some of them.

Special training and behavior modification can improve the skills and quality of life for retarded people, many of whom are cared for in the community rather than in institutions. Family support and counseling are essential in preserving stability in the lives of retarded persons.

Current social policy favors retention of retarded individuals in their own homes or in homelike community settings when possible. This policy has led to the development of ancillary programs that enhance the care of mentally retarded persons. These programs are concerned with mental health and social services, living arrangements, education and prevocational and vocational training. Physicians should counsel mentally retarded patients and their families on how to gain access to appropriate facilities and obtain such services. Caring for a mentally retarded child or young adult is a stressful situation for families. Gentle but open communication between all family members and the physician is essential.

Preventive measures include genetic counseling, the elimination of infections such as rubella, reducing intake of alcohol and drugs during pregnancy and the early identification of fetal abnormalities.

For information, contact:

American Association on Mental Deficiency (AAMD)
1719 Kalorama Road NW
Washington, D.C. 20009
Phone: (202) 387-1968

Association for Retarded Citizens (ARC)
P.O. Box 6109
Arlington, TX 76005
Phone: (817) 640-0204

National Down Syndrome Congress
1800 Dempster
Park Ridge, IL 60068-1146
Phone: (708) 823-7550

See also INTELLIGENCE; LEAD POISONING; MENTAL RETARDATION in BIBLIOGRAPHY.

American Psychiatric Association. *Diagnostic and Statistical Manual of Mental Disorders,* 3d ed., rev. Washington, D.C.: APA, 1987.

Clayman, Charles B., Ed. *The American Medical Association Encyclopedia of Medicine.* New York: Random House, 1989.

Grossman, Herbert J., et al., eds. *AMA Handbook on Mental Retardation.* Chicago: American Medical Association, 1987.

mentor   An older, more experienced and higher-ranking individual in an organization or field who promotes the career of a younger, lower-ranking person with assistance and advice. Mentors serve as teachers and role models and have been shown to be a key element in the rise to success. Although they are not necessarily close friends of their proteges, friendships may develop. They serve to make the protege comfortable in the field or corporate structure. A mentor may also use his or her influence directly to promote the protege's career. For this reason, mentors are rarely in a direct line of authority over the protege because of the problems of jealousy and resentment from colleagues. The mentor offers support to the protege in terms of professional decisions or crisis.

Most mentor relationships grow somewhat spontaneously out of work situations and usually start with requests for advice or help. Frequently neither side is precisely aware when the relationship started. A mentor is usually drawn to a younger employee because of his or her talent, ambition and interest in the field or organization. Although the benefits to the protege are obvious, there are also definite benefits to the mentor, most obviously a sense of generosity and satisfaction. A mentor may also be at a point in her career when she has reached the pinnacle but feels the need for further accomplishment. In acquiring a protege, a mentor also gains support for her ideas or programs within the organization. She may also accumulate information from the lower-ranking person about problems or other matters within the organization that could not be acquired through more formal methods.

Mentor relationships may also benefit the organization. For example, proteges are integrated into the organization in a way that enhances formal training and are groomed for higher positions. Relationships with mentors provide for longevity and lower employee turnover and promote communication and understanding among the different levels in an organization.

With all of their benefits, there are also problems inherent in the mentor-protege relationship. For example, a male-female relationship may turn into a romance or at least give the appearance of doing so. Even without this element, the relationship may promote envy or charges of favoritism. A mentor-protege relationship is inherently temporary, since the object for the protege is advancement in the organization; but one of the two may hang on and become dependent on the relationship in a destructive way. The protege may also experience difficulties if the relationship is interrupted because the mentor is transferred or becomes ill or unable to function for some other reason. Either side may also fall in the corporate opinion if one makes a blunder or performs poorly.

Collins, Nancy W. *Professional Women and Their Mentors.* Englewood Cliffs, N.J.: Prentice-Hall, 1983.

meperidine The generic name for an analgesic (pain-relieving) drug (trade name: Demerol). It has effects similar to those of morphine and is widely used in anesthetic premedication, in balanced anesthesia and with caution in obstetric analgesia. The dosage of meperidine should be reduced when antipsychotic agents, sedative-hypnotics or other drugs that depress the central nervous system are given concurrently. There can be adverse reactions in individuals who use meperidine at the same time as monoamine oxidase inhibitors.

meprobamate The generic name for an antianxiety drug (trade names: Equanil, Me-

prospan and Miltown). While useful in treatment of anxiety, it is less effective than the benzodiazepine drugs.

See also BENZODIAZEPINE MEDICATIONS.

Meprospan Trade name under which the antianxiety drug meprobamate is marketed.

See also ANXIETY; MEPROBAMATE.

mercury poisoning Inhalation of mercury vapor is a common cause of mercury poisoning that may result in shortness of breath and later brain and kidney damage. Mercury poisoning in the brain may cause uncoordination, tremors, excitability and, in severe cases, impairment of vision and a type of irreversible dementia. Mercury encephalopathy is a type of brain damage that can occur.

The expression "mad as a hatter" arose because many hatmakers often suffered from mental confusion, slurred speech and tremors as a result of inhaling poisonous mercury-laden vapors while making felt hats.

Treatment of mercury poisoning includes use of agents to help the body excrete the mercury rapidly; in some cases dialysis (to purify the blood) is performed.

See also DEMENTIA.

mescaline A hallucinogenic drug obtained from the Mexican peyote (peyotl) cactus. Effects of the drug generally last for four to eight hours and include changes in thought and mood, a sense of being in touch with the unknown and an altered sense of time. Frightening experiences or thoughts may lead an individual to panic and injury. Use of mescaline can be addictive.

See HALLUCINOGENS; PEYOTE; SUBSTANCE ABUSE.

metabolic dysfunctions Irreversible dementias can occur with diseases of the thyroid, parathyroid, adrenal and pituitary glands. Pulmonary diseases can cause dementia from hypoxia (lack of oxygen in the blood) or hypercapnia (excess of carbon dioxide in the blood). Chronic or acute renal failure each may cause irreversible dementia, as can liver failure (i.e., hepatic encephalopathy). Dementia also occurs in diabetic individuals, often as a result of hypoglycemic coma.

The electroencephalogram (EEG) is used to determine if the individual's cognitive symptoms are due to some type of metabolic disorder.

See also DEMENTIA.

methadone   A synthetic pain-killing narcotic that resembles morphine. It is used to relieve withdrawal symptoms in individuals undergoing a supervised morphine or heroin detoxification program, as it causes only mild symptoms when withdrawn.

methamphetamines   Stimulants available by prescription for limited medical purposes such as narcolepsy and certain cases of obesity. In some cases these drugs are diverted from the legitimate market. The most common forms are white powders, pills or "rock." This class of stimulants is swallowed, injected into veins or inhaled through a tube into the nose. Ice is a rock form of methamphetamines that is ingested via smoking, which magnifies the drug's effects.

These stimulants affect the central nervous system to produce feelings of increased alertness and an enhanced sense of well-being. Best known for their appetite suppressant abilities, stimulants also increase blood pressure and respiratory rates. Some individuals use these drugs to stay awake for long periods of time. Significant adverse effects include dizziness, headaches, blurred vision, loss of coordination, nervousness, irritability and tremors. Acute anxiety and paranoia are not uncommon. The "crash" following amphetamine use can lead to suicidal behavior. Street names include speed, uppers, pep pills, bennies, dexies, meth, crystal, black beauties and crank.

See also SUBSTANCE ABUSE.

Media Resource Guide on Common Drugs of Abuse. Public Relations Society of America, National Capital Chapter, Fairfax, Va., September 1990.

MHPG test   See 3-METHOXY-4-HYDROXYPHENYLGLYCOL.

mid-life crisis   A term given to life stresses that occur at or around middle age. Men and women both may experience mid-life crises. In a sociological sense, these occur as individuals realize that they have reached the prime of their lives and begin to question whether or not they have achieved their goals, reset goals and, in some cases, turn their lives in new directions. In physiological terms, mid-life crises occur as people realize that they no longer have the physical strength and stamina that they had when they were younger. For women, menopause marks the end of their childbearing years. Many men and women begin to fear that they are losing their attractiveness and sex appeal. Many turn to cosmetic surgery to relieve aging lines, give more character to their chins or remove excess body fat. Some people focus more on their body shape and embark on strenuous courses of exercise at health clubs and gyms in an effort to retard effects of aging.

The term "mid-life crisis" is really a misnomer for many psychological stresses that occur in the 45–60 age range. Such stressors include children growing up and leaving home, married children returning home with their own children, facing job loss, facing forced retirement, divorce, widowhood, loss of a sex life because of lack of a partner, seeking a new partner and adjusting to a second marriage and a set of secondhand problems with another's children or parents and caring for aging parents. While some blame psychological distress in women on decreasing hormonal levels, these psychosocial factors should not be discounted.

See also CLIMACTERIC; EMPTY NEST SYNDROME; MENOPAUSE; STRESS.

Kahn, Ada P., and Holt, Linda Hughey. *Midlife Health: A Woman's Practical Guide to Feeling Good.* New York: Avon Books, 1989.

migraine headaches   See HEADACHES.

migration   Migration has a profound impact on an individual's mental health. Leaving one's country sets in motion a mourning process similar to that which occurs after losing a person.

Sigmund Freud stated: "Mourning is regularly the reaction to the loss of a loved person, or to the loss of some abstraction which has taken the place of one, such as one's country, liberty, an ideal, and so on." The loss of one's country resembles the death of a person, and depending on the age at the time of loss, it may even more closely parallel a developmental loss, particularly the emotional detachment from parents in late adolescence.

The mourning process may include three stages. The first is dominated by separation anxiety, grief and efforts to recover the object. Retrieval has been given up in the second stage, when the focus is no longer on the lost object. It is accompanied by pain, despair and even depression. The third phase heralds reorganization, which may include maintaining values and pursuing goals that have developed in association with the lost object.

As early as 421 B.C., Euripides, in *Medea*, wrote: "There is no sorrow above the loss of a native land." At first sight, loss of country might appear clearer and less complicated in the event of involuntary emigration; however, it is no less true of the voluntary emigrant. The latter may, through a reversal mechanism, feel abandoned. The feeling of abandonment may be reinforced at times by relatives and friends who feel abandoned themselves and resent the person leaving. Although the newcomer may appear to adjust to a new life in the new country more and more, at the same time he or she may be longing for the old country and idealize it as a result.

He may have fantasies of "bringing it back," in this case taking himself back to it. The disillusionment may be intense when the immigrant decides to return to live in his homeland and finds that the country he left is no longer there. His relationship with the country is fixated at the time of his emigration. Subtle external signs of this fixation may include dated use of the language. Return to the homeland may be the moment of truth when disavowal of the loss no longer works, and depression may follow.

Culture Shock   Another aspect of migration is culture shock, which can be described as the result of a sudden change of an average, expectable environment to a strange and unpredictable one. The impact of the violent encounter with the new environment, combined with the mourning process set in motion by the loss, causes a threat to the newcomer's identity. The sense of the continuity of the self, as well as the sense of self-sameness, is threatened. Concomitantly, the consistency of one's own interpersonal interactions is disrupted. No longer is there the same confirmation of one's identity in interaction with the environment. One's national identity is hardly thought of as an issue while in one's own country, but an American in a hostile country would be likely to be acutely aware of his nationality. National symbols such as the flag and national anthem would take on added significance. But even in a more friendly foreign country, one's sense of national identity is heightened and may be threatened. Many environmental clues that normally confirm one's identity are absent and have been replaced by unfamiliar phenomena, including language, architecture, manner of dress, food, music and smell.

One means of coping is to try to translate the unfamiliar into the familiar. For example, an individual from a forested country may look at tall buildings in a city and say that tall buildings look like the forest. A similar mechanism may have been at work when early settlers chose an area that was physically like the one they left, thus reducing the psychologically "unsettling" effect of beginning new life in a strange environment.

The country and its physical environment—the nonhuman aspect—constitute a separate object the person relates to, and a separate object that needs to be mourned when it is left behind. Common usage confirms its object status; one speaks of one's fatherland or motherland. In 63 B.C., Cicero already recognized this when he said, "Our country is the common parent of all." The process of mourning one's country may be the focal point in the migration process and may be parallel to—or at times interchangeable with, depending on the developmental level—the late-adolescent developmental process of decreasing dependency and preoccupation with idealization of the parents of childhood. Idealization of the lost object, be it a dead parent or a lost country, is common.

Certain cultural or basic aspects of the native country, such as food, may be glorified. Social gatherings with compatriots, at which traditional foods are eaten, have a quality of the funeral meal after the death of a mother or father, at which siblings gather and reminisce about that parent. In this case, they reminisce about the beloved country. These gatherings thus become part of a life-long mourning process.

Returning to visit the lost country turns one into a visitor, in many ways similar to visiting the parental home when one is no longer a child. Moreover, just as an adolescent may begin to see his own family more clearly when he gets to know other families, the immigrant may see his native country in a different light once he becomes familiar with the new country.

It is tempting to use the image of adoption, particularly when birth mother and country of birth so closely parallel each other. Yet in some ways, what happens is more like entering a stepfamily. Unlike an adoptive family that may be eagerly awaiting the arrival of the adopted child, a stepfamily is more likely to have strong ambivalent feelings about the new arrival. The latter is also true of the receiving country, which may be quite ambivalent about new arrivals.

See also NOSTALGIA.

De Vryer, Miepje A. "Leaving, Longing, and Loving: A Developmental Perspective of Migration." *Journal of American College Health* 38 (Sept. 1989).

milieu therapy   A complex approach to the care of individuals using environment or aspects of the environment in ways to promote mental health and change behaviors of clients involved. It includes a structuring of the physical and social environment of a mental health treatment program so that every interaction and activity is as therapeutic as possible for the patient. Milieu therapy is used in a variety of community and institutional settings.

Milieu therapy revolves around the idea that an individual's mental health difficulties in relating to others often contribute to the development of problems in responding and adapting to the environment. An increasing awareness of basic psychosocial principles can aid the individual in making more positive adaptations.

Milieu therapy stresses the patients' responsibilities not only in their own care but also in the care of their peers. Whether milieu therapy is used in a facility depends on the resources of the facility, type of client population and their length of stay. Milieu programs are generally characterized by commitment, democracy, engagement, communalism and humanitarianism.

See also BEHAVIORAL THERAPY.

Miltown   A trade name under which the antianxiety drug meprobamate is marketed.

See also ANXIETY; MEPROBAMATE.

minor tranquilizers Drugs used to reduce low levels of anxiety. An example is the benzodiazepine class of drugs. See also SUBSTANCE ABUSE.

miscarriage Spontaneous loss of a pregnancy before the fetus is capable of surviving outside the uterus; it is also known as spontaneous abortion. Many women who experience miscarriage experience symptoms of grief and depression for a period of time after the event. A woman will feel the loss, even though the child was never born and she never saw the child. Family and friends seem less sympathetic toward women who have suffered miscarriages than those whose babies are stillborn or die in early infancy. Many are encouraged to try to achieve another pregnancy very soon. Those who do often overcome their depressed feelings; but with those for whom another pregnancy is difficult to achieve, regrets about the lost pregnancy may linger. Women who experience miscarriage can mentally accept the situation better when they understand the physiology involved in the process. Early miscarriages are usually the result of defects in the fetus. Later miscarriages, which occur in the middle trimester, are more likely to be caused by an incompetent cervix, uterine abnormalities, toxemias or preexisting chronic material disease.

Normal exercise does not usually induce miscarriage. Most women who have been tennis players, hikers or swimmers are advised by their obstetricians to continue exercising throughout their pregnancy (or until the last two months). Women who miscarry after some strenuous activity may feel guilty and believe that they induced the miscarriage. Usually this is not the case.

Habitual abortion is a term used when a woman has miscarried three or more consecutive times. The first sign of the possibility of miscarriage is vaginal bleeding, with or without cramping. Not all vaginal bleeding indicates miscarriage. Some bleeding may be associated with implantation, or it may come from the vagina, vulva or cervix. If bleeding occurs from the uterus without any dilation of the cervix, and usually without pain, the situation is termed threatened abortion. Treatment includes rest and waiting to see what happens. With appropriate medical care, cases of threatened abortion can be salvaged, and many women have healthy babies who were in the "threatened" stage during pregnancy.

In a later miscarriage, when the placenta and embryo are totally evacuated, the term used is complete abortion. When placental tissue remains in the uterus, the term is incomplete abortion, and the tissue must be removed by curettage. Late miscarriage may be the most difficult for a woman (and the infant's father) to accept. If she has had good medical care and has taken good care of herself, she should not feel that anything she did or did not do induced the miscarriage.

See also POST-PARTUM DEPRESSION; PREGNANCY.

mitral valve prolapse (MVP) A heart defect that has sometimes been linked with anxiety. In this condition, the mitral valve does not close sufficiently and blood is forced back into the atrium as well as through the aortic valve. About 40 percent of normal adults have MVP.* The condition can lead to a feeling of palpitations, anxiety and difficult breathing. Research to study the relationship between anxiety disorders and mitral valve prolapse has unequivocally demonstrated that MVP is not a precursor to, cause of or even related to panic and agoraphobia. While there is some symptom overlap, the overwhelming majority of MVP reactors do not develop panic or anxiety. However, individuals who have an anatomic vulnerability of their mitral valves may develop prolapse as a result of increased demands placed on their cardiovascular systems by anxiety.

See also PANIC ATTACK.

*Marks, Isaac M. *Fears, Phobias and Rituals.* New York: Oxford University Press, 1987.

Mazza, Dominic, et al. "Prevalence of Anxiety Disorders in Patients with Mitral Valve Prolapse." *American Journal of Psychiatry* 143, no. 3 (Mar. 1986).

modeling A behavioral therapy technique in which the individual learns by observation without reinforcement from a therapist. The troubled individual watches someone else perform a particular action, such as riding up and down in an elevator (in the case of an elevator phobic person), and then gradually becomes able to perform the action without fear. In a traditional learning sense, modeling is a form of social learning; children learn appropriate culturally acceptable behaviors in this way from their parents.

See also BEHAVIORAL THERAPY; ANXIETIES AND ANXIETY DISORDERS in BIBLIOGRAPHY.

money Money is such a practical matter and so consistently present in daily life that many people never identify their real feelings about it and what it symbolizes. For some, money arouses feelings of envy, possibly one reason that those who have it may be reluctant to discuss it and those who lack it may pretend that they are well off. Parents may be reluctant to reveal financial matters to their children, which may lead them to fantasize that they are quite well off or in serious financial straits or simply lead to the impression that money is a taboo subject.

Western tradition offers two conflicting messages: self-denial, generosity, spirituality and antimaterialism; and the opposite spectrum, the capitalistic, materialistic, hardworking influence of the Protestant work ethic. The practical solution seems to be that it is good to have money but not to flaunt it or overly discuss it.

In 1913 Sigmund Freud wrote, "Money questions will be treated by cultured people in the same manner as sexual matters, with the same inconsistency, prudishness and hypocrisy." As the end of the 20th century approaches, society has lost a good deal of reluctance to discuss sex openly and honestly, but issues involving money are still handled carefully. For example, a question about the price of a friend's coat or furniture might be asked indirectly or with elaborate apologies or not asked at all, even though owning clothes and furniture is really not as personal and private a matter as sexual activity.

Money may not bring happiness, but it is strongly associated with powerful forces of love, freedom and power. To some extent, fear of success may be a fear of giving up love. Some people associate being on their own financially with giving up a childlike, dependent role in which someone cares for them and loves them to such an extent that they may sabotage or ignore their own abilities in favor of letting someone else be the boss or handle their finances. Shopaholics, people who are addicted to purchasing and spending, often try to overcome depression and buy love for themselves to compensate for not being loved or for actual abuse early in their lives.

Money buys freedom from daily cares and from the fear of economic disaster. However, it may make some people feel constricted and unworthy to the extent that they may embark on spending sprees because they feel undeserving of inherited wealth or even money that they themselves have earned.

Immortality, the ultimate power, is frequently associated with money. In addition to the power that money bestows in normal day-to-day life, a man or woman who is wealthy enough to endow social institutions, build a lavish home and pass money along to heirs really does seem to live beyond physical death.

The very rich are a minority and may experience the same feelings of isolation and alienation that other minorities experience. Middle- and upper-middle-class children sense that both rich and poor children are different and may reject them for that reason. Marriage among the wealthy is often riddled with divorce and extramarital affairs, possibly because the marriages are frequently entered into for financial rather than emotional reasons. If both spouses are affluent, each may go his or her own way and never have to form the cooperative team of middle-class life. By "marrying down" a wealthy person may acquire a more attractive spouse than he might reasonably expect if only relying on his own personal qualities; but day-to-day living may make some of the challenges this type of relationship difficult.

Children of the wealthy may experience a conflicted type of upbringing in which one or both parents may be absent or preoccupied a good deal of the time. The child may be looked down upon if she seems less than likely to live up to the larger-than-life achievements and reputation of her family. Further complicating the life of the "poor little rich girl"—or boy—is that when help with psychological problems is sought, it may be less effective because of a variety of difficulties than for a person of average background. Mental health professionals may be somewhat envious or intimidated when dealing with a wealthy family. A "fast-track" life is not conducive to consistent treatment. Additionally, the patient or his family has the resources to shop around for a therapist who tells them what they want to hear, since the truth is often as difficult for other family members as for the patient to accept.

See also SHOPAHOLISM.

Damon, Janet. *Shopaholics*. Los Angeles: Price Stern Sloan, 1988.

Krueger, David, ed. *The Last Taboo*. New York: Brunner/Mazel, 1986.

monoamine oxidase (MAO) An enzyme that breaks down neurotransmitter molecules into inactive substances. It destroys biogenic amines and intercepts the message that tells a brain cell to activate. Once the cell has been triggered, it receives enough monoamine oxidase to stop the triggering message.

See also ANTIDEPRESSANT MEDICATIONS; MONOAMINE OXIDASE INHIBITORS.

monoamine oxidase inhibitors (MAOIs) A class of antidepressant drugs that reduce excessive emotional fluctuations and may stabilize brain chemistry by inhibiting action of monoamine oxidase, which in turn inactivates norepinephrine. The more mood is elevated, the more norepinephrine becomes available in the sympathetic nervous system. Examples of MAOIs include isocarboxazid, phenelzine sulfate and tranylcypromine sulfate. Persons taking MAOIs should avoid foods containing tyramine.

Tricyclic antidepressants are a newer form of antidepressant medication, but MAOIs are in widespread use, too.

See also ANTIDEPRESSANT MEDICATIONS; NOREPINEPHRINE; SYMPATHETIC NERVOUS SYSTEM.

mononucleosis See INFECTIOUS MONONUCLEOSIS.

mood An emotion that determines how a person feels. Examples of moods include sad, glad, angry or happy. According to the American Psychiatric Association (in *Diagnostic and Statistical Manual of Mental Disorders,* 3d ed., rev.), moods can be characterized as follows:

Dysphoric: An unhappy or sad mood, such as depressed, anxious or irritable.

Elevated: A more cheerful than usual mood.

Euphoric: A feeling of extreme well-being; this occurs in manic-depressive disorder. This type of mood is beyond what most people rate as simply "feeling good."

Euthymic: Feeling good; absence of depressed or elated mood, and feeling able to cope with life.

Irritable: A feeling of internal tension and being easily annoyed and provoked to anger.

See also AFFECTIVE DISORDERS; DEPRESSION; MANIC-DEPRESSIVE ILLNESS.

American Psychiatric Association. *Diagnostic and Statistical Manual of Mental Disorders,* 3d ed., rev. Washington, D.C.: APA, 1987.

mood disorders   See AFFECTIVE DISORDERS; MANIC-DEPRESSIVE ILLNESS.

morals   Accepted and excepted norms of behavior and social values within a culture. Mental health professionals believe that a child's moral sense is at first simply a response to authority and to his feelings that what he is told about right and wrong is quite fixed and almost sacred. At early stages a child is unable to comprehend that others have the feelings that he has and is unable to discipline himself or anticipate the outcome of his actions. Moral development continues through childhood as the child gradually comes to recognize that others feel pain and deprivation as he does until he actually develops an ability to put himself in the situation of others and to supply his own set of rules to govern his behavior. The development of the capacity to feel guilty for wrongdoing parallels this tendency to internalize feelings of morality.

According to a 1989 Gallup poll, the American public is becoming more concerned with morals. As part of a survey of social values, participants were asked to rate the importance of following a strict moral code. The number of participants who felt that it was very important to follow a strict moral code climbed from 47 percent in 1981 to 60 percent in 1989. Of the women surveyed, 66 percent thought that a strict moral code was important, as compared with 54 percent of the men.

The survey did not attempt to define specific areas of morality, which are outgrowths of cultural values and may actually be in conflict in the same culture. Even as basic an issue as preservation of life is open to moral conflict. For example, controversy has arisen over the right of terminally ill patients to die and to request painless methods of euthanasia from physicians. Advocates and opponents of birth control and abortion continue to argue the sanctity of life against the mental and physical welfare of the mother and the environmental and social problems presented by added unwanted children to the population.

Kohlberg, Lawrence. "Moral Development," in Sills, David S., ed., *International Encyclopedia of the Social Sciences,* vol. 10. New York: Macmillan, 1968.

Leach, Penelope. "Discipline and Self-Discipline," in *The Child Care Encyclopedia.* New York: Knopf, 1984.

"Social Values, Public Values and Intangible Assets More Than Material Possessions." *Gallup Report* (Mar./Apr. 1989).

morning sickness   The nausea and vomiting that some women experience during early pregnancy. While many women go through pregnancy without any discomfort, some have nausea all day long, and some throughout the entire pregnancy.

See also PREGNANCY.

mothers   Qualities of mothers traditionally include protecting and caring for offspring. Mothers give the infant and child emotional warmth as well as sensory stimulation, both of which are necessary for the child to develop a sense of self-worth and an ability to deal effectively with the environment. Mother love is the natural protective and possessive affection a mother displays toward her child. This feeling may be instinctive, but it is also reinforced by pressures of the social group, which expects mothers to nurture their offspring with tenderness.

If television situation comedies reflect reality, mothers have changed, or possibly the audience has grown more realistic and tolerant—even admiring—of different types of mothers. For example, in the 1950s and early 1960s, television mothers were always present in the home, dispensing maternal wisdom and feminine charm while well dressed and adorned with neat pearl necklaces. Title roles in the mid-1990s are occupied by wisecracking, tougher, thoroughly flawed but likable characters. Some fit unwed motherhood into their life-styles with help from friends and colleagues. Typically, television mothers in the 1990s are working mothers.

Many women undertake the double role of having a career as well as family out of economic necessity. However, a Gallup poll measured a growing tendency to perceive this as desirable despite the conflicts. Between 1975 and 1987 the percentage of women polled who felt that having marriage, children and a full-time job was not only possible but also a preferable way of life rose from 32 percent to 43 percent. However, women still tend to be saddled with family and social responsibilities. Even men who are willing to stay home with a sick child or leave work punctually because of a family obligation may not be met with an understanding or positive attitude from an employer or colleagues. Working mothers must not only get themselves to work; they quite often have to adapt their schedules to getting their child to a care facility or home. Some mothers of school-age children may have to deal with the uncertainties of having "latch key" children. Careers may have to be adapted to eliminate travel and situations that keep the mother inaccessible by telephone. Hobbies, interests or just having time for oneself are almost nonexistent on such a schedule. Faced with these pressures, more women are expressing an interest in limiting their family to one child. Beginning in the late 1970s many women tried to "have it all"—meaning marriage, family and career—but later felt constantly pressured by all factors. During the 1990s, some working women have opted for less aggressive career tracks so that they can spend more time with their families and have better mental health.

Motherhood may serve many purposes other than the simple desire for a child. A child may seem to be the solution for a troubled marriage, or even a less than certain suitor. Women may expect their child to succeed where they have failed and may live vicariously through their offspring. Faced with her older children maturing and the threat of no longer being needed, some women will have another child rather than explore the next phase of life. Women may also work out conflicts and problems in the relationships with their own parents through their children.

Regardless of how good the relationship between mother and child, a mother must at times scold, correct and attempt to control the child's behavior. Many mental health professionals feel that the legendary "wicked stepmother" is actually a veiled symbol for the angry disciplinarian that all mothers must at some time seem to be to their children.

In her landmark work *The Second Sex,* Simone de Beauvoir succinctly summarized the experience of motherhood as "a strange mixture of narcissism, altruism, idle daydreaming, sincerity, bad faith, devotion and cynicism," adding her observation of the still stranger paradox that while women have generally been considered less talented, emotionally stable and more frivolous and petty than men, the education and training of the next generation has been left almost entirely in their hands.

See also ADOPTION; MARRIAGE; OEDIPUS COMPLEX; REMARRIAGE; STEPFAMILIES; SURROGACY; UNWED MOTHERS; COURTSHIP, LOVE, ROMANCE, RELATIONSHIPS and MOTHERHOOD in BIBLIOGRAPHY.

Beauvoir, Simone de. *The Second Sex.* New York: Modern Library, 1968.
Leach, Penelope. *The Child Care Encyclopedia.* New York: Knopf, Alfred A. 1984.
"U.S. Women Endorse Jobs, Marriage and Children." *Gallup Report* (Dec. 1987).

mothers-in-law   In some families, mothers-in-law present in-law problems, with conflict often arising between daughter-in-law and husband's mother. In other young couples, the conflict is between husband and wife's mother because of the young bride's continuing dependence on her mother. In some cases, sources of these conflicts may be children's repressed resentments of their own parents being projected toward in-laws; ethnic, social and religious differences; or the mother-in-law's own difficulty in adjusting to the departure of her children and the aging process.

Mother-in-law jokes abound. While some jokes probably reflect some underlying social truths, many people actually have excellent relationships with their in-laws, particularly as the in-laws become grandparents and share in the joy of childrearing.

See also MOTHERS; PARENTING.

Kahn, Ada P., and Holt, Linda Hughey. *The A to Z of Women's Sexuality.* Alameda, Calif.: Hunter House, 1992.

motion sickness A feeling of queasiness, nausea and dizziness that occurs when one is on a moving vehicle, such as a car, boat or airplane. About a third of the population develops motion sickness during a car trip on a bumpy road. Another third requires more unstable conditions, such as a ride aboard a pitching boat, to become upset. The other third sometimes thinks that motion sickness is all in the sufferer's mind; these individuals are not very sympathetic to sufferers.

Motion sickness is a very real event for sufferers and seems to happen when the central nervous system cannot reconcile conflicting signals coming from the inner ear, the eyes and the rest of the body. There may be heat rushes and cold sweats, headaches, drowsiness and vomiting, followed by lethargy and dehydration. Symptoms usually disappear shortly after one leaves the moving vehicle. Many individuals have experienced motion sickness while on a boat, but shortly after they get on land, they are able to enjoy eating a normal meal.

For those who suffer from motion sickness, here are some helpful hints:

- Keep your eyes on the horizon.
- Take deep breaths of fresh air.
- Avoid drinking alcohol before a trip.
- Do not overeat before a trip.
- If you are in a car, stop occasionally, get out and stretch.

A number of over-the-counter medications are available to help prevent motion sickness. They work by depressing signals from the inner ear and by quieting the gastrointestinal tract and decreasing nausea. Most of these preparations should be taken an hour or so before departure.

For some, the power of suggestion is helpful. Keeping busy is also helpful. Often the same individual who feels ill as the passenger does not develop motion sickness if he is the driver. If a person has suffered from motion sickness before, she will become apprehensive about going on the same vehicle again. Just the fear of developing motion sickness and the concentration on waiting for symptoms to occur may be enough to trigger an attack.

See also CENTRAL NERVOUS SYSTEM.

mourning See GRIEF.

MPD See MULTIPLE PERSONALITY DISORDER.

MRI See BRAIN IMAGING; MAGNETIC RESONANCE IMAGING.

multi-infarct dementia The second most common cause of dementia, after Alzheimer's disease. It differs from Alzheimer's disease in its history and concomitant symptoms. Symptoms of vascular disease, both within and outside the brain, are characteristic of multi-infarct dementia. Characteristics are variable among individuals and may include aphasia, amnesia, agnosia, apraxia or slowness, depression, emotional liability, forgetfulness and reduced cognitive function. There may be a past or recent history of transient ischemic episodes (small strokes), high blood pressure and cerebrovascular disease.

In some cases, infarctions may be visible on computerized tomograms of the head, but they may be too small to be radiologically visualized. In cases of vascular dementia, electroencephalography may be useful in revealing multifocal slowing.

No therapy has proved efficacious for this disorder. However, treatment is usually directed at improving the underlying condition; speech and language therapy may help improve dysarthria and aphasia.

Because of the vascular nature of this disorder, there are several theoretical implications. If predisposing conditions can be diminished, the progression of dementia may be slowed, if not stopped. In the future, studies may give some clues about possibilities of pharmacologic agents to enhance cerebrovascular circulation or decrease the propensity for thrombotic or embolic episodes that may alter the course of this type of dementia.

See also ALZHEIMER'S DISEASE; DEMENTIA.

Cummings, Jeffrey L. *Clinical Neuropsychiatry.* Orlando: Grune & Stratton, 1985.

David, Kenneth; Klar, Howard; and Coyle, Joseph T. *Foundations of Psychiatry.* Philadelphia: W. B. Saunders, 1991.

multiple personality disorder (MPD)

A severe chronic dissociative disorder characterized by a disruption of memory and identity. Dissociation is the process during which a set of ideas and feelings loses most of its relationship with the rest of the personality, functioning somewhat independently.

Bennett G. Braun, M.D., director of the Dissociative Disorders Unit, Rush North Shore Medical Center, Skokie, Illinois (an affiliate of Rush Presbyterian–St. Luke's Medical Center, Chicago), explains MPD as the demonstration in one person of two or more personalities, each of which possesses identifiably distinctive, consistently ongoing characteristics and a relatively separate memory of individual life history.

According to Dr. Braun, executive control of the body is transferred from one personality to another, but the total individual is never out of touch with reality. Some or all of the personalities frequently experience periods of time loss, or amnesia. Amnesia for thoughts and actions of other personalities often occurs in the host personality, which is the one that has executive control of the body most of the time.

In the United States, between 25,000 and 250,000 people may have MPD. More women than men have been diagnosed with it. MPD was first described 150 years ago and has been an often used and misused theme in fiction. However, it has only been recognized as a separate and distinct mental disorder since 1980 when it was so classified in the *Diagnostic and Statistical Manual of Mental Disorders* by the American Psychiatric Association. The MPD diagnosis is a relatively new one and is unfamiliar to many people.

Diagnosing MPD According to Dr. Braun, more than 95 percent of patients who come for treatment of MPD have been severely and traumatically abused as children, either physically, sexually or emotionally. Uncontrolled dissociation is viewed as an abused child's principal defense mechanism. Such children experience severe, repeated abuse by parents or family members who intersperse abuse with expressions of love. They grow up with a double bind of confusing messages and a powerfully enforced rule that the abuse and the double bind cannot be openly addressed. Many are threatened with their lives if they tell anyone about what they have been subjected to and/or observed. When viewed in this way, MPD is a form of post-traumatic stress disorder that arises because of abuse that was administered in an inconsistent way and because of the double bind messages.

Diagnosis of MPD is difficult because it is designed to maintain secrecy both internally and externally, especially about the abuse. However, "switching" of personalities produces diverse physical appearances such as different facial expressions, differences in body posture and body language, changes in handedness, voice changes, reversals in outward gender presentation and significant weight gain or loss over short periods of time; different personalities may speak in different accents or languages, which helps to make the diagnosis. Some of the personalities may have symptoms not experienced by the others. For example, some have headaches, anxieties, unpredictable responses to medications, chest pain, extreme sensitivity or extreme tolerance to pain, gastrointestinal problems and allergies. Some feel physically ill even though a doctor cannot find anything wrong with them. They may feel depressed, angry or fearful and not know why.

The term ''splitting'' is given to the creation of a new personality entity by the splitting off of energy that forms the nucleus of a separate personality or fragment. The term ''switching'' applies to going back and forth between already existing personalities or fragments. Switching may be brought about by external or internal stimuli.

Some MPD patients have severe phobic symptoms and avoid certain kinds of activities that they cannot tolerate. The phobia may be transferred into an alternate personality. Many MPD patients report difficulty sleeping. This is typical because many childhood abuses occurred late at night when the child was thought to be sleeping. Moreover, many abuses are remembered through dreams. Nightmares often leave the person in a state of terror that makes further sleep that night impossible and results in fatigue.

Several diagnoses are frequently confused with MPD. These include substance abuse, schizophrenia, paranoia, anxiety, somatoform and borderline personality disorders. Some patients who withhold information either intentionally or because of memory gaps may guide the therapist in misdirections.

There is no evidence that MPD comes from a physical or chemical imbalance in the person's body. However, some people are more likely to dissociate, and these people may be more likely to develop MPD if they were badly abused or frightened as children.

Treatment The most important part of psychotherapy is the building of trust between the therapist and the individual. The therapist becomes acquainted with the different parts inside the MPD person and gets the different parts inside the MPD person to talk to one another. Once they start talking to one another, they usually start remembering what happened to one another and can begin to work better together. The work is designed to gradually integrate the parts into ultimately one whole personality. Pacing is critical. The most common mistake is to go too fast, uncovering too much before the material is processed. Integration, the process of bringing parts together, contains the fusion of the appropriate parts into a new combined part, not the exclusion of a part or its being taken over by another.

Expressive therapies, such as art, music, movement therapy and psychodrama, help some MPD patients who are reluctant or afraid to talk about their experiences express useful information without specifically telling. The therapist integrates such information into more traditional psychotherapy.

Family therapy is helpful in treating an individual with MPD. Family therapy may include interventions to stop abuse of a child or interrupt a family abuse cycle, marital therapy, parenting programs, incest groups for support of past victims, assertiveness training groups, peer networks and alcohol and drug abuse groups.

Group therapy involves bringing together several people with MPD and therapists. Together they explore their similarities, differences and the possibilities for helping one another with their problems. The group experience is usually used in conjunction with individual therapy and provides an opportunity for people who are characteristically secretive to learn communications skills of interaction, acceptance and tolerance.

Hospitalized treatment is recommended for some cases, such as for those who have suicidal or homicidal ideation. Hospitalization may also be necessary if the individual has a severe inability to function or is experiencing severe rage reactions or to undertake special therapeutic procedures safely. Hospitalization for MPD ranges from three days to many months. Patients who require stays of six months or longer usually have a mixed diagnosis including multiple personality disorder and depression and/or anxiety and/or borderline personality disorder, and symptoms including suicidal/homicidal ideas, severe issues of trust, inability to care for themselves and concurrent medical problems.

Medication   Pharmacologic therapy can be helpful during crises. However, the use of medication can be problematic because different personality states have different responses and tolerances for a given amount of a drug. There is potential for the patient to unconsciously overmedicate; one personality may take a medication and not be aware that another personality already took a similar dose. In addition, the use of antipsychotic drugs may further impair the MPD sufferer's reality testing skills and promote further switching and splitting. However, in some cases, a single dose of an antipsychotic drug is helpful to reestablish control during a crisis.

During the early 1990s, propranolol and clonidine are two drugs used in some tertiary settings under close supervision to reduce anxiety, switching and impulsivity in dissociative disorder patients, enabling them to benefit more from psychotherapy. In some patients, the effects of these drugs can complement effects of benzodiazepine drugs. When unusual medication regimens are used, the patient must be fully informed and understand what is being undertaken and why.

International Society for the Study of Multiple Personality & Dissociation   The International Society for the Study of Multiple Personality & Dissociation (ISSMP & D) is a nonprofit, professional association organized to promote research and training in the identification and treatment of multiple personality and other dissociative states, to provide professional and public education, to catalyze international communication and cooperation among clinicians and investigators working in the field and to promote development of local societies for study, education and referral.

The ISSMP & D publishes a newsletter, membership directory and bibliographies and provides consultations regarding setting up local affiliate societies. To date, there are more than 20 local affiliates throughout the United States.

For information, contact:

International Society for the Study of
   Multiple Personality & Dissociation
5700 Old Orchard Road, First Floor
Skokie, IL 60077
Phone: (708) 966–4322

An International Conference on Multiple Personality/Dissociative States is sponsored every year by Rush-Presbyterian–St. Luke's Medical Center, Chicago, and is held in conjunction with the annual meeting of the ISSMP & D.

For information on the annual conference, contact:

Dissociative Disorders Program
Rush North Shore Medical Center
9600 Gross Point Road
Skokie, IL 60076
Phone: (708) 933–6685

See also DISSOCIATIVE DISORDERS; PSYCHOTHERAPY; MULTIPLE PERSONALITY DISORDER in BIBLIOGRAPHY.

Braun, Bennett G. ''The BASK Model of Dissociation.'' *Dissociation* 1, no. 1 (Mar. 1988).

Braun, Bennett G. "The BASK Model of Dissociation: Part II: Treatment." *Dissociation* 1, no. 2 (June 1988).

Braun, Bennett G. "Unusual Medication Regimens in the Treatment of Dissociative Disorder Patients: Part I. Noradrenergic Agents." *Dissociation* 3 no. 3 (Sept. 1990).

Braun, Bennett G., ed. *Treatment of Multiple Personality Disorder*. Washington, D.C.: American Psychiatric Press, 1986.

multiple sclerosis (MS) A progressive disease of the central nervous system in which scattered patches of the protective covering of nerve fibers in the brain and spinal cord are destroyed, causing symptoms ranging from numbness and tingling to paralysis and incontinence. Severity of the disease varies among individuals. Although causes are unknown, it is thought to be an autoimmune disease, in which the body's defense system treats some of its own parts as foreign matter and destroys them. Another theory is that it is a virus picked up by a susceptible person during early childhood and develops later on.

There may be a genetic factor in the disease, as relatives of affected people are eight times more likely than others to contract the disease. It is five times more common in temperate zones than in the tropics. The ratio of women to men with the disease is three to two.

Researchers are still seeking a cure for MS, and sufferers are encouraged to lead as active a life as their disabilities allow and to keep a positive mental attitude. Physical therapy helps many maintain their mobility. For some individuals, corticosteroid drugs are prescribed to relieve symptoms of an acute attack.

MS is a disease that affects families and family relationships, as other individuals may be called on to become a caregiver at any time. A good communication system within the family network is essential as the disease progresses, so that understanding and empathy can be expressed openly.

See also CAREGIVERS; CENTRAL NERVOUS SYSTEM; CHRONIC ILLNESS; PAIN.

Munchausen's syndrome A form of chronic disorder in which the individual complains of physical symptoms that are pretended or self-induced; the disorder is also known as factitious disorder. Such individuals want attention and want to be taken care of. Many are repeatedly hospitalized for investigation of a variety of ailments.

The name for the syndrome comes from the 19th-century Baron von Munchausen, who was known for tall tales and fanciful exaggeration.

Individuals with this syndrome may complain of dizziness, pain in the abdomen, skin rashes and fever. They usually invent a dramatic history to gain attention and entry into a hospital; many have detailed medical knowledge on which to base their stories. Physicians must be aware of this syndrome to help such individuals avoid having surgery and other unnecessary procedures performed that ultimately might be harmful.

The incidence of this syndrome is unknown, probably because many cases go undetected. In one study involving fever of unknown origin, up to 10 percent of the fevers were diagnosed as factitious. Factitious symptoms can occur in almost any organ system, and the various symptoms produced are limited only by the imagination of the patient.

music therapy Music therapists admit they do not know precisely why music produces such powerful effects, but they contend the benefits are unmistakable. According to Donna Devall, a social worker in Washington, D.C., "music is a way to connect" and of "getting through" to people who are otherwise unreachable. Songs embody life experiences and bring back memories of courtship, a wedding or even wartime. In many nursing homes, individuals who have been very untalkative and unresponsive may start to tap their foot, hum or sing to music, particularly live music that they are watching being performed.

According to Oliver Sacks, an American neurologist, author of *The Man Who Mistook His Wife for a Hat* and pioneer in developing therapies, music organizes motor functions, thus smoothing out, for example, the uncontrolled movements that afflict patients with Parkinson's disease or enabling people with speech losses to sing the words to familiar melodies.

Using music as a healer is not new. According to Greek mythology, Apollo was god of both music and medicine. His son, Aesculapius, who became god of medicine, cured mental diseases with song and music. Plato, the Greek philosopher, believed that music influenced a person's emotions and character. According to the Bible, David's harp playing relieved King Saul's melancholy (depression). During the Middle Ages, music was used to exhaust crowds of people suffering from mass hysteria; the music probably encouraged them to continue dancing until they were exhausted. In his plays, Shakespeare referred to the healing powers of music. The first English-language book on music as therapy, *Medicina Musica,* was written in the early 1700s by Richard Browne, an apothecary. Browne said music could ''soothe turbulent affections'' and calm ''maniacal patients who did not respond to other remedies.''

Music therapy was used in the early part of the 19th century in the form of brass bands for patients with the then-identified mental disorders, including anxiety. In the 20th century, particularly during World War II, many American psychiatric hospitals began active music therapy programs. In 1950 the National Association for Music Therapy (NAMT) was organized; in 1954, the NAMT recommended a curriculum for preparation of music therapists. Subsequent organizations of music therapists were formed in Europe, South America and Australia.

Music is no substitute for conventional treatment. Its benefits may end almost as soon as the music ends. However, when used in conjunction with other therapies, it may be useful and get results other therapies cannot.

See also ALTERNATIVE THERAPIES.

Crowley, Susan L. ''The Amazing Power of Music.'' *Bulletin,* American Association of Retired Persons (Feb. 1992).

mutism   Inability or refusal to speak, which may occur as a symptom of severe manic-depressive illness, catatonic schizophrenia and a rare form of conversion disorder.

As a childhood disorder, elective mutism may start before the child is five years old. Although the child understands language and is able to speak properly, he only nods his head and gestures. Mild mental retardation or the anxiety of leaving home for school may contribute to the condition.

Treatment for mutism varies, depending on the underlying cause.

See also DEPRESSION; SCHOOL PHOBIA; SEPARATION ANXIETY.

myalgic encephalomyelitis   An alternative name for chronic fatigue syndrome; used more in Europe than in the United States.

See also CHRONIC FATIGUE SYNDROME.

N

nail biting   One of a group of habits including thumb sucking and hair pulling that may continue because of their routine, unconscious nature without a real continuing underlying cause. Nail biting is a difficult habit to break. Many nail biters are embarrassed by their habit.

Mental health professionals say that nail biting is a soothing or stimulating habit that helps children deal with anxiety or boredom, but exact causes are not known. Nail biting does not really correlate with specific personality qualities despite the stereotype of the nervous nail biter. There seems to be a slight hereditary tendency to nail biting, but this is difficult to establish because family members are prone to mimic one another's habits. A nail-biting parent is likely to have trouble correcting a nail-biting child. Nail biting is a somewhat universal habit that seems to have no relationship to sex, race or intelligence, although more women than men seek help to break the habit. It is estimated that over 50 percent of the population has had the nail-biting habit at some point in life. About 20 to 25 percent of adults are nailbiters. Nail biting usually starts in childhood after the age of three and frequently ends in adolescence when peer pressure and personal grooming become important.

See also ANXIETY; PEER GROUP; PEER PRESSURE.

narcissism   An exaggerated feeling of self-love. A narcissistic person may overestimate her capacities, so that she feels omnipotent and demands extreme amounts of attention and admiration from others. The term comes from Narcissus, a character in Greek mythology who fell in love with his own image reflected in the water. Excessive narcissism is termed narcissistic personality disorder.

See also EGO; PERSONALITY.

narcolepsy   Dropping off to sleep at inappropriate times, such as while walking, driving a car, eating or carrying on a conversation. Narcolepsy occurs three or four times more often among men than women. The causes are unknown, but it is suspected that narcolepsy is related to some malfunction of the sleep-controlling centers of the hypothalamus, a part of the brain. Narcolepsy may follow sudden emotional experiences, such as laughter or crying. The narcoleptic person may have a few or dozens of sleep episodes every day, becoming unconscious for two or three minutes or for hours. There are no ill effects unless the sleep attacks cause an accident.

Methylphenidate (Ritalin) is considered one standard medication for this condition. It increases alertness and reduces sleep attacks.

See also SLEEP.

narcotic drugs   Drugs prescribed by physicians to produce sleep and relieve pain. Alcohol, cocaine and opium, plus its derivatives, heroin, morphine and codeine (the opiates), are all narcotics. When used to excess, they produce euphoria, addiction and both physical and psychological dependence. Unconsciousness caused by narcotics is known as narcosis.

See also SUBSTANCE ABUSE.

Nardil   See PHENELZINE.

National Alliance for Research on Schizophrenia and Depression (NARSAD)   A privately funded organization that raises and distributes funds for scientific research regarding prevention, causes, treatments and cures of severe mental illnesses, primarily schizophrenias and depressions.

Formed in 1986, the NARSAD complements federal funding efforts of the National Institute of Mental Health (NIMH). For example, NARSAD has established an award process to identify promising research and enable investigators to obtain necessary funding to initiate research rather quickly. The group's Scientific Council, composed of distinguished psychiatric researchers, solicits and evaluates research proposals and responds to grant requests.

For information, contact:

National Alliance for Research on Schizophrenia and Depression

208 S. LaSalle St., Suite 1438
Chicago, IL 60604
Phone: (312) 641–1666

National Alliance for the Mentally Ill

A national organization composed of family members of patients with serious mental illnesses. Chapters of AMI provide local forums for sharing information with members who give one another encouragement and support and raise hopes through diminishing feelings of isolation.

For information, contact:

National Alliance for the Mentally Ill
2101 Wilson Boulevard, Suite 302
Arlington, VA 22201
Phone: (703) 524–7600

National Depressive and Manic-Depressive Association (NDMDA)

A national association that recognizes the biochemical nature of bipolar and unipolar affective disorders and the disruptive psychological impact of the illnesses on patients and families. Its purpose is to provide personal support and direct service to persons with major depression or manic-depression and their families; to educate the public concerning the nature and management of these disorders; and to help patients suffering with depression and manic-depression gain access to effective care.

Membership in the group provides not only information and support but also a source of realized self-esteem and dignity for those suffering from depressive disorders and their families.

In addition to the service aspect of local chapters, the national organization fights the stigma associated with mental illness, promotes funding for research to improve diagnosis and treatment and lobbies for adequate insurance coverage for the treatment of these disorders. The association also gives an annual research award to a research investigator contributing to improved treatments, as well as the Dr. Jan Fawcett Humanitarian Award to individuals who have contributed to the goals of the organization.

There are chapters throughout the United States and Canada.

For information contact:

NDMDA
730 North Franklin Street, Suite 501
Chicago, IL 60610
Phone: (312) 642–0049

See also AFFECTIVE DISORDERS; BIPOLAR DEPRESSION; DEPRESSION; MANIC-DEPRESSIVE ILLNESS.

National Foundation for Depressive Illness

A group of lay and professional people organized to advance private and public education about depression and its treatment. There is an 800 number that gives a recorded message concerning symptoms of depression and offering to send a list of local referrals and literature.

For information, contact:

National Foundation for Depressive Illness, Inc.
P.O. Box 2257
New York, NY 10116
Phone: (212) 620–7637 or (800) 248-4344

See also DEPRESSION; MANIC-DEPRESSIVE ILLNESS.

National Institute of Mental Health (NIMH)

A U.S. government agency that supports and conducts research concerning prevention, diagnosis and treatment of mental illnesses. Studies bring hope to individuals with mental health problems, to those at risk of developing problems and to concerned families and friends. NIMH is part of the Alcohol, Drug Abuse and Mental Health Administration, a component of the U.S. Department of Health and Human Services.

For information, contact:

National Institute of Mental Health
5600 Fishers Lane, Room 15C–05

Rockville, MD 20857

Phone: (301) 443–3673

National Institute of Mental Health Epidemiologic Catchment Area (ECA) Program

One of a series of epidemiologic research studies carried out by independent research teams in collaboration with staffs of the Division of Biometry and Epidemiology of the National Institute of Mental Health (NIMH). Goals of the program include estimating rates of prevalence and incidence of specific mental disorders and rates of mental health services use. The program also studies factors influencing development and continuance of disorders and use of services.

Through a survey of about 20,000 individuals in six major cities, it has provided the most authoritative data on the incidence and prevalence of various mental disorders in the United States.

National Institute of Mental Health Treatment of Depression Collaborative Research Program (TDCRP)

The first multisite study carried out by the National Institute of Mental Health (NIMH) concerning psychotherapy research. This project studied the effectiveness of specific forms of brief psychotherapy (16 weeks) for treating nonbipolar, nonpsychotic depressed outpatients. The two forms of psychotherapy studied were interpersonal psychotherapy (IPT), as described by Gerald Klerman, Myrna Weissman and colleagues in Boston and New Haven, and cognitive behavior therapy (CBT), as described by Aaron T. Beck and colleagues in Philadelphia. These therapies were compared with the antidepressant drug imipramine. A double-blind study involved a pill-placebo group, the two pharmacotherapy conditions and clinical management. Initial results indicated that both specific psychotherapies and drug treatment can help reduce depressed symptoms. Continuing studies are aiming to understand

for which patients each of these treatments may be most helpful. Some patients may benefit from a combination of antidepressant drugs and some form of therapy.

See also ANTIDEPRESSANT MEDICATIONS; DEPRESSION; MANIC-DEPRESSIVE ILLNESS.

National Institute on Drug Abuse

A part of the U.S. Alcohol, Drug Abuse and Mental Health Administration (ADAMHA). Its function is to provide leadership, policies and goals for governmental work in preventing, controlling and treating narcotic addiction and drug abuse and in rehabilitating affected individuals.

For further information, contact:

National Institute on Drug Abuse
5600 Fishers Lane
Rockville, MD 20857
Phone: (301) 443–6487

National Mental Health Association

A voluntary nongovernmental organization for the prevention of mental illness and promotion of mental health, with more than 650 chapters nationwide. Goals of the organization include protecting the rights of people with mental health problems, educating the public about mental health and promoting research concerning all aspects of mental health.

For information, contact:

National Mental Health Association
1021 Prince Street
Alexandria, VA 22314–2971
Phone: (703) 684–7722

See also DEPRESSION; MANIC-DEPRESSIVE ILLNESS.

nausea   A feeling of sickness in the stomach as if one may have to vomit. There may be dizziness, lightheadedness or sweating along with nausea. Some individuals experience nausea when coming into contact with a food associated with an anxiety-producing experience recalled from the past. Other individuals experience nausea before certain events, such as before a public appearance for speaking or performing. Some develop nausea before playing in a sports event or before taking tests. Such nausea can be overcome with behavioral therapy techniques. However, in all cases of repeated nausea, physical causes should first be ruled out. Some medications may produce nausea as a side effect in susceptible individuals.

See also BEHAVIORAL THERAPY.

Marks, Isaac M. *Fears, Phobias, and Rituals.* New York: Oxford University Press, 1987.

near-death experiences   Certain sensations and out-of-body experiences are common to many people who have come close to dying but have been revived. After observing similar phenomena in several patients and hearing reports of other near-death situations, Raymond Moody, a physician, coined the phrase ''near-death experience'' and described his findings in his work *Life after Life,* published in 1975. His work encouraged people to talk more freely about such experiences.

In 1982, a Gallup poll showed that 8 million adult Americans had survived what they considered to be a near-death experience. There are common elements in many of these near-death experiences. Many subjects describe a sensation of floating above their own body watching attempts to resuscitate. Some have convincingly described visiting their families in other parts of the hospital and have recounted details of their clothing and conversations that they could not have known without a genuine out-of-body experience.

A common element is a sense of peace, joy, freedom from pain and reluctance to return to life to the extent that some become angry at their physician for reviving them. Many describe an experience of entering a lighted tunnel and of contact with beings who are surrounded by light, some of whom are family and loved ones who have died. Some recount a nonjudgmental review of their life and an encounter with a supreme being who is a projection of their religious beliefs. Despite a sense of reluctance to return to life, many later see the experience as a glimpse into another world that they accept with gratitude. The experience seems to be as common to the nonreligious as to the religious but frequently results in an increased interest in spiritual, metaphysical matters. Many report a stronger belief in the afterlife and an increase in psychic abilities.

Skeptics of the near-death experience point to the fact that these sensations take place when the body is in the grip of its own chemical response to stress and also frequently influenced by drugs such as pain killers, tranquilizers and anesthetics. To refute near-death experience claims, some researchers have reproduced similar sensations in laboratory situations using drugs. One researcher concerned with psychological similarities among subjects of near-death experiences found a high incidence of childhood abuse and neglect.

Moody, Raymond. *The Light Beyond.* Toronto: Bantam Books, 1988.
''Near Death Experience,'' in Guiley, Rosemary Ellen. *Harper's Encyclopedia of Mystical and Paranormal Experience.* San Francisco: Harper, 1991.

nervous   A nonmedical term and form of anxiety referring to feelings of restlessness, apprehension, irritability, fearfulness and tension. The word ''nervous'' derives from Sigmund Freud's theory that neurological weaknesses (neurasthenias) develop as a result of unconscious conflicts. When people say they have ''nervous symptoms,'' they usually mean that they have anxieties. Nervousness is a normal symptom under many circumstances, such as the first day of school, the first day of a new job, approaching the platform to deliver a speech, trying to catch a train at the last minute, having an important meeting with a boss or walking into a room full of strangers. Nervousness is related to social phobia in that social phobics display nervousness about certain situations; the phobic, however, carries the nervousness and anxieties to such an extreme that he begins to avoid the circumstances that make him fearful and nervous.

Individuals who occasionally have bouts of nervousness need not fear that they are having a nervous breakdown. As long as they feel that they are coping well with their situation and keep their emotions under control, their equilibrium will probably return soon.

A "nervous stomach" refers to feelings of abdominal discomfort, nausea and diarrhea that happen to many people when they feel nervous or anxious. Nervous stomach is also a common symptom of irritable bowel syndrome and panic attack.

A "nervous habit" refers to involuntary twitches and facial tics and voluntary habits such as nose picking, thumb sucking and nail biting. These habits are thought to be a means of relieving stress and anxieties. Nervous habits increase during periods of stress.

See also ANXIETY; ANXIETY DISORDERS; IRRITABLE BOWEL SYNDROME; STRESS.

nervous breakdown   A nonmedical term applied to any one of several mental health disorders in an acute phase. The term applies when one loses control of his emotions so that he is no longer able to control his behavior. Popularly, the term is applied to severe anxieties as well as more severe psychoses. The individual suffering the breakdown feels that his emotions are out of control, and perhaps a better term would be "emotional breakdown." The individual may be unable to sleep, will have little interest in eating, may cry frequently and may become fearful or severely depressed. Physical symptoms may be fast heartbeat, dizziness, headaches, fainting and sweating palms. These symptoms will interfere with activities of daily living as well as work.

Many individuals experience some of these symptoms for brief periods of time. It is when they last for a long time that they produce a breakdown.

Avoiding an emotional breakdown can be best accomplished by developing an ability to share one's feelings and emotions with another person. Just talking to another person helps many people get their life situations in a better focus before their emotional system goes on overload and breaks down. Many breakdowns occur at times of transition and change, such as adolescence, middle age, entering or graduating from school, marriage, divorce and parenthood. At times of transition a person is more insecure and hence more vulnerable to emotional swings.

See also ANXIETY DISORDERS; DEPRESSION; STRESS.

nervous system   See BRAIN; CENTRAL NERVOUS SYSTEM.

networking   A term that describes using individual contacts to gain important information, employment, power or some type of financial advantage. The contacts used in networking are generally mutually advantageous to all parties and may be arrived at informally, even socially. Networking involves an exchange of favors and usually breaks down if an individual is always on the receiving or giving end. An example of networking in action is when a young woman gets a job or information about a job possibility through relatives, friends, friends of friends or teachers rather than going through the more organized route of registering with an employment agency or contacting employers listed in help-wanted ads.

Networks may be drawn together by certain similarities of their members' goals. For example, women's networks have coalesced in fields such as business and politics to counteract the hold of the "old boy network" of white males on such institutions. Networking has been used in sales techniques, to market creative work and ideas and to put forward social programs.

Individuals who are withdrawn and are not social minglers have more trouble networking than those who are joiners and have large circles of friends and acquaintances, both business and social. Being a successful "networker" involves extroverted personality traits such as meeting new people easily and a willingness to become involved in a cause or activity or a group.

Boe, Anne, and Youngs, Bettie B. *Is Your "Net" Working?: A Complete Guide to Building Contacts and Career Visibility.* New York: Wiley, 1989.

Steinem, Gloria. "Networking," in *Outrageous Acts and Everyday Rebellions.* New York: New American Library, 1983.

neuroimaging See BRAIN IMAGING; POSITRON EMISSION TOMOGRAPHY.

neuroleptic A medication that helps to relieve psychotic symptoms (antipsychotic drugs) such as delusions or hallucinations, schizophrenia and mania.

See also ANTIPSYCHOTIC MEDICATIONS; HALLUCINATION; SCHIZOPHRENIA.

neurological examination To help physicians diagnose conditions affecting the nervous system, brain and spinal cord, several types of imaging techniques may be used after a complete general physical examination. These techniques include magnetic resonance imaging and computerized axial tomography (CAT). Angiography (X-ray imaging to show blood vessels) may also be used.

See also ALZHEIMER'S DISEASE.

neurology The branch of science that studies the human nervous system, including the brain and the spinal cord. The medical specialist within this field is a neurologist. In the last few decades, advances have been made in neurology, and now, with improved understanding of the biochemical and struc-

tural bases of neurological disorders, new treatments have been developed, including drug treatment for some forms of dementia, surgical removal of tumors and repair of damaged nerves.

See also PARKINSON'S DISEASE.

neuromyasthenia Disease of the nerves and muscles. The term is sometimes used synonymously with chronic fatigue syndrome.

See also CHRONIC FATIGUE IMMUNE DYSFUNCTION SYNDROME; CHRONIC FATIGUE SYNDROME.

neuron A nerve cell. The central nervous system has billions of neurons that act in various combinations to initiate all human actions and thoughts. Neurons trigger the release of neurotransmitters, which may then cause an endocrine gland to release a hormone, or a muscle cell to contract. Different stimuli activate different types of neurons. For example, sensory neurons may be aroused by a physical stimulus, such as a bright light or intense cold.

Babies are born with their total number of neurons, and the number decreases thereafter. Neurons can be damaged or obliterated by disease, injury or persistent alcohol abuse. Consequently, loss of neurons interferes with mental as well as physical capacities.

See also NEUROTRANSMITTERS.

neuropsychiatry The branch of medicine dealing with the relationship between symptoms of mental illness and distinct neurological disorders. Such disorders are usually forms of brain disease, such as temporal lobe epilepsy, tumors or infections. Neuropsychiatry emphasizes the interplay of neurological, psychodynamic, genetic and environmental factors. New neurodiagnostic technology has allowed psychiatric diagnoses and treatment to become more specific, while providing a means for testing neurobiologic hypotheses. Neuropsychiatry uses diagnostic techniques drawn from neurology, behavioral neurology and neuropsychology in combination with traditional methods of interviewing and mental status evaluation to study mental health conditions associated with brain abnormalities. Basic sciences related to neuropsychiatry include neuroanatomy, neurochemistry, neurophysiology, neuropathology, neuroimmunology and behavioral genetics. Clinical sciences related to neuropsychiatry include general psychiatry, psychopharmacology, behavioral neurology, neuropsychology, neuroendocrinology and neuroimaging.

See also NEUROPSYCHOLOGICAL TESTING.

neuropsychological testing A method of further evaluating a patient's cognitive functioning. A neuropsychologist (specialist trained in neuropsychology) administers a group of cognitive tests to the patient. Reasons for neuropsychological testing may include gathering additional data in support of a possible diagnosis, localizing cognitive deficits picked on another examination, determining a cognitive baseline against which future testing can be compared to document improvement or deterioration, or to determine the severity of an injury or deficit. Testing is also used to facilitate rehabilitation plans, to assess treatment effect and to determine whether preexisting deficits could be contributing to a current clinical problem.

Common neuropsychological tests used in evaluating adults include intelligence tests, achievements test, attention surveys and tests relating to abstraction, memory, language ability, calculation ability, visual-spatial thought and motor skills.

See also NEUROPSYCHIATRY.

neurosis An old term for a variety of mental health disorders including agoraphobia, anxiety, panic attacks, panic disorder, phobias, depression, dysthymia, hypochondria and obsessive-compulsive disorder. Historically, some of these conditions have been referred to as neurotic disorders (now an obsolete term).

See AGORAPHOBIA; ANXIETY DISORDERS; DEPRESSION; DYSTHYMIA; HYPOCHONDRIASIS; OBSESSIVE-COMPULSIVE DISORDER; PANIC ATTACK; PANIC DISORDER; PHOBIA.

neurosurgery The medical specialty concerned with the surgical treatment of disorders of the central nervous system, including otherwise untreatable pain. Conditions more commonly treated by neurosurgery include tumors of the brain, spinal cord or meninges (membranes that surround the brain and spinal cord); certain abnormalities of the blood vessels that supply the brain, such as an aneurysm (bulge in a weak point of an artery); and bleeding inside the skull. Neurosurgery is also sometimes used in certain types of epilepsy and nerve damage caused by accidents or illness.

See also BRAIN.

neurosyphilis When syphilis is untreated, it can result in an infection of the brain or spinal cord. Symptoms may include poor coordination of leg movements when walking, urinary incontinence and pains in the limbs and abdomen. Brain damage may result in dementia, muscle weakness and extensive neurological damage, which is sometimes referred to as general paralysis of the insane.

Syphilis is considered a sexually transmitted disease (formerly known as venereal disease) and contracted through sexual intercourse and can also exist at birth (congenital syphilis). The drug of choice for treatment of syphilis is penicillin, although other medications are also used. However, organ damage already caused by the disease cannot be reversed.

See also SEXUALLY TRANSMITTED DISEASES.

neurotransmitters Chemical messengers released by neurons. The neurotransmitters norepinephrine and serotonin have been closely linked with depression. Neurotransmitters help transfer nerve impulses from one cell to another.

See also BRAIN CHEMISTRY.

nicotine dependence   Nicotine is the main substance responsible for dependence on tobacco. Nicotine in tobacco smoke passes into the bloodstream after inhaling; in chewing tobacco the nicotine is absorbed through the lining of the mouth. In habitual smokers, nicotine increases the heart rate, narrows blood vessels, raises blood pressure, stimulates the central nervous system, reduces fatigue, increases alertness and improves concentration. Regular smoking results in tolerance, and a higher intake is required to bring about the desired effects.

See also SMOKING; SUBSTANCE ABUSE.

nightmare   A dream during the night characterized by frightening elements. Usually people awaken immediately after a nightmare with a clear recollection of the dream and a feeling of intense uneasiness. Many normal children have nightmares after witnessing a frightening movie or after a day filled with great excitement, such as a first day of school or an important community event. Usually children outgrow nightmares and, when they do occur, can distinguish a dream from reality and are less frightened.

Individuals who have witnessed a crime, been a victim of a crime or served in a battle (among many causes) may experience post-traumatic stress disorder and also experience nightmares as part of that disorder. They may relive their experience in the nightmare and wake up just as frightened as they felt when the event or period of time was happening.

Nightmares usually occur during REM (rapid-eye-movement) sleep and during the later part of the sleep period during the night.

Children are more likely to experience nightmares when they have a cold or other infection, if their breathing is impaired or when they are separated from their parents. Adults taking certain medications, such as beta blockers and benzodiazepine drugs, have been known to have nightmares as a side effect.

Nightmares can usually be remembered upon awakening the next morning, whereas night terrors tend to be forgotten.

See also BEHAVIORAL THERAPY; DREAMING; NIGHT TERROR; POST-TRAUMATIC STRESS DISORDER.

Marks, Isaac. *Fears, Phobias and Rituals*. New York: Oxford University Press, 1987, p. 393.

night terror (sleep terror)   An intense nightmare from which the sleeper, usually a child, awakens screaming in terror, disoriented, agitated and difficult to comfort. Episodes usually occur about half an hour to three and a half hours after falling asleep. These may occur between age four and seven and usually diminish in early adolescence. Such episodes are frightening to parents and should be discussed with the pediatrician. Usually the dreamer does not recall the event upon awakening the next morning.

When adults experience night terrors, the episodes may be part of an anxiety disorder. In addition, nightmares of people who have post-traumatic stress disorder may at times be classified as terrors because they are so vivid and frightening.

See also DREAMING; NIGHTMARE; SLEEP.

NIMH   See NATIONAL INSTITUTE OF MENTAL HEALTH.

nocturnal emission   An involuntary male orgasm during sleep that results in ejaculation; it is also known as a wet dream. Nocturnal emissions are usually accompanied by dreams. Sex researchers say that a small percentage of women also experience nocturnal orgasms. Babylonians believed in a "maid of the night" who visited men in their sleep and a "little night man" who visited women as they slept. Later, the concept of Incubus—a demon who seduced women—and Succubus—a demon who seduced men—became somewhat widespread.

See also WET DREAM.

nocturnal erection Penile erection that occurs during sleep. This is normal, especially during dreaming sleep (irrespective of the content of the dream) even in young boys. In treating impotence, a sex therapist will ask about nocturnal erections, since their occurrence means that many of the important vascular and neurological systems involved in an erection are intact and rules out some of the physical causes of impotence. This can be measured mechanically in sleep laboratory studies.

See EJACULATION; IMPOTENCE; NOCTURNAL EMISSION; WET DREAM.

nominfensine An antidepressant medication (trade name: Merital). Common side effects may include restlessness, mild insomnia, nausea and some cardiac side effects. This medication was found effective by some patients who had depression that did not improve with other medications. However, the occurrence of dangerous blood abnormalities related to its use in Europe led its manufacturer to abruptly remove it from the world market for safety reasons, leaving many patients unable to benefit from this medication. It is no longer available.

See also ANTIDEPRESSANT MEDICATIONS; DEPRESSION.

noncompliance The simple behavioral act of either not doing what is one element of a regimen, or doing that which is proscribed. In the American Psychiatric Association's *Diagnostic and Statistical Manual of Mental Disorders* (3d ed., rev.), noncompliance is mentioned under the heading ''codes for conditions not attributable to a mental disorder that are a focus of attention or treatment.'' As examples, noncompliance is a major causal factor of the ''revolving door'' mental hospital patient; the bipolar affective disorder patient not taking his or her lithium;

and the schizophrenic not taking his or her antipsychotic medication.

Compliance is extremely important in mental health care because of the complications that may result from the presence of a chronic mental illness that is not treated in an optimal manner. For example, some people deviate from their prescription regimen or do not take their medication at all. Mental health care practitioners face a challenge to increase patients' informed decision making as well as compliance. They constantly strive to determine methods for measuring compliance as well as to develop more acceptable treatments.

According to Raymond A. Ulmer, Ph.D., director of the Noncompliance Institute of Los Angeles (established in 1976), the 10 problem areas of compliance (noncompliance) are:

1. Meeting medical appointments with physician
2. Reporting for diagnosis and treatment
3. Proper taking of medications
4. Avoiding drug abuse
5. Avoiding alcohol use
6. Following smoking recommendations
7. Following dietary suggestions
8. Following work recommendations
9. Conforming to exercise suggestions
10. Proper rest

The Noncompliance Institute of Los Angeles is an organization that works with patients and health care professionals to achieve greater compliance. According to a study conducted by the institute, noncompliant patients have twice as many complications as a compliant patient and cost four times as much to treat.

For further information, contact:

Noncompliance Institute of Los Angeles
6411 W. Fifth Street
Los Angeles, CA 90048
Phone: (213) 553–7387

Greengard, Samuel. ''When Patients Don't Follow Doctor's Orders.'' *Los Angeles Times,* Sept. 16, 1986.

McFarland, Gertrude K., and Thomas, Mary Durand. *Psychiatric Mental Health Nursing.* Philadelphia: J. B. Lippincott, 1991.

non-REM sleep   See SLEEP.

nonverbal communications   See BODY LANGUAGE.

norepinephrine   One of several neurotransmitters (also known as noradrenaline). Norepinephrine is a biogenic amine that transmits electrochemical signals from one brain cell to another. It is responsible for signaling many major functions, including wakefulness, learning, memory and eating. Norepinephrine can signal excitation or inhibition; it causes increased pulse and blood pressure. The level of norepinephrine in the brain may be associated with depression and manic states. One theory is that depression may result from too little norepinephrine and mania results from too much. Serotonin, another neurotransmitter, may also bring about depression when in short supply.

See also BIPOLAR DISORDER; DEPRESSION; NEUROTRANSMITTERS; SEROTONIN.

normal depression   Many people experience feelings of low mood as a reaction to life's circumstances. There may be extreme feelings of discouragement, disappointment, anger and conflict, but the mood lifts, as opposed to a clinical depression, in which the feelings are pervasive, last longer and interfere with the individual's normal functioning. While no medications are given for normal depression, psychological counseling can help in many cases.

See also DEPRESSION; PSYCHOTHERAPY.

Norpramin   Trade name for desipramine, an antidepressant drug, considered as effective as imipramine in the treatment of depression. Anticholinergic and sedative actions are less pronounced than those produced by imipramine.

See also ANTIDEPRESSANT MEDICATIONS; DEPRESSION; DESIPRAMINE; DEPRESSION AND AFFECTIVE DISORDERS in BIBLIOGRAPHY.

nortriptylene   A tricyclic antidepressant drug, marketed under the trade names Aventyl and Pamelor. Nortriptylene is as effective as imipramine in the treatment of depressive episodes of major depression and bipolar disorder; it also may be useful in the depressive periods of dysthymic disorder and in atypical depression.

See also ANTIDEPRESSANT MEDICATIONS; DEPRESSION.

Griest, J. H., and Jefferson, J. W. *Depression and its Treatment: Help for the Nation's #1 Mental Problem.* Washington, D.C.: American Psychiatric Association, 1984.

nostalgia   A longing to return to a place where one may have emotional ties, for example, to a home or to a native country. Nostalgia is related to feelings of isolation in the adopted location. According to Miepje DeVryer, writing in the *Journal of American College Health* (Vol. 39, Sept. 1989), nostalgia should be distinguished from homesickness, which tends to be resolved by returning "home." By contrast, in nostalgia, the longing or yearning is for a lost past without a desire to actually return. It is characterized by a bittersweet feeling, painful on the one hand, pleasurable and soothing on the other; these feelings combine with memories of the past. In nostalgia, the memories are consistently of places and nonhuman experiences, not of people.

See also MIGRATION.

nutrition   Good mental and physical health depends on good nutrition. The body and mind need many nutrients to function optimally. Factors that affect one's nutrition involve emotional, biologic, cognitive and sociocultural aspects. However, at times of certain mental or physical illnesses, nutrition may be less than optimal. For example, a severely depressed individual may have little interest in eating and lose weight, or an individual with a chronic illness such as cancer may have little appetite because of chemotherapy.

Alcoholism and substance abuse can suppress the appetite, leading to a decrease in food intake. Additionally, excessive alcohol intake impairs liver and pancreatic functioning and often results in gastric inflammation. There may be nutrients taken in by the alcohol abuser that are malabsorbed; vitamin B complex, magnesium, zinc, folic acid and vitamin K are just a few examples.

Severe anxiety and stress can interfere with an individual's ability to meet optimal nutritional needs. For example, severe anxiety increases the release of epinephrine and norepinephrine. These hormones shunt blood from the digestive organs to the muscles, heart and brain. In addition, during stress, the body prepares itself for fight or flight. The body's response to stress is to fuel itself for this response, and the body increases its release of glucocorticoids as well as growth hormone. Glucocorticoids increase glucose production, while growth hormone decreases the effectiveness of insulin in glucose metabolism. Decreased blood flow, along with the increased glucose production, creates a state of anorexia in which the individual has a decreased intake of essential nutrients.

Psychotropic medications can contribute to inadequate nutrition for some individuals. For example, dry mouth, a side effect of some medications, may make eating less pleasurable than usual. Other side effects that interfere with one's ability to maintain good nutrition include glossitis (inflammation of the tongue), nausea, abdominal pain, vomiting and diarrhea.

Mental impairment, caused by organic mental disorders, alcohol and other drug use or mental retardation, can result in an inability to make decisions about eating. The lack of judgment may be reflected in inappropriate selection or preparation of meals. Memory impairment associated with some

of these disorders may cause one to forget to eat—even after frequent reminders—or forget that one has already eaten, and eat a second meal.

In today's society, many homeless and destitute individuals do not have adequate nutrition. Social isolation, inadequate financial resources and lack of food storage and preparation facilities offer the potential for inadequate nutrition.

Emphasis on thinness in our society has led many to poor nutritional habits in an effort to lose weight. Hence one's perception of body image may also interfere with proper nutritional intake.

See also ANOREXIA NERVOSA; EATING DISORDERS; HOMELESSNESS; ANOREXIA, BULIMIA AND EATING DISORDERS in BIBLIOGRAPHY.

nutritional disorders Some psychiatric symptoms can be brought on by nutritional disorders. For example, thiamine deficiency may lead to Wernicke-Korsakoff syndrome and Korsakoff's syndrome, an amnestic disorder. Pernicious anemia can also produce dementia. Pellagra (niacin deficiency), a major problem in underdeveloped countries, shows a dramatic response to niacin, even when mental changes have been present for a long time.

See also NUTRITION; WERNICKE-KORSAKOFF SYNDROME; KORSAKOFF'S SYNDROME.

nymphomania A female compulsion including an excessive or insatiable desire for sexual stimulation and gratification. This desire may be expressed not only in seeking frequent sexual intercourse but also in frequent masturbation. Psychoanalytic explanations for this disorder include denial of homosexual tendencies, attempts to disprove frigidity, a reaction to seduction in childhood or an outlet for emotional tension.

Feminists say that nymphomania is a sexist term for women who have an excessive desire for sexual activity.

See also SEXUAL DYSFUNCTION.

Kahn, Ada P., and Holt, Linda Hughey. *The A to Z of Women's Sexuality.* Alameda, Calif.: Hunter House, 1992 .

O

obesity Obesity, a state of being overweight, affects an individual's self-esteem, feeling of attractiveness and one's mental well-being. Obesity can lead to social withdrawal or to constant binge-dieting. Many psychological factors are often associated with an individual's obesity. For example, one might overeat because of persistent emotional tension, use food as a substitute for satisfaction in a sexual relationship or because of sexual frustration.

Obesity can result from certain endocrine diseases (for example, hypothyroidism or hyperadrenal function, also known as Cushing's disease). There is an ongoing controversy about whether subtle biochemical or metabolic differences not yet specified may lead to obesity in some individuals.

Obesity can affect a woman's or man's enjoyment of sexual activities, as some grossly overweight individuals have difficulty in finding a comfortable position during a sexual relationship.

Obesity is also a risk factor for many diseases, including diabetes, heart and kidney disease and some forms of cancer.

See also BODY IMAGE; EATING DISORDERS; SELF-ESTEEM; BODY IMAGE in BIBLIOGRAPHY.

object relations A psychiatric term referring to the emotional bonds between one person and another, as contrasted with interest in and love for the self. The term is usually used with regard to the capacity to love and react appropriately to others' love.

obscenity Words, gestures, drawings, stories, films or sexual behavior (such as exhibitionism and voyeurism) that are considered repulsive and revolting because they grossly violate the norms of "good taste" in a particular society or group of individuals. Historically, many jokes regarding sexuality have been considered obscene. However, general ideas of obscenity change with cultures, the times and the setting. In the 1950s, television broadcasts could not portray a couple in a double bed; anything closer than a married couple in twin beds was considered "obscene." Some people consider nudity obscene; others do not. Bare breasts might seem obscene in a "girly" show but not on a sculpture in an art museum. Hence, obscenity is defined by cultural standards.

See also OBSCENITY-PURITY COMPLEX.

obscenity-purity complex Also known as puritan complex. A set of self-imposed moral standards about "impure" or obscene actions, feelings or thoughts. An individual who has this complex may dread violating these standards.

See also OBSCENITY; VICTORIANISM.

obsessive-compulsive disorder (OCD) A relatively common mental health disorder in which an individual has both obsessions and compulsions. Obsessions are persistent ideas, thoughts, impulses or images that come into one's consciousness irresistibly. The most common obsessions are repetitive negative and repeated thoughts of violence, e.g., killing one's child, contamination (such as becoming infected by shaking hands) and doubt (such as repeatedly wondering whether one has performed some act, such as locking the car door.) Compulsions are repetitive, purposeful and intentional behaviors performed in response to obsessions, such as ritualistic checking, counting, correcting, etc., usually in a certain order or style. The individual engages in the compulsive behavior to neutralize or to prevent discomfort or some dreaded situation or event. The activity is not usually connected with what it is planned to prevent, or it is excessive. There is a sense of compulsion coupled with a desire to resist the compulsion. The individual does not derive pleasure from carrying out the compulsive behavior but does find a release of anxieties by doing so.

Most people check to see that their doors are locked or that they have turned off the coffee pot. It is only when these obsessions and compulsions become so severe and frequent that they affect the individual's life that a diagnosis of obsessive-compulsive disorder (OCD) is made.

Victims of obsessions spend hours preoccupied with thoughts or fears about dirt, germs, fire, death, lucky/unlucky numbers or symmetry/exactness. They act out continuous rituals such as checking lights, appliances and homework, showering or bathing or arranging articles of clothing or tableware. They know these thoughts and rituals are senseless but cannot stop them.

Mental rituals can be so disabling that the patient suffers from depression, panic attacks and phobias. Many sufferers quit their jobs and cannot leave their homes.

OCD affects between 4 million and 7 million Americans, a third of whom are children and adolescents. OCD comes on suddenly, beginning often in early childhood, around age eight to 10. The disorder is twice as prevalent in the general population as panic disorder or schizophrenia.

According to John Zajecka, M.D., clinical director of the Department of Psychiatry's Treatment Research Unit, Rush-Presbyterian–St. Luke's Medical Center, Chicago, OCD is a disorder of secrecy because people are reluctant to talk about their symptoms; they think they are crazy and the only ones with these problems. The disorder is often unrecognized because patients underreport and hide their symptoms from friends and even close family members. The average time from the onset of the illness to its recognition is 7.5 years. There is no significant sex difference in the incidence of OCD. Onset of the disease is usually in the early twenties but can occur at a later age and in children of any age.

Diagnosis may be missed because the patient may complain of anxiety as a prominent feature rather than report the behavior causing the anxiety. According to Veeraindar Goli, M.D., and colleagues, writing in *Canadian Family Physician* (June 1991), patients who have excessive concern regarding certain blood tests or physical findings (excessive fear of AIDS, etc.) and who request repeated tests with no rational explanation should be investigated further for evidence of OCD.

The clinical course of OCD may take one of three forms: episodic, continuous or progressive. Secondary changes, such as major depression and anxiety disorders or alcohol and drug abuse, are frequently seen. According to the Canadian authors, about 25 percent of patients with OCD develop major depression. At one time it was believed that these patients might develop a pattern similar to schizophrenia, but delusions and hallucinations are very rarely seen in OCD. Other conditions known to be associated with OCD include Tourette syndrome and simple phobia. It has been reported that the familial incidence of Tourette syndrome is higher in patients with OCD; there may be a genetic vulnerability for both disorders.

Biologic Basis of OCD There is growing acceptance of the genetic tie in OCD. Researchers have found that 21 to 25 percent of family members who suffer from OCD also have children with the disorder. Scientists are also beginning to pinpoint lesions in certain areas of the brain that may cause OCD symptoms; other researchers are studying serotonin because they believe abnormal levels of this neurotransmitter may be a possible cause of OCD.

Because of biologic implications of this disorder, medications have become the most effective and safe treatment. Some antidepressant drugs work specifically to regulate the serotonin system. During the early 1990s, the antidepressant clomipramine (trade name:

Anafranil) is the only medication approved in the United States for the treatment of OCD. However, it is not effective in all patients with OCD and, in some patients, only helps them for a short time. Dr. Zajecka's department, like many other research-based institutes, is studying medications in combination. One drug may alleviate or partially alleviate some symptoms, but in combination with another, it may totally eradicate all OCD symptoms.

Researchers at Rush-Presbyterian–St. Luke's Medical Center are also following patients on a long-term basis to see what the course of illness is. Many patients report that as children they had some obsessional thoughts and performed checking or washing rituals.

Another research interest at the same institution is trichotillomania, or excessive hair pulling. Some people actually pull hair out of their scalps, leaving patches of baldness. Trichotillomania is like a compulsive symptom in that patients do not want to do it but feel that if they do not do it, they will go crazy. Therapy with antiobsessional drugs can reduce the urge to pull out hair, but as with OCD, the proven antidepressant drugs do not work for all patients.

According to Dr. Zajecka, few obsessive-compulsives benefit greatly from psychoanalysis because the more information that is uncovered during therapy, the more patients start obsessing about it. Psychosurgery is 70 percent effective but is hazardous.

Historically, OCD patients have been treated with neuroleptic (antipsychotic) drugs because their anxiety seemed intractable, because they lost insight and seemed psychotic or because they were misdiagnosed as psychotic. There is little evidence that these drugs work, and their long-term side effects can be serious. According to the Harvard Medical School Mental Health Letter (Sept. 1988), these should be tried only if everything else fails, and continued if there is clear-cut improvement within a few weeks.

The Harvard Medical School Mental Health Letter reported that there is little evidence for the usefulness of lithium, the anticonvulsant drug carbamazepine or such stimulants as dextroamphetamine and methylphenidate, although an occasional patient with OCD seems to benefit from one of these drugs. Diazepam (trade name: Valium), chlordiazepoxide (trade name: Librium) and other benzodiazepine antianxiety drugs have also proved to be largely ineffective. One possible exception is alprazolam (trade name: Xanax).

According to the Harvard Medical School Mental Health Letter, even the best antiobsessional drugs are only partially effective. On various rating scales, the average reduction in symptoms ranges from 30 to 60 percent, and the patient usually relapses when the drug is discontinued if no other treatment has been provided. For patients with compulsive rituals as well as obsessive thoughts, behavior therapy can be useful along with drugs.

Behavioral Therapy for OCD   According to the Canadian research group, behavioral techniques generally help more than 70 percent of patients with OCD. Behavioral therapy techniques expose patients to their fears and prevent them from performing their compulsive behavior. In the case of hand washing, for example, sufferers are commonly afraid of dirt, contamination and disease. Behavioral therapy requires motivation and is sometimes distressing to the patient. It is not often used often in young children.

The Canadian researchers say that behavior therapy is more effective for compulsions than for obsessions, and for cleaning compulsions than for checking compulsions. Behavioral techniques used in OCD include exposure therapy (exposing the individual for extended periods to situations that provoke the compulsions); response prevention (preventing the compulsive rituals for extended periods); use of imagery (or image flooding); participant modeling; and thought stopping (interrupting undesirable thoughts). Image flooding extends the techniques to imagined situations and is useful as a beginning point for patients too anxious to cope with exposure therapy. For example, a patient afraid to handle knives would be asked merely to imagine holding a knife and then to imagine the worst things that could happen. The patient notes the feelings of anxiety aroused and discusses them with the therapist. Once the patient realizes that his fears are unfounded, he can be exposed to real-life situations. A combination of drug therapy and behavioral therapy may achieve the best level of symptom reduction in many OCD patients.

Diagnosing OCD in Minority Populations After a 1990 study of major centers treating patients with OCD, Freda Lewis-Hall, M.D., of the Howard University College of Medicine, Washington, D.C. observed that OCD is often underdiagnosed in minority populations.

She cited differential utilization of mental health resources, potential differences in presentation and cultural influences as possible reasons for overlooking OCD in black populations. In her study of 1,500 patients diagnosed as having OCD, only 30 were black. The average number of total patients per center was 65, and approximately 39 percent of all centers had treated black patients (at least one or two patients at each center).

Hall observed that the language barrier can be a major difficulty in diagnosing, and she cited possible misdiagnosis as a reason for underreporting of OCD in black populations who receive health care in community mental health centers. For example, some black patients who relate bizarre ideas may receive a diagnosis of schizophrenia; once they are diagnosed, changing the diagnosis in those settings may be difficult. Moreover, some minority and rural populations may have different perspectives regarding behaviors because of varied cultural beliefs and thus may not notice compulsions as they are detected in other populations. Families, friends and the individuals themselves may not recognize ritualistic behaviors that are unreasonable, excessive and designed to neutralize obsessions because of their perspectives.

Comorbidity (other diseases at the same time) plays a part in overlooking OCD di-

Behavioral Therapy for OCD

Technique	Action	Anticipated Effect
Exposure	Patient is gradually exposed to the feared thought or object	Reduces anxiety; decreases obsessions and compulsions
Response prevention	Patient gradually delays performance of rituals for longer intervals	Helps reduce compulsions
Thought stopping	Patient tries to voluntarily interrupt obsessive thoughts	Helps decrease obsessions
Imagery	Patient is encouraged to imagine being exposed to feared situation and preventing an unwanted response	Helps decrease obsessions and anxiety
Modeling	Therapist actively models response behaviors; patient follows	Alters patient's unwanted responses to more acceptable ones

SOURCE: Adapted from *Canadian Family Physician* (June 1991).

agnosis in general. Many OCD patients have concomitant disorders and may be treated for phobias, major depressive episodes, alcohol abuse, substance abuse and panic disorders. Many are placed in treatment programs for these disorders, and their OCD is overlooked.

Common cognitive compulsions and rituals, such as counting and repeating, are well known in OCD. However, the most common cognitive rituals observed among black OCD patients studied by Lewis-Hall generally involved religious rituals, particularly praying rituals. According to Lewis-Hall, this is a frequently overlooked obsessive behavior.

At a meeting of the Anxiety Disorders Association of America (ADAA) in conjunction with the Chicago Consortium for Psychiatric Research, Inc., held in Chicago in April 1991, Lewis-Hall emphasized a need for better diagnosis and treatment of OCD in minorities, citing the statistic that 30 percent of the U.S. population will be made up of minorities in 10 years. She recommended modifications of current diagnostic and therapeutic techniques to make appropriate interactions with one-third of the population.

Self-help Groups The Obsessive-Compulsive Disorder Foundation is a nonprofit organization formed by sufferers and other concerned individuals. They publish a newsletter and a list of available treatment centers in a given area. Individuals interested in these materials or in learning about local support groups for OCD may contact:

Obsessive-Compulsive Disorder Foundation
P.O. Box 60
Vernon, CT 06066
Phone: (203) 772–0565

Anxiety Disorders Association of America
6000 Executive Boulevard, Suite 200
Rockville, MD 20852–3801
Phone: (301) 231–9350

See also ANTIDEPRESSANT MEDICATIONS; ANXIETY DISORDERS; BEHAVIORAL THERAPY; TOURETTE SYNDROME.

American Psychiatric Association. *Diagnostic and Statistical Manual of Mental Disorders,* 3d ed., rev. Washington, D.C.: APA, 1987.

Excerpts from Goli, Veeraindar; Krishnam, Ranga, and Ellinwood, Everett. "Obsessive Compulsive Disorder." *Canadian Family Physician* 37 (June 1991).

Excerpts from "Is There a Drug Treatment for Obsessive-Compulsive Disorder?" *Harvard Medical School Mental Health Letter,* Boston (Sept. 1988).

Kahn, Ada P. "OCD Said to Be Underdiagnosed in Minority Populations." *Psychiatric News* (July 19, 1991).

Excerpts from Redeker, Mary-Ann. "Understanding OCD." *Insights,* Rush-Presbyterian–St. Luke's Medical Center, Chicago, vol. 13, no. 3 (1990).

obstructive sleep apnea syndrome (OSAS) See SLEEP; SNORING.

Oedipus complex The Oedipus complex, originally described by Sigmund Freud, is a crucial component of Freudian thinking. The concept comes from the Greek myth about Oedipus, who unwittingly killed his father and married his mother. Freud saw this myth as representing every small boy's unconscious sexual attachment and desire for his mother and jealousy and rivalry with his father.

Freud believed that a boy who does not successfully rechannel such urges may be tormented, leading to anxieties and other mental health problems. He also hypothesized that as children develop, they come to identify with the parent of the same sex and are later able to make sexual attachments with members of the opposite sex outside the family. A young child represses these feelings and keeps them in the unconscious out of fear of displeasure or punishment by the parent of the same sex.

In its original use, the term applied only to a boy or man and his relationship with his mother. The term "Electra complex" applied to girls and women and their relationships with their fathers.

The Oedipus complex may influence young men in their choice of wives. Some choose women just like their mothers, and some choose the exact opposite. Other men look for older women in whom they see a mother figure. Overall, the Oedipus complex is one of the most well known terms left in the legacy of Freudian thinking.

See also ELECTRA COMPLEX; FREUD, SIGMUND.

Stone, Evelyn M., ed. *American Psychiatric Glossary,* 6th ed. Washington, D.C.: American Psychiatric Press, 1988.

old boy network   See NETWORKING.

only children   The concentrated attention and love that an only child usually receives from parents has both advantages and disadvantages. Only children have a strong sense of security and all family resources devoted to developing their talents, but they may be handicapped when the need to become independent and strike out for themselves arises. The only child may have less privacy, the burden of trying to fulfill high expectations and an unrealistic sense of what the world is like because of undivided parental attention. Only children rarely get away with behavioral transgressions because there is no one else to blame for mundane events such as mud on the carpet, but they are never blamed for what someone else did. Adult life—in which it is very possible to be blamed for things done by others but also to get way with undesirable behavior—may come as a shock to only children.

On the other hand, some only children experience a type of deprivation because the home remains adult-centered. Parents may continue a romantic, exclusive relationship because one child requires less change than two or more. For example, adult standards of cleanliness, quiet and neatness that would be difficult to preserve with two or more children may stay intact. Parents of one child may be less likely to plan vacations and other recreation around the child because they are in the majority.

Only children frequently not only live in an adult-centered home but in many cases have relatively older parents. The fact that the child has to learn early to be a "little adult" helps to prepare for adult life but may make the child quieter and more sophisticated, and therefore such a child may seem somewhat unusual to other children.

While their parents age, only children are in a unique position. They have to deal with their aging problems with no help from siblings. The problems may burden such children while their own families and occupational responsibilities are at their peak.

Only children share some attributes with older children. They have parents who have no experience in parenting. As more children arrive, parents may become more realistic and mellow regarding childlike behavior, but the only child does not get the benefit of this attitude. First-borns and only children tend to be achievers and score higher on intelligence tests, particularly in the area of verbal ability. Other children in the family constellation may share the only child experience. Mental health professionals believe that any child with an age difference of seven years or more from the closest sibling or even a single girl in a family of boys or vice versa may have the experience and outlook of an only child.

Despite possible disadvantages of being an only born, the only child usually learns to tolerate and even enjoy solitude and to develop inner resources. Only children frequently enter fields that require them to work in an independent, solitary manner. In many cases, only-born women seem to adapt to widowhood better than women who had many siblings. As an only child, the young women learned to fill their time without others around.

Fictional only children such as Dennis the Menace and Eloise are entertaining. However, only children may be more limited by the stereotypes attached to them than by the actual circumstances of being an only born. Even the stereotypes conflict. Only children have been considered to be passive, introverted and tied to mother's apron strings yet also driven, aggressive and quarrelsome.

Numbers of only children are increasing and will probably continue to do so in the Western world. A number of factors have contributed to the increasing number of couples who produce only one child. Improved birth control techniques and legal abortions have given couples control of family size. More frequently than in the past, divorce brings the growth of a family to a halt. It has become less common for a financially established man to marry a younger woman with many childbearing years ahead of her. In general, couples are marrying later; the emphasis on women's education and careers means that a woman may postpone childbearing until one child is the only biologic possibility. Additionally, women often feel that juggling career and motherhood is easier with only one child. The simple cost of raising and educating more than one child may be prohibitive, particularly in urban areas where comfortably housing a family of more than three can be quite costly.

Limiting families to one child is not an entirely new phenomenon. During the Depression, one out of four children were only children. During the Baby Boom, the ratio dropped to one in 10. In the 1980s, the Census Bureau found that the number of married women expecting to have only one child was 11 percent of the population, compared with 7 percent in 1960.

See also BIRTH ORDER.

open marriage   An arrangement in which both partners agree to accept the freedom of their spouse to have extramarital sexual activity. Success of an open marriage depends on an equal desire by both partners to maintain the arrangement. Each partner in an open marriage may have sexual and emotional needs that cannot be satisfied within a monogamous relationship.

The concept of open marriage increased in popularity during the 1960s but decreased during the 1980s along with the spread of sexually transmitted diseases (STDs) and acquired immunodeficiency syndrome (AIDS).

See also MARRIAGE.

opioid substance abuse   In 1980s, there were nearly 500,000 opioid addicts in the United States. Opioid substances include many opium-related compounds. In addition to the natural alkaloids of opium, morphine and codeine, there are important synthetic derivatives such as heroin, hydromorphone hydrochloride (trade name: Dilaudid), oxycodone (trade name: Percocet) and oxymorphone hydrochloride (trade name Numorphan), as well as purely synthetic opioids such as meperidine (trade name: Demerol), methadone (trade name: Dolopine), pentazocine (trade name: Talwin) and dextropropoxyphene hydrochloride (trade name: Darvon). Men outnumber women by three to one among narcotic addicts, and addiction is more prevalent among people between the ages of 18 and 25. Few addicts manage to break the habit, and recidivism is estimated to be as high as 90 percent. Some health care professionals who have ready access to narcotics become addicted to them.

Serious complications of opioid addiction include infection, suicide and homicide. In the 1990s, the spread of the AIDS virus through shared needles has made heroin addiction a major risk factor for contracting the virus.

Mental health professionals treat many addicts for their addictions in hospital emergency rooms when they are experiencing overdose or withdrawal symptoms as well as in outpatient settings.

See also SUBSTANCE ABUSE.

oral character   A psychoanalytic term for personality patterns that derive from experiences during the oral phase of psychosexual development. This theory suggests that a child who experiences adequate sucking satisfaction and attention from the mother during this period will develop a friendly, optimistic, cooperative and generous outlook on life. However, if the child is not satisfied during the oral sucking and biting stage, the individual may become hostile, overly competitive, aggressive and critical.

See also PSYCHOSEXUAL DEVELOPMENT.

Orestes complex   A psychiatric term referring to a son's repressed impulse to kill his mother, or the actual act of killing his mother (matricide). The term is derived from the myth of Orestes, who killed his mother, Clytemnestra, and her lover.

See also COMPLEX.

organic approach   A concept that mental and physical disorders have a biochemical or biologic basis. For example, those who hold this view point to evidence that manic-depressive illness, schizophrenia and anxiety disorders occur because of biochemical disturbances in the nervous or glandular system. While there may be growing evidence of organic or biologic factors in certain forms of mental illness, it is understood by most psychiatrists that most organic disorders represent an interaction of psychological factors or stresses with a biologic vulnerability, which is also true of many medical disorders such as myocardial infarction (heart attack).

See also BIOLOGICAL MARKERS; BRAIN CHEMISTRY; DEPRESSION.

organic brain syndrome   See BRAIN SYNDROME, ORGANIC.

orgasm   The climax or peak of intense pleasure during sexual activity. It is the third stage of the sexual response cycle, after excitement and the plateau stage. Orgasm is the culmination of sexual tension in muscle contractions, which force out accumulated blood from erect and engorged genital tissues. This is usually accompanied by a feeling of intense pleasure. There may be a momentary feeling of clouding of consciousness.

In women, an orgasm usually involves a series of rhythmic muscular contractions, each lasting about a second, of the lower vagina and surrounding tissues and may involve uterine contractions. In males, ejaculation from the penis occurs. The focus of the male orgasm is the penis, prostate gland and seminal vesicles. During orgasm, blood pressure and heart rate usually increase.

Orgasm is a very individual experience. Feelings based on mutual warmth and understanding between the two individuals are important factors for women in achieving sexual gratification. Variations in orgasm are reported by different women, and the experience differs in one woman at different times. With sexual stimulation, some women experience more than one orgasm; such multiple orgasms may occur as close together as only a few minutes. Although there is wide variation among individuals, according to sex researchers Masters and Johnson, women take longer on average to reach orgasm than men, 15 minutes as opposed to three minutes.

For some women, penile thrusting is not enough to bring them to the point of orgasm; many achieve orgasm most easily by stimulation of the clitoris either by hand (hers or her partner's) or during oral or vaginal intercourse. A woman's partner often cannot tell if a woman's orgasm is occurring. With communication between partners, they can achieve mutual intensification of the experience.

According to Freud's dual-orgasm theory, there are two types of female orgasm, the "mature" vaginal orgasm and the "immature" clitoral orgasm. In their 1966 work, Masters and Johnson reported that there is only one type of female orgasm, with the clitoris as the center of sensation. Since that time, some sex researchers agreed that the most likely stimulation to create arousal to orgasm is direct stimulation of the clitoris. Other researchers say women achieve orgasm without direct stimulation of the clitoris, and not all women respond to only clitoral stimulation.

According to E. R. Mahoney, in *Human Sexuality* (1983), orgasm by clitoral stimulation is typically described as very intense, sharp and ecstatic, while orgasm by means of deep vaginal penetration is described as more internal, soothing, subtle and full.

Some women report that regular sexual stimulation that stops short of orgasm results in pelvic discomfort. However, many women enjoy sexual activity without orgasm. Some women who have lost sensation in the lower part of their body enjoy sexual stimulation of various erogenous areas of their body. Other women report that orgasm can relieve the pelvic congestion associated with menstrual cramps.

The term "frigidity" is used to refer to the condition of never achieving an orgasm during sexual activity. The term "female orgasmic dysfunction" is currently used to refer to difficulty in achieving orgasm.

See also CLITORIS; FRIGIDITY.

Kahn, Ada P., and Holt, Linda Hughey. *The A to Z of Women's Sexuality.* Alameda, Calif.: Hunter House, 1992.

orgasmic dysfunction Inability to reach orgasm through physical stimulation. Masters and Johnson, in their major 1966 work *Human Sexual Response,* described two types. Primary orgasmic dysfunction meant that the woman never had an orgasm through any physical contact, including masturbation. Situational orgasmic dysfunction meant that the woman had at least one instance of orgasm through physical contact. Orgasmic dysfunction is not limited to females.

See also MALE SEXUAL DYSFUNCTION; ORGASM; ORGASMIC RECONDITIONING.

Stone, Evelyn M., ed. *American Psychiatric Glossary,* 6th ed. Washington, D.C.: American Psychiatric Press, 1988.

orgasmic peak The moment of climax or orgasm when an individual feels the maximum intensity of sexual excitement and gratification.

See also ORGASM.

orgasmic platform A term used by Masters and Johnson in conjunction with their belief that female orgasms originate in the vagina. They classified structures such as the clitoral bulbs, urethral sponge, inner labia, perineal sponge and blood vessels as "the outer third of the vagina" or "orgasmic platform."

See also JOHNSON, VIRGINIA; MASTERS, WILLIAM H.; ORGASM; SEXUAL RESPONSE CYCLE.

Kahn, Ada P., and Holt, Linda Hughey. *The A to Z of Women's Sexuality.* Alameda, Calif.: Hunter House, 1992.

orgasmic reconditioning (orgasmic reorientation) A technique used in sex therapy in which fantasies or illustrative representations are used to arouse the patient, who then engages in masturbation until sexual climax is reached. Later, these stimuli are replaced by more conventional heterosexual representations just before orgasm and at progressively earlier points, in order to develop normal arousal patterns.

See also MASTURBATION; ORGASM; SEX THERAPY.

Kahn, Ada P., and Holt, Linda Hughey. *The A to Z of Women's Sexuality.* Alameda, Calif.: Hunter House, 1992.

orthopsychiatry An interdisciplinary approach to mental health emphasizing child development and family life. Social workers, pediatricians, psychiatrists, psychologists, sociologists and nurses collaborate in studying and treating emotional and behavioral problems before they become severe and disabling.

orthostatic   A term relating to standing erect. For example, orthostatic hypotension refers to a drop in blood pressure when one rises from a lying or sitting position. The individual may experience dizziness or lightheadedness; falls are sometimes attributed to orthostatic hypotension.

See also BLOOD PRESSURE.

Othello syndrome   See DELUSIONAL JEALOUSY.

outpatient   An individual who receives care without hospitalization. Such care for mental health concerns may be in a neighborhood or community mental health clinic or in a hospital. Care received in a hospital is referred to as inpatient care.

See also MENTAL HOSPITAL.

over-the-counter medications (OTC)   Medications that may be purchased without a prescription from a physician. Many remedies for colds, headaches and minor pains are available without a prescription. Medications that require prescriptions are known as ethical drugs.

See also ETHICAL DRUG.

P

pain   A sensation that can range from mild discomfort to an unbearable and excruciating experience. How one perceives pain is a very individual matter. The term "pain threshold" applies to the level at which individuals become very uncomfortable from a similar level of unpleasant stimulation. Fear and anxiety are often associated with pain, because a pain may signal a problem of unknown origin and unknown outcome. Unexplained pain seems more stressful than a pain for which a diagnosis can be made.

How individuals relate to pain and express pain may be affected by their upbringing and culture. For example, in Western society, many men were raised to endure mild pain, such as athletic injuries, while women were asked to rest upon the slightest suggestion of pain. Men were told that uncomplaining endurance of pain was "manly."

Drugs that relieve pain are known as analgesic drugs. They usually help in relieving mild pain such as headache, toothache or dysmenorrhea (menstrual pain). The most widely used drugs in this group are acetaminophen and aspirin. Mild to moderate pain, such as that caused by sports injuries or arthritis, is often treated with a nonsteroidal anti-inflammatory drug (NSAID). Severe pain caused by kidney stones, a serious injury, a surgical procedure or cancer may be treated with a narcotic analgesic. Nondrug treatments include massage, ice packs or hot packs. Recurrent or chronic pain is sometimes relieved by acupuncture, acupressure or hypnosis; biofeedback also helps some individuals. Laughter has been known to ease pain. People who are depressed are more likely to interpret pain as more serious than those who feel good about themselves and their life situations.

See also DEPRESSION; HEADACHES; LAUGHTER.

palpitations   An awareness that the heart is beating faster than normal or skipping beats. This occurs during and after exercise or in stressful or feared situations. If the feeling lasts for several hours or recurs over several days, or if it causes chest pain, breathlessness or dizziness, a physician should be consulted as soon as possible. Palpitations may be caused by a cardiac arrhythmia, usually premature ventricular beats or contractions (PVB) or mitral valve prolapse, which usually do not require treatment; if severe, these may require further diagnosis or treatment. If palpitation episodes are brief, they are probably within the range of normal. Rarely, some medications can produce palpitations from PVBs. Some cases of mitral valve prolapse require treatment. Persistent palpitations or tachycardia can be evaluated by a family physician, general internist or specialist in cardiology.

Palpitations often occur during panic attacks or as a phobic reaction to a feared stimulus. For example, a person who is phobic about dogs may experience palpitations just at the sight of a dog walking on the street. Although the dog is on a leash and does not seem aggressive, the phobic individual may experience palpitations along with sweaty palms, weak knees and dizziness.

Those who experience palpitations may fear that they are having a heart attack or that they are going to die. Just thinking these thoughts and becoming afraid of imagined consequences can cause the palpitations to increase.

Symptoms of anxiety, such as palpitations, are treated with behavioral therapy, cognitive therapy and, in some cases, drug therapy.

See also ANXIETY DISORDERS; ANXIOLYTIC DRUGS; PHARMACOLOGIC THERAPY in BIBLIOGRAPHY.

Pamelor   Trade name for nortriptylene hydrochloride, an antidepressant drug.

See also ANTIDEPRESSANT DRUGS; NORTRIPTYLENE; PHARMACOLOGIC THERAPY in BIBLIOGRAPHY.

panic attack   A short period (five to 20 minutes) of suddenly occurring intense fear or extreme discomfort, usually for no apparent reason. To be diagnosed as a panic attack, the incident must have at least four of more than a dozen characteristic symptoms, which might include fear of dying, fear of going crazy, fear of losing control, shortness of breath, dizziness, faintness, choking, palpitations or rapid heartbeat, trembling or shaking, sweating, nausea or abdominal distress, numbness or tingling sensations, hot flashes or chills and chest pain or discomfort. Attacks involving fewer than four symptoms are known as limited symptom attacks. Panic attacks are considered one of several anxiety disorders.

A diagnosis of panic attack is made when organic factors are ruled out as the cause of the disturbance. According to the *Diagnostic and Statistical Manual of Mental Disorders* (3d ed., rev., 1987), panic attacks usually last minutes or, more rarely, hours. Typically, the first attack may occur during the late teens. The attacks last from five minutes to an hour, averaging 15 to 20 minutes, with minor attacks much shorter.

Initially, attacks are unexpected and do not occur immediately before or on exposure to a situation that usually causes anxiety, such as a simple phobia. Additionally, attacks are not triggered by situations in which the individual is the focus of others' attention and scrutiny, as is the case with a social phobia. Later in the course of the disorder, one may associate certain situations, such as crossing a bridge or being on an escalator, with having a panic attack. Once a panic attack has occurred in a particular setting, the individual may become fearful that it will happen again and may tend to avoid the situation whenever possible.

Because such individuals tend toward avoidance behaviors, many also have agoraphobia. However, not all agoraphobics have panic attacks or panic disorder. The average age for onset of panic attacks is in the late twenties.

Many individuals who have panic attacks also have anxieties and depression; often they fear having another attack and feel some degree of hopelessness and helplessness regarding their life circumstances.

The word ''panic'' evolved from the name Pan, the god the Greeks worshiped as their god of flocks, herds, pastures and fields.

Humans depended on Pan to make flocks fertile; Pan himself was a lustful creature known for his ability to reproduce. Pan's shape was that of a goat that could traverse fields and dart through herds of cattle. Pan loved to scare people—often in dark forests and at night—and would dart out of the woods and make eerie noises to frighten passersby. The fright he aroused was known as "panic." Pan later fell out of favor, because his two horns seemed to portray the devil.

When severe panic attacks recur frequently and disrupt one's life, the condition is known as panic disorder. The average panic disorder sufferer may have attacks two to four times a week, but people have been known to get as many as several a day and as few as one a year. Panic disorder occurs in 1 to 2 percent of the population.

See also AGORAPHOBIA; ANXIETY DISORDERS; MITRAL VALVE PROLAPSE; PANIC DISORDER; PHOBIA.

panic disorder A diagnosis of panic disorder is made when at least four panic attacks have occurred within a four-week period, or when one or more attacks have been followed by a period of at least a month of persistent fear of having another attack.

According to the *Diagnostic and Statistical Manual of Mental Disorders* (3d ed., rev.), panic disorder without agoraphobia is equally common in males and in females; panic disorder with agoraphobia is about twice as common in females as in males. Panic disorder usually begins during periods of choices, transitions, separation and added responsibility. The mean age of onset is in the mid-twenties. Panic disorder occurs in 1 to 2 percent of the population. Panic disorder patients often show a family history of panic disorders. For example, first-degree relatives of patients with panic disorder are at a markedly higher risk of developing the disorder (15 to 20 percent compared with 1 percent in the general population). Recent research, has suggested that panic disorder patients

have a higher incidence of suicide attempts (20 to 30 percent).

In the 1950s, panic disorder was sometimes referred to as "atypical depression"; in the 1960s, "phobic anxiety"; and, in the 1970s, "endogenous anxiety." The syndrome was described in 1959 as separate from anxiety disorders by Donald Klein, M.D. In 1989, the World Health Organization in its *International Classification of Diseases,* for the first time, named panic disorder as a separate syndrome.

According to H. Michael Zal, D.O., F.A.C.N., a board-certified psychiatrist and author of *Panic Disorder, the Great Pretender* (1990), individuals who have panic disorder are at greater risk for death from unnatural causes—especially suicide—over the course of the illness.

Personality characteristics of those who have panic disorder vary considerably. However, Dr. Zal, a clinical professor of psychiatry at the Philadelphia College of Osteopathic Medicine, has observed some common factors. Cross-sectional studies of persons with panic disorder or agoraphobia have demonstrated personality traits of dependency, avoidance, low self-esteem and interpersonal sensitivity. One common attribute of the panic-prone persons may include placing a great value on control. Any loss or threatened loss of control causes them to feel anxious. According to Dr. Zal, changes in their life that upset their balance may make them feel as if they will lose control. Additionally, panic-prone individuals overvalue their independence and feel great discomfort in acknowledging their dependency needs. They are often reluctant to accept help and prefer to help others. They tend to repress feelings and feel anxious when their emotions surface. They tend to be perfectionist, compulsive individuals, with high expectations of themselves and others.

Panic Disorder in Men At a conference on men's health sponsored by the American Osteopathic Association in Chicago in 1990, Dr. Zal explained that panic disorder is "the great pretender'' because it tends to mimic physical and psychological syndromes, making diagnosis more difficult.

Many men attempt to mask symptoms of panic disorder, sometimes through self-medication with alcohol. Because of these factors, it is difficult to estimate how many men suffer from panic disorder. Some men experience severe symptoms, either alone or in combination. Many men complain of lower gastrointestinal problems, which are a symptom of panic disorder. He believes that some patients with irritable bowel syndrome also have panic attacks and vice versa. In many cases, if the panic disorder is treated, gastrointestinal symptoms disappear.

Many men go to family physicians, see multiple specialists or end up in emergency rooms thinking they have physical disorders, such as a heart attack, a neurological problem or irritable bowel syndrome; but medical results find no organic pathology. Appropriate medical and laboratory work-ups should be performed that focus on target systems to rule out physical problems as the cause of fast heartbeat, trembling, shaking, fainting, dizziness, numbness, tingling and other complaints.

According to Dr. Zal, clinicians should be on the lookout for accompanying physical disorders when diagnosing panic disorder, such as substance abuse and depression. Many patients with panic attacks drink ''to settle their nerves,'' and this type of self-medication can develop into a secondary problem.

At one time, hypoglycemia (low blood sugar) was thought to be the cause of panic attacks. In the 1980s, researchers suggested the possibility that mitral valve prolapse (MVP), was a cause, or at least a contributing factor. There is still ongoing controversy regarding the role of MVP in panic disorder. Many panic disorder patients also have MVP, but no conclusive research evidence has shown that MVP causes panic disorder.

In panic attacks and anxiety, researchers now say there may be an actual vulnerability, an abnormality of the parahippocampus, in the brains of some persons who have panic attacks. Researchers suspect that certain events, perhaps stressful, lead to stimulation of the locus coeruleus to cause the parahippocampal abnormality to overreact. This initiates an anxiety attack by sending signals to the parts of the brain that control heart palpitations, shortness of breath and other symptoms of panic attacks.

Treatment   Treatment for panic disorder may involve behavioral therapy, such as cognitive therapy, psychotherapy or medical psychopharmacology. Often a combination of treatments is specifically chosen for each individual patient. Usually treatment begins with education about the illnesses and encouragement to reenter situations about which the individual has become avoidant. For some individuals, cognitive therapy (changing how they think) helps. For others, behavioral therapy (changing how the individual acts in response to certain situations) is helpful. Behavioral therapy in the form of behavior modification helps many anxious individuals. Behavioral therapists use desensitization techniques in which they gradually expose sufferers to the situations they have avoided.

Cognitive therapy focuses on getting sufferers to change their original way of thinking (a misappraisal of the significance of body sensations) about and dealing with their sensations of anxiety. They learn to focus on challenging thoughts that tell them they are having a heart attack or will die. One technique of this therapy is learning to experience the panic and see that nothing bad happens. Patients learn to control their breathing to prevent hyperventilation and to use relaxation techniques, such as visualizing places or situations that make them feel calm.

There are types of psychotherapies that are effective for overcoming panic disorder. For many, short-term psychotherapy—lasting a few weeks to a year—is enough to bring about improvement.

In mid-1992, alprazolam (trade name: Xanax) became the first and only medication approved in the United States for panic disorder. It is also widely used for the treatment of patients suffering from clinical anxiety and anxiety associated with depression.

In the late 1980s a study, known as the Cross-National Collaborative Panic Study, was conducted to evaluate the clinical efficacy and safety of alprazolam. Its first phase involved more than 600 patients in the United States, Canada and Austria. In the second phase, more than 1,100 patients in 15 countries were involved. Alprazolam is currently the only medication approved by the U.S. Food and Drug Administration for the treatment of panic attacks.

Prior to this research, various studies indicated that the tricyclic antidepressant drugs (e.g., imipramine) provided an effective, safe treatment for panic disorder. However, those medications typically take three to six weeks for noticeable improvement, and researchers found that side effects, including anxiety symptoms, occur in up to one-third of the patients.

For some individuals, there is a problem of relapse after drug therapy. Even after a year of treatment, 75 to 80 percent of patients will get some recurrence within three to four months after the drug is stopped. In some cases there is a rebound effect, in which panic attacks return in even greater numbers and intensity. Gradually reducing the dosage is crucial to successfully withdrawing patients from drugs while preventing rebounding panic attacks.

Three-quarters of patients who have to take drugs will need long-term drug therapy; another 25 percent will not be helped regardless of how long they take drugs. Overall, a quarter of the patients who do take drugs are helped permanently and will not have to continue them.

How Families Can Help Panic Disorder Sufferers Family members can learn to recognize panic disorders by being alert to the masked appearances of anxiety, because to a large degree, symptoms are hidable. Repeated avoidance of situations is often the best clue.

Treatment for panic disorder is not limited to medical or psychotherapeutic interven-tion. Family members can help one another cope with panic disorder by giving thoughtful support, being good listeners and talking openly and constructively with one another. Instead of enabling the person to avoid a situation, family members can help the sufferer negotiate a small step forward. According to Sally Winston, director of the Anxiety Disorder Program at Sheppard Pratt Hospital, Towson, Maryland, family members should find something positive in every experience and help the sufferer in the present and avoid "catastrophizing" about the future. Winston advises family members to be patient and accepting but not to "settle" for a lifelong disorder within the family and not to sacrifice their own lives and build resentment toward the sufferer. Treatment is available, and many sufferers are helped by one or more available therapies.

For information on panic disorder as well as other anxiety disorders, contact:

Anxiety Disorders Association of America
6000 Executive Boulevard, Suite 200
Rockville, MD 20852-3801
Phone: (301) 231-9350

National Mental Health Association
1021 Prince Street
Alexandria, VA 22314
Phone: (703) 684-7722

See also ALPRAZOLAM; ANXIETY DISOR-DERS; MITRAL VALVE PROLAPSE; PHOBIA.

Kahn, Ada P. "Panic Attacks" and "Family Members Can Help Sufferers Cope with Attacks." *Chicago Tribune,* June 23, 1991.
Zal, H. Michael. *Panic Disorder: The Great Pretender.* New York: Insight Books, Plenum Press, 1990.

paranoia A pervasive and unwarranted tendency to interpret the actions of others as deliberately demeaning or threatening. For example, a paranoid person may question loyalty of employees or friends. In new situations, a paranoid individual may read hidden meanings into remarks or events. These individuals are quick to anger and are reluctant to confide in others because they fear that information may be used against them.

Many normally healthy individuals have paranoid tendencies at certain times and under certain circumstances, some of which may be warranted. However, when carried to extreme, paranoid tendencies are considered paranoid personality disorder. This term is applied to persistent, nonbizarre delusions that are not due to any other mental disorder, such as schizophrenia or a mood disorder. Common types of delusions are erotomanic, grandiose, jealous and persecutory. Erotomanic delusions are that one is loved by another, usually a famous or important person. Grandiose delusions commonly take the form of the person's being convinced that he or she possesses some great talent or has made some important discovery for which he or she will be recognized. Jealous delusions involve feelings that one's spouse or lover is unfaithful (Othello syndrome).

Persecutory delusions are the most common type and usually involve a single theme or series of themes, such as being spied on, cheated, followed, poisoned or drugged. Small slights may be exaggerated and become the focus of a delusional system. Elderly patients with dementia, as they see themselves losing control of their life and decisions, may accuse loyal and helpful children of stealing their funds or savings.

Additionally, there are somatic delusions (or paranoias) in which individuals have a delusion about their body or parts of their body, for example, that they have a foul odor emanating from their breath, that certain parts of the body are not functioning or that they have an internal parasite.

Paranoid disorders are slightly more common in females than males. They usually begin in middle or late adult life but can begin at a younger age. In most studies, average age of onset has been found to be between 40 and 55.

Paranoid schizophrenia is a type of schizophrenia in which extreme delusions are related to a single theme; unlike undifferentiated schizophrenia, paranoid schizophrenia may develop in the late twenties or thirties.

See also AGORAPHOBIA; BODY IMAGE; DELUSION; IDEAS OF REFERENCE; SCHIZOPHRENIA.

paraphilias Psychosexual disorders in which an individual requires unusual or bizarre acts or images for sexual excitement. They include specific types, such as coprophilia (feces), exhibitionism, fetishism, frotteurism (rubbing), klismaphilia (enema), mysophilia (filth), necrophilia (corpses), pedophilia (children), sexual masochism, sexual sadism, telephone scatalogia (lewdness), transvestitism, voyeurism, urophilia (urine) and zoophilia (animals).

Imagery may take one of many forms, including preference for inhuman objects, such as animals or clothes of the other sex; sexual activity involving real or simulated humiliation or suffering, such as bondage or whipping; or repetitive sexual activity with nonconsenting partners.

Some cultures view any form of paraphilia as abnormal; other cultures are accepting of forms that do not involve victimization of others or interfere with satisfying sexual relationships. For example, many men who are transvestites (cross-dressers into women's clothes) may enjoy perfectly satisfying sex lives. In a sexually permissive society this may not be problematic behavior, whereas in a restrictive culture this could be considered abnormal behavior. However, behavior patterns such as pedophilia can lead to molestation of young children; such victimization that can result in long-term damage to the child is not a harmless sexual variant.

See also SEXUAL DYSFUNCTION.

parapsychology A branch of psychology concerned with events and experiences that cannot be explained by scientific method; also known as extrasensory perception (ESP). Examples of such phenomena are paranormal experiences, such as telepathy—in which one communicates thoughts to another—or clairvoyance, an ability to mentally see events from afar.

parasexuality Any form of sexual behavior considered abnormal or out of the normal range of sexual activities, such as paraphilias.

See also PARAPHILIAS.

parasomnia A type of sleep disorder including conditions such as nightmares, sleep terrors and sleepwalking. These conditions are particularly common in children.

See also NIGHTMARE; NIGHT TERROR; SLEEP; SLEEPWALKING.

parenting Caring for and nurturing children. The term "parenting" is also applied to the situation when middle-aged adults care for their own aging parents. Of all the roles in life, parenting is one of the most important, yet one for which there is the least preparation. Individuals become parents at the time of the birth of their infant (or at the time of adoption), usually with little instruction or experience. Parenting roles and relationships never stop, no matter how old the children are.

Parenting skills throughout life include the basics of feeding and bathing as well as the psychological nurturing necessary to encourage the child to grow into a communicative, socially adjusted individual. As the child ages, parents become role models. They provide basic teaching about moral and ethical values held by the family and the culture within which the family lives. They must also be disciplinarians, which involves daily training by actions, words and examples to influence their children's behavior. Rewarding acceptable behavior helps reinforce good conduct on the children's part; withholding rewards helps reduce unwanted behaviors if conduct is unacceptable. Teaching compliance with rules begins as soon as an infant gets out of his or her crib. When the baby begins to crawl, safety rules must be enforced. At the toddler stage, information regarding social skills has to be communicated.

Parenting involves dealing with family disputes, including sibling rivalry. While parents try to avoid playing favorites by treating all their children alike, sometimes they do not treat the children the same without conscious effort. Birth order may affect the way children are treated, as well as family circumstances when the child arrives.

Parenting involves responding to problems and concerns of children, both physical and mental. One example of coping with children's concerns is dealing with troubling nightmares. Usually nightmares of small children can be related to some exciting event, such as going to a frightening movie or having started a new school or in a new classroom. If a parent does not respond with comfort to the cries of a child with a nightmare, just the sound of his or her own voice will add to the terror the child feels upon awakening. Permitting a child to keep a small light on may allay many fears of young childhood.

As children grow, parents teach them about sexuality. Parents should be open to questions and give children the amount of information they can assimilate at the time. Children are naturally curious and may ask questions about sexuality as soon as they can talk. As they grow older, they can understand more information. With young people becoming sexually active at an early age plus the spread of AIDS and sexually transmitted diseases, it is imperative that children receive as much information about their bodies and sexuality as soon as they are interested and able to understand. Although still controversial, the topic of sex education is still taught in many schools, starting from kindergarten on up.

As children become adults, the parenting role often becomes one of friend and companion. Many adult children and their parents enjoy sports activities, traveling and hobbies, whether they live nearby or in distant cities. Characteristics of their relationship while the children were young, such as open and honest communication, carry over into late life. These qualities make for good relationships between adult children and their parents.

When young people leave home, some parents are faced with the "empty nest" and no longer feel needed. While this may be a time of loneliness for some parents, it is also a time in which the parents can explore their own interests, further their educations and enjoy the intimacy they shared as newlyweds.

Since the mid-1980s, in the United States, there has been a trend concerning grown children who leave home and then return, some divorced and with children; for many, this is occurring out of economic necessity. Some families cope well with this multigenerational situation, but others find that it produces constant stresses and strains. Generally, if communication between the child and parents was good before he or she left home, problems occurring in the new situation can be dealt with happily. Parents in this situation need to remember that the children are adults and should not be treated like children.

See also BIRTH ORDER; EMPTY NEST SYNDROME; SIBLING RIVALRY; STRESS; WORKING MOTHERS.

paresthesia   Numbness or tingling. This symptom may occur during a panic attack or phobic reaction, along with dizziness and weakness in the knees. It can also occur as the result of vitamin deficiencies.

See also ANXIETY DISORDERS; PANIC ATTACK; PANIC DISORDER.

Parkinson's disease (PD)   A disease in which individuals lack the substance dopamine, which is involved in the control of muscle activity by the nervous system. Tremor, stiffness and slowness are characteristic features of Parkinson's disease. Speech may be slow, and movement may be difficult to initiate. Late in the course of the disease some individuals develop dementia. According to the Alzheimer's Disease and Related Disorders Association, some Parkinson patients develop Alzheimer's disease and some Alzheimer patients develop Parkinson symptoms. Drugs for PD may improve the motor symptoms but may not improve the mental changes that occur. Research on drugs for PD has also encouraged research on Alzheimer's disease.

See also ALZHEIMER'S DISEASE.

partial hospitalization   Treatment at a mental hospital or another treatment facility for a number of hours each day but without an overnight stay. Many mental health services are offered through partial hospitalization, also referred to as day treatment or partial care.

passive-aggressive personality disorder   A disorder characterized by being aggressive in a quietly passive way. For example, while outward aggression shows itself in a loud voice and possibly with physical force, passive aggression is more calculated and done quietly. A passive-aggressive act may be one in which a person gives another directions to find a place but purposely leaves out an important detail. Another such act might be deliberately being late, causing others to wait and miss a train or other important opportunity. Characteristics of this personality disorder include putting off or forgetting to do a chore or being purposefully inefficient. This procrastination or inefficiency gets in the way of job promotion and social acceptability.

Passive-aggressive characteristics may be caused by hidden aggression.

See also AGGRESSION; DEPRESSION; PERSONALITY.

pathological gambling   An inability to resist the impulse to gamble, despite the outlook for serious adverse consequences.

See GAMBLING.

Pavlov, Ivan Petrovich (1849–1936)
Russian physiologist known for learning theories based on conditioning techniques.

In experiments with dogs, Pavlov gave them food (unconditioned stimulus) and simultaneously range a bell. The dogs, in an unconditioned response, salivated at the scent of food. After many trials, the dogs salivated at the sound of the bell. They had learned a conditioned response to a conditioned stimulus. This became known as Pavlovian conditioning and became the basis for teaching and reinforcing behavior. According to Pavlovian theory, learning is the response to an external event, or stimulus, to which a person or animal becomes accustomed or conditioned.

PCP   Phencyclidine, a hallucinogen. It was first developed as a human anesthetic, but human use was discontinued because of severe side effects. Later it became commercially available for veterinary use; however, this was discontinued in the late 1970s. Thus, virtually all PCP available in the United States is produced clandestinely.

PCP's effects vary based on the amount ingested. Sensory changes are often accompanied by slurred or blocked speech and a loss of coordination that may be accompanied by a sense of strength and invincibility. PCP can produce psychoses indistinguishable from schizophrenia. Because PCP causes disorientation, some users suffer accidents—even fatally—and others become violent.

Available in tablets and capsules, PCP is most widely used in powder and liquid forms, applied to leafy materials such as parsley, mint, oregano and marijuana and then smoked. PCP is known by many street names. The most common are angel dust, supergrass, killer weed, K.J. crystal, embalming fluid, rocket fuel and sherms.

See also SUBSTANCE ABUSE.

Media Resource Guide on Common Drugs of Abuse. Public Relations Society of America, National Capital Chapter, Fairfax, Va., September 1990.

peer group   A like-age group that influences one's self-concept, self-esteem, attitudes and behavior. Peer group relationships are important to children as well as adults. While teenagers look to one another for acceptance and approval, so do adults seeking to make new friends, and same-level employees in a workplace.

Although peer relationships are most obviously important to adolescents, peers are actually crucial to psychological development throughout life. Children were once thought to be most highly influenced by adults; however, modern thinking recognizes the importance of the peer group to childhood. Through peer relationships, children learn to cooperate, work together, handle aggressive impulses in nondestructive ways and explore differences between themselves and their friends. Children who do not learn to combat loneliness by fitting into a peer group may develop emotional problems later in life. For adults, the increasing mobility that often cuts them off from family and longtime friends has made the development of peer relationships through work or other activities extremely important.

See also PEER PRESSURE.

peer pressure   Peer pressure begins to dominate life in adolescence. Teenagers want to "fit in" and feel that they belong to the group they choose. They react to the confusing physical changes and approaching adult responsibilities by extremely close bonding with members of their own age group. Fads in music, language and clothing become extremely important and are accepted and discarded quickly as teenagers try to meet conventions established by their peer group. The rallying cry of teenagers is often "everybody's doing it" (or "everyone has it"). Parents frequently become distressed by this peer influence. They may feel left out of activities and decisions from which their child now excludes them in favor of peers. They may also fear that the influence of friends may lead to genuinely damaging activities such as experimenting with drugs, smoking, drinking, criminal behavior, irresponsible sexual activity or dropping out of school.

Some children who feel "different" from their peers have some difficulties "fitting in." Such children may be those who are in recently divorced families, in recently "merged" families with two sets of parents, or adopted children of single parents.

See also ADOPTION; PARENTING; PEER GROUP; REMARRIAGE; SELF-ESTEEM; STEP-FAMILIES; UNWED MOTHERS.

John, D. W., and Johnson, R. T. "Peer Influences," in Corsini, Raymond J., ed., *Encyclopedia of Psychology,* vol. 2. New York: Wiley, 1984.
Leach, Penelope. *The Child Care Encyclopedia.* New York: Knopf, 1984.

peer review   The procedure by which physicians, psychiatrists, psychologists and other professionals review the writing as well as clinical work of others in their profession. For example, articles in some journals published for mental health professionals are reviewed by a committee of "peers" before selection for publication. In addition, medical records of mental health patients (as are records for all other patients) are reviewed by a committee of peers of the psychiatrist or psychologist in an institution, health care organization or health insurance provider.

See also MEDICARE.

peptides   Fragments of protein consisting of two or more amino acids. Peptides result in the linkage of amino acids by chemical bonds between the amino and carboxyl groups of adjacent acids. There are peptides in the endocrine system and nervous system. Many hormones are peptides, such as some gastrointestinal hormones and several pituitary hormones. Examples are oxytocin and ACTH (adrenocorticotropic hormone). In the nervous system, there are peptides in nerve cells throughout the brain and spinal cord. Ex-amples are endorphins and substances involved in the control of the pituitary gland.

Larger peptides, consisting of many linked amino acids, are referred to as polypeptides. Longer chains of amino acids, composed of linked polypeptides, are called proteins.

See also ENDOCRINE SYSTEM; ENDOR-PHINS; PITUITARY GLAND.

perception   One's mental attitudes of sensations about the environment interpreted through the five senses of tasting, smelling, hearing, seeing and touching. False perceptions can occur when there is no sensory stimulation. These may take the form of hallucinations. Perception is usually based on an ability to organize information into some framework or pattern. For example, the individual must be able to recognize objects as separate from their background and as stationary or moving, such as a chair or a person. Such differentiation requires the use of memory. Finally, interpretation depends on one's attitudes, current mood and expectations. For example, a hungry person will pay attention to food sooner than a person who has just finished a meal.

Some mental health disorders, such as Alzheimer's disease and schizophrenia, involve distortions in perception.

Perception can also relate to one's feelings of fear or danger. What appears dangerous to one person may seem like a thrilling challenge to another. The individual who has a phobia of heights will react with sweaty palms, shaky knees and nausea when faced with climb to the top of a mountain, but another person may view the climb as exciting.

Perception also relates to one's attitudes. For example, a teenager's perception of appropriate behavior or wearing apparel may be what his or her peer group views as the current fad, but that perception may differ from the parents' idea of behavior or wearing apparel.

See also ALZHEIMER'S DISEASE; PEER GROUP; SCHIZOPHRENIA.

perphenazine A phenothiazine-type antipsychotic drug used to relieve symptoms in certain psychiatric disorders, such as schizophrenia. Perphenazine is also sometimes used to relieve nausea and vomiting (antiemetic drug) caused by chemotherapy, radiation therapy or anesthesia.

Adverse effects may include abnormal movements of the face and limbs, blurred vision, drowsiness and headache. Parkinsonism may result from long-term use of the drug.

See also ANTIPSYCHOTIC MEDICATIONS; SCHIZOPHRENIA.

perseveration A tendency to emit the same verbal response again and again to different questions or stimuli. This may involve constant repetition of one word or phrase or an inability to shift conversation away from a particular topic. It is a disorder of thought process, which refers to the way a person puts ideas together, the associations between ideas and the form and flow of thoughts in conversation.

See also SCHIZOPHRENIA.

personality All of one's traits, habits, experiences, ways of emotionally responding (including temperament,) and motivation. Personality development seems to depend on the interaction of many complex factors, including interaction of heredity and environment. While many theorists hold that genetics is more important than environment, many take the opposite view.

Personality tests are questionnaires designed to determine various traits, to assist in psychological research and at times to determine the suitability of an individual for a particular field of work or job assignment. Personality tests measure many aspects of an individual's being, such as how one relates to people and one's degree of extroversion or introversion.

See also EXTROVERSION; INTROVERSION; PERSONALITY DISORDERS.

personality disorders A group of disorders involving behaviors or traits that are characteristic of a person's recent and long-term functioning. Patterns of perceiving and thinking are not usually limited to isolated episodes but are deeply ingrained, inflexible, maladaptive and severe enough to cause the individual mental stress or anxieties or to interfere with interpersonal relationships and normal functioning. Personality disorders are often recognizable by adolescence or earlier, continue through adulthood and become less obvious in middle or old age. An individual may have more than one personality disorder at a time.

The common factor among individuals who have personality disorders, despite a variety of character traits, is the way in which the disorder leads to pervasive problems in social and occupational adjustment. Some individuals with personality disorders are perceived by others as overdramatic, paranoid, obnoxious or even criminal, without an awareness of their behaviors. Such qualities may lead to trouble getting along with other people, as well as difficulties in other areas of life and often a tendency to blame others for their problems. Other individuals with personality disorders are not unpleasant or difficult to work with but tend to be lonely, isolated or dependent. Such traits can lead to interpersonal difficulties, reduced self-esteem and dissatisfaction with life.

Causes of Personality Disorders Different mental health viewpoints propose a variety of causes of personality disorders. These include Freudian, genetic factors, neurobiologic theories and brain wave activity.

Freudian Sigmund Freud believed that fixation at certain stages of development led to certain personality types. Thus, some disorders as described in the *Diagnostic and Statistical Manual of Mental Disorders* (3d ed., rev.) are derived from his oral, anal and phallic character types. Demanding and dependent behavior (dependent and passive-aggressive) was thought to derive from fixation at the oral stage. Characteristics of obsessionality, rigidity and emotional aloofness were thought to derive from fixation at the anal stage; fixation at the phallic stage was thought to lead to shallowness and an inability to engage in intimate relationships. However, later researchers have found little evidence that early childhood events or fixation at certain stages of development lead to specific personality patterns.

Genetic Factors Researchers have found that there may be a genetic factor involved in the etiology of antisocial and borderline personality disorders; there is less evidence of inheritance of other personality disorders. Some family, adoption and twin studies suggest that schizotypal personality may be related to genetic factors.

Neurobiologic Theories In individuals who have borderline personality, researchers have found that low cerebrospinal fluid 5-hydroxyindoleacetic acid (5-HIAA) negatively correlated with measures of aggression and a past history of suicide attempts. Schizotypal personality has been associated with low platelet monoamine oxidase (MAO) activity and impaired smooth pursuit eye movement.

Brain Wave Activity Abnormalities in electroencephalograph (EEG) have been reported in antisocial personality for many years; slow wave is the most widely reported abnormality. A study of borderline patients reported that 38 percent had at least marginal EEG abnormalities, compared with 19 percent in a control group.

Types of Disorders According to the American Psychiatric Association's *Diagnostic and Statistical Manual of Mental Disorders* (3d ed., rev., 1987), or DSM-III-R, personality disorders are categorized into three major clusters:

Cluster A: Paranoid, schizoid and schizotypal personality disorders. Individuals who have these disorders often appear to have odd or eccentric habits and traits.

Cluster B: Antisocial, borderline, histrionic and narcissistic personality disorders.

Individuals who have these disorders often appear overly emotional, erratic and dramatic.

Cluster C: Avoidant, dependent, obsessive-compulsive and passive-aggressive personality disorders. Individuals who have these disorders often appear anxious or fearful.

The DSM-III-R also lists another category, "personality disorder not otherwise specified," that can be used for other specific personality disorders or for mixed conditions that do not qualify as any of the specific personality disorders.

Individuals with diagnosable personality disorders usually have long-term concerns, and thus therapy may be long-term.

See also AVOIDANT PERSONALITY DISORDER; BORDERLINE PERSONALITY DISORDER; DEPENDENT PERSONALITY DISORDER; OBSESSIVE-COMPULSIVE DISORDER; PARANOID; PASSIVE-AGGRESSIVE PERSONALITY DISORDER.

American Psychiatric Association. *Diagnostic and Statistical Manual of Mental Disorders,* 3d ed., rev. Washington, D.C.: APA, 1987.
Andreasen, Nancy C., and Black, Donald W. *Introductory Textbook of Psychiatry.* Washington, D.C.: American Psychiatric Association, 1991.

Pertofrane See DESIPRAMINE.

perversion, sexual A psychiatric term for a culturally, morally or legally unacceptable form of sexual behavior. The term applies to practices that deviate widely from the norm, such as sadomasochism, exhibitionism, necrophilia, coprophilia, zoophilia and pedophilia. However, the preferred term is paraphilia, because it seems less judgmental.

See also PARAPHILIAS.

pets Pets reduce loneliness, provide companionship and give the owner a sense of order to his or her life. No matter how the owner may feel about other events in his life, the routine of caring for a pet provides a distraction from life's stresses problems and draws the owner out of himself. Dog owners often find that no matter how little they may feel like exercising, the dog's need for walks forces them out. They end up feeling better for it and possibly meet neighbors and other dog walkers along the way.

Pets have been found to be so important to mental health that nursing homes and other institutions may have pets in residence or programs through which pets visit residents or patients. It has been observed that simply stroking a dog or cat can reduce blood pressure.

The world may not really be divided into "dog people" and "cat people," but sometimes it seems that way. Cat owners admire their pets' independence, graceful shape and movements and wild instincts. Since cats tend to require less human companionship than dogs, they are ideal for busy people who must be away from home for long periods of time. However, their owners must be people who can enjoy providing food and other care to animals that may seem to be aloof. Dogs, on the other hand, have been called the "yes men of the animal world." With their affectionate, emotional nature and appetite for food (regardless of whether they are really hungry or it is really good for them), they offer unconditional love and act out human behavior that their more inhibited masters can enjoy vicariously.

The death of a pet can be a devastating experience for one's mental health. Although a child who has lost a pet may be inconsolable for a time, in the end it may be an experience that leads to the child's maturity, since it is frequently the child's first brush with genuine loss. Adults who lose pets are often reluctant to express themselves freely about their sorrow because they fear that others will think their behavior is childlike and self-indulgent. However, the fact that veterinary hospitals now frequently send a sympathy card or letter of condolence on the death of a pet is an indication of the increasing awareness of the effect of an animal's loss.

PET scan   See BRAIN IMAGING; POSITRON EMISSION TOMOGRAPHY.

peyote   The primary active ingredient of the peyote cactus is the hallucinogen mescaline. Peyote can be found in the fleshy parts of this cactus plant; it is ground into a powder and then taken orally. Mescaline can also be produced synthetically. A typical dose of mescaline will produce illusions and hallucinations that last from five to 12 hours.

See also HALLUCINATION; HALLUCINOGENS; MESCALINE.

Media Resource Guide on Common Drugs of Abuse. Public Relations Society of America, National Capital Chapter, Fairfax, Va., September 1990.

Phaedra complex   Sexual love of a mother for her son. The term is derived from the Greek myth about Phaedra, daughter of Minos and wife of Theseus, who was in love with her stepson, Hippolytus; when he rejected her, she accused him of violating her and hanged herself.

See also OEDIPUS COMPLEX.

phallic stage   The third stage of psychosexual development (according to psychoanalytic thinking), which occurs between ages three and six. At this time the child first focuses sexual feeling on the genital organs; masturbation becomes a source of pleasure. According to Sigmund Freud, the penis becomes the center of attention, for both boys and girls. During the phallic phase or stage, boys experience sexual fantasies toward mothers and rivalry toward fathers; they eventually give up both because of fear of castration. Similarly, girls experience sexual fantasies toward fathers and hostility toward mothers, because of rivalry and blaming mothers for depriving them of penises. Girls usually give up these feelings out of fear of losing the love of both parents. The American psychoanalyst Erik H. Erikson (1902–) suggested that when a child does not advance beyond the phallic stage to the genital stage, he or she may experience later guilt, role fixation and inhibition, which may lead to anxieties about sexual activity and sexual dysfunction.

See also ELECTRA COMPLEX; OEDIPUS COMPLEX.

phallic symbol   According to psychoanalytic theory, any object that resembles or represents the penis may be considered a phallic symbol. In dreams or in everyday life, structures that are longer than they are wide may be phallic symbols. Examples include trees, sticks, cigars, pencils, snakes, flutes and other musical instruments, such as clarinets or trombones.

See also PHALLIC STAGE; SEXUAL FEARS.

phallic woman   Traditionally, in psychoanalytic terms, a woman who is fixated at the phallic stage of development, who consciously seeks to deny that she lacks a penis or unconsciously wishes to castrate all men so that they will also be deprived of a penis. Feminist theorists tend to discount the entire concept, viewing women who are angry at men as reacting to a male-dominated social structure rather than to an anatomical difference.

See also CASTRATION; FREUD, SIGMUND.

phantom limb pain; phantom pain
According to the American Cancer Society, individuals who have had a limb (or a breast) surgically removed may experience pain as if it were coming from the absent limb. While physicians are not sure why this occurs, phantom limb pain exists and is not imaginary. Individuals experiencing this kind of pain become anxious, irritable and nervous because they often do not understand what is happening to them. There is no single method of relieving phantom pain in individuals who experience it. However, relaxation techniques are effective for many people.

phantom lover syndrome   A type of schizophrenic delusion in which a woman believes that an unknown man is in love with her.

See also SCHIZOPHRENIA.

pharmacokinetics   A term relating to how the body deals with a medication, such as how the drug is absorbed into the bloodstream, distributed to different tissues, broken down and excreted from the body. This is important in determining appropriate dosage and anticipating side effects and possible adverse drug effects. Pharmacokinetics of medications used for mental health disorders are important considerations for the prescribing physician.

pharmacotherapy   See PSYCHOPHARMACOLOGY.

phencyclidine   See PCP.

phenelzine   An antidepressant drug of the monoamine oxidase inhibitor (MAOI) class; known by the trade name Nardil. Phenelzine is sometimes prescribed for relief of moderate to severe depression in adults and in treatment of panic attacks and panic disorder, but it is not used for mild depression or depression that results from temporary stress. Individuals taking phenelzine (and other drugs in the MAOI class) must be careful to avoid foods containing tyramine, which is present in hard cheese, red wines and many other foods and beverages, because high blood pressure may result from the interaction of tyramine and MAO inhibitors.

See also ANTIDEPRESSANT MEDICATIONS; DEPRESSION; MONOAMINE OXIDASE INHIBITORS; PANIC ATTACK; PANIC DISORDER; TYRAMINE.

Greist, J. H., and Jefferson, J. W. *Depression and Its Treatment: Help for the Nation's #1 Mental Problem.* Washington, D.C.: APA, 1984.

phenobarbital A medication known as a barbiturate drug used mainly as an anticonvulsant drug, although its usage has largely been replaced by newer anticonvulsant drugs. It is still used in children who have epilepsy along with phenytoin. In some cases, it is prescribed as a sedative and may be combined with antispasmodic drugs for treating irritable bowel syndrome.

See also EPILEPSY; IRRITABLE BOWEL SYNDROME.

phenothiazine drugs The name of a group of drugs classed as antipsychotics; they are sometimes called major tranquilizers.

These medications, which became available in the mid-1950s, created a pharmacologic revolution because they suppressed delusions, hallucinations, regression, withdrawal and agitated behavior that resulted in the chronic hospitalization of schizophrenics. In the mid-1950s, state hospitals were increasing their inmate population by 10 percent each year, this rate decreased by 10 percent a year after the introduction of these medications.

While helpful in both acute and chronic psychotic states from any cause (schizophrenia, psychotic depression, mania, organic brain syndrome and some cases of Alzheimer's disease), they are often only partially effective and have significant side effects.

Although phenothiazine drugs were once thought to be safe, permanent neurological symptoms (tardive dyskinesia) have been linked to their long-term use. Examples of such drugs include chlorpromazine, thioridazine and trifluoperazine. They are currently indicated for psychotic behaviors rather than anxiety or agitation.

See also ANTIDEPRESSANT MEDICATIONS; TRICYCLIC ANTIDEPRESSANT MEDICATIONS.

phobia A persistant and irrational fear of a specific object or situation. Usually the phobia causes the individual to avoid the object or situation. Commonly, the term "phobia" is misused to refer to people who merely have a distaste for certain things or situations, such as snakes or crowded rooms. In a true phobia, there are physiological reactions that occur, despite the individual's attempts at controlling them. Some individuals are actually incapacitated by their phobias; for example, those who will not ride elevators cannot work in high-rise buildings, and those who fear dust live in sealed environments.

Phobias are included in a group of disorders known as anxiety disorders. These also include generalized anxiety disorder, panic disorders, obsessive-compulsive disorders and post-traumatic stress disorder.

Phobias are defined by psychological as well as physiological reactions. Symptoms may include feeling irrational panic or terror when in a harmless situation, recognizing that the fear goes beyond normal boundaries and the real threat of danger and that others do not perceive a danger. The reaction is automatic, uncontrollable and pervasive. The individual suffers from many physical reactions associated with extreme fear and has an overwhelming desire to avoid or escape from the situation. Avoidance is a characteristic of the lives of phobic people.

According to a recent study by the National Institute of Mental Health (NIMH), people of all ages, at all income levels and in all geographic locations suffer from phobias. Estimates are that between 5 and 12 percent of Americans suffer from phobias. They are more common among women than men.

Phobias can be divided into three basic categories. Simple, or specific, phobias are the most common and involve fear of particular things, such as one type of animal (dogs, cats, snakes), or of particular situations (such claustrophobia, fear of being in an enclosed place,or acrophobia, fear of heights).

Social phobias include a wide variety of situations most people encounter in everyday life. Most people become somewhat anxious in certain situations, such as interviewing for a new job, having dinner at the boss's home or meeting new in-laws. However, for some people, these situations cause more than simple nervousness. They become so upset that they eventually begin to avoid the kinds of situations that cause them distress. The most prevalent social phobia seems to be a fear of public speaking. Fears of meeting new people, of being seen while eating or writing or of using public toilets are also common social phobias. Social phobias seem to stem from a fear of being scrutinized and possibly criticized by others. Social phobias affect men and women equally. Often a person with one social phobia will also have other social phobias, as most social phobias relate to a fear of embarrassment.

Another type of phobia is agoraphobia. This condition is really a fear of fear, although technically the word comes from the Greek term meaning "fear of the marketplace." Agoraphobia involves fear of having a panic attack and being far from a source of help or assistance. There are aspects of fears of embarrassment; many agoraphobics fear throwing up in public or fainting. Some agoraphobics will venture out with the company of a trusted companion, in some cases a child or a dog.

Agoraphobia seems to be more prevalent in individuals from families where other members also have the disorder. Agoraphobia is often accompanied by alcoholism. Most agoraphobics develop symptoms between the ages of 19 and 35. More women than men have agoraphobia.

Causes of Phobias   Some phobias may result from learned responses; for example, children brought up by parents who fear dogs may learn to fear dogs themselves. Others result from a traumatic experience. For example, if a young child receives a painful bite from a dog, he or she may fear all dogs. However, for many individuals, there is no learned component, and there may actually be an aspect of brain chemistry that makes one individual more susceptible to acquiring phobias than others.

Often phobic people are also depressed. It is difficult to generalize whether the depression comes first or the phobia, but it is understandable that the person who reacts with unwanted extreme fear to certain situations and feels helpless may also feel depressed.

According to the American Psychiatric Association, phobias may develop as result of panic attacks. After a panic attack, the individual may fear a situation associated with the attack and begin to avoid it. Not all phobic people experience panic attacks.

Treatment   Individuals with phobias should understand that greater knowledge of phobias has been gained during the last few decades and that help is available and seek treatment. Many forms of therapy are used to treat phobic individuals, ranging from behavioral therapy to psychoanalysis. In behavioral therapy, the therapist focuses on the symptoms and attempts to change the physiological reactions, enabling the sufferer to face the feared situation. Many phobic people have good results with exposure therapy and desensitization to the feared object or situation. In psychoanalysis, the analyst may delve into the individual's past to determine the roots of the current problem. Relaxation therapy and psychopharmacotherapy are used in conjunction with other therapies. In some individuals, antianxiety drugs help them reduce the panic they feel when even thinking about a feared situation. With medication, such individuals can learn to face their phobic situation and overcome it. A variety of medications are used to treat phobic individuals. Some help some people, while others are useful to others. Pharmacologic treatment for phobias is a very individual matter.

In many cases, those with social phobias can improve themselves by concentrating on improving their social skills. When they gain confidence, they will not think so much about their possible blushing, sweating or appearing nervous to others.

Phobias can be treated by a qualified psychiatrist, psychologist, social worker or other mental health professional.

Reading material in the form of pamphlets are available from several sources.

For further information, contact:

Anxiety Disorders Association of America
6000 Executive Boulevard, Suite 200
Rockville, MD 20852
Phone: (301) 231-9350

National Mental Health Association
1021 Prince Street
Alexandria, VA 22314-2971
Phone: (703) 684-7722

See also AGORAPHOBIA; ANXIETY DISORDERS; BEHAVIORAL THERAPY; SCHOOL PHOBIA.

phobic disorders See ANXIETY DISORDERS.

Pick's disease A rare brain disease that closely resembles Alzheimer's disease and is usually difficult to diagnose clinically. Disturbances in personality, behavior and orientation may precede and initially be more severe than memory defects. Like Alzheimer's disease, a definitive diagnosis is usually obtained at autopsy.

See also ALZHEIMER'S DISEASE.

pineal gland A pea-sized endocrine organ. It is located in the brain at the entrance to an important canal for the circulation of spinal fluid and has a role in controlling the flow of cerebrospinal fluid. The gland secretes the hormone melatonin for a fixed period every 24 hours, during darkness. The period is set by a biological clock that is light-sensitive. If there are eight hours of darkness, it can produce its quota. If there are only six, it falls short. Some researchers have tied seasonal affective disorder to melatonin because of the way the hormone is produced in the dark, particularly during winter.

See also SEASONAL AFFECTIVE DISORDER.

pituitary gland A pea-sized endocrine gland near the base of the brain known as the master gland of the endocrine system because it is a source of a number of hormones, including the gonadotropic hormones. The gonadotropins which stimulate the gonads (ovaries in women and testicles in men) are LH (luteinizing hormone) and FSH (follicle stimulating hormone). In women, LH and FSH regulate ovulation; in men they regulate production of testosterone. The pituitary is a fairly remarkable gland, as it also regulates thyroid function and adrenal function in addition to playing a role in regulation of nursing and fluid balance in the body. The pituitary is in turn regulated by the hypothalamus, a portion of the brain involved in primitive functions.

Pituitary problems, such as benign growths that produce prolactin, another pituitary hormone, are quite common and can cause menstrual irregularities or amenorrhea, abnormal breast secretions and infertility problems, which may lead to stress and anxieties.

See also BRAIN; ENDOCRINE SYSTEM; HORMONES; HYPOTHALAMUS.

placebo; placebo effect A substance used as a treatment that has no pharmacologic medicinal effect but that superficially resembles an active drug and is administered either as a control in testing new drugs or as a psychotherapeutic agent. Sometimes placebos induce reactions because of the power of suggestion. Individuals in a "double-blind" study do not know if they are taking a placebo or the real drug. The "placebo effect" refers to the therapeutic benefit of the chemically inactive substance. The word is derived from the Latin word meaning "I shall please."

play therapy Use of play activities and materials, such as dolls, puppets, clay and finger paint in child psychotherapy. Such activities mirror children's emotional life and fantasies, enabling them to play out their feelings and problems and to test out new approaches and relationships in action. Play therapy is also referred to as analytical play therapy and ludotherapy.

pleasure principle A psychiatric term referring to the inner force that motivates individuals to seek immediate gratification of instinctual impulses such as hunger, thirst, elimination and sex. According to Sigmund Freud, when these needs are not satisfied, people are in a state of tension. When they are fulfilled, reduction in tension evokes the experience of pleasure. The pleasure principle dominates the early life of the child but is later modified by the reality principle. The development of maturity has a great deal to do with the capacity to delay instant gratification.

PMS See PREMENSTRUAL SYNDROME.

politically correct A term coined in the early 1990s to refer to a sensitivity about many causes, including the needs and problems of minorities, avoidance of sexist and racist terms and attitudes and respect for animals and the environment. In an effort to be "politically correct," politicians, government officials and organizational leaders are adding an additional stress to their activities as well as those of their constituents.

Although these causes are considered worthwhile by many people, the term is often applied in a derisive, pejorative manner. Like many liberal movements and concepts, political correctness seems to have evolved from academic life and therefore may be held in contempt by segments of the population who feel that professors and students live in an ivory tower of theories and impractical ideas. What may also be offensive about political correctness is a sense of uniformity, smugness and humorlessness that seems to accompany this constellation of attitudes. Columnist Mike Royko complained that "among the politically correct, everything has to have some social significance."

Kilian, Michael. "To All Women Interested in the Look for Spring: Happy Birthday Suite to You." *Chicago Tribune,* Dec. 4, 1991.

Royko, Mike. "Proof That It's Not Over until the Verdict's In." *Chicago Tribune,* Dec. 12, 1991.
Stewart, Thomas A. "How to Be a Politically Correct Person." *Fortune* 123 (Jan. 14, 1991).

polysubstance dependence Repeated use of three or more compounds by an individual. Usually no single agent predominates. Use of one substance greatly increases the chance of that person using another. Some compounds are deliberately combined to produce a desired effect, such as cocaine, amphetamines and heroin.

See also SUBSTANCE ABUSE.

pornography Writing or drawing that some individuals find sexually arousing. The term is derived from the Greek, meaning "writing of harlots." Pornography is also known as psychological aphrodisiacs.

Throughout history, there have been laws about printing and distributing pornography, but this has always been fraught with the subjectivity in deciding what is or what is not pornography. However, in a general way, pornography can be divided into erotica—which is generally graphic about "normal" heterosexual love—and exotica, which centers on sexual practices outside the cultural norm, such as sadism, masochism and fetishism.

Pornography appears in the Old Testament and in the plays of Aristophanes. The term "pornography" is probably derived from the name Porneius, a character in Greek legend.

See also VICTORIANISM.

Hendrickson, Robert. *Facts On File Encyclopedia of Word and Phrase Origins.* New York: Facts On File, 1987.

positive reinforcement A term used in behavioral therapy referring to rewards that strengthen responses. On the other hand, a negative reinforcer, such as a punishment, diminishes the response. Positive reinforcement is more effective in sustaining behavior than is negative reinforcement. Failure to provide reinforcements will usually extinguish a behavior, and variable and unpredictable schedules of reinforcement may be more effective in maintaining behavior than fixed regular reinforcements. An example is the pathological gambler who receives the positive reinforcement of winning only occasionally but continues to gamble and is rarely deterred by loss of financial assets.

positron emission tomography (PET)
A brain imaging technique to measure blood flow in areas of the brain using radioactive tracers or isotopes. The technique became available in the middle to late 1970s. A major application of PET is to the study of the neurochemical systems within the brain. For example, PET is useful in assessing the amount of a psychoactive drug in various parts of the brain, as well as physiological abnormalities.

PET is used with Alzheimer's disease patients; 70 to 80 percent of such patients show a characteristic decrease in metabolic function or cerebral blood flow in posterior temporoparietal regions. Schizophrenia, major depression, manic-depression, anxiety disorders and obsessive-compulsive disorders have all been found to show decreases or increases in blood flow and sugar metabolism in various areas of the brain.

PET may be particularly useful in differentiating Alzheimer's disease from other disorders that are present with confusion and intellectual deterioration.

See also ALZHEIMER'S DISEASE; BRAIN IMAGING.

Andreasen, Nancy C., and Black, Donald W. *Introduction to Psychiatry.* Washington, D.C.: American Psychiatric Association, 1991.

postambivalent stage   The ultimate stage of object love and psychosexual development, when a genital-love relationship becomes important to the individual. This type of love is usually unmixed with destructive feelings, as in earlier stages in which the achievement of satisfaction involves destroying the object by methods such as swallowing or biting.

See also PSYCHOSEXUAL DEVELOPMENT.

postpartum "blues"   Depression following childbirth.

See also POSTPARTUM DEPRESSION.

postpartum depression   Some women experience postpartum depression, sometimes referred to as "maternity blues," after childbirth. While the new mother may be elated with her new baby, some of the mild depression may be attributed to the letdown after months of eager anticipation. Hormonal changes after the birth of a baby may also affect a woman's mood. For example, rapidly plummeting estrogen and progesterone can lead to hot flashes and irritability, similar to the phenomena associated with menopause. Sleep deprivation caused by a crying baby can also lead to irritability and depression.

Some women become depressed after childbirth because they fear being a parent, fear being a failure as a parent, feel less loving toward the baby than they think they should and feel less sexually attractive to their mates because their bodies have not regained their normal shape. Women may also feel a loss of self-esteem if they go from careers outside the home into full-time motherhood. Because of demands of new babies, women may feel exhausted, overwhelmed with chores and chronically fatigued. In addition, any stresses within marriage that existed before the birth of a baby may worsen after the baby's arrival.

The extent to which women experience postpartum depression may also depend on their support systems, including husbands, families and additional helpers in the household. A significant number of persistent, severe postpartum depressions become recurrent major depression or bipolar (manic-depressive) disorders requiring psychiatric treatment.

See also ANTIDEPRESSANT MEDICATIONS; CHILDBIRTH; DEPRESSION; PREGNANCY.

Holt, Linda H., M.D., Skokie, Ill. (personal interview).

postpartum psychosis When postpartum depression expands from mild depression to severe thought disorders and complete dissociation, the situation is called postpartum psychosis; it is also referred to as puerperal psychosis. A psychotic episode during the month after childbirth may be schizophrenic or depressive, not uncommonly the beginning of a depressive disorder brought about by the stresses of the pregnancy and delivery. It may be caused or aggravated by factors such as preexisting personality defects, marital instability and financial burdens.

See also POSTPARTUM DEPRESSION.

post-traumatic stress disorder (PTSD)
An anxiety disorder produced by an unusual and extremely stressful event, such as assault, flood, military combat or a threatening experience as in a car accident. Individuals with prior mental health difficulties such as depression, personality disorders or substance abuse problems are more likely to develop PTSD. Sufferers characteristically reexperience the trauma in painful recollections or recurrent dreams or nightmares. Some have diminished emotional responsiveness (''numbing''), feelings of estrangement from others, disturbed sleep, recurrent dreams of the trauma, difficulty in concentrating or remembering, guilt about surviving when others did not, avoidance of activities that cause recollection of the traumatic event and intensive thoughts related to the event.

Individuals who have survived disasters such as earthquakes, airplane crashes, war and the effects of abuse or neglect as children or adults may be affected by PTSD. (In addition, living in poverty and in high-crime areas can produce anxiety as a form of PTSD.) PTSD is also known as shell shock, battle fatigue and war neurosis.

In wartime, veterans of heavy combat are most likely to suffer from PTSD. Psychiatrists estimate that several hundred thousand of the 3.5 million men and women who served in the Vietnam War are affected by PTSD.

Often PTSD surfaces several months or even years later, although its symptoms can occur soon after the event. Some PTSD sufferers reexperience their trauma in nightmares that awaken the person screaming in terror. Individuals with PTSD often develop insomnia in an attempt to avoid dreaded dreams. Sometimes the reexperience comes as a sudden, painful rush of emotions that seem to have no cause. These emotions are sometimes of anger or intense fear. Some PTSD sufferers endure anxiety and panic attacks as a result of their experiences.

In PTSD, a flashback of the traumatic situation can be so strong a recollection that the individual thinks he or she is actually experiencing the traumatic event again. When a person has a severe flashback, he or she is in a dissociative state, which sometimes can be mistaken for sleepwalking. During panic attacks, their throats tighten, breathing and heart rate increase and they may feel dizzy and nauseated. Avoidance behavior also occurs. This affects the individual's relationships with others, because he or she often avoids close emotional ties with family, colleagues and friends. At first the person feels numb, has diminished emotions and can complete only routine, mechanical activities. Later, when reexperiences of the event begin, the individual alternates between the flood of emotions caused by the reexperience and the inability to feel or express emotions at all. Some individuals who have PTSD often say they cannot feel emotions, especially toward those to whom they are closest; or, if they can feel emotions, often they cannot express them. As the avoidance continues, the person appears to be bored or preoccupied.

PTSD sufferers also might avoid situations that remind them of the traumatic event.

For example, a survivor of an airplane crash might overreact in another plane as it seems to descend too rapidly. Others who have PTSD may have poor work records and poor relationships with their family and friends. Some have trouble concentrating or remembering current information.

War veterans and others who have PTSD may be constantly on guard for danger and, as a result, have exaggerated startle reactions. War veterans may revert to their war behavior upon hearing noises, such as backfiring cars or fireworks, which sound similar to battle noises. Individuals who have PTSD can learn to work through the trauma and pain and resolve their anxieties. Among the treatments is individual psychotherapy. PTSD results in part from the difference between the individual's personal values and the reality that he witnessed during the traumatic event. Psychotherapy helps the individual examine his values and how his behavior and experience during the traumatic event violated them. The goal is a resolution of the conscious and unconscious conflicts that were thus created. Additionally, the individual works to build his self-esteem and self-control, develop a good and reasonable sense of personal accountability and renew his sense of integrity and personal pride.

In many cases, therapy is recommended because spouses' and children's behavior may affect and be affected by the PTSD sufferer. Some spouses and children report that their loved ones do not communicate, show affection or share in family life. Thus, a therapist can help family members learn to recognize and cope with the range of emotions each feels. They do this by improving communication skills and learning parenting and techniques for stress management.

A newer technique for PTSD involves ''rap'' groups, in which survivors of similar traumatic events are encouraged to share their experiences and reactions. In doing so, group members help one another realize that many people have done the same thing and felt the same emotions. That in turn helps the individual realize that she is not uniquely unworthy or guilty. Over time, the individual changes her opinion of herself, improves self-image and self-esteem and creates a new view of the world. Antidepressant medications have also been reported to reverse symptoms of PTSD.

See also ANTIDEPRESSANT MEDICATIONS; ANXIETY; ANXIETY DISORDERS; DISSOCIATION; FEAR; POST-TRAUMATIC STRESS DISORDER in BIBLIOGRAPHY.

Adapted from material provided by the American Psychiatric Association.

powerlessness   The perception that one's own actions will not significantly affect an outcome. A person who feels powerless may be unable to set goals and unable to follow through on activities relating to school, work or family life. For some individuals, feelings of powerlessness may underlie depression, suspiciousness and aggressive behavior. Powerlessness is associated with withdrawal, passivity, submissiveness, apathy and, in some individuals, increasing frustration, agitation, anxiety, aggression, acting-out behavior and even violence.

Powerlessness can be induced by illness and hospitalization, because such events compromise one's sense of independence and control. Powerlessness also arises from interpersonal interactions and life-style. Strategies to help an individual who feels powerless include enabling him or her to have control of a situation, to increase knowledge and to promote a sense of well-being.

McFarland, Gertrude K., and Thomas, Mary Durand. *Psychiatric Mental Health Nursing.* Philadelphia: J. B. Lippincott, 1991.

prefrontal system   One of the largest cortical subregions of the human brain, also known as the prefrontal cortex. It may constitute nearly a third of the human brain and receives connections from all over it.

The prefrontal areas have to do with motivation and initiative, as well as appreciation of the future consequences of behaviors or acts. Damage to the frontal lobes via head trauma, brain degeneration, tumors, strokes or chronic alcohol toxicity can cause marked behavioral changes and symptoms of apathy, with lack of spontaneous behavior. It can also cause a state of euphoria, with a deterioration of behavior including inappropriate sexual behavior or deterioration of personal habits.

See also BRAIN.

pregenital phase   A term for the stages of psychosexual development before the stages when the penis and clitoris become the central erogenous zones and when the sex organs begin to exert a dominant influence. The pregenital phase includes the first stages of sexuality, when the individual concentrates on the mouth, anus and urethra rather than the genital organs.

See also PSYCHOSEXUAL DEVELOPMENT.

pregnancy   Pregnancy evokes many mental health and physiological issues. Some women experience frequent mood swings, ranging from crying to euphoria, and many have exciting or frightening dreams, sometimes involving the unborn child. Emotional changes are due to hormonal as well as emotional adjustments involved in pregnancy.

Both parents as well as extended family make many psychological adaptations to pregnancy. An important influence on the progress of the pregnancy is the presence of a supportive emotional environment. For example, if there have been multiple previous pregnancies, the attitude toward the current pregnancy will be affected. The parents' attitude toward the pregnancy will also be influenced by factors such as whether the child was wanted or not, if an abortion had been attempted or considered or if there are hereditary disorders in the family. However, these anxieties usually are replaced by positive feelings as signs of life are experienced and the pregnancy progresses.

For many women, an early symptom of pregnancy is morning sickness, which is sometimes considered ''imaginary'' but is a very real problem for sufferers. Nausea during the first months of pregnancy may be due to a low level of vitamin B6 or may occur because of the natural slowing down of a pregnant woman's digestive process. When food remains undigested in the stomach for longer periods than normal, nausea and the urge to vomit occur. Morning sickness usually diminishes or disappears by the time the pregnancy is in the fourth month.

How a woman copes with pregnancy depends largely on the woman and her husband's attitude toward pregnancy. While most couples have a positive outlook, sometimes pregnancy occurs to please others, such as grandparents, or with the wish to be nurtured oneself. In some cases, conception occurs in an attempt to save a marriage that is dysfunctional or to deal with anxiety about sterility. At the time the new mother begins to feel the infant's movement, ambivalence about becoming pregnant may become apparent.

Many women cope with the psychological stresses of pregnancy better when they begin participating in ''prepared childbirth'' classes offered by many hospitals, which teach prospective parents about the physiological changes that occur during pregnancy and labor. Some classes provide exercises to help the new mothers learn to relax and reduce tension. For example, the Lamaze method, named for a French obstetrician, involves learning breathing, relaxing and massage routines for the mother and her coaching partner.

Men and Pregnancy   Couvade (from the French word for hatching) is the term applied to the range of sympathetic physical changes men go through during their wives' pregnancy. Some men actually experience symptoms such as nausea, fatigue, backache and weight gain as a result of the emotional conflicts of imminent fatherhood. Some cultures developed elaborate rituals to help men through these difficult times. In Western cultures, however, men have a role in pregnancy and often participate in prenatal education classes and the birth event itself.

Assisted Pregnancy Pregnancy and motherhood without marriage has become more culturally acceptable in some Western countries. Couples who cannot conceive can now become parents with the use of "assisted reproductive" techniques, including in vitro fertilization and artificial insemination. Surrogate motherhood is also gaining some degree of acceptance, despite legal complications. Women who delay motherhood into their late thirties or early forties because of their own or their husbands' careers or because of the attraction of the single life face diminished fertility and greater anxiety about the possibility of birth defects that come with increased maternal age. However, amniocentesis (testing the amniotic fluid to detect abnormalities in the fetus) allays some fears of women who postpone motherhood.

Baby Blues Subsequent endocrine changes after childbirth, as well as fatigue from being awakened during the night to feed the newborn, often lead to postpartum depression or "baby blues." Some women become weepy a few days after giving birth. Some who experience clinical depressive symptoms may feel withdrawn and partially reject the infant. This response may become evident in difficulties in feeding and patterns of mother-child interaction. In most cases, postpartum depression does not last more than two weeks. However, if it persists longer, professional help should be sought. A woman may develop irrational fears, despair and hopelessness and may have ideas involving violent anger toward the new baby.

Fears Involving Pregnancy Fears of pregnancy stem from both psychological and physical sources. Some examples include unmarried women who fear conceiving and bearing a child out of wedlock; married

women who do not want the burden of a child; women who fear the pain of childbirth or fear that they might die during pregnancy; and some who fear the interruption in their work and physical activity. Some women fear that their pregnant physical appearance will be unattractive to their husbands, and some fear that they will never return to their original physical appearance.

Many women become anxious and embarrassed by the physical symptoms associated with pregnancy. Morning sickness, food cravings, frequent urination, water retention, bloating and swollen breasts are frequent complaints. First-time mothers fear that they may not be able to recognize the first movements of the fetus and as a result may worry that the baby is abnormal or dead. While some mothers fear weight gain during pregnancy, others feel that they are not gaining enough. Recent findings about effects on the fetus of the mother's smoking and alcohol consumption have caused many pregnant women to abstain out of fear that they will have an unhealthy baby.

Teenage Pregnancy Twenty percent of all live births in the United States are to adolescent mothers. The adolescent pregnancy rate in the United States is greater than in any other Western country. Infants of teenage mothers are at significantly higher risk for "failure to thrive" syndrome, physical abuse, school failure and behavioral disturbances. Many teenage mothers are unmarried and will face difficulties in continuing with their education and finding employment. Unfortunately, most adolescent fathers do not provide assistance or maintain contact with their young families.

Some adolescent girls who become pregnant may have had the fantasy of becoming autonomous and independent from their families. These ideas quickly disappear as the young women face the reality of reinforced dependence, helplessness and hopelessness. Many such young women both before and after the pregnancy have persistent low mood and poor self-esteem. Usual developmental landmarks, including separation and disengagement from the family of origin and pursuit of academic and career goals may be missed, as the adolescent girl must increasingly rely on her family throughout the pregnancy and often beyond.

Pregnancy and Sexual Intercourse
Psychological stress arises for many couples during pregnancy when they become concerned about the advisability of continuing sexual intercourse during pregnancy. Although this is an individual matter for each couple, it causes stress in many relationships, as both partners may fear hurting the fetus, and the male may fear hurting the woman. However, depending on the course of the pregnancy, gynecologists usually allow women who have no unusual vaginal discharges, pain or other symptoms to continue sexual relations until the seventh month. In later months, modifications of coital position are suggested to assure that intercourse will not harm the baby or cause a miscarriage.

See also BONDING; CHILDBIRTH; COUVADE; POSTPARTUM DEPRESSION.

Davis, Kenneth; Klar, Howard; and Coyle, Joseph T. *Foundations of Psychiatry.* Philadelphia: W. B. Saunders, 1991.

Eisenberg, Arlene; Murkoff, Heidi Eisenberg; and Hathaway, Sandee Eisenberg. *What to Expect When You're Expecting.* New York: Workman Publishing, 1984.

Rockwell, Beverly. "Expectant Fathers: Changes and Concerns." *Canadian Family Physician* 35 (May 1989).

premenstrual depression   Many women experience irritability and depressed feelings before menstrual periods. In recent years, researchers have been considering premenstrual depression as part of premenstrual syndrome (PMS) and are looking into causes and relationships to depressive disorders. Researchers at the National Institute of Mental Health have noted that in some women, premenstrual depression is a cyclical prob-

lem, as is seasonal affective disorder (SAD), which is more common among women than men. Both may be biologically linked. Symptoms of premenstrual syndrome (PMS) and SAD are similar, in that women feel lethargic and may oversleep or overeat. Some have more premenstrual symptoms seasonally, primarily during the winter, during which time they are depressed only when they are premenstrual. Light therapy that helps sufferers of SAD may also be helpful for premenstrual depression.

See also ANTIDEPRESSANT MEDICATIONS; DEPRESSION; PREMENSTRUAL SYNDROME; SEASONAL AFFECTIVE DISORDER.

premenstrual syndrome (PMS)   The recurrence of symptoms in the 14 days (or less) prior to menstruation with absence of symptoms after menstruation. Discomforts that may occur before a menstrual period include water retention, tender breasts, headaches, body aches, food cravings, lethargy and depression. Asthma, herpes, acne, baby battering, epilepsy and mood swings have little in common, but they all have a connection if they recur at the same time in each menstrual cycle. Until the 1970s or 1980s, many women experiencing these symptoms were told that they were imagining them. The medical profession did not recognize the constellation of symptoms as a "syndrome"; consequently, many women became even more stressed by lack of help from physicians and lack of understanding by family members.

There is no single definitive test to diagnose PMS, but there are ways to determine if it is present. Mainly, it is the perception of the woman and her family and a confirmation of the cyclical nature of the symptoms by "charting" them each month. The severity of symptoms may vary from one cycle to the next, but the main symptoms will remain the same.

Causes of premenstrual syndrome have not been determined and vary from woman to woman. Symptoms occurring several days before menstruation seem to be related to the interrelationships of hormones between ovulation and the beginning of menstruation.

The medical profession's attitude that the discomfort of PMS was "all in the mind" increased anxiety for many women. Attitudes are changing and PMS is now a recognized physical condition, but there is still some reluctance to take it seriously. Although there is no single successful treatment for PMS, many doctors now regard it as a challenging problem in need of solution. A variety of treatments, such as hormones, vitamins, analgesics and diuretics, have been tried with varying degrees of success.

During the 1980s and 1990s, many women suffering from PMS have found practitioners within women's health centers sympathetic and interested in treating these problems. Women who once worried that they were "going crazy" before their menstrual period have now learned new ways of coping with their symptoms through a combination of diet, medication, exercise and counseling.

See also MENSTRUATION.

Lever, Judy, and Brush, Michael G. *Pre-menstrual Tension.* New York: McGraw-Hill, 1981.

premenstrual tension The irritability, bloating and abdominal discomfort that many menstruating women notice about a week before their menstrual period. These discomforts occur because of progesterone secretion and fluid retention. Symptoms usually diminish when the menstrual period begins.

See also PREMENSTRUAL DEPRESSION; PREMENSTRUAL SYNDROME.

prevalence A term used by statisticians and epidemiologists to refer to the total number of cases of a disorder or disease at a given time. For example, the prevalence of depression includes all the existing cases in a given year. Prevalence is different from incidence, which counts the number of new cases of, for example, depression, in a defined population during a defined time period.

See also ANXIETY; PHOBIA.

primal anxiety A psychiatric term referring to the most basic form of anxiety that the infant first experiences during separation from the mother when he faces new stimuli in the real world.

primal fantasies Children often fantasize about conception, birth, sexual intercourse by their parents and castration. Children do this to fill the gaps in their knowledge. Many such unconscious fantasies are revealed in dreams and daydreams.

primal scene The sexual act between parents. Early psychoanalysts believed that witnessing the parent in a sex act would trigger a crisis in sexuality in the child. However, more recent theories have discounted the significance of this experience, pointing out that in most places in the world entire families share a room, with little evidence that children suffer sexual trauma or confusion resulting from this lack of privacy. Nonetheless, Western culture usually downplays parental sexuality in front of children.

See also PRIMAL THERAPY.

primal scream therapy See PRIMAL THERAPY.

primal therapy Primal therapy (also known as primal scream therapy) is used to treat some mental dysfunctions, including anxieties about sexuality, by encouraging the individual to relive basic or "primal" traumatic events and let go of associated painful emotions. Such events may have led to development of anxieties and frequently involve feelings of abandonment or rejection experienced in infancy or early childhood. The technique was developed by Arthur Janov (1924–), an American psychologist and author of *The Primal Scream* (1970). During therapy, the individual may scream or cry and afterward feel that the "primal pain" has been released.

See also PRIMAL SCENE.

primal trauma   An event or situation that the individual perceived as painful in early life.

See also PRIMAL THERAPY.

primary depression   Depression in which one's mood is unrelated to a preexisting mental disorder or to a physical condition, substance abuse disorder or a medication. Primary depressions occur in individuals with no previous history of any other mental illness. Primary depression is divided into unipolar and bipolar depressions. Some individuals with primary depression complain of a sad, blue, low mood; others also complain of hopelessness, helplessness, irritability, fearfulness and anxiety.

Sufferers complain of loss of interest in normal activities, diminished pleasurable experiences, withdrawal from other people and recurrent thoughts of death or suicide. Individuals who have primary depression may also have physical symptoms such as headache, fatigue, palpitations, gastrointestinal disturbances and weight loss.

procreation fantasy   Imagined or fantasized participation in sexual reproduction, for example, by women who experience a false pregnancy. In men, a common procreation fantasy is playing the role of a father who begets a famous offspring.

See also FANTASY.

prodrome   An early symptom of a mental or physical illness that serves as a warning sign that may lead to preventive measures. The word comes from the Greek word *prodromos,* which means "running before." An example of a prodrome, or prodromal sign, is the beginning of withdrawal from social activities by a depressed person. A prodromic dream is one that contains a warning of impending disorder.

prognosis   Prediction of the future course, severity, duration and outcome of a disease or mental disorder. A prognostic test forecasts results of education or training for a specific skill.

projection   A defense mechanism one uses unconsciously that involves blaming somebody else for one's own thoughts or actions. The individual unknowingly rejects emotionally unacceptable thoughts, attributing (projecting) them to others.

See also DEFENSE MECHANISMS.

prolactin   A substance secreted by the anterior pituitary, possibly with a circadian rhythm. It is released in response to suckling, physical and emotional stress, hypoglycemia and estrogen administration. Prolactin inhibitory factors (PIF) and prolactin releasing factors (PRF) are secreted at the hypothalamic level. Dopamine stimulates PRF secretion, whereas serotonin inhibits it. Studies of PRF secretion have been used to research the pathophysiology of affective disorders and schizophrenia.

Some women experience amenorrhea because of increased prolactin thought to be produced in the pituitary gland. This condition may also be caused by psychotropic medications such as neuroleptics. When occurring simultaneously, it can be diagnosed and treated by a general physician or specialist in endocrinology.

See also PITUITARY GLAND; SEROTONIN; PHARMACOLOGIC THERAPY, SCHIZOPHRENIA in BIBLIOGRAPHY.

pro-life and pro-choice   Terms for individuals who oppose abortion (pro-life) and those who favor giving women the option of abortion (pro-choice.) Pro-life advocates believe in a general set of values regarding the value of all human life. Pro-choice advocates believe their position supports a woman's civil rights. During the 1990s, controversy between these groups continues.

See also ABORTION; ROE V. WADE.

Prolixin   Trade name for fluphenazine, an antipsychotic drug.

See also PHENOTHIAZINE DRUGS.

promazine   An antipsychotic drug of the phenothiazine class used in some patients as a sedative. In some cases, after anesthesia, it is used to relieve nausea and vomiting (antiemetic).

See also PHENOTHIAZINE DRUGS.

promiscuity   The term given to certain sexual behavior of men or women; the term is somewhat judgmental, and the definition has changed over a period of years, particularly after the "sexual revolution" of the 1960s. In the United States today, however, the most commonly held attitude is that a person is generally considered promiscuous if he or she has sexual intercourse with several casual acquaintances over a short period of time. Premarital intercourse with one partner is not considered promiscuous. Promiscuous behavior has been discouraged to a great extent because of the increase in sexually transmitted diseases and AIDS. It appears that since the emergence of the AIDS epidemic, promiscuous sexual behavior among homosexual people has reduced.

See also ACQUIRED IMMUNODEFICIENCY SYNDROME; PEER GROUP; SAFE SEX; SEXUALLY TRANSMITTED DISEASES.

propranolol   A medication in the family of beta blocking agents commonly used to treat high blood pressure, migraine headaches and some heart conditions. In some individuals, it is prescribed to reduce rapid heartbeat (tachycardia) and general nervousness associated with anxiety disorders. In other cases, it is prescribed to help control symptoms of stage fright and fears of public appearances. Many patients tolerate it well because it has few side effects. However, possible side effects include dizziness, slow pulse, sleep difficulties, diarrhea, coldness, numbness and/or tingling of fingers or toes. Individuals who have chronic lung disease, asthma, diabetes or certain heart diseases and those who are severely depressed should not take propranolol.

See also HEADACHES.

proprietary   A medication for which one company holds a patent for production. This differs from a generic drug, which may be manufactured by other companies without a patent.

See also ETHICAL DRUG.

prostitution   A service providing sexual activity based on payment of money or exchange of other property or valuables. The term can apply to male and female, heterosexuals and homosexuals. The service may be sexual intercourse or performance of acts that gratify sexual deviations, or paraphilias.

Fear of prostitutes is known as cyprianophobia. At the end of the 20th century, this fear has increased because of the risk of contracting a sexually transmitted disease or the AIDS virus. In many parts of the world, these diseases are found in epidemic proportions among prostitutes.

See also PARAPHILIAS.

Kahn, Ada P., and Holt, Linda Hughey. *The A to Z of Women's Sexuality*. Alameda, Calif.: Hunter House, 1992.

protriptyline   An antidepressant drug (tricyclic) that seems to cause less drowsiness than some other antidepressant drugs. In some cases, it is also used to reduce symptoms of headaches.

See also ANTIDEPRESSANT MEDICATIONS; HEADACHES.

Prozac   Trade name for fluoxetine.

See also FLUOXETINE HYDROCHLORIDE.

pseudodementia   A condition that sometimes accompanies depressive illness, which should be differentiated from dementia. In this disturbance, the depressed person seems to be demented. He or she is unable to remember correctly, cannot calculate well and complains of lost cognitive abilities and skills. The pseudodemented person has a treatable illness and is not truly demented. The "dementia" is usually caused by the depressive illness.

See also DEMENTIA; DEPRESSION.

psyche   A term derived from the ancient Greek word for soul or spirit. It refers to the mind as opposed to the body. According to Sigmund Freud, the psyche could be divided into the conscious and the unconscious. The prefix "psych-" is derived from this word.

See also PSYCHIATRIST; PSYCHOLOGIST; PSYCHOLOGY.

psychiatrist   A physician (medical doctor with an M.D. degree) who specializes in the diagnosis and treatment of mental health and emotional disorders. Psychiatrists can prescribe medications and can admit patients to hospitals.

In 1982, there were an estimated 30,642 psychiatrists in the United States, and the number has been increasing since then. Slightly more than eight out of 10 U.S. psychiatrists in 1982 were men, yet psychiatry ranked first among medical specialties in the proportion of women and third in the number of women practitioners. The number of women physicians choosing psychiatric careers has increased in recent years, as suggested by the greater proportion of women than men in psychiatry who are younger than 40 years of age.

The distribution of psychiatrists varies considerably within the United States, ranging from four per 100,000 resident population in Idaho to more than 28 per 100,000 in Massachusetts and New York and 77 per 100,000 in the District of Columbia. Generally, the New England and the Middle Atlantic states have the most psychiatrists per population; the least are in the East South Central and the West South Central states.

Psychiatrists practice within several theoretical frames of reference. Various approaches offer differing explanations of how symptoms or disorders develop, how they interfere with an individual's functioning and how and why they can be altered by interventions. (For example, some are influenced by Sigmund Freud, while others are influenced by Heinz Kohut.)

Today most psychiatrists are trained in a variety of diagnostic possibilities and treatments, including psychodynamic psychotherapy. There is also a stronger medical emphasis because of the rapid development of techniques of psychopharmacology, which require a knowledge of pharmacology, physiology, cardiology and endocrinology, all subjects taught in medical training. Recent advances in neuroscience as it relates to behavior have provided a strong medical as well as psychosocial focus for psychiatry, which now spans these areas of knowledge. According to data collected by the American Medical Association on the Physician's Professional Activities Census, approximately 6 percent of all U.S. physicians designate their specialty as psychiatry or child and adolescent psychiatry. As of January 1, 1988, there were 33,679 general psychiatrists and 4,107 child and adolescent psychiatrists in the United States. In the latter half of the 1980s, the number of general psychiatrists increased by 10 percent, and the number of child and adolescent psychiatrists increased by 14 percent. The number of all physicians increased by 12.7 percent.

In addition to providing direct patient care, many general and child and adolescent psychiatrists devote some time to other professional activities such as administration, medical teaching and research, and many work in more than one setting. Many psychiatrists are likely to devote at least part of their practice hours to salaried and managed care settings, including health maintenance organizations, preferred provider organizations and large hospital systems. The percentage of nonfederal psychiatrists in group practice increased from 9 percent in 1980 to 15 percent in 1988.

Cooperation and consultation between psychiatrists, primary care physicians and other providers continues to be important for the provision of comprehensive care to patients. Especially in rural areas, primary care providers are critical gatekeepers for the diagnosis and treatment of mental health problems. The detection of mental disorders and the treatment of the less severe disorders, including the prescription of medications, often take place in a primary medical setting. Primary care physicians, however, are less likely than psychiatrists to treat patients with serious or complex mental disorders, such as patients with dual diagnoses or coexistence of psychiatric and medical illnesses. Primary care physicians are more likely to prescribe medications for anxiety, while psychiatrists are more likely to prescribe drugs for depression.

See also RURAL MENTAL HEALTH CARE.

Council on Long Range Planning and Development. ''The Future of Psychiatry.'' *Journal of the American Medical Association* 264, no. 19 (Nov. 21, 1990).

National Institute of Mental Health. *Mental Health, United States, 1990.*

Manderscheid, R. W., and Sonnenschein, M. A., eds. DHHS Pub. No. (ADM) 90-1708. Washington, D.C.: USGPO, 1990.

psychic vaginismus   A painful vaginal spasm that prevents sexual intercourse, due to psychological rather than physiological causes.

See also DYSPAREUNIA; VAGINISMUS; SEXUAL DYSFUNCTION in BIBLIOGRAPHY.

psychoactive drug   One of many chemical compounds that affect thought processes and mood. These drugs have been subject to both appropriate and inappropriate uses. Psychoactive drugs may make one more relaxed or more active. Antidepressant drugs and tranquilizers are two examples of psychoactive drugs. Alcohol is also considered a psychoactive drug. Psychoactive drugs are prescribed for a wide range of mental health disorders, including depression, anxieties and phobias.

It is possible to develop a dependency on one or more psychoactive substances prescribed by a physician. Close monitoring by a physician is necessary when taking psychoactive drugs.

See also ANTIDEPRESSANT MEDICATIONS.

psychoanalysis   The original mode of treatment for mental health disorders developed by Sigmund Freud and his followers. It aims to reorganize character structure, with an emphasis on self-understanding and a correction of developmental lags. Symptom relief usually occurs as a result of this understanding, but it is usually not the immediate goal of the treatment.

Psychoanalysis is practiced by clinicians who have undergone specialized training in this after residency training. Individuals who practice psychoanalysis are not necessarily medical doctors, but they must pass certain examinations given by many centers throughout the world. Analysts use features of free association, dream analysis and the development and working through of transference distortions in the relationship with the analyst. Sessions are usually held four or five times a week, and a completed analysis generally takes three to five years, but length of treatment varies considerably with the nature of the problems being treated.

The American Psychoanalytic Association has more than 3,000 members, and the International Psychoanalytical Association numbers over 7,500.

According to a report in *Psychiatric News* (Sept. 6, 1991), the nature of psychoanalysis is changing to include multiple theoretical viewpoints that work synergistically. There is a proliferation of psychoanalytic publications dealing with clinical and theoretical issues, as well as the application of psychoanalytic study to other fields such as history, literature, anthropology and art.

See also FREUD, SIGMUND; PSYCHOTHERAPY.

psychogenic A disorder caused by a mental rather than a physical disturbance. For example, some sexual dysfunctions are of psychogenic origins.

See also SEX THERAPY.

psychogenic amnesia Memory loss from psychological causes. The disorder is defined as a single episode of sudden inability to recall important information, a loss too extensive to be explained by ordinary forgetfulness. This has been reported to occur after severe physical or psychosocial stressors, for example after war or a fire. In a study of combat veterans, 5 to 10 percent were amnestic for their combat experiences, and 5 to 14 percent of all military psychiatric casualties have amnestic syndromes.

See also AMNESIA; POST-TRAUMATIC STRESS DISORDER.

Andreasen, Nancy C., and Black, Donald W. *Introductory Textbook of Psychiatry.* Washington, D.C.: American Psychiatric Association, 1991.

psychogenic fugue A mental health disorder in which there is sudden unexpected travel away from home or customary workplace with the assumption of a new identity and an inability to recall the previous identity. The disturbance is not due to multiple personality disorder or to an organic mental disorder. The fugue may follow a severe psychosocial stress, is usually brief (hours or days) and involves only limited travel, but rarely it may extend for months and involve complex travel. Significant alcohol use seems to predispose to this disorder.

This disorder should be distinguished from multiple personality disorder, which more typically involves repeated shifts of identity—more than a single episode—and a history of identity disturbances since childhood. Psychogenic amnesia usually lacks purposeful travel or the assumption of a new identity.

See also PSYCHOGENIC AMNESIA.

Amchin, Jess. *Psychiatric Diagnosis: A Biopsychosocial Approach Using DSM-III-R.* Washington, D.C.: American Psychiatric Press, 1990.

psycho-imagination therapy (PIT) A process with major emphasis on subjective meaning through use of waking imagery and imagination to effect personality changes. The basic proposition of psycho-imagination therapy recognizes the individual's needs to become aware of how he defines himself in relation to others and how he thinks others define him. A person's imagery, more than any other mental function, indicates how he or she views the world. Use of systematically categorized imagery can open up the inner world to both patient and therapist. The technique was developed in 1965 by Joseph E. Shorr, an American psychologist, and is theoretically related to the interpersonal school of psychoanalysis that stems from the work of Harry Stack Sullivan (1892–1949), an American psychiatrist and dissenter of Sigmund Freud. Many psychotherapists use aspects from several different schools of thought.

See also PSYCHOTHERAPY.

psychological aphrodisiacs Pictures, words and imagery, in print or on film, that stimulate sexual desire; also known as pornography.

See also PORNOGRAPHY.

psychological tests There are many tests commonly used for diagnostic purposes. Some are used by therapists, while others are used by human resource departments as part of preemployment screening of applicants.

Usually devised by psychologists, such tests are designed to determine qualities of the applicant's or client's personality and the suitability of the individual for the assignment.

See also PSYCHOLOGIST; PSYCHOLOGY.

psychologist A nonmedical specialist in diagnosing and treating mental health concerns. In most states, a psychologist has a Ph.D. degree from a graduate program in psychology. Psychologists are licensed, receive insurance reimbursement, have hospital privileges and act as expert witnesses in court cases.

Prior to World War II, psychologists were primarily involved in academic institutions, with only a few individuals employed outside universities and actively engaged in mental health services. Not until 1977—with the passage of the Missouri psychology licensure act—did all 50 states and the District of Columbia grant statutory recognition to the profession. Since that time, the number of licensed psychologists has grown, rising from an estimated 20,000 in 1975 to almost 46,000 only 10 years later.

Along with this dramatic growth in the population of practitioners was a significant expansion in psychologists' role as direct mental health providers. Today, psychologists are involved in almost every type of mental health setting, including institutional or community-based, research- or treatment-oriented and general health– or mental health–focused. Within these environments, psychologists' roles have also expanded beyond traditional activities of diagnostic assessment and psychotherapy to include primary prevention, community-level intervention strategies, assessment of service delivery systems and client advocacy.

Within psychology, there are many subspecialties. These include child, developmental, school, clinical, social and industrial. Many psychologists have private practices, are employed by a health care facility and teach in universities.

Psychologists cannot prescribe medications. They usually refer patients requiring medication to a physician.

See also PSYCHOLOGY.

psychology   The study of all processes of the mind, such as memory, feelings, thought and perception, as well as intelligence, behavior and learning. Within the field, many different approaches are applied. For example, behavioral psychology studies the way people react to events and adapt accordingly; neuropsychology relates human behavior to brain and body functions; and psychoanalytic psychology emphasizes the role of the unconscious and experiences of childhood.

Subdivisions in the American Psychological Association's designated areas of specialization include medical, child, industrial, social and animal-experimental psychology.

See also BEHAVIORAL THERAPY; PSYCHOLOGIST.

National Institute of Mental Health. *Mental Health, United States, 1990.*
Manderscheid, R. W., and Sonnenschein, M. A., eds. DHHS Pub. No. (ADM) 90-1708. Washington, D.C.: USGPO, 1990.

psychometry   The measurement of psychological functions, using devices such as intelligence tests, personality tests and specific aptitude tests. While such tests have been refined since the earlier versions, the validity of such tests is still questionable.

See also INTELLIGENCE; PERSONALITY.

psychoneuroimmunology   A relatively new branch of science that studies the relationship of mental health to the immune process and how emotional stress can lead to ill health.

See also STRESS.

psychoneurosis   A term used interchangeably with neurosis, which relates to mental disorders associated with many psychological symptoms. In neurosis, the individual does not lose touch with reality but realizes that he or she is not mentally healthy. In psychosis, the individual loses touch with reality and believes that he or she does not have any illness.

See also NEUROSIS; PSYCHOSIS.

psychopathology   The study of abnormal mental processes. There are two major approaches, the descriptive and the psychoanalytic. In descriptive psychopathology, the clinician records symptoms that make up a diagnosis, such as delusions, hallucinations or mood disturbances. In the psychoanalytic approach, the clinician delves into the individual's unconscious motivations.

The terms "psychopathic personality" and "sociopathic personality" have been applied to the condition of antisocial personality disorder, which was first recognized during the 19th century as "moral insanity." It applied to immoral or guiltless behavior that was not accompanied by impairments in reasoning.

See also PSYCHOANALYSIS.

psychopharmacology Treatment of mental disorders with medications. Generally, medications used to treat psychiatric illnesses are known as psychotropic medications. There are several major categories of these drugs, including neuroleptic (or antipsychotic) medications, antiparkinsonian medications, lithium, antidepressant drugs and antianxiety medications, as well as many other drugs that are known to be efficacious in some mental health conditions.

See also ANTIANXIETY MEDICATIONS; ANTICHOLINERGIC MEDICATIONS; ANTIDEPRESSANT MEDICATIONS; BENZODIAZEPINE MEDICATIONS; LITHIUM CARBONATE; NEUROLEPTIC.

psychosexual development A psychoanalytical term for the effects of sexual maturation on the development of personality; also called libidinal development. Freud viewed this development as a stage-by-stage expression of the libido, or source of energy. In the first stage (oral), the mouth is the prime erotic zone, with sucking and biting the characteristic expressions. In the next stage (anal), the infant derives pleasure in expelling or retaining feces. In the phallic stage, the libido focuses on the genital organs, with masturbation the major source of pleasure. The Oedipus complex may develop at this time. Next is the latency stage, in which overt sexual interest is repressed and sublimated into peer activities. The genital stage is reached in puberty, when one focuses erotic interest and activity on a sexual partner.

See also PSYCHOSEXUAL DISORDERS.

psychosexual disorders A group of sexual dysfunctions that arise from psychological rather than physical factors. These include gender identity disorders, paraphilias and psychosexual dysfunctions, such as disturbances in sexual desire or response.

See also PARAPHILIAS.

psychosexual dysfunctions Disorders in which there is no known organic cause for an interference with the normal process of sexual response. Conditions termed "sexual dysfunctions" include lack of sexual desire, impotence, premature ejaculation, painful intercourse and lack of orgasm. These dysfunctions are common in men and women, often start in early adult life and, in many people, disappear with experience, increased confidence and personality maturation.

Many people respond well to sex therapy, which can be done with an individual or a couple.

See also DYSPAREUNIA; IMPOTENCE; SEXUAL RESPONSE CYCLE; VAGINISMUS.

psychosexual trauma A frightening sexual experience in early life that may relate to a current psychologically induced sexual dysfunction. Examples include child abuse, incest or rape.

See also INCEST; RAPE, RAPE PREVENTION AND RAPE TRAUMA SYNDROME.

psychosis A severe mental disorder in which the individual loses contact with reality. This differs from neurosis, which is a more mild group of mental disorders. Psychotic individuals have a distorted ability to think, perceive and judge clearly; they do not realize that they are ill. Neurotics, on the other hand, generally know they are ill.

A psychotic episode can involve hallucinations, delusions, disorientation and extremely aggressive behavior. Schizophrenic and manic-depressive psychoses are examples of functional psychosis. In toxic psychosis, psychoticlike behavior results from impairment of brain cell function.

Many people recover from psychotic episodes with appropriate treatment, often involving use of psychotropic medications, carefully monitored by their physicians.

See also PSYCHOPHARMACOLOGY; PSYCHOTROPIC DRUGS.

psychosomatic (psychosomatic illness)
A term that refers to physical problems that may either be imagined or made worse by psychological factors. Some examples of conditions that sometimes have psychosomatic components include headache, nausea, asthma, irritable bowel syndrome, ulcers and certain types of eczema.

See also MUNCHAUSEN'S SYNDROME.

psychosurgery Any operation on the brain as a treatment for symptoms of mental disorders, usually performed when all other treatments have been ineffective. Although psychosurgery has helped some people, successes with the operations have been inconsistent, with highly unpredictable results, and remain a controversial form of treatment for mental illness. At one time, prefrontal lobotomy was the most widely used form of psychosurgery but, as it often resulted in harmful side effects, has been replaced by other safer operations.

The term "neurosurgery" is preferred when referring to the relief of pain due to organic diseases.

See also BRAIN.

psychotherapy Treatment of a mental health concern through an experience resulting from an interaction between a trained therapist (psychotherapist) and the individual. When one thinks he or she cannot cope with emotional swings and strong feelings of low self-esteem and wants to get help, one should share these feelings either with an understanding friend or professional counselor. There are many types of psychotherapists available.

One can choose a therapist who is personally recommended by a friend. If one does not want to talk with friends about a need for emotional therapy, one can consider asking a family physician or local community mental health center for a recommendation.

When choosing a therapist, one should check out credentials. Know whether the therapist is a psychiatrist, psychologist or psychiatric social worker. Determine where the person received training and check with that institution. There are also professional societies for many specialties. Check with an appropriate organization to see that the therapist has the appropriate accreditation to counsel in your community.

Good mental health is a continuum. Everyone has good days and bad, stresses brought on by work and home life, and moods that seem down from one's usual feeling of well-being. People with mental health problems who realize they need help may be faced with the question of whether they need a trained medical doctor or not for their emotional problem.

If one recognizes what the problems are and there are just occasional periods of feeling in a low mood, one probably does not require therapy by a psychiatrist. One also probably does not need a psychiatrist if:

- The end of the problem is in sight, but one just can't get there by oneself
- One realizes that symptoms are of short duration and that the stress that brought them on can be identified

However, if one has tried going to a nonmedical therapist regarding symptoms and has not found relief, one may need an M.D. One will also want an M.D. if:

- Medications are necessary. M.D.s are the only mental health therapists who can prescribe medications. For certain emotional illnesses, medications are helpful.

- If one has incapacitating or debilitating symptoms
- If one has concurrent other medical problems for which care and medications are being received
- There is a history of mental illness in the family, if other family members have ever been hospitalized for mental illness or if one requires hospitalization for a mental problem

Many therapies have been used historically, and many are used today. Some are client-centered, some therapist-centered and others take a mixed approach. Some are directed to conscious awareness and others to the unconscious, while still others are mixed. Some approaches go into the individual's past, some into the present. Others are future-oriented. Some systems aim for limited results, while others have aspirations of changing the whole personality. Some systems approach cognition, others emotions and still others, behavior. Some are a combination of these three. Some systems see the human being as strictly determined, some as having free will and some as determined by a combination of heredity, environment and self.

See also BEHAVIORAL THERAPY; PSYCHOLOGY.

psychotropic drugs Prescription medications that have effects on behavior, experience or other psychological functions. Psychotropic drugs include antidepressant drugs, sedatives, hypnotics, narcotics, stimulants, tranquilizer drugs and psychedelic drugs. Substances that have mind-altering effects that are not their primary function are not considered psychotropic drugs.

Psychotropic medications usually require highly individualized dosage schedules and are often prescribed to individuals who are receiving more than one drug at a time.

Special attention should be given to the possibilities of drug interactions.

See also ANTIDEPRESSANT MEDICATIONS; PSYCHOPHARMACOLOGY.

PTSD See POST-TRAUMATIC STRESS DISORDER.

puberty The period during which adult sexual characteristics develop. Puberty normally occurs between age 10 and 14 in girls and one to two years later in boys, although precocious or delayed puberty can occur in both sexes. The onset of puberty is known as pubarche.

In females, puberty usually starts with breast budding and/or the appearance of pubic hair. Over the next year or so, the breast tissue underlying the initial "buds" enlarges, the hips widen and pubic and axillary hair thickens. Soon menarche, the first menstruation, occurs. When regular cyclic menses have been established, puberty is considered completed.

The high levels of estrogens that occur during puberty generally "seal" a girl's leg bones, so little additional height growth will occur after puberty. Occasionally, a girl can conceive if sexual intercourse predates full pubertal development and ovulation occurs at this time. Increasingly intense interest in the opposite sex occurs in young women and men, and though neither sex is ready for the responsibilities of parenthood, it is usually possible for a young man to impregnate a young woman and for a young woman to become pregnant and bear a child.

Puberty occurs earlier in well-nourished populations, and the average age of menarche has declined in the developed world over the past few generations to age 12. The occurrence of the normal adolescent tendency to try to establish independence; deteriorating social structures, such as church and family; and early sexual development have made adolescence a time of great turmoil for both children and their parents.

Precocious puberty is the premature development of functioning gonads in young women and young men; women ovulate and men produce mature spermatozoa. Precocious puberty may occur as early as the age of eight in girls and the age of 10 in boys; such young people also have adult levels of sex hormones and the secondary sex characteristics of their gender.

Sexual awakening is a term for the period of psychological change that accompanies puberty. During this time, young people undergo changes in attitudes, emotions and interests that are appropriate for approaching sexual maturity. Physical experimentation, including increased masturbation and petting, occurs during this phase.

See also MASTURBATION; MENSTRUATION; PUBERTY RITES.

puberty rites In some societies, ceremonies are performed to mark the arrival of puberty and the beginning of adulthood; the rites are also known as initiation rites.

Formal rites may include teaching of legends and laws as well as sexual practices and responsibilities expected of an adult in the particular society.

See also PUBERTY.

puritan complex See OBSCENITY-PURITY COMPLEX.

puritanism An English movement inspired by the French reformer John Calvin (1509–1564), emphasizing the doctrine of "original sin" and the "total depravity of fallen humanity." The attitude of puritanism led to the enactment of laws relating to sexual activity as well as subsequent anxieties and feelings of guilt. The term "puritanical attitude" is derived from this movement and is characteristic of individuals with compulsive personalities.

See also VICTORIANISM.

R

racing thoughts See THOUGHT DISORDERS.

randomized clinical trial An experiment designed to test the safety and/or efficacy of an intervention, such as a prescription drug, in which people are randomly allocated to experimental or control groups and outcomes are compared. Many new pharmaceutical products are extensively tested in this way.

rape, rape prevention and rape trauma syndrome Rape is forcible sexual intercourse against the will of the partner. There is some variation among states as to the actual definition; in many states sexual assault need not involve either force, actual penetration or ejaculation. In some places genital contact under the heat of force or even implied threat of force meets the legal definition.

In the majority of cases the perpetrator is male and the victim female, but it is possible for the victim to be male. In many states, sexual contact between an adult and an underage child or adolescent is automatically considered rape.

Traditionally women have most feared violent sexual assault by a stranger. However, society has increasingly recognized that forced intercourse can occur with perpetrators known to the victim—even a husband. The incidence of "date rape" (rape by a person with whom one has had a social engagement) is increasingly reported.

Rape is now recognized as more a crime of violence than one of sexuality; rapists often have a history of other types of violent crime. As courts and law enforcement agencies have been more sympathetic toward victims, the number of reported rapes in the United States has increased dramatically.

Fear of rape, known as virgivitiphobia, underlies the entire female experience of sexuality. In early adolescence, girls are taught to be distrustful of men and fearful of being victimized. Adult women are often fearful of going out without a male escort out of fear of sexual harassment and possible assault.

Although public support and sympathy for rape victims have recently improved, society continues to hold a "blaming the victim" mentality toward rape victims. Often victims are blamed for being in the wrong place or dressed in a seductive fashion, and the role of the criminal is downplayed. In recent years, the efforts of rape victim advocacy groups have helped place rape in the violent context in which it belongs.

Immediate dangers of rape include direct injury, pregnancy and sexually transmitted disease (STD). Rape victims may be shot, knifed or beaten. The rape itself can cause perineal bruising or lacerations, particularly if the victim is very young, if anal penetration occurs or if dangerous objects are used in the assault. Cultures are taken for gonorrhea and other sexually trans-mitted diseases, and appropriate antibiotics may be recommended. For the victim exposed to herpes or AIDS, there is at present no effective way of preventing these diseases.

After the attack, the victim's body and clothing will be examined for traces of semen, hair or clothing of the rapist. Recent development of DNA "fingerprints" from semen and blood will allow for very accurate identification of the person responsible.

Women at risk for pregnancy may be offered "morning after" contraception. Unfortunately, many victims fail to press charges, either out of fear of having to relive the incident in court, out of fear of shame or other reprisal or actual fear of the assailant. In later years, many victims suffer depression and post-traumatic stress reactions, which can adversely affect their professional, personal and sexual lives.

Prevention of rape will depend on major restructuring of the way society views violence against women and prevention of the drug, alcohol and poverty problems that lead to violent crimes. To a lesser extent, self-defense and assertiveness training for women can decrease the risk to those women but fails to address the underlying psychopathology of the rapist.

Rape trauma syndrome is a term used to describe the results of sexual victimization against the victim's consent. The trauma that develops from this attack or attempted attack may include an acute phase of disorganization of the victim's life-style and, in some cases, a long-term traumatization with symptoms similar to post-traumatic stress disorder. Many factors influence the process of recovery from rape trauma syndrome, including the type of assault, the victim's coping style and level of self-esteem, the type of social support available, additional life stressors and additional history of victimization.

See also SEXUAL FEARS.

Becker, Judith V.; Skinner, Linda J.; Abel, Gene G.; and Cichon, Joan. "Level of Postassault Sexual Functioning in Rape and Incest Victims." *Archives of Sexual Behavior* 15, no. 1 (1986).

Clark, Stephanie. "Perspectives on Sexual Assault." *Canadian Family Physician* 35 (Jan. 1989).

Edmonds, Ed M., and Cahoon, Delwin D. "Attitudes Concerning Crimes Related to Clothing Worn by Female Victims." *Bulletin of the Psychonomic Society* 24, no. 6 (1986).

Gordon, Margaret T., and Riger, Stephanie. *The Female Fear.* New York: Free Press, 1989.

Kahn, Ada P., and Holt, Linda Hughey. *The A to Z of Women's Sexuality.* Alameda, Calif.: Hunter House, 1992.

Koss, Mary P.; Gidycz, Christine A.; and Wisniewski, Nadine. "The Scope of Rape: Incidence and Prevalence of Sexual Aggression and Victimization in a National Sample of Higher Education Students." *Journal of Consulting and Clinical Psychology.* 55, no. 2 (1987).

Leland-Young, Jan, and Nelson, Joan. "Prevention of Sexual Assault Through the Resocialization of Women: Unlearning Victim Behavior." *Women and Therapy* 6, no. 1–2 (Spring-Summer 1987).

Masters, William H. "Sexual Dysfunction as an Aftermath of Sexual Assault of Men by Women." *Journal of Sex and Marital Therapy* 12, no. 1 (Spring 1986).

rapid cycling A mood disorder in which episodes of mania or depression occur at least four times within a year.

See also DEPRESSION; MANIA; MANIC-DEPRESSIVE ILLNESS.

regression A defense mechanism involving reversion to immature behavior when one feels threatened or overwhelmed by internal conflicts. Some individuals may regress on an ongoing basis, and others do it on a temporary basis in specific situations. Examples of regression include crying or temper tantrums to gain attention. In psychoanalysis, individuals are sometimes encouraged to temporarily regress to help them remember some childhood events, their feelings and their methods of coping. In some alternative therapies, including primal therapy, individuals are also encourage to regress during therapy.

See also PSYCHOTHERAPY.

reinforcement Strengthening of good habits (or bad habits such as addictions) or behaviors by positive rewards (positive reinforcement). For good mental health, individuals have a need for positive self-regard, much of which comes from approval (or disapproval) from significant others. When good habits are praised and rewarded, they are reinforced; when bad habits are ignored and rewards are withheld or punished (negative reinforcement), presumably they will diminish. In daily life as well as in therapy, individuals can be motivated to change behavior patterns to include more adaptive responses and more socially acceptable behaviors. Methods of reinforcement may include rewards such as privileges or increased social interactions. There is evidence suggesting that in humans positive reinforcement works better than negative reinforcement to change behavior.

relaxation training A procedure that teaches individuals control over their mental state and body. In a training program, individuals are instructed to move through the muscle groups of the body, making them tense and then completely relaxed. Through repetitions of this procedure, individuals learn how to be in voluntary control of their feelings of tension and relaxation. Some therapists provide individuals with instructional audio tapes that can be listened to for practice, while other therapists go through the procedure repeatedly with their clients. Relaxation training is used by individuals who suffer from pain and its accompanying anxieties, or along with various techniques of behavioral therapy. Relaxation training itself is a form of behavioral therapy.

To determine the effectiveness of relaxation training, some therapists use biofeedback to determine an individual's degree of relaxation and absence of anxiety.

Also known as autogenic training or progressive relaxation, relaxation therapy was developed during the 1930s and refined during the 1950s. Joseph Wolpe, a pioneer in systematic desensitization, described and recommended progressive relaxation.

See also IMAGERY.

Turin, A. C., and Lynch, S. N. "Comprehensive Relaxation Training," in Corsini, R. J., ed., *Handbook of Innovative Psychotherapies*. New York: Wiley, 1981.

religion Systems of beliefs regarding oneself and the universe. Religion gives many people a sense of security, a feeling of meaning and order and an ethical pattern for living. Religious beliefs offer help, support and strength to those with both external and internal mental health concerns. Religious programs and rituals facilitate social interaction, which is important in an age when contact with lifelong friends and extended family is the exception rather than the rule and when urban anonymity has produced a sense of alienation for many.

Religious beliefs and practices satisfy mystical and illusory needs for many individuals. For example, the image of a divine being or beings meets a longing evident in many civilizations for a higher power in control of the universe. Prayer and meditation are comforting and helpful to many people. Modern psychotherapeutic discoveries have confirmed the benefits of breath control and mental centering practiced for centuries in Zen Buddhism and yoga. Religion has also focused the energies of important artists by giving them an outlet and inspiration for their creativity. Certain religions such as the Pentecostal movement in Christianity and Native American religions have fostered ecstatic, visionary states that satisfy a need for an experience that transcends reality.

Religious attitudes have been of concern to mental health professionals since the 1800s, but the relationship between the disciplines has not always been congenial, despite the fact that the meaning of the word "psychology" ("the science of the soul") implies a strong relationship between the fields. Members of the clergy, psychologists, psychiatrists and psychotherapists meet some overlapping needs in that they offer support, advice and wisdom and in many cases serve as confessors.

There is a sharp division in the mental health field regarding the role of religion in preserving a healthy state of mind. For example, Sigmund Freud (1856–1939) considered religion to be an "illusion" and an extension of childlike attitudes toward parents. Carl Jung (1875–1961) believed that proving or disproving the existence of God was not within the framework of psychology but that psychologists should accept thoughts

and feelings related to religious beliefs as real and significant. In *Modern Man in Search of a Soul* (1933) Jung wrote, "Among all my patients in the second half of life, that is to say over 35, there has not been one whose problem in the last resort was not that of finding a religious outlook on life."

In the period from 1930 to 1960, theologian Paul Tillich (1886–1965), philosopher Martin Buber (1878–1965) and psychoanalyst Rollo May (1909–) published important works attempting to synthesize religion, psychology and modern philosophical movements. An interest in combining the mental health disciplines with the influence of religion has encouraged the development of training in pastoral counseling in recent years. In the early 1970s, priest-sociologist Andrew Greeley (1928–) in his book *Unsecular Man: The Persistence of Religion* (1974) described a conservative, religious social trend that recently has become more obvious in movements such as the creationist opposition to secular humanism in education, in the political influence of religious leaders and in celebrities publicizing their "born again" experiences.

Religion contains elements that are both supportive and damaging to good mental health. The Christian promise of reward in the afterlife has inspired and comforted many, but it has also been held responsible for making believers passive or accepting of hardships and inequities that they could overcome through their own efforts. Highly disturbed psychotic patients have been known to literally accept biblical passages as commands leading to self-mutilation. Others with obsessional disorders literally live a hellish life struggling with guilt and behaviors to undo what they feel are sinful (obsessive) thoughts. Many experience religion as being constraining and supportive of narrow-minded behavior. For example, Abraham Lincoln abandoned what he believed to be the pettiness of organized religion while adhering to the high aspirations of religious thoughts. Religious movements have brought about bloodshed and dissension, as in the Protestant-Catholic conflict in Northern Ireland in the latter part of the 20th century. Historically, religious visions and thoughts have been part of unstable behavior, particularly in such religious leaders as Martin Luther, John Wesley and Saint Ignatius. More recently, reports of fraud and sexual abuse by religious leaders have shown that the power that society gives religious leaders can corrupt.

Two recent surveys, one completed in 1991 for *Time* and one taken by the Gallup poll, indicate that while religion is a strong influence in the United States, there seems to be a lack of confidence or awareness of its importance. For example, the *Time* survey showed that 78 percent of those surveyed felt that children should be allowed to say prayers in public schools. Sixty-three percent said that they would not vote for a presidential candidate who did not believe in God. Fifty-five percent said that there was too little religious influence in American life, and 65 percent felt that religious influence was decreasing. The latter opinion can be both supported and contradicted by the Gallup poll, depending on one's point of reference. The percentage of those surveyed who felt that religion was "very important" or "fairly important" to them personally, about 85 percent, has remained fairly constant since the 1970s. Attendance at church or synagogue during the previous week had actually risen slightly from a low of 40 percent in the 1970s to 43 percent in 1989, while actual membership had dropped from 73 percent in 1965 to 68 percent in 1989.

The Gallup survey further defined the religious in the population. Female nonwhite adults over the age of 50, southerners and those with annual incomes under $20,000 are most likely to place importance on religion. On the other hand, the wealthy have a high rate of church attendance and membership.

An earlier survey of World War II veterans offered interesting insights into the religious state of mind of men who had experienced warfare. About 26 percent said that the war made them more religious; 19 percent that it made them less so. Fifty-eight percent of those surveyed said that even though their religious conviction may have increased, decreased or remained the same, their war experiences made them more interested in the subject of religion. The veterans exhibited an even stronger tendency when describing their religious attitudes during battle. Most were of the opinion that everyone prays in combat. The interesting variation was the comment "There were atheists in fox holes, but most of them were in love," implying that the thought of a loved one might carry a man through danger almost as well as an appeal to a higher power.

See also CULTS.

remarriage Widowed and divorced men and women remarry at a high rate. In 1987, 46 percent of all marriages were remarriages for the bride or groom or both. More widows than widowers remarry, but divorced men are more likely to remarry than divorced women. Nineteen percent of divorced men remarry within a calendar year of their divorce; 8 percent of widowed men marry within a year of the death of their wives. Divorced men have good reason to remarry. Death rates for divorced men who remain single are far higher than for divorced women who do not remarry.

Although the divorced and widowed remarry at a high rate, the divorce rate for these unions is higher than for first marriages. Responses to a survey concerning the failure rate of second marriages consistently listed two leading causes: children and money. Friction between stepparents and stepchildren is common. In remarriages, the husband is frequently several years older than the wife and may not want more children, while she may be eager for a family. The financial strains of a man called on to support two families are very often disruptive.

Other major obstacles are a reflection of the reasons for the second marriage. Some divorced men and women marry a person very similar to their first spouse and encounter similar difficulties; others try so hard to find a quality that was lacking in their first spouse that they may marry a person who has that particular quality and become blind to the fact that in other ways they are actually incompatible. Divorced or widowed persons may remarry out of emotional and financial need without fully establishing themselves or sifting through and resolving their feelings about their previous marriage. Some carry feelings of guilt about how the second marriage affects their children or previous spouse. The ex-wife or husband may interfere in the marriage, and family members may make it obvious that they preferred the previous spouse.

How well one is accepted by the extended remarriage family may relate to the circumstances of the courtship. For example, if a woman was the "other woman" while the new husband was still married, relatives may regard her as a "homewrecker." If she knew him before he was widowed and marries him soon after his wife's death, relatives may think the marriage was too hasty and disrespectful to the deceased. Many mid-life women grew up dependent on their families or their husbands. Until the 1950s, most women's mindset when entering marriage was "until death do us part." Having to seek a second, or third, husband weighs heavily on the self-esteem of divorced women.

In the 1990s, some individuals, after meeting a lovable other who loves them, choose not to marry for a variety of reasons ranging from not wanting to lose alimony payments, to waiting for vesting in a pension plan, to fear of making a mistake. Many older individuals who are past childbearing and child-rearing years opt for a "living together" arrangement instead of remarriage.

See also DIVORCE; MARRIAGE; STEPFAMILIES; COURTSHIP, LOVE, ROMANCE, RELATIONSHIPS in BIBLIOGRAPHY.

Belovitch, Jeanne. *Making Remarriage Work.* Lexington, Mass.: Lexington Books, 1987.

Kahn, Ada P., and Holt, Linda Hughey. *Midlife Health: A Woman's Practical Guide to Feeling Good.* New York: Avon Books, 1989.

U.S. Department of Commerce. *Statistical Abstract of the United States, 1991.* Washington, D.C.: USGPO, 1991.

Wilson, Barbara Foley. "The Marry-Go-Round." *American Demographics* (Oct. 1991).

remembering   See MEMORY.

REM (rapid-eye-movement) sleep   A stage of sleep in which dreams occur. A sleep cycle consists of stages (known as Stages I, II, III and IV) in a cycle lasting about 90 minutes followed by the period of REM sleep for about 10 minutes. With each cycle, REM periods lengthen. During the last cycle, REM sleep may last for 30 to 60 minutes. REM sleep onset has been found to occur earlier in individuals with symptoms of depression and may be a biological marker for depression or vulnerability to depression.

See also DEPRESSION; DREAMING; SLEEP.

repression   In psychoanalysis, the basic defense mechanism, which excludes painful experiences and unacceptable impulses from consciousness. Repression operates on an unconscious level against anxiety often produced by objectionable sexual feelings and feelings of hostility.

residential treatment center (RTC)   In this treatment setting, patients with substance abuse and mental health disorders participate in a 24-hour therapeutically planned group living and learning situation in which individualized treatment takes place. RTCs are designed for those for whom outpatient treatment is not appropriate but for whom a protected and structured environment is necessary. Adaptive skills are taught to help the patient function successfully at home, at school and in the community.

resistance   The feelings, thoughts, attitudes and behaviors on the part of the patient that oppose therapeutic goals in a psycho-therapeutic setting. Sigmund Freud viewed resistance as a defense mechanism, while behavioral therapists now explain resistance as part of avoidance learning; certain thoughts repeatedly associated with painful experiences, such as situations that produce anxieties or fears, become aversive. For best results, psychotherapists plan tactics to help overcome the patient's resistance to the therapist, to the process of treatment and to the loss of symptoms. An examination of resistance by the therapist may suggest certain diagnoses as well as whether the patient is amenable to certain modes of psychotherapy.

See also BEHAVIORAL THERAPY; DEFENSE MECHANISMS; FREUD, SIGMUND; PSYCHO-ANALYSIS.

retardation, mental   See MENTAL RE-TARDATION.

retirement   Withdrawing from the work force, usually at an older age. Retirement is highly sought by some, but it produces mental health problems including anxieties, boredom and feelings of lack of productivity for others. Many retired people feel that they are not contributing members of society and become depressed and withdrawn. Some feel the lack of prestige they formerly received from their position.

Retired people who adjust the best to retirement seem to be those who enjoy getting into new activities and making new acquaintances. Most retired people enjoy having more time for family and friends, for travel and for pursuit of long-standing hobbies.

Those who enjoy their freedom from work usually have planned ahead by starting an interest or form of recreation before retirement that they pursue with additional vigor when additional time is available. For example, some individuals learn a musical instrument, while others pursue woodworking or sewing as a hobby. Others do volunteer work to help others in their previous profes-

sion. Some U.S. cities have "job corps" of senior citizens willing to use their knowledge in business and industry.

Many retired people enjoy going back to school and taking classes at local colleges and universities. Some participate in Elderhostel activities, traveling to a distant college campus for a week or two to study a favorite topic.

Many people who retire actually go back to a paid position. According to researchers at the University of Southern California, retirement is no longer a once-in-a-lifetime happening. They tracked 2,816 American men who turned 55 between 1966 and 1976. Approximately one-third went back to work for an average of two more years after they retired.

Other significant findings indicated that the average American male retires between age 61 and 62, that white-collar workers stay on the job about two years longer than blue-collar workers and that blue-collar workers spend an average of 10 years in retirement. White collar workers average 12 years of retirement.

Wives of retired men are sometimes affected by their mates' retirement. A research project reported in *Modern Maturity* (Dec. 1990–Jan. 1992) indicated that most women polled reported satisfaction with their husbands' retirement. Effects of retirement on 413 upper-middle-class women married to men retired an average of 16 years were examined. More than one-third of the women had no problems with their husbands' retirement, and two-thirds said they were fully prepared for it. Only 12 percent said they felt some loss of personal freedom, and 5 to 6 percent reported an increase in household chores. Among those who said they would have done things differently, the majority mentioned the need to be better prepared financially for retirement.

See also AGING.

right to die   See LEGAL ISSUES.

Ritalin   A trade name for a drug (methylphenidate hydrochloride) sometimes used to treat hyperactivity in children. It is a mild stimulant to the central nervous system that may help some children increase their ability to concentrate in school and perform homework and other expected chores. Use of the drug has been controversial. Newer medications have been developed and have replaced the use of Ritalin to some extent.

See also ATTENTION-DEFICIT HYPERACTIVITY DISORDER.

rites of passage   See PUBERTY RITES.

ritual   See OBSESSIVE-COMPULSIVE DISORDER.

Roe v. Wade   A 1973 ruling by the U.S. Supreme Court in which previous antiabortion laws enacted by individual states were struck down, making abortion legal in the United States and spelling out legal concerns about abortion during the three trimesters of pregnancy.

See also ABORTION; PREGNANCY; PRO-LIFE AND PRO-CHOICE; WOMEN'S LIBERATION MOVEMENT.

Rorschach test (inkblot test)   A standardized test in which an individual responds to a set of inkblot pictures. Presumably, the individual reveals his or her attitudes, emotions and feelings by interpreting the pictures. The test was developed by Hermann Rorschach (1884–1922), a Swiss psychiatrist and psychoanalyst.

See also PSYCHOLOGICAL TESTS.

runner's high   A feeling of physical and mental well-being, which may occur during or after a period of exercise that makes the cardiovascular system work harder for longer than it usually does. For example, about 30 to 40 minutes of jogging may produce the feeling in many individuals. There is a common misconception that runner's high is caused exclusively by the release of endorphins, brain chemicals that can reduce pain and elevate mood in a manner similar to that of opiate drugs. In addition to release of endorphins, exercise causes the body to release many neurochemicals that in turn trigger physiological reactions. For example, stimulation of the sympathetic nervous system, along with activation of the endocrine system's adrenal medulla, causes the heart rate to increase and more oxygen to be delivered to the brain, all of which contribute to "runner's high."

See also ENDORPHINS.

rural mental health care   The prevalence of mental health disorders in rural Americans is similar to that in urban areas. Despite similarity in mental health problems, it appears that rural areas have substantially fewer mental health resources than urban areas. Where resources exist, they are likely to be narrower in scope.

Mental health facilities face problems in serving populations spread over vast distances. Additionally, they are caught between competing needs for services for the chronically mentally ill and services for acute and less serious conditions. Because recent federal and state policies have tended to emphasize the former, the ability of many rural mental health providers to offer services such as suicide prevention, education, crisis intervention, support groups and individual counseling for less severe mental health conditions has waned. Other sources of services, such as from nonprofit foundations, are less available to fill needs in rural than in urban areas.

Rural mental health professionals face problems similar to those of other rural health professionals. For example, they have fewer training opportunities, fewer colleagues with whom to consult and to discuss professional issues and more diverse demands on their time than their urban counterparts. Primary care physicians provide much of the mental health care in both urban and rural areas, yet they receive relatively little training in mental health diagnosis and treatment. Master's level mental health professionals and paraprofessionals and volunteers are also vital providers of rural health services.

According to *Health Care in Rural America,* a publication of the Office of Technology Assessment, U.S. Congress, the severe shortage of psychiatrists and doctoral-level psychologists in rural areas, the proportion of mental health care provided by nonpsychiatric physicians and the types of services likely to be most acceptable to rural residents all suggest that integrating mental health and other health care is especially important in rural areas. Social workers, psychologists, clinical psychiatric nurse specialists and paraprofessionals play an important role in extending rural mental health services to those in need, and in linking these services with physical health services. These linkages may include features such as health and mental health clinics sharing a single service site, routine consultation between physicians and mental health center staff or a full-time social worker providing counseling and educational services in a community health clinic or physician's office. Recent legislation has expanded the reimbursement available for certain "linkage" services, namely the mental health services provided by clinical social workers and psychologists in community health centers.

A problem in rural mental health service is the lack of awareness among rural residents that mental health services exist and can be helpful. In addition, transportation for both clients and professionals is a serious mental health service issue. Although catchment areas are no longer used for federal purposes, many states continue to use them for funding and service requirements. The average size of a rural catchment area ranges from 5,000 to 17,000 square miles (depending on the definition of rural). Some rural distances are so great that continuity of care and follow-up services are virtually impossible to provide.

Difficulties in obtaining mental health care confidentially can also act as a barrier to services, particularly for rural youth. A survey of adolescents in a small town in the Midwest showed a preference for specialized clinics over private physicians' offices for particularly sensitive matters such as contraception and substance abuse. Adolescents also prefer not to be accompanied by parents when they seek health care for problems like depression.

U.S. Congress, Office of Technology Assessment. *Health Care in Rural America.* OTA-H-434. Washington, D.C.: USGPO, 1990.

S

SAD   See SEASONAL AFFECTIVE DISORDER.

sadism   A sexual deviation (paraphilia) in which an individual needs to inflict pain on another in order to achieve sexual satisfaction. The term "sadism" is named for the Marquis de Sade (1740–1814), a French novelist whose works described his own bizarre sexual activities. Works such as *The Story of Juliette* (1797) and *The Bedroom Philosophers* (1795) were long banned for obscenity; de Sade spent many years in prison for his views.

Sadistic acts may include physical cruelty, such as beating or tying up the victim, or mental cruelty, as in humiliating the partner. Such acts may be inflicted on either a consenting or a nonconsenting person and may range from mild injury to raping, torturing or even killing the victim. Masochism is the term applied to instances in which an individual must be subjected to pain in order to achieve such satisfaction.

The term "sadism" was first used by Baron Richard von Krafft-Ebing (1840–1902), a German author and neurologist, in his classic work *Psychopathia Sexualis* in 1882. He described the forms that sadism might take following unsatisfying intercourse, sadistic acts that increase desire and acts that brought about orgasm without intercourse in cases of impotence.

Mental health professionals say that sadism as a psychological syndrome alone is rare. Most cases of sadism have been reported by prostitutes. Sadism is most frequently combined with masochistic behavior, a tendency to derive sexual pleasure from being dominated or injured by the sexual partner. A study of individuals who showed some type of sadomasochistic behavior showed that while men tended toward sadism and women toward masochism, both sexes derived pleasure from some behavior patterns of each type.

See also MASOCHISM; PARAPHILIAS; SADOMASOCHISM; SEXUAL DYSFUNCTION in BIBLIOGRAPHY.

sadomasochism Two forms of sexual preference, one in which a person derives pleasure and sexual gratification from inflicting pain (sadism), and the other being when one becomes sexually aroused by experiencing pain (masochism). This practice is abbreviated as SM. Many sadomasochistically oriented people center their activities around reading magazines featuring photographs of women dressed in leather and spike-heeled shoes while they chain, whip and torture their victims; others actually practice this behavior. Some normal couples enjoy acting out sadomasochistic fantasies during lovemaking; the behavior becomes aberrant when it crosses into inflicting pain or humiliation on either individual.

See also PARAPHILIAS; SADISM; SEXUAL DYSFUNCTION in BIBLIOGRAPHY.

Katchadourian, Herant A., and Lunde, Donald T. *Fundamentals of Human Sexuality*. New York: Holt, Rinehart and Winston, 1972.

SADS See SCHEDULE FOR AFFECTIVE DISORDERS AND SCHIZOPHRENIA.

"safe sex" A term coined during the 1980s as the AIDS (acquired Immunodeficiency syndrome) epidemic heightened and was known to involve the heterosexual population of men and women. The term "safe sex" means avoiding behaviors in which the AIDS virus can be transmitted. Anal intercourse seems to carry the highest risk for infection of all sexual techniques.

Safe sex practices involve avoiding sexual intercourse with known drug users and those who test positive for the HIV virus (known to cause AIDS), knowing about one's partner's sexual background, using condoms as well as a spermicide and becoming involved in a monogamous relationship. Safe sex practices can also help avoid transmission of many sexually transmitted diseases.

See also ACQUIRED IMMUNODEFICIENCY SYNDROME; SEXUALLY TRANSMITTED DISEASES; SEXUALLY TRANSMITTED DISEASES in BIBLIOGRAPHY.

Kahn, Ada P., and Holt, Linda Hughey. *Midlife Health: A Woman's Practical Guide to Feeling Good*. New York: Avon Books, 1989.
Paalman, M. E. M. "Safer Sex." *World Health* (Nov. 1988).

"sandwich" generation The generation of mid-life adults who are involved in their adult children's (and in some cases grandchildren's) lives while still caring for aging parents. Estimates are that women in particular will spend more time caring for aging parents than they did in raising their own children.

"Sandwich" generation adults have many stresses in their lives because of their multiple roles. For many, financial considerations are important, as they begin to face the possibility of requiring nursing home care for aging parents when they have just finished paying off college tuitions. Many find that just as their children have left home, parents' needs increase, and an increasing amount of time and energy is spent in caring for them.

In many homes during the 1990s, adult children have returned to what parents thought would be an empty nest. With two (and sometimes three) generations in the home, as well as an elderly parent either in the home or elsewhere, adults find that they need to stretch their adaptive skills in family dynamics. Their children are no longer children, but in returning home they seem to have put themselves in that role.

Those who adapt well in this new dimension of parenting become good listeners, but not critics, helpers and supporters in emotional and financial ways (to the extent possible) without becoming domineering. Just as when the children were younger, the goal of most parents is to encourage personal growth and independence in their children. In most cases, the younger generation wants to be on their own as soon as possible, and successful parents patiently encourage that goal.

See also ELDERLY PARENTS; EMPTY NEST SYNDROME; PARENTING.

Zal, H. Michael. *The Sandwich Generation*. New York: Plenum Press, 1992.

Schedule for Affective Disorders and Schizophrenia (SADS)   A structured interview to aid in the diagnostic process as well as for use in research projects. Available since the 1970s, it covers symptoms and past history. The first section evaluates the current condition; the second evaluates symptoms occurring during the patient's lifetime. It differs from other such standard research diagnostic interview formats in that it records the severity of each symptom (on a 1–6 scale).

schizoaffective disorder   A category of illness used when a differential diagnosis between affective disorders and schizophrenia or schizophreniform disorder cannot be made. Elements of mood swings associated with bipolar disorder as well as psychotic symptoms associated with schizophrenia occur. Patients with the manic form of schizoaffective disorder have been found to have increased likelihood of relatives with bipolar disorder.

See also AFFECTIVE DISORDERS; SCHIZOPHRENIA; SCHIZOPHRENIFORM DISORDER.

schizoid personality disorder   A personality characterized by social withdrawal, hypersensitivity, absence of tender feelings for others, indifference to praise or criticism, close friendships with only one or two persons and sometimes unusual thoughts or beliefs. Usually eccentricities of behavior, thought and speech are not present.

See also SCHIZOPHRENIA; SCHIZOPHRENIFORM DISORDER; SCHIZOPHRENIA in BIBLIOGRAPHY.

schizophasia   Jumbled speech characteristic of advanced schizophrenia. It is also known as word salad.

See also SCHIZOPHRENIA; SCHIZOPHRENIA in BIBLIOGRAPHY.

schizophrenia   A group of mental illnesses or related disorders characterized in a general way by distortions of perception, speech and thoughts. Although symptoms vary among individuals, common symptoms include disturbances in affect, inappropriate affect, withdrawal from reality, hallucinations and delusions. Schizophrenia causes pervasive dysfunction in many areas of behavior and is one of the most catastrophic mental illnesses because of its chronicity and the devastating effects it has on family members.

Individuals whose symptoms involve feelings of persecution and fixed delusions are said to have paranoid schizophrenia, despite the capacity to function socially and occupationally at some level; those who have incoherent thought and speech but do not have delusions are said to have disorganized schizophrenia. Approximately 150 out of every 100,000 persons in the United States have schizophrenia; men and women of all races are affected equally. The U.S. government estimates the cost of schizophrenia at more than $40 billion annually in direct medical costs and lost productivity. It is the fourth most costly diagnosis for Medicaid nationally.

Historical Background In the late 1800s, Emil Kraepelin (1856–1926), a German psychiatrist, combined "hebrephrenia" and "catatonia" with certain paranoid states and called the condition "dementia praecox." Kraepelin said the condition consisted of large irreversible intellectual deterioration that began around or shortly after adolescence. Eugene Bleuler (1857–1939), a Swiss psychiatrist, modified Kraepelin's conception in the early 1900s to include cases with better outlook and in 1911 renamed the condition schizophrenia. The word "schizophrenia" is derived from the New Latin terms for "split mind" *(schizo* and *phrenia).*

Diagnostic criteria in the *Diagnostic and Statistical Manual of Mental Disorders* (3d ed., rev.) may include: (1) delusions, prominent hallucinations, incoherence/loosening of associations, catatonic behavior, inappropriate/flat affect (at least two); or (2) bizarre delusions; or (3) prominent hallucinations, for at least one week.

Gradual Onset of Symptoms Schizophrenia usually begins gradually during adolescence or young adulthood, except for the paranoid variety, which may develop in the late twenties or after. Early symptoms may not be detected by family and friends for a while. Initially, the sufferer may feel tense, is unable to sleep or concentrate and may become socially withdrawn, and there is general deterioration of job performance and self-appearance. Symptoms become increasingly bizarre as the disease progresses. Some individuals talk in nonsensical terms, and others have unusual perceptions. The condition improves (remission or residual stage) and worsens (relapses) in cycles. Sometimes sufferers may appear relatively normal, while other patients in remission may appear strange because they speak in a monotone, have odd speech habits, appear to have no emotional feelings and are prone to have "ideas of reference" (the idea that random social behaviors are directed at them).

During an acute phase, schizophrenics suffer from hallucinations, delusions or thought disorders.

The most commonly noted hallucination is hearing voices that give commands, comment on behavior or insult the patient. Hallucinations also occur in visual or tactile form. Visual hallucinations may include having nonexistent perceptions, such as walls bending in and out as they breathe. Tactile hallucinations may include itching or burning sensations or a sense that "unhealthy" processes are affecting the body.

Delusions are bizarre thoughts that have no basis in reality. Some sufferers believe that someone can hear their thoughts, put thoughts into their heads or control their feelings. Some believe that others are spying on or planning to harm them, while others have delusions that they are a famous person from history or that they are part of some religious process.

Thought disorders involve loosely associated thoughts, shifting from one topic to other, unrelated topics with no logical connection. Some substitute rhymes or make up their own words that mean nothing to others.

Because of their illness, schizophrenics have a distorted ability to determine whether a situation or event they perceive is real, because while they are doing one activity, they may hear a voice talking about something totally unrelated. For example, while trying to read, they may hear a voice they attribute to Martians telling them to do something else.

Diagnosis and Causes Psychiatrists diagnose schizophrenia when the condition has lasted at least six months and has included a psychotic phase. Although there are no accepted laboratory tests for schizophrenia, studies of brain metabolism during a task requiring mental concentration have shown lack of normal increases in the frontal lobes of the brain.

Some scientists believe that there may be an inherited susceptibility to schizophrenia, because the illness does run in families.

According to the American Psychiatric Association, if one identical twin has the disease, there is a 50 to 60 percent chance that the sibling (identical genetic makeup) also has schizophrenia. With one parent suffering from schizophrenia, a child has an 8 to 18 percent chance of developing the illness. If both parents have the disease, the child has a risk of between 15 and 50 percent.

There are many theories regarding schizophrenia. The onset of schizophrenia in most cases seems to be during puberty, as the body undergoes structural and biochemical changes. It may be that a schizophrenic's brain is more sensitive to certain biochemicals or that it produces excessive or inadequate biochemicals necessary for good mental health, that the brain does not develop normally or that the brain may not effectively screen stimuli when processing information that healthy people easily handle.

Some researchers have suggested that schizophrenia may have similarities to some "autoimmune" diseases, which are disorders caused when the body's immune system attacks itself. Another theory is that the mother of a schizophrenic suffered with a viral infection while he or she was in the uterus. A recent finding of MRI (magnetic resonance imaging) abnormalities in nonconcordant identical twins with schizophrenia not present in the normal twin supports the possibility of intrauterine influence. The virus could have infected the baby in such a way that changes occurred many years after birth. Several factors put together, such as the genetic predisposition, the immune system and the virus, may interact to cause an individual to develop the disease.

Treatment Treatment involves use of medication, hospitalization in some cases and psychotherapy for the individual as well as the sufferer's family members. Treatment plans are individualized according to the patient's condition and the needs of the families involved.

New medical technology enables researchers to use several tools to diagnose or confirm diagnosis of schizophrenia and plan a treatment approach. One such technique is computerized axial tomography (CAT scan), which shows subtle abnormalities in the brains of some sufferers; ventricles (fluid-filled spaces within the brain) are larger in some schizophrenics' brains. Enlarged ventricles are also seen in bipolar disorder, and CAT findings are therefore not diagnostic.

In some schizophrenics, the prefrontal cortex in the brain appears to have either atrophied (shrunk, dried out) or developed abnormally.

Medications that interfere with the brain's production of dopamine (a biochemical) are successful with schizophrenics because their brains are either extraordinarily sensitive to dopamine or produce too much dopamine.

A number of antipsychotic medications help bring biochemical imbalances closer to normal in a schizophrenic. Medications reduce delusions, hallucinations and incoherent thoughts and reduce or eliminate chances of relapse.

According to the American Psychiatric Association, 60 to 80 percent of those who did not take medication as part of their treatment had a relapse the first year after leaving the hospital, while only 20 to 50 percent of those who took medication were rehospitalized the first year. When patients continued taking medication beyond the first year, relapse rates were reduced to 10 percent.

Antipsychotic drugs have some side effects, including dry mouth, blurred vision, drowsiness, constipation and dizziness upon standing up; in a few weeks, these side effects usually disappear. A more serious possible side effect is tardive dyskinesia (TD), a condition that affects 20 to 30 percent of people taking antipsychotic drugs. TD involves small tongue tremors, facial tics and abnormal jaw movements, and spasmodic movements of the hands, feet, arms, legs, neck and shoulders. TD symptoms are relieved in many cases when medication is stopped.

Psychotherapy for the individual as well as family members helps all involved cope with the disease and its processes. Family members need reassurance and suggestions for handling the emotional aspects of the disorder. Suggestions may also be made regarding changes in the patient's living and working environment that will reduce stress and anxieties.

A variety of other therapies are useful for many schizophrenics, including dance therapy, art therapy, psychodrama and occupational therapy.

The following are some resources for information on schizophrenia:

American Mental Health Fund
2735 Hartland Road (#302)
Falls Church, VA 22043
Phone: (703) 573-2200

American Psychiatric Association
1400 K Street NW
Washington, D.C. 20005
Phone: (202) 797-4900

National Alliance for the Mentally Ill
1901 North Fort Myer Drive, Suite 500
Arlington, VA 22009-1604
Phone: (703) 524-7600

National Alliance for Research on Schizophrenia and Depression
208 South LaSalle Street, Suite 1438
Chicago, IL 60604
Phone: (312) 641-1666

National Mental Health Association
1021 Prince Street
Alexandria, VA 22314-2971
Phone: (703) 684-7722

See also AFFECTIVE FLATTENING; ANTI-PSYCHOTIC MEDICATIONS; CLOZAPINE; PSYCHOSIS; TARDIVE DYSKINESIA; THOUGHT DISORDERS.

Facts About Schizophrenia. Washington, D.C.: American Psychiatric Association, 1988.

schizophrenic depression The term applied to a mental illness that is characterized by the combined symptoms of schizophrenia and depression.

See also DEPRESSION; SCHIZOPHRENIA.

schizophreniform disorder A disorder that meets the criteria of schizophrenia but is of shorter duration, generally lasting two weeks to six months. Although the onset is acute rather than gradual, there is a greater chance of recovery from schizophreniform disorder than from schizophrenia. The term was first used in 1939 to describe an acute disorder that occurred in persons with normal personalities.

See also SCHIZOPHRENIA.

schizotypal personality disorder A pattern of peculiar behavior, odd speech and thinking and unusual perceptual experiences; a mild form of schizophrenia without psychotic symptoms. Treatment often centers on issues that disturb the patient, such as mild feelings of paranoia or ideas of reference. A supportive approach and training in social skills help many individuals feel more comfortable in social situations.

See also PERSONALITY DISORDERS; SCHIZOPHRENIA.

school phobia In children, one of the most common anxiety disorders; also known as school refusal or school absenteeism. There is some controversy whether refusal to go to school is related to separation anxiety, truancy secondary to conduct disorder or a fear of failure. Fear of going to school may begin as early as kindergarten, but it usually develops during grade or junior high school. In many cases, the child begins to devise reasons for staying home from school. Some develop symptoms, such as nausea, stomachache or headache. Others leave home for school but then return without their parents knowing that they are absent from school, or spend their day elsewhere.

School avoidance should be evaluated and treated as soon as it is detected to prevent future personal, academic and social consequences. A therapist, along with teachers, parents and the child, should try to determine the underlying reasons for the school avoidance. Reasons may include low self-esteem, being teased or bullied by others, being criticized by others or feeling inferior to others. Situations surrounding actual school issues should be considered, such as riding on the school bus, eating in the school lunchroom, using the public washrooms and undressing in the gym locker rooms. Issues of body image may be involved. Often the child's mother covertly remembers her own phobic behavior or has anxieties about the child and needs supportive help to not convey her anxieties to the child.

Treatment of a child who avoids school should be regarded as a crisis intervention. The goal should be to get the child back in school as soon as possible and attending regularly with less fear and more confidence to meet the daily challenges, whether in the classroom, the playground or the gym.

With appropriate counseling and conferences with teachers or other school officials, children and parents can develop a new understanding of the anxieties regarding school attendance. There is some evidence linking early history of school phobia with later occurrences of panic disorder and agoraphobia.

Fear of school, or school phobia, is known as didaskaleinophobia.

See also ANXIETY DISORDERS; PHOBIA.

Andreasen, Nancy C., and Black, Donald W. *Introductory Textbook of Psychiatry*. Washington, D.C.: American Psychiatric Association, 1991.

seasonal affective disorder (SAD)
Seasonal affective disorder is characterized by severe mood swings corresponding to the change of seasons. Typically, depression occurs more often during the winter months and remissions or changes from depression to mania during the spring. A diagnosis can be made once the individual has exhibited this pattern of illness in three separate years, and when seasonally timed episodes outnumber nonseasonal episodes by three to one.

Therapy may include bright lights that extend the hours of bright illumination during short winter days, in addition to psychotherapy and possible medication.

See also AFFECTIVE DISORDERS; DEPRESSION; MOOD; DEPRESSION AND AFFECTIVE DISORDERS in BIBLIOGRAPHY.

Waldinger, Robert J. *Psychiatry for Medical Students,* (2d ed.) Washington, D.C.: American Psychiatric Press, 1991.

secondary depression
A depression occurring in an individual who has another illness—either mental or physical—that precedes the depression. Depression may accompany psychiatric disorders, such as obsessive-compulsive disorder, alcohol abuse or alcoholism (most common), and it may occur after or along with a medical illness. Careful evaluation of secondary depression is essential to determining the cause and course of treatment.

See also ANTIDEPRESSANT MEDICATIONS; DEPRESSION; DEPRESSION AND AFFECTIVE DISORDERS in BIBLIOGRAPHY.

security object
A special object, such as a blanket or a favorite toy, that gives a young child reassurance and comfort. Many children sleep with their security object or take it with them wherever they go. If the item is lost or taken away, the child will become extremely distressed until it is returned.

sedative drug
One of many substances that tend to moderate or tranquilize (sedate) a person's state of mind and help induce sleep. Many drugs have sedative side effects; examples include antianxiety drugs, antipsychotic drugs, some antidepressant drugs and some sleeping medications. Many sedative side effects decrease as the patient takes the medication over time, and the patient accommodates to the side effects. Many

people receive sedative drugs before surgery.

See also BARBITURATE DRUGS; CENTRAL NERVOUS SYSTEM; HYPNOTIC DRUGS.

seizures A sudden episode of uncontrolled electrical activity in the brain. Symptoms may be as subtle as a twitching of a small area of the body—such as the face or an arm or leg—or more severe, causing a convulsion of the body. Consciousness is almost always lost during a seizure. Recurrent seizures are known as epilepsy. Seizures can occur because of infection, head injury, brain tumor or stroke (cerebrovascular accident) or may be alcohol-related.

See also ANTICONVULSANT MEDICATIONS; CONVULSIONS; EPILEPSY.

selegiline A medication (trade name: Deprenyl) that slows the progress of Parkinson's disease. It was approved for use in the United States in 1989. It is a monoamine oxidase (MAO) Type B inhibitor at low doses that increases brain dopamine level; at higher doses it inhibits MAO Type A and may be useful for depression.

See also PARKINSON'S DISEASE.

self-esteem Liking, respecting and accepting oneself and appreciating one's self-worth. In the 1990s, self-esteem has been targeted as a major characteristic of good mental health. Low self-esteem can lead to mental and physical disorders, such as depression, poor appetite, sleeplessness and headaches.

People tend to compare themselves with others, their own standards and standards set for them by others. If they think they do not measure up, they have low self-esteem. Such individuals may feel inferior, either intellectually or physically, while individuals with high self-esteem feel confident and capable. People with low self-esteem often depend on approval from others. Some become

workaholics, and some become totally dependent on outside approval.

Lack of self-esteem can be life threatening, particularly in young people when it is a major factor in suicide. Lack of self-esteem has been pointed to as a cause for many social ills, including juvenile delinquency, crime and substance abuse. While it may not be the most important causative factor, it usually plays a role.

Causes of low self-esteem vary among individuals, but there are many common themes. For example, many people have low self-esteem because of physical appearance. Obesity is a common situation; this can be overcome by seeking counseling regarding a diet and exercise program. Some adults have lifelong low self-esteem because of a prominent facial feature, such as a misshapen nose or ear; with counseling and possibly cosmetic surgery, improvements can be made in both outlook and appearance. But some people have obsessional ideas about unattractive body features (dysmorphophobia), which seems to be a subtype of obsessive-compulsive disorder; this should be understood and treated.

There are other common physical causes of low self-esteem. Child abuse, whether sexually or psychological, can be a major factor. Abused spouses and lovers also suffer from low self-esteem. Being bullied or criticized in school can also harm a child's confidence and self-worth.

Some children lose their self-esteem on the athletic fields because they do not compete well or do not have the physical ability to keep up with others. Other children lose self-esteem in the classroom when they find doing math or science difficult and are advised to pursue other avenues of career choice. Simple comments by teachers can ruin a child's self-esteem; for example, when a child is told that he cannot sing well and should just mouth the words, he may lose his confidence in ever trying to sing again. A high school student criticized because of lack of public speaking ability may become afraid of standing up in front of a crowd. In such cases, lack of self-esteem can lead to social fears and phobias.

In a Gallup poll in early 1992, 612 adults were interviewed by telephone. Respondents were asked about situations that would make them feel very bad about themselves. Situations included not being able to pay bills, being tempted into doing something immoral, having an abortion, getting a divorce, losing a job, feeling they had disobeyed God, being noticeably overweight, doing something embarrassing in public and being criticized by someone they admire. People over 50 years of age were more likely to feel bad about these situations than younger people. However, overall, 63 percent said that time and effort spent on self-esteem is worthwhile; only 34 percent said that time and effort could be better spent on work.

Extreme over-inflation of self-esteem is a characteristic of manic behavior. An individual may feel extremely powerful and influential and may even experience delusions. Narcissistic individuals act as if they feel very important, but in fact they rely constantly on external support for money, clothes, important friends and success to counteract their inner emptiness and low self-esteem.

See also BODY IMAGE; CODEPENDENCY; CRITICISM; DEPRESSION; INFERIORITY COMPLEX; SCHOOL PHOBIA; SUICIDE.

Kahn, Ada P., and Kimmel, Sheila. *Self-Esteem.* New York: Avon Books. In press.

self-help groups   These consist of people who share a common experience and wish to assist one another with or without the use of a trained mental health professional. Such groups became popular during the 1970s and continue to be so. Central to a self-help group is the idea of sharing feelings, perceptions and problems with others who have had the same experience. The group can pass on practical advice to new members, such as what life is like after divorce or how to cope with aging parents.

The National Self-Help Clearinghouse can provide information about groups throughout the United States, as well as books and pamphlets on how to start a group and what to look for in an existing group.

For information, contact:

National Self-Help Clearinghouse
33 West 42nd St.
New York, NY 10036
Phone: (212) 642-2944

self-help techniques   During the 1990s, American society has been offered self-help in the form of magazine articles, radio call-in shows, television talk shows, speakers, support groups, audio and video tapes. Self-help can work if the individual is motivated to make it work. In fact, even with psychotherapy under the guidance of a mental health professional, much of the improvement in a person's mental health actually comes from self-help.

Self-help techniques include meditation and progressive relaxation. Both are skills that can be learned and applied to relieve many mental health concerns, such as stress, anxiety and phobias.

Many individuals join self-help groups or support groups to learn various techniques for particular situations.

See also ANXIETY; MEDITATION; STRESS.

self psychology   A term for the psychological system propounded by Heinz Kohut (1913–1981), an Austrian-born American psychoanalyst. This theory holds that all behavior can be interpreted in reference to the self. He proposed that the young child has tendencies toward assertiveness and ambition as well as tendencies toward idealization of parents and the beginnings of ideals and values. Both groups of tendencies contribute to strong ties between the infant and parent. He believed that the real mover of psychic development is the self, rather than sexual and aggressive drives, as Sigmund Freud suggested. Kohut used the term ''self-object'' to describe an object in an infant's surrounding that the infant regards as part of him- or herself. People with narcissistic personality disorder cannot separate adequately from the selfobject and thus cannot perceive or respond to the individuality of others. Kohut believed that lack of emphatic response between parent and infant is the cause of later psychological disorders in the growing child.

Kohut developed his major theories in several publications, including *The Analysis of the Self* (1971), *The Restoration of the Self* (1977) and *The Search for the Self* (1978).

self-talk   See AFFIRMATION.

senile dementia   See DEMENTIA; SENILITY.

senility   Changes in mental ability brought on by old age, including impaired memory and reduced ability to concentrate. Dementia affects about one in five individuals over age 80.

See also DEMENTIA; MEMORY.

sensate-focus-oriented therapy   The approach developed by Masters and Johnson to overcome sexual difficulties involving training sessions in which both partners learn to think and feel sensually by progressively touching, stroking, fondling, kissing and massaging all parts of their mate's body. The therapy also includes a complete history of each partner's attitudes, steps toward improvement in communication between the partners and at-home practice.

See also SEX THERAPY; SEXUAL DYSFUNCTION.

sense of humor   See LAUGHTER.

separation anxiety   A distressed feeling one experiences when separated from parents or individuals with whom one has an attachment. Infants and toddlers normally experience anxiety about separation from parents or caregivers, but the intensity usually diminishes by the time the child is four to five years old. Children who fear separation cry, cling to the parent and demand to be held and cuddled.

In childhood, symptoms of separation may be headaches, stomachaches and other vague complaints in an effort to keep the parent from leaving or to keep the child from going off to school. School phobia, or school refusal, is sometimes a case of separation anxiety rather than a fear of being bullied or a fear of failure. What some children fear is that something dreadful will happen to their parent(s) if they are away or that the parent will not be there when the child returns.

Sometimes the parent (usually the mother) has fears of danger when her child is away from her, which gets transmitted to the child and augments the child's fears. This means that often the mother of a child with separation anxiety may need supportive psychotherapy to help the child. There is some evidence that a child who has a history of separation anxiety is associated with panic attacks and agoraphobia as an adult.

See also AGORAPHOBIA; SCHOOL PHOBIA; SECURITY OBJECT.

serotonin   A neurotransmitter (also known as hydroxytryptamine, 5-hydroxytryptamine or 5-HT) found in the central nervous system, in many tissues, in the lining of the digestive tract and in the brain. Serotonin influences sleep and emotional arousal and is indirectly involved in the psychobiology of depression and impulsive behavior. It may be that low levels of serotonin are a factor in the development of depression and impulsive, sometimes violent behavior. Some antidepressant drugs increase the levels of serotonin and norepinephrine, another neurotransmitter. Serotonin is derived from tryptophan, an essential amino acid found throughout the body and in the brain. Serotonin stimulates smooth muscles (involuntary muscles such as in the intestinal wall) and constricts blood vessels. Serotonin was identified in the 1950s.

See also ANTIDEPRESSANT MEDICATIONS; DEPRESSION; NEUROTRANSMITTERS.

sertraline hydrochloride An antidepressant drug (trade name: Zoloft). This medication is indicated for the symptomatic relief of depressive illness. It should not be taken along with monoamine oxidase inhibitors.

See also ANTIDEPRESSANT MEDICATIONS; DEPRESSION; SEROTONIN.

sex addiction According to Joel Z. Spike, D.D., associate professor and director of Education and Drug Prevention, Southeastern College of Osteopathic Medicine, North Miami Beach, Florida, sex addiction meets the criteria of addiction that we tend to use, including compulsive behavior, loss of control and continuing behavior despite knowing the negative consequences.

Men are more affected with sexual addictions than women; Dr. Spike reports the ratio as being about eight to one. Sexual addictions occur in all socioeconomic groups; concurrent psychopathology may or may not be present. About 90 percent of sex addicts have other types of addictions. In a study from the Sexual Dependency Unit of Golden Valley Health Care Center, Golden Valley, Minnesota, in which 85 percent of patients were male, 42 percent of whom had incomes above $30,000, 58 percent were college graduates, and half were married. According to Dr. Spike, "These people are totally preoccupied with sex. They feel a compulsion to have sexual activity, which while not pleasurable for them, is a way of relieving stress and anxiety. They repeatedly have sexual activity followed by guilt, shame and depression. It is not unusual for these men

to have literally thousands of partners in a year."

About 87 percent of male sex addicts come from dysfunctional families in which some addictions or substance abuse occurred. Many male sex addicts have backgrounds of childhood physical, sexual or emotional abuse. Many were victims of sexual trauma, such as seductions or incest.

Lives of sex addicts revolve around compulsivity, having experiences and recovering from the experiences. Addicts spend large amounts of time every day with their activity; many have financial problems, spending thousands of dollars on massage parlors, prostitutes, phone sex and pornography. Very often there are also major family issues, causing these men to seek relationship counseling.

Recognizing Sex Addiction in Men   The most notable signs are presence of a sexually transmitted disease, urinary tract symptoms and depression. Sex addicts want help, even though they show excessive reliance on denial. Sex addicts express cognitive distortions including denial, minimization, rationalization, suspicion, paranoia and self-delusion. Addicts work hard to maintain their secret and believe that they are the only one who feels such severe pain.

Most sex addicts have feelings of low self-esteem and isolation, and some may come in for treatment with ideas of suicide. They have basic beliefs about themselves that they are bad and unworthy people and feel unlovable as they are. They suffer from "stroke hunger" and want attention. They feel a major conflict with their own role system, values and morals.

Sex addiction involves a continuum of compulsive behavior and loss of control. Behavioral abnormalities may include reduced community involvement and social interactions, as well as family, employment and legal problems. Risking increasing consequences to achieve more exciting highs indicates an escalation of a sexual addiction. Individuals often escalate within their own levels. Level I addiction involves exaggeration of behaviors considered normal, acceptable or tolerable. Such behaviors, however, are carried out compulsively; there is anonymous sexual behavior.

Level II addictions involve even greater risks of social, moral and legal sanctions. The addict may be a "nuisance" offender, such as a voyeur or "flasher"; he may be perceived by others as pathetic. Escalation may place him at risk of inflicting damage to others and of legal consequences for himself in committing incest, rape or pedophilia.

Treatment To treat a sex addiction, the patient must be drug-free. According to Dr. Spike, "Any substance abuse or dependency must be treated before beginning active treatment of the sex addiction." Sexual addiction is more difficult to treat than drug dependency or alcoholism. One must help the patient develop communication skills, deal with the issues of truth and improve cognitive distortions. Behavioral therapy may help in treating sexually dysfunctional individuals as they come out of other addictions.

Treatment for sex addiction may consist of abstinence, education, medication and group, co-joined and individual therapy. Group therapy helps because it breaks down denial more than can be done in individual therapy. In some programs, addicts enter into an eight-week celibacy contract, avoiding all forms of sexual expression, including masturbation and fantasy, that may act as a bridge between their past and future.

See also SEXUAL DYSFUNCTION in BIBLIOGRAPHY.

Sex Anxiety Inventory (SAI)
A questionnaire used by therapists with individuals in counseling for sexual anxieties. Responses to the SAI give some indications of the individual's sexual attitudes, experiences and possible basis for anxieties. Developed in 1974, the 25-item questionnaire permits the respondent to select alternative answers.

See also SEX THERAPY; SEXUAL FEARS.

Janda, L. H., and O'Grady, K. E. "Development of a Sex Anxiety Inventory." *Journal of Consulting and Clinical Psychology* 48 (1980).

Kleinknecht, Ronald A. *The Anxious Self.* New York: Human Sciences Press, 1986.

Klorman, R.; Weerts, T. C.; Hastings, J. E.; Melamed, B. G.; and Lang, P. J. "Psychometric Description of Some Specific-Fear Questionnaires." *Behavior Therapy* 5 (1974).

sex appeal Attractiveness to the opposite sex, including some arousal of sexual interest and desire. A person who has sex appeal may be said to be "sexy" based on cultural patterns and personal tastes. In Western society, standards of what constitutes sex appeal are often established by film and media. Many Americans find men who are muscular and athletic sexy, while many men find relatively slim women attractive. Healthy, good-looking faces, attractive hair and an attractive body shape are generally the attributes of sex appeal in the United States today. Individuals with these characteristics are pictured in advertisements and in films. At other periods in history, such as during the Renaissance, plumper women were considered attractive. This tendency was shown in the paintings of Peter Paul Rubens, a Flemish painter, whose nudes gave our vocabulary the term "Rubenesque" to refer to the well-developed and heavier body shape.

See also BODY IMAGE; EATING DISORDERS; BODY IMAGE in BIBLIOGRAPHY.

sex drive The desire to have sexual activity. This drive varies in strength in different women and men and at different ages and stages of life in the same individual. Differences may be due to inhibitions about sexual activity produced by parental attitudes toward sex and those of peer groups. One's expression of sex drive may differ also, according to whether or not one has a partner. For example, sex researchers have found that some widowed postmenopausal women who have no partner do not believe that their sex drive is very strong, while women in the same peer group who date and have regular, attractive male companions feel a strong sex drive.

Although some researchers believe that sex drive decreases with age, many senior adults will attest to the fact that sex drive can persist throughout all stages of life. Good health, freedom from chronic disease and companionship with others of the opposite sex stimulate the sex drive to continue until older age.

See also LIBIDO; SEX THERAPY.

sexism   An attitude or belief that one sex is superior to the other for certain situations. Usually the term refers to male attitudes about women, such as "women in public office might cry if they are upset" or "a woman shouldn't be trained for a highly paying job because she will leave to have children." To a large extent the women's liberation movement during the latter half of the 20th century fought and overcame sexism.

See also SEXUAL HARASSMENT; WOMEN'S LIBERATION MOVEMENT; SEXISM AND SEX DISCRIMINATION in BIBLIOGRAPHY.

sex object   A person or object (such as a fetish) toward which one's sexual attractions are drawn. In common use, the term is considered derogatory, as many women (and sometimes men) resent being considered primarily as objects for arousal and gratification.

See also WOMEN'S LIBERATION MOVEMENT; SEXISM AND SEX DISCRIMINATION in BIBLIOGRAPHY.

sex therapy   Counseling and treatment of sexual difficulties that are not due to physical causes. Many people are helped by a combination of sex therapy and marital counseling. The purpose of sex therapy is to reduce anxieties the couple has about sexual activity and increase their enjoyment of their relationship. In sex therapy, couples learn about normal sexual behavior and to reduce their anxieties about sex by gradually engaging in increasingly intimate activities. Couples learn to communicate better with each other regarding sexual matters and preferences and to retrain their approaches and response patterns.

Sex therapists use several techniques. One is sensate-focus therapy, in which the couple explores pleasurable activities in a relaxed manner without sexual sensations. The couple might start with massage of nonerogenous areas of the body. Gradually, as anxieties diminish, the couple progresses to stimulation of sexual areas and finally to sexual intercourse.

Other techniques sex therapists use are directed toward reducing premature ejaculation, relieving vaginismus (muscle spasm of the vagina) and helping both partners reach orgasm.

For sexual problems related to physical causes or illness, individuals should consult a physician, particularly specialists in gynecology or urology.

See also ANORGASMIA; DYSPAREUNIA; EJACULATION; ORGASM; SENSATE-FOCUS-ORIENTED THERAPY; SEXUAL FEARS; SEXUAL FULFILLMENT.

Kahn, Ada P., and Holt, Linda Hughey. *The A to Z of Women's Sexuality*. Alameda, Calif.: Hunter House, 1992.

sexual abuse   The forced participation of an unwilling individual in sexual activity by use of direct or implied threats. Abuse may involve actual physical contact, acts of exhibitionism or indecent exposure between adults and children. Fear of sexual abuse is known as agraphobia or contrectophobia. Sexual abuse occurs at all ages, from infants through older-age adults.

See also ABUSE; DISSOCIATION; DOMESTIC VIOLENCE; FAMILY VIOLENCE; INCEST; MULTIPLE PERSONALITY DISORDER; RAPE, RAPE PREVENTION AND RAPE TRAUMA SYNDROME.

Matas, M., and Marriott, A. "The Girl Who Cried Wolf: Pseudologia Phantastica and Sexual Abuse.'' *Canadian Journal of Psychiatry* 32 (May 1987).

Walker, Edward, et al. ''Relationship of Chronic Pelvic Pain to Psychiatric Diagnoses and Childhood Sexual Abuse.'' *American Journal of Psychiatry* 145, no. 1 (Jan. 1988).

sexual anxiety   See COITUS; SEX THERAPY; SEXUAL FEARS.

sexual disorders   Abnormalities of sexuality, which could include physical maldevelopment of the sexual organs but most commonly refers to abnormalities of sexual function.

See also SEX THERAPY.

sexual dysfunction   Any condition that interferes with the process leading to and including coitus. Masters and Johnson estimated that 50 percent of American marriages were affected by some form of sexual dysfunction. Individuals may have temporary dysfunctions or situations that persist throughout life. Use of some prescription drugs may cause sexual dysfunction for some individuals; in some cases, other similar drugs may be substituted by a physician that do not have these unpleasant side effects.

To some extent, sexual dysfunction is culturally defined; for example, anorgasmia in women was considered proper and even desirable in the Victorian era but is considered a dysfunction at present. Homosexuality and masturbation have at different times been considered abnormal and at other times normal behavior. Present forms of female sexual dysfunction include anorgasmia, painful sexual intercourse (dyspareunia) and vaginismus. Examples of male sexual dysfunctions include impotence, difficulty in maintaining erection, premature ejaculation and retarded ejaculation.

See also ANORGASMIA; DYSPAREUNIA; IMPOTENCE; ORGASM; SEX THERAPY; SEXUAL RESPONSE CYCLE; VAGINISMUS.

Avery-Clark, Constance. ''Sexual Dysfunction and Disorder Patterns of Working and Non-

working Wives.'' *Journal of Sex and Marital Therapy* 12, no. 2 (Summer 1986).

Brown, Pamela. ''Sexual Dysfunction in Women.'' *Canadian Family Physician* 35 (June 1989).

Buffum, John. ''Pharmacology Update: Prescription Drugs and Sexual Function.'' *Journal of Psychoactive Drugs* 18, no. 2 (April–June 1986).

De Amicis, Lyn A., et al. ''Clinical Follow-up of Couples Treated for Sexual Dysfunction.'' *Archives of Sexual Behavior* 14, no. 6 (1985).

Newman, Amy S., and Bertelson, Amy D. ''Sexual Dysfunction in Diabetic Women.'' *Journal of Behavioral Medicine* 9, no. 3 (1986).

Pinhas, Valerie. ''Sexual Dysfunction in Women Alcoholics.'' *Medical Aspects of Human Sexuality* (June 1987).

sexual fears   Many people have fears that impair or weaken their sexual responses to partners. For example, some women are afraid of experiencing pain during intercourse or that they will not experience orgasm. Some men fear that they will not be able to achieve or maintain an erection long enough for a satisfactory experience.

Ill health can cause people to fear that they will not be able to enjoy sexually fulfilling experiences. For example, some people after surgery fear being hurt by their partner or hurting their partner during sexual activity.

The threat of acquiring a sexually transmitted disease (STD) or the HIV virus (known as the cause of AIDS) is a contemporary fear of many people who are not in monogamous relationships. These fears can largely be overcome by the use of ''safe sex'' practices.

See also BEHAVIORAL THERAPY; DYSPAREUNIA; SAFE SEX; SEX THERAPY; SEXUAL DYSFUNCTIONS.

sexual fulfillment   A feeling of contentment after a pleasurable and satisfying sexual encounter. An individual has a feeling of intense fulfillment in the orgasmic and resolution phases of the sexual response cycle. This is accompanied by a feeling of extreme relaxation, sometimes a "high" feeling and emotional closeness with the partner.

See also ORGASM.

sexual harassment   Unwanted and uninvited sexual attentions whether from men toward women, women toward men or toward same-sex individuals. Such attentions may include jokes and remarks, questions about the other's sexual behavior, "accidental" touching and repeated and unwanted invitations for a date or for a sexual relationship.

In 1980, a U.S. Supreme Court decision *(Meritor v. Vinson)* declared that sexual harassment is a form of sex discrimination and therefore a violation of Title VII of the 1964 Civil Rights Act.

In 1991, sexual harassment received national attention when Anita Hill, a female lawyer, accused Judge Clarence Thomas, a nominee for the U.S. Supreme Court, of sexual harassment and the federal hearing was nationally televised.

During the 1980s American society became increasingly aware of sexual harassment. For example, in the study by the U.S. Merit Systems Protection Board reported in 1988, federal workers were more inclined to define certain types of behavior as sexual harassment than in 1980. In 1987, 42 percent of women and 14 percent of men employed by the federal government said they experienced some form of uninvited and unwanted sexual attention. Federal workers in the survey believed that sexual harassment was not worse in the federal government than in the private sector.

Federal workers reported that the most frequently experienced type of uninvited sexual attention was "unwanted sexual teasing, jokes, remarks or questions." The least frequently experienced type of harassment, "actual or attempted rape or assault," is also arguably the most severe. When victims of sexual harassment took positive action in response to unwanted sexual attention, it was largely informal action and, in many cases,

Cost of Sexual Harassment

Item	Total (million)
Job turnover	$36.7
Sick leave	26.1
Individual productivity	76.3
Work group productivity	128.2
Total	$267.3

SOURCE: *Sexual Harassment in the Federal Government: An Update.* U.S. Merit Systems Protection Board, Washington, D.C., June, 1988.

was judged to be effective. For both sexes, simply asking or telling the offender to stop improved the situation most frequently. Threatening to tell others or telling others was the second most effective action for women, while avoiding the person(s) was the second most effective action for men.

Sexual harassment during the survey period of May 1985 through May 1987 cost the federal government an estimated $267 million. The accompanying chart indicates these costs.

sexual identity   An individual's biologically determined sex orientation.

See also GENDER IDENTITY.

sexuality   The ability to think and behave as a sexual being; also, any aspect of human thought or behavior that has sexual meaning. Sexuality implies a self-concept of oneself as a sexual being as well as having the capacity to respond to erotic stimuli and sexual activity. Sexuality encompasses being comfortable with sexual fantasies and erotic zones of the body as well as with one's own gender identity, although no specific set of behaviors or sexual preference is necessary to have a good sense of one's own sexuality. There are social, psychological and biologic dimensions to human sexuality.

sexually transmitted diseases (STDs)   Sexually transmitted diseases is the term given to a group of diseases that affect both men and women and are generally transmitted during sexual intercourse. These diseases cause discomfort, may lead to infertility and may be life threatening. They cause psychological distress for many reasons, including a need to communicate one's problem to one's partner and a need to disclose information about past sexual activities. The term "safe sex" relates to prevention of STDs as well as AIDS.

Historically, syphilis and gonorrhea were referred to as venereal diseases long before the term STD was coined during the latter part of the 20th century. Several STDs became notably widespread during the 1980s. These include herpes, chlamydia, hepatitis B, pubic lice, genital warts and other vaginal infections. Syphilis and gonorrhea are still prevalent, and some sources say they are on the increase owing to the upswing in other concurrent STDs.

Concerns about STDs are prevalent among individuals who are widowed or divorced and who begin seeking new partners after their loss, as well as among never-married individuals. Fears of acquiring STDs have led many formerly sexually active people to seek fewer sexual partners. Such concerns have also increased the use of condoms, as they are thought to reduce the likelihood of spreading most STDs (as well as AIDS).

Herpes   Herpes (technically known as Herpes simplex or herpes virus hominus) outbreaks cause either single or multiple blisters that occur on mucous membranes such as lips or the vagina. Herpes simplex I causes most oral "cold sores." Herpes simplex II causes most genital herpes. Transmission can occur when a herpes blister comes in contact with any mucous membrane or open cut or sore. Herpes is most often transmitted through sexual intercourse and can also be transmitted during mouth-genital contact or with manual contact during heterosexual or homosexual relations.

Herpes can be debilitating in an active stage. Herpes recurs and often attacks when the previously infected individual is under stress, fatigued or has another illness. Women who know that they have the herpes infection are concerned about giving birth to a baby who may also have herpes, as the infection can be transmitted to the baby during the birth process. Women who have active vaginal herpes blisters are routinely given cesarean sections.

Many individuals who have herpes take drugs to relieve the pain of the blisters and prophylactically (as a preventive) to reduce the severity of future attacks. A medication in the form of a cream is also available.

Chlamydia   Chlamydia is two or three times more common than gonorrhea but less well known. It is only in the latter quarter of the 20th century that information about this disease has appeared in the medical and popular press. Chlamydia is feared because untreated infections in women can lead to infections in the fallopian tubes and uterus (pelvic inflammatory disease). The disease affects men and women, but women are less likely to notice symptoms in early stages. The signs in women are unusual vaginal discharge, irregular bleeding, bleeding after intercourse or deep pain during and after intercourse. Men may notice clear, mucus-like discharge from the penis and burning during urination. Chlamydia is treated with antibiotics, and sexual partners must be treated to avoid a ping-pong effect of reinfection. Thus, when one individual discovers that he or she has it, psychological concerns arise regarding telling the partner(s) and encouraging treatment for both.

Hepatitis B   This infection may develop about two months after sexual activity. It is usually acquired during sexual intercourse with an infected individual. Hepatitis B is common in underdeveloped countries and among intravenous drug users in the United States. People who are concerned about getting Hepatitis B can obtain an immunization against it; the immunization is recommended for health care workers and for household and sexual contacts of infected individuals.

Pubic Lice   These are tiny bugs, also known as "crab lice" or "crabs," that burrow into the skin and suck blood. They thrive on hairy parts of the body, including the pubic mound, outer lips of the vulva, underarms, the head and even eyebrows and eyelashes. Eggs take from seven to nine days to hatch; persons infected may notice itching one to three weeks after exposure. The most direct way of acquiring pubic lice is through sexual or close physical contact with an infected person's body. However, pubic lice can also be transmitted by shared towels or bed sheets. Pubic lice is commonly treated with a standard pesticide (known in the United States as Kwell) that is also used for head lice. Those who have pubic lice (or live in the same household with someone who has them) can reduce risks of spread by washing towels and bedding with disinfectant, such as household bleach, in boiling water and drying the items in a hot dryer to be sure of killing off the unhatched eggs of the lice.

Genital Warts   Warts, or small bumps, on the mucous membrane of the vulva, the clitoral hood, in the perineum, inside the vagina, in the anus, on the penis or in the urinary tract may be genital warts. They cause discomfort and anxiety to the sufferer and may be particularly painful during sexual intercourse or when the sufferer wears tight clothing. Genital warts are caused by a sexually transmitted virus and can be removed by a physician. Certain strains of the wart virus have been implicated as a cause of cervical cancer. If either partner has a history of genital warts, a condom should be used during sexual intercourse to reduce transmission of the wart virus.

Gonorrhea and Syphilis   Gonorrhea is caused by a bacterium that can infect the genital organs and spread to other parts of the body. Gonorrhea can cause complications including pelvic inflammatory disease, joint pains, heart disease, liver disease, meningitis and blindness. Gonorrhea has been referred to as the "dose," "clap" or "drip." Gonorrhea is treated with large doses of penicillin, usually injected, often with follow-up doses of oral antibiotics. During the latter part of the 20th century, many cases of penicillin-resistant gonorrhea have appeared, making the disease more fearsome than during the years when penicillin was hailed as the "magic bullet" against the disease. Because there are fewer symptoms in women than men, gonorrhea is usually detected later in women. In a woman, the gonorrhea germs travel to the uterus, fallopian tubes and ovaries. As the disease advances, she may notice abdominal pain. Males may notice painful urination and pus discharging from the penis.

Syphilis, though less common than gonorrhea, can result in serious complications when untreated. Syphilis—also known as "lues," "syph," "pox" and "bad blood"— is caused by a microorganism from the spirochete family. An initial outbreak (primary syphilis) causes a large punched-out lesion called a chancre. After this initial outbreak, symptoms may not recur for several months, when a skin rash, or secondary syphilis, occurs. Years later, central nervous system symptoms in the form of mental aberrations and a stumbling gait may occur (tertiary syphilis). Treatment with penicillin or other antibiotics is usually effective during the early stages of the disease and will prevent complications. Treatment is difficult in the later stages of the disease.

Acquired Immunodeficiency Syndrome (AIDS)   This has become a widely known disease during the latter part of the 20th century. The AIDS virus is known to be transmitted by direct exchange of body fluid, such as semen or blood.

Other Diseases   One commonly known infection is trichomonas, which is caused by microscopic parasitic organisms that live in small numbers in the vagina. The organisms, known as trichomonads, also live under the foreskin of a man's penis or in the urethra, usually without producing any symptoms. Medications are available to combat this infection. However, a treated individual must inform his or her sexual partner so that the partner can also be treated.

Yeast infections (monilia) are not necessarily sexually transmitted diseases, but the organisms also live in the vagina and under the foreskin of the penis and can be transmitted during sexual intercourse. Many women, however, have yeast infections without having had sexual intercourse. Taking antibiotics can trigger a yeast infection by destroying the balance of organisms in the vagina.

Bacterial infections can also be transmitted during sexual intercourse; these are treatable with sulfa creams or oral antibiotics.

Reducing Risks of Acquiring an STD
Although some STDs seem to be increasing in prevalence, people can reduce their risk of these diseases by taking certain precautions:

1. Have a monogamous relationship. Have sexual contact with only one partner who limits contact to you only.
2. Look your partner over. Ask about any suspicious-looking discharges, sores or rashes.
3. Be clean. Partners should bathe before and after sexual intercourse. Wash with soap and water.
4. Use condoms. Condoms provide some (though not complete) protection against STDs. However, the condom must be put on before sexual activity begins and not removed until the end of the activity.
5. Use foam, a diaphragm with spermicides, or sponge spermicides, which kill many infectious agents; these should be used in addition to the condom.
6. Avoid the ping-pong effect of infection. If one partner has an STD, the other partner must be informed and treated at the same time to avoid reinfection.

See also ACQUIRED IMMUNODEFICIENCY SYNDROME.

Kahn, Ada P., and Holt, Linda Hughey. *The A to Z of Women's Sexuality.* Alameda, Calif.: Hunter House, 1992.

sexual response Physiological reaction to sexual stimulation and arousal. In women, vaginal lubrication is an early sign in the sexual response cycle. In men, erection of the penis occurs. Responsiveness is a highly individual matter, largely determined by mutual feelings of love and affection between the partners and a wide variety of emotional and physical circumstances. Levels of responsiveness vary among individuals and vary within the same individual at different times. Many people become anxious about their responses, not realizing that a wide range of differences are considered normal.

See also SEX THERAPY.

sexual revolution Changes in sexual attitudes and behaviors during the 1960s, 1970s and early 1980s. These included more liberal attitudes toward premarital sexual activity, changes in the sexual double standard in which sexual activity is seen as more acceptable for men than for women and more open discussion of women's sexual needs. Changes in the double standard and increases in premarital activity evolved in part as a result of development of better and easier means of birth control, including oral contraceptives during the late 1950s.

For many young people, dating habits during the sexual revolution included sexual intercourse early in the relationship. However, with the recognition of the increase of sexually transmitted diseases and acquired immunodeficiency syndrome (AIDS) in the heterosexual population in the 1980s, many people became more cautious and selective about their choice of sexual partners and monogamy regained favor.

The sexual revolution was closely tied with the Women's Liberation Movement. Many college dormitories became coeducational, offering women more options regarding housing. There was wider acceptance of unmarried adults "living together."

Movies and plays during the sexual revolution included more sexually explicit scenes, and sexuality was discussed more openly in the media.

See also ACQUIRED IMMUNODEFICIENCY SYNDROME; WOMEN'S LIBERATION MOVEMENT.

shell shock   A term that referred to mental disorders that occurred as a result of battle. This term, as well as ''combat fatigue,'' was used during World War I. A newer term for the same syndrome or effects is post-traumatic stress disorder (PTSD). There are still some elderly veterans in Veterans Administration hospitals who are there because of lifelong mental difficulties ensuing after shell shock.

See also POST-TRAUMATIC STRESS SYNDROME.

shift work   Many psychological factors related to adaptation to night-shift work are based on how well the individual handles the interruption of the circadian rhythm. The break in circadian rhythm can affect mental ability, alertness and temperament. Some night-shift workers experience anxiety and lapses in memory as a result of sleep deprivation. Coping mechanisms to combat fatigue, and later to induce sleep, may include overeating, alcohol consumption and use of sedatives and stimulants.

Social needs of night-shift workers are a consideration. For example, the rest of the world operates on a 9 to 5 schedule, with most socialization occurring after work and on weekends. For night-shift people to have a family or social life, they must schedule creatively.

Hurley, Margaret, and Neidlinger, Elizabeth A. *Schumpert Medical Quarterly*, Schumpert Medical Center, Shreveport, La., vol. 9, no. 2 (Oct. 1991).

shock therapy   See ELECTROCONVULSIVE THERAPY.

shopaholism   Stress reduction by shopping that can create a compulsive syndrome. Excessive shopping shares some character-istics with obsessive-compulsive disorder, in which people perform certain rituals to relieve tension. In this way, compulsive shopping is similar to the problems of alcoholics or compulsive gamblers.

Compulsive shoppers buy things in order to make themselves forget the pressures of their lives and make themselves feel good. However, what happens is that it takes more and more spending and buying to improve their moods.

According to Thomas C. O'Guinn of the University of Illinois, probably 2 percent of Americans can be described as compulsive buyers, and another 2 or 3 percent are on the verge. Advertising suggests that shopping is a good way to relieve anxiety.

In a symposium on compulsive buying during a conference of the American Psychological Association in San Francisco in September 1991, advertisers and store owners drew some blame for encouraging irresponsible spending, as did credit card companies. Stores that are most tempting to compulsive buyers feature soft lights and music, in which reality is shut out and the customers can indulge in fantasy; some gambling casinos have similar characteristics. After studying hundreds of compulsive buyers, O'Guinn concluded that such buyers have a knack for deluding themselves when they want to buy something. They believe that they will have the money to pay for the items when the bills come, but they really will not.

Many people who are normally good about balancing their budget overbuy around holidays. According to Dr. James Jefferson, director of the Center for Affective Disorders, University of Wisconsin Hospital and Clinics and professor of psychiatry at the University of Wisconsin Medical School, for people who are compulsive shoppers, the problem can be magnified during holidays. Excessive shopping can be attributed in part to an attempt to promote a better self-image through buying multiple or expensive gifts. For others, gift giving is seen as a way to change people's perceptions about the giver, to make an economic statement or to serve as a substitute for other, weaker aspects of the relationship.

Evan Steffans, consulting therapist for Shopper Stoppers, a support group for addictive spenders in Dayton, Ohio, has some tips for shopaholics:

Work Out Your Stress Most people with addictive illnesses do not know how to cope with stress. Learn alternatives to blotting out the stress, which is what the shopping does.

Develop Social Outlets Cultivate groups of friends with whom you can share activities as a healthful alternative to shopping.

Exercise Physical exercise is a good stress reliever and will clear the mind for better concentration later on.

While it is impossible to give up shopping entirely, compulsive shoppers who understand their addiction can help themselves by following a few reminders:

- Shop with a list and buy only what is on the list.
- Shop with a partner who will help you resist temptations.
- Do not browse.
- Avoid sales. The excitement can trigger a shopping spree.
- Avoid use of credit cards. Use them only for business, if you need to.

Debtors Anonymous is a Chicago-area support group for overspenders based on the 12-step recovery program of Alcoholics Anonymous. DA members work toward financial solvency the way AA members work toward abstinence. Experienced DA members review new members' finances and help them formulate an action plan for resolving debts and a spending plan for the future. DA members look to one another for support, hope and strength in dealing with the stresses of indebtedness.

For information, contact:

Debtors Anonymous
Phone: (312) 274-DEBT.
or

Debtors Anonymous
P.O. Box 20322
New York, NY 10025–9992

See also OBSESSIVE-COMPULSIVE DISORDER; OBSESSIVE-COMPULSIVE DISORDER in BIBLIOGRAPHY.

Moore, Judy Kay. "Holiday Shopping Can Be Compulsive For Some: UW Expert." *Feature Story,* Center for Health Sciences, University of Wisconsin—Madison (Nov. 1991).

Nilsson, Pam. "No, It Won't Kill You . . . But Shopaholism Will Murder Your Bank Account." *Today's Chicago Woman,* November 1991.

"shotgun" wedding   See UNWED MOTHERS.

sibling rivalry   Competition between brothers and/or sisters is normal. The first situation occurs after the birth of a new baby, when an older sibling feels "displaced" and constantly seeks to command the parents' attention. Feelings of rivalry may persist throughout life. One child may be continuously compared with another in the family, and the parents may influence the feeling of rivalry by showing one child as the better example. Throughout school, brothers and sisters may feel competitive with one another in order to gain more affection from their parents.

Personality differences may account for sibling rivalry. For example, while one child may be extroverted, have an outgoing personality and make friends easily, another child in the family may be more introspective and find it difficult to mingle in new groups of children. The quieter child may be jealous of the other child, even though he excels in academic skills, while the child with many friends may be jealous of her sibling's academic achievements.

Sibling rivalry may persist even after the death of parents, when brothers and sisters become jealous over uneven distribution of their parents' possessions.

See also JEALOUSY.

sick building syndrome Symptoms experienced by people who work in office buildings, including headaches, itchy eyes, nose and throat and tiredness. These symptoms may be caused by air conditioning systems, fluorescent lighting systems and not enough ventilation. More important, the symptoms may be caused by the frustration of feeling closed in and not being able to control the amount of heat or light in the immediate environment.

When one employee in such a building starts complaining, the situation takes on a "ripple effect," with others believing that they too have headaches as a result of the workplace. The notion of becoming ill from the building in which one works is not entirely farfetched, when one considers the outbreak of Legionnaire's disease—a form of pneumonia—that occurred among American Legion conventioneers in a Philadelphia hotel during the 1970s from bacteria in the air conditioning system. Tests identified the organisms responsible for the disease as a contaminant of water systems that had been responsible for earlier epidemics of pneumonia, although the cause had not been understood earlier.

side effects of drugs Results that occur after taking medications that are unrelated to the hoped-for effect. Not all individuals experience the same side effects. Usually individuals are warned about possible side effects of medications, such as dry mouth as a common side effect of some antidepressant drugs. Other common side effects of some drugs include dizziness, nausea and constipation. Sometimes side effects occur because of synergism between drugs (additive effects) or an individual's allergies.

When an individual experiences side effects of a prescription medication, this situation should be discussed with the prescribing physician. Some people choose to stop taking their medication because of a side effect, and when this occurs, they are putting themselves at risk for the more severe consequences of their unmedicated condition.

SIDS See SUDDEN INFANT DEATH SYNDROME.

sign An objective indication of a disorder that is observed or detected by a physician or another person as opposed to indications reported by the individual, which are known as symptoms. For example, repeated bruises on a child may be a sign to a physician that the child is a victim of child abuse. On the other hand, headaches, which the physician cannot see, may be reported by a patient and may be a symptom of underlying disease.

See also SYMPTOM.

Sinequan Trade name for doxepin hydrochloride, a tricyclic antidepressant drug. The usefulness of Sinequan is comparable to that of imipramine in the treatment of depressive episodes of major depression and bipolar disorder. It may also be effective in the depressive periods of dysthymic disorder and in atypical depression.

See also ANTIDEPRESSANT MEDICATIONS; DEPRESSION.

SK-Pramine See IMIPRAMINE HYDROCHLORIDE.

sleep Recurring periods of relative physical and psychological disengagement from one's environment. Sleep-related problems are among the most common complaints individuals have when they visit physicians or other therapists. Depression seems to be a major factor that interferes with sleep, causing some individuals to sleep too much and preventing others from getting to sleep or sleeping through the night. Sleep in individuals with a chronic illness or pain is often interrupted.

Sleep patterns vary with age, state of health, medication and psychological state. Sleeping habits affect most people's moods. Many feel somewhat irritable and short-tempered without adequate sleep. According to Rosalind Cartwright, Ph.D., director of the Sleep Disorder Service at Rush-Presbyterian–St. Luke's Medical Center, Chicago, people who can't fall asleep are usually the complainers and worriers, those who don't learn how to relax before sleeping and those whose minds don't stop to let them relax.

The old adage "early to bed and early to rise" is too generalized a plan for most people, says Dr. Cartwright. There are many individual patterns of sleep that work well. Some elderly people don't go to bed until 4:00 A.M. They stay awake until then, reading, knitting or doing some creative work. They wake up at 8:00 A.M. when everyone else does and they feel good. Such individuals once went to bed at midnight and worried about staying awake for hours; now they turn those hours into doing something constructive.

Stages of sleep differ in proportion to how we spend our time during the day. People who do hard physical work do not necessarily need more sleep than sedentary office workers, but their sleep is deeper. According to Dr. Cartwright, they have more prolonged stage 4 sleep at the beginning of the night.

There are some sleep differences between men and women. One difference is that men lose their ability for deep sleep (delta sleep) as they age sooner than women, even though more women complain about insomnia and light sleeping. Men begin to lose their deep sleep in their late forties and fifties, while women continue to have deep sleep later in life.

Sleep Disorders   There are two basic categories of sleep disorders. One is known as DIMS, or disorders of initiating or maintaining sleep. These include difficulty getting to sleep or staying asleep or waking too early. The second category is known as DOES, or disorders of excessive sleep. Characteristics may include falling asleep inappropriately and difficulty in awakening. Such individuals are known as hypersomniacs.

Another common and more serious disorder of sleep is sleep apnea. This consists of brief periods of ceasing to breathe. There may be at least 250,000 people in the United States who cease breathing so often or for such long periods of time at night that they are tired all day and are likely to drift off into sleep at any moment. They must walk around often to fight off sleep. Such individuals can't drive safely.

Signs of sleep apnea are loud snoring, prolonged periods between breaths (apnea), weight gain and elevated blood pressure. Diagnosis of sleep apnea can be made from a tape recording at the bedside of the snorer. If there are repeated pauses of more than 10 seconds between snores, it may mean that the oxygen level in the brain is going down. The person must wake himself to restart the brain. There is treatment for sleep apnea, and it is important that such people be treated because this disorder causes a strain on the heart.

Repetitive Nocturnal Myoclonus   This involves involuntary jerky motions of the legs, episodes of muscle spasms and twitching that disturb sleep. This is an uncomfortable sensation that occurs just before falling asleep. The individual feels an urge to get up and walk around. This sensation may increase with age and, according to some researchers, frequently runs in families. It is more common in individuals age 50 to 60 than in younger people.

Sleep Difficulties of Menopausal Women   Many women experience changes in their sleep patterns around menopause. Some changes may be due to hot flashes or to many other factors involving other individual psychosocial stresses. According to Dudley Dinner, M.D., director of the Sleep Disorders Center, the Cleveland Clinic Foundation, while women may have slept seven to eight hours at age 20, they may decrease up to six or six and a half hours between age 55 and 60. In addition, sleep tends to become more "fragmented." Women in this age group may awaken more often and spend more time awake during the night, although the total time in bed may increase.

Sleep Disturbance Related to Medication Because many medications can cause sleepiness in some individuals, all such medications should be taken only under a physician's supervision. Some medications may make sleep apnea worse.

Medications Used for Inducing Sleep Many individuals have sleeping medications prescribed for them at some time during their life. Often at a time of great bereavement, such as after the death of a spouse or parent, an individual will have difficulty sleeping and can be helped with the assistance of an appropriately prescribed medication for short-term use.

Dreaming Most dreaming takes place during the REM (rapid-eye-movement) stage. Nightmares of being unable to move have a real basis during this phase of sleep because of the limpness of the muscles. Most people forget dreams unless they awaken during a REM period or within 10 minutes afterward.

According to Dr. Cartwright, dreaming has a role in our mental health. This is indicated by the fact that people in poor mental health are distinctly different. ''Dreaming doesn't cause mental illness, but when dreams work well, they help process our emotions of the day. We put our emotions to rest during sleep. When we are upset, our dreaming does not serve us well,'' Dr. Cartwright said.

Research Evaluation of individuals' problems as well as sleep research is carried out in many sleep laboratories across the United States. Sessions for a troubled sleeper in a sleep laboratory depend on the diagnosis and how complex the problem is. Some tests, such as those for narcolepsy—a disorder of excessive daytime sleepiness—are done during the day, with a series of five short naps. However, most sleep lab evaluations are done during the night. Patients are monitored for many things, including naso-oral air flow and heart rate. Insomniacs are tested to determine how much they really

sleep. Typically, many physiological parameters are measured on a 16-channel machine. One person can be measured on 16 channels, or two people on eight channels. There is an intercom from the control room, and researchers can talk to any sleeper in a room or tape-record from any room.

With use of an electroencephalogram (EEG), a graphic depiction of the brain's electrical potentials recorded by scalp electrodes, sleep is divisible into two categories: nonrapid-eye-movement sleep (NREM) and rapid-eye-movement (REM) sleep. Dreaming sleep is another term for REM sleep. There are four stage of NREM sleep. Stage I occurs immediately after sleep begins with a pattern of low amplitude and fast frequency. Stage II has characteristic waves of 12 to 16 cycles per second known as sleep spindles. Stages III and IV have progressive further slowing of frequency and increase in amplitude of the wave forms. After the beginning of sleep, over a period of 90 minutes, a person goes through the four stages of NREM sleep and goes from them into the first period of REM sleep. Dreaming usually occurs during REM sleep, and short cycles (20 to 30 minutes) of REM sleep recur about every 90 minutes throughout the night. This type of sleep is so named because of the coordinated rapid eye movements that occur.

Sleep and Sex Research Sex researchers test individuals' capabilities for sexual arousal while they are asleep to determine if sexual dysfunctions are caused by physiological problems. In males, a penile plethysmograph indicates changes in blood flow and size of the penis as it undergoes erection. In females, a vaginal plethysmograph records vaginal blood flow during sexual arousal. When individuals show indications of high sexual arousal during sleep, psychotherapy often helps them achieve improved sexual function during waking hours.

Snoring Snoring is a serious problem for more than 10 million Americans. It is a problem for the snorer as well as their bed partner or roommate, often causing the other

How to Get a Good Night's Sleep

It takes most people about 15 minutes or less to fall asleep. If you have trouble getting to sleep and staying asleep long enough to feel good throughout the day, try some of these suggestions:

- Drink a cup of warm milk before bedtime. Eat a light snack. Avoid stimulating beverages that contain caffeine, such as coffee, cola beverages and chocolate.
- Take a warm, relaxing bath.
- Relax in bed and read something you enjoy. As your mind becomes engrossed, your muscles will relax. When your body is relaxed, you are likelier to become sleepy and ready for sleep. Watching television may have the same effect.
- Read something you find very dull. When your mind cannot handle what you present, your internal coping mechanism of falling asleep may take over. Watching television may have the same effect.
- Experiment by changing your environment. Make the room warmer or colder. Use different combinations of covers. Some people like the feeling of the "weight" of blankets, while others do not. If you like warmth without weight, use an electric blanket. Some have dual controls so that each bed partner can have individual arrangements.
- Avoid stressful situations before bedtime. Postpone discussions of problems until morning when possible. Avoid lengthy telephone conversations that may upset you before bedtime.
- If you have an argument or tension-filled discussion late at night, don't go to bed mad.
- If you are alone and feel hostile, call a friend and talk. Venting may help you unload and you will sleep better.
- Avoid using sleeping pills. People build up a tolerance to them, and some have daytime hypnotic effects. Some pills induce sleep apnea.
- If you must take a sleeping pill during times of extreme stress, such as after the death of a loved one, after surgery or during extreme jet lag, take short-acting sleeping medications.
- Nightly use of a sleeping medication may not be effective after a while. If you have to use them at all, use them only every other night, or every third night.
- Avoid taking naps during the day; go to bed a little later each night.

---

to awaken tired and irritable after many awakenings throughout the night. Snoring is the cause of many marital arguments.

Heavy snoring accompanied by slowed breathing patterns may indicate the presence of sleep apnea.

See also DREAMING; JET LAG; REM SLEEP; SNORING.

Kahn, Ada P., and Holt, Linda Hughey. *Midlife Health: A Woman's Practical Guide to Feeling Good*. New York: Avon Books, 1989.

sleep apnea   See SLEEP; SNORING.

sleep disorders   See SLEEP.

sleep paralysis   A sensation of being unable to move at the moment of waking up or going to sleep. This feeling may last for only a few seconds and be accompanied by frightening hallucinations. This occurs in some people who have narcolepsy but also occasionally happens in normally healthy people as well.

See also NARCOLEPSY; SLEEP.

sleep therapy   A treatment sometimes used for depression in which the individual is monitored in a sleep laboratory and the sleep-wake cycle is altered. For example, the individual might be kept awake during one full night or during specific hours of several nights. This is termed sleep deprivation therapy. Russian psychiatrists have used sedative drugs to promote sleep for several days as a form of therapy. This type of sleep therapy is not used in the United States as a standard treatment.

See also DEPRESSION; PSYCHOTHERAPY; SLEEP.

sleepwalking (somnambulism) Walking while asleep during NREM (nonrapid-eye-movement) sleep; this affects about 5 percent of adults and many more children. For unknown reasons, boys are more likely to sleepwalk than girls. A child may sleepwalk after awakening from a nightmare or night terror and may scream, talk or even urinate in an inappropriate place.

It is difficult to awaken a sleepwalker; the best approach is to calmly lead him or her back to bed. However, in a household where an individual is known to sleepwalk, it is best to close off stairwells and remove loose objects in the possible pathway to prevent injury.

Since somnambulism occurs during stage IV sleep, it frequently responds to benzodiazepine medications, such as flurazepam (Dalmane) or temazepam (Restoril).

slips of the tongue Also known as "lapsus lingae," slips of the tongue occur when one says one thing but means another. Most people do this at times, and doing so does not mean that one is losing one's memory. These are mistakes that grouped together with other errors such as mislaying objects, memory lapses and writing errors are known as symptomatic acts. Sigmund Freud theorized that these acts have a subconscious basis with some motivation that is not recognized by the person who commits them. This type of behavior is temporary and correctable. Although undesirable, it tends to fall within normal limits and is not considered pathological.

Campbell, Robert Jean. *Psychiatric Dictionary.* New York, Oxford University Press, 1981.

smoking The actual physiological effects of smoking are somewhat at odds with the sensations that smokers report. When nicotine enters the bloodstream, it raises the heart rate, blood pressure and blood flow and dilates the arteries. It also raises the level of glucose in the blood. However, smokers report a sense of tranquillity, despite the stimulating effects of nicotine.

Smoking is generally experienced as an uncomfortable, negative experience the first time it is attempted, but it soon becomes a habit that is difficult to break despite its link with cancer and heart disease.

The habit of smoking is usually started in adolescence and seems to be a function of a desire to conform to peer pressure. Rebellious attitudes, lower socioeconomic status, desire for tension relief and patterns of family smoking also seem to be factors that contribute to teenage smoking.

According to a 1989 Gallup poll, 63 percent of smokers would like to quit the habit and many of those have made a serious but unsuccessful effort to stop. Although the survey showed a decline in smoking, down to a low of 27 percent from a peak of 45 percent in 1954, smoking is still prevalent among adolescents and has actually increased slightly to 13 percent of 13- to 17-year-olds, up from 10 percent in previous years.

Possibly a reflection of the importance of athletics to teenagers is the fact that more teenage girls (14 percent) smoke than teenage boys (11 percent). In the general population, men have traditionally smoked more than women, although these figures are now somewhat even at 28 percent of men and 26 percent of women. Although their numbers have decreased, men are still heavier smokers than women. One-fourth of men smoke more than a pack of cigarettes a day, while only 14 percent of the women surveyed exceed a pack a day. Light smoking of less than a pack a day is common among the population in the 18- to 29-year-old age bracket.

Smoking is now regarded as an addiction. Many stop-smoking programs exist to help cigarette addicts. However, for the programs to be helpful, the individual must attend regularly and follow the rules set forth. For many, unfortunately, this is easier said than done. Dr. Alexander Gussman of the Psychiatric Institute, Columbia Medical School, has shown that smokers have a significantly higher past history of depression and may reexperience depression when trying to withdraw from smoking, requiring antidepressant treatment.

Since antismoking laws have been passed in the United States during the 1980s and early 1990s, there are frequent incidents of anger and hostility between smokers and nonsmokers. Although scientists have documented harmful effects of smoking to smokers as well as those who are forced to breathe secondhand smoke, many smokers still believe that it is their ''right'' to smoke when and where they want to. Nonsmokers maintain the same ''right'' to clean air. Increasingly, workplaces are adopting nonsmoking policies and setting up outdoor smoking areas for smokers. Most restaurants have nonsmoking areas, but there are some that do not. For those that do not, ventilation systems are not always effective, and nonsmokers are frequently offended by smoke in the air. For many nonsmokers, smoke in the air is more than an annoyance; for asthmatics and those with other respiratory disorders, being forced to breathe in secondhand smoke can bring on an attack and cause them to be ill.

Because of the known health effects of smoking (credited as a factor in 500,000 deaths per year), the United States may eventually become a smokeless society. However, in Third World countries, numbers of smokers are increasing and cigarette consumption is increasing, especially as American tobacco manufacturers have turned elsewhere in the world to market their products.

Blau, T. H. ''Smoking Behavior,'' in Corsini, Raymond J., ed., *The Encyclopedia of Psychology,* vol. 3. New York: Wiley, 1984.
''Smoking: Cigarette Smoking at 4-Year Low.'' *Gallup Report* (July 1989).

snoring   An annoying condition that results when the soft palate vibrates because an air passage is blocked during sleep. Snoring frequently results when one sleeps on his or her back; the tongue slides back into a position that partially blocks the nasal passage, forcing one to breathe through the mouth, particularly in a deep sleep. Snoring may deprive both the snorer and the bed partner of necessary sleep, possibly resulting in irritability and tension the next day.

Snoring is more common in overweight people, in part because they are more likely to sleep on their backs and because fatty tissue in their throat may cause blockage. Snoring may also be caused by enlarged tonsils and nasal problems. Heavy drinking, smoking or eating just before sleep may also cause snoring.

Snoring is more common in men than in women and tends to increase with age. A significant number of snorers can be heard in the next room. Measurements of snoring volume have recorded decibel levels as high as the sound of a jack hammer or pneumatic drill. Robert W. Hart, M.D., writing about snoring in *Chicago Medicine* (Dec. 21, 1991), characterized it as ''mild, moderate, severe or heroic.'' According to Hart, the incidence of habitual snoring in an unselected population has been estimated near 20 percent. However, in overweight males between the ages of 30 and 59, that incidence reaches 60 percent. Some sources estimate that 40 million Americans snore.

Snoring and Sleep Apnea   Many individuals who report chronic fatigue and irritability are victims of sleep apnea, known as obstructive sleep apnea syndrome (OSAS). If untreated, OSAS can have lethal consequences when daytime sleepiness leads to automobile and industrial accidents, as well as consequences for interpersonal relationships because of short tempers due to tiredness.

OSAS is characterized by repetitive episodes of complete (apnea) or incomplete (hypopnea) obstruction of the upper airways

Tips for Snorers

- Learn to sleep on your side or stomach.
- Attach something to the back of your pajamas or nightgown to awaken yourself when you lie on your back.
- Avoid having an alcoholic nightcap, because it aggravates snoring; alcohol causes too much relaxation in the oralpharynx region. The same thing happens after taking tranquilizers and sleeping pills.
- Elevate the head of your bed several inches. This may alleviate the tendency to snore.
- Devices are available that help. One is a vinyl molded tooth guard, much like an athletic mouth guard, that captures and holds the tongue so that it doesn't fall to the back of the throat. It makes the airway stay open.
- Masks are available for really heavy snorers. These prevent snoring by supplying positive air pressure and keeping the throat open.
- Surgical techniques may be a last resort for an individual with severe and serious snoring problems. One procedure involves tightening up the tissues in the back of the throat. Another procedure involves making a permanent hole in the breathing system before the voice box. The hole bypasses the throat area when open and prevents the movement of the tissues that lead to snoring.

during sleep. OSAS is more common in males and postmenopausal females, with its frequency increasing with age and weight. The OSAS sufferer may complain of feelings of choking or suffocating during the night or feel panicky because of an inability to take in enough air.

Treatment options for OSAS include general measures, such as weight loss, abstinence from alcohol and other offending substances, pharmacologic approaches for limited periods of time, devices (such as oral and orthodontic devices) and surgical procedures (such as nasal surgery or uvulopalatopharyngoplasty).

OSAS syndrome is linked to hypertension, ischemic heart disease and cerebrovascular disease and may have consequences for an individual's physical as well as mental health.

See also CHRONIC FATIGUE SYNDROME; SLEEP.

Borbely, Alexander. *Secrets of Sleep*. New York: Basic Books, 1984.

Hales, Dianne. *The Complete Book of Sleep*. Reading, Mass.: Addison-Wesley, 1981.

Hart, Robert W. "Snoring and Sleep Apnea: A Clinical Approach." *Chicago Medicine* 94, no. 24 (Dec. 21, 1991).

social anxiety   See ANXIETY DISORDERS; PHOBIA.

social phobia   See PHOBIA.

Social Security disability   Individuals incapacitated by a mental health disability may be entitled to a monthly stipend under the provisions of the Social Security Administration disability program. For example, some people with schizophrenia, chronic depression and chronic fatigue syndrome meet standards for such benefits. Eligibility standards are strict, however.

A person is considered disabled when she has a severe physical or mental impairment or combination of impairments that prevents her from working for a year or more or that is expected to result in death. The work does not necessarily have to be the kind of work done before disability; it can be any gainful work found in the national economy. This definition requires total disability.

To be eligible for this benefit, a person must have worked long enough and recently enough to be insured under the system that is funded by Social Security taxes paid by employers, employees and self-employed persons. To apply, an individual should begin by contacting the local office of the Social Security Administration. Documentation must be complete, including letters from physicians and mental health professionals, possibly laboratory test results and test results of various psychometric tests, which measure psychological or cognitive damage. Letters from previous employers, friends and relatives can be helpful, as can letters from congressional representatives and attorneys. Social Security will want to know how one's impairment limits function.

Following written application, the process will include personal interviews with a case worker. If the first application is rejected, there is a process of appeal, and many cases are granted disability status after one or more appeals.

The Clearinghouse on Disability Information is a centralized source of information about federal, state and local programs. It also follows related legislations and can make referrals on a local basis. The clearinghouse publishes a newsletter on federal activities affecting people with mental as well as physical disabilities and several small guidebooks.

Clearinghouse on Disability Information
Office of Special Education and Rehabilitative Services
U.S. Department of Education
Switzer Building, Room 312
Washington, DC 20202
Phone: (202) 732–1723

The National Organization of Social Security Claimants' Representatives (NOSSCR) is a membership organization of attorneys who represent individuals applying for Social Security disability. They can answer questions about the process of application and appeal and can make referrals to local attorneys.

NOSSCR
6 Prospect Street
Midland Park, NJ 07432
Phone: (800) 431–2804 or
(201) 444–1415

See also MEDICARE.

social support system   An individual's relationships with others and with the environment. This includes significant others, job, community, church and material resources. An individual with a mental health problem may have inadequate social support because family members do not understand why certain regimens are important and thus may not offer the assistance or encouragement that would help the person comply. An inadequate support system may encourage noncompliance and interfere with the individual's improvement.

See also NONCOMPLIANCE.

social work   Social workers have been major providers of mental health services since the early 1920s, when they were an integral part of the beginning of the child guidance movement. Social workers are trained to have expertise concerning community resources available for various types of support and therapy, as well as to intervene when the individual and the environment do not mesh smoothly, causing discomfort or disruption for the individual or family.

Social workers are found in the public and private sectors. Many work in publicly funded health and mental health clinics, public schools, family agencies, clinics, hospitals and private practices. Some work in employee assistance programs (EAP), alcohol and chemical dependency programs and in religious settings.

Social workers early identified the importance of the family as a central focus rather than an individual in isolation. Much early professional literature emphasized the importance of the family and identified it as the unit for treatment. This had an impact on the early child guidance movement, as well as other mental health efforts, and influenced the development of family therapy.

In the 1960s and 1970s, with the establishment and development of comprehensive community mental health centers, clinical social workers were heavily utilized and provided a major proportion of outpatient mental health treatment services. In the 1980s, an increasing number of clinical social workers moved into full- or part-time private practice. In the 1990s, private practice is the fastest-growing setting for clinical social workers.

As of June 1990, there were 129,092 members of the National Association of Social Workers (NASW), an organization limited to those persons who have a bachelor's, master's or doctoral degree from a university program accredited by the Council on Social Work Education.

See also RURAL MENTAL HEALTH CARE.

National Institute of Mental Health. *Mental Health, United States, 1990*. Manderscheid, R. W., and Sonnenschein, M. A., eds. DHHS Pub. No. (ADM) 90–1708. Washington, D.C.: USGPO, 1990.

socioeconomic factors and cardiovascular disease   Living alone and being poor are factors that seem to influence deaths from cardiovascular disease, although specific reasons are unknown. According to two studies reported in the *Journal of the American Medical Association* (Jan. 21, 1992), people living alone and poor people do less well after heart attacks than more affluent people or people who do not live alone.

In one study, people who lived alone did worse after a heart attack than people who lived with someone. "Living alone . . . is an independent risk factor for prognosis after heart attack when compared with all other known risk factors," Robert B. Case, M.D., Department of Medicine, St. Luke's–Roosevelt Hospital, New York, said. In a multicenter trial, 1,234 patients who had suffered heart attacks were studied. Age range of the patients was 25 to 75 years; they were followed for one to four years. At six months after myocardial infarction, the cumulative rate of recurrent cardiac events for those living alone was almost double the rate for those living with others (15.8 percent vs. 8.8 percent).

The researchers said that they did not know which factor or factors are responsible for the hazard from living alone. It may include items as simple as the unavailability of quick medical assistance.

Patients with a significant other did better than unmarried persons living alone. According to the study, unmarried patients without a confidant had a more than threefold increase in the risk of death within five years compared with patients who were either married or had a close confidant.

In another study at Duke Medical Center, patients with higher household incomes had better survival after cardiovascular disease. Those with annual household incomes of $40,000 or greater had an average five-year survival rate of 0.91, while in patients with incomes below $10,000 the five-year survival rate was 0.76. In relative terms, those with low incomes were almost twice as likely to die within five years of entry into the study as those with high incomes.

One possible adverse effect of low economic resources is reduced access to a broad spectrum of medical care, such as reduced ability to pay for expensive medications, fewer physician visits and reduced access to expensive surgical procedures. Reduced social support has been found to affect health behaviors in what could increase risk.

In an editorial accompanying reports of these studies, William Ruberman, M.D., of the Institute of Environmental Medicine, New York University School of Medicine, New York, commented that in humans, adverse social circumstances might enhance the likelihood of encountering stressful life experiences in the absence of social support adequate to mitigate such stress.

See also ANGINA PECTORIS.

Journal of the American Medical Association 267, no. 4 (Jan. 22–29, 1992).

socioeconomic trends in mental health care   According to estimates from a major National Institute of Mental Health (NIMH) study of mental health in three U.S. communities, an estimated 9.6 million people, or 4.3 percent of the civilian noninstitution-alized population, had one or more ambulatory mental health visits in 1980. Of those persons with one or more mental health visits, approximately 25 percent were seen by psychiatrists in office practice; another 25 percent were seen by psychologists in office practice; 40 percent were seen in office settings by other providers, such as nonpsychiatrist physicians or social workers; and the remainder were seen in organized settings, such as hospital outpatient departments, emergency departments and specialty mental health clinics.

According to estimates derived from studies of several communities by the NIMH, within any one-month period, approximately 15 percent of adults meet the diagnostic criteria for psychiatric disorders in the United States. Almost 20 percent of those surveyed in the NIMH study had one or more psychiatric disorders in the preceding six months. Of those with a psychiatric disorder, anxiety disorders (29.4 percent) and substance abuse (24.4 percent) were the most prevalent. Phobias and affective disorders such as depression were most common in women. Alcohol abuse/dependence and phobias were most common in men.

In children, an estimated 12 percent of the population have psychiatric disorders, which vary in severity and do not all require treatment. Each year, over 25,000 children are hospitalized for more than 90 days for psychiatric disorders, and there are more than 10,000 children with major psychotic disorders who are not hospitalized.

Between 1977 and 1987, admissions to nonfederal psychiatric hospitals increased by approximately 9 percent, but the average length of stay declined sharply from 131 days in 1977 to 81 days in 1987, reducing inpatient days in psychiatric hospitals by 32 percent in the 10-year period. In 1987, the number of patients discharged from short-stay hospitals was 73.7 per 10,000 population for mental disorders and 13.9 per 10,000 for alcohol dependence syndrome.

See also HOMELESSNESS; COMMUNITY MENTAL HEALTH in BIBLIOGRAPHY.

"The Future of Psychiatry." *Journal of the American Medical Association* 265, no. 19 (Nov. 21, 1990).

sodium lactate infusions Intravenous infusions of sodium lactate will provoke a panic attack in most patients with panic disorder but not in normal subjects. The mechanism by which this occurs is not clear, and researchers hope that future test results may provide keys to biochemical factors in the causes of panic attacks.

The mechanism for sodium lactate precipitation of panic attacks is not clear, but it is also known that increased carbon dioxide (CO_2) accumulation can precipitate panic attacks, leading to a theory that the change in acid-base balance may also be affected by carbon dioxide levels.

See also PANIC DISORDER.

solvent abuse Glue sniffing or inhaling fumes of industrial solvents and aerosol sprays containing hydrocarbons, which can produce feelings of intoxication. These substances can produce a state of euphoria followed by depression of the central nervous system. Results of this habit can damage the brain, liver and kidneys. Occasionally death occurs as the result of a direct toxic effect on the heart or asphyxiation.

See also SUBSTANCE ABUSE.

somatic A term that means related to the body (soma) or related to body cells, as opposed to germ cells (eggs and sperm). The term "somatic" also relates to the body wall as opposed to the viscera (internal organs). The psyche relates to the mind. Somatic treatments in psychiatry include the use of medications and electroconvulsive therapy (ECT).

See also SOMATIC FIXATION; SOMATIZATION.

somatic fixation A process whereby a physician or patient or family focuses exclusively and inappropriately on physical or biomedical aspects of a complex problem. This can occur in any illness, especially chronic illness, when there is a one-sided emphasis on the biomedical aspects of a multifaceted problem. Somatically fixated patients tend to have anxiety, depression, trouble coping and numerous physical symptoms.

Some individuals have been raised in an environment in which they receive considerable attention for physical pain and little, if any, attention for emotional pain. Families operate on a continuum from full encouragement of emotional and physical experience to complete lack of acceptance of emotional experience. Emotionally repressed families condition children to experience any need or problem as physical. Thus physical symptoms may become their language for a range of experiences, from physical to emotional.

According to Susan McDaniel, M.D., and colleagues from the University of Rochester School of Medicine, Rochester, New York, physicians should evaluate both the biomedical and psychosocial elements of a patient's problem, elicit the patient's and family's understanding of the problem and learn about any recent stressful events or unresolved crises in the lives of family members.

Treatment of a patient with a somatic fixation should involve medical treatment as well as extensive emotional support for the patient and family members.

Somatization disorder (Briquet's syndrome) is seen in people who have numerous physical symptoms without abnormal tests or medical findings who have repeated medical evaluations and increased amounts of surgery compared with others. Studies have shown that such people live long lives but persist in having numerous physical symptoms and medical treatment.

See also HYPOCHONDRIASIS; SOMATIZATION.

McDaniel, Susan; Campbell, Thomas; and Seaburn, David. ''Treating Somatic Fixation: A Biopsychosocial Approach.'' *Canadian Family Physician* 37 (Feb. 1991).

somatization The term for a feeling of physical symptoms in the absence of disease or out of proportion to a given ailment. From a public health point of view, somatization is important. According to the *Harvard Health Letter* (Apr. 1992), in any given week almost 80 percent of basically healthy people have symptoms that are not caused by physical disease. About one in five health care dollars is spent on patients with somatization. Nearly half of the patients seen in physicians' offices are the ''worried well.''

People who have ongoing somatic complaints may undergo uncomfortable invasive procedures that may cause complications. For example, it is possible that a person who repeatedly reports chest pains could eventually undergo coronary angiography to rule out serious arterial narrowing. These individuals may also be taking many medications needlessly, some with serious side effects.

Individuals who ''somatize'' are said to have somatoform disorders.

somatoform disorders See SOMATIC; SOMATIC FIXATION; SOMATIZATION.

somnambulism See SLEEPWALKING.

spectator role A term referring to a behavior pattern in which one's natural sexual responses are blocked by observing oneself closely and worrying about how well or poorly one is performing rather than participating freely. The term was introduced by William H. Masters (1915–), an American physician and sex researcher, and Virginia Johnson (1925–), an American psychologist and sex researcher.

See also SEX THERAPY.

spinal tap See BRAIN.

split personality An inappropriate term for multiple personality disorder. It is sometimes also erroneously used to refer to schizophrenia; Bleuler used the term "split personality" to refer to the separation of thought and emotion in this disorder.

See also DISSOCIATION; DISSOCIATIVE DISORDERS; MULTIPLE PERSONALITY DISORDER; SCHIZOPHRENIA.

splitting See DISSOCIATION; DISSOCIATIVE DISORDERS; MULTIPLE PERSONALITY DISORDER.

spouse abuse See BATTERED WOMEN; DOMESTIC VIOLENCE: FAMILY VIOLENCE.

stage fright A feeling of nervous anticipation that individuals experience before giving a public speech, making an appearance on a stage (as in a theatrical production), playing a musical instrument or singing publicly, being on a radio or television program or being videotaped.

Those who go out of their way to avoid public speaking and public appearances may actually have a phobia about public appearances. Symptoms of stage fright and public speaking phobia may include becoming dizzy and nauseated when getting near the stage, having sweaty palms, weak knees and difficulty breathing and feeling a rapid heartbeat. While most people feel these symptoms in a very mild manner, phobic people will suffer so much that they momentarily fear they will die because of their rapid heartbeat and difficulty in getting enough air to breathe comfortably. (They may be overbreathing but not realize it.)

Some people have these symptoms for a few moments before going on stage, and as soon as they walk onto the stage, their fears disappear as they focus all of their attention and energy on their performance.

Those who do not lose their fears hold on to them for many reasons, including fear of criticism, fear of making a mistake, fear of being a failure or believing that they are not adequate for the task. Behavioral therapy techniques can help people overcome stage fright. By systematically becoming accustomed to being in front of people, many individuals learn to lose their fear and become successful public figures.

See also ANXIETY DISORDERS; PHOBIA.

STDs See SEXUALLY TRANSMITTED DISEASES.

stepfamilies Relationships in stepfamilies are far more complex than in traditional nuclear families. Stresses and challenges arise partly from the fact that society does not define the role of the stepparent as well as that of the natural parent. As a result, everyone may have a different set of ideas regarding how stepparent and stepchild get along. Frequently, a stepparent may feel that he or she should assume the role of an actual parent, but this may be very uncomfortable and objectionable to the child, especially as he may continue to have a strong relationship with his own natural parent. Children who live with a single parent may have had a partial sense of being the center of attention in the household and may have difficulty giving up that role when the stepparent arrives.

When two families merge, the living arrangements may cause stresses and challenges to the mental health of all involved. For example, some children may be in residence, and others may visit. Living arrangements may change during the course of the marriage in some anticipated way. A child who had been living with the other parent may suddenly decide he wishes to leave that parent, possibly because of a stepparent in that household, and move in. If conflicts erupt between stepsiblings, parents usually side with their own child rather than being peacemakers as in the traditional marriage. Children may also feel that their inheritance rights are threatened by the arrival of a stepfather or -mother, especially in cases involving older couples and adult children.

There may be a highly charged sexual atmosphere in the home because the couple are actually newlyweds but with children present. This may arouse real or potential relationships between stepsiblings that are technically, although not biologically, incestuous. There is also a potential for technical incest between stepparent and stepchild, particularly if the stepparent is young, even close to the age of the child. Stepparents sometimes even encourage these feelings in children by their attempts to be warm and friendly.

See also DIVORCE; REMARRIAGE; COURTSHIP, LOVE, ROMANCE, RELATIONSHIPS in BIBLIOGRAPHY.

Belovitch, Jeanne. *Making Re-marriage Work.* Lexington, Mass.: Lexington Books, 1987.
Wald, Esther. *The Remarried Family.* New York: Family Service Association of America, 1981.

steroids A group of chemical compounds with similar structure that act as chemical activators and regulators. They are secreted by various glands and activate various body functions. An example of a steroid is cortisol, which is higher in individuals who have depression and lessens as they are recovering. Anabolic steroids (synthetic compounds) are misused by some athletic trainers to stimulate muscle development. Anabolic steroids can be legally obtained in the United States only with a physician's prescription.

See also ANABOLIC STEROIDS; BRAIN CHEMISTRY; CORTISOL.

stillbirth The death of a fetus between the 20th week of gestation and delivery. The major cause of stillbirth appears to be loss of oxygen to the baby, because of either a problem with the placenta or an umbilical cord accident before or during labor. However, there is no known cause for more than half of stillbirths. A stillbirth causes a special kind of grief for the parents. Although they have never seen their child, they have imagined how he or she would look, what they would use for a name and how the child would interact with others in the family. After the stillbirth, there are no "real" memories, such as photographs or items the child actually used or touched. Friends and others in the family do not share the grief with the parents in the way that they might with an older infant who died, making grief even more difficult for the parents.

Even though another child may arrive a year or more later, most parents of a stillborn never fully recover from their loss. Some remember the "due date" for years and observe it with sadness and revival of the feeling of loss.

See also GRIEF; MISCARRIAGE; PREGNANCY.

stimulant drugs (stimulants) Drugs that stimulate the central nervous system and increase the activity of the brain or the spinal cord. Examples of stimulant drugs include amphetamines, cocaine, caffeine and nicotine. As these agents produce a feeling of euphoria and may temporarily increase alertness, they are often overused and abused; this occurs particularly with amphetamines and cocaine.

See also AMPHETAMINE DRUGS; COCAINE; METHAMPHETAMINES; SUBSTANCE ABUSE.

stress A major factor in achieving a feeling of well-being and ongoing mental wellness. Stress is an everyday part of life and can be a source of energy or a source of impaired mental health. Everyone feels a sense of emotional strain, tension and anxiety at times. Different individuals can cope with differing levels of stress. Sometimes individuals feel completely overloaded by what is going on in their lives. Because each individual experiences life in unique ways, circumstances that one enjoys may be stressful to others.

Events that cause stress for different individuals vary. Some find happy events, such as starting a new job or planning a trip, sources of stress. Others find that trouble at home or on the job causes stress. Major life changes, such as the death of a loved one, divorce, loss of a job or moving to a new city, cause stress. At all stages of life, individuals sometimes find their personal agenda too full for comfort and feel overwhelmed. Stress increases when they feel a lack of support from those around them.

Stress is an internal response to circumstances known as "stressors." These include difficulty in getting along with people, feeling trapped or inadequate, finding little pleasure in life and feeling distrustful. Stress can lead to depression, frustration and anxiety.

When an individual feels stressed, chemical changes take place in the body. The adrenaline starts flowing and the nervous system is activated, which causes a fight or flight response. During extreme stress, some people notice that they have a faster heartbeat and a sick feeling in their stomach; it is hard to work or function efficiently at such times.

Stress affects all aspects of life. Some individuals find that stress actually raises their energy level and helps them focus their mind better on their work or on a sports activity. Some thrive on many kinds of stressors. People who do are often attracted to high-stress occupations and professions.

Stress that starts at work can affect home life, and the reverse is also true for many people. Stress within a family causes tension and difficulty in communicating with one another. In some cases, interpersonal stresses develop when an individual has two feelings at the same time, such as wanting to be an independent adolescent yet feeling dependent on parents. As life is a series of progressions through emotional stages, it is helpful to remember that change and growth always involve some degree of stress. In a family, several people are trying to cope with their own stress and the stress of others about whom they care.

Diet and exercise can help relieve stress. Normal eating of three meals a day reduces effects of stress for some people. "Crash diets" and "fad diets" can lead to anxiety, depression and an inability to maintain a good weight. Well-balanced meals provide a slow release of necessary nutrients throughout the day. For some people, too much caffeine causes additional stress by bringing on symptoms of anxiety.

Many people find that regular physical workouts involving running, walking or exercising in a gym, health club or on exercise equipment at home help them relieve stress and get ready to effectively face challenges of the day ahead. Using muscles is a way to use up some of the fight or flight readiness in the body.

Some people use massage or soothing music as stress relievers. Sources of relaxation are very individual matters. What allows one person to relax may actually cause stress for another. An example is noise level in the workplace or at home. Each individual should try to create an environment in which to work and live that is the least stressful and concentrate on reaching peak performance and feeling of well-being.

Individuals who have been exposed to sudden and unexpected events, such as seeing someone attacked or beaten, seeing a suicide or death or surviving a natural disaster (such as an earthquake or flood), may have a pattern of stress known as post-traumatic stress disorder. Over a period of weeks, months or even years, the mind and body may continue to react in many ways. The individual may have bad dreams, flashbacks and feelings that the event is recurring. With support from family, friends and mental health professionals, these individuals can find help.

See also ANXIETY; DEPRESSION; FLASHBACKS; FRUSTRATION; HEADACHES; POST-TRAUMATIC STRESS DISORDER; SLEEP.

Adapted with permission from Kahn, Ada P. *Stress* (booklet), Mental Health Association of Greater Chicago, 1989.

stroke   A unit of positive recognition or love, which may take the form of a kind word, compliment, reinforcing feedback or a physical "pat on the back." Individuals need frequent doses of good strokes to maintain their good mental health.

Stroke also refers to damage to the brain caused by interruption to its blood supply. Movement, sensation or function controlled by the damaged area is often impaired. Intellectual impairment is often permanent.

According to Robert W. Teasell, M.D., assistant professor of Medicine, University of Western Ontario, and chief of Physical Medicine and Rehabilitation, University Hospital, London, Ontario, clinically significant depression occurs in more than 30 percent of stroke patients. This depression reduces motivation and, with an adverse effect on activities of daily living and socialization, often adds to family problems and stresses.

Treatment should include positive feedback, emotional support and psychological counseling. Some antidepressant drugs can be appropriately used under careful supervision following a stroke.

One person's stroke affects the well-being of others in the family. Those providing care to a stroke victim face their own adjustment problems, as their personal needs are often sacrificed to meet the needs of the stroke patient. With limited opportunities for rest, caregivers are often under great stress and themselves suffer a higher rate of depression and deterioration of health.

See also CAREGIVERS; CHRONIC ILLNESS; REINFORCEMENT.

Teasell, Robert W. "Long Term Sequelae of Stroke." *Canadian Family Physician* 38 (Feb. 1992).

stupor A mental state in which there is marked decrease in eactivity to the environment and reduction of spontaneous movements and activity. The individual may be totally unresponsive to any stimulus. Stupor may occur as a result of epilepsy, brain disease, serious depression or many other causes such as catatonia. In catatonic stupor the patient may seem totally unresponsive but later show awareness of everything that happened around her during the catatonic stupor.

See also BRAIN; EPILEPSY.

stuttering A speech disorder involving repeated hesitation and delay in saying words or in which certain sounds are unusually prolonged. Also known as stammering, it usually starts in early childhood and may be a temporary situation. About half of the children whose stuttering persists after age five continue to do so throughout adulthood.

Some people who have a stammer find it more pronounced when they become anxious or fearful. For example, some individuals who are fearful of public speaking (a common social phobia) have difficulty getting words out if they have to stand up in a crowd and say something. These same individuals have no difficulty in reading or singing in unison.

For many, stuttering is a source of embarrassment. Some stutterers become socially withdrawn because they fear ridicule from others. Some individuals improve their speech pattern through speech therapy, which may include learning to give equal weight to each syllable.

Causes of stuttering are not understood; theories suggest that it may be due to a subtle form of brain damage or may be related to a psychological problem.

subconscious According to psychoanalytic theory, the subconscious is the part of the mind through which information passes on its way from the unconscious to the conscious mind. The subconscious contains thoughts, feelings or ideas that one is temporarily unaware of but that can be recalled under certain circumstances.

sublimation A process by which individuals redirect impulses into socially acceptable forms of behavior. For example, aggressive urges may be channeled into sports activities. Sublimation is also regarded as a defense mechanism.

See also FREUD, SIGMUND; PSYCHOANALYSIS.

substance abuse   An addiction or a problem with alcohol or other drugs. Many people look to alcohol and drugs to help them cope with stress, anxiety or depression. Other people misuse substances they obtain with a physician's prescription. Some people develop a dependence on drugs, which means that they have a compulsion to continue using the substance because it gives them a feeling of well-being. One can be psychologically dependent on a drug and not physically dependent; the reverse is also true. Dependence can occur after periodic or prolonged use of a drug, and the characteristics of dependence vary according to the drug involved.

The toll exacted on society, health and the economy by substance abuse remains staggering in the early 1990s. In the inner cities in the United States, the drug problem appears to be worsening, with a concomitant increase in violent crime. For example, in 1989, the number of murders in Washington, D.C. averaged more than one a day, and more than 70 percent were drug related.

In a comprehensive economic analysis conducted in 1983, costs of alcohol problems in the United States were estimated to exceed $70 billion per year, with the majority of these costs attributed to reduced productivity. An additional $44 billion in economic costs were attributed to drug problems. Alcohol is implicated in nearly half of all deaths caused by motor vehicle crashes and fatal intentional injuries such as suicides and homicides; victims are intoxicated in approximately one-third of all homicides, drownings and boating deaths.

Adolescents who use alcohol and other drugs are much more likely than their non-using peers to experience other serious problems. An estimated one in four adolescents is at very high risk of alcohol and other drug problems, school failure, early unwanted pregnancy and/or delinquency.

An estimated 21.2 million Americans have tried cocaine at least once. Use of crack cocaine, which appears to be even more addictive than the powdered form, has become increasingly widespread, especially in some urban centers. Among serious consequences of cocaine use is the incidence of developmental disabilities among infants of crack-addicted mothers.

Substance abuse significantly increases the risk of transmitting the human immunodeficiency virus (HIV). This can occur directly through the sharing of contaminated needles, sexual contact with intravenous drug abusers or other drug injectors or via in utero infection and indirectly through adverse effects on immune system functioning and the increased risk of unsafe sexual practices.

Recognition of the gravity of the substance abuse problem in the United States is evidenced on almost every national opinion poll that places substance abuse as a priority concern. The national effort to prevent these problems has mobilized government, schools, communities, businesses and families.

The combination of increased public resolve, advanced scientific understanding and treatments available for those who seek help gives some small degree of optimism for overcoming the national substance abuse problem in the United States.

See also ADDICTION; ALCOHOLISM: BOARDER BABIES; COCAINE; EMPLOYEE ASSISTANCE PROGRAMS.

U.S. Department of Health and Human Services, Public Health Services. *Healthy People 2000.* DHHS Publication No. (PHS) 91–50212. Washington, D.C.: USGPO, 1990.

sudden infant death syndrome (SIDS) SIDS, or ''crib death,'' is the sudden death of an infant that cannot be explained by prior medical history or postmortem examination. Victims of SIDS are infants, usually between the ages of two and four months, who stop breathing during a normal sleeping period. Ninety percent of all victims die within the first four months, but it may strike children as old as one year. Although causes of SIDS are unknown, it is not caused by childhood vaccines, suffocation, vomiting and choking. Many research projects are under way to determine predictive factors that may prevent some deaths in the future.

According to Phipps Cohe, public affairs director, National SIDS Alliance, one infant every hour or one out of every 500 babies born in the United States succumbs to SIDS. Out of 36 industrialized nations, the United States ranks 20th in infant mortality; a large number of these deaths are attributed to SIDS.

A SIDS death can affect as many as a hundred people, among them parents, siblings, grandparents, extended family, co-workers, neighbors, baby-sitters and day-care workers. A SIDS death produces an intense reaction for many of these people. After the initial shock wears off, many parents find themselves experiencing feelings of guilt and depression. Support groups can be helpful for parents who have lost a child to SIDS.

For information on SIDS, contact:

National SIDS Alliance
10500 Little Patuxent Parkway
Columbia, MD 21044
Phone: (800) 221–SIDS

See also GRIEF; SUPPORT GROUPS.

suicide Killing oneself voluntarily and intentionally. Many people do not like to talk about suicide or acknowledge its existence. A diagnosis of suicide is usually not one that the family wants to hear. When a high possibility of suicide exists within a family, certain measures should be taken. Suicidal tendencies should be explained to family members as a manifestation of depression that can be successfully treated. In an acute suicidal crisis, the family should be instructed to remove all weapons and all lethal means from the home, including prescription drugs. They should be told not to leave the individual alone at any time. Friends or loved ones who show signs of depression or express hopelessness or suicidal impulses should be helped to get immediate professional help before a suicidal crisis develops.

Associated with the word ''suicide'' are the terms suicidal ideation (having thoughts of committing suicide or thoughts of methods by which to commit suicide), suicide attempt (self-destructive behavior that could be lethal), suicidal gesture (self-destructive behavior that is usually not lethal and is often viewed by others as manipulative behavior) and self-destructiveness (behavior by which one damages himself immediately, impulsively or chronically).

Suicide is the eighth leading cause of death in the United States and the second most frequent cause of death for young people in the 15 to 25 age bracket. About 12 percent of those who threaten or attempt suicide actually kill themselves. Current statistics may understate the actual occurrence of suicide. Many auto and other accidents may have suicidal intention. Because of social stigma, insurance coverage issues and legal criteria for classifying cause of death, suicide may not be recorded as the cause in many cases.

Prevention of Suicide One of the most difficult challenges clinicians face is the prevention of suicide by their patients. Such psychiatric clinicians routinely deal with patients whose diagnoses are associated with a high risk for suicide; assessment and intervention always make such cases a high priority.

The physician, psychotherapist or mental health worker is sometimes the only person with the opportunity of recognizing suicidal intent. Studies have shown that from 40 to 75 percent of suicidal individuals will see physicians within six months to a year preceding their self-destructive acts. A number of studies have pointed out that even while receiving psychiatric treatment, psychiatric

Suicide Potential: Risk Factors and Characteristics

The possibility that the individual will kill him- or herself voluntarily and intentionally is referred to as suicide potential.

Risk Factors	Characteristics
Depression	Ambivalence
Other mood disorders	Withdrawn, isolative behavior
Schizophrenia	
Other psychoses	Impaired concentra-
Neurological disorders	tion
Delirium	Constricted thought
Use or withdrawal of alcohol or other substances	processes, tunnel vision
	Psychomotor agitation
Organic brain disorders	Psychomotor retarda-
Hallucinations, delusions	tion
	Anxious
Stress, acute or chronic	Attentive to internal
Isolation	stimuli
Loss of significant other	Verbalizes suicidal
Loss of self-esteem	thoughts, feelings,
Loss of physical health, function	plan
	Verbalized references
Cultural factors	to dealth, dying
Spiritual anxiety	Gives away posses-
Personality disorders	sions
Impulse control disorders	Anger, hostility
	Impulsive behaviors
Internal conflicts, guilt	Depressed mood
Family dysfunction, crisis	Appetite disturbances
	Hopeless-helpless
Loss of resources, social and economic	Disturbed sleep patterns
Unmet needs	

hospitalization or treatment with psychotropic drugs, patients do commit suicide.

Although suicide rarely can be a logical, rational decision based on an individual's situation, evidence seems to support the contention that most suicides occur in the context of psychiatric illness. However, the absence of psychiatric treatment at the time of suicide does not necessarily preclude the existence of a serious mental disturbance. It has been observed that severely depressed patients may appear symptom-free just prior to suicide. This may lead to an erroneous assumption that the individual is "normal" at the time of suicide. While suicidal behavior may manifest itself in patients fitting any psychiatric diagnostic category, it has been found most prevalent in depression, especially manic-depression and psychotic depression, as well as in alcoholism, substance abuse and schizophrenia, especially in younger age groups.

Typically, the high-risk patient is one with symptoms of a serious depressive syndrome manifesting signs such as sleep disturbance, weight loss, dry mouth, loss of sexual drive, gastrointestinal discomfort, complete loss of interest, impairment of function, delusional guilt, neglect of personal appearance and cleanliness, inability to make decisions, a feeling of emptiness, psychomotor retardation or agitation in a depressed mood, feelings of hopelessness and helplessness and severe anxiety or panic attacks. Generally, the risk of suicide appears to be greatest in the early course of depressive illness (first three episodes) and decreases as drive and affect are "burned out" and life becomes a kind of partial death, without ambition and seemingly without purpose.

The Chronically Suicidal Individual
Repeated communication of a wish to die or suicidal thoughts is a characteristic of the chronically suicidal person. However, this in itself is not sufficient to distinguish the high- from the low-risk individual, since it has also been observed that the majority of the much larger group of patients who attempt but do not complete suicide also convey intent in advance.

Intense dependency is often an underlying dynamic in the suicidal individual. This dependency has been observed throughout all spheres of the suicidal individual's life-style, where inordinately excessive demands are made on others for constant attention, affection and approval. The individual also feels unable to cope by himself, thereby needing continual supervision and guidance. Others

Chronic Pre-lethal Features*

1. Suicidal communications
2. Symbiotic dependency and reliance on external controls
3. Rigid thinking
4. Paranoid traits
5. Externalized anger
6. Intermittent loss of control
7. Chronic stimulus seeking
8. Impaired personal coping

have independently observed this basic feeling of helplessness in patients who commit suicide.

Tendencies toward rigid thinking that does not allow for alternatives in a crisis—and thinking in opposites—have been observed in the personalities of many suicidal individuals. Perfectionism as a personality trait is carried to a pathological state, and this finds expression in the form of an anxious striving toward perfection in all undertakings.

A less commonly recognized characteristic repeatedly associated with a high risk of suicide is paranoia. While paranoia can serve as a temporary defense against depression, unrecognized suicidal impulses may result when this defense fails.

Sigmund Freud viewed suicide and depression as unconscious rage toward a lost loved object turned back on oneself; however, cases have suggested a high frequency of externalized anger and even violent tantrums in the histories of patients who commit suicide or make serious attempts.

Perhaps the most important characteristic of the chronically high-risk individual is that of impaired capacity for interpersonal relating. One study showed that 91 percent of those who completed suicide made no attempt to communicate their intent just prior to their suicide, but the suicide-gesture group contacted a significant other 73 percent of the time.

Assessing Acute Pre-lethal Factors Mental health professionals are often placed

in a difficult position regarding a patient's family or friends when they believe that suicide is a strong imminent possibility. However, there are a number of acute behavioral and situational factors found with the greatest frequency in seriously attempted and completed suicides.

Suicide in Major Affective Disorder A study reported during 1990 indicated that among 954 patients with major affective disorders, nine clinical features were associated with suicide. Six of these—panic attacks, severe psychic anxiety, diminished concentration, global insomnia, moderate alcohol abuse and severe loss of interest or pleasure—were associated with suicide within one year. Three others—severe hopelessness, suicidal ideation and history of previous suicide attempts—were associated with suicide occurring after one year. These findings drew attention to the importance of: (1) standardized prospective data for studies of suicide; (2) assessment of short-term suicide risk factors; and (3) anxiety symptoms as modifiable suicide risk factors within a clinically relevant period.****

Situational Precursors of Suicide The most commonly understood instances of increased suicidal risk in the depressed individual are situations associated with separation or loss. The loss does not necessarily have

Acute Pre-lethal Features*

1. Specific suicidal plan
2. Abrupt clinical change
3. Decreasing fear of death concomitant with an increasingly positive attitude toward death
4. Failure of psychological defenses (severe anxiety or panic attacks)
5. Mental regression
6. Delusional hopelessness
7. Loss of future perspective
8. Sudden decline of interpersonal relating, with help negation
9. Dreams of symbolic peaceful scenes of dying in which death is looked upon as exciting or euphoric

Situational Precursors of Suicide*

1. Threatened or actual loss of relationship
2. Failure situation
3. Real or perceived physical illness

to be the final loss or death of a loved one as Freud emphasized, but it may be simply a temporary loss to the individual who is in a depressive crisis. For example, losses may be spouse, home, job, hospital discharge, temporary separation from therapist, money, love, and so on.

The "failure situation" ranks high as a precursor of suicide. This situation may occur after a hospital discharge when a patient is trying to regain or attain higher levels of function, such as successfully starting a job or returning to college. This factor also ranks high when individuals try to meet higher expectations of themselves or others.

Additionally, the presence of real or perceived physical illness may be significant in the assessment of suicidal risk. In malignant or incurable illness, two critical suicidal periods seem to be those of: (1) uncertainty while diagnosis and prognosis are still at issue, and (2) shock following the first realization of the upheavals and suffering, actual or fantasized, that are to follow.*

Suicide in Youth* There are some clues to predicting suicide among youngsters or adolescents. They are more likely to communicate with those in their peer group than their parents. They may give away a prized possession with the comment that they will not be needing it any more. They may be more morose and isolated than usual. Although there may be signs of insomnia, worry and anorexia, the youngster may not have all the classical signs of depression.

One study listed symptoms occurring in 25 college-age suicides in order of their frequency: despondency, futility, lack of interest in schoolwork, a feeling of tenseness around people, insomnia, suicidal communications, fatigue and malaise without apparent organic cause, feelings of inadequacy or unworthiness and brooding over the death of a loved one.

According to an article published in December 1991 in the *Journal of the American Medical Association,* having a gun at home may increase the risk that a psychologically troubled teen will commit suicide.*** David A. Brent, M.D., Western Psychiatric Institute and Clinic, Pittsburgh, Pennsylvania, and colleagues noted that the odds that potentially suicidal adolescents will kill themselves are up 75-fold when a gun is kept in the house. They commented on the differences between teen suicides and that of adults. For teens, they said, a suicide attempt may be an attempt to communicate that they are in great pain, although they may be ambivalent about wanting to die. For such adolescents, ready access to a firearm may guarantee that their plea for help will not be heard.

In a study, the authors matched 47 adolescents who had committed suicide in Pennsylvania from July 1986 through February 1988 with 47 adolescents who had attempted suicide and 47 never-suicidal psychiatric controls. All three groups were similar with respect to age, gender, race and socioeconomic status. (The study population was predominantly white, male and 15 to 17 years of age.)

Researchers found that guns (handguns and long guns) were twice as likely to be found in the homes of suicide victims as in the homes of attempters or psychiatric controls. There was no difference in the methods of storage of firearms among the three groups, so that even guns stored locked or separated from ammunition were associated with suicide by firearms.

The authors commented that it is clear that firearms have no place in the homes of psychiatrically troubled youngsters. Physicians who care for psychiatrically disturbed adolescents with any indicators of suicidal risk, such as depression, conduct problems, substance abuse or suicidal thoughts, have a responsibility to make clear and firm recommendations that firearms be removed from the homes of these at-risk youths. In an accompanying editorial, Mark L. Rosenberg, M.D., Division of Injury Control, National Center for Environmental Health and Injury Control, Centers for Disease Control, Atlanta, Georgia, commented that today the relationship between guns access and suicide is all but ignored.*

Assisted Suicide In 1991, *Final Exit,* a "how-to" book by Derek Humphry, executive director of the Hemlock Society—a group aimed at promoting death with dignity—was published. His premise was that his book, for the terminally ill, is not meant to be a book for unhappy or depressed people.

Many mental health professionals worried that this book and others might legitimize suicide for troubled people with undiagnosed depression who could be treated if their illnesses were diagnosed correctly. Many expressed fear that such books could push up suicide rates, particularly among the elderly who are not terminally ill. However, according to David Clark, president of the American Society of Suicidology—an organization dedicated to preventing suicide—many people are extraordinarily glad when they recover from an attempt that someone did not help them die.**

In March 1990, a group of physicians writing in the *New England Journal of Medicine,* in an article entitled "The Physician's Responsibility Toward Hopelessly Ill Patients," held that "it is not immoral for a physician to assist in the rational suicide of a terminally ill person."**** Two of the 12 authors of the paper dissented from this statement.

Later in 1990, Dr. Jack Kevorkian assisted in the suicide of Janet Adkins, an Oregon woman said to have Alzheimer's disease. He provided her with a device that she activated to administer a lethal dose of drugs. Questions were raised about Dr. Kevorkian's ability to confirm the patient's diagnosis, about the patient's ability to make an informed decision and about the circumstances. The event took place in a van parked on a side road in Michigan, far from the patient's family and outside any institution.****

Suicide Rates Among the Aging Population A federal study published during 1991 showed that from 1980 to 1986, suicides by Americans aged 65 and older jumped 23 percent for the men, and 42 percent for black men. The rate for white women rose 17 percent, while there were too few suicides among black women to show a meaningful trend. A study in Illinois using a grant from the American Association of Retired People Andrus Foundation showed that the great majority of the elderly who committed suicide were physically healthy. However, 79 percent had shown symptoms of a major treatable psychiatric illness, usually depression or alcoholism.**

For further information:

American Psychiatric Association
1400 K Street, NW
Washington, DC 20005
Phone: (202) 797-4900

American Academy of Child and Adolescent Psychiatry
3615 Wisconsin Avenue, NW
Washington, DC 20016
Phone: (202) 966-7300

American Academy of Pediatrics
141 Northwest Point Boulevard
P.O. Box 927
Elk Grove Village, IL 60007
Phone: (708) 228-5005

American Association of Suicidology
2459 South Ash Street
Denver, CO 80222
Phone: (303) 763-5958

National Alliance for the Mentally Ill
2101 Wilson Blvd., Suite 302
Arlington, VA 22201
Phone: (703) 524-76000

National Committee on Youth Suicide
Prevention
65 Essex Road
Chestnut Hill, MA 02167
Phone: (617) 738-0700

National Depressive and Manic Depressive Association
730 North Franklin Street
Chicago, IL 60601
Phone: (312) 642-0049

National Institute of Mental Health
5600 Fishers Lane
Rockville, MD 20857
Phone: (301) 443-3673

National Mental Health Association
1021 Prince Street
Alexandria, VA 22314-2932
Phone: (703) 684-7722

See also ALCOHOLISM; DEPRESSION; SUICIDE in BIBLIOGRAPHY.

***Brent, David A., et al. "The Presence and Accessibility of Firearms in the Homes of Adolescent Suicides." *Journal of the American Medical Association* 266, no. 21 (Dec. 4, 1991).
Fawcett, Jan, et al. "Time-Related Predictors of Suicide in Major Affective Disorder." *American Journal of Psychiatry* 147, no. 9 (Sept. 1990).
*Fawcett, Jan, and Susman, Paul. "A Clinical Assessment of Acute Suicidal Potential: A Review." *Rush-Presbyterian–St. Luke's Medical Bulletin* 14, no. 2 (Apr. 1975).
**Katz, Marvin. "Critics Fear Misuse of Suicide Books." *Bulletin, American Association of Retired Persons* 32, no. 11 (Dec. 1991).
****"Should the Doctor Ever Help?" *Harvard Health Letter* 16, no. 10 (Aug. 1991).

sundowning; sundown syndrome   Increased symptoms of confusion during the late afternoon or evening hours, as exhibited by patients with dementia usually in nursing homes or long-term care institutions. Manifestations of sundowning include increased confusion, disorientation, agitated behavior and an increase in verbal behavior. Such spells can extend into the night, resulting in restlessness and sleeplessness.

See also AGING; ALZHEIMER'S DISEASE; AGING, ALZHEIMER'S DISEASE in BIBLIOGRAPHY.

superego   A psychoanalytic term for the aspect of personality that represents the standards of parents and society and determines the individual's own sense of right and wrong as well as aspirations and goals. The more common term for superego is conscience.

See also CONSCIENCE.

superiority complex   The unrealistic and exaggerated belief that one is better than others. In some people, this develops as a way to compensate for unconscious feelings of low self-esteem or inadequacy. For example, bullies who push other children around act like they are stronger and smarter than others their age. The reality is that they have low self-esteem. In adults, even business executives may put on a tough facade and try to make others think well of them, but inside they feel inadequate and do not respect themselves.

See also BULLIES; SELF-ESTEEM.

support groups   Also known as self-help groups, support groups consist of individuals with the same mental health disorder or concern for the disorder who join together to help one another by sharing experiences and advice and providing emotional support for one another.

Support groups exist for patients themselves, as well as for spouses and family members. For example, individuals with manic-depressive illness began an organization that has now become nationwide, with chapters in many cities. Individuals with chronic fatigue syndrome (CFS) have done the same, with the result that sufferers no longer need feel alone and that they are the only individuals with the problems. Another example is Y-ME, a national organization of women who have had breast cancer.

There are support groups for parents of children with specific mental health concerns, as well as groups for middle-aged people who care for aging parents.

Many physicians recommend that patients join support groups because they realize that help with the anger and confusion can augment any therapies provided by medical means.

An additional benefit of belonging to a support group for a particular concern is than one can stay up to date on research progress being made as researchers work toward cures and better treatments. Many groups circulate articles from popular and scientific publications and bring in experts to discuss their latest findings.

According to Karyn Feiden, author of *Hope and Help for Chronic Fatigue Syndrome,* the work of support groups generally falls into three interlinked areas:

* Informing and educating the general public, and particularly patients, their families and the medical community.
* Counseling and consoling those who have been diagnosed with the particular disorder.
* Organizing and advocating for the cause at both the local and the national level.

See also BEHAVIORAL THERAPY; CHRONIC FATIGUE SYNDROME; DEPRESSION; EXPOSURE THERAPY; SELF-HELP GROUPS.

supra-additive effect   See SYNERGY.

surrogacy   Any person who substitutes or takes the place of another. The term ''surrogacy'' may be used by mental health professionals for purely emotional or social family relationships. A child who lacks a parent may develop a relationship with a friend, teacher or relative and make that person his surrogate mother or father. An only child may adopt a surrogate brother or sister from her extended family or circle of friends.

Surrogacy gained a more physical, clinical meaning in recent years as science developed techniques whereby a woman could carry and give birth to a child for a woman who was incapable of normal pregnancy and childbirth. This technique has aroused religious opposition and seems to some unnatural or the first step toward a futuristic society that might take an overly clinical, calculating attitude toward reproduction.

Emotional as well as legal problems have arisen from the fact that the surrogate mother may become attached to the child she is carrying and be reluctant to give it up. Surrogate mothers at first were women who agreed to be artificially inseminated with the sperm of the prospective father. Advances in in vitro fertilization later offered the possibility of natural parenthood for both wife and husband for cases in which the wife produced normal eggs but had some other physical problem that made pregnancy difficult, dangerous or impossible. The egg and sperm are brought together outside the parents' bodies and then implanted in a surrogate mother for a normal pregnancy.

An unusual 1991 case of surrogate motherhood involved a woman who agreed to give birth to her own grandchildren. The grandmother was of childbearing age and in good health. Her daughter, who was born without a uterus, was capable of producing normal eggs but not of carrying a child. Eggs from the daughter fertilized with her husband's sperm were successfully implanted in her mother and resulted in twins.

Sex surrogates have also become a controversial issue in recent years. Surrogate sexual partners have been known to act as therapists by engaging in sex with people who have severe sexual dysfunctions. Rape victims, nonorgasmic men and women and people who have remained virgins well into adult life are thought to be appropriate candidates for this type of therapy. Because of a lack of trained therapists and a lack of standards or licensing for the field, it is vulnerable to quacks and practitioners whose motives are dubious. A serious problem in treatment by a sex surrogate is that an attraction may develop that makes the relationship unprofessional or that the patient may become emotionally dependent on the surrogate.

See also INFERTILITY; SEX THERAPY; SURROGATE ACT.

Goldenson, Robert M. "Surrogate," in *The Encyclopedia of Human Behavior,* vol. 2. Garden City, N.Y.: Doubleday and Co., 1970.
"How Safe Are Surrogates?" *Cosmopolitan* (Nov. 1990).
Singer, Peter, and Wells, Deane. *Making Babies.* New York: Scribner's, 1985.

Surrogate Act   In 1991, the Health Care Surrogate Act was signed into law in the state of Illinois. Typical of acts in other states, the law in some instances permits a surrogate to make decisions concerning medical care, including such life-sustaining treatment as artificial nutrition and hydration, for a person unable to make such decisions. For example, in some instances the act authorizes surrogates, including a person's spouse or adult children, to make certain health care decisions when the person has a terminal condition, is in a state of permanent unconsciousness or has an incurable or irreversible condition as defined by the act. The act does not apply if a person has a valid living will or durable power or attorney for health care.

See also LEGAL ISSUES; SURROGACY.

survivor guilt   See HOSTAGES; POST-TRAUMATIC STRESS DISORDER.

switching   Swings of mood from high energy, increased confidence, increased assertiveness and decreased need for sleep to periods of lethargy, fatigue, loss of confidence and increased need for sleep. Symptoms of switching are diagnosed as cyclothymia, a mild form of bipolar depression. In bipolar disorder, mania with exaggerated confidence, grandiosity and sometimes psychosis is alternated with severe depression. Sudden changes from one arousal state

to the other can occur dramatically and rapidly, without necessary environmental stresses.

See also BIPOLAR DISORDER; DEPRESSION; MANIA; MANIC-DEPRESSIVE ILLNESS.

symbolism   In dreams, phobias and the unconscious mind, an object or idea that may signify something else, based on a resemblance between the original and its substitute.

See also DREAMING; FREUD, SIGMUND; PHALLIC SYMBOL.

sympathetic nervous system (SNS)
One of two divisions of the autonomic nervous system. The SNS controls many involuntary activities of the glands, organs and other parts of the body. For example, the SNS is responsible for preparing people for fighting, fleeing, action or sexual climax. Among many effects, the SNS speeds up contractions of blood vessels, slows those of the intestines and increases heartbeat.

See also AUTONOMIC NERVOUS SYSTEM.

SYMPATHOLYTIC DRUGS   Drugs that block actions of the sympathetic nervous system. These include beta blocker drugs, guanethidine, hydralazine and prazosin. They work either by reducing the release of the stimulatory neurotransmitter norepinephrine from nerve endings or by occupying the receptors that the neurotransmitters normally bind to, thus preventing their normal actions.

See also NEUROTRANSMITTERS; NOREPINEPHRINE.

symptom   An indication of a disease or disorder that is noticed by the sufferer, such as a headache. A symptom is different from a sign, which is an indication of a disorder noticed on an objective basis by another person, such as a physician. A group of symptoms as well as signs are sometimes referred to as a syndrome. An example is post-traumatic stress disorder, in which the individual may experience a wide range of symptoms, such as nightmares, feelings of claustrophobia and an inability to concentrate. The physician may notice increased heartbeat, rapid breathing and other signs during examination.

See also SIGN; SYNDROME.

synapse   A microscopic gap between the neurons in the chemical network of the brain. Billions of neurons send and receive electrical messages across synapses through specific amounts of neurotransmitters.

See also BRAIN; NEUROTRANSMITTERS.

syndrome   A group of symptoms or signs occurring together that make up a particular mental or physical disorder. For example, the syndrome that leads a physician to diagnose depression in an individual may include difficulty sleeping, loss of weight, lack of interest in previously enjoyed activities, inability to concentrate, lack of interest in sexual activity and other factors. Another example is post-traumatic stress disorder, a syndrome with many different symptoms experienced by different individuals.

See also SIGN; SYMPTOM.

synergy   The cooperation or joint action of two drugs that when taken together are more effective than when used individually. Because of this phenomenon, an amount of a drug that might be safe under normal circumstances can have a harmful effect if taken with a drug that acts synergistically. An example is a small amount of alcohol combined with a small dose of a barbiturate drug, which can have a much greater effect than either alcohol or a barbiturate taken alone.

How the Synergistic Process Works   In *The Encyclopedia of Drug Abuse,* Robert O'Brien and Sidney Cohen write: "The synergistic process begins in the liver, which metabolizes ingested material. When two drugs are taken together, the enzyme system that processes them is overwhelmed because it does not have the capacity to metabolize both at the same time. In the case of alcohol and a barbiturate drug, which compete for the same enzymes, alcohol is always processed first. The barbiturate, meanwhile, accumulates in the blood, where it has an exaggerated effect on the body and the mind. This delayed metabolization of the barbiturate can result in a tripling or quadrupling of its potency when it enters the central nervous system."

The Third Special Report to the U.S. Congress on Alcohol and Health defined an interaction between alcohol or other central nervous system depressants, and a drug as "any alteration in the pharmacologic properties of either due to the presence of the other." The report classified three different types of interactions:

1. Antagonistic, in which the effects of one or both drugs are blocked or reduced. This can be hazardous when the therapeutic effects of one drug are reduced by the presence of the other.
2. Additive, in which the effect is the sum of the effects of each.
3. Supra-additive (synergistic or potentiating), in which the effect of the two drugs in combination is greater than it would be if the effects were additive. This effect is the most dangerous because at times it can prove fatal.

Half-life of Drugs   Drugs also have a half-life; this is the amount of time it takes for the body to remove half of the drug from the system. For example, Valium has a half-life of 24 hours; half of the first dose may still be in the body when the next is taken. After several days, the buildup can be large, and when alcohol or other central nervous system depressants are taken, the result can be deleterious.

O'Brien, Robert, and Cohn, Sidney. *The Encyclopedia of Drug Abuse.* New York: Facts On File, 1984.

T

tachycardia Rapid beating of the heart. A rapid heartbeat is often associated with anxiety and panic attacks. Individuals who are already feeling anxious or fearful may become even more so when they realize that their heart is beating rapidly. Under such circumstances they may fear that they are having a heart attack. Individuals who are experiencing a panic attack with physical symptoms of rapid heartbeat, difficulty breathing and dizziness may fear that they are going to die. Rapid heartbeat is normal under some conditions, such as exercise or sexual activity.

See also ANXIETY; ANXIETY DISORDERS; PANIC ATTACK; PANIC DISORDER; PHARMA-COLOGIC THERAPY in BIBLIOGRAPHY.

"talking" treatment Psychotherapy by means other than medication. A wide variety of therapies involve the troubled individual talking to the psychotherapist and the therapist listening attentively with empathy and understanding and available to make constructive suggestions. When modern anti-depressant drugs became available in the latter half of the 20th century, some feared that the "old-fashioned" talking treatment would be abandoned. However, when medications are given, they are usually given in combination with psychotherapy and some verbal contact.

More recently, studies comparing short-term therapy (interpersonal or cognitive psychotherapy) with medication treatment or the combination have shown that this combined means of therapy can be successful in treating outpatients with mild to moderate depression.

See also PSYCHOTHERAPY.

Talwin The trade name for pentazocine, a purely synthetic opioid used as a strong painkiller. It is useful for medical purposes but also has a strong potential for the development of tolerance, as well as psychological and physiological dependence. Many addicts seek treatment for their addiction but also sometimes turn to hospital emergency rooms if they are experiencing acute symptoms of overdose or withdrawal.

See also SUBSTANCE ABUSE; SUBSTANCE ABUSE in BIBLIOGRAPHY.

tangentiality See THOUGHT DISORDERS.

tantrums Angry physical outbursts may occur at any time in life, but they are most common in childhood and are thought to be a normal part of a child's developmental process. Tantrums may take many forms, usually involving some combination of screaming, rushing around madly, writhing on the floor and breaking available objects or using them as a weapon. Small children's tantrums are usually triggered by frustration and are beyond the child's control. Mental health professionals feel that the emotional flood that constitutes a tantrum may be just as terrifying for the child as for the adult, because the child fears his own loss of control.

A child may be angered by a new experience or obstacle that she cannot successfully master. Toys or other objects that the child wishes to handle that are either too large or too complex or intricate can trigger an outburst but may also provide a learning experience. There is some evidence that brighter children who are more eager to learn and explore may actually have more tantrums. Tantrums may also be started by the child's inability to understand that the adult world does not always revolve around him as he has come to expect. Most children grow out of their tantrums as they develop a better understanding of their role in the family and learn how people interact on a more mature level.

Leach, Penelope. "Tantrums," in *The Child Care Encyclopedia,* New York: Knopf, 1984.

tardive dyskinesia   Uncontrolled, involuntary facial tremors and grimacing and jerky movements of the arms and legs caused as a side effect of the use of some neuroleptic drugs. This syndrome develops late in treatment (after six months to 20 years) and is estimated to occur in about 20 percent of chronic schizophrenic patients. It is most likely to occur in postmenopausal females with depressive features. This condition may continue after withdrawal of the medications and may become worse after treatment.

It is believed that tardive dyskinesia is caused by chronic blockage of dopamine receptors, resulting in a prolonged supersensitivity of dopamine receptors to normal levels of dopamine. However, this theory does not explain why some patients get tardive dyskinesia and others who must take chronic neuroleptic medications do not.

The best prevention for tardive dyskinesia is using antipsychotics only when indicated and in the lowest effective doses. Patients taking them should be monitored frequently with trials off medication to assess their ongoing need for the medication.

See also SCHIZOPHRENIA; THORAZINE; PHARMACOLOGIC THERAPY, SCHIZOPHRENIA in BIBLIOGRAPHY.

Tay-Sachs disease   A genetic disorder that leads to progressive central nervous system damage. Approximately one in 3,600 infants among eastern European Jewish populations is born with Tay-Sachs disease, while only one in 360,000 non-Jewish infants is affected. The frequency of the abnormal gene for Tay-Sachs disease in the former populations is quite high. There is normal development for three to six months, followed by severe neurological deterioration, blindness, deafness and seizures. Individuals who believe they carry an abnormal gene should obtain genetic counseling before they have children. Tay-Sachs disease is considered a form of mental retardation.

See also MENTAL RETARDATION; MENTAL RETARDATION in BIBLIOGRAPHY.

teenage mothers   See ABORTION; MOTHERS; UNWED MOTHERS.

Tegretol   The trade name for carbamazepine, a commonly used antiepileptic drug, especially for temporal lobe epilepsy. Carbamazepine is chemically related to tricyclic antidepressant drugs. It is now used to treat patients with manic-depressive illness who are not helped by lithium treatment, especially rapidly cycling mania, or patients with dysphoric mania. It will probably not receive approval from the Food and Drug Administration for this use because it is no longer protected by patent from generic distribution, and therefore there is no incentive to fund the cost of studies to demonstrate its efficacy in manic-depressive illness.

See also EPILEPSY; PHARMACOLOGIC THERAPY in BIBLIOGRAPHY.

temperament   One's usual manner of reacting to things. For example, some people are usually calm and passive, and others are active and excitable. Traits of temperament are often noticeable in newborns and become obvious within a few days. Temperament traits may be inherited and become a part of personality, and they usually follow a lifelong pattern.

See also PERSONALITY.

temporal lobe epilepsy (TLE)   Also known as psychomotor epilepsy, this disorder manifests itself with personality changes such as extreme and excessive interest in religion, hypergraphia (writing prolifically), hyposexuality, temper outbursts and, occasionally, mood disorders. It is due to an electrical and functional disturbance in the brain and is best evaluated by laboratory tests using neurophysiology and functional neuroimaging, as well as the electroencephalogram (EEG). Individuals with this condition may experience temporal lobe illusions (temporal lobe hallucinations, temporal hallucinations).

See also EPILEPSY.

temporomandibular joint (TMJ) syndrome Symptoms, including pain, that affect the jaw, face and head. TMJ occurs when the ligaments and muscles that control and support these areas do not work together properly. A spasm of the chewing muscles can bring on the disorder. In some individuals, this occurs because of bruxism (teeth grinding) or clenching of the teeth as a response to stress and tension. Treatment may include relieving pain by applying moist heat to the face, taking muscle-relaxant drugs and using a bite splint at night to prevent teeth clenching and grinding. Some individuals resort to surgery on their jaw; others undergo orthodontia to correct their bite. Psychological counseling is often recommended to help the individual overcome the underlying causes of tension that may have led to the disorder.

See also BRUXISM; STRESS.

TENS (transcutaneous nerve stimulation) See PAIN; TRANSCUTANEOUS NERVE STIMULATION.

tension headache See HEADACHES.

terminal illness An illness from which medical experts have agreed there will be no recovery. Since modern medicine has prolonged the final stages of illnesses, the mental and physical state of dying patients has received increased attention. In 1969, Elisabeth Kubler-Ross (1926–) described the final stages of terminal illness as denial, anger, bargaining, depression and acceptance. These attitudes and feelings may take different forms and may overlap, but they do seem to form a common experience among dying patients. Kubler-Ross observed that most patients find their death incomprehensible and the product of some intentional, destructive force, no matter what the actual cause. Terminally ill patients, in addition to fearing their own annihilation, fear the withdrawal of loved ones, real or imagined, and their own growing dependence and inability to cope with daily life. Patients frequently suffer from a loss of self-esteem and may express fears that they are being abandoned or persecuted. On the other hand, elderly patients approaching death may seem to experience it as a sort of summing up and end, a natural part of life.

A frequent problem in dealing with dying patients is that while they may wish to talk about their situation, listeners are hard to find because of the common resistance among those in good health to be confronted with the possibility of their own eventual annihilation.

Mental health professionals have found certain techniques and attitudes useful in dealing with dying patients. For example, it has been helpful to imagine the person without his illness, so that the illness does not become the most important thing about him, and to dwell on the patient's traits and talents in normal life. It is also important for the professional to be aware of her own fears and to maintain a balanced attitude between gloom and unrealistic optimism.

Professionals in health care have also found it helpful to combat the patient's fears about the potential pain and suffering as his illness reaches its final stages by informing him that those approaching death usually do not experience suffering.

See also ACQUIRED IMMUNODEFICIENCY SYNDROME; CAREGIVERS; CHRONIC ILLNESS; DEATH; HOSPICE.

Felner, R. D. "Terminally Ill People," in Corsini, Raymond J., ed., *Encyclopedia of Psychology*, vol. 3. New York: Wiley, 1984.
Zimmerman, Jack McKay. *Hospice*. Baltimore: Urban & Schwarzenberg, 1986.

terrorism In a 1986 public report issued by then Vice President George Bush's Task Force on Combating Terrorism, terrorism was defined as: "The unlawful use or threat of violence against persons or property to further political or social objectives. It is usually intended to intimidate or coerce a government, individuals or groups to modify their behavior or politics.''

Worldwide terrorism interferes with many people's feeling of mental well-being, as it makes them fearful and apprehensive about traveling and trusting strangers.

Terrorists are usually young men who are fanatical about their cause to the extent that they have no concern for their victims or for their own lives. Boys as young as 14 or 15 have been used for dangerous missions. Some terrorist groups are self-supporting through activities such as bank robbery or selling drugs, but most are supported by governments who find terrorism and hostage taking effective and inexpensive in comparison with the costs of conventional military force. Terrorism aimed at U.S. diplomats increased dramatically in the 20 years before the Bush report.

See also HOSTAGES; POST-TRAUMATIC STRESS DISORDER; POST-TRAUMATIC STRESS DISORDER in BIBLIOGRAPHY.

testosterone A male androgenic sex hormone that stimulates muscles, bones and sexual development. During puberty it leads to deepening of the voice and growth of facial hair. The most important of the androgen hormones, testosterone is produced in the testes (and in very small amounts in a woman's ovaries). Testosterone in medicinal form is sometimes used to treat infertility in males who have disorders of the testes or pituitary gland. Since related androgenic hormones promote muscle development and strength, they have been self-administered by athletes to improve their function. Not only may this promote the development of cardiac disease, but increases in aggression and impulsive behavior (including homicide) have also occurred. Androgenic drugs are outlawed by all athletic leagues and organizations.

See also INFERTILITY; PITUITARY GLAND.

thalamus See BRAIN.

therapeutic alliance The trusting rapport and understanding between the psychotherapist and the patient. In order to derive benefit from the psychotherapeutic consultations, the patient must trust the therapist and believe the therapist can help. The therapist, in turn, must communicate respect, interest and empathic understanding in order to facilitate the patient's trust.

See also PSYCHOTHERAPY.

therapeutic contract See CONTRACT (THERAPEUTIC CONTRACT).

therapeutic foster care A type of mental health care for children and adolescents, ideally involving the following features:

1. Placement of a child with foster parents who have specifically been recruited to work with an emotionally disturbed child or adolescent.
2. Provision of special training to the foster parents to assist them in working with the child.
3. Placement of only one child in each special foster home (with occasional exceptions).
4. A low staff-to-patient ratio, thereby allowing clinical staff to work very closely with each child, with the foster parents and with the biologic parents if they are available.
5. Creation of a support system among the foster parents.
6. Payment of a special stipend to the foster parents for working with the emotionally disturbed child or adolescent and for participating in the training and other program activities.

This type of care is regarded as the least restrictive of residential mental health services.

See also MENTAL RETARDATION.

U.S. Congress, Office of Technology Assessment. *Adolescent Health, Volume 1: Summary and Policy Options*. OTA-H-468. Washington, D.C.: USGPO, 1991.

therapy   See PSYCHOTHERAPY.

thiamine deficiency   Thiamine deficiency may lead to Wernicke-Korsakoff syndrome (also known as alcohol amnestic disorder) and Korsakoff's psychosis (usually caused by alcohol abuse), an amnestic disorder (inability to remember recent events). In some cases, malabsorption or dietary inadequacy can lead to these disorders. Individuals with Korsakoff's syndrome often fabricate answers to questions in an attempt to fill in details they do not recall (confabulation). The most common memory impairment involves difficulty in learning new information. Korsakoff's syndrome improve in about 75 percent of people who stop alcohol abuse and who maintain an adequate diet for more than six months.

See also ALCOHOLISM.

thioridazine   An antipsychotic medication (trade name: Mellaril) used primarily to treat schizophrenia and other psychoses. The use of thioridazine has also been suggested to relieve anxiety, agitation and depression associated with mood disorders. The drug is used in conjunction with psychotherapy, but its use for anxiety alone is limited because it carries with it the risk of tardive dyskinesia.

See also ANTIPSYCHOTIC MEDICATIONS; ANXIETY DISORDERS; DEPRESSION; SCHIZOPHRENIA.

Thorazine   Trade name for chlorpromazine hydrochloride, the first antipsychotic agent marketed; it is a phenothiazine derivative also referred to as a neuroleptic medication. It was used primarily to treat schizophrenia, other psychoses or mania. For a while during the 1950s it was used to treat anxiety disorders, but it has been replaced with newer anxiolytic agents because of its serious side effects and limited efficacy in anxiety. The primary indication for chlorpromazine and related medications is the treatment of psychosis.

Prior to the introduction of chlorpromazine around the mid-1950s, the population of state mental hospitals was increasing at a rate of 10 percent per year. After the introduction of chlorpromazine, the population decreased at the rate of 10 percent per year.

Psychiatrists, pharmacologists and neuroscientists have not solved the problem of schizophrenia, but the neuroleptics which have been developed do suppress hallucinations, delusions and symptoms of withdrawal seen in schizophrenia, organic psychoses, psychotic depression and other psychotic disorders. They do not by themselves restore schizophrenic patients to normal function and cause a range of side effects that limit compliance and their use. Related drugs (Prolixin and thioridazine) are examples of other phenothiazines. Side effects include extrapyramidal effects, Parkinsonian symptoms such as muscle rigidity, akathisias (a state of physical agitation often producing anxiety) and sedation. Acute administration may cause neuroleptic malignant syndrome, associated with rigidity, disorientation and high fever with possible chronic neurological damage. Long-term use carries a 4 percent per year risk of tardive dyskinesia. For these reasons, chlorpromazine and related medications are used in severe psychotic disorders.

See also ANTIPSYCHOTIC MEDICATIONS; TRANQUILIZER DRUGS; PHARMACOLOGIC THERAPY in BIBLIOGRAPHY.

thought disorders   Disturbance of thought processes or thought content. Thought process refers to the way an individual puts ideas together, to the associations between ideas and to the form and flow of thoughts in conversation. Thought content refers to the ideas the person communicates.

Disorders of thought processes include racing thoughts, a situation in which the individual is flooded with ideas and is unable to keep up with them. This is seen in some people who have schizophrenia and also in manic states. Another is circumstantiality, which involves thinking that is indirect in reaching a goal or getting to the point. People who are obsessional sometimes have this characteristic. Blocking is a sudden interruption or obstruction in the spontaneous flow of thoughts, considered by the individual as an absence of thought. This occurs in severe anxiety states and schizophrenia. Perseveration is a tendency for an individual to respond with the same sound or words to varied stimuli, and also an inability to shift the trend of conversation away from one specific topic.

Other thought process disorders include flight of ideas, verbally skipping from one related idea to another; tangentiality, in which the person replies to questions in irrelevant ways; clanging, which involves using the sound of a word, instead of its meaning (such as rhymes) to communicate; word salad, which is a jumble of words and phrases lacking comprehensive meaning or logical coherence; and echolalia, parrotlike repetition of another's speech (seen in organic brain syndrome and in mania). Loose associations involve transitions from one idea to another, unrelated idea.

Disorders of thought content include delusions, false beliefs firmly held despite incontrovertible and obvious proof to the contrary. There may be delusions of grandeur or delusions of persecution. Some individuals who have delusions of control believe that one's feelings and actions are imposed by some external source. Somatic delusions are beliefs about body image or body function. Thought broadcasting is the belief that other people can read one's thoughts. Ideas of reference involve incorrectly interpreting casual incidents and external events as having direct personal reference. These ideas are usually delusions. Depersonalization is a sense of unreality or strangeness concerning oneself and feeling detached from and being an outside observer

of one's mental processes or body. Derealization refers to feeling detached from one's environment so that a sense of reality of the external world is lost. Depersonalization and derealization are fairly common in severe anxiety states and also in borderline personality disorder.

Another thought disorder is preoccupation (persistent ideas), which includes obsessions, compulsions and phobias. Some depressed people have morbid preoccupations about guilt or death.

See also ANXIETY DISORDERS; DELUSION; DEPRESSION; OBSESSIVE-COMPULSIVE DISORDER; PHOBIA; SCHIZOPHRENIA.

thought stopping   A behavioral therapy technique in which the individual imagines hearing the word ''stop'' whenever an undesirable thought occurs. Developed by Joseph Wolpe (1915–   ), an American psychiatrist, this technique is sometimes useful in treating anxieties, phobias, smoking and sexual deviations.

See also BEHAVIORAL THERAPY; REINFORCEMENT; BEHAVIORAL THERAPY in BIBLIOGRAPHY.

3-methoxy-4-hydroxyphenylglycol (MHPG)   The major metabolite of norepinephrine in the central nervous system. Urinary excretion of MHPG is usually decreased in individuals with bipolar disorder while they are in the depressed mode as compared with the manic state. Levels of this substance are also increased during episodes of extreme anxiety or fear. Levels of MHPG diminish after use of imipramine or clonidine or after anxiety episodes diminish. Measurements of the substance help determine effectiveness of some antianxiety medications.

See also ANXIETY; LABORATORY TESTS; ANXIETIES AND ANXIETY DISORDERS in BIBLIOGRAPHY.

thyroid gland   A gland located at the back of the neck, which may have a biologic link to depression. Normally the pituitary gland generates a hormone at night that stimulates the thyroid, but sleep suppresses this action. In individuals who cycle to mania or in depressed persons deprived of sleep, levels of the thyroid-stimulating hormone fluctuate between highs and lows. Increased levels of thyroid disease occurs in some manic-depressive individuals, especially those with rapid cycles of the highs and lows.

See also THYROTROPIN-RELEASING HORMONE TEST.

thyrotropin-releasing hormone test
A test used as an aid in diagnosing depressions and assessing the status of the thyroid gland. Some clinicians and researchers believe that some individuals who suffer from a subclinical form of hypothyroidism should be monitored for thyroid function as a diagnostic tool. The thyroid-stimulating hormone (TSH) is measured after infusion of protirelin (thyrotropin-releasing hormone, TRH). Manics seem to have a blunted response compared with that of normal controls. Thus the thyroid-stimulating hormone (TSH) response to the thyrotropin-releasing hormone (TRH) infusion has indicated that the TRH test can be useful for both diagnosis and treatment.

Studies suggest that a significant proportion of individuals with depression may have early hypothyroidism. Many researchers also believe that both depressed inpatients and outpatients may be appropriate candidates for a comprehensive thyroid evaluation, including the TRH test. This evaluation is especially important if the patient is taking, or being considered for treatment with, lithium carbonate, which is known to cause hypothyroidism in some individuals.

See also BIOLOGICAL MARKERS.

Roesch, Roberta. *The Encyclopedia of Depression*. New York: Facts On File, 1991.

tic   Rapid, repetitive movements of individual muscle groups. Most noticeable tics involve the facial muscles, such as the lips or eyelids. Tics may also be vocal. In some cases, tics are associated with anxiety and stress. Tics are also a characteristic of Tourette syndrome, a disorder of the nervous system.

See also BEHAVIORAL THERAPY; TOURETTE SYNDROME.

tiredness   See CHRONIC FATIGUE SYNDROME.

titration   A technique physicians use to determine the optimum dose of a drug required to produce a desired effect in a particular individual. Dosage may be gradually increased until the patient notices an improvement or decreased from a level that is excessive because of side effects. For example, antidepressant drugs are titrated for each individual. Certain blood tests of serum drug concentration levels are also used for this purpose. Because titration of many medications is essential, it is important for people who start drug therapy to be closely supervised by their physician.

See also ANTIDEPRESSANT MEDICATIONS; ANTIPSYCHOTIC MEDICATIONS; PSYCHOPHARMACOLOGY.

TM   See TRANSCENDENTAL MEDITATION.

TMJ   See TEMPOROMANDIBULAR JOINT (TMJ) SYNDROME.

tobacco   The active ingredient in tobacco is nicotine, which is addictive. It affects the central nervous system through routes that differ from other drugs, but it produces very similar results, such as pleasurable euphoria, dependency and withdrawal symptoms when stopped suddenly.

Nicotine acts as both a stimulant and a depressant. Shallow puffs seem to increase alertness, but deep ones are relaxing. Smokers sense their nicotine levels and tend to self-regulate them by varying inhalation patterns, as well as their frequency of smoking.

In regular smokers, nicotine improves short-term memory, intellectual performance and concentration. Although smoking speeds up the heart rate and raises blood pressure, it also seems to relieve stressful feelings for some smokers. Nicotine consumption also appears to control weight to some extent, probably by lowering circulating insulin levels and thus decreasing smokers' craving for sweets and tendency to store fat. This particular aspect of nicotine makes smoking appeal to those who are afraid of gaining weight.

Smokers who quit may experience genuine physical discomfort and cravings. Withdrawal symptoms from nicotine include headaches, irritability, upset stomach, breathing and circulation problems, trouble sleeping, dizziness and numbness.

During pregnancy, smoking increases the risk of miscarriage, fetal death, premature delivery and low birth weight. Infants of mothers who smoked during pregnancy also have a 50 percent greater chance of sudden infant death syndrome (SIDS) than infants whose mothers did not smoke.

See also ADDICTION; SMOKING.

Media Resource Guide on Common Drugs of Abuse. Public Relations Society of America, National Capital Chapter, Fairfax, Va., September 1990.

Tofranil   Trade name for imipramine hydrochloride, a tricyclic antidepressant drug, used in treatment of depressive episodes of major depression and bipolar, dysthymic panic and phobic disorders. It is also used to treat bedwetting in children and urinary incontinence in elderly individuals.

See also ANTIDEPRESSANT MEDICATION; IMIPRAMINE HYDROCHLORIDE; PHARMACOLOGIC THERAPY in BIBLIOGRAPHY.

toilet training   Learning to use the toilet presents the first great potential conflict between mother and child. Some mental health professionals connect toilet training that is too early or too harsh with later behavior that is obedient but resentful. On the other hand, a child whose toilet training was delayed may develop a self-indulgent, narcissistic personality. A strong atmosphere of conflict surrounding toilet training may cause feelings of guilt, self-doubt and rage.

Modern child development professionals say that toilet training can best be accomplished when a child is ready for it and has some sense of assuming responsibility for the functions of his own body that will make him like the adult world. Parents are usually most successful in presenting toilet training as an interesting idea and avoiding an authoritarian manner. One difficulty that must be surmounted in toilet training is that small children have little or no ability to connect the bodily sensation from the bladder or the intestines with the necessity of heading for the bathroom. Some awareness of the function does begin to develop between the 12th and 18th month, but usually at this point the child exhibits some interest but does not anticipate. Even children who are trained have so little ability to anticipate that their need to use the toilet is usually instantaneous. Once children are partly trained, parents can begin to rely on the child's own resistance to soiling himself rather than constantly reminding him, which may actually delay the time when he is fully trained.

Freeman, Lucy, and Kupfermann, Kerstin. *The Power of Fantasy.* New York: Continuum, 1988.
Leach, Penelope. ''Toilet Training,'' *The Child Care Encyclopedia.* New York: Knopf, 1984.

Tourette syndrome   A neurological syndrome characterized by rapid, repeated and purposeless involuntary movements of various muscle groups (motor tics) and by grunts, barks and sniffing sounds (vocal tics). It is the most debilitating of several tic disorders. It often begins before age 21 with one or more vocal tics. Behavioral difficulties such as attentional problems, compulsions and obsessions are commonly observed in TS patients.

Until the 1970s, TS was frequently misdiagnosed as schizophrenia, obsessive-compulsive disorder, epilepsy or nervous habits. Once thought to be rare, TS is now considered a relatively common disorder affecting up to one person in every 2,500 in its complete form and three times that number in its partial expressions that include chronic motor tics and some forms of obsessive-compulsive disorder.

TS was first described in 1885 by Georges Gilles de la Tourette, a French physician. The cause of the disorder is unknown; however, there is recognition that TS is familial and genetic. Researchers are actively engaged in searching for the chromosomal location of the TS gene of affected individuals. There is not yet a genetic or biochemical test to determine if a person with TS or an unaffected individual carries the gene; there is no prenatal test for the vulnerability to TS.

An inability to control one's own body and even one's own thoughts is taken for granted by most people and is often a source of anxiety, guilt, helplessness and depression. TS patients react in individual ways; some become withdrawn, others become overly aggressive and still others become perfectionists. Self-esteem problems are common. Psychotherapy can be helpful to the individual as well as to the family involved. There is evidence that Tourette syndrome may be associated with symptoms of obsessive-compulsive disorder.

Medications help some individuals who have TS. Among those used are haloperidol (trade name: Haldol), pimozide (trade name: Orap), phenothiazine drugs (particularly fluphenazine) and clonidine (trade name: Catapres).

For additional information, contact:

Tourette Syndrome Association
42-40 Bell Boulevard
Bayside, NY 11361
Phone: (718) 224-2999

See also CHRONIC ILLNESS; FAMILY THERAPY; OBSESSIVE-COMPULSIVE DISORDER; TIC.

toxic shock syndrome See MENSTRUATION.

trait A long-lasting aspect of one's personality, such as dependence, independence, introversion or extroversion, that helps to predict how a person will respond in a variety of situations.

See also PERSONALITY.

tranquilizer medications Anxiety-reducing medications that act on the brain and nervous system and may have sedative side effects. Tranquilizer medications are generally divided into two categories: major tranquilizers (or antipsychotic drugs) and minor tranquilizers (known as antianxiety drugs). The sedative effect may promote tranquilizing effects but is not necessary for the later effect.

See also ANTIANXIETY MEDICATIONS; ANTIPSYCHOTIC MEDICATIONS.

transactional analysis (TA) A type of group or individual therapy in which the goal is to develop one's identity and independence and to better one's means of coping with interactions with others. TA was developed by Eric Berne, a Canadian-born American psychologist (1910–1970), and described in 1967 by Thomas A. Harris in the book *I'm OK, You're OK.* In TA, all behavior, thinking, feeling and experience is categorized into three ego states: parent (critical and/or loving); adult (practical and evaluative); and child (feelings, such as dependency, or fun-loving and caring). These ego states can be identified by nonverbal changes, changes in voice tone, expressions and words. All three states are considered to serve a valuable purpose. Individuals can learn to identify which ego state is in control.

TA analyzes transactions to gain insight into the dynamics of interpersonal problems. When the lines of the transaction are parallel, the transaction is complementary. When the lines of the transaction cross, communication stops.

See also GROUP THERAPY.

transcendental meditation (TM) A technique for meditation based on ancient Hindu writings, developed by Maharishi Maheh Yogi and introduced in the United States in the early 1960s. Typically, the meditator spends two 20-minute periods a day sitting quietly with eyes closed and attention focused totally on the verbal repetition of a special sound or "mantra." Repetition of the mantra blocks distracting thoughts. The effect achieved is better relaxation and relief from stress. TM has also been referred to as mystic union.

See also ALTERNATIVE THERAPIES; MEDITATION.

transcutaneous nerve stimulation (TENS) A method for relieving pain using tiny electrical impulses to nerve endings under the skin. TENS seems to work by blocking pain messages to the brain by providing alternative stimuli. TENS is usually recommended for individuals who do not respond to analgesic medications. Careful monitoring by a physician is required when an individual uses this type of therapy.

See also PAIN.

transference The unconscious process during psychotherapy in which a person displaces emotional feelings and attributes of a significant attachment figure from the past—usually a parent—to the therapist. During psychoanalytic therapy, an understanding and resolution of this process must be achieved to understand how old conflicts could be resolved more satisfactorily.

Transference often occurs between patient and physician, worker and boss, student and teacher, but is not often recognized. Transference may be positive (trusting, feelings of strength and support) and negative (distrust, anger, anticipation of criticism, etc.), often depending on the individual's experience with parent figures. The process is often unconscious and unrecognized except in psychotherapy with a well-trained therapist. It can lead to very intense pervasive feelings.

See also COUNTERTRANSFERENCE; FREUD, SIGMUND; PSYCHOANALYSIS.

transgenderism A gender-identity disorder in which an individual identifies strongly with the opposite sex and may cross-dress but does not desire a sex-change operation. Such confusion of sex roles may develop when the individual does not receive adequate sex-role modeling from one or both parents.

See also GENDER IDENTITY.

transsexualism A feeling that exists when a person feels that she or he is a member of one gender trapped in a body that has sexual characteristics associated with the other gender, usually evident to that person since childhood. The term "transsexualism" was coined by Harry Benjamin in 1966. The first well-known case of transsexualism was Christine Jorgensen, who had a sex change operation from male to female in 1952.

See also GENDER IDENTITY.

transvestitism Individuals who wear the clothing of the other sex, a practice known as cross-dressing. Transvestitism takes many forms. For example, pseudotransvestites try cross dressing for fun and not to fulfill any need. The fetishistic transvestite cross-dresses episodically because women's clothes are fetish objects and create sexual arousal.

tremor An involuntary movement of muscles (shaking) in part of the body, most commonly the hands. Individuals who are extremely anxious may experience tremors at times of excitement or fear. Many elderly people have a slight tremor not related to any disease. Essential tremor is a disorder that sometimes runs in families but seems to have no known cause.

Some tremors are associated with neurological diseases such as Parkinson's disease. Other disorders in which tremor is a characteristic include multiple sclerosis, mercury poisoning and hepatic encephalopathy. Some drugs may cause tremors in some individuals; among them are amphetamine drugs, antidepressant drugs and lithium. Alcohol withdrawal may produce tremors.

See also ALCOHOLISM; PARKINSON'S DISEASE.

tricyclic antidepressant medications A group of antidepressant drugs. A commonly used tricyclic antidepressant is imipramine, which is also widely used in treating panic disorder. Tricyclic drugs are so named because their molecular structure is characterized by three fused rings.

See also ANTIDEPRESSANT MEDICATIONS; DEPRESSION.

trisomy 21 See DOWN'S SYNDROME.

twin studies Studies of twins have revealed a great deal about the possible genetic causes of certain mental health disorders. For example, studies of the incidence of depressive illness in twins, in families and in the general population have established a genetic basis for at least some depressive disorders. Relatives of people with unipolar depressive illness have a higher frequency of depression than the general population. The prevalence of unipolar depression is greatest among first-degree relatives of unipolar depressive individuals. Moreover, monozygotic twins (same genes) have a 65 to 75 percent concordance rate for bipolar depression, while dizygotic twins (different eggs, different genes) have only a 14 to 19 percent concordance rate for the illness. That means that if one twin suffers from depression, it is much more likely that the other twin will also suffer from depression if he or she is identical rather than fraternal.

There have been at least four well-known twin studies of alcoholism. In one, a Swedish investigator found that identical twins were significantly more concordant for alcoholism than fraternal twins, and the more severe the alcoholism, the greater the difference. A Finnish study reported that younger identical twins shared alcohol problems more often than older identical twins, but there was no difference in the total sample. Another study showed no difference at all between American identical and fraternal twins. A Veterans Administration study supported a finding that identical twins were more often concordant for alcoholism than fraternal twins. Differences in these studies may be accounted for by differences among cultures, sampling, information gathering and definitions of alcoholism.

Twin studies show the concordance for panic disorder among monozygotic twins to be five times that among dizygotic twins. However, there are still confounding environmental variables, such as the possibility that parents treat identical and fraternal twins differently.

Twin studies show higher concordance of schizophrenia among identical twins than among fraternal twins. When one twin is schizophrenic, the other is much more likely to be schizophrenic if the twins have identical genetic makeup.

See also ADOPTION STUDIES; DEPRESSION; SCHIZOPHRENIA.

Type A personality A designation that usually relates to a life-style, and style of work and performance, characterized by competitive feelings, drive, ambition, impatience, goal orientation, anxiety, worry or hostility. Such individuals may tend to emphasize speed and quantity over quality of work. They may take on multiple commitments and become preoccupied with meeting deadlines. Their behavior may be characterized by abrupt gestures, and they may express themselves explosively. They tend to feel guilty if not working and take little pleasure in other activities. Many of these individuals neglect family responsibilities in favor of working and tending to business interests.

Some researchers believe that Type A people have individualistic traits that set them apart from others and that they tend to be suspicious people who lack the emotional support that comes from close relationships.

Type A personalities have sometimes been associated with high incidence of coronary heart disease. Many individuals make efforts to change their personality traits after a serious illness and, as a result, relax more and learn to spend their leisure time in enjoyable ways instead of working or competing. Studies involving Type A individuals have shown that this kind of behavior can be changed through learning relaxation techniques, development of a sense of humor and other life-style changes. They thus become a combination of Type A and Type B personalities.

See also TYPE B PERSONALITY.

Type B personality Personality traits that enable an individual to enjoy activities that are not competitive. These individuals usually work without agitation or a sense of urgency and are not particularly goal-oriented, as are Type A personalities.

At one time A and B personality traits were thought to be strongly related to achievement and health and were also seen as being more rigid. However, more recent research indicates that the single trait of hostility is more strongly related to heart disease than the whole spectrum of traits known as Type A. It has also been found that Type A behavior is not as strong a predictor of achievement as once thought. Successful executives have actually been found to be people who can move back and forth between the Type A and Type B char-

acteristics, depending on appropriateness to the situation. A and B personality types have been found to be scattered fairly evenly among top and middle management. For optimal mental health, it seems that a combination of the A and B traits may be best, so that an individual can enjoy a balanced life, with aspects of work, family, love, friends, recreation and fun.

See also FRIENDS.

Armand, M., Jr., ed. *The New Harvard Guide to Psychiatry.* Cambridge: Belknap Press of Harvard University, 1988.
Pelletier, Kenneth. *Healthy People in Unhealthy Places.* New York: Delacorte Press, 1984.

tyramine A substance found in some foods that may interfere with the effectiveness of certain antidepressant drugs because it affects constriction and expansion of blood vessels. It is generally recommended that individuals who take MAO (monoamine oxidase) inhibitors as mood elevators for depression avoid ripe cheeses, anything fermented, pickled or marinated foods (such as herring), sour cream, yogurt, nuts, peanut butter, seeds, pods of broad beans (lima, navy, pinto, garbanzo and pea), chocolate, vinegar (except white vinegar) and any foods containing large amounts of monosodium glutamate (such as some Oriental foods).

Individuals who suffer from migraine headaches are also advised to avoid foods containing tyramine.

See also ANTIDEPRESSANT MEDICATIONS; HEADACHES; MONOAMINE OXIDASE INHIBITORS.

Kahn, Ada P. *Headaches.* Chicago: Contemporary Books, 1983.

U

unconscious The area of the mind in which memories, perceptions or feelings are stored; the individual is not aware of this store and cannot willfully recollect them.

See also FREUD, SIGMUND; PSYCHOANALYSIS.

unconsciousness   Loss of awareness of self and surroundings. Unconsciousness may be normal—as during sleep—or very brief, as in fainting. After a concussion, unconsciousness may be brief. More prolonged unconsciousness is known as coma.

underachiever   A student or other individual who is of average or superior ability but performs poorly in school. Underachievement may be applied to specific areas such as arithmetic or reading ability if the child has shown potential beyond his achievement in that area. Underachievement affects the student's mental health as well as that of his parents.

Educational factors may contribute to underachievement. Teachers who have personality conflicts with certain students can contribute to poor performance by ignoring or contributing to their difficulties. Large class size or school systems that lack the personnel and techniques to delve into the causes of poor performance may cause or exacerbate a child's learning problems. Underachievement, particularly in very bright students, may result from boredom when classroom activities do not stimulate them or challenge their abilities. Average or bright students with short attention spans can also appear to be below normal.

A child's relationship with her parents may also cause underachievement. Parents who are high achievers themselves may have unrealistic expectations of their children, which causes a child who already has low self-esteem to suffer from an ever poorer performance. Parents with average abilities who produce a child with exceptional intelligence or other ability may not understand and even discourage their child's superior performance. Family problems such as divorce, conflict, death or serious illness of a parent may also hold a child back.

Children may also become underachievers because they are perceived as different and are not socially well-adjusted to their peer group. Factors such as exceptionally high intelligence, ethnic or religious difference, a financial status that is far above or below classmates or very mature or immature behavior patterns may set a child apart, limit her friendships and lower her school performance. Achievement is also reduced when a child desires to become a member of a gang so badly that he associates with troublemakers or other students who perform poorly in school.

Sex role expectations also influence a child's performance. For example, girls may respond to social conditioning that they are not supposed to be as bright as boys, particularly in subjects such as math or science. These expectations may adversely affect some boys as well. If their families expect consistently superior performance from them, they may become so frustrated that the results are the opposite.

See also PEER GROUP; SELF-ESTEEM.

Thiel, Ann; Thiel, Richard; and Grenoble, Penelope B. *When Your Child Isn't Doing Well in School*. Chicago: Contemporary Books, 1988.
''Underachievement,'' in Dejnozka, Edward, *American Educator's Encyclopedia*. Westport, Conn.: Greenwood Press, 1982.

unipolar disorder (unipolar depression)   An affective illness (mood disorder) in which only depressive episodes occur. This is contrasted with bipolar disorder, in which episodes of depression as well as mania occur.

See also BIPOLAR DISORDER; DEPRESSION; RAPID CYCLING.

unwed mothers   A woman who becomes pregnant out of wedlock faces many psychological stresses in making many decisions. In most cases, there are several options to consider. She may either choose to terminate the pregnancy with a legal abortion or have the child and choose between single parenthood and giving the child up for adoption. Depending on her relationship with the father, she may also choose marriage. Research on the latter option has shown various results. It was once believed that a "shotgun" marriage was a poor choice, both because of the failure rate of such marriages and because the wife frequently dropped out of school. Some studies of this type of marriage in the 1980s showed a fairly high success rate, often dependent on the father being older than the mother and having finished school. A study of such marriages involving low-income black teenagers in Baltimore showed that one-third were still married 17 years later. Some researchers believe that these marriages may be of some benefit even if they do not last. In another study, women who had married under these circumstances and had stayed married for five years were found to be better off financially.

The typical unwed mother in the United States is in her late teens or early twenties. Statistics for 1988 show that 31.1 percent of births to unmarried women were to women in the 15 to 19 age range and that 34.9 percent were to women whose ages ranged from 20 to 24. Some of these women who choose to have their babies and relinquish them for adoption may opt for the more traditional procedure in which the birth mother severs all ties and responsibilities for the child. Others may choose a system called "open adoption," which allows the birth mother some participation in decision making and some continuing contact even though the child is legally adopted by a couple. Changing social standards and even the examples of celebrities have encouraged unwed mothers to keep and raise their babies, but they still must face problems of providing financial support, coping with illness and other childhood disasters while working, and taking the responsibility for child rearing alone.

Often grandparents participate very actively in decision making about an out-of-wedlock pregnancy and also in rearing the child, with more or less favorable results depending on the flexibility of their attitudes. However, having one's child reared by one's parents brings several stressors into the picture. The young woman and her parents may have different ideas of appropriate behavior with the result of giving mixed messages to the child. In addition, the grandparents may be at an age and life-style at which having a young child around interferes with their long-planned activities.

In addition to women who unintentionally become pregnant out of wedlock, an increasing number of single women choose unwed motherhood. Some single women "feel the biological time clock ticking," meaning that they are in their late thirties and want to have children, although they have not yet found a man to marry. Some single women choose adoption; others choose to become impregnated by a man whom they know they will not marry, sometimes even retaining a friendly relationship with the man. Still others choose artificial insemination; however, these women often must work around the reluctance of some doctors to inseminate single women and the psychological difficulties of knowing very little about the father of their child. In all of these cases, even though social standards are changing, unwed mothers must still eventually cope with the possibility that their child may feel different because he or she lacks a father. Such a child may face many questions as he or she grows up in a peer group of children who have two known parents, even though many of them will be in stepfamilies or merged families.

Legal abortion is still an option for women whose duration of pregnancy and religious and philosophical outlook allow for terminating a pregnancy. In the 1980s, about 40 percent of teen pregnancies were ended by abortion. Between 1972 and 1987 the number of legal abortions increased from 44,588 to 57,964. Although the absolute number of abortions has increased, the ratio of abortions to live births peaked in 1983 at 436 per 1,000 live births and dropped to 406 per 1,000 live births in 1987.

See also ABORTION; ADOPTION.

Chance, Paul. "Return of the Shotgun Wedding." *Psychology Today* 21 (Sept. 1987).
Kantrowitz, Barbara. "Mothers on Their Own." *Newsweek* (Dec. 23, 1985).
Statistical Abstract of the United States, 1991. "Births to Unmarried Women by Race of Child and Age of Mother: 1970 to 1988" p. 67; "Legal Abortions—Estimated Number, Rate, and Ratio by Race: 1972 to 1987," p. 71.

upper The street name for amphetamine drugs. These are central nervous system stimulants with actions that resemble those of the naturally occurring substance adrenaline. Until recent years, physicians prescribed amphetamines for obesity, depression and narcolepsy. Amphetamines have also been widely misused by students studying for examinations and truck drivers on long trips in an attempt to stay alert for long periods of time.

Amphetamines are commercially produced but are limited by the Controlled Substances Act of 1972.

See also AMPHETAMINE DRUGS; SUBSTANCE ABUSE.

urethral phase A stage of psychosexual development representing transition from the anal to the phallic stage, involving conflicts about urethral control, resolution of which leads to self-competence and gender identity.

See also GENDER IDENTITY.

urolagnia A paraphilia (sexual aberration) in which the women or man has a morbid attraction for urine or the urinary processes of the sex partner or someone else. Such individuals may obtain sexual stimulation by watching the partner urinate, by sniffing garments smelling of urine during intercourse or masturbation, by drinking the partner's urine or by yielding to one's desire or the partner's desire to be urinated upon.

See also PARAPHILIAS; UROPHILIA.

urophilia A psychosexual disorder marked by interest in urine and urination as a source of sexual excitement.

See also UROLAGNIA.

uteromania An obsolete term for nymphomania, a female condition marked by an excessive or insatiable desire for sexual stimulation and gratification.

See also NYMPHOMANIA.

V

vaginismus An involuntary muscle spasm of the vaginal opening that makes vaginal penetration and hence sexual intercourse painful. Vaginismus is one of the more common sexual dysfunctions that women experience. It is often triggered by a distasteful or painful early sexual problem such as rape or being the victim of sexual molestation. It can also be caused by physical problems such as chronic vaginitis or an imperforate hymen. At times vaginismus treatment requires intensive psychotherapy to search into its causes; in other cases, simply correcting a physical problem will alleviate vaginismus. Behavioral modification techniques have proven highly successful in treatment, based on a woman and her partner practicing stretching the vaginal opening, often with vaginal dilators.

See also BEHAVIORAL THERAPY; SEXUAL DYSFUNCTION.

Valium An antianxiety drug. Chemically known as diazepam, Valium is in a class of drugs called benzodiazepines. It has been used more extensively and for more conditions than any of the other benzodiazepines.

Valium is effective in the management of generalized anxiety disorder and panic disorder in appropriately selected patients. It is also used for skeletal muscle relaxation, for seizure disorders, for preanesthetic medication or intravenous anesthetic induction and for alleviating abstinence symptoms during alcohol withdrawal.

Valium is subject to abuse and may produce physical dependence after prolonged administration.

See also ANTIDEPRESSANT MEDICATIONS; BENZODIAZEPINE MEDICATIONS; DEPRESSION.

verbal slips   See SLIPS OF THE TONGUE.

vertigo   An illusion that one is spinning around or that one's surroundings are spinning around. The term is incorrectly used to describe dizziness or faintness. Some people who have agoraphobia or other phobias experience vertigo.

Healthy people experience vertigo when in boats, on amusement park rides or even when watching certain types of movies. Vertigo is caused by a disturbance of the semicircular canals in the inner ear or the nerve tracts leading from them. Severe vertigo may be an indicator of several medical disorders, such as ear infections, influenza or Meniere's disease. Severe vertigo may be accompanied by ringing in the ears (tinnitus), jerky eye movements (nystagmus) and unsteadiness.

If symptoms of vertigo persist, the individual should seek medical treatment; pharmacologic therapies are available that help many people.

See also ANXIETY DISORDERS; DIZZINESS.

Veterans Administration   The number of Veterans Administration Medical Centers (VAMCs) that provide psychiatric services increased slowly from 115 in 1970 to 136 in 1980, then dipped to 129 in 1982, climbed

to 139 in 1984 and remained there through 1986. During the same period, the number providing inpatient and/or residential treatment psychiatric services increased from 110 to 124, the number providing outpatient services increased from 100 to 137 and the number providing partial care services rose from 48 in 1970 to 69 in 1976 and then dropped slowly to 63 in 1986.

Although the number of VAMCs with psychiatric inpatient and/or residential treatment services increased between 1970 and 1986, the number of beds decreased considerably. From a base of 50,688 beds in 1970, the number consistently decreased throughout the 1970–84 period to 23,546, before increasing to 26,874 in 1986. The corresponding rate per 100,000 civilian population decreased from 26 in 1970 to 10 in 1984, before growing to 11 in 1986.

Outpatient additions to psychiatric services of VAMCs rose more than sevenfold from 16,790 in 1969 to 120,243 in 1979, decreased to 103,377 in 1983 and reached a peak of 125,280 in 1986. By contrast, the rate of outpatient additions reached a peak of 56 per 100,000 civilian population in 1979, which exceeded the rate of 52 in 1986.

The number of partial care additions more than doubled from 3,500 in 1970 to 7,888 in 1975. Since then the number has hovered around 7,000, except for a peak of 10,189 in 1983.

National Institute of Mental Health. *Mental Health, United States, 1990.* Manderscheid, R. W., and Sonnenschein, M. A., eds. DHHS Pub. No. (ADM) 90-1708. Washington, D.C.: USGPO, 1990.

Victorianism   In the United States, habits practiced during the years 1865 to 1918. The term comes from the name of Queen Victoria, who reigned in England from 1819 to 1901. Victorian attitudes held that women were weak and without sexual feeling and that female sexual activity was primarily to serve male needs for gratification. Married women were considered the guardians of children. Prostitutes, not wives or mothers, were considered the ideal "bad women." A proper middle-class woman did not dress in a provocative or revealing manner. Skirts were an inch off the ground, with many petticoats; a bustle extended up to three feet from the back of the dress, and her body was firmly held by a corset outfitted with tight strings and metal stays.

Although strict public standards of purity and decency were enforced, there was considerable prostitution and pornography. Laws relating to sexual interests included the Comstock Law (1873), regarding the mailing of obscene matter within the United States.

Sigmund Freud's view that sexuality affected every aspect of life had an effect on Victorianism. Freud said that repression of sexual instincts in men could lead to neuroticism and other harmful results. Freud also allowed that women were also sexual, but they were simply imperfect men because they lacked a penis. Freud put forth his theory of two types of female orgasm, the vaginal and clitoral (dual-orgasm theory), which tied in with his theory of developmental stages, which held that female development moved away from the clitoris to the vagina as the center of sexual pleasure. He considered failure to transfer the focus from the clitoris to the vagina as immature. Freud's theory indirectly argued that the male is not only sexually superior, but that women are dependent on a male penis inserted into the vagina for a "mature" sexual response. Freud viewed female masturbation as a sign of immaturity and ill health. Many agreed with Freud's views, including the dual-orgasm theory, until the 1960s when sex researchers, including Kinsey, debunked these notions.

During the Victorian era, female masturbation was generally thought to result in many ailments, including a harmful effect on reproduction. To cure adolescent female masturbation, vaginal mutilation and removal of the clitoris was at times carried out.

In public places, genitals on statues were covered with fig leaves. It was considered improper to talk about sexuality publicly. Books and plays (including those of Shakespeare) were censored.

Dissenters from Victorian views saw sexuality as healthy and natural. Writers such as Emerson and Thoreau advocated a return to nature and appreciation of human relationships, including sexuality. Many women's leaders attacked the sexual repression of women. Victorian outlooks and habits changed around the time the United States entered World War I.

See also DUAL-ORGASM THEORY; FREUD, SIGMUND.

Kahn, Ada P., and Holt, Linda Hughey. *The A to Z of Women's Sexuality*. Alameda, Calif.: Hunter House, 1992.

Masson, Jeffrey Moussaieff. *A Dark Science: Women, Sexuality and Psychiatry in the Nineteenth Century*. New York: Farrar, Straus and Giroux, 1986.

violence   See DOMESTIC VIOLENCE; FAMILY VIOLENCE.

volunteerism   There are more people giving their time and energy without direct compensation to improve the quality of life in the United States than ever before. Estimates are that there are 80 million volunteers in the United States, contributing more than 19.5 billion hours of voluntary effort worth $150 billion in 1987 alone (according to the 1987 Gallup survey "Giving and Volunteering in the U.S.").

Deciding to volunteer is a personal commitment and covers the vast range of causes, concerns, beliefs, attitudes and needs of the diverse American population. A wide variety of options are open to volunteers, making it possible for people to find something to do that meets a real need and at the same time fits what they like to do or want to learn.

This "right match" is what most often brings real fulfillment and joy to the volunteer.

It is often during life's major transitions, such as loss of a loved one, moving to a new community, loss of a job or divorce, that individuals experience great loneliness. According to Marlene Wilson's book *You Can Make a Difference!* volunteering can be a very helpful and healing experience during these times, because it is in the reaching out to others that people "get out" of themselves.

For information on volunteerism, contact:

Volunteer Management Associates
320 South Cedar Brook Road
Boulder, CO 80304
Phone: (303) 447–0558

Wilson, Marlene. *You Can Make a Difference!* Boulder: Volunteer Management Associates, 1990.

voyeurism   A sexual disorder in which an individual (male: voyeur, female: voyeuse) derives sexual satisfaction from secretly observing people's nude bodies in the act of undressing or during sexual activity. When this is the person's preferred or exclusive method of sexual excitement, the practice is considered a paraphilia. Voyeurism is also known as inspectionalism and "peeping Tomism." Voyeurism is considered a crime in many states in the United States.

W

wandering uterus   According to Hippocrates' theory, hysteria—now known as conversion disorder—was attributed to a uterus that had wandered to different parts of the body in search of a child. Medically, it is a uterus that is not fixed in the same position at all times. Normally, the uterus changes position—varying with the posture of the woman—but does not "wander."

warehousing   A popular term used in the mid-20th century for the practice of confining mentally ill patients to large institutions for long-term and, in many cases, lifetime custodial care.

war neurosis   A term largely replaced with post-traumatic stress disorder. War neurosis referred to a traumatic neurosis caused by wartime experiences, including bombings, exposure to combat conditions and internal conflicts over killing. Symptoms included anxiety, nightmares, irritability, depression and fears.

See also POST-TRAUMATIC STRESS DISORDER.

weekend depression   A type of depression that some individuals experience when away from their work. Particularly for some individuals who live alone, facing solitude creates emotional difficulties. To overcome the dislike and fear of being alone, as well as the change in mood from the workweek when one is surrounded by people, individuals may schedule pleasurable activities with friends or like-minded others so that they will not spend the entire weekend alone. Weekend depression should be distinguished from chronic depression.

See also DEPRESSION.

weight gain and loss   Concern about one's weight is often related to one's mental perception of body image and self-esteem. Weight gain and loss are also sometimes related to eating disorders such as anorexia nervosa or bulimia. Some individuals who fear gaining weight practice bulimia, the "bingeing and purging" syndrome, in which they gorge themselves and then induce vomiting. Many individuals become worried and impose stress on themselves because of their weight. Acceptance of oneself and one's body shape contributes to better mental health.

See also ANOREXIA NERVOSA; BODY IMAGE; BULIMIA; EATING DISORDERS.

Wellbutrin A brand name for an antidepressant drug, known generically as bupropion hydrochloride.

See also BUPROPION HYDROCHLORIDE.

weltanschauung A German word literally meaning "world outlook." The term refers to the totality of an individual's conception of reality, or philosophy of human life, society and the world at large.

Weltanschauung is a broader concept but roughly similar to the cognitive triad of negative view of the self, the future and the world, believed to underlie depression according to cognitive behavior theory.

Wernicke-Korsakoff syndrome An episode of encephalopathy, a neurological disease marked by confusion, disorientation, ataxia and nystagmus, followed by alcohol amnestic disorder also known as Korsakoff's disease. Both are believed to be due to thiamine deficiency. It is most common in men 40 to 60 years old; although prognosis is poor, recovery can occur over a period of months. Thiamine is the best treatment, as it prevents progression, but it does not necessarily cause improvement.

See also ALCOHOLISM; NUTRITION; NUTRITIONAL DISORDERS.

Western blot test A blood test for HIV (human immunodeficiency virus). The first-line serum test used to detect HIV is known as the enzyme-linked immunosorbent assay (ELISA). If the result is positive, the serum is then subjected to the more accurate Western blot test, because false positives may occur with ELISA. Persons should not be notified of a positive result until the Western blot test has been performed. In some states, all positive results are reported to public health authorities.

See also ACQUIRED IMMUNODEFICIENCY SYNDROME; ENZYME-LINKED IMMUNOSORBENT ASSAY.

wet dream In the adult male, a sleep period in which ejaculation occurs (often characterized by dreams with sexual content). Wet dreams are common during adolescence and are considered normal even in adult males with regular sexual partners. Wet dreams sometimes cause embarrassment for young men.

See also EJACULATION; NOCTURNAL EMISSION.

will to survive The mental fortitude and determination to live despite an adverse state such as a severe illness, disabling disorder or extreme environmental conditions, such as lack of water and food. Will to survive, or will to live, is often mentioned when survivors are found in mine shafts. Will to survive is credited with prolonging some terminal patients' lives.

See also HOSTAGES.

wish fulfillment According to Sigmund Freud's wish-fulfillment theory of dreams, dreams express fulfilled wishes. The theory assumed that dreams have psychological meaning, that the hallucinatory quality of dreams enables the dreamer to represent as fulfilled wishes those that would otherwise have awakened him and that the wishes expressed are usually ones unacceptable to the sleeper's waking self. Only a small proportion of one's dreams are manifestly wish-fulfilling. The wish-fulfillment theory has been challenged by later psychiatrists and psychologists.

See also DREAMING; FREUD, SIGMUND.

womb envy A mental characteristic of a transsexual or transvestite male whose gender identity is female.

See also GENDER DYSPHORIA; GENDER ROLE.

women's health movement As part of the women's liberation movement of the 1970s, women in many parts of the United States started their own health centers and hired their own physicians. The aim of these centers is to increase knowledge about feminine anatomy and physiology, with strong emphasis on preventive health care and better patient-practitioner communications.

When possible, women's health centers have hired women physicians. Proponents of the women's health movement advocate more self-help groups and women helping women. During the 1980s, many hospitals reorganized their facilities to include "women's centers," in which women can obtain necessary health care in one place. Incorporated into the philosophy of such centers is better understanding of women's needs and health concerns and respect for women's rights to information about their health care.

See also WOMEN'S LIBERATION MOVEMENT.

women's liberation movement Activities undertaken during the 1960s, 1970s, and early 1980s with intent to elevate women from total responsibility for child rearing and homemaking and from inferior positions in business, the professions and social clubs; to gain equal pay as men in the same work; and to gain freedom from the sexual double standard. In general, the movement worked toward less overall dominance by men and against the traditional stereotype of women as dependent, passive and fragile. The movement has enabled a generation of women to follow career paths not open to their mothers or grandmothers, to enjoy motherhood at the same time and to participate in previously male-dominated professional and social organizations. The "sexual revolution," during which women began to express sexuality with an increase in premarital and extramarital relationships, was an outgrowth of the women's liberation movement.

Significant steps in the women's liberation movement include publication of *The Feminine Mystique* (1963) by Betty Freidan, which exploded the myth of the happy housewife; the passage of the Equal Pay Act by the U.S. Congress in 1963; the founding of the National Organization for Women (1966); the first accredited women's studies course at Cornell University (1969); publication of *Sexual Politics* (1970) by Kate Millett; the founding of the National Women's Political Caucus (1971); the historic *Roe v. Wade* decision by the U.S. Supreme Court legalizing abortion (1973); the election of the first woman governor in her own right (Ella Grasso, Connecticut, 1974); the declaration of 1975 as the International Year of the Woman by the United Nations; the First National Women's Conference in Houston (1977); the march in 1978 of nearly 100,000 women in Washington to support extension of the Equal Rights Amendment; the appointment of Sandra Day O'Connor as the first woman to become an associate justice of the U.S. Supreme Court; and the candidacy of Geraldine Ferraro as the U.S. Democratic candidate for vice president in 1984.

See also SEXISM; SEXUAL HARASSMENT; WOMEN'S HEALTH MOVEMENT; WORKING MOTHERS.

Cott, Nancy F. *The Grounding of Modern Feminism.* New Haven: Yale University Press, 1989.

women's roles The functions of women in society that traditionally were homemaking and child rearing were expanded in the later 20th century to include increasing participation in business, the military, government and other fields previously considered "men's fields." The change in women's roles has led in many cases to stress for women and the men in their lives; as competition between the sexes increases, jealousies over being the provider in the family occur, and males feel an increasing loss of power and control over women in their personal and professional lives.

See also WOMEN'S LIBERATION MOVEMENT.

word blindness See LEARNING DISABILITIES.

work addiction (workaholism) A compulsive dependence on work as the most important means of maintaining one's self-esteem; the term "workaholic" refers to a person addicted to his or her work and who works excessively long hours, even when not necessary.

See also ADDICTION.

workaholism See WORK ADDICTION.

working mothers Mothers of young children who are in the civilian labor force. At the end of the 20th century, 57.3 percent of American women work outside the home, in many cases creating role conflicts between home and work, especially for mothers. Despite these conflicts, many working mothers have feelings of self-fulfillment and realize economic advantages. Many working mothers find cooperation from their husbands or other family members helpful. Because of so many working mothers, day-care facilities have become widespread. For many women, placing children in day-care facilities is a guilt-ridden experience that they must work through to come to terms with the reality of trying to be in the work force as well as raise a family.

See also WOMEN'S LIBERATION MOVEMENT.

working through Exploration of a problem by an individual and therapist until a satisfactory solution is found or until a symptom has been traced to its unconscious sources. During the working-through process, the individual learns to understand the full implications of some interpretation or insight. Working through involves getting used to a new stage in life or getting over a loss or painful experience. As an example, the state of mourning requires some working through, as it involves the recognition that the deceased person is no longer available in many contexts in which he or she previously was a central figure.

worry A state of mental uneasiness, distress or agitation due to concern for a past, impending or anticipated event, threat or danger. Some degree of worrying is a common, everyday occurrence for most people. For some people, however, excessive worry interferes with mental health. Individuals who have anxiety disorders tend to worry more than others; for example, one with agoraphobia may worry about what will happen if he or she goes out, or one with a phobia may worry about what will happen if the phobic object or situation is encountered. Various forms of psychotherapy and self-helps relieve excessive worrying for many people.

See also ANXIETY.

worry beads Along with other types of beads, worry beads became the stylish way to relieve anxiety in the 1960s. Initially, the term "worry" was more nearly equivalent to the sense of the term meaning to shake or manipulate, but through usage it began to be associated with anxiety relief.

The modern source for worry beads is a peasant custom in Greece. Greeks customarily fingered sets of beads called *komboloi*. The habit is associated with the inclinations to use beads such as rosaries for religious purposes in other cultures, but in Greece it was simply a secular custom satisfying the tendency to want to do something with one's hands. A flood of tourism to Greece aroused an interest in Greek folk art, including *komboloi*. The beads became an international fad, were produced in ever more expensive and attractive styles and materials and ultimately were used by members of the Greek upper class who had looked down upon them.

See also ANXIETY; ANXIETY DISORDERS; WORRY.

Kulukundis, Elias. "Worry, Worry, Worry, the Greeks Have a Cure for It." *Holiday* (Apr. 1969).

X

Xanax Trade name for alprazolam, a triazolobenzodiazepine compound with antianxiety and sedative-hypnotic actions. It is efficacious in agoraphobia, has approval by the U.S. Food and Drug Administration for use in panic disorders and is also used to treat generalized anxiety disorder. Studies suggest that alprazolam also has antidepressant activity in moderate depression.

See also AGORAPHOBIA; ANTIDEPRESSANT MEDICATIONS; ANXIETY DISORDERS; DEPRESSION; PANIC DISORDER.

X-linked disorders Genetic disorders in which the abnormal gene or genes are located on the X chromosome and in which almost all those affected are males. Examples of this type of disorder are color vision deficiency and hemophilia.

See also CHROMOSOME; GENE.

X-linked mental retardation (XLMR) X-linked mental retardation (XLMR) accounts for approximately 20 to 25 percent of all known mental retardation. XLMR is also thought to cause the male excess observed in the mentally retarded population. The most well known XLMR is the fragile X syndrome, which is identified by the presence of a cytogenetic abnormality seen on chromosome analysis.

Males with fragile X syndrome frequently demonstrate behavioral problems, including hyperactivity and autistic behavior. Fragile X syndrome is the most common transmissible form of mental retardation. Approximately one-quarter to one-third of females who carry the fragile X genetic abnormality are also mentally retarded, generally in the mild range of severity.

XYY syndrome Down's syndrome in most cases is due to chromosomal defects resulting in three copies of chromosome number 21. Down's syndrome produces a variety of physical abnormalities and various degrees of mental retardation from relatively mild to quite severe. Among normal males, only 0.13 percent have two Y chromosomes. Compared with other males, XYY individuals are taller, often have severe acne and generally have low intelligence, although rarely in the retarded range.

See also CHROMOSOME; DOWN'S SYNDROME; MENTAL RETARDATION.

Davis, Kenneth; Klar, Howard; and Coyle, Joseph T. *Foundations of Psychiatry.* Philadelphia: W. B. Saunders, 1991.

Y

yoga A method of attaining a higher level of consciousness that eliminates anxiety-producing thought patterns. Yoga is a mental and physical discipline intended to help one get in touch with one's true nature and mystical feelings outside everyday existence and improve mental health.

There are several types of yoga practice and varying emphasis on physical, mental and social activity. Some yoga disciplines are more spiritual and metaphysical. The most commonly practiced yoga in the West is Hatha Yoga; it concentrates on spiritual improvement through the practice of physical exercise, which consists of postures called asanas. Mantras, or sacred sounds, are used in Mantra yoga. Still another branch of yoga practice concentrates on the kundalini or serpent power, which is thought to lie at the base of the spine and which can be released through postures, mantras and meditation. In some yoga practice, various forms are combined.

Yoga is an extremely ancient practice that influenced and was in turn influenced by Brahminism, Jainism, Buddhism and Hinduism. Yoga practice started to move westward as a result of the Muslim invasions of India, but only the colonial expansion of the British brought Europeans in contact with yoga.

Critics of yoga say that it can be physically dangerous if practiced without supervision and that it may lead to introversion or a hedonistic philosophy. The degree to which adherents depend on their teacher or guru may decrease a sense of independence in the student and may give the teacher too strong a sense of his own power.

"Kundalini" and "Yoga," in Guiley, Rosemary Ellen, *Harper's Encyclopedia of Mystical and Paranormal Experience*. San Francisco: Harper, 1991.

yohimbine A substance considered by some as an aphrodisiac, or an erotic potion to increase capacity for and interest in lovemaking. Yohimbine is an alkaloid chemical derived from the bark of the African yohimbe tree. Its use was first observed by Europeans among natives in the 19th century; samples were brought back to Germany for study. The drug stimulates the nervous system and can cause anxiety. It is danger-ous in large doses. It is sold under the trade name Yocon in the United States for sexual performance disorders. There is controversy concerning its effectiveness.

youngest children See BIRTH ORDER; SIBLING RIVALRY.

Z

zidovudine (AZT) A drug currently approved for use in patients with AIDS that has been shown to improve longevity and quality of life and may delay progression from ARC (AIDS-related complex) to the full-blown disease. AZT has also been demonstrated to ameliorate cognitive impairment in some individuals.

See also ACQUIRED IMMUNODEFICIENCY SYNDROME.

Vella, Stefano. "Zidovudine May Improve Survival for AIDS Patients." *Journal of the American Medical Association* (Mar. 3, 1992).

Zoloft A new antidepressant drug (generic name: sertraline hydrochloride). It is indicated for the symptomatic relief of depressive illness. It is one of a category of medications known as selective serotonin reuptake inhibitors (SSRIs).

See also ANTIDEPRESSANT MEDICATIONS; DEPRESSION; SEROTONIN.

APPENDIX OF ORGANIZATIONS

The following organizations/societies/support/self-help groups will be of interest to readers.

Addiction

(See SUBSTANCE ABUSE)

Adoption

Reunite, Inc.
P.O. Box 694
Reynoldsburg, OH 43068
Phone: (614) 861-2584

WAIF (Adoption)
67 Irving Place
New York, NY 10003
Phone: (212) 533-2558

Yesterday's Children
P.O. Box 1554
Evanston, IL 60204
Phone: (708) 545-6900

Aging

(See also GERONTOLOGY; RETIREMENT)

American Society on Aging
833 Market Street, Suite 512
San Francisco, CA 94103
Phone: (415) 882-2910

Gray Panthers
1424 16th Street NW, Suite 602
Washington, DC 20036
Phone: (202) 387-3111

Health Promotion Institute
% National Council on the Aging
600 Maryland Avenue SW, W. Wing 100
Washington, DC 20024
Phone: (202) 479-1200

AIDS

American Foundation for AIDS Research
5900 Wilshire Boulevard, 2nd floor
Los Angeles, CA 90036
Phone: (213) 857-5900

Gay Men's Health Crisis (AIDS)
129 W. 20th Street
New York, NY 10011
Phone: (212) 807-6664

Names Project Foundation (AIDS)
2362 Market Street
San Francisco, CA 94114
Phone: (415) 863-5511

National AIDS Clearinghouse
P.O. Box 6003
Rockville, MD 20849-6003
Phone: (310) 217-0023

National Association of People with AIDS
1413 K Street NW, 10th floor
Washington, DC 20005
Phone: (202) 898-0414

Pediatric AIDS Foundation
2407 Wilshire Boulevard, Suite 613
Santa Monica, CA 90403
Phone: (213) 395-9051

San Francisco AIDS Foundation
P.O. Box 6182
San Francisco, CA 94101-6182
Phone: (415) 864-5855

World Hemophilia AIDS Center
10 Congress Street, Suite 340
Pasadena, CA 91105
Phone: (818) 577-4366

Alzheimer's Disease

Alzheimer's Association
919 North Michigan Avenue, Suite 1000
Chicago, IL 60611
Phone: (312) 335-8700

Anxiety Disorders

Anxiety Disorders Association of America
6000 Executive Boulevard, Suite 200
Rockville, MD 20852
Phone: (301) 231-9350

Birth Defects

(See MENTAL RETARDATION)

Codependency

Co-Dependents Anonymous
P.O. Box 33577
Phoenix, AZ 85067-3577
Phone: (602) 277-7991

Love-N-Addiction
P.O. Box 759
Willimantic, CT 06226
Phone: (203) 423-2344

Depression

Depression and Related Affective Disorders
   Association
Johns Hopkins Hospital, Meyer 3-181
600 North Wolfe Street
Baltimore, MD 21205
Phone: (410) 955-4647

Depression Awareness, Recognition and
   Treatment Project
National Institute of Mental Health
Room 15-C-05
5600 Fishers Lane
Rockville, MD 20857
Phone: (301) 443-4513

Depressives Anonymous: Recovery From
   Depression
329 East 62nd Street
New York, NY 10021
Phone: (212) 689-2600

Foundation for Depression and Manic-
   Depression
7 East 67th Street
New York, NY 10021
Phone: (212) 772-3400

National Depressive and Manic Depressive
   Association (NDMDA)
730 North Franklin Street, Suite 501
Chicago, IL 60610
Phone: (312) 642-0049

National Foundation for Depressive Illness
P.O. Box 2257
New York, NY 10116
Phone: (212) 268-4260 or (800) 248-4344

Domestic Violence

Amend Network (Domestic Violence)
777 Grant Street, Suite 600
Denver, CO 80203
Phone: (303) 832-6363

Batterers Anonymous
16913 Lerner Lane
Fontana, CA 92335
Phone: (714) 355-1100

Clearinghouse on Family Violence Infor-
   mation
P.O. Box 1182
Washington, DC 20013
Phone: (703) 385-7565

National Assault Prevention Center
P.O. Box 02005
Columbus, OH 43202
Phone: (614) 291-2540

National Coalition Against Domestic Vio-
   lence
P.O. Box 34103
Washington, DC 20043-4103
Phone: (202) 638-6388

National Woman Abuse Prevention Project
1112 16th Street NW, Suite 920
Washington, DC 20036
Phone: (202) 857-0216

Wives Self-Help Foundation
Smyulie Times Building, Suite 205
8001 Roosevelt Boulevard
Philadelphia, PA 19152
Phone: (215) 332-2311

Eating Disorders

The Obesity Foundation
5600 South Quebec, Suite 160-D
Englewood, CO 80111
Phone: (303) 850-0328

Employee Assistance

(See also SUBSTANCE ABUSE)

Employee Assistance Society of America
2728 Phillips
Berkley, MI 48072
Phone: (313) 545-3888

Epilepsy

American Epilepsy Society
638 Prospect Avenue
Hartford, CT 06105-4298
Phone: (203) 232-4825

Epilepsy Foundation of America
4351 Garden City Drive
Landover, MD 20785
Phone: (301) 459-3700

International League Against Epilepsy
National Institutes of Health
Building 31, Room 8A52
Bethesda, MD 20892
Phone: (301) 496-3167

Gay/Lesbian/Homosexuality

National Center for Lesbian Rights
1663 Mission Street, 5th floor
San Francisco, CA 94103
Phone: (415) 621-0674

National Gay and Lesbian Task Force
1734 14th Street NW
Washington, DC 20009–4309
Phone: (202) 332–6483

Genetic Disorders

(See also MENTAL RETARDATION)

National Fragile X Foundation
1441 York Street, Suite 215
Denver, CO 80206
Phone: (303) 333-6155

Support Organization for Trisomy 18/13
2982 S. Union Street
Rochester, NY 14624
Phone: (716) 594-4621

Gerontology

(See also AGING; RETIREMENT)

American Geriatrics Society
770 Lexington Avenue, Suite 300
New York, NY 10021
Phone: (212) 308-1414

Gerontological Society of America
1275 K Street NW, Suite 350
Washington, DC 20005
Phone: (202) 842-1275

Incest

Incest Survivors Anonymous
P.O. Box 5613
Long Beach, CA 90805-0613
Phone: (310) 428-5599

Learning Disabilities

Learning Disabilities Association of America
4156 Library Road
Pittsburgh, PA 15234
Phone: (412) 341-1515

National Center for Learning Disabilities
99 Park Avenue, 6th Floor
New York, NY 10016
Phone: (212) 687-7211

Mental Health

American Mental Health Foundation
2 East 86th Street

New York, NY 10028
Phone: (212) 737–9027

American Mental Health Fund
2735 Hartland Road, Suite 302
Falls Church, VA 22043
Phone: (703) 573–2200

National Alliance for the Mentally Ill
2101 Wilson Boulevard, Suite 302
Arlington, VA 22201
Phone: (703) 524-7600

National Institute of Mental Health
Public Information Branch
5600 Fishers Lane
Rockville, MD 20857
Phone: (301) 443-3673

National Mental Health Association
1021 Prince Street
Alexandria, VA 22314-2971
Phone: (703) 684-7722

World Federation for Mental Health
1021 Prince Street
Alexandria, VA 22314
Phone: (703) 684-7722

Mental Retardation

(See also GENETIC DISORDERS)

American Association on Mental Retardation
1719 Kalorama Road NW
Washington, DC 20009
Phone: (202) 387-1968

Association for Children with Retarded
Mental Development
162 5th Avenue, 11th floor
New York, NY 10010
Phone: (212) 741-0100

Association for Retarded Citizens of the
U.S.
500 East Border Street, Suite 300
Arlington, TX 76010
Phone: (817) 261-6003

Mental Retardation Association of America
211 East 300 South, Suite 212

Salt Lake City, UT 84111
Phone: (801) 328-1575

National Association for Down Syndrome
P.O. Box 4542
Oak Brook, IL 60522-4542
Phone: (708) 325-9112

National Down Syndrome Congress
1800 Dempster Street
Park Ridge, IL 60068-1146
Phone: (708) 823-7550

National Down Syndrome Society
666 Broadway
New York, NY 10012
Phone: (212) 460-9330

Parents of Down Syndrome Children
% Montgomery County Association for
Retarded Citizens
11600 Nebel Street
Rockville, MD 20852
Phone: (301) 984-5792

Multiple Personality and Dissociation

International Society for the Study of Multiple Personality and Dissociation
5700 Old Orchard Road
Skokie, IL 60077-1024
Phone: (708) 966-4322

Obsessive-Compulsive Disorder

Obsessive-Compulsive Anonymous
P.O. Box 215
New Hyde Park, NY 11040
Phone: (516) 741-4901

Obsessive-Compulsive Disorder Foundation
#9 Depot
Milford, CT 06460
Phone: (203) 878-5669

Psychiatry

American Academy of Child and Adolescent Psychiatry
3615 Wisconsin Avenue NW
Washington, DC 20016
Phone: (202) 966-7300

American Academy of Clinical Psychiatrists
P.O. Box 3212
San Diego, CA 92163
Phone: (619) 298-0538

American Academy of Psychoanalysis
30 East 40th Street, Suite 206
New York, NY 10016
Phone: (212) 679-4105

American Association for Geriatric Psychiatry
P.O. Box 376-A
Greenbelt, MD 20768
Phone: (301) 220-0952

American Board of Psychiatry and Neurology
500 Lake Cook Road, Suite 335
Deerfield, IL 60015
Phone: (708) 945-7900

American College of Psychiatrists
P.O. Box 365
Greenbelt, MD 20768
Phone: (301) 345-3534

American Orthopsychiatric Association
19 West 44th Street, Suite 1616
New York, NY 10036
Phone: (212) 354-5770

American Psychiatric Association
1400 K Street NW
Washington, DC 20005
Phone: (202) 682-6000

American Society for Adolescent Psychiatry
4330 East West Highway, Suite 1117
Bethesda, MD 20814
Phone: (301) 718-6502

Group for the Advancement of Psychiatry
P.O. Box 28218
Dallas, TX 75228
Phone: (214) 388-1310

International Association for Child and Adolescent Psychiatry and Allied Professions

University of California, San Francisco
401 Parnassus Avenue
San Francisco, CA 94143-0984
Phone: (415) 476-7232

International Transactional Analysis Association
1771 Vellejo Street
San Francisco, CA 94123
Phone: (415) 885-5992

National Association of Psychiatric Treatment Center for Children
2000 L Street NW, Suite 200
Washington, DC 30036
Phone: (202) 955-3828

Psychiatry Research Institute
150 East 69th Street
New York, NY 10021
Phone: (212) 628-4800

Society of Biological Psychiatry
University of Texas
Southwestern Medical Center
5323 Harry Hines Boulevard
Dallas, TX 75235
Phone: (214) 688-8766

World Association for Social Psychiatry
696 Ladera Lane
Santa Barbara, CA 93108
Phone: (805) 969-1376

Psychoanalysis

American College of Psychoanalysts
2006 Dwight Way, Number 304
Berkeley, CA 94704
Phone: (415) 845-7957

American Psychoanalytic Association
309 East 49th Street
New York, NY 10022
Phone: (212) 752-0450

American Society of Psychoanalytic Physicians
4804 Jasmine Drive
Rockville, MD 20853
Phone: (301) 929-1623

Association for Applied Psychoanalysis
116 Village Walk Drive
Royal Palm Beach, FL 33411
Phone: (407) 793-0686

Association for Child Psychoanalysis
P.O. Box 5935
Washington, DC 20016
Phone: (202) 363-7849

Association for Psychoanalytic Medicine
4560 Delafield Avenue
New York, NY 10021
Phone: (212) 288-2297

Karen Horney Clinic
329 East 62nd Street
New York, NY 10021
Phone: (212) 838-4333

National Association for the Advancement
  of Psychoanalysis and the American
  Board for Accreditation and Certification
  (NAAPABAC)
80 8th Avenue, Suite 1501
New York, NY 10011-1501
Phone: (212) 741-0515

National Psychological Association for
  Psychoanalysis (NPAP)
150 W. 13th Street
New York, NY 10011
Phone: (212) 924-7440

Sigmund Freud Archives
23 The Hemlocks
Roslyn, NY 11576
Phone: (516) 621-6850

Psychology

Alfred Adler Institute (AAI)
1841 Broadway
New York, NY 10023
Phone: (212) 974-0431

American Board of Professional Psychology (ABPP)
2100 East Broadway, Suite 313
Columbia, MO 65201
Phone: (314) 875–1267

American Psychological Association
1200 17th Street NW
Washington, DC 20036
Phone: (202) 955-7600

American Psychological Practitioners Association
3801 Bridge Road, Suite 5A
Sarasota, FL 34239
Phone: (813) 925-1278

American Psychology-Law Society (AP-
  LS)
University of Massachusetts Medical
  Center
Department of Psychology
55 Lake Avenue North
Worcester, MA 01655
Phone: (508) 856-3625

Association for Advancement of Psychol-
  ogy (AAP)
P.O. Box 38129
Colorado Springs, CO 80937
Phone: (719) 520-0688

Association for Humanistic Psychology
  (AHP)
1772 Vallejo, Suite 3
San Francisco, CA 94123
Phone: (415) 346-7929

Association for Women in Psychology
  (AWP)
Haverford College
370 Lancaster Avenue
Haverford, PA 19041-1392
Phone: (215) 896-1000

C. G. Jung Foundation for Analytical Psychology
28 East 39th Street
New York, NY 10016
Phone: (212) 697-6430

Center for Applications of Psychological
  Type (CAPT)
2720 NW 6th St., Suite A
Gainesville, FL 32609
Phone: (904) 375-0160

Psychotherapy

American Art Therapy Association
1202 Allanson Road
Mundelein, IL 60060
Phone: (708) 949-6064

American Association for Music Therapy
355 Crossfield
King of Prussia, PA 19406
Phone: (215) 265–4006

American Board of Medical Psychotherapists
Physicians' Park B, Suite 11
300 Twenty-first Avenue North
Nashville, TN 37203
Phone: (615) 327-2984

American Dance Therapy Association
2000 Century Place, Suite 108
Columbia, MD 21044
Phone: (301) 997-4040

American Group Psychotherapy Association
25 East 21st Street, 6th floor
New York, NY 10010
Phone: (212) 477-2577

Association for Advancement of Behavior Therapy
15 West 36th Street
New York, NY 10018
Phone: (212) 279-7970

Institute for Rational-Emotive Therapy (IRET)
45 East 65th Street
New York, NY 10021
Phone: (212) 535-0822

National Association for Drama Therapy
19 Edwards Street
New Haven, CT 06511
Phone: (203) 498-1515

National Association for Music Therapy
8455 Colesville Road, Suite 930
Silver Spring, MD 20910
Phone: (301) 589-3300

National Coalition of Arts Therapy Associations
1819 Bradburn Drive
St. Louis, MO 63131
Phone: (314) 822-8635

Retirement

(See also AGING; GERONTOLOGY)

American Association of Retired Persons (AARP)
601 East Street NW
Washington, DC 20049
Phone: (202) 434-2277

Association of Retired Americans
P.O. Box 610286
Dallas, TX 75261
Phone: (800) 622-8040

Schizophrenia

American Schizophrenia Association
900 North Federal Highway, Suite 330
Boca Raton, FL 33432
Phone: (407) 393-6167

National Alliance for Research on Schizophrenia and Depression
60 Cutter Mill Road, Suite 200
Great Neck, NY 11202
Phone: (516) 829-0091

Schizophrenics Anonymous
1209 California Road
Eastchester, NY 10709
Phone: (914) 337-2252

Self-help Organizations

International Network for Mutual Help Centers
% Edward J. Madara
St. Charles–Riverside Medical Center
Pocono Road
Denville, NJ 07834
Phone: (201) 625-9565

National Mental Health Consumer Self-Help Clearinghouse

311 South Juniper Street, Room 902
Philadelphia, PA 19107
Phone: (215) 735-6367

National Self-Help Clearinghouse
25 West 43rd Street, Room 620
New York, NY 10036
Phone: (212) 642-2944

Sexual Addiction

Sex Addicts Anonymous
P.O. Box 3038
Minneapolis, MN 55403
Phone: (612) 338-0217

Sex and Love Addicts Anonymous
P.O. Box 119
Newton, MA 02258
Phone: (617) 332-1845

Sexaholics Anonymous
P.O. Box 300
Simi Valley, CA 93062
Phone: (805) 581-3343

Sexual Health

American Association of Sex Education,
   Counselors and Therapists
435 North Michigan Avenue, Suite 1717
Chicago, IL 60611
Phone: (312) 644-0828

American Social Health Association
P.O. Box 13827
Research Triangle Park, NC 27709
Phone: (919) 361-8400

Council for Sex Information and Education
   (CSIE)
444 Lincoln Boulevard, Suite 107
Venice, CA 90291

Sex Information and Education Council of
   the U.S. (SIECUS)
130 West 42nd Street, Suite 2500
New York, NY 10036
Phone: (212) 819-9770

Sleep

American Narcolepsy Association
425 California Street, Suite 201
San Francisco, CA 94104
Phone: (415) 788-4793

American Sleep Disorders Association
1610 14th Street NW, Suite 300
Rochester, MN 55901
Phone: (507) 287–6006

Narcolepsy and Cataplexy Foundation of
   America
445 East 68th Street, Suite 12L
New York, NY 10021
Phone: (212) 628-6315

Substance Abuse

Addiction Research and Treatment Corporation
22 Chapel Street
Brooklyn, NY 11201
Phone: (718) 260-2900

Al-Anon Family Group Headquarters
P.O. Box 862, Midtown Station
New York, NY 10018
Phone: (212) 302-7240

Alcoholics Anonymous World Services
475 Riverside Drive
New York, NY 10163
Phone: (212) 686-1100

Alcoholism Center for Women
1147 South Alvarado Street
Los Angeles, CA 90006
Phone: (213) 381-8500

National Institute on Drug Abuse
5600 Fishers Lane
Rockville, MD 20857
Phone: (301) 443-6487

Women's Drug Research Project (Substance Abuse)
University of Michigan
School of Social Work
1065 Frieze Building

Ann Arbor, MI 48109-1285
Phone: (313) 763-5958

Sudden Infant Death Syndrome (SIDS)

National SIDS Clearinghouse (NSIDSC)
8201 Greensboro Drive, Suite 600
McLean, VA 22102
Phone: (703) 821-8955

SIDS Alliance
10500 Little Patuxent Parkway, Suite 420
Columbia, MD 21044
Phone: (410) 964-8000

Suicide

American Association of Suicidology
2459 South Ash Street S
Denver, CO 80222
Phone: (303) 692-0985

American Suicide Foundation
1045 Park Avenue
New York, NY 10028
Phone: (212) 410-1111

National Committee on Youth Suicide Prevention
65 Essex Road

Chestnut Hill, MA 02167
Phone: (617) 738-0700

Seasons: Suicide Bereavement
P.O. Box 187
Perk City, UT 84060
Phone: (801) 649-8327

Surrogate Parenthood

Center for Surrogate Parenting
8383 Wilshire Boulevard, Suite 750
Beverly Hills, CA 90211
Phone: (213) 655-1974

Donor's Offspring (Surrogate Parenthood)
P.O. Box 37
Sarcoxie, MO 64862
Phone: (417) 548-3679

National Association of Surrogate Mothers
8383 Wilshire Boulevard, Suite 750D
Beverly Hills, CA 90211
Phone: (213) 655-2015

Parents of Surrogate-Borne Infants and
   Toddlers in Verbal Exchange
P.O. Box 204
East Meadow, NY 11554
Phone: (516) 794-5772

BIBLIOGRAPHY

Acquired Immunodeficiency Syndrome (AIDS)

Bateson, Mary Catherine, and Goldsby, Richard. *Thinking AIDS*. Reading, Mass.: Addison-Wesley, 1988.

Broder, Samuel, ed. *AIDS, Modern Concepts and Therapeutic Challenges*. New York: M. Dekker, 1987.

Corless, Inge B., and Pittman-Lindeman, Mary. *AIDS: Principles, Practices and Politics*. New York: Hemisphere Publishing Corporation, 1988.

Gong, Victor, and Rudnick, Norman, eds. *AIDS: Facts and Issues*. New Brunswick, N.J.: Rutgers University Press, 1986.

Hardsfield, H. H. "Heterosexual Transmission of Human Immunodeficiency Virus." *Journal of the American Medical Association* 260 (Oct. 7, 1988):1943–1944.

Havarkos, H. W., and Edelman, R. "The Epidemiology of Acquired Immunodeficiency Syndrome Among Heterosexuals." *Journal of the American Medical Association* 260 (1988):1922–1929.

Hearst, N., and Hulley, S. B. "Preventing the Heterosexual Spread of AIDS: Are We Giving Our Patients the Best Advice?" *Journal of the American Medical Association* 259 (Apr. 22–29, 1988):2428–2432.

Langone, John. *AIDS: The Facts*. Boston: Little, Brown, 1988.

Masters, William H. *Crisis: Heterosexual Behavior in the Age of AIDS*. New York: Grove Press, 1988.

Nadler, J. L., and Battery, C. M. G. "Premarital Screening for HIV." *Journal of the American Medical Association* 259 (June 3, 1988):3127–3128.

Norwood, Christopher. *Advice for Life: A Woman's Guide to AIDS Risks and Prevention*. New York: Pantheon Books, 1987.

Padian, N., et al. "Male to Female Transmission of Human Immunodeficiency Virus." *Journal of the American Medical Association* 258 (Aug. 14, 1987):788–790.

Raymond, C. A. "Pilot Project: Preventing Further AIDS Spread Among Women, General Heterosexual Population." *Journal of the American Medical Association* 259 (June 24, 1988):3224–3225.

Adolescence

Anderson, J. C., et al. "DSM-III Disorders in Preadolescent Children—Prevalence in a Large Sample from the General Population." *Archives of General Psychiatry* 44 (1987):69–76.

Bailey, G. W. "Current Perspectives on Substance Abuse in Youth." *Journal of the American Academy of Child and Adolescent Psychiatry* 28 (1989):151.

Barglow, P.; Bornstein, M.; and Exum, D. "Psychiatric Aspects of Illegitimate Pregnancy in Early Adolescents." *American Journal of Orthopsychiatry* 38 (1968):672.

Baumrind, D., and Moselle, K. A. "A Developmental Perspective on Adolescent Drug Abuse." *Advances in Alcohol and Substance Abuse* 4 (1985):41.

Bernet, W. "The Technique of Verbal Games in Group Therapy with Early Adolescents." *Journal of the American Academy of Child Psychiatry* 21 (1982):496–501.

Blos, P. "The Second Individuation Process of Adolescence." *Psychoanalytic Study of the Child* 22 (1967):162.

Clayton, R. R., and Ritter, C. "The Epidemiology of Alcohol and Drug Abuse Among Adolescents." *Advances in Alcohol and Substance Abuse* 4 (1985):69.

Corder, G. F.; Whiteside, L.; and Haizlip, T. "A Study of Curative Factors in Group Psychotherapy with Adolescents." *International Journal of Group Psychotherapy* 31 (1981):345–354.

Kandel, D. B. "Epidemiological and Psychosocial Perspectives on Adolescent Drug Use." *Journal of the American Academy of Child Psychiatry* 21 (1982):328.

Kay, R. L., and Kay, J. "Adolescent Conduct Disorders." *Annual Review of Psychiatry* 5 (1986):480.

Lewis, D. O., et al. "Violent Juvenile Delinquents: Psychiatric, Neurological, Psychological and Abuse Factors." *Journal of the American Academy of Child Psychiatry* 18 (1979):307.

Offer, D. "Adolescent Development: A Normative Perspective." *Annual Review of Psychiatry* 5 (1986):404.

Offer, D.; Ostrov, E..; and Howard, K. "The Mental Health Professional's Concept of the Normal Adolescent." *Archives of General Psychiatry* 38 (1981):149–152.

Paton, S.; Kessler, R.; and Kandel, D. "Depressive Mood and Adolescent Illicit Drug Use." *Journal of Genetic Psychology* 131 (1977):267.

Ryan, N. D., and Puig-Antioch, J. "Affective Illness in Adolescence." *Annual Review of Psychiatry* 27 (1988):675.

Strober, M., and Carlson, G. "Bipolar Illness in Adolescents with Major Depression." *Archives of General Psychiatry* 39 (1982):549.

Tanner, J. M. "Issues and Advances in Adolescent Growth and Development." *Journal of Adolescent Health Care* 8 (1987):470.

Affective Disorders

(See DEPRESSION AND AFFECTIVE DISORDERS)

Aggressive Behavior

Brizer, D. A.; Convit, A.; Krakowski, M.; and Volavka, M. "A Rating Scale for Reporting Violence on Psychiatric Wards." *Hospital and Community Psychiatry* 38, no. 7 (1987):769.

Eichelman, B. "Neurochemical Bases of Aggressive Behavior." *Psychiatric Annals* 17, no. 6 (1987):371.

Fawcett, J., ed. *Dynamics of Violence.* Chicago: American Medical Association, 1972.

Felthous, A. R., and Kellert, S. R. "Childhood Cruelty to Animals and Later Aggression Against People: A Review." *American Journal of Psychiatry* 144 (1987):710.

Green, R. G., and Donnerstein, E. I., eds. *Aggression: Theoretical and Empirical Reviews.* Vols. 1 and 2. New York: Academic Press, 1983.

Silver, J. M., and Yudofsky, S. C. "Aggressive Behavior in Patients with Neuropsychiatric Disorders." *Psychiatric Annals* 17, no. 6 (1987):367.

Valzelli, L. *Psychobiology of Aggression and Violence.* New York: Raven Press, 1981.

Aging

Baruch, Grace, et al. *Lifeprints: New Patterns of Love and Work for Today's Woman.* New York: McGraw-Hill, 1983.

Brown, Judith K., and Kerns, Virginia, eds. *In Her Prime: A New View of Middle-Aged Women.* South Hadley, Mass.: Bergin and Garvey, 1985.

Porcino, Jane. *Growing Older, Getting Better.* Reading, Mass.: Addison-Wesley, 1983.

Ransohoff, Rita M. *Venus after Forty: Sexual Myths, Man's Fantasies, and Truths About Middle-Aged Women.* Far Hills, N.J.: New Horizon Press, 1987.

Renshaw, Domeena C. "Sex, Intimacy and the Older Woman." *Women and Health* 8, no. 4 (Winter 1983):43–54.

Agitation/Patient Violence

Cavanaugh, S. V. "Psychiatric Emergencies." *Medical Clinics of North America* 70 (1986):1185–1202.

Jessor, R., et al. *Society, Personality and Deviant Behavior.* Huntington, N.Y.: Kreiger Publishing, 1975.

Risse, S. C., and Barnes, R. "Pharmacologic Treatment of Agitation Associated with Dementia." *Journal of the American Geriatrics Society* 34 (1986):368–376.

Roth, L. H., (ed.) *Clinical Treatment of the Violent Person.* Rockville, Md.: U.S. Department of Public Health and Human Services, NIMH, Publication no. (ADM) 85-1425, 1985.

Struble, L. M., and Sivertsen, L. "Agitation: Behaviors in Confused Elderly Patients." *Journal of Gerontological Nursing* 13, no. 11 (1987):40–44.

Tanke, E. D., and Yesavage, J. A. "Characteristics of Assaultive Patients Who Do and Do Not Provide Visible Cues of Potential Violence." *American Journal of Psychiatry* 142 (1985):1409–1413.

Young, G. P. "The Agitated Patient in the Emergency Department." *Emergency Medicine Clinics of North America* 5 (1987):765–781.

Alcoholism

Berner, P.; Lesca, O. M.; and Walter, H. "Alcohol and Depression." *Psychopathology* 19, supp. (1987):177–183.

Brolsma, J. K. "Family Therapy in the Treatment of Alcoholism," in Estes, N. K., and Heinemann, M. E., eds., *Alcoholism: Development, Consequences and Interventions.* St. Louis: C. V. Mosby, 1986.

Brown, R. L.; Carter, W. B.; and Gordon, M. J. "Diagnosis of Alcoholism in a Simulated Patient Encounter by Primary Care Physicians." *Journal of Family Practice* 25 (1987):260.

Bulik, C. M. "Drug and Alcohol Abuse by Bulimic Women and Their Families." *American Journal of Psychiatry* 144 (1987):12.

Cadoret, R. J., et al. "Alcoholism and Antisocial Personality: Interrelationships, Genetic and Environmental Factors." *Archives of General Psychiatry* 42 (1985):161–167.

Carstensen, L. L.; Rychtarik, R. G.; and Prue, D. "Behavioral Treatment of the Geriatric Alcohol Abuser: A Long-Term Follow-up Study." *Addictive Behaviors* 10 (1985):307–310.

Clancy, J.; Vanderhuth, E.; and Campbell, P. "Evaluation of an Aversive Technique as a Treatment for Alcoholism-controlled Trial with Succinylcholine-induced Apnea." *Journal of Studies on Alcohol* 28 (1967):476–485.

Cloninger, C. R. "Neurogenic Adaptive Mechanisms in Alcoholism." *Science* 236 (1987):410–416.

Cohen, M.; Kern, J. C.; and Hassett, C. "Identifying Alcoholism in Medical Patients." *Hospital and Community Psychiatry* 37 (1987):399.

Cohen, S., and Callahan, J. F. *The Diagnosis and Treatment of Drug and Alcohol Abuse.* New York: Haworth Press, 1986.

Douglas, S. S., and Pesheau, G. "Evaluation of an Inpatient Women's Addiction Group," in *Alcohol, Drugs and Tobacco: An International Perspective—Past, Present, Future.* Calgary, Alberta: Alberta Alcohol and Drug Commission, 1985.

Eckardt, M. J., et al. "Health Hazards Associated with Alcohol Consumption." *Journal of the American Medical Association* 246 (1981):648–666.

Ewing, J. A. "Detecting Alcoholism: The CAGE Questionnaire." *Journal of the American Medical Association* 14 (1984):1905–1907.

Fawcett, J., et al. "A Double-blind, Placebo Controlled Trial of Lithium Carbonate Therapy for Alcoholism." *Archives of General Psychiatry* 44 (1986):248–258.

Frances, R. J.; Bucke, S.; and Alexopoulous, G. S. "Outcome Study of Familial and Nonfamilial Alcoholism." *American Journal of Psychiatry* 141 (1984):1469–1471.

Goodwin, D. W. "Alcoholism and Genetics." *Archives of General Psychiatry* 42 (1985):171–174.

Grant, I.; Adams, K. M.; and Reed, R. "Aging, Abstinence, and Medical Risk Factors in the Prediction of Neuropsychologic Deficit Among Long-Term Alcoholics." *Archives of General Psychiatry* 41 (1984):710–718.

Helzer, J. E.; Canino, G. J.; Yeh, E. K.; et al. "Alcoholism—North America and Asia: A Comparison of Population Surveys with the Diagnostic Interview Schedule." *Archives of General Psychiatry* 47 (1990):313–319.

Helzer, J. E., and Pryzbeck, T. R. "The Co-occurrence of Alcoholism with Other Psychiatric Disorders in the General Population and Its Impact on Treatment." *Journal of Studies on Alcohol* 49 (1098):219–224.

Helzer, J. E.; Robins, L. N.; Taylor, J. R.; et al. "The Extent of Long-Term Moderate Drinking Among Alcoholics Discharged from Medical and Psychiatric Treatment Facilities." *New England Journal of Medicine* 312 (1985):1678–1682.

Hesselbrock, M. M.; Neyer, R. E.; and Keener, J. J. "Psychopathology in Hospitalized Alcoholics." *Archives of General Psychiatry* 42 (1985):1050–1055.

Holden, C. "Is Alcoholism Treatment Effective?" *Science* 236 (1987):20–22.

Irwin, M.; Schuckit, M.; and Smith, T. L. "Clinical Importance of Age at Onset in Type I and Type II Primary Alcoholics." *Archives of General Psychiatry* 47 (1990):320–324.

Judd, L. L., and Huy, L. Y. "Lithium Antagonizes Ethanol Intoxication in Alcoholics." *American Journal of Psychiatry* 141 (1984):1517–1521.

Kalant, H. "Tolerance and Its Significance for Drug and Alcohol Dependence," in *Problems of Drug Dependence, 1986*. Rockville, Md.: National Institute on Drug Abuse, 1987.

Light, W. J. H. *Psychodynamics of Alcoholism*. Springfield, Ill.: Charles C. Thomas, 1986.

Malcolm, R., et al. "Double-blind Controlled Trial Comparing Carbamazepine to Oxazepam Treatment of Alcohol Withdrawal." *American Journal of Psychiatry* 146 (1989):617–621.

Metzger, L. *From Denial to Recovery*. San Francisco: Jossey-Bass, 1988.

Pickens, R. W., et al. "Relapse by Alcohol Abusers." *Alcoholism* 9 (1985):244–247.

Alcoholism and Sexuality

Klassen, Albert D., and Wilsnack, Sharon C. "Sexual Experience and Drinking Among Women in a U.S. National Survey." *Archives of Sexual Behavior* 15, no. 5 (1986):363–392.

Pinhas, Valerie. "Sexual Dysfunction in Women Alcoholics." *Medical Aspects of Human Sexuality* 21, no. 6 (June 1987):97–101.

Shrestha, K., et al. "Sexual Jealousy in Alcoholics." *Acta Psychiatrica Scandinavica* 72, no. 3 (Sept. 1985):283–290.

Turner, Sandra, and Coloa, Flora. "Alcoholism and Sexual Assault: A Treatment Approach for Women Exploring Both Issues." *Alcoholism Treatment Quarterly* 2, no. 1 (Spring 1985):91–103.

Alzheimer's Disease

Beck, C., and Heacock, P. "Nursing Interventions for Patients with Alzheimer's Disease." *Nursing Clinics of North America* 23 (1988):95–123.

Geriatrics Panel Discussion. "Practical Considerations in Managing Alzheimer's Disease: I." *Geriatrics* 42 (Sept. 1987):78–98.

Geriatrics Panel Discussion. "Practical Considerations in Managing Alzheimer's Disease: II." *Geriatrics* 42 (Oct. 1987):55–65.

Group for the Advancement of Psychiatry. *The Psychiatric Treatment of Alzheimer's Disease*. New York: Brunner/Mazel, 1988.

Pagel, M. D.; Becker, J.; and Coppel, D. B. "Loss of Control, Self-blame, and Depression: An Investigation of Spouse Caregivers of Alzheimer's Disease Patients." *Journal of Abnormal Psychology* 94 (1985):169–182.

Pajk, M. "Alzheimer's Disease: Inpatient Care." *American Journal of Nursing* 84 (1984):217–228.

Palmer, M. H. "Alzheimer's Disease and Critical Care." *Journal of Gerontological Nursing* 9 (1983):86–91.

Pomara, N., and Stanley, M. "The Cholinergic Hypothesis of Memory Dysfunction in Alzheimer's Disease: Revisited." *Psychopharmacology Bulletin* 22, no. 1 (1986):110–118.

Schneck, M. K.; Reisberg, B.; and Ferris, S. "An Overview of Current Concepts of Alzheimer's Disease." *American Journal of Psychiatry* 139 (1982):165–173.

Anger

Antai-Otong, D. "When Your Patient Is Angry." *Nursing* 18, no. 2 (1988):45.

Benson, B.; Rice, C. J.; and Miranti, S. V. "Effects of Anger Management Training with Mentally Retarded Adults in Group Treatment." *Journal of Consulting Clinical Psychology* 54 (1986):728–729.

Rothenberg, A. "On Anger." *American Journal of Psychiatry* 128 (1971):454–460.

Anorexia, Bulimia and Eating Disorders

Abraham, Suzanne. *Eating Disorders: The Facts.* New York: Oxford University Press, 1984.

Bruch, Hilde. *Eating Disorders: Obesity, Anorexia Nervosa, and the Person Within.* New York: Basic Books, 1973.

Bruch, Hilde. *The Golden Cage: The Enigma of Anorexia Nervosa.* New York: Vintage Books, 1974.

Crisp, A. H., et al. "Clinical Features of Anorexia Nervosa: A Study of 102 Cases." *Journal of Psychosomatic Research* 24 (1980):179–191.

Devlin, M. J., et al. "Metabolic Abnormalities in Bulimia Nervosa." *Archives of General Psychiatry* 47 (1990):144–148.

Drewnowski, A.; Hopkins, S. A.; and Kessler, R. C. "Prevalence of Bulimia Nervosa in the U.S. College Student Population." *American Journal of Public Health* 78 (1988):1322–1325.

Fairburn, C. "A Cognitive-Behavioral Approach to the Treatment of Bulimia." *Psychological Medicine* 11 (1981):707–711.

Fava, M., et al. "Neurochemical Abnormalities of Anorexia Nervosa and Bulimia Nervosa." *American Journal of Psychiatry* 146 (1989):963–971.

Heater, Sandra Harvey. *Am I Still Visible?: A Woman's Triumph over Anorexia Nervosa.* White Hall, Va.: White Hall Books, 1983.

Hsu, G. "The Treatment of Anorexia Nervosa." *American Journal of Psychiatry* 143 (1986):573–581.

Hudson, J. I., et al. "Phenomenologic Relationship of Eating Disorders to Major Affective Disorder." *Psychiatric Resident* 9 (1983):345–354.

Hughes, T. L., et al. "Treating Bulimia with Desipramine." *Archives of General Psychiatry* 43 (1986):182–186.

Liebman, R.; Minuchin, S.; and Baker, L. "An Integrated Treatment Program for Anorexia Nervosa." *American Journal of Psychiatry* 43 (1986):182–186.

Logue, C. M.; Crowe, R. R.; and Bean, J. A. "A Family Study of Anorexia Nervosa and Bulimia." *Comprehensive Psychiatry* 30 (1989):179–188.

Mitchell, James E., ed. *Anorexia Nervosa and Bulimia: Diagnosis and Treatment.* Minneapolis: University of Minnesota Press, 1985.

Mitchell, J. E., Pyle, R. L.; and Eckert, E. D. "A Comparison Study of Antidepressants in Structured, Intensive Group Psychotherapy in the Treatment of Bulimia Nervosa." *Archives of General Psychiatry* 47 (1990):149–157.

Monaghan, M. "Fluoxetine's Anorexic Effects." *Psychiatric Pharmacy Newsletter,* Creighton School of Pharmacy, Omaha, vol. 1, no. 4 (1988):2.

Neuman, Patricia A. *Anorexia Nervosa and Bulimia: A Handbook for Counselors and Therapists.* New York: Van Nostrand Reinhold, 1983.

Orbach, Susie. *Hunger Strike: An Anorexic's Struggle as a Metaphor for Our Age*. New York: Norton, 1986.

Pope, H. G.; Judson, J. I.; Johas, J. M.; et al. "Bulimia Treated with Imipramine: A Placebo Controlled Double Blind Study." *American Journal of Psychiatry* 140 (1983):554–558.

Pope, H. G.; Keck, P. E.; McElroy S.; et al. "A Placebo Controlled Study of Trazodone in Bulimia Nervosa." *Journal of Clinical Psychopharmacology* 9 (1989):254–259.

Romeo, Felicia F. *Understanding Anorexia Nervosa*. Springfield, Ill.: C. C. Thomas, 1986.

Sacker, Ira M. *Dying to Be Thin*. New York: Warner Books, 1987.

Steinhausen, H. C., and Glanville, K. "Follow-up Studies of Anorexia Nervosa: Review of Research Findings." *Psychological Medicine* 13 (1983):239–249.

White, Marlene B. *Bulimarexia: The Binge/Purge Cycle*. New York: Norton, 1983.

Woodman, Marion. *The Owl Was a Baker's Daughter: Obesity, Anorexia Nervosa, and the Repressed Feminine, a Psychological Study*. Toronto: Inner City Books, 1980.

Yates, W. R., et al. "Comorbidity of Bulimia Nervosa and Personality Disorder." *Journal of Clinical Psychiatry* 50 (1989):57–59.

Anxieties and Anxiety Disorders

Barlow, D. H. *Anxiety and Its Disorders—The Nature and Treatment of Anxiety and Panic*. New York: Guilford, 1988.

Breslau, N., and G. C. Davis. "Post-traumatic Stress Disorder: The Etiologic Specificity of War Time Stressors." *American Journal of Psychiatry* 144 (1987):578–583.

Davidson, J., et al. "Treatment of Post-traumatic Stress Disorder with Amitriptyline and Placebo." *Archives of General Psychiatry* 47 (1990):259–266.

Fyer, A. J., et al. "Familial Transmission of Simple Phobias and Fears: A Preliminary Report." *Archives of General Psychiatry* 47 (1990):252–256.

Gorman, J. M., et al. "A Neuroanatomical Hypothesis for Panic Disorder." *American Journal of Psychiatry* 146 (1989):148–161.

Greist, J. H.; Jefferson, J. W.; and Marks, I. M. *Anxiety and Its Treatment—Help Is Available*. Washington, D.C.: American Psychiatric Press, 1986.

Heimberg, R. G., and Barlow, D. H. "Psychosocial Treatments for Social Phobias." *Psychosomatics* 29 (1988):29–37.

Lee, M. A., et al. "Anxiogenic Effects of Caffeine in Panic and Depressed Patients." *American Journal of Psychiatry* 145 (1988):632–365.

Marks, I. M. "Behavioral Aspects of Panic Disorder." *American Journal of Psychiatry* 144 (1987):1160–1165.

Marks, I. M. *Fears, Phobias, and Rituals: Panic, Anxieties, and Their Disorders*. New York: Oxford University Press, 1987.

Marks, I. M. *Living with Fear*. New York: McGraw-Hill, 1978.

Ross, R. J., et al. "Sleep Disturbance as the Hallmark of Post-traumatic Stress Disorder." *American Journal of Psychiatry* 146 (1989):697–707.

Shaw, D. M., et al. "Criminal Behavior and Post-traumatic Stress Disorder in Vietnam Veterans." *Comprehensive Psychiatry* 28 (1987):403–411.

Battered Women

Limandri, B. J. "The Therapeutic Relationship with Abused Women." *Journal of Psychosocial Nursing and Mental Health Services* 25 (1987):9–16.

Sonkin, D. J.; Martin, D.; and Walker, L. E. A. *The Male Batterer.* New York: Springer Publishing, 1985.

Walker, L. E. *The Battered Woman Syndrome.* New York: Springer Publishing, 1984.

Behavioral Therapy

Bellack, A. S., and Hersen, M., eds. *Dictionary of Behavioral Therapy Techniques.* New York, Pergamon Press, 1985.

Cantela, J. R., and Kearney, A. *The Covert Conditioning Handbook.* New York: Springer Publishing, 1986.

Hersen, M., ed. *Pharmacological and Behavioral Treatment: An Integrative Approach.* New York: Wiley 1986.

Krug, R., and Cass, A. R. *Behavioral Sciences.* New York: Springer-Verlag, 1987.

Milne, D. *Training Behavior Therapists: Methods, Evaluation and Implication with Parents, Nurses and Teachers.* Cambridge, Mass.: Brookline Books, 1986.

Body Image

Gillies, D. A. "Body Image Changes Following Illness and Injury." *Journal of Enterostomal Therapy* 11, no. 5 (1984):186–189.

Glynn, Prudence. *Skin to Skin: Eroticism in Dress.* New York: Oxford University Press, 1982.

Janelli, L. M. "Body Image in Older Adults: A Review of the Literature." *Rehabilitation Nursing* 11, no. 4 (1986):6–8.

Lasry, J. C., et al. "Depression and Body Image Following Mastectomy and Lumpectomy." *Journal of Chronic Diseases* 40, no. 6 (1987):592–534.

Leon, G.; Lucas, A.; Colligan, R.; Ferdinande, R.; and Kamp, J. "Sexual, Body-Image and Personality Attitudes in Anorexia Nervosa." *Journal of Abnormal Child Psychology* 13, no. 2 (1985):245–258.

Noles, S.; Cash, T.; and Winstead, B. "Body Image, Physical Attractiveness and Depression." *Journal of Consulting and Clinical Psychology* 53, no. 1 (1985):88–94.

Sacks, O. *The Man Who Mistook His Wife for a Hat.* New York: Harper & Row, 1987.

Borderline Personality Disorder

Chopra, H. D., and Beatson, J. A. "Psychotic Symptoms in Borderline Personality Disorder." *American Journal of Psychiatry* 143, no. 12 (1986):1605–1607.

Cowdry, R. W. "Current Overview of the Borderline Diagnosis." *Journal of Clinical Psychiatry* 48, supp., no. 8 (1987):15–22.

Gunderson, J. G.; Kolb, J. E.; and Austin, V. "The Diagnostic Interview for Borderline Patients." *American Journal of Psychiatry* 138 (1981):896–903.

Jonas, J. M., and Pope, H. G. "Personality Disorders." *Psychotherapy and Psychosomatics* 46 (1987):58–66.

Boredom

Farmer, R., and Sundberg, N. "Boredom Proneness—The Development and Correlates of a New Scale." *Journal of Personality Assessment* 50, no. 1 (1986):4–17.

Frick, S. "Diagnosing Boredom, Confusion, and Adaptation in School Children." *Journal of School Health* 55, no. 7 (1985):254–257.

Leckart, B., and Weinberger, L. G. *Up from Boredom, Down from Fear.* New York: Richard Marek Publishers, 1980.

Morrant, J. C. A. "Boredom in Psychiatric Practice." *Canadian Journal of Psychiatry* 29 (1984):431–434.

Perkin, R. E., and Hill, A. B. "Cognitive and Affective Aspects of Boredom." *British Journal of Psychology* 76, pt. 2 (1985):221–234.

Rediger, G. L. *Lord, Don't Let Me Be Bored.* Philadelphia: Westminster Press, 1986.

Savitz, J., and Friedman, M. "Diagnosing Boredom and Confusion." *Nursing Research* 30, no. 1 (1981):16–19.

Taylor, G. "Psychotherapy with the Bored Patient." *Canadian Journal of Psychiatry* 29 (1984):217–222.

Chemical Dependency

Ganguli, H. G. L. "Meditation Subculture and Drug Use." *Human Relations* 38 (1985):953.

Gorsuch, R. L., and Butler, M. C. "Initial Drug Abuse: A Review of Predisposing Social Psychological Factors." *Psychological Bulletin* 83 (1986):120–137.

Mulry, J. T. "Drug Use in the Chemically Dependent." *Postgraduate Medicine* 83 (1988):279–283.

Newcomb, M. D.; Maddolician, E.; and Bealter, P. M. "Risk Factors for Drug Use Among Adolescents: Concurrent and Longitudinal Analysis." *American Journal of Public Health* 76 (1986):525–531.

O'Malley, D. M.; Johnston, L. D.; and Bachman, J. G. "Cocaine Use Among American Adolescents and Young Adults," in Kogel, N. J., and Adams, E. H., eds., *Cocaine Use in America: Epidemiological and Clinical Perspectives.* Rockville, Md.: National Institute on Drug Abuse, 1985.

Rounsaville, B. J.; Kosten, T. R.; Weissman, M. W.; and Keeber, H. D. *Evaluating and Treating Depression in Opiate Addicts.* Rockville, Md.: National Institute on Drug Abuse, 1985.

Textor, M. R. "Family Therapy with Drug Addicts: An Integrated Approach." *American Journal of Orthopsychiatry* 57 (1987):495–507.

Zackon, F.; McAuliffe, W. E.; and Ch'ien, S. M. N. *Addict Aftercare Recovery and Self Help.* Rockville, Md.: National Institute on Drug Abuse, 1985.

Child Abuse

(See CHILDREN AND CHILD ABUSE)

Childhood

August, G. J., and Stewart, M. A. "Familial Subtypes of Childhood Hyperactivity." *Journal of Nervous and Mental Disease* 171 (1983):362–368.

Campbell, M.; Green, W. H.; and Deutsch, S. I. *Child and Adolescent Psychopharmacology.* Beverly Hills, Calif.: Sage, 1985.

Gittleman, R. *Anxiety Disorders of Childhood.* New York: Guilford, 1986.

Puig-Antioch, J. "Major Depression and Conduct Disorder in Prepuberty." *Journal of the American Academy of Child Psychiatry* 21 (1982):118–128.

Rapoport, J. L.; Conners, C. K.; and Reatig, N. "Rating Scales and Assessment Instruments for Use in Pediatric Psychopharmacology Research." *Psychopharmacology Bulletin* 21 (1985):713–1125.

Stewart, M., and Kelso, J. "A Two-Year Follow-up of Boys with Aggressive Conduct Disorder." *Psychopathology* 20 (1987):296–304.

Children and Child Abuse

Bittner, S., and Newberger, E. H. "Pediatric Understanding of Child Abuse and Neglect." *Pediatric Review* 2 (1981):197–207.

Doyle, A. H.; Gold, D.; and Moskowitz, D. *Children in Families under Stress.* San Francisco: Jossey-Bass, 1979.

Erikson, E. *Identity: Youth and Crisis.* New York: Norton, 1986.

Gelfand, D. M., and Peterson, L. *Child Development and Psychopathology.* Beverly Hills: Sage, 1985.

Graham, P. *Child Psychiatry: A Developmental Approach.* Oxford: Oxford University Press, 1986.

Harris, P. L. *Children and Emotion: The Development of Psychological Understanding.* New York: Basil Blackwell, 1989.

Kellam, S. G., et al. *Mental Health and Going to School.* Chicago: University of Chicago Press, 1975.

Light, P. "Piaget and Egocentrism: A Perspective on Recent Developmental Research." *Early Child Development and Care* 12 (1983):7–18.

Osofsky, J., ed. *Handbook of Infant Development.* New York: Wiley, 1987.

Ross, S. D., and Edelson, J. L. *Working with Children and Adolescents in Groups.* San Francisco: Jossey-Bass, 1987.

Selman, R., and Selman, A. "Children's Ideas About Friendship: A New Theory." *Psychology Today* 13 (1979):70–80, 114.

Chronic Fatigue Syndrome

Behan, P. O., et al. "The Postviral Fatigue Syndrome—An Analysis of the Findings in 50 Cases." *Journal of Infection* 10 (1988).

Brody, Jane E. "Chronic Fatigue Syndrome: How to Recognize It and What to Do About It." *New York Times,* July 28, 1988.

Brooks, Barbara, and Smith, Nancy. *CFIDS: An Owner's Manual.* Self-published (Box 6456, Silver Spring, Md. 20906), 1988.

Fackelmann, K. A. "The Baffling Case of Chronic Fatigue." *Science News* 135 no. 1 (Jan. 1989):4.

Feiden, Karyn. *Hope and Help for Chronic Fatigue Syndrome.* New York: Prentice-Hall, 1990.

Hellinger, Walter C., et al. "Chronic Fatigue Syndrome and the Diagnostic Utility of Antibody to Epstein-Barr Virus Early Antigen." *Journal of the American Medical Association* 260, no. 7. (Aug. 19, 1988).

Holmes, Gary. "Chronic Fatigue Syndrome: A Working Case Definition." *Annals of Internal Medicine* 108, no. 3 (Mar. 1988).

Holmes, Gary, et al. "A Cluster of Patients with Chronic Mononucleosis-like Syndrome: Is Epstein-Barr Virus the Cause?" *Journal of the American Medical Association* 257, no. 17 (May 1, 1987).

Manu, Peter, et al. "The Frequency of the Chronic Fatigue Syndrome in Patients with Symptoms of Persistent Fatigue." *Annals of Internal Medicine* 109, no. 7 (Oct. 1, 1988).

Marsa, Linda. "Newest Mystery Illness: Chronic Fatigue Syndrome." *Redbook* (Apr. 1988).

Swartz, Morton N. "The Chronic Fatigue Syndrome—One Entity or Many?" *New England Journal of Medicine* 319, no. 26 (1988).

Tierney, Lawrence M. "Chronic Fatigue Syndrome: Current Recommendations for Diagnosis and Management." *Consultant* 29, no. 3 (Mar. 1989).

Zoler, Mitchel L. "Chronic Fatigue: Taking the Syndrome Seriously." *Medical World News* 29, no. 23 (Dec. 12, 1988).

Community Mental Health

(See also RURAL MENTAL HEALTH CARE)

Bachrach, L. L. "The Challenge of a Service Planning for Chronic Mental Patients." *Community Mental Health Journal* 22 (1986):170–174.

Bellack, A. S., and Mueser, K. T. "A Comprehensive Treatment Program for Schizophrenia and Chronic Mental Illness." *Community Mental Health Journal* 22 (1986):175–189.

Berkman, L. F. "The Assessment of Social Networks and Social Support in the Elderly." *Journal of American Geriatric Society* 31 (1983):743–749.

Clark, R. F. "The Costs and Benefits of Community Care: A Perspective from the Channeling Demonstration." *Pride Institute Journal* 6, no. 2 (1987):3–12.

Cordes, C. "The Plight of the Homeless Mentally Ill." *APA Monitor* 15 (1985):1–13.

Goldman, H. H.; Adams, N. H.; and Taube, C. A. "Deinstitutionalization: The Data Demythologized." *Hospital and Community Psychiatry* 34 (1983):129–134.

Coping Skills/Defense Mechanisms

(See also STRESS AND STRESS MANAGEMENT)

Bond, M.; Gardner, S. T.; Christian, J.; and Sigal, J. J. "Empirical Study of Self Rated Defense Styles." *Archives of General Psychiatry* 40 (1983):333–338.

Bond, M. P., and Vaillant, J. S. "An Empirical Study of the Relationship Between Diagnosis and Defense Style." *Archives of General Psychiatry* 43 (1986):285–288.

Coelho, G. V.; Hamburg, D. A.; and Adams, J. E. *Coping and Adaptation.* New York: Basic Books, 1974.

Cohen, F., and Lazarus, R. S. "Active Coping Processes, Coping Dispositions and Recovery from Surgery." *Psychosomatic Medicine* 35 (1973):375–389.

Folkman, S., and Lazarus, R. S. "An Analysis of Coping in a Middle-aged Community Sample." *Journal of Health and Social Behavior* 21 (1980):219–239.

Lazarus, R. S., and Folkman, S. *Stress, Appraisal and Coping.* New York: Springer Publishing, 1984.

Norris, J., and Kunes-Connell, M. "Self Esteem." *Nursing Clinics of North America* 20 (1985):745–761.

Pearlin, L. I., and Schoolar, C. "The Structure of Coping." *Journal of Health and Social Behavior* 19 (1978):2–21.

Saxon, D. F., and Haring, P. W. *Care of Patients with Emotional Problems.* St. Louis: C. V. Mosby, 1979.

Selye, H. *Stress Without Distress.* New York: Lippincott & Crowell, 1974.

Viney, L. L., and Westbrook, M. T. "Coping with Chronic Illness: Strategy Preferences, Changes in Preferences and Associated Emotional Reactions." *Journal of Chronic Diseases* 34 (1984):489–502.

Courtship, Love, Romance, Relationships

Andelin, Helen B. *Fascinating Womanhood: A Guide to a Happy Marriage.* Santa Barbara, Calif.: Pacific Press, 1974.

Beck, Aaron T. *Love Is Never Enough: How Couples Can Overcome Misunderstandings, Resolve Conflicts, and Solve Relationship Problems Through Cognitive Therapy.* New York: Harper & Row, 1988.

Benghis, Ingrid. *Combat in the Erogenous Zone.* New York: Knopf, 1972.

Bernard, Jessie Shirley. *The Future of Marriage.* Toronto: Bantam Books, 1972.

Botwin, Carol. *Is There Sex after Marriage?* New York: Pocket Books, 1986.

Brown, Helen Gurley. *Sex and the Single Girl.* New York: Bernard Geis Associates, 1962.

Cassell, Carol. *Swept Away: Why Women Fear Their Own Sexuality.* New York: Simon & Schuster, 1984.

Derenski, Arlene, and Landsburg, Sally B. *The Age Taboo: Older Women–Younger Men Relationships.* Boston: Little, Brown, 1981.

Dolesh, Daniel J., and Lehman, Sherelynn. *Love Me, Love Me Not: How to Survive Infidelity.* New York: McGraw-Hill, 1985.

Ellis, Havelock. *Sex and Marriage: Eros in Contemporary Life.* New York: Random House, 1952.

Eskapa, Shirley. *Woman Versus Woman: The Extramarital Affair.* New York: Franklin Watts, 1984.

Forward, Susan, and Torres, Joan. *Men Who Hate Women and the Women Who Love Them.* Toronto: Bantam Books, 1986.

Gordon, Barbara. *Jennifer Fever: Older Men/Younger Women.* New York: Harper & Row, 1988.

Grosskopf, Dianne. *Sex and the Married Woman.* New York: Simon & Schuster, 1983.

Norwood, Robin. *Women Who Love Too Much: When You Keep Wishing and Hoping He'll Change.* New York: Pocket Books, 1985.

Richardson, Laurel. *The New Other Women: Contemporary Single Women in Affairs with Married Men.* New York: Free Press, 1985.

Rubin, Lillian B. *Intimate Strangers: Men and Women Together.* New York: Harper & Row, 1983.

Russell, Bertrand. *Marriage and Morals*. London: Allen & Unwin, 1929.

Schickel, Richard. *Singled Out: A Civilized Guide to Sex and Sensibility for the Suddenly Single Man—or Woman*. New York: Viking Press, 1981.

Weitzman, Lenore. *The Divorce Revolution: The Unexpected Social and Economic Consequences for Women and Children in America*. New York: Free Press, 1985.

Westermarck, Edward A. *The Future of Marriage in Western Civilisation*. London: Macmillan, 1936.

Westheimer, Ruth. *Dr. Ruth's Guide for Married Lovers*. New York: Warner Books, 1986.

Wolfe, Linda. *Playing Around: Women and Extramarital Sex*. New York: Morrow, 1975.

Zola, Marion. *All the Good Ones Are Married: Married Men and the Women Who Love Them*. New York: Times Books, 1981.

Cultural Influences

Buunk, Bram, and Hupka, Ralph B. "Cross-cultural Differences in the Elicitation of Sexual Jealousy." *Journal of Sex Research* 23, no. 1 (1987):12–22.

Caplan, Patricia, and Bujra, Janet M., eds. *Women United, Women Divided: Comparative Studies of Ten Contemporary Cultures*. Bloomington: Indiana University Press, 1979.

Driver, Edwin D., and Driver, Aloo E. "Gender, Society and Self-Conceptions: India, Iran, Trinidad-Tobago and the United States." *International Journal of Comparative Sociology* 24, no. 3–4 (1983):200–217.

Escobar, J. I. "Cross-cultural Aspects of the Somatization Trait." *Hospital and Community Psychiatry* 38 (1987):174–180.

Flaskerud, J. H. "The Effects of Culture-Compatible Intervention on the Utilization of Mental Health Services by Minority Clients." *Community Mental Health Journal* 22 (1986):127–141.

Friedl, Ernestine. *Women and Men: An Anthropologist's View*. New York: Holt, Rinehart and Winston, 1975.

Furnham, Adrian, and Karani, Roshni. "A Cross-cultural Study of Attitudes to Women, Just World and Locus of Control Beliefs." *Psychologia* 28 (1985):11–20.

Hite, Shere. *The Hite Report: A Nationwide Study of Female Sexuality*. New York: Macmillan, 1976.

Jones, B. E., and Gray, B. A. "Problems in Diagnosing Schizophrenia and Affective Disorders Among Blacks." *Hospital and Community Psychiatry* 37 (1986):61–65.

Kinsey, Alfred C.; Pomeroy, Wardell B.; Martin, Clyde E.; and Gebhard, Paul H. *Sexual Behavior in the Human Female*. Philadelphia: W. B. Saunders, 1953.

Kirkpatrick, Martha, ed. *Women's Sexual Experience: Explorations of the Dark Continent*. New York: Plenum Press, 1982.

Kitzinger, Sheila. *Woman's Experience of Sex*. New York: Putnam, 1983.

Koss, J. D. "Expectations and Outcomes for Patients Given Mental Health Care of Spiritist Healing in Puerto Rico." *American Journal of Psychiatry* 144 (1987):56–61.

Leacock, Eleanor Burke. *Myths of Male Dominance: Collected Articles on Women Cross-culturally*. New York: Monthly Review Press, 1981.

Leininger, M. M. "Transcultural Eating Patterns and Nutrition: Transcultural Nursing and Anthropological Perspectives." *Holistic Nursing Practice* 3 (1988):16–25.

Littlewood, R., and Lipsedge, M. "The Butterfly and the Serpent: Culture, Psychopathology and Biomedicine." *Culture, Medicine and Psychiatry* 11 (1987):289–335.

Masson, Jeffrey Moussaieff. *A Dark Science: Women, Sexuality and Psychiatry in the Nineteenth Century*. New York: Farrar, Straus & Giroux, 1986.

Masters, William H., and Johnson, Virginia. *The Pleasure Bond: A New Look at Sexuality and Commitment*. Boston: Little, Brown, 1974.

Matheson, L. "If You Are Not an Indian, How Do You Treat an Indian?" in Lefley, H. P., and Pederson, P. B., eds., *Cross-cultural Training for Mental Health Professionals*. Springfield, Ill.: Charles C. Thomas, 1986.

Miller, Patricia Y., and Fowlkes, Martha R. "Social and Behavioral Constructions of Female Sexuality." *Signs* 5 (Summer 1980):783–800.

Morgan, Elaine. *The Descent of Woman*. New York: Bantam, 1973.

Munroe, Robert L.; Munroe, Ruth H.; and Whiting, John W. M. "The Couvade: A Psychological Analysis." *Ethos* 1, no. 1 (1973):30–74.

Robinson, Paul A. *The Modernization of Sex: Havelock Ellis, Alfred Kinsey, William Masters and Virginia Johnson*. New York: Harper & Row, 1976.

Sanday, Peggy Reeves. *Female Power and Male Dominance: On the Origins of Sexual Inequality*. New York: Cambridge University Press, 1981.

Delusional and Other Psychotic Disorders

Kendler, K. S.; Masterson, C.; and Davis, K. "Psychiatric Illness in First Degree Relatives of Patients with Paranoid Psychosis, Schizophrenia, and Medical Illness." *British Journal of Psychiatry* 147 (1985):524–531.

Kendler, K. S.; Spitzer, R. L.; and Williams, J. B. W. "Psychotic Disorders in DSM-III-R." *American Journal of Psychiatry* 146 (1989):953–962.

Levitt, J. J., and Tsuang, M. T. "The Heterogeneity of Schizoaffective Disorder: Implications for Treatment." *American Journal of Psychiatry* 145 (1988):926–936.

Maj, M. "Lithium Prophylaxis in Schizoaffective Disorder—A Prospective Study." *Journal of Affective Disorders* 14 (1988):129–135.

Sacks, M. H. "Folie a Deux." *Comprehensive Psychiatry* 29 (1988):270–277.

Watt, J. A. G. "The Relationship of Paranoid States to Schizophrenia." *American Journal of Psychiatry* 142 (1985):1456–1458.

Weinberger, D. L., et al. "Computed Tomography in Schizophreniform Disorder and Other Acute Psychiatric Disorders." *Archives of General Psychiatry* 39 (1982):778–783.

Winokur, G. "Familial Psychopathology and Delusional Disorder." *Comprehensive Psychiatry* 26 (1985):241–248.

Dementia

Cummings, J. L., and Benson, D. F. *Dementia: A Clinical Approach*. Boston: Butterworths, 1983.

Katzman, R., and Terry, R. *The Neurology of Aging*. Philadelphia: F. A. Davis, 1983.

Depression and Affective Disorders

Akiskal, H. S. "The Clinical Significance of the 'Soft' Bipolar Spectrum." *Psychiatric Annals* 16 (1986):667–671.

Akiskal, H. S., and Webb, W. L. "Affective Disorders: Recent Advances in Clinical Conceptualization." *Hospital and Community Psychiatry* 34 (1983):695–702.

Andreasen, N. C.; et al. "Familial Rates of Affective Disorder: A Report from the National Institute of Mental Health Collaborative Study." *Archives of General Psychiatry* 44 (1987):461–469.

Angst, J., et al. "Bipolar Manic-Depressive Psychoses: Results of a Genetic Investigation." *Human Genetics* 55 (1980):237–254.

Billings, A. G., and Moos, R. H. "Psychosocial Stressors, Coping, and Depression," in Beckham, E. E., and Leber, W. R., eds., *Handbook of Depression: Treatment, Assessment and Research.* Homewood, Ill.: Dorsey, 1985.

Bruss, C. R. "Nursing Diagnosis of Hopelessness." *Journal of Psychosocial Nursing and Mental Health Services* 26 (1988):28–31.

Campbell, L. "Hopelessness: A Concept Analysis." *Journal of Psychosocial Nursing and Mental Health Services* 25 (1987):18–22.

Chaisson, M.; Butler, L.; Yost, E.; and Allender, J. "Treating the Depressed Elderly." *Journal of Psychosocial Nursing and Mental Health Services* 22 (May 1984):25–30.

Coppen, A. J., and Doogan, D. P. "Serotonin and Its Place in the Pathogenesis of Depression." *Journal of Clinical Psychiatry* 49 supp. 8 (1988):4–11.

Field, W. E. "Physical Causes of Depression." *Journal of Psychosocial Nursing and Mental Health Services* 23 (Oct. 1985):7–11.

Flomenbaum, N. E.; Freedman, A. M.; Levy, N. B.; Simpson, G. M.; and Talley, J. "Treatment of Depression in the Physicaly Ill: Multidisciplinary Viewpoints in a Roundtable Discussion." *Emergency Medicine* 17 (1984):2–20.

Fogelson, D. L.; Bystritsky, A.; and Sussman, N. "Interrelationships Between Major Depression and Anxiety Disorders: Clinical Relevance." *Psychiatric Annuals* 18 (1988):158–167.

Fopma-Loy, J. "Depression and Dementia: Differential Diagnosis." *Journal of Psychosocial Nursing and Mental Health Services* 24 (Feb. 1986):27–29.

Gillin, J. C., and Byerley, W. A. "Sleep: A Neurobiological Window on Affective Disorders." *Trends in Neuroscience* 8 (1985):537–542.

Glazebrook, C. K., and Munjas, B. A. "Sex Roles and Depression." *Journal of Psychosocial Nursing and Mental Health Services* 24 (Dec. 1986):9–12.

Goldwyn, R. M. "Educating the Patient and Family About Depression." *Medical Clinics of North America* 72 (1988):887–895.

Gordon, V. C., and Ledray, L. E. "Depression in Women: The Challenge of Treatment and Prevention." *Journal of Psychosocial Nursing and Mental Health Services* 23 (Jan. 1985):26–34.

Greist, John H., M.D., and Jefferson, James W., M.D. *Depression and Its Treatment: Help for the Nation's #1 Mental Problem.* Washington, D.C.: American Psychiatric Press, 1984.

Holmes, T., and Rahe, R. "Social Readjustment Rating Scale." *Journal of Psychosomatic Research* 11 (1976):213–218.

James, M. E., and Cohen-Cole, S. A. "Major Depression: Current Perspectives." *Emory University Journal of Medicine* 3 (1989):110.

Jarrett, R. B., and Rush, J. A. "Psychotherapeutic Approaches for Depression," in Cavenar, J. O., ed., *Psychiatry,* vol 1. Philadelphia: Lippincott, 1988.

Jimerson, D. C. "Role of Dopamine Mechanisms in the Affective Disorders," in Meltzer, H. Y., ed., *Psychopharmacology: The Third Generation of Progress.* New York: Raven, 1987.

Klerman, Gerald, M.D. *Suicide and Depression Among Adolescents and Young Adults.* Washington, D.C.: American Psychiatric Press, 1986.

Klerman, G. L., et al. "Birth Cohort Trends in Rates of Major Depressive Disorder Among Relatives of Patients with Affective Disorder." *Archives of General Psychiatry* 42 (1985):689–693.

Kolata, G. "Manic-Depression: Is It Inherited?" *Science* 232 (1986):575–576.

Lehman, H. E. "Affective Disorders: Clinical Features," in Kaplan, H. L., and Sadock, B. J., eds., *Comprehensive Textbook of Psychiatry/IV.* Baltimore: Williams & Wilkins, 1985.

Lewinsohn, P. M.; Hoberman, H. M.; Teri, L.; and Hautzinger, M. "An Integrative Theory of Depression," in Reiss, S., and Bootzin, R., eds., *Theoretical Issues in Behavior Therapy.* New York: Academic Press, 1985.

Lum, T. L. "An Integrated Approach to Aging and Depression." *Archives of Psychiatric Nursing* 2 (1987):211.

Meller, W., et al. "HPA Axis Abnormalities in Depressed Patients with Normal Response to the DST." *American Journal of Psychiatry* 145 (1988):318–324.

Meltzer, H. Y. "Lithium Mechanisms in Bipolar Illness and Altered Intracellular Calcium Functions." *Biological Psychiatry* 21 (1986):492–510.

Mitchell, J., et al. "Phenomenology of Depression in Children and Adolescents." *Journal of the American Academy of Child and Adolescent Psychiatry* 27, no. 1 (1988):12–20.

Pakel, E. S., ed. *Handbook of Affective Disorders.* New York: Guilford, 1982.

Peterson, C., and Seligman, M. E. P. "The Learned Helplessness Model of Depression: Current Status of Theory and Research," in Beckham, E. E., and Leber, W. R., eds., *Handbook of Depression: Treatment, Assessment and Research.* Homewood, Ill.: Dorsey, 1985.

Plumlee, A. A. "Biological Rhythms and Affective Illness." *Journal of Psychosocial Nursing and Mental Health Services* 24 (Mar. 1986): 12–17.

Rosenthal, N.; Carpenter, C. J.; James, S. P.; et al. "Seasonal Affective Disorders in Children and Adolescents." *American Journal of Psychiatry* 143 (1986):356–358.

Rosenthal, N.; Sack, D. A.; Carpenter, C. J.; et al. "Antidepressant Effects of Light in Seasonal Affective Disorder." *American Journal of Psychiatry* 142 (1985):163–170.

Rothschild, A. J. "Biology of Depression." *Medical Clinics of North America* 72 (1988):765–790.

Ryan L.; Montgomery, A.; and Meyers, S. "Impact of Circadian Rhythm Research on Approaches to Affective Illness." *Archives of Psychiatric Nursing* 1 (1987):236–240.

Ryan, N. D., et al. "The Clinical Picture of Major Depression in Children and Adolescents." *Archives of General Psychiatry* 44 (1987):854–861.

Sacco, W. P., and Beck, A. T. "Cognitive Therapy of Depression," in Beckham, E. E., and Leber, W. R., eds., *Handbook of Depression: Treatment, Assessment, and Research.* Homewood, Ill.: Dorsey, 1985.

Schleifer, S. J., et al. "Major Depressive Disorder and Immunity: Role of Age, Sex, Severity, and Hospitalization." *Archives of General Psychiatry* 46 (1989):81–87.

Siever, L. J., and Davis, K. L. "Overview: Toward a Dysregulation Hypothesis of Depression." *American Journal of Psychiatry* 142 (1985):1017–1031.

Simmons-Alling, S. "New Approaches to Managing Affective Disorders." *Archives of Psychiatric Nursing* 1 (1987):219–224.

Thompson, C., and Issacs, G. "Seasonal Affective Disorder—A British Sample Symptomatology in Relation to Mode of Referral and Diagnostic Subtype." *Journal of Affective Disorders* 14 (1988):1–11.

Todd, B. "Depression and Antidepressants." *Geriatric Nursing* 8 (Jul./Aug. 1987):302.

Wehr, T.; Sack, D. A.; Rosenthal, N. E.; et al. "Rapid Cycling Affective Disorders: Contributing Factors and Treatment Responses in 51 Patients." *American Journal of Psychiatry* 145 (1988):179–184.

Wehr, T.; Skwerer, R. G.; Jacobsen, F. M.; et al. "Eye Versus Skin Phototherapy of Seasonal Affective Disorder." *American Journal of Psychiatry* 144 (1987):753–757.

Weissman, M. M. "Advances in Psychiatric Epidemiology: Rates and Risks for Major Depression." *American Journal of Public Health* 77 (1987):445–451.

Weissman, M. M.; Gammon, D.; John, K.; Merikangas, K. R.; Prusoff, B. A.; and Sholomskas, D. "Children of Depressed Parents: Increased Psychopathology and Early Onset of Major Depression." *Archives of General Psychiatry* 44 (1987):847–853.

Weissman, M. M.; Kidd, K. K.; and Prusoff, B. A. "Variability in Rates of Affective Disorders in Relatives of Depressed and Normal Probands." *Archives of General Psychiatry* 39 (1982):1397–1403.

Weissman, M. M.; Leaf, P. J.; Bruce, M. L.; et al. "The Epidemiology of Dysthymia in Five Communities: Rates, Risks, Comorbidity, and Treatment." *American Journal of Psychiatry* 145 (1988):815–819.

Whybrow, P. C.; Akiskal, H. S.; and McKinney, W. T., Jr. *Mood Disorders: Toward a New Psychobiology*. New York: Plenum Press, 1984.

Winokur, G. *Depression: The Facts*. New York: Oxford University Press, 1981.

Dissociative Disorders

(See also MULTIPLE PERSONALITY DISORDER)

Bliss, E. L. *Multiple Personality, Allied Disorders, and Hypnosis*. New York: Oxford University Press, 1986.

Braun, B. G. "Dissociation: Behavior, Affect, Sensation, Knowledge," in Braun, ed., *Dissociative Disorders 1985: Proceedings of the Second International Conference on Multiple Personality/Dissociative States*. Chicago: Rush University, 1985.

Braun, B. G. "The Transgenerational Incidence of Dissociation and Multiple Personality Disorder," in Kluft, R. P., ed., *Childhood Antecedents of Multiple Personality*. Washington, D.C.: American Psychiatric Press, 1985.

Coons, P. M., and Bradley, K. "Group Psychotherapy with Multiple Personality Patients." *Journal of Nervous and Mental Disorders* 173 (1985):515–521.

Fahy, T. A. "The Diagnosis of Multiple Personality Disorder: A Critical Review." *British Journal of Psychiatry* 153 (1988):597–600.

Horevitz, R. P., and Braun, B. G. "Are Multiple Personalities Borderline?" *Psychiatria Clinica North America* 7 (1984):69–88.

Kluft, R. P. "An Update on Multiple Personality Disorder." *Hospital and Community Psychiatry* 38 (1987):363–373.

Putnam, F. W., and Guroff, J. J. "A Clinical Phenomenology of Multiple Personality Disorder: Review of 100 Recent Cases." *Journal of Clinical Psychiatry* 47 (1986):285–293.

Schenk, L., and Bear, D. "Multiple Personality and Related Dissociative Phenomena in Patients with Temporal Lobe Epilepsy." *American Journal of Psychiatry* 138 (1981):1311–1315.

Schreiber, F. R. *Sybil*. Chicago: Henry Regnery, 1973.

Thigpen, C. H., and Cleckley, H. M. *The Three Faces of Eve*. New York: McGraw-Hill, 1957.

Eating Disorders

See ANOREXIA, BULIMIA, AND EATING DISORDERS.

Elderly

Berezin, M. A. "Psychotherapy of the Elderly: Introduction." *Journal of Geriatric Psychiatry* 16, no. 3 (1983):3–6.

Buckwalter, K. C. "Integration of Social and Mental Health Services for the Elderly." *Family Community Health* 8, no. 4 (1985):76–87.

Cohen, P. M. "A Group Approach for Working with Families of the Elderly." *Gerontologist* 23, no. 3 (1983):248–250.

Copstead, L. E., and Patterson, S. "Families of the Elderly," in Carnevali, D., and Patrick, M., eds., *Nursing Management for the Elderly,* 2d ed. Philadelphia: Lippincott, 1986.

Evans, L. K. "Sundown Syndrome in Institutionalized Elderly." *Journal of the American Geriatrics Society* 35 (1987):101–108.

Gelfand, D. E.; Olson, J. K.; and Block, M. R. "Two Generations of Elderly in the Changing American Family: Implications for Family Services." *Family Coordinator* 27 (1978):395–403.

Hussian, R. A. *Geriatric Psychology: A Behavioral Perspective*. New York: Van Nostrand Reinhold, 1981.

Kahana, R. J. "Psychotherapy of the Elderly: A Miserable Old Age—What Can Therapy Do?" *Journal of Geriatric Psychiatry* 16, no. 1 (1983):7–32.

Liston, E. G. "Delirium in the Aged." *Psychiatria Clinica North America* 5 (1982):49–66.

Lund, D., et al. "Identifying Elderly with Coping Difficulties after Two Years of Bereavement." *Omega* 16, no. 3 (1985–86):213–224.

Oberleder, M. "Psychotherapy with the Aging: An Art of the Possible?" *Psychotherapy* 3 (1966):139–142.

Paulmeno, S. R. "Psychogeriatric Care: A Specialty Within a Specialty." *Nursing Management* 2 (1987):39–42.

Reisberg, B. "An Ordinal Functional Assessment Tool for Alzheimer-type Dementia." *Hospital and Community Psychiatry* 36 (1985):593–595.

Reubin, A.; Bierman, E. L.; and Hazzard, W. R. *Principles of Geriatric Medicine*. New York: McGraw-Hill, 1985.

Rosen, W. G.; Mohs, R. C.; Davis, K. L. "A New Rating Scale for Alzheimer's Disease." *American Journal of Psychiatry* 141 (1984):1356–1364.

Seelback, W. C. "Correlates of Aged Parents' Filial Responsibility, Expectations and Relations." *Family Coordinator* 27 (1978):241–250.

Storandt, M. *Counseling and Therapy with Older Adults*. Boston: Little, Brown Series on Gerontology, 1983.

Terry, R. D. *Aging and the Brain*. New York: Raven Press, 1988.

Wan, T., and Odell, B. "Major Role Losses and Social Participation of Older Males." *Research on Aging* 5, no. 2 (1983):173–196.

Family Interaction/Therapy

Carter, E. A., and McGoldrick, M., eds. *The Family Life Cycle: A Framework for Family Therapy*. New York: Gardner Press, 1980.

Combrinck-Graham, L. "A Developmental Model for Family Systems." *Family Process* 24 (1985):139–150.

Falloon, I. R. H.; Boyd, J. L.; and McGill, C. W. *Family Care of Schizophrenia: A Problem-solving Approach to the Treatment of Mental Illness*. New York: Guilford Press, 1984.

Ferreira, A. "Psychosis and Family Myth." *American Journal of Psychotherapy* 21 (1967):186–197.

Goldstein, M. J., and Doane, J. A. "Family Factors in the Onset, Course and Treatment of Schizophrenic Disorders: An Update on Current Research." *Journal of Nervous and Mental Disease* 170 (1982):692–700.

Gottlieb, B. H. "Social Support and the Study of Personal Relationships." *Journal of Social and Personal Relations* 2 (1985):351.

Gray-Price, H., and Szczesny, S. "Crisis Intervention with Families of Cancer Patients: A Developmental Approach." *Topics in Clinical Nursing* 7 (1985):58–70.

Heinrichs, D. W., and Carpenter, W. T. "The Coordination of Family Therapy with Other Treatment Modalities for Schizophrenia," in McFarlane, W. R., ed., *Family Therapy in Schizophrenia*. New York: Guilford Press, 1983.

Hogarty, G. E.; Anderson, C. M.; and Reiss, D. J. "Family Psychoeducation, Social Skills, Training, and Maintenance Chemotherapy in the Aftercare Treatment of Schizophrenia." *Archives of General Psychiatry* 43 (1986):633–642.

Kanter, J.; Lamb, H. R., and Loeper, C. "Expressed Emotion in Families: A Critical Review." *Hospital and Community Psychiatry* 38 (1987):374–380.

Satir, V. *Conjoint Family Therapy*, rev. ed. Palo Alto, Calif.: Science and Behavior Books, 1967.

Terkelsen, K. G. "Schizophrenia and the Family, II: Adverse Effects of Family Therapy." *Family Process* 22 (1983):191–200.

Walsh, R., ed. *Normal Family Processes*. New York: Guilford Press, 1982.

Wright, L. M., and Leahey, M., eds. *Families and Chronic Illness*. Springhouse, Pa.: Springhouse Corp., 1987.

Fears and Phobias

Doctor, Ronald M., and Kahn, Ada P. *The Encyclopedia of Phobias, Fears and Anxieties.* New York: Facts On File, 1989.

Ferrari, M. "Fears and Phobias in Childhood: Some Clinical and Developmental Considerations." *Child Psychiatry and Human Development* 17 (1986):75–87.

Foa, E. B., and Kozak, M. J. "Emotional Processing of Fear: Exposure to Corrective Information." *Psychological Bulletin* 99 (1986):20–35.

Goldstein, Alan J. *Overcoming Agoraphobia: Conquering Fear of the Outside World.* New York: Viking, 1987.

Lentz, K. A. "The Expressed Fears of Young Children." *Child Psychiatry and Human Development* 16 (1985):3–13.

Marks, I. M. "Genetics of Fear and Anxiety Disorders." *British Journal of Psychology* 149 (1986):406–418.

Moores, A. "Facing the Fear." *Nursing Times* 83 no. 13 (1987):34–38.

Paolino, Adele. *Agoraphobia: Are Panic and Phobias Psychological or Physical?* Winona, Minn.: Apollo Books, 1984.

Seidenberg, Robert, and De Crow, Karen. *Women Who Marry Houses: Panic and Protest in Agoraphobia.* New York: McGraw-Hill, 1983.

Sipes, G.; Rardin, M.; and Fitzgerald, B. "Adolescent Recall of Childhood Fears and Coping Strategies." *Psychological Reports* 57 (1985):1215–1223.

Vose, Ruth Hurst. *Agoraphobia.* London: Faber & Faber, 1981.

Gender Identity

Bolin, Anne. *In Search of Eve: Transsexual Rites of Passage.* South Hadley, Mass.: Bergin & Garvey, 1988.

Lothstein, Leslie Martin. *Female-to-Male Transsexualism: Historical, Clinical and Theoretical Issues.* Boston: Routledge & Kegan Paul, 1983.

Morris, Jan. *Conundrum.* New York: New American Library, 1975.

Richards, Renee. *Second Serve: The Renee Richards Story.* New York: Stein & Day, 1983.

Stoller, Robert J. *Sex and Gender, Volume 1: The Development of Masculinity and Femininity.* New York: Aronson, 1974.

Stoller, Robert J. *Sex and Gender, Volume 2: The Transsexual Experiment.* New York: Aronson, 1975.

Genetics

Fieve, R. R.; Rosenthal, D.; and Brill, H., eds. *Genetic Research in Psychiatry.* Baltimore: Johns Hopkins University Press, 1975.

Fuller, J. L., and Thompson, W. R. *Foundations of Behavior Genetics.* St. Louis: C. V. Mosby, 1978.

Goodwin, D. W. "Genetic Factors in the Development of Alcoholism." *Psychiatria Clinica North America* 9 (1986):427–433.

Pardes, H., et al. "Genetics and Psychiatry: Past Discoveries, Present Dilemmas, and Future Directions." *American Journal of Psychiatry* 146 (1989):435–443.

Grief

Bowlby, J. *Loss: Sadness and Depression—Attachment and Loss,* vol 3. New York: Basic Books, 1980.

Collison, C., and Miller, S. "Using Images of the Future in Grief Work." *Image* 19 (1987):9–11.

Engel, G. L. "Grief and Grieving." 64, no. 9 (1964):93–98.

Fulton, R., and Gottesman, D. "Anticipatory Grief: A Psychosocial Concept Reconsidered." *British Journal of Psychiatry* 137 (1980):45–54.

Hampe, S. O. "Needs of the Grieving Spouse in a Hospital Setting." *Nursing Research* 24 (1975):113–120.

Johnson, S. E. *After a Child Dies: Counseling Bereaved Families.* New York: Springer Publishing, 1987.

Kubler-Ross, E. *On Death and Dying.* New York: Macmillan, 1969.

Lindemann, E. *Beyond Grief: Studies in Crisis Intervention.* New York: Aronson, 1979.

Martocchio, B. C. "Grief and Bereavement: Healing Through Hurt." *Nursing Clinics of North America* 29 (1985):327–341.

Osterweis, M.; Solomon, F.; and Green, M., eds. *Bereavement: Reactions, Consequences, and Care.* Washington, D.C.: National Academy Press, 1984.

Parkes, C. M., and Weiss, R. S. *Recovery from Bereavement.* New York: Basic Books, 1983.

Pollock, G. H. "The Mourning-Liberation Process in Health and Disease." *Psychiatria Clinica North America* 10 (1987):345–354.

Rees, W. D. "The Bereaved and Their Hallucinations," in Schoenberg, B., et al., eds., *Bereavement: Its Psychosocial Aspects.* New York: Columbia University Press, 1975.

Stephenson, J. S. *Death, Grief, and Mourning: Indiidual and Social Realities.* New York: Macmillan, 1985.

Stewart, T., and Shields, C. R. "Grief in Chronic Illness: Assessment and Management." *Archives of Physical Medicine and Rehabilitation* 66 (1985):447–450.

Vachon, M. L. S. "Unresolved Grief in Persons with Cancer Referred for Psychotherapy." *Psychiatria Clinica North America* 10 (1987):467–486.

Welch, D. "Anticipatory Grief Reactions in Family Members of Adult Patients." *Issues in Mental Health Nursing* 4 (1982):149–158.

Worden, W. J. *Grief Counseling and Grief Therapy.* New York: Springer Publishing, 1982.

Group Dynamics/Group Therapy

Cronenwett, L. R. "Network Structure, Social Support, and Psychological Outcomes of Pregnancy." *Nursing Research* 34 (1985):93–99.

Festinger, L. "Informal Social Communication," in Cartwright, D., and Zander, A., eds., *Group Dynamics.* New York: Harper & Row, 1968.

Lieberman, M. A.; Yalom, I. D.; and Miles, M. B. *Encounter Groups: First Facts.* New York: Basic Books, 1972.

Loomis, M. E. "Levels of Contracting." *Journal of Psychosocial Nursing and Mental Health Services* 23 (1985):9–14.

Norbeck, J. S. "Types and Sources of Social Support for Managing Job Stress in Critical Care Nursing." *Nursing Research* 34 (1985):225–230.

Yalom, I. D. *The Theory and Practice of Group Psychotherapy,* 3d ed. New York: Basic Books, 1985.

Headaches

Adler, C. S.; Adler, S. M.; and Packard, R. C. *Psychiatric Aspects of Headache.* Baltimore: Williams & Wilkins, 1987.

Bakal, D. A.; Demjen, S.; and Kaganov, J. A. "Cognitive Behavioral Treatment of Chronic Headache." *Headache* 21 (1981):81–86.

Bakal, D. A., and Kaganov, J. A. "Muscle Contraction and Migraine Headache, Psychophysiologic Comparison." *Headache* 17 (1977):208–215.

Barlow, C. F. *Headache and Migraine in Childhood.* Philadelphia: Lippincott, Oxford Blackwell Scientific Publications, 1984.

Benson, H. *Beyond the Relaxation Response.* New York: Berkeley, 1984.

Blau, J. N. "Adult Migraine: The Patient Observed," in Blau, J. N., (ed.), *Migraine: Clinical and Research Aspects.* Baltimore: Johns Hopkins University Press, 1987.

Blau, J. N.; Path, F. R. C.; and Thavapalan, M. "Preventing Migraine: A Study of Precipitating Factors." *Headache* 28 (1988):481–483.

Dalton, K. "Food Intake Prior to a Migraine Attach—Study of 2,313 Spontaneous Attacks." *Headache* 15 (1975):188–193.

Edmeads, J. "The Cervical Spine and Headache." *Neurology* 38 (1988):1874–1878.

Kahn, A. P. *Headaches.* Chicago: Contemporary Books, 1983.

Kudrow, L. *Cluster Headache: Mechanisms and Management.* New York: Oxford University Press, 1980.

Labbe, E. E. "Childhood Muscle Contraction Headache." *Headache* 28 (1988):430–434.

Lance, J. W. *Mechanism and Management of Headache,* 4th ed. Boston: Butterworth Scientific, 1982.

Langemark, M.; Olesen, J.; Poulsen, D. L.; and Beck, P. "Clinical Characterization of Patients with Chronic Tension Headache." *Headache* 28 (1988):590–596.

Sacks, O. *Migraine: Understanding a Common Disorder.* Los Angeles: University of California Press, 1985.

Sandler, M., and Collins, G. M. eds. *Migraine: A Spectrum of Ideas.* New York: Oxford University Press, 1990.

Selby, G. *Migraine and Its Variants.* Boston: ADIS Health Science Press, 1983.

Shinnar, S., and D'Souza, B. J. "The Diagnosis and Management of Headaches in Childhood." *Pediatric Clinics of North America* 29 (1982):79–94.

Solomon, Seymour, M.D., and Fraccaro, Steven. *The Headache Book.* Mount Vernon, N.Y.: Consumer Reports Books, 1991.

Solomon, S.; Guglielmo-Cappa, K.; and Smith, C. R. "Common Migraine: Criteria for Diagnosis." *Headache* 28 (1988):124–129.

Sorbi, M. *Psychological Intervention in Migraine.* Delft, The Netherlands: Eburon, 1988.

Takeshima, T., and Takahashi, K. "The Relationship Between Muscle Contraction Headache and Migraine: A Multivariate Analysis Study." *Headache* 28 (1988):272–277.

Van den Bergh, V.; Amery, W. K.; and Waelkens, J. "Trigger Factors in Migraine: A Study Conducted by the Belgium Migraine Society." *Headache* 27 (1987):191–196.

Homelessness

(See also COMMUNITY MENTAL HEALTH)

Axelrod, S., and Toff, G. *Outreach Services for the Homeless Mentally Ill People.* Intergovernmental Health Policy Project, George Washington University, No. 278-86-0006. Washington, D.C.: National Institute for Mental Health, 1987.

Bassuk, E. "The Homeless Problem." *Scientific American* 251, no. 1 (1984):40–45.

Bassuk, E., and Rubin, L. "Homeless Children: A Neglected Population." *American Journal of Orthopsychiatry* 57 (1986):2.

Bassuk, E.; Rubin, L.; and Lauriat, A. "Is Homelessness a Mental Health Problem" *American Journal of Psychiatry* 141, no. 12 (1984):1546–1550.

Bassuk, E. L.; Rubin, L.; and Lariat, A. S. "Characteristics of Sheltered Homeless Families." *American Journal of Public Health* 76 (1986):9.

Goldman, H., and Morrissey, J. "The Alchemy of Mental Health Policy: Homelessness and the Fourth Cycle of Reform." *American Journal of Public Health* 75 (1985):727–731.

Lenehan, G.; McInnis, G.; O'Donnell, D.; and Hennessey, M. "A Nurses' Clinic for the Homeless." *American Journal of Nursing* 85 (1985):11.

Levine, I. S., and Haggard, L. K. "Homelessness as a Public Health Mental Health Problem," in Rochefort, D., ed., *Handbook on Mental Health Policy in the United States.* New York: Greenwood Press, 1989.

Long, M. *What Are the Health Needs of the Homeless? The Homeless: Findings from the Ohio Study.* Presented at a special meeting on the homeless with alcohol-related problems. Rockville, Md.: National Institute on Alcohol Abuse and Alcoholism, 1986.

Marin, P. "Helping and Hating the Homeless." *Harper's* (Jan. 1987):39–49.

Stark, L. "Blame the System, Not Its Victims," in *Homelessness: Critical Issues for Policy and Practice.* Boston: Boston Foundation, 1987.

Homosexuality and Lesbianism

Abbott, Sidney, and Love, Barbara. *Sappho Was a Right-On Woman: A Liberated View of Lesbianism.* New York: Stein & Day, 1973.

Bozett, Frederick W. *Gay and Lesbian Parents.* New York: Praeger Publishers, 1987.

Clunis, D. Merilee, and Green, G. Dorsey. *Lesbian Couples.* Seattle: Seal Press, 1988.

Curb, Rosemary, and Manahan, Nancy, eds. *Lesbian Nuns: Breaking Silence.* Tallahassee, Fla.: Naiad Press, 1985.

Faderman, Lillian. *Surpassing the Love of Men: Romantic Friendship and Love Between Women from the Rennaissance to the Present.* New York: Morrow, 1981.

Furnell, Peter J. "Lesbian and Gay Psychology: A Neglected Area of British Research." *Bulletin of the British Psychological Society* 39 (Feb. 1986):41–47.

Gardner-Loulan, JoAnn. *Lesbian Sex.* San Francisco: Spinsters Ink, 1984.

Golomobk, Susan; Spencer, Ann; and Rutter, Michael. "Children in Lesbian and Single-Parent Households: Psychosexual and Psychiatric Appraisal." *Journal of Child Psychology* 24, no. 4 (1983):551–572.

Grier, Barbara, and Reid, Colletta, eds. *Lesbian Lives: Biographies of Women from the Ladder.* Baltimore: Diana Press, 1976.

Groves, Patricia A., and Ventura, Lois A. "The Lesbian Coming Out Process: Therapeutic Considerations." *Personnel and Guidance Journal* 62, no. 3 (1983):146–149.

Harris, Mary B., and Turner, Pauline. "Gay and Lesbian Parents." *Journal of Homosexuality* 12, no. 2 (1985–86):101–113.

Jay, Karla, and Young, Allen. *The Gay Report: Lesbians and Gay Men Speak Out About Sexual Experience and Lifestyles*. New York: Summit Books, 1979.

Johnston, Jill. *Lesbian Nation: The Feminist Solution*. New York: Simon & Schuster, 1973.

Katz, Jonathan. *Gay American History: Lesbians and Gay Men in the USA*. New York: Crowell, 1976.

Lewis, Sasha Gregory. *Sunday's Women: A Report on Lesbian Life Today*. Boston: Beacon Press, 1979.

Owen, William F., Jr. "Medical Problems of the Homosexual Adolescent." *Journal of Adolescent Health Care* 6, no. 4 (1985):278–285.

Polikoff, Nancy. "Lesbian Mothers, Lesbian Families: Legal Obstacles, Legal Challenges." *Review of Law and Social Changes* 14 (1986):907–914.

Sisley, Emily L., and Harris, Bertha. *The Joy of Lesbian Sex: A Tender and Liberating Guide to the Pleasures and Problems of a Lesbian Lifestyle*. New York: Crown, 1977.

Vida, Ginny, ed. *Our Right to Love: A Lesbian Resource Book*. Englewood Cliffs, N.J.: Prentice-Hall, 1978.

Wolf, Deborah Goleman. *The Lesbian Community*. Berkeley: University of California Press, 1979.

Wolfe, Susan J., and Stanley, Julia Penelope. *The Coming Out Stories*. Watertown, Mass.: Persephone Press, 1980.

Wolff, Charlotte. *Love Between Women*. New York: Harper & Row, 1972.

Wyers, Norman L. "Homosexuality in the Family: Lesbian and Gay Spouses." *Social Work* 32, no. 2 (1987):143–148.

Illness and Disability: Psychosexual Effects

Bos, Gerjanne. "Sexuality of Gynecological Cancer Patients: Quantity and Quality." *Journal of Psychosomatic Obstetrics and Gynaecology* 5, no. 3 (1986):217–224.

Comfort, Alex. *Sexual Consequences of Disability*. Philadelphia: George F. Strickley, 1978.

Farber, Martin, ed. *Human Sexuality: Psychosexual Effects of Disease*. New York: Macmillian, 1985.

Johnson, Warren R., and Kempton, Winifred. *Sex Education and Counseling of Special Groups: The Mentally and Physically Disabled, Ill and Elderly*, 2d ed. Springfield, Ill.: Thomas, 1981.

Mooney, Thomas O.; Cole, Theodore M.; and Chilgren, Richard A. *Sexual Options for Paraplegics and Quadriplegics*. Boston: Little, Brown, 1975.

Newman, Amy S., and Bertelson, Amy D. "Sexual Dysfunction in Diabetic Women." *Journal of Behavioral Medicine* 9, no. 3 (1986):261–270.

Woods, Nancy Fugate. *Human Sexuality in Health and Illness,* 3d ed. St. Louis: C. V. Mosby, 1984.

Illness and Disability in the Family

Boss, P., and Greenberg, J. "Family Boundary Ambiguity: A New Variable in Family Stress Theory." *Family Process* 23 (1984):535–546.

Byng-Hall, J. "Scripts and Legends in Families and Family Therapy." *Family Process* 27, no. 2 (1988):167–181.

Campbell, T. L. "Family's Impact on Health: A Critical Review." *Family Systems Medicine* 4, nos. 2&3 (1986):135–328.

Carter, E. A., and McGoldrick, M., eds. *The Changing Family Life Cycle: A Framework for Family Therapy,* 2d ed. New York: Allyn & Bacon, 1989.

Chilman, C. S.; Nunnally, E. W.; and Cox, F. M., eds. *Chronic Illness and Disability: Families in Trouble Series.* Beverly Hills: Sage, 1988.

Eisenberg, M. G.; Sutkin, L. C.; and Jansen, M. A., eds. *Chronic Illness and Disability Through the Life Span: Effects on Self and Family.* New York: Springer Publishing, 1984.

Glenn, M. L. "Toward Collaborative Family-oriented Health Care." *Family Systems Medicine* 3, no. 4 (1985):466–475.

Gonzales, S.; Steinglass, P.; and Reiss, D. "Putting the Illness in Its Place: Discussion Groups for Families with Chronic Medical Illnesses." *Family Process* 28, no. 1 (1989):69–89.

Herz, F. "The Impact of Death and Serious Illness on the Family Life Cycle," in Carter, E. A., and McGoldrick, M., eds., *The Changing Family Life Cycle: A Framework for Family Therapy,* 2d ed. New York: Gardner Press, 1988.

Penn, P. "Coalitions and Binding Interactions in Families with Chronic Illness." *Family Systems Medicine* 1, no. 2 (1983):16–25.

Ramsey, C. N., Jr., ed. *Family Systems in Medicine.* New York: Guilford Press, 1989.

Reiss, D.; Gonzales, S.; and Kramer, N. "Family Process, Chronic Illness, and Death." *Archives of General Psychiatry* 43 (1986):795–804.

Rolland, J. S. "Anticipatory Loss: A Family Systems Developmental Framework." *Family Process* 29, no. 3 (1990):229–244.

Rolland, J. S. "Chronic Illness and the Life Cycle," in Carter, E. A., and McGoldrick, M., eds., *The Changing Family Life Cycle: A Framework for Family Therapy,* 2d ed. New York: Gardner Press, 1988.

Rolland, J. S. "Chronic Illness and the Life Cycle: A Conceptual Framework." *Family Process* 26, no. 2 (1987):203–221.

Rolland, J. S. "A Conceptual Model of Chronic and Life-threatening Illness and Its Impact on the Family," in Chilman, C.; Nunnally, E.; and Cox, F., eds., *Chronic Illness and Disability: Families in Trouble.* Beverly Hills: Sage, 1988.

Rolland, J. S. "Toward a Psychosocial Typology of Chronic and Life-threatening Illness." *Family Systems Medicine* 2, no. 3 (1984):245–263.

Strauss, A. L. *Chronic Illness and the Quality of Life.* St. Louis: C. V. Mosby, 1975.

Strong, M. *Mainstay: For the Well Spouse of the Chronically Ill.* Boston: Little, Brown, 1988.

Walker, G. "The Pact: The Caretaker-Parent/Ill Child Coalition in Families with Chronic Illness." *Family Systems Medicine* 1, no. 4 (1984):6–30.

Wolin, S. J., and Benett, L. A. "Family Rituals." *Family Process* 23, no. 3 (1984):401–420.

Incest

Armstrong, Louise. *Kiss Daddy Goodnight: A Speak-Out on Incest.* New York: Pocket Books, 1979.

Brady, Katherine. *Father's Days: A True Story of Incest.* New York: Seaview Books, 1979.

Gelinas, D. J. "The Persisting Negative Effects of Incest." *Psychiatry* 46 (1983):312–332.

Herman, Judith Lewis, and Hirshman, Lisa. *Father-Daughter Incest.* Cambridge: Harvard University Press, 1981.

Russell, Diana E. H. *The Secret Trauma: Incest in the Lives of Girls and Women.* New York: Basic Books, 1986.

Vidman, Lou Ann Lalani. "A Multidimensional Psychotherapy for Women Incest Victims." *Dissertation Abstracts International* 46, no. 10 (1985):1–230.

Ward, Elizabeth. *Father-Daughter Rape.* New York: Grove Press, 1985.

Infertility

Bellina, Joseph H. *You Can Have a Baby: Everything You Need to Know About Fertility.* New York: Crown, 1985.

Corson, Stephen L. *Conquering Infertility.* Norwalk, Conn.: Appleton-Century-Crofts, 1983.

Daya, Salim. "Investigation of the Infertile Couple." *Canadian Family Physician* 35 (June 1989):1379–1383.

Harkness, Carla. *The Infertility Book: A Comprehensive Medical and Emotional Guide.* San Francisco: Volcano Press, 1987.

Manning, Barbara Eck. *Infertility: A Guide for the Childless Couple.* Englewood Cliffs, N.J.: Prentice-Hall, 1988.

Mazor, Miriam D., and Simons, Harriet F., eds. *Infertility: Medical, Emotional and Social Considerations.* New York: Human Sciences Press, 1984.

Mishell, Daniel R., Jr., and Davajan, Val, eds. *Infertility, Contraception and Reproductive Endocrinology,* 2d ed. Oradell, N.J.: Medical Economics Books, 1986.

Legal Issues

Brakel, S. J.; Parry, J.; and Waner, B. A. *The Mentally Disabled and the Law,* 3d ed. Chicago: American Bar Foundation, 1985.

Riskin, L. "Sexual Relations Between Psychotherapists and Their Patients: Toward Research and Restraint." *California Law Review,* 67 (1979):1000–1027.

Simon, J. T. *Clinical Psychiatry and the Law.* Washington, D.C.: American Psychiatric Press, 1987.

Weisstub, D. N., ed. *Law and Mental Health International Perspectives.* Toronto: Pergamon Press, 1986.

Loneliness

Fromm-Reichmann, F. "Loneliness." *Psychiatry* 22 (1959):1–15.

Gordon, S. *Lonely in America.* New York: Simon & Schuster, 1976.

Moustakas, C. E. *Loneliness.* Englewood Cliffs, N.J.: Prentice-Hall, 1961.

Moustakas, C. E. *Loneliness and Love.* Englewood Cliffs, N.J.: Prentice-Hall, 1972.

Peplau, H. E. "Loneliness." *American Journal of Nursing* 55 (1955):1476–1481.

Perlman, D., and Peplau, L. A. "Toward Psychology of Loneliness," in Gilmour, R. G., and Duck, S., eds., *Personal Relationships in Disorder.* London: Academic Press, 1981.

Rubenstein, C., and Shaver, P. "The Experience of Loneliness," in Peplau, L. A., and Perlman, D., eds., *Loneliness: A Sourcebook of Theory, Research, and Therapy.* New York: Wiley, 1982.

Welt, S. R. "The Developmental Roots of Loneliness." *Archives of Psychiatric Nursing* 1 (1987):25–32.

Memory

Atkinson, R. C., and Shiffrin, R. M. "The Control of Short-Term Memory." *Scientific American* 225 (1971):82–90.

Baas, L. "Memory Error." *Nursing Clinics of North America* 20 (1985):731–743.

Baddeley, A. D. *The Psychology of Memory*. New York: Basic Books, 1976.

Galizia, V. "Pharmacotherapy of Memory Loss in the Geriatric Patient." *Drug Intelligence and Clinical Pharmacy* 18 (1984):784–790.

Gillis, D. "Patients Suffering from Memory Loss Can Be Taught Self-care." *Geriatric Nursing* 41, no. 10 (Sept.-Oct. 1986):257–261.

Glisky, E. "Remediation of Organic Memory Disorders: Current Status and Future Prospects." *Journal of Head Trauma Rehabilitation* 1, no. 3 (1986):54–63.

Klatzky, R. L. *Human Memory: Structure and Processes*. New York: W. H. Freeman, 1980.

Larson, E.; Larue, A.; and Wyma, D. "Memory Loss: Is It Reversible?" *Patient Care* 21 no. 8 (Apr. 30, 1987):54–66.

Markson, E. "Gender Roles and Memory Loss in Old Age: An Exploration of Linkages." *International Journal of Aging and Human Development* 22, no. 3 (1985–86):205–214.

Moss, M.; Alber, M.; Butters, N.; and Payne, M. "Differential Patterns of Memory Loss Among Patients with Alzheimer's Disease, Huntington's Disease, and Alcoholic Korsakoff's Syndrome." *Archives of Neurology* 43 (1986):239–246.

Pedersen, B., and Dam, M. "Memory Disturbances in Epileptic Patients." *Acta Neurologica Scandinavica* 74, supp. 109 (1985):66–70.

Squire, L. R. *Memory and Brain*. New York: Oxford University Press, 1987.

Thompson, R. F. "The Neurobiology of Learning and Memory." *Science* 233 (1986):941–947.

Mental Health Promotion

Antonovsky, A. *Unraveling the Mystery of Health*. San Francisco: Jossey-Bass, 1987.

Aubrey, L. "Health as a Social Concept." *British Journal of Sociology* 4 (1953):109–124.

Clark, C. C. *Wellness Nursing: Concepts, Theory, Research, and Practice*. New York: Springer Publishing, 1986.

Dunn, H. L. "Points of Attack for Raising the Level of Wellness." *Journal of the National Medical Association* 49 (1975):223–235.

Faden, R. R. "Ethical Issues in Government-Sponsored Health Campaigns." *Health Education Quarterly* 14 (1987):27–37.

Greiner, P. A. "Nursing and Worksite Wellness: Missing the Boat." *Holistic Nursing Practice* 2 (1987):53–60.

Jahoda, M. *Current Concepts of Positive Mental Health*. New York: Basic Books, 1958.

McBride, A. B. "Mental Health Effects of Women's Multiple Roles." *Image* 20 (1988):41–47.

Marlatt, G. A., and Gordon, J. R. *Relapse Prevention*. New York: Guilford Press, 1985.

Menninger, K. A. *The Human Mind,* 3d ed. New York: Knopf, 1945.

Nemcek, M. A. "Research Trends in the Health Promotion of Well Adults." *AAOHN (American Association of Occupational Health Nurses) Journal* 34 (1986):470–475.

Oelbaum, C. H. "Hallmarks of Adult Wellness." *American Journal of Nursing* 74 (1974):1623–1625.

Pender, N. J. *Health Promotion in Nursing Practice*, 2d ed. Norwalk, Conn.: Appleton-Lange, 1987.

U.S. Department of Health, Education, and Welfare. *Healthy People: The Surgeon General's Report on Health Promotion and Disease Prevention.* DHEW Publication No. 79-55071A. Washington, D.C.: USGPO, 1979.

Mental Retardation

Abel, E. L., and Sokol, R. "Incidence of Fetal Alcohol Syndrome and Economic Impact of FAS-related Anomalies." *Drug and Alcohol Dependence* 19 (1987):51–70.

Akesson, H. O. "The Biological Origin of Mild Mental Retardation." *Acta Psychiatrica Scandinavica* 74 (1986):3–7.

Beavers, J.; Hampson, R. B.; Hulgus, Y. F.; and Beavers, W. R. "Coping in Families with a Retarded Child." *Family Process* 25 (1986):365–377.

Grossman, H. *Manual of Terminology and Classification in Mental Retardation.* Washington, D.C.: American Association of Mental Deficiency, 1977.

Lubetsky, M. "The Psychiatrist's Role in the Assessment and Treatment of the Retarded Child." *Child Psychiatry and Human Development,* 16 (1987):261–271.

Matson, J., and Frame, C. *Psychopathology Among Mentally Retarded Children and Adolescents.* Beverly Hills: Sage, 1986.

Munro, J. D. "Epidemiology and the Extent of Mental Retardation." *Psychiatria Clinica North America* 9 (1986):591–624.

Payton, J. B.; Burkhart, J. E.; Hersen, M.; and Helsel, W. J. "Treatment of ADDH in Mentally Retarded Children: A Preliminary Study." *Journal of the American Academy of Child and Adolescent Psychiatry* 28 (1989):761–767.

Reiss, A. L., and Freund, L. F. "Fragile X Syndrome." *Biological Psychiatry* 27 (1990):223–240.

Rutter, M., and Schopler, E. "Autism and Pervasive Developmental Disorders: Concepts and Diagnostic Issues." *Disorders* 17 (1987):159–186. *Journal of Autism and Developmental Disorders* 17 (1987):159–186.

Steele, S. "Assessment of Functional Wellness Behavior in Adolescents Who Are Mentally Retarded." *Issues in Comprehensive Pediatric Nursing* 9 (1986):331–340.

Motherhood

Bernard, Jessie Shirley. *The Future of Motherhood.* New York: Penguin Books, 1974.

Frank, Diana, and Vogel, Marta. *The Baby Makers.* New York: Carroll and Graf Publishers, 1988.

Hammer, Signe. *Daughters and Mothers: Mothers and Daughters.* New York: New American Library, 1976.

Leifer, Myra. *Psychological Effects of Motherhood: A Study of First Pregnancy.* New York: Praeger, 1980.

McKaughan, Molly. *The Biological Clock: Reconciling Careers and Motherhood in the 1980's.* Garden City, N.Y.: Doubleday, 1987.

O'Neill, Onora, and Ruddick, William, eds. *Having Children: Philosophical and Legal Reflections on Parenthood.* New York: Oxford University Press, 1979.

Payne, Karen, ed. *Between Ourselves: Letters Between Mothers and Daughters, 1750–1982.* Boston: Houghton Mifflin, 1983.

Peck, Ellen, and Senderowitz, Judith. *Pronatalism: The Myth of Mom and Apple Pie.* New York: Crowell, 1974.

Rich, Adrienne. *Of Woman Born: Motherhood as Experience and Institution.* New York: Norton, 1976.

Multiple Personality Disorder

(See also DISSOCIATIVE DISORDERS)

Adityanjee, R., et al. "Current Status of Multiple Personality Disorder in India." *American Journal of Psychiatry* 146, no. 12 (Dec. 1989):1607–1610.

Braun, B. G. *Treatment of Multiple Personality Disorder.* Washington, D.C.: American Psychiatric Press, 1986.

Horevitz, R. P. "Hypnosis for Multiple Personality Disorder: A Framework for Beginning." *American Journal of Clinical Hypnosis* 28 (1983):138–145.

Kluft, R. P. "Hypnotherapeutic Crisis Intervention in Multiple Personality." *American Journal of Clinical Hypnosis* 28 (1983):73–83.

Kluft, R. P. "Multiple Personality." *International Journal of Family Therapy* 5 (1984):283–302.

Spiegel, D. "Multiple Personality as a Post-traumatic Stress Disorder." *Psychiatric Clinics of North America* 7 (1984):101–110.

Obsessive-Compulsive Disorder (OCD)

Ballantine, H. T., et al. "Treatment of Psychiatric Illness by Stereotactic Cingulotomy." *Biological Psychiatry* 22 (1987):887–897.

Black, A. "The Natural History of Obsessional Neurosis," in Beach, H. R., ed., *Obsessional States.* London: Methuen, 1974.

Black, D. W., and Noyes, R. "Comorbidity in Obsessive-Compulsive Disorder," in Maser, J. D., and Cloninger, C. R., eds., *Comorbidity in Anxiety and Mood Disorders.* Washington, D.C.: American Psychiatric Press, 1990.

DeVeaugh-Geiss, J.; Landau, P.; and Katz, R. "Treatment of Obsessive-Compulsive Disorder with Clomipramine." *Psychiatric Annals* 19 (1989):97–101.

Hamburger, S. D., et al. "Growth Rate in Adolescents with Obsessive-Compulsive Disorder." *American Journal of Psychiatry* 146 (1989):652–655.

Hollander, E., et al. "Signs of Central Nervous System Dysfunction in Obsessive-Compulsive Disorder." *Archives of General Psychiatry* 47 (1990):27–32.

Karno, M., et al. "The Epidemiology of Obsessive-Compulsive Disorder in Five U.S. Communities." *Archives of General Psychiatry* 45 (1988):1094–1099.

Marks, I. M. "Review: Obsessive-Compulsive Disorders," in Marks, I. M., ed., *Fears, Phobias, and Rituals: Panic, Anxiety and Their Disorders.* New York: Oxford University Press, 1987.

Perse, T. L., et al. "Fluvoxamine Treatment of Obsessive-Compulsive Disorder." *American Journal of Psychiatry* 144 (1987):1543–1548.

Rapoport, J. L. *The Boy Who Couldn't Stop Washing: The Experience and Treatment of Obsessive-Compulsive Disorder*. New York: Dutton, 1989.

Rapoport, J. L. "The Neurobiology of Obsessive-Compulsive Disorder." *Journal of the American Medical Association* 260 (1988):2888–2890.

Panic Disorder

(See ANXIETIES AND ANXIETY DISORDERS)

Personality Disorders

Akhtar, S., and Thompson, J. A. "Full Review: Narcissistic Personality Disorder." *American Journal of Psychiatry* 139 (1982):12–20.

Beck, Aaron T., et al. *Cognitive Therapy of Personality Disorders*. New York: Guilford Press, 1990.

Black, D. W., et al. "The Importance of Axis II in Patients with Major Depression—A Controlled Study." *Journal of Affective Disorders* 14 (1988):115–122.

Kernberg, O. *Severe Personality Disorders*. New Haven: Yale University Press, 1984.

Lewis, G., and Appleby, L. "Personality Disorders: The Patients Psychiatrists Dislike." *British Journal of Psychiatry* 153 (1988):44–49.

Perry, J. C., and Flannery, R. B. "Passive-Aggressive Personality Disorder—Treatment Implications for a Clinical Typology." *Journal of Nervous and Mental Disease* 170 (1982):164–173.

Siever, L. J., et al. "Psychobiology of Personality Disorders: Pharmacologic Implications." *Psychopharmacology Bulletin* 23 (1987):333–336.

Soloff, P. H.; Ansom, G.; and Nathan, R. S. "The Dexamethasone Suppression Test in Patients with Borderline Personality Disorders." *American Journal of Psychiatry* 139 (1982):1621–1623.

Tarnepolsky, A., and Berelowitz, M. "Borderline Personality—A Review of Recent Research." *British Journal of Psychiatry* 151 (1987):724–734.

Thompson, D. J., and Goldberg, D. "Hysterical Personality Disorder." *British Journal of Psychiatry* 150 (1987):241–245.

Torgerson, S. "Genetic and Nosologic Aspects of Schizotypal and Borderline Personality Disorders: A Twin Study." *Archives of General Psychiatry* 14 (1984):546–554.

Tucker, L., et al. "Long-Term Hospital Treatment of Borderline Patients." *American Journal of Psychiatry* 144 (1987):1443–1448.

Zanarini, M. C., et al. "Childhood Experiences of Borderline Patients." *Comprehensive Psychiatry* 30 (1989):18–25.

Pharmacologic Therapy

Black, J. L.; Richelson, E.; and Richardson, J. W. "Antipsychotic Agents: A Clinical Update." *Mayo Clinic Proceedings* 60 (1985):777–789.

Busto, U., et al. "Withdrawal Reaction after Long-Term Therapeutic Use of Benzodiazepines." *New England Journal of Medicine* 315 (1986):854–859.

Chiarello, R. J., and Cole, J. O. "The Use of Psychostimulants in General Psychiatry: A Reconsideration." *Archives of General Psychiatry* 44 (1987):286–295.

Clary, C., and Schweizer, E. "Treatment of MAOI Hypertensive Crisis with Sublingual Nifedipine." *Journal of Clinical Psychiatry* 48 (1987):249–250.

Cole, J. O.; Chiarello, R. J.; and Merzela, P. C. "Psychopharmacology Update: Long-Term Pharmacotherapy of Affective Disorders." *McLean Hospital Journal* 11 (1986):106–138.

Cooper, G. L. "The Safety of Fluoxetine—An Update." *British Journal of Psychiatry* 153, no. 3 (1988):77–86.

Dilsaver, S. C. "Antidepressant Withdrawal Syndromes: Phenomenology and Pathophysiology." *Acta Psychiatrica Scandinvica* 79 (1989):113–117.

Fawcett, J., and Kravitz, H. M. "The Long-Term Management of Bipolar Disorders with Lithium, Carbamazepine, and Antidepressants." *Journal of Clinical Psychiatry* 46 (1985):58–60.

Hyman, S. E., and Arana, G. W. *Handbook of Psychiatric Drug Therapy.* Boston: Little, Brown, 1987.

Jones, K. L. et al. "Pattern of Malformations in the Children of Women Treated with Carbamazepine During Pregnancy." *New England Journal of Medicine* 320 (1989):1661–1666.

Kane, J., et al. "Clozapine for the Treatment-Resistant Schizophrenic—A Double Blind Comparison with Chlorpromazine." *Archives of General Psychiatry* 45 (1988):789–796.

Kocsis, J. H., et al. "Imipramine Treatment for Chronic Depression." *Archives of General Psychiatry* 45 (1988):253–257.

Kramlinger, K. G., and Post, R. M. "Adding Lithium Carbonate to Carbamazepine: Antimanic Efficacy of Treatment-Resistant Mania." *Acta Psychiatrica Scandinavica* 79 (1989):378–385.

Kupfer, D. T.; Carpenter, L. L.; and Frank, E. "Possible Role of Antidepressants in Precipitating Mania and Hypomania in Recurrent Depression." *American Journal of Psychiatry* 145 (1988):804–808.

Olajide, D., and Lader, M. "A Comparison of Buspirone, Diazepam, and Placebo in Patients with Chronic Anxiety States." *Journal of Clinical Psychopharmacology* 75 (1987):148–152.

Quitkin, F. M., et al. "Phenelzine Versus Imipramine in the Treatment of Probable Atypical Depression: Defining Syndrome Boundaries of Selective MAOI Responders." *American Journal of Psychiatry* 145 (1988):306–311.

Richelson, E. "Synaptic Pharmacology of Antidepressants: An Update." *McLean Hospital Journal* 13 (1988):67–88.

Rickels, K., et al. "Clorazepate and Lorazepam: Clinical Improvement and Rebound Anxiety." *American Journal of Psychiatry* 145 (1988):312–317.

Roose, S. P., et al. "Tricyclic Antidepressants in Depressed Patients with Cardiac Conduction Disease." *Archives of General Psychiatry* 44 (1987):273–275.

Rosebush, P., and Stewart, T. "A Prospective Analysis of 24 Episodes of Neuroleptic Malignant Syndrome." *American Journal of Psychiatry* 146 (1989):717–725.

Yudofsky, Stuart, M.D.; Hales, Robert, M.D.; and Ferguson, Tom, M.D. *What You Need to Know About Psychiatric Drugs.* Chicago: Grove Weidenfeld, 1991.

Post-traumatic Stress Disorder (PTSD)

Burgess, A. W., and Holmstrom, L. L. "Rape Trauma Syndrome." *American Journal of Psychiatry* 131 (1974):981–986.

Card, J. "Epidemiology of PTSD in a National Cohort of Vietnam Veterans." *Journal of Clinical Psychology* 43 (1987):6–17.

Catherall, D. R. "The Support System and Amelioration of PTSD in Vietnam Veterans." *Psychotherapy* 23 (1986):472–482.

Chodoff, P. "The German Concentration Camp as a Psychological Stress." *Archives of General Psychiatry* 22 (1970):78–87.

Dollinger, S. J. "Lightning-strike Disaster Among Children." *British Journal of Medical Psychology* 58 (1987):375–383.

Foy, D. W.; Carroll, E. M.; and Donahoe, C. P. "Etiological Factors in the Development of PTSD in Clinical Samples of Vietnam Combat Veterans." *Journal of Clinical Psychology* 43 (1987):17–27.

Horowitz, M. J. "Stress-Response Syndromes: A Review of Post-traumatic and Adjustment Disorders." *Hospital and Community Psychiatry* 37 (1986):241–248.

Lazarus, R., and Folkman, S. *Stress, Appraisal and Coping.* New York: Springer Publishing, 1984.

Lifton, R. J. *Death in Life: Survivors of Hiroshima.* New York: Vintage Books, 1969.

Logue, J. N.; Melick, M. E.; and Struening, E. L. "A Study of Health and Mental Health Status Following a Major Natural Disaster." *Research in Community and Mental Health* 2 (1980):217–274.

Niederland, W. G. "Survivor Syndrome: Further Observations and Dimensions." *Journal of the American Psychoanalytical Association* 29 (1981):413–416.

Psychology and Psychiatry

Adams, Paul L. "The Mother Not the Father." *Journal of the American Academy of Psychoanalysis* 15, no. 4 (1987):465–480.

Al-Issa, Ihsan. *The Psychopathology of Women.* Englewood Cliffs, N.J.: Prentice-Hall, 1980.

Bardwick, Judith M. *Psychology of Women: A Study of Bio-cultural Conflicts.* New York: Harper & Row, 1971.

Bardwick, Judith M., ed. *Readings on the Psychology of Women.* New York: Harper & Row, 1972.

Chesler, Phyllis. *Women and Madness.* New York: Avon, 1972.

Chessick, R. "Thirty Unresolved Psychodynamic Questions Pertaining to Feminine Psychology." *American Journal of Psychotherapy* 42, no. 1 (1988):86–95.

Coward, Rosalind. *Female Desires, How They Are Sought, Bought and Packaged.* New York: Grove Press, 1985.

Cox, Sue, ed. *Female Psychology: The Emerging Self.* New York: St. Martin's, 1981.

de Castillejo, Irene Claremont. *Knowing Woman: A Feminine Psychology.* New York: Harper & Row, 1974.

Dervin, Daniel. "Matricentric Narratives: A Report on the Psychoanalysis of Gender Based on British Women's Fiction." *Journal of Psychoanalytic Anthropology* 9, no. 4 (1986):393–446.

Deutsch, Helene. *The Psychology of Women.* New York: Bantam Books, 1973.

Dinnerstein, Dorothy. *The Mermaid and the Minataur.* New York: Harper & Row, 1976.

Douglas, Ann. *The Feminization of American Culture.* New York: Avon Books, 1977.

Ehrenreich, Barbara, and English, Deirdre. *For Her Own Good: 150 Years of Expert Advice to Women.* Garden City, N.Y.: Anchor Press/Doubleday, 1978.

Eichenbaum, Luise, and Orbach, Susie. *Understanding Women: A Feminist Psychoanalytic Approach.* New York: Basic Books, 1983.

Ellis, Havelock. *Psychology of Sex.* New York: Emerson Books, 1944.

Ellis, Havelock. *Studies in the Psychology of Sex.* New York: Random House, 1942.

Ernst, Sheila, and Goodson, Lucy. *In Our Own Hands: A Woman's Guide to Self-help Therapy.* Los Angeles: J. P. Tarcher, 1981.

Freud, Sigmund. "Civilized Sexual Morality and Modern Nervous Illness," in Freud, Sigmund, *The Standard Edition of the Complete Psychological Works of Sigmund Freud,* vol. 9, pp. 177–204. London: Hogarth Press and the Institute of Psycho-Analysis, 1959.

Freud, Sigmund. "Female Sexuality," in Freud, Sigmund, *The Standard Edition of the Complete Psychological Works of Sigmund Freud,* vol. 21, pp. 221–243. London: Hogarth Press and the Institute of Psycho-Analysis, 1961.

Freud, Sigmund. "Femininity (New Introductory Lecture on Psycho-Analysis No. 33)," in Freud, Sigmund, *The Standard Edition of the Complete Psychological Works of Sigmund Freud,* vol. 22, pp. 112–135. London: Hogarth Press and the Institute of Psycho-Analysis, 1964.

Freud, Sigmund. "Fragment of an Analysis of a Case of Hysteria," in Freud, Sigmund, *The Standard Edition of the Complete Psychological Works of Sigmund Freud,* vol. 7, pp. 1–122. London: Hogarth Press and the Institute of Psycho-Analysis, 1953.

Freud, Sigmund. "Observations on Transference-Love (Further Recommendations on the Technique of Psycho-Analysis III)," in Freud, Sigmund, *The Standard Edition of the Complete Psychological Works of Sigmund Freud,* vol. 12, pp. 157–171. London: Hogarth Press and the Institute of Psycho-Analysis, 1958.

Freud, Sigmund. "On the Universal Tendency to Debasement in the Sphere of Love (Contributions to the Psychology of Love II)," in Freud, Sigmund, *The Standard Edition of the Complete Psychological Works of Sigmund Freud,* vol. 11, pp. 177–190. London: Hogarth Press and the Institute of Psycho-Analysis, 1957.

Freud, Sigmund. "The Psychogenesis of a Case of Homosexuality in a Woman," in Freud, Sigmund, *The Standard Edition of the Complete Psychological Works of Sigmund Freud,* vol. 18, pp. 146–174. London: Hogarth Press and the Institute of Psycho-Analysis, 1961.

Freud, Sigmund. "Some Psychical Consequences of the Anatomical Distinction Between the Sexes," in Freud, Sigmund, *The Standard Edition of the Complete Psychological Works of Sigmund Freud,* vol. 19, pp. 241–258. London: Hogarth Press and the Institute of Psycho-Analysis, 1961.

Freud, Sigmund. "The Taboo of Virginity (Contributions to the Psychology of Love III)," in Freud, Sigmund, *The Standard Edition of the Complete Psychological Works of Sigmund Freud,* vol. 11, pp. 191–208. London: Hogarth Press and the Institute of Psycho-Analysis, 1957.

Freud, Sigmund. *Three Essays on the Theory of Sexuality.* London: Hogarth Press, 1974.

Freud, Sigmund, and Breuer, Josef. "Studies on Hysteria," in Freud, Sigmund, *The Standard Edition of the Complete Psychological Works of Sigmund Freud,* vol. 2. London: Hogarth Press and the Institute of Psycho-Analysis, 1955.

Friday, Nancy. *Jealousy.* New York: Morrow, 1985.

Gillespie, William H. "Women and Her Discontents: A Reassessment of Freud's View on Female Sexuality." *International Review of Psychoanalysis* 2, no. 1 (1975):1–9.

Gilligan, Carol. *In a Different Voice: Psychological Theory and Women's Development.* Cambridge: Harvard University Press, 1982.

Greenspan, Miriam. *A New Approach to Women and Therapy.* New York: McGraw-Hill, 1983.

Horney, Karen. *Feminine Psychology.* New York: Norton, 1967.

Hyde, Janet Shibley. *Half the Human Experience: The Psychology of Women,* 3d ed. Lexington, Mass.: D. C. Heath, 1985.

Janda, L. H., and O'Grady, K. E. "Development of a Sex Anxiety Inventory." *Journal of Consulting and Clinical Psychology* 48 (1980):169–175.

Jung, Carl Gustav. "Mind and Earth," in Jung, C. G., *The Collected Works of C. G. Jung* vol. 10, pp. 29–49. New York: Random House, 1964.

Jung, Carl Gustav. "The Relations Between the Ego and the Unconscious," in Jung, C. G., *The Collected Works of C. G. Jung,* vol. 7, pp. 123–244. Princeton, N.J.: Princeton University Press, 1966.

Jung. Carl Gustav. "Woman in Europe," in Jung, C. G., *The Collected Works of C. G. Jung,* vol. 10, pp. 113–133. New York: Random House, 1964.

Miller, Jean Baker. *Toward a New Psychology of Women,* 2d ed. Boston: Beacon Press, 1986.

Mitchell, Juliet. *Psychoanalysis and Feminism: Freud, Reich, Laing and Women.* New York: Random House, 1975.

Moulton, Ruth. "Early Papers on Women: Horney to Thompson." *American Journal of Psychoanalysis* 35 (1975):207–223.

Strouse, Jean, ed. *Women and Analysis: Dialogues on Psychoanalytic Views of Femininity.* New York: Grossman, 1974.

Walker, Edward, et al. "Relationship of Chronic Pelvic Pain to Psychiatric Diagnoses and Childhood Sexual Abuse." *American Journal of Psychiatry.* 145, no. 1 (1988):75–80.

Westerlund, Elaine. "Freud on Sexual Trauma: An Historical Review of Seduction and Betrayal." *Psychology of Women Quarterly* 10 (1986):297–310.

Williams, Juanita H. *Psychology of Women: Behavior in a Biosocial Context,* 3d ed. New York: Norton, 1987.

Williams, Juanita H. *Psychology of Women: Selected Readings,* 2d edition. New York: Norton, 1985.

Psychosocial Treatment

(See PSYCHOLOGY AND PSYCHIATRY)

Psychotherapies

(See PSYCHOLOGY AND PSYCHIATRY)

Rape

Burgess, A. W., and Holmstrom, L. L. *Rape: Crisis and Recovery.* Bowie, Md.: Robert J. Brady, 1978.

Burgess, A. W., and Holmstrom, L. L. "Rape Trauma Syndrome." *American Journal of Psychiatry* 131 (1974):981–986.

Burt, M. "Cultural Myths and Supports for Rape." *Journal of Personality and Social Psychology* 38 (1980):217–230.

Finkelhor, D. *Child Sexual Abuse: New Theory and Research.* New York: Free Press, 1984.

Foley, T. S., and Davies, M. A. *Rape: Nursing Care of Victims.* St. Louis: C. V. Mosby, 1983.

Kilpatrick, D. G.; Veronen, L. J.; and Resnick, P. A. "Assessment of the Aftermath of Rape: Changing Patterns of Fear." *Journal of Behavioral Assessment* 1 (1979):133–148.

Russell, D. *Rape in Marriage.* New York: Macmillan, 1982.

Russell, D. *Sexual Exploitation: Rape, Child Sexual Abuse, and Sexual Harassment.* Beverly Hills: Sage, 1984.

Sanday, P. "The Socio-cultural Context of a Rape: A Cross Cultural Study." *Journal of Social Issues* 37 (1981):5–27.

Rural Mental Health Care

(See also COMMUNITY MENTAL HEALTH)

Ambrosius, G. R. "To Dream the Impossible Dream: Delivering Coordinated Services to the Rural Elderly," in Kim, P. K. H., and Wilson, C. P. eds., *Toward Mental Health of the Rural Elderly,* Washington, D.C.: University Press of America, 1981.

Daniels, D. N. "The Community Mental Health Center in the Rural Area: Is the Present Model Appropriate?" *American Journal of Psychiatry* 124, supp. (1967):32–37.

Harbert, Harbert, A. S., and Wilkinson, C. W. "Growing Old in Rural America." *Aging* (Jan.–Feb. 1979):36–40.

McCormick, J. "America's Third World." *Newsweek,* Aug. 8, 1988, pp. 20–24.

Schizophrenia

Andreasen, N. C. "The Diagnosis of Schizophrenia." *Schizophrenia Bulletin* 13 (1987):9–22.

Baribeau-Braun, J.; Picton, T. W.; and Gosselin, J-Y. "Schizophrenia: A Neurophysiological Evaluation of Abnormal Information Processing." *Science* 219 (1983):874–876.

Baron, M. "Genetics of Schizophrenia." *Biological Psychiatry* 21 (1986):1051–1066.

Black, D. W., and Boffeli, T. J. "Simple Schizophrenia: Past, Present, and Future." *American Journal of Psychiatry* 146 (1989):1267–1273.

Bleuler, M. *The Schizophrenic Disorders: Long-Term Patient and Family Studies.* Clemens, S., trans. New Haven: Yale University Press, 1978.

Casanova, M. F., and Kleinman, J. E. "The Neuropathology of Schizophrenia: A Critical Assessment of Research Methodologies." *Biological Psychiatry* 27 (1990):353–362.

Cutting, J. "Outcome in Schizophrenia: Overview," in Kerr, T. A., and Snaith, R. P., eds., *Contemporary Issues in Schizophrenia.* Washington, D.C.: American Psychiatric Press, 1986.

Falloon, I. R. H.; Boyd, J. L.; and McGill, C. W. *Family Care for Schizophrenia: A Problem-solving Approach to Mental Illness.* New York: Guilford Press, 1984.

Freedman, R., et al. "Neurobiological Studies of Sensory Gating in Schizophrenia." *Schizophrenia Bulletin* 13 (1987):669–678.

Geyer, M. A., and Braff, D. L. "Startle Habituation and Sensorimotor Gating in Schizophrenia and Related Animal Models." *Schizophrenia Bulletin* 13 (1987):643–668.

Johnson, D. R. "Representation of the Internal World in Catatonic Schizophrenia." *Psychiatry* 47 (1984):299–314.

Kane, J., et al. "Clozapine for the Treatment of Resistant Schizophrenia." *Archives of General Psychiatry* 45 (1988):789–796.

Kendler, K. S. "Overview: A Current Perspective of Twins Studies of Schizophrenia." *American Journal of Psychiatry* 140 (1983):1413–1425.

Lanin-Kettering, I., and Harrow, M. "The Thought Behind the Words: A View of Schizophrenic Speech and Thinking Disorders." *Schizophrenia Bulletin* 11 (1985):1–15.

Leete, E. "The Treatment of Schizophrenia: A Patient's Perspective." *Hospital and Community Psychiatry* 38 (1987):5.

Levitt, J. J., and Tsuang, M. T. "The Heterogeneity of Schizoaffective Disorder: Implications for Treatment." *American Journal of Psychiatry* 145 (1988):926–936.

Loranger, A. W. "Sex Difference in Age at Onset of Schizophrenia." *Archives of General Psychiatry* 41 (1984):157.

Pao, P-N. *Schizophrenic Disorders*. New York: International Universities Press, 1979.

Parker, G.; Johnston, P.; and Hayward, L. "Parental 'Expressed Emotion' as a Predictor of Schizophrenic Relapse." *Archives of General Psychiatry* 45 (1988):806.

Pyke, J., and Page, J. "Long-Term Care for the Chronic Schizophrenic Patient." *Canadian Nurse* 78 (1982):37–44.

Rabins, P.; Pauker, S.; and Thomas, J. "Can Schizophrenia Begin After Age 44?" *Comprehensive Psychiatry* 25 (1984):290.

Tanguay, P. E., and Cantor, S. L. "Schizophrenia in Children," *Journal of the American Academy of Child and Adolescent Psychiatry* 25, no. 5 (1986):591–594.

Torrey, E. F. *Surviving Schizophrenia: A Family Manual*. New York: Harper & Row, 1983.

Tsuang, M. T., and Simpson, J. C. "Schizoaffective Disorder: Concept and Reality." *Schizophrenia Bulletin* 10 (1984):14.

School Phobia

Berg, I. "School Phobia in Children of Agoraphobic Women." *British Journal of Psychiatry* 128 (1976):86–89.

Bernstein, G. A., and Garfinkel, B. D. "School Phobia: The Overlap of Affective and Anxiety Disorders." *Journal of the American Academy of Child and Adolescent Psychiatry* 25, no. 2 (1986):235–241.

Last, C. G., et al. "Separation Anxiety and School Phobia: A Comparison Using DSM-III Criteria." *American Journal of Psychiatry* 144 (1987):653–657.

Self-esteem

Bell, Meisenhelder, J. "Self-esteem: A Closer Look at Clinical Interventions." *International Journal of Nursing Studies* 22, no. 2 (1985):127–135.

Brunngraber, L. "Father-Daughter Incest: Immediate and Long-Term Effects of Social Abuse." *Advances in Nursing Science* 8, no. 4 (1986):15–35.

Miller, A. *Thou Shalt Not Be Aware: Society's Betrayal of the Child*. New York: Farrar, Straus, Giroux, 1984.

Reasoner, R. "Enhancement of Self-esteem in Children and Adolescents." *Family and Community Health* 6 (1983):51–64.

Sexism and Sex Discrimination

Bank, Mirra. *Anonymous Was a Woman*. New York: St. Martin's, 1979.

Bird, Carolyn. *Born Female: The High Cost of Keeping Women Down*. New York: Pocket Books, 1966.

Chicago, Judy. *Through the Flower: My Struggle as a Woman Artist*. Garden City, N.Y.: Doubleday, 1975.

Gornick, Vivian, and Moran, Barbara K., eds. *Woman in Sexist Society*. New York: New American Library, 1971.

Greer, Germaine. *The Obstacle Race: The Fortunes of Women Painters and Their Work*. New York: Farrar, Straus & Giroux, 1979.

Hays, H. R. *The Dangerous Sex: The Myth of Feminine Evil*. New York: Putnam, 1964.

Lakoff, Robin. *Language and Woman's Place*. New York: Harper & Row, 1975.

Miller, Casey, and Swift, Kate. *Words and Women: New Language in New Times*. Garden City, N.Y.: Anchor Press, 1977.

Nilsen, Alleen Pace; Bosmajian, Haig; Gershuny, H. Lee; and Stanley, Julia P. *Sexism and Language*. Urbana, Ill.: National Council of Teachers of English, 1977.

Reed, Evelyn. *Sexism and Science*. New York: Pathfinder Press, 1978.

Riemer, Jeffrey W. *Hard Hats: The Work World of Construction Workers*. Beverly Hills, Calif.: Sage, 1979.

Roberts, Joan I., ed. *Beyond Intellectual Sexism: A New Woman, a New Reality*. New York: David McKay, 1976.

Ruether, Rosemary Radford. *New Woman, New Earth: Sexist Ideologies and Human Liberation*. New York: Seabury Press, 1975.

Reuther, Rosemary Radford. *Religion and Sexism: Images of Women in the Jewish and Christian Traditions*. New York: Simon & Schuster, 1974.

Sacks, Karen Brodkin, and Remy, Dorothy, eds. *My Troubles Are Going to Have Trouble with Me: Everyday Trials and Triumphs of Women Workers*. New Brunswick, N.J.: Rutgers University Press, 1984.

Schur, Edwin M. *Labeling Women Deviant: Gender, Stigma and Social Control*. New York: Random House, 1984.

Stacey, Judith; Bereaud, Susan, and Daniels, Joan, eds. *And Jill Came Tumbling After: Sexism in American Education*. New York: Dell, 1974.

Walshok, Mary Lindenstein. *Blue Collar Women: Pioneers on the Male Frontier*. Garden City, N.Y.: Anchor Press/Doubleday, 1981.

Sexual Abuse and Sexual Assault

(See also BATTERED WOMEN; CHILDREN AND CHILD ABUSE)

Amir, Menachem. *Patterns in Forcible Rape*. Chicago: University of Chicago Press, 1971.

Benedict, Helen. *Recovery: How to Survive Sexual Assault for Women, Men, Teenagers, Their Friends and Families*. Garden City, N.Y.: Doubleday, 1985.

Beneke, Timothy. *Men on Rape*. New York: St. Martin's, 1982.

Brownmiller, Susan. *Against Our Will: Men, Women and Rape*. New York: Simon & Schuster, 1975.

Chapman, Jane Roberts, and Gates, Margaret, eds. *The Victimization of Women*. Beverly Hills, Calif.: Sage, 1978.

Costa, Joseph J. *Abuse of Women: Legislation, Reporting and Prevention*. Lexington, Mass.: D. C. Heath, 1983.

Delacoste, Frederique, and Newman, Felice, eds. *Fight Back! Feminist Assistance to Male Violence*. Minneapolis, Minn.: Cleis Press, 1981.

Edmonds, Ed M., and Cahoon, Delwin D. "Attitudes Concerning Crimes Related to Clothing Worn by Female Victims." *Bulletin of the Psychonomic Society* 24, no. 6 (1986):444–446.

Grossman, Rochel, and Sutherland, Joan, eds. *Surviving Sexual Assault*. New York: Congdon & Weed, 1983.

Masters, William H. "Sexual Dysfunction as an Aftermath of Sexual Assault of Men by Women." *Journal of Sex and Marital Therapy* 12, no. 1 (1986):35–45.

Matas, M., and Marriott, A. "The Girl Who Cried Wolf: Pseudological Phantastica and Sexual Abuse." *Canadian Journal of Psychiatry* 32, no. 4 (1987):305–309.

Russell, Diana E. H. *Rape in Marriage*. New York: Macmillan, 1982.

Russell, Diana E. H. *Sexual Exploitation and Rape, Child Sexual Abuse and Workplace Harrassment*. Beverly Hills, Calif.: Sage, 1984.

Schwendinger, Julia R., and Schwendinger, Herman. *Rape and Inequality*. Beverly Hills, Calif. Sage, 1983.

Silbert, Mimi H. "Pornography and Sexual Abuse of Women." *Sex Roles* 10, no. 11–12 (1984):857–868.

Stanko, Elizabeth A. *Intimate Intrusions: Women's Experience of Male Violence*. Boston: Routledge & Kegan Paul, 1985.

Walker, Lenore E. *The Battered Woman Syndrome*. New York: Springer Publishing, 1984.

Sexual Dysfunction

Berlin, F. S., and Meinecke, C. F. "Treatment of Sex Offenders with Anti-androgenic Medication." *American Journal of Psychiatry* 138 (1981):601–607.

Buffum, John. "Pharmacosexology Update: Prescription Drugs and Sexual Function." *Journal of Psychoactive Drugs* 19, no. 2 (1986):97–106.

De Amicis, Lyn A., et al. "Clinical Follow-up of Couples Treated for Sexual Dysfunction." *Archives of Sexual Behavior* 14, no. 6 (1985):467–489.

Fagan, P. J., et al. "Distressed Transvestites—Psychometric Characteristics." *Journal of Nervous and Mental Disease* 176 (1988):626–632.

Fuller, A. K. "Child Molestation and Pedophilia—An Overview for the Physician." *Journal of the American Medical Association* 261 (1989):602–606.

Gaffney, G. R., and Berlin, F. S. "Is There a Gonadal Dysfunction in Pedophilia?: A Pilot Study." *British Journal of Psychiatry* 145 (1984):657–660.

Gaffney, G. R.; Lurie, S. F.; and Berlin, F. S. "Is There Familial Transmission of Pedophilia?" *Journal of Nervous and Mental Disease* 172 (1984):546–548.

Hayashi, Judy; Hoon, Peter; Amberson, Jan; and Murphy, William D. "The Reliability of Nocturnal Vaginal Blood Flow." *Journal of Psychotherapy and Behavioral Assessment* 8, no. 4 (1986):281–288.

Herman, J., and LoPiccolo, J. "Clinical Outcome of Sex Therapy." *Archives of General Psychiatry* 40 (1983):443–449.

Kaplan, Helen Singer. *Disorders of Sexual Desire and Other New Concepts and Techniques in Sex Therapy.* New York: Simon & Schuster, 1979.

Kaplan, Helen Singer, ed. *The Evaluation of Sexual Disorders: Psychological and Medical Aspects.* New York: Brunner/Mazel, 1983.

LoPiccolo, Joseph, and Stock, Wendy E. "Treatment of Sexual Dysfunction." *Journal of Consulting and Clinical Psychology* 54, no. 2 (1986):158–167.

Masters, William H., and Johnson, Virginia. *Human Sexual Inadequacy.* Boston: Little, Brown, 1970.

Meyer, J. K., and Reter, D. J. "Sex Reassignment Follow-up." *Archives of General Psychiatry* 36 (1979):1010–1015.

Money, John. *Varnuses Penases: Sexology, Sexosophy and Exigency Theory.* New York: Prometheus Books, 1986.

Offit, Avodah K. *Night Thoughts: Reflections of a Sex Therapist.* New York: Congdon & Lattes, 1981.

Offit, Avodah K. *The Sexual Self.* Philadelphia: Lippincott, 1977.

Pietropinto, Anthony. "Male Contributions to Female Sexual Dysfunction." *Medical Aspects of Human Sexuality* 20, no. 12 (1986):84–91.

Schover, Leslie R. "Sexual Dysfunction: When a Partner Complains of Low Sexual Desire." *Medical Aspects of Human Sexuality* 20, no. 3 (1986):108–116.

Segraves, R. J. "Effects of Psychotropic Drugs on Human Erection and Ejaculation." *Archives of General Psychiatry* 46 (1989):275–284.

Sexual Harassment

Benard, Cheryl, and Schlaffer, E., eds. "The Man in the Street: Why He Harasses?" *Ms.* 9, no. 11 (May 1981):18–19.

Berger, Gilda. *Women, Work and Wages.* New York: Franklin Watts, 1986.

Collins, Eliza G. C., and Blodgett, Timothy B. "Sexual Harassment: Some See It . . . Some Won't." *Harvard Business Review* 59 (Mar.–Apr. 1981):76–95.

Dziech, Billie Wright, and Weiner, Linda. *The Lecherous Professor: Sexual Harrassment on Campus.* Boston: Beacon Press, 1984.

Hoffman, Jan. "Digging in Hell: The Story of Women Coal Miners." *Mademoiselle* 89 (May 1983):166–167.

Horn, Patrice D., and Horn, Jack C. *Sex in the Office.* Reading, Mass.: Addison-Wesley, 1982.

Jensen, Inger W., and Gutak, Barabara A. "Attributions and Assignments of Responsibility in Sexual Harassment." *Journal of Social Issues* 38 (Winter 1982):121–136.

MacKinnon, Catherine A. *Sexual Harassment of Working Women: A Case of Sex Discrimination.* New Haven: Yale University Press, 1979.

Meyer, Mary Coeli; Berchtold, Inge M.; Oestrich, J. L.; and Collins, Frederick J. *Sexual Harassment*. New York: Petrocelli Books, 1981.

Neugarten, Dail Ann, and Shafritz, Jay M., eds. *Sexuality in Organizations: Romantic and Coercive Behaviors at Work*. Oak Park, Ill.: Moore, 1980.

Teague, Bob. *Live and Off-Color: New Biz*. New York: A & W Publishers, 1982.

United States Merit Systems Protection Board. *Sexual Harassment in the Federal Workplace: Is It a Problem?* Washington, D.C.: USGPO, 1981.

Sexuality

Adams, Henry E., and Chiodo, June. "Sexual Deviation," in Adams, Henry E., and Sutker, Patricia B., eds., *Comprehensive Handbook of Psychology*. New York: Plenum Press, 1984.

Ayalah, Daphna, and Weinstock, Issac J. *Breasts: Women Speak About Their Breasts and Their Lives*. New York: Summit Books, 1979.

Barbach, Lonnie Garfield. *The Fulfillment of Female Sexuality*. Garden City, N.Y.: Anchor Press/Doubleday, 1976.

Bonaparte, Marie. *Female Sexuality*. New York: International Universities Press, 1953.

Britton, Bryce, and Dumont, Belinda. *The Love Muscle: Every Woman's Guide to Experiencing Sexual Pleasure*. New York: New American Library, 1981.

DeFries, Zira; Friedman, Richard C.; and Corn, Ruth, eds. *Sexuality: New Perspectives*. Westport, Conn.: Greenwood Press, 1985.

Elia, Irene. *The Female Animal*. New York: A Donald Hutter Book/Henry Holt & Company, 1988.

Ellis, Havelock. *Man and Woman: A Study of Human Secondary Sexual Characteristics*. London: Walter Scott Publishing Company, 1904.

Fisher, Seymour. *The Female Orgasm: Psychology, Physiology, Fantasy*. New York: Basic Books, 1973.

Gebhard, Paul H.; Raboch, Jan; and Giese, Hans. *The Sexuality of Women*. New York: Stein & Day, 1970.

Geer, James H., and O'Donohue, William T., eds. *Theories of Human Sexuality*. New York: Plenum Press, 1987.

Goldberg, Steven. *The Inevitability of Patriarchy*. New York: Morrow, 1973.

Hacker, Neville F., and Moore, J. George. *Essentials of Obstetrics and Gynecology*. Philadelphia: W. B. Saunders, 1986.

Halbert, David S. *Your Breast and You*. Abilene, Tex.: Askon Corporation, 1985.

Heiman, Julia, and LoPiccolo, Joseph. *Becoming Orgasmic: A Sexual and Personal Growth Program for Women*, rev. ed. Englewood Cliffs, N.J.: Prentice-Hall, 1988.

House, W. C., and Pendleton, L. "Sexual Dysfunction in Diabetes." *Postgraduate Medicine* 79 (1986):227–235.

Hutt, Corinne. *Males and Females*. Baltimore: Penguin Books, 1972.

Hyde, Janet Shibley. *Understanding Human Sexuality*. New York: McGraw-Hill, 1982.

Kapland, H. S. *Disorders of Sexual Desire*. New York: Simon & Schuster, 1979.

Kassorla, Irene. *Nice Girls Do—And Now You Can Too!* Los Angeles: Stratford Press, 1980.

Key, Mary Richie. *Male/Female Language*. Metuchen, N.J.: Scarecrow Press, 1975.

Kinsey, A. C.; Pomeroy, W. B.; and Martin, C. W. *Sexual Behavior in the Human Female.* Philadelphia: W. B. Saunders, 1953.

Kinsey, A. C.; Pomeroy, W. B.; and Martin, C. W. *Sexual Behavior in the Human Male.* Philadelphia: W. B. Saunders, 1948.

Kirkpatrick, Martha, ed. *Women's Sexual Development: Explorations of Inner Space.* New York: Plenum Press, 1980.

Kline-Graber, Georgia, and Graber, Benjamin. *Woman's Orgasm: A Guide to Sexual Satisfaction.* New York: Warner Books, 1975.

Kolodny, Robert C.; Masters, William H.; and Johnson, Virginia E. *Textbook of Sexual Medicine.* Boston: Little, Brown, 1979.

Ladas, Alice Kahn; Whipple, Beverly; and Perry, John D. *The G Spot and Other Recent Discoveries about Human Sexuality.* New York: Holt, Rinehart & Winston, 1982.

LaFerla, J. J. "Inhibited Sexual Desire and Orgasmic Dysfunction in Women." *Clinical Obstetrics and Gynecology* 27 (1984):738–749.

Lance, Kathryn, and Agardy, Maria. *Total Sexual Fitness for Women.* New York: Rawson, Wade, 1981.

Llewellyn-Jones, Derek. *Everywoman: A Gynaecological Guide for Life.* London: Faber & Faber, 1986.

Lowry, Thomas Power. *The Classic Clitoris: Historic Contributions to Scientific Sexuality.* Chicago: Nelson-Hall, 1978.

Maccoby, Eleanor Emmons, and Jacklin, Carol Nagy. *The Psychology of Sex Differences.* Stanford, Calif.: Stanford University Press, 1974.

Meshorer, Marc, and Meshorer, Judith. *Ultimate Pleasure: The Secrets of Easily Orgasmic Women.* New York: St. Martin's, 1986.

Money, John, and Ehrhardt, Anke. *Man and Woman, Boy and Girl: The Differentiation and Dimorphism of Gender Identity.* New York: Mentor Books, 1974.

Sagatun, Inger Johanne. "Sex Differences in Attribution." *Scandinavian Journal of Psychology* 22 (1981):51–57.

Shephard, Bruce D., and Shephard, Carroll A. *The Complete Guide to Women's Health.* Tampa, Fla.: Mariner Publishing Company, 1982.

Slag, M. F..; Morley, J. E.; and Elson, M. K. "Impotence in Medical Clinic Outpatients." *Journal of the American Medical Association* 249 (1983):1736–1740.

Sloane, Ethel. *Biology of Women.* New York: Wiley, 1980.

Steege, J. F. "Dyspareunia and Vaginismus." *Clinical Obstetrics and Gynecology* 27 (1984):750–759.

Thompson, W. L. "Sexual Problems in Chronic Respiratory Disease." *Postgraduate Medicine* 79 (1986):41–44, 47, 50–52.

Woods, N. F. *Human Sexuality in Health and Illness,* 3d ed. St. Louis: C. V. Mosby, 1984.

Zilbergeld, B. *Male Sexuality.* Boston: Little, Brown, 1978.

Sexually Transmitted Diseases

Brandt, Allen M. *A Social History of Venereal Disease in the United States Since 1880.* New York: Oxford University Press, 1985.

Breitman, Patti. *How to Persuade Your Lover to Use a Condom and Why You Should.* Rocklin, Calif.: Prime Publishing and Communications, 1987.

Freudberg, Frank. *Herpes: A Complete Guide to Relief and Reassurance*. Philadelphia: Running Press, 1982.

Kilby, Donald. *A Manual of Safe Sex: Intimacy Without Fear*. Toronto: B. C. Decker, 1986.

Sleep

Gilberg, M., and Akerstedt, T. "Body Temperature and Sleep at Different Times of Day." *Sleep* 5 (1985):378–388.

Hauri, P., and Almstead, E. "What Moment of Sleep Onset for Insomnia?" *Sleep* 6 (1983):10–15.

Knab, B., and Engle, R. "Perception of Waking and Sleeping: Possible Implications for Evaluation of Insomnia." *Sleep* 11 (1988):265–272.

Ruler, A., and Lack, L. "Gender Differences in Sleep." *Sleep Research* 17 (1988):244.

Snyder, F. "Changes in Respiration, Heart Rate, and Systolic Blood Pressure in Human Sleep." *Journal of Applied Physiology* 19 (1964):417–422.

Stress and Stress Management

(See also COPING SKILLS/DEFENSE MECHANISMS)

Allen, R. *Human Stress Response: Its Nature and Control*. Minneapolis: Burgess Publishing Co, 1983.

Berdanier, C. D. "The Many Faces of Stress," *Nutrition Today* 20, no. 2 (1987):12–17.

Cobb, S. "Social Support as a Moderator of Life Stress." *Psychosomatic Medicine* 38 (1976):300–314.

Davis, M.; Eshelman, E.; and MacKay, M. *The Relaxation and Stress Reduction Workbook*. Oakland: New Harbinger Publications, 1982.

Elliott, G. R., and Eisendorfer, C. *Stress and Human Health*. New York: Springer, 1982

Holmes, T., and Rahe, R. "The Social Readjustment Rating Scale." *Journal of Psychosomatic Research* 11 (1968):213–218.

Mason, L. *Guide to Stress Reduction*. Culver City, Calif.: Peace Press, 1980.

Schafer, W. *Stress Management for Wellness*. New York: Holt, Rinehart & Winston, 1987.

Selye, H. *The Stress of Life,* New York: McGraw-Hill, 1978.

Substance Abuse

Busto, U., et al. "Withdrawal Reaction After Long-Term Therapeutic Use of Benzodiazepines." *New England Journal of Medicine* 315 (1986):854–859.

Charney, D. S.; Henninger, G. R.; and Kleber, H. D. "A Combined Use of Clonidine and Naltrexone as a Rapid, Safe, and Effective Treatment of Abrupt Withdrawal from Methadone." *American Journal of Psychiatry* 143 (1986):831–837.

Council on Scientific Affairs. "Marijuana—Its Health Hazards and Therapeutic Potentials." *Journal of the American Medical Association* 246 (1981):1823–1827.

Council on Scientific Affairs. "Methaqualone—Abuse Limits Its Usefulness." *Journal of the American Medical Association* 250 (1983):3052.

Cregler, L. L., and Mark, H. "Medical Complications of Cocaine Abuse." *New England Journal of Medicine* 315 (1986):1495–1500.

Dinwiddie, S. H.; Zorumski, C. F.; and Rubin, E. H. "Psychiatric Correlates of Chronic Solvent Abuse." *Journal of Clinical Psychiatry* 48 (1987):334–337.

Gawin, F. H.; Allen, D.; and Humblestone, B. "Outpatient Treatment of 'Crack' Cocaine Smoking with Flupenthixol Decanoate." *Archives of General Psychiatry* 46 (1989):322–325.

Gawin, F. H., and Kleber, H. D. "Cocaine Abuse Treatment." *Archives of General Psychiatry* 41 (1984):903–909.

Gawin, F. H.; Kleber, H. D. "Cocaine Abuse Treatment." *Archives of General Psychiatry* 41 (1984):903–909.

Gawin, F. H.; Kleber, H. D.; Byck, R; et al. "Desipramine Facilitation of Initial Cocaine Abstinence." *Archives of General Psychiatry* 46 (1989):117–121.

Gossop, M., et al. "What Happens to Opiate Addicts Immediately after Treatment: A Prospective Follow-up Study." *British Medical Journal* 293 (1986):103–104.

Kozel, N. J., and Adams, E. H. "Epidemiology of Drug Abuse: An Overview." *Science* 234 (1986):970–974.

Nicholi, A. M. "The Non-therapeutic Use of Psychoactive Drugs—A Modern Epidemic." *New England Journal of Medicine* 308 (1983):925–933.

Verebey, K., and Gold, M. S. "From Coca Leaves to Crack: The Effects of Dose and Routes of Administration in Abuse Liability." *Psychiatric Annals* 18 (1988):513–520.

Suicide

Asberg, M.; Nordstrom, P.; and Traskman-Benz, L. "Biological Factors in Suicide," in Roy, A., ed., *Suicide*. Washington, D.C.: American Psychiatric Association, 1987.

Beck, A. T., et al. "Hopelessness and Eventual Suicide: A 10-Year Prospective Study of Patients Hospitalized with Suicidal Ideation." *American Journal of Psychiatry* 142 (1985):559–563.

Blythe, M. M., and Pearlmutter, D. R. "The Suicide Watch: A Reexamination of Maximum Observation." *Perspectives in Psychiatric Care* 21 (1983):3.

Bouknight, R. R. "Suicide Attempt by Drug Overdose." *American Family Physician* 33 (1986):4.

Boyd, J. H., and Moscicki, E. K. "Firearms and Youth Suicide." *American Journal of Public Health* 76 (1986):1240–1242.

Brent, D. A., et al. "Alcohol, Firearms and Suicide Among Youth." *Journal of the American Medical Association* 257 (1987):3369–3372.

Brent, D. A., et al. "Risk Factors for Adolescent Suicide." *Archives of General Psychiatry* 45 (1988):581–588.

Bunney, W. E., and Fawcett, J. A. "Biochemical Research in Depression and Suicide," in Resnik, H. L. P., ed., *Suicidal Behaviors*. Boston: Little, Brown, 1968.

Bunney W. E., and Fawcett, J. A. "Possibility of a Biochemical Test for Suicide Potential." *Archives of General Psychiatry* 13 (1965):212.

Clayton, P. J. "Suicide." *Psychiatric Clinica North America* 8, no. 2 (1985):203–204.

Eisenberg, L. "The Epidemiology of Suicide in Adolescents." *Psychiatric Annuals* 13 (1984):47.

Fawcett, T. J., et al. "Clinical Predictors of Suicide in Patients with Major Affective Disorders: A Controlled Prospective Study." *American Journal of Psychiatry* 144 (1987):35–40.

Hatton, C. L.; Valente, S. M.; and Rink, A. *Suicide: Assessment and Intervention*. New York: Appleton-Century-Crofts, 1977.

Hawton, K. *Suicide and Attempted Suicide Among Children and Adolescents.* Beverly Hills: Sage, 1986.

Miles, C. P. "Conditions Predisposing to Suicide: A Review." *Journal of Nervous and Mental Disease* 164 (1977):231–246.

Mullis, M. R., and Byers, P. H. "Social Support in Suicidal Patients." *Journal of Psychosocial Nursing and Mental Health Services* 25, no. 4 (1987):16.

Murphy, G. E. "Suicide in Alcoholism," in Roy, A., ed., *Suicide.* Baltimore: Williams & Wilkins, 1986.

Murphy, G. E., and Wetzel, R. D. "The Lifetime Risk of Suicide and Alcoholism." *Archives of General Psychiatry* 47 (1990):383–392.

O'Brien, P.; Caldwell, C.; and Transeau, G. "Destroyers: Written Treatment Contracts Can Help Cure Self Destructive Behaviors of the Borderline Patient." *Journal of Psychosocial Nursing and Mental Health Services* 23, no. 4 (1985):19.

Pallikkathayil, L., and McBride, A. B. "Suicide Attempts: The Search for Meaning." *Journal of Psychosocial Nursing and Mental Health Services* 24, no. 8 (1986):13–18.

Phillips, D. P., and Carstonson, L. L. "Clustering of Teenage Suicides after Television News Stories About Suicide." *New England Journal of Medicine* 55 (1986):685–689.

Piotrowski, Z. A. "Psychological Test Prediction of Suicide," in Resnik, H., ed., *Suicidal Behaviors.* Boston: Little, Brown, 1968.

Pokorny, A. D. "Prediction of Suicide in Psychiatric Patients." *Archives of General Psychiatry* 40 (1983):249–257.

Roy, A. "Suicide in Schizophrenia," in Roy, A., ed., *Suicide.* Baltimore: Williams & Wilkins, 1986.

Sainsbury, P. "The Epidemiology of Suicide," in Roy, A., ed., *Suicide.* Baltimore: Williams & Wilkins, 1986.

Schmidtke, A., and Hafner, H. "The 'Werther' Effect after Television Films: New Evidence for an Old Hypothesis." *Psychological Medicine* 18 (1988):665–676.

Shaffer, D., et al. "Preventing Teenage Suicide: A Critical Review." *Journal of the American Academy of Child and Adolescent Psychiatry* 27 (1988):675.

Shaffi, M., et al. "Psychological Autopsy of Completed Suicide in Children and Adolescents." *American Journal of Psychiatry* 142 (1985):1061.

Shafii, M.; Steltz-Lenarsky, J.; Derrick, A. M.; et al. "Comorbidity of Mental Disorders in the Postmortem Diagnoses of Completed Suicide in Children and Adolescents." *Journal of Affective Disorders* 15 (1988):227–233.

Whitlock, F. A. "Suicide and Physical Illness," in Roy, A. ed., *Suicide.* Baltimore: Williams & Wilkins, 1986.

Wolk-Wasserman, D. "The Intensive Care Unit and the Suicide Attempt Patient." *Acta Psychiatrica Scandinavica* 71 (1985):581–595.

Wright, N., and Adam, K. S. "Changing Motivation in Severely Suicidal Patients." *Canadian Medical Association Journal* 135 (1986):1361–1363.

Tourette Syndrome

Cohen, D.; Bruun, R.; and Leckman, J. *Tourette's Syndrome.* New York: Wiley, 1991.

Pauls, D. L., and Leckman, J. F. "The Inheritance of Gilles de la Tourette's Syndrome and Associated Behaviors." *New England Journal of Medicine* 315 (1986):993–997.

INDEX

Boldface numbers indicate main headings

A

AA *See* Alcoholics Anonymous
AAI *See* Alfred Adler Institute
AAMD *See* American Association on Mental Deficiency
AAMI *See* age-associated memory impairment
AAP *See* Association for the Advancement of Psychology
AARP *See* American Association of Retired Persons
AAS *See* American Association of Suicidology
aberration **1**
ABMP *See* American Board of Medical Psychotherapists
abnormal **1**
abnormal psychology **1**
abortifacients **1–2**
abortion **1–3**, 306
ABPP *See* American Board of Professional Psychology
Abraham, Karl 133
abstract thought **3**
abuse **3** *See also* domestic violence; family violence; substance abuse
acceptance **3**
access to care **3**
accommodation **3–4**
acetaldehyde 44
acetylcholine **4**, 33, 45, 96
acquired immunodeficiency syndrome (AIDS) **4–9**, 339
    AIDS-related complex 25–26
    drugs used for 8, 65, 390
    HIV virus 202–203
    infants with HIV 78
    organizations concerned with 8, 391
    preventing through "safe sex" 4, 113, 324
    tests for 155, 386
acrophobia **9**
ACTH (adrenocorticotrophic hormone) 13, 74
acting out **9**
action therapy **9**
active analytic psychotherapy **9**
actualization **9**
acupuncture 159, 194
acute depression **10**

acute dystonia *See* dystonic reaction
ADAA *See* Anxiety Disorders Association of America
Adapin *See* doxepin hydrochloride
adaptation **10**
adaptational approach **10**
addiction **10** *See also* alcoholism; dependency; sex addiction; substance abuse; work addiction
Addiction Research and Treatment Corporation 398
addictive personality **10**
Addison's disease 158
additive effect **10–11**, 367
ADHD *See* attention-deficit hyperactivity disorder
adjustment disorders **11**
Adkins, Janet 363
Adler, Alfred 41, 76, 172
adolescents
    with AIDS 5
    anxiety disorders 56–57
    as bullies and victims 87–88
    conduct disorders 113–114
    depression 135
    eating disorders 44, 87
    peer groups 289–290
    pregnancy 303–304
    puberty 314–315
    suicide 362
adoption **11–12**, 381, 391
adoption studies **12–13**
ADRDA *See* Alzheimer's Disease and Related Disorders Association
adrenal cortex **13**
adrenal-cortical hyperfunction 13
adrenal gland **13**, 82
adrenaline (epinephrine) **13**, 14, **163**, 168
adrenal medulla 13
adrenergic blocking agents **13–14**
adrenergic drugs **14**
adrenergic system **14**
adrenocorticotrophic hormone (ACTH) 13, 74
Adrian, Edgar 85
affairs, extramarital **14**
affect **14**
affective disorders **14–17** *See also specific affective disorders (e.g., depression)*
affective flattening (blunting) **17**

affirmation **17–18**
Africa 4, 105, 171, 232, 390
Afterloss (newsletter) 184
agape (agapism) **18**
age-associated memory impairment (AAMI) 31–32, 236–237
age factors **18**
aggression **18–19**, 288
aging **19–20** *See also* elderly parents; retirement
    abandonment during 183
    constipation during 115
    depression during 181
    organizations concerned with 391, 393, 397
    psychiatry specializing in 181–182
    suicide related to 363
agitation **20**
agnosia **20**, 33
agonist **20–21**
agoraphobia 18, **21–25**, 55, 296
agraphia 58
AHP *See* Association for Humanistic Psychology
AIDS *See* acquired immunodeficiency syndrome
AIDS-related complex (ARC) **25–26**
akathisia 20, **26**, 50
Alameda County (California) 20
Al-Anon (organization) **26**
Al-Anon Family Group Headquarters 398
Alateen (organization) **26**
Alcoholics Anonymous (AA) 26, **27**
Alcoholics Anonymous World Services 398
alcoholism **26–29**
    agoraphobia and 25
    delirium resulting from 128
    drugs used to deter 44–45
    fetus affected by 76, 168–169
    nutrition affected by 271
    organizations concerned with 398
    studies of 13, 378
Alcoholism Center for Women 398
alexia 58
alexithymia 9, **29**
Alfred Adler Institute (AAI) 396
algolagnia **29**

445